Nepal
a travel survival kit

Tony Wheeler
Richard Everist

W9-BJL-436

Nepal - a travel survival kit
1st edition

Published by
Lonely Planet Publications
Head Office: PO Box 617, Hawthorn, Vic 3122, Australia
US Office: PO Box 2001A, Berkeley, CA 94702, USA

Printed by
Singapore National Printers Ltd, Singapore

Photographs by
Sonia Berto (SB)
Richard Everist (RE)
Catherine Griffiths (CG)
James Lyon (JL)
John Radford (JR)
Tony Wheeler (TW)

Front cover: Swayambhunath Stupa, Sonia Berto

See page 345 for descriptions of the feature photo pages

Published
October 1990

National Library of Australia Cataloguing in Publication Data

Wheeler, Tony
    Nepal - a travel survival kit.

    1st ed.
    Includes index.
    ISBN 0 86442 024 2.

    1. Nepal – Description and travel – Guide-books.
    I. Everist, Richard. II. Title.

915.4960452

text & maps © Lonely Planet 1990
photos © photographers as indicated 1990

Tony Wheeler

Born in England, Tony spent most of his younger days overseas due to his father's airline occupation. Those years included a lengthy spell in Pakistan, a shorter period in the West Indies and all his high school years in the USA. He returned to England to do a university degree in engineering, worked for a short time as an automotive design engineer, returned to university again and did an MBA, then dropped out on the Asia overland trail with his wife Maureen. They set up Lonely Planet in the mid-70s and have been travelling, writing and publishing ever since. Travel for Tony and Maureen is now considerably enlivened by their daughter Tashi and son Kieran.

Richard Everist

Richard grew up in Geelong, Australia. His chequered career includes such highlights as painting ships (not an artistic endeavour) in Geelong, a brief run-in with the law (as a student of) in Melbourne, marble polishing (not the little round ones) in London, and working as a tripping counsellor (not that kind) in Connecticut. In between travelling and spending as much time as possible around the Otway Ranges he has been involved with the print media as a cleaner, freelance writer, copy-writer, sub-editor and editor. He started work with Lonely Planet in 1985.

Lonely Planet Credits

Editors	Tom Smallman
	Sue Mitra
Design, cover design & illustrations	Margaret Jung
Maps	Greg Herriman
	Margaret Jung
	Chris Lee-Ack
	Ralph Roob

Thanks also to Sharan Kaur and Lindy Cameron for copy-editing; to Diana Saad and Michelle de Kretser for copy-editing and proofing; and to Richard Nebesky for additional photographs.

THIS EDITION

The first five editions of Lonely Planet's guide to Nepal were the work of Nepalese writer Prakash A Raj, first under the title of *Nepal – A Traveller's Guide* and then as *Kathmandu & the Kingdom of Nepal*. With this sixth edition it was time for a title change, to bring it into line with other Lonely Planet travel survival kits, and a complete rewrite.

Tony Wheeler and Richard Everist, both regular visitors to Nepal since the early '70s, travelled to Nepal and covered the country from end to end with the intention of making this the most thoroughly researched guidebook to Nepal available. Along the way they visited hundreds of temples, trekked in the Himalaya, drove the length of the Terai, rode everything from mountain bikes to elephants and sampled all the favourite Kathmandu restaurants from Freak St to Thamel. Not only did they cover all the familiar sites and attractions, but a great deal of new information was added, nearly every map in the book was redrawn and many additional maps were created. There is a map legend on page 344.

Acknowledgements

Special thanks in Nepal must go to Stan Armington, author of Lonely Planet's *Trekking in the Nepal Himalaya* and the resourceful and helpful staff of Malla Treks for their superb assistance and advice during the research of this book and their instant fax replies to countless questions while it was being written. Special thanks to Daniel Tamang for his research and to the Chitwan Jungle Lodge for their assistance in the Chitwan.

Richard would also like to thank Badri Adhikari from Kanchanjunga Travel, and Vijaya Kumar Aryal (BJ) from Adventure Jungle Camp who also gave generous hospitality, help and advice. Others who made especially significant contributions were Bishnu Shrestha from Dialad Graphics, who drew the temple illustrations in the Kathmandu, Bhaktapur & Patan chapter, Anju Babbar from Tiger Mountain, and Roland Van Asch.

See page 343 for the names of travellers who wrote in with corrections, suggestions and additions.

A Warning & A Request

Things change – prices go up, schedules change, good places go bad, bad places go bankrupt – nothing stays the same. So if you find things better, worse, cheaper, more expensive, recently opened or long since closed, please write and tell us and help make the next edition better!

Your letters will be used to help update future editions and, where possible, important changes will also be included as a Stop Press section in reprints.

All information is greatly appreciated and the best letters will receive a free copy of the next edition, or any other Lonely Planet book of your choice.

Contents

Introduction

Draped along the greatest heights of the Himalaya the kingdom of Nepal is a land of eternal fascination, a place where one visit is rarely enough. It's a land of ancient history, colourful cultures and people, superb scenery and some of the best walking on earth.

Nepal's history is closely related to its geographical location – separating the fertile plains of India from the desert-like plateau of Tibet. Its position between India and China meant the country was able at times to play the role of intermediary, a canny trader between two great powers, while at other times it faced the threat of invasion. Internally the history was just as colourful with city-states in the hills vying with each other for power until one powerful king, Prithvi Narayan Shah, overran them all. That history is very visible today where the three great towns of the Kathmandu Valley – Kathmandu, Patan and Bhaktapur – still bear witness to their days as fiercely competitive mediaeval mini-kingdoms. Indeed in Nepal it's often possible to suspend belief and mentally roll the clock right back to the mediaeval era.

Behind the time-worn temples and palaces of the Kathmandu Valley, above and beyond the hills that ring the valley, another 'kingdom' rises skyward. 'The abode of snows', which is what *Himalaya* means in Sanskrit, is a natural 'kingdom' and a magnet to mountaineers from all over the world. Fortunately you don't have to be a Sherpa and your surname doesn't have to be Messner or Hillary in order for you to get in amongst these great mountains. With a dash of enterprise and a modicum of fitness most

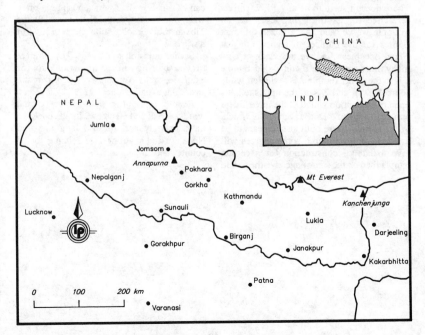

travellers can walk the trails that lead into the roadless heights of the Himalaya. One trek, the term for a long walk in Nepal, is rarely enough and, after what was intended to be the experience of a lifetime, many visitors soon find themselves planning to return.

Fascinating old towns, magnificent temples and great walking are not all Nepal has to offer.

Many visitors come to Nepal expecting to find these things but also discover how outstandingly friendly the Nepalese people are.

Nor is trekking the only activity which draws visitors – Nepal also has some superb white-water rafting opportunities, mountain biking is becoming more and more popular, and down in the jungle lowland in the south of the country, safaris on elephant-back into the Royal Chitwan National Park are another not-to-be-missed part of the Nepal experience.

Warning about Figures, Dates & Names

There doesn't seem to be any 100% correct reference for anything in Nepal. As an example we've seen half a dozen different figures for the number of square km that Nepal occupies. And we lost track of how many times sources A, B and C said Temple 1 is to the right, Temple 2 is to the left while sources X, Y and Z said the opposite. It's open to contention which of the three Taleju temples in Patan's Durbar Square is which. When temples were built also appears to be a matter of speculation: some sources will give a date of construction for a certain temple then on the same page give the period of reign for the king who built it and the two will not agree.

Many temples in Nepal have alternative names. For example, the Vishnu Temple in Patan's Durbar Square is referred to as the Jagannarayan or Charnarayan Temple; the great Shiva Temple in Kathmandu's Durbar Square is sometimes called the Maju Deval, at others simply the Shiva Temple. Where possible, alternative names that are commonly used have been given.

Mandir simply means 'temple' and generally we have used the English word except in cases where mandir is always used, as with the Krishna Mandir in Patan.

Further confusion can be caused by different systems of transliteration from Sanskrit – the letter 'h' appears in some systems, but doesn't appear in others so you may see Manjushri and Manjusri, Machhendranath and Machendranath. The letters 'b' and 'v' are also used interchangeably in different systems – Shiva's fearsome manifestation can be Bhairab or Bhairav, Vishnu is often written as Bishnu and the Nepali word for the Tibetan thunderbolt symbol can be a *bajra* or a *vajra*.

Some confusion is also caused by different places having the same name; so for example, in the Annapurna region there are two villages called Phedi.

Finally, texts differ in their use of the words Nepali and Nepalese. In this book we have used Nepali for the language and Nepalese for anything else relating to the country and its people.

Facts about the Country

HISTORY

Nepal's history as a crossroads has been a long and colourful one. Culturally and linguistically the country formed a boundary between the Mongoloid people of Tibet and their Tibeto-Burmese language and the people of the Indian plains and their Indo-European languages. To this day Nepal remains a trading centre where profits are made from a strategic position. In earlier times Nepal's importance was as the conduit for trade between India and China. Today the country continues to exploit its strategic position between uneasy giants.

Over the centuries the boundaries of Nepal have extended to include huge tracts of neighbouring India, or contracted to little more than the Kathmandu Valley and a handful of surrounding city-states. Long before recorded history made its mark on the land, legends recount that the Kathmandu Valley was a great lake and that Manjushri came from China and with a magical sword sliced open the valley wall to drain the water and create the Kathmandu Valley we know. Or perhaps it wasn't Manjushri at all; he was, after all, a Buddhist and the Hindus claim it was Krishna who performed the mighty deed, hurling a thunderbolt to create the Chobar Gorge. Choose whichever legend you prefer, but scientists agree that the valley was submerged at one time and the rivers of the valley do indeed flow southward through the narrow Chobar Gorge.

The Kiratis

Recorded history came with the Kiratis who arrived in Nepal from the east around the 7th or 8th century BC. Although they are the first known rulers of the Kathmandu Valley and Yalambar, the first of their kings, is mentioned in the Hindu epic the *Mahabharata*, very little more is known about them. It was during the Kirati period that Buddhism first arrived in the country; indeed it is claimed that during the reign of the seventh of the 28 Kirati kings

Buddha, together with his disciple Ananda, visited the valley and stayed for a time in Patan.

Other accounts of the Kirati period are more positive including a 4th century BC description of their sheep breeding and agricultural activities. Around the 2nd century BC the great Buddhist Indian emperor Ashoka visited Nepal and erected a pillar at the Buddha's birthplace at Lumbini, south of Pokhara near the present-day Indian border. Ashoka also visited the Kathmandu Valley and evidence of four stupas he erected around Patan can still be clearly seen. Ashoka may have also enlarged the stupas at Bodhnath and Swayambhunath. His daughter Charumati was said to have founded Chabahil, a village now swallowed up by Kathmandu which lies on the road between the capital and Bodhnath. There is a stupa, a smaller version of Bodhnath, and a monastery here which are claimed to date back to her time in Nepal.

The Kirati period ended around 300 AD but the Rai and Limbu people of eastern Nepal are said to be descendants of the Kiratis.

The Licchavis

Buddhism faded and Hinduism reasserted itself with the Licchavis who invaded from north India about 300 AD and overthrew the last Kirati king. They brought with them the caste divisions which continue in Nepal to this day but also ushered in a golden age of Nepalese art and architecture. Manadeva I also established the Licchavis' political and military might and a valley inscription dated to 476 AD tells of his prowess; it can be seen at the beautiful Changu Narayan Temple in the eastern part of the Kathmandu Valley. His successor, Manadeva II, left numerous stone inscriptions around his kingdom, most of them commenting on what a wonderful mother he had and how he wouldn't have got anywhere without her!

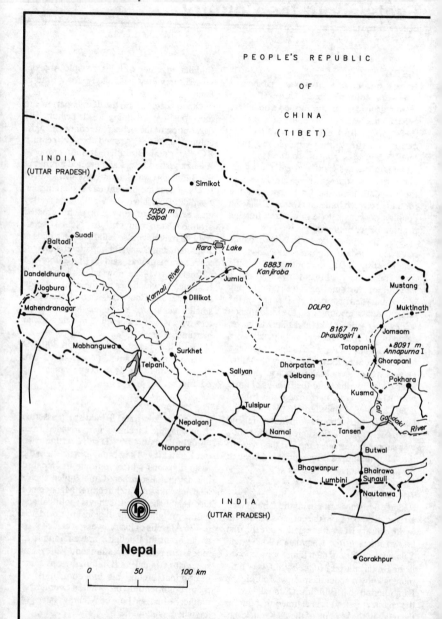

Nepal

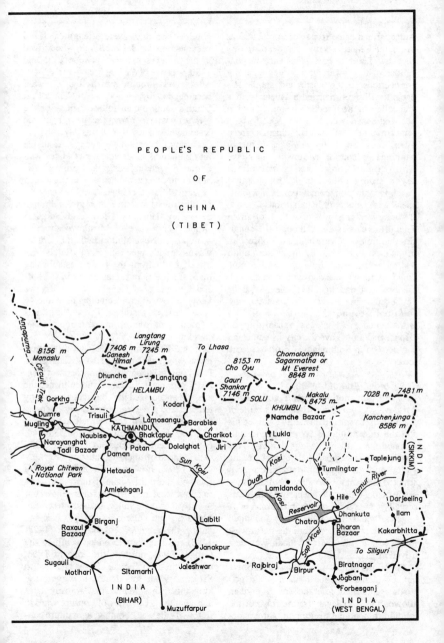

The Thakuris

Amsuvarman came to power in 602 AD as the first Thakuri king, succeeding his Licchavi father-in-law. Amsuvarman consolidated his power with strategic family connections to the north and south. His daughter Bhrikuti married a Tibetan prince and collected the Buddha's begging bowl in her wedding dowry. She was said to be a reincarnation of Tibetan Buddhism's Green Tara, seen on many *thangkas* (Tibetan paintings on cotton). Meanwhile in Nepal Amsuvarman constructed a marvellous seven storey palace at Deopatan near Pashupatinath and contemporary accounts speak with wonder of his luxurious life.

Amsuvarman's was the first of three Thakuri dynasties and although the centuries that followed were a time of confusion, invasions and turmoil, the Kathmandu Valley's strategic location ensured the kingdom's survival and growth even through this Nepalese dark age. It is believed that the city of Kantipur, today's Kathmandu, was founded around the 10th century by Gunakamadeva. His Kasthamandap or 'House of Wood' gave the city its name and can be seen in Kathmandu's Durbar Square today.

The Golden Age of the Mallas

In 1200, so another legend goes, King Ari-deva was wrestling when news came of the birth of his son. He instantly awarded his son the title Malla or 'Wrestler' and thus founded the illustrious Malla dynasty. This golden age saw great wealth flow to the valley and the kingdom's architects constructed many of the wonderful buildings we see in Nepal today, but the early Malla years actually saw a series of terrible disasters. A huge earthquake shook the valley and killed thousands, an invasion from the north-west followed and the town of Patan was destroyed in 1311.

The Hindu Mallas were followers of Shiva but considered to be incarnations of the god Vishnu and their tolerance of Buddhism allowed the Himalayan Tantric form of the religion to continue to flourish. An aristocracy grew up under the Malla rulers and the Hindu caste rules were strengthened and became more rigid. Hari Singh, who arrived in the valley sometime between 1325 and 1330, was one of the best known early Malla rulers and through him Taleju Bhawani became the royal goddess of Nepal. Hari Singh's south Indian followers may be the Newaris whose name the people of the Kathmandu Valley take to this day.

During this period Nepal began to divide into numerous independent city-states with frequently feuding kings and princes. The hill country began to be more densely settled as agricultural techniques improved but a Muslim invasion from Bengal swept through the valley damaging Hindu and Buddhist shrines. The wave of Muslim destruction soon passed Nepal, but in India the damage was more widespread and many Hindus were driven north from the plains, establishing more small Rajput principalities in the hills and mountains of Nepal. The country we know today was divided at that time into 46 separate small states. These kingdoms minted their own coins and maintained standing armies.

In the Kathmandu Valley the three great towns which remain to this day – Kathmandu, Patan and Bhaktapur – were independent kingdoms with powerful kings who cultivated the arts and encouraged the construction of many temples and the creation of many enduring works of art. Each city centred around the king's palace with the nobility and high castes concentrated close to the centre. City walls fended off their neighbours.

In 1372, however, Jayasthiti Malla founded the third Malla dynasty and took first Patan and then, 10 years later, Bhaktapur to unify the whole valley. In the 15th century Malla art and culture was at its peak and during the reign of Yaksha Malla (1428-1482) the kingdom extended south to the Ganges River, north to the edge of Tibet, west to the Kali Gandaki River and east to Sikkim. With his death, however, the kingdom again split into small warring states and another 2 centuries of conflict were to follow. Trade was booming, agriculture continued to improve and the valley towns enjoyed an orgy of temple and palace construction, but the constant squabbling of the Malla kingdoms opened the door to a new dynasty.

The Shah Dynasty Unifies Nepal

From the tiny kingdom of Gorkha, halfway between modern Kathmandu and Pokhara, the Shah kings had gradually strengthened and extended their power and dreamed of eventually conquering the rich Kathmandu Valley. In 1768 Prithvi Narayan Shah, ninth of the Shah kings, conquered the valley and moved his capital to Kathmandu. The Malla period had ended and the Shah dynasty, which continues to this day, was established.

From this new base the kingdom's power continued to expand until a clash with the Chinese in Tibet led to an ignominious defeat. The Nepalese had first fought the Chinese in 1790, but by 1792 the Chinese army had struck back and in the ensuing treaty the Nepalese had to stop their attacks on Tibet and pay tribute to the Chinese emperor in Beijing; the payments continued until 1912.

British power on the subcontinent was growing at this time and a British envoy arrived in Kathmandu in 1792, too late to aid the Nepalese against the Chinese invasion. Despite treaties with the British the expanding Nepalese boundaries, stretching all the way from Kashmir to Sikkim by the early 19th century, were bound to cause problems with the Raj, and disputes over the Terai, the lowlands south of the Himalayan foothills, led to a war with the British. In 1810 Nepal was approximately twice its current size but the 1816 'Treaty of Friendship' with the British ended the growth. Britain took Sikkim, Nepal's present-day eastern and western borders were established and most of the Terai was lost to the British Raj. Some of the land was restored to Nepal in 1858, in reward for Nepalese support during the 'Indian Mutiny'.

The treaty opened the door for Indian business influence in Nepal and when, a century later, new direct trade routes were estab-

lished between India and Tibet the Nepalese also began to lose their influence as an intermediary in trade between the two countries. A British resident was sent to Kathmandu to keep an eye on things. The Nepalese, less than entranced with the British, allotted him a piece of land which they considered to be disease-prone and a haven for evil spirits but the British stiff upper lip prevailed. In fact the defeat so rankled with the Nepalese that they decided to shut off all foreign contact and from 1816 right through until 1951 the country's borders were firmly closed to outsiders. The British residents in Kathmandu were the only Westerners to set eyes on Nepal for over 100 years.

Many Nepalese eyes were, however, viewing the outside world. The British were so impressed by the fighting qualities of the Nepalese that they brought 'Gurkhas' into the British army. Gurkha mercenaries have fought in the British army ever since, even spreading fear amongst the Argentinians during the Falklands War in 1982. Gurkha earnings are an important element in Nepal's income today and although the importance of Gurkha troops to Britain is diminishing various other nations are only too happy to pay for their soldiering abilities. The Sultan of Brunei, for example, has a contingent of Gurkha troops.

The Ranas

Although the Shah dynasty continued in power a curious palace revolt occurred in 1846 when Jung Bahadur Rana engineered the 'Kot massacre' and took on the role of prime minister. Later he extended his title to Maharajah and then made the title hereditary. The Ranas became a second 'royal family' within the kingdom and held the real power, treating the Shah kings almost as puppets.

For over a century the hereditary family of Rana prime ministers held power and although development in Nepal stagnated, the country did manage to preserve its independence during the period when the European colonial powers were snatching up virtually every country unable to defend itself. Nepal was never ruled by a colonial power, but it was almost completely isolated from the outside world right through the Rana period. Only on rare occasions were visitors allowed into Nepal and even then they were only allowed to visit a very limited part of the country.

Jung Bahadur Rana travelled to Europe in 1850 and brought back a taste for neoclassical architecture (examples of it can be seen in Kathmandu today). To the Ranas' credit *suttee* (the Hindu practice of casting widows on their husband's funeral pyre) was abolished, forced labour was ended and a school and a college were established in Kathmandu, but overall Nepal during the century of Rana power was in a time warp. While the Ranas and their relations lived luxurious lives in huge Kathmandu palaces the peasants in the hills were locked in a mediaeval existence.

Elsewhere in the region dramatic changes were taking place. After WW II India gained its independence and a revolution took place in China. Tibetan refugees fled into Nepal when the new People's Republic of China annexed Tibet and Nepal became a buffer zone between the two Asian giants. The turmoil naturally spread over Nepal's closed borders and while one Rana made moves towards liberalising the country's moribund political system another attempted to move towards even stronger central control. Under B P Koirala the Nepali Congress Party, supported by the ruling Indian Congress Party, was established by many Nepalese and even by some Rana family members. At the same time King Tribhuvan, forgotten in his palace, was being primed to overthrow the Ranas.

Modern Nepal

In late 1950 the king escaped from his palace to the Indian Embassy and from there to India. Meanwhile B P Koirala's forces managed to take most of the Terai from the Ranas and established a provisional government which ruled from the border town of Birganj. Nepal was in turmoil, but there was no clear victor and it was India which finally exerted its influence and negotiated an end to the Rana period. King

Tribhuvan returned to Nepal in 1951 and set up a new government comprised of Ranas and commoners from Koirala's Congress Party.

Although Nepal gradually reopened its long-closed doors and established relations with many other nations, dreams of a new democratic system were not permanently realised. King Tribhuvan died in 1955 and was followed by his son Mahendra, a new constitution provided for a parliamentary system of government and in 1959 Nepal held its first general election. The Nepali Congress Party won a clear victory, somewhat to the king's surprise, and Koirala became the new prime minister. Democracy was to last less than 2 years for in late 1960 the king decided it wasn't working to his taste and had the cabinet arrested. Political parties were banned and the king swapped his ceremonial role for real control.

In 1962 King Mahendra decided that a partyless, indirect *panchayat* system of government was more appropriate to Nepal. Local panchayats (councils) chose representatives to district panchayats which in turn were represented in a national panchayat. The real power, however, remained with the king who directly chose 16 members of the 35 member national panchayat, and appointed the prime minister and his cabinet. Political parties were banned.

In 1972 Mahendra died and was followed by his Eton and Harvard educated son, Birendra. The colourful coronation followed after astrologers had chosen a suitably auspicious date in February 1975. King Birendra's view that Nepal now had the correct and appropriate political system was not supported by everybody, however. Popular discontent with slow development, corrupt officials and rising costs simmered and bubbled in the '70s. Finally in 1979 the smouldering anger turned into rioting and violence in Kathmandu and King Birendra announced that a referendum would be held to choose between the current system and one that would permit political parties to operate.

Koirala, who had been in jail or in self-imposed exile since 1960, was allowed to campaign but the referendum in 1980 was 55:45 in favour of the partyless system.

Nevertheless, the king had already declared that whichever way the vote went the people would elect the country's legislature on a 5 year term and in turn it would elect the prime minister. He, however, would continue to directly appoint 20% of the legislature, and all candidates would have to be members of one of six government-approved organisations and stand under their own name, not as a representative of any party.

The first elections under this system were held in 1981. In 1986, Marich Man Singh Shrestha became prime minister after elections that were preceded by protests from the antimonarchist United Front. Parties had remained politically active despite being banned, but most of them totally boycotted the elections. Nevertheless, some national panchayat members were elected on a platform calling for reform of the partyless system.

On the surface, the panchayat system, which allowed a secret vote and universal suffrage, did not appear to be dictatorial: the constitution theoretically guaranteed freedom of speech and peaceful assembly, and the right to form unions and associations (so long as they were not motivated by party politics).

The reality was somewhat different. The military/police apparatus was one of the least publicly accountable in the world and there was strict censorship. The Indian press was banned and from time to time local papers were closed or seized. Mass arrests and beatings of suspected activists are well documented. And the leaders of the main opposition, the Nepali Congress Party, have spent the years between 1960 and 1990 in and out of prison.

Until early 1990, the king wielded considerable power. It is difficult to know quite how much – the inner workings of the palace and the king's relationships with members of the cabinet were not made public – but the constitution guaranteed his supremacy. The aristocracy, in general, managed to retain its influence and wealth (the king and his brothers are all married to Ranas) and the panchayat system did not seem to cramp their style.

In 1989 the opposition parties formed a coalition to fight for a multiparty democracy with the king as constitutional head. It seems likely that popular support was motivated in part by the economic problems caused by the Indian blockade (see the Economy section

following) and widespread discontent with blatant corruption.

In February 1990 the government responded to nonviolent protest meetings with bullets, tear gas, mass arrests and torture. However, after several months of intermittent rioting, curfews, a successful strike, and pressure from various foreign aid donors the government was forced to back down. The people's victory did not come cheaply. Estimates of the number who died range from 50 to 300.

On 9 April the king announced on national radio that he was lifting the ban on political parties and on 16 April he asked the opposition to lead an interim government prior to holding elections in spring 1991. He also announced his readiness to accept a role as a constitutional monarch. A new constitution is, at the time of writing, being drafted to reflect these changes. It must be said that the king (for many, an incarnation of Vishnu) still retains considerable popularity and his government's behaviour is often blamed on those who surround him. Despite this however, the Nepali Congress Party, led by Ganesh Man Singh, is likely to re-emerge as the country's major political force. Congress was the senior partner in the successful opposition coalition (which was also toughened, some say, by the inclusion of seven small communist factions).

Whatever does happen in the spring elections, the country's problems are likely to prove extremely difficult for any political party to solve. Nepal's ethnically and religiously fragmented population is continuing to grow at a frightening rate, the economy can only be described as fragile and its precarious position between India and China will continue to be a mixed blessing. Both local superpowers seem increasingly prepared to lean heavily on smaller neighbours if they move in what they perceive to be the wrong direction.

GEOGRAPHY

In two of the three dimensions, length and breadth, Nepal is just another small country. In the third, height, it's number one in the world. Nepal stretches from north-west to south-east about 800 km and varies in width from around 90 km to 230 km. This gives it a total area of just 147,181 sq km according to the official figures. Within that small area, however, is the greatest range of altitude to be seen on this earth because Nepal stretches from the lowland Terai, only 100 metres or so above sea level, all the way to the top of 8848 metre Mt Everest, the highest point on earth.

In cross section Nepal can be divided into four distinct bands. Starting at the bottom by the Indian border there is the low-lying Terai. This fertile band of jungle was a disease-ridden wilderness until the 1950s when malaria control programmes prompted a rapid increase in population, with devastating results for the jungle and its previously prolific wildlife.

Band two includes the succeeding ranges of foothills, first the green-clad Siwalik Hills and then the higher, barer Mahabharat Range. This band of hills separates the low-

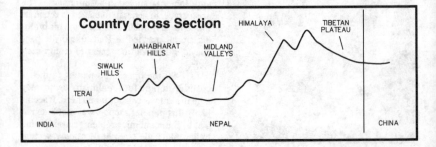

Country Cross Section

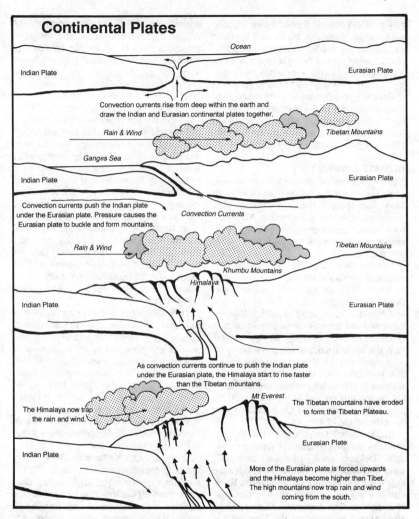

Continental Plates

Ocean

Indian Plate

Eurasian Plate

Convection currents rise from deep within the earth and draw the Indian and Eurasian continental plates together.

Rain & Wind

Tibetan Mountains

Ganges Sea

Indian Plate

Eurasian Plate

Convection currents push the Indian plate under the Eurasian plate. Pressure causes the Eurasian plate to buckle and form mountains.

Convection Currents

Rain & Wind

Tibetan Mountains

Khumbu Mountains

Himalaya

Indian Plate

Eurasian Plate

As convection currents continue to push the Indian plate under the Eurasian plate, the Himalaya start to rise faster than the Tibetan mountains.

The Himalaya now trap the rain and wind.

Mt Everest

The Tibetan mountains have eroded to form the Tibetan Plateau.

Indian Plate

Eurasian Plate

More of the Eurasian plate is forced upwards and the Himalaya become higher than Tibet. The high mountains now trap rain and wind coming from the south.

lying Terai from the midland valleys which shelter a large proportion of the country's population. This third band is principally between 1000 and 2000 metres above sea level. Finally the fourth band encompasses the high peaks of the Himalaya, forming a barrier between the subcontinent and the high plateau of Tibet.

Nepal is a zone of massive geological change as the Indian and Asian plates collide. The Indian plate continues to push under the Asian plate, with the result that the Himalaya is increasing in height at a rate of about 2 mm a year! The mountains rise steeply on the southern side then slope gradually away on the northern, Tibetan, side. Most of the

Nepal-Tibet border is formed by the highest peaks of the Himalaya. Mt Everest actually sits astride the border and numerous other peaks can be seen to lie right on the border. Nepal is widest in the west and at one point the country's mysterious Mustang Province is actually a geographic part of the desert-like Tibetan plateau. In the west there is also a stretch near Nepalganj where the southern border with India is actually on the Siwalik Hills and there is effectively no Terai.

CLIMATE & WHEN TO GO

Nepal has a typical monsoonal two season year. There's the dry season from October to May and there's the wet season, the monsoon, from June to September. Although the monsoon can be thought of as simply one season, the dry season can usefully be split into three periods.

October-November, the start of the dry season, is in many ways the best time of year in Nepal. With the monsoon only recently finished the countryside is green and lush and Nepal is at its most beautiful. Rice is harvested and there are some important and colourful festivals to enjoy. At this time of year the air is sparkling clean, visibility is unexcelled and the Himalayan views are as near perfect as you can ask. Furthermore the weather is still balmy, neither too hot (as it can be towards the end of the dry season or during the monsoon) nor too cold (as it can be at the height of winter).

In December-January the climate and visibility are still good, though it can get very cold. Trekkers need to be well prepared, snow can even be encountered on high altitude treks and heading for the Everest Base Camp at this time of year can be a real feat of endurance. The Annapurna Circuit trek is often closed by snow on the Thorong La pass. Down in Kathmandu the cheaper hotels, where heating is nonexistent, are often chilly and gloomy in the evenings. There's sometimes a brief 'winter monsoon', lasting just a day or two in January.

February-March-April, the tail end of the dry season, is a good second-best time. The weather gets warmer so high altitude treks are no longer as arduous, although by the end of the dry season, before the monsoon breaks, it starts to get too hot for comfort. Visibility is not so good as the country is now very dry and dust in the air reduces that crystal Himalayan clarity. In compensation Nepal's wonderful rhododendrons and other flowers are in bloom so there's plenty of colour to be seen along the trekking trails.

May and the early part of June are not the best months as it is extremely hot and dusty and the coming monsoon hangs over you like a threat. Finally the monsoon comes from mid-June to September and this is the least popular time to visit Nepal. The rains wash the dust out of the air, but the clouds obscure the mountains so you're unlikely to enjoy more than a rare glimpse of the Himalaya. Although it doesn't rain all day it usually does rain every day and the trails (and the roads in most Nepalese towns) will be muddy and unpleasant. Many trails will be plagued by leeches making trekking even less pleasant.

Despite leeches and slippery trails it is possible to trek during the monsoon, although high rivers may further complicate matters and it's certainly not as pleasant as other times of year. Landslides sometimes block roads during the monsoon but many visitors come to Nepal from India as the weather is even less pleasant down on the plains. The latter part of the monsoon, the months of August-September, are a time of festivals which will certainly enliven a visit to Kathmandu at that time of year.

In the summer Kathmandu can get very hot with temperatures often in the 30°Cs. Even in the winter the bright sunny days often reach 20°C although with nightfall the mercury may plummet to near freezing. It never actually snows in the Kathmandu Valley and higher up the coldest weather is also the driest weather so snow is unusual. Due to its lower altitude Pokhara is warmer and more pleasant than Kathmandu in the winter, but hotter when the temperature builds up and wetter during the monsoon.

Surprisingly Kathmandu is actually further south than New Delhi, on about the same latitude as Cairo, Miami or Taipei. Nepal is about 1500 km closer to the equator than the Alps in Europe so the snow line is much higher.

How Long to Visit

If you are visiting during the monsoon, and your stay is restricted to the Kathmandu Valley, a week is probably quite enough. During the dry season you really need more like a month to enjoy the country: a week or two for Kathmandu and the surrounding area, a week for a short trek, and a week for Pokhara and a visit to the Royal Chitwan National Park. If you want to walk some of the longer trekking routes then you had better extend your visit – it takes 3 weeks to walk the Annapurna Circuit.

NATIONAL PARKS & CONSERVATION AREAS

Nepal has eight national parks and three wildlife reserves that give good representation of every significant ecological system in the country – from the tropical plains of the Terai, to the fertile midland valleys, to the highest mountains in the world.

Altogether, over 10,000 sq km are protected, or 7% of the country's area, and you can add another 2600 sq km if you include the Annapurna Conservation Area. Considering the strength of the demand for land, there has been a particularly impressive commitment to conservation.

Travellers are almost certain to visit a protected area – the Sagarmatha National Park includes Mt Everest, the Annapurna Conservation Area includes many of the most popular treks around the Annapurna Himal, and the Royal Chitwan National Park is famous for its elephant-back safaris in search of Royal Bengal tigers and rhinoceroses.

All visitors are charged Rs 250 (or around US$10) for entering a park or reserve, except for the Annapurna Conservation Area where the entry fee is Rs 200. Organised groups will find the fee is included in the cost of their package, trekkers pay it when they apply for their trekking permit, and individuals visiting Chitwan will pay it every time they cross

the river from Sauraha. The Department of National Parks & Wildlife Conservation (tel 2-20912) has a number of brochures on individual parks and can be contacted through PO Box 860, Babar Mahal, Kathmandu. Babar Mahal is a well-known complex of government offices on the main road to the airport.

The problems that Nepal has faced in setting aside areas for conservation are more acute than those faced in most industrially developed countries, but the Nepalese are responding by developing new management concepts – it is not possible or desirable to set aside areas of land that are totally untouched by humans.

Firstly, very little of Nepal can be accurately described as wilderness. Most of the country is, in some way, used by humans. Virtually every possible cm of arable land is used for farming; the remaining forests are utilised for firewood, hunting and grazing; the high country is used for hunting and grazing; and the whole country is criss-crossed with trade routes. The only exceptions are several royal hunting reserves, some of the Terai (large parts of which were untouched until the 1950s), and mountain peaks at high altitude.

Secondly, developing national parks and conservation areas by following the Western model would have meant totally blocking local people's access to a resource that might literally mean the difference between life and death. In most cases, therefore, the Nepalese have attempted to marry the competing interests between conservation (and tourist attractions?) on the one hand and farming (and food?) on the other.

For instance, the Sagarmatha National Park is the traditional home to several thousand Sherpas whose ancestors settled the area 500 years ago. Banishing them from their homeland would have been unthinkable, so the park management has been responsible for encouraging sustainable economic development, as well as controlling the impact of a growing number of tourists.

In another example, although thousands of recent settlers were actually moved outside

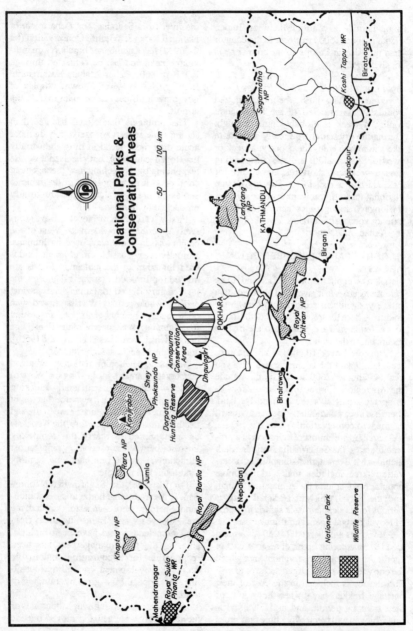

the park's boundary when it was declared, the Royal Chitwan National Park is still used by them as an important source for thatching grass, which is harvested every year.

Despite these essential compromises, there have been some notable successes. The magnificent Royal Bengal tiger was saved in Chitwan and there have been impressive achievements in the Sagarmatha National Park and the Annapurna Conservation Area – in forestry, agriculture, health and education, as well as in protecting some of the most spectacular scenery in the world.

Koshi Tappu Wildlife Reserve

The Koshi Tappu Wildlife Reserve is a small (6.5 sq km) reserve that lies on the beautiful floodplain of the Sapt Kosi (one of the three largest tributaries to the Ganges) in eastern Nepal. It runs north from the massive Kosi Barrage and the Indian border.

The reserve is often flooded during the monsoon, although mostly to shallow depths only. It is, nonetheless, home to the last surviving group of wild buffalo and several species of deer. The vegetation is mainly grassland with some scrub forest and mixed riverine forest. A total of 280 different species of birds – including many migrants – have been recorded. Local villages harvest grasses for thatching as well as fish and edible fruits and ferns.

The Mahendra Highway skirts the reserve, but there is no nearby accommodation. See the Terai chapter for complete details.

Sagarmatha National Park

North-east of Kathmandu and bordering the Tibetan border the Sagarmatha National Park covers 114.8 sq km, all above 3000 metres in altitude. Mt Everest is the single main attraction, but there are a number of other well-known peaks, including Lhotse and Ama Dablam. The mountains are broken by deep gorges, glacial valleys and lakes.

Tree species include pine, fir, juniper and birch, as well as numerous species of rhododendron. Amongst the animals, there are musk deer, Himalayan tahr, black bears, wolves, and there is fascinating birdlife. The most famous would be the beautiful Impeyan pheasant, the national bird of Nepal, but there are choughs, snow pigeons and Himalayan griffons among 130 others.

Over 3500 Sherpas use the park for cropping and grazing (their villages are not included in the park proper) and their unique culture provides yet another reason to visit. There are several important monasteries. For detailed information on this park try to find a copy of *Sagarmatha, Mother of the Universe – The Story of Mt Everest National Park* by Margaret Jefferies (Cobb/Horwood Publications, Auckland, New Zealand) an excellent book that gives fascinating background information, as well as some magnificent photos.

This is one of the most popular trekking regions in the country, but it's only accessible by foot, with the nearest airstrip at Lukla and the roadhead at Lamosangu. Many trekkers visit, lured by the highest and most spectacular mountain scenery in the world and Sherpa culture. See the Trekking chapter for information on trekking in general, and treks in this region in particular.

Royal Chitwan National Park

South-west of Kathmandu, near the Indian border on the tropical Terai, the Royal Chitwan National Park and contiguous Parsa Wildlife Reserve cover just over 98 sq km. The park includes much of the Churia hills and the Rapti, Narayani and Reu valleys.

Sal forest covers 70% of the parks, with the remaining consisting of grasslands and riverine forests. This is home to the only significant number of rhinoceroses surviving in Nepal, and other endangered species like the Royal Bengal tiger, Gangetic dolphin and gharial crocodile. Altogether, there are over 50 species of large mammals and over 400 species of birds. There are no human communities actually in the park, but the surrounding countryside is intensively cultivated.

The park is easily accessible by road, and accommodation ranges from five-star and expensive, to zero-star and cheap. Many people visit for 2 or 3 days (especially if they are going to or from India) to take advantage of elephant safaris through the forest. See the Terai chapter for complete details.

Annapurna Conservation Area

North of Pokhara and extending to the Tibetan border, the Annapurna Conservation Area covers 260 sq km. It includes the Annapurna peaks, the famous Annapurna Sanctuary and a significant section of the Kali Gandaki Valley.

The conservation area is run by a non-governmental, non-profit organisation (the Annapurna Conservation Area Project, or ACAP) which is funded by various trusts. Its primary objectives are to improve local standards of living, to protect the environment and develop more sensitive forms of tourism.

This is the most popular trekking region in Nepal, especially for individual trekkers, and this influx of visitors has added to the pre-existing problems in the mountains. The trekkers' demands for heating and hot water have led to increased deforestation, there are litter and sanitation problems, and wildlife has been driven away from many parts.

In response, ACAP has started work on a number of projects, like forestry nurseries, introducing wood-saving technologies (eg efficient stoves), banning fires altogether in certain areas, and building rubbish tips and latrines. Many problems still remain, and it is vital that trekkers cooperate with these and other initiatives. If you would like more information on ACAP activities, contact the King Mahendra Trust (tel 2-23229), PO Box 3712, Babar Mahal, Kathmandu.

The treks around the Annapurna Himal are undoubtedly some of the best in the world – not only for the grandeur of the mountains, but also for the variety of fascinating cultures that you can visit (Bhotiya, Tibetan, Tamang, Magar, Gurung, Thakali and others). The area is easily accessible from Pokhara and there is an airstrip at Jomsom. See the Trekking chapter for more information on trekking in general and this region in particular.

Langtang National Park

This is the nearest national park to Kathmandu, extending from 32 km north of Kathmandu to the Tibetan border, and covering 171 sq km. The park encloses the catchments for two major rivers – the Trisuli and the Sun Kosi – and several 7000 metre mountains.

The complex topography and geology of the area together with the varied climatic patterns means there is a wide variety of vegetation types and animals. There are small areas of subtropical forest below 1000 metres, then temperate oak and pine forests, subalpine juniper, larch and birch, and finally alpine scrub, rocks and snow. The fauna includes, pandas, muntjacs, musk deer, black bear, ghoral, serows and monkeys.

About 45 villages lie within the park boundaries (although they do not come under park jurisdiction). In total, around 18,000 people depend on the park's resources, mainly for wood and pasture land. There are several ethnic groups, but the majority are Tamangs (settlers from Tibet and followers of the pre-Buddhist Bon-po religion).

There are a number of popular treks in the park, ranging in length and difficulty. There is road access to Dhunche (the park head-quarters) from Kathmandu, or you can walk in from Sundarijal, Panchkal, or from Chautara or Tatopani on the Kodari road. See the Trekking chapter for more details.

Dhorpatan Hunting Reserve

The 132.5 sq km Dhorpatan Hunting Reserve lies in the Dhaulagiri Himal in western Nepal. It is characterised by a dry climate in the north and well-developed mixed hardwood forests at lower elevations.

The reserve is one of the prime habitats for the blue sheep, a highly prized trophy animal. Other 'game' animals include ghoral, serow, Himalayan thar, Himalayan black bear, pheasants and partridges. I imagine trekkers would also make good sport.

The only access, unless you have a helicopter, is by foot from Jelbang.

Shey Phoksundo National Park

The Shey Phoksundo National Park is the largest park in Nepal at 355 sq km. It encompasses the Kanjiroba Himal in western Nepal and runs north to the Tibetan border.

The park includes representative examples of the complete range of environments that can be found in Nepal – from the luxuriant forest of the lower Himalaya to the near desert of the Tibetan Plateau. Typical animals include the Tibetan hare, Himalayan weasel and the beautiful snow leopard. Lake Phoksundo and Shey Monastery are the two main attractions in the park, but the entire region has been little touched by the 20th century.

Very few people visit this region, partly because access has, in the past, been officially restricted and it is a very long (14 days) and dangerous trek from Pokhara. Permits can now be arranged through trekking companies. See *Trekking in Hidden Land of Dolpa-Tarap & Shey Poksumdo* by Paolo Gondini (Tiwari's Pilgrims Book House, Kathmandu) for more detailed information. According to information from the department, it takes 2 days to walk to the entrance gate for Sumduwa from Dunai, the district headquarters for Dolpo.

Rara National Park

In little-visited western Nepal, the 10 sq km Rara National Park was established to preserve the catchment and surrounds of the beautiful Rara Lake – a clear high altitude lake ringed with pine, spruce and juniper forests and snow-capped peaks. The lake is the largest in Nepal and is an important habitat for resident and migratory water birds.

The only way to get to Rara Lake is a strenuous 4 day walk from the airstrip at Jumla, or from the roadhead at Surkhet. Trekking in this area is much more difficult than in east or central Nepal: some areas are still closed and there are frequent food shortages. See *Trekking in the Nepal Himalaya* by Stan Armington for more details.

Royal Bardia National Park

In the western Terai, bordering the Karnali River, this 96.8 sq km reserve is reminiscent in many ways of the Royal Chitwan National Park. The difficulty of access, however, means it is much less popular. And there is a higher likelihood of seeing a Royal Bengal tiger.

The reserve is bordered to the north by the Siwalik Hills, but is predominantly flat and dominated by sal forests and grasslands. Apart from tigers there is a small herd of introduced rhinoceroses, blue bull, a variety of deer and at least one wild elephant. If you're lucky you might also see Gangetic dolphin in the river.

The park is 4 hours by road from Nepalganj and there is comfortable (though expensive) accommodation available. See the Terai chapter for complete details.

Khaptad National Park

Another rarely visited park, Khaptad covers 22.5 sq km in far western Nepal. Lying at around 3000 metres it is largely a rolling plateau with grasslands, and oak and coniferous forests.

Royal Sukla Phanta Wildlife Reserve

This 15.5 sq km reserve lies in the far south-western corner of Nepal on the border with India. It covers a riverine flood plain, dominated by sal forest, but like both the Chitwan and Bardia there are also grasslands which make it ideal for wildlife observation.

Sukla Phanta is one of the last strongholds for the endangered swamp deer, but there are also tigers and possibly a wild elephant or two.

Access to the park is by road from Mahendranagar and it is possible to stay in comfortable tents. See the Terai chapter for details.

ECONOMY

Judged by Western standards, Nepal is one of the poorest countries in the world with an estimated annual Gross Domestic Product (GDP) of only US$170 per person. To a certain extent, this suggests an overly bleak picture because more than 90% of the population is basically, and will almost certainly remain, subsistence farmers operating outside the cash economy.

Agriculture

At present, most farmers succeed in meeting their basic needs and producing a small surplus for cash sales. Indeed, aid workers on the Terai have been known to bemoan the fact that they can't convince peasant farmers to work harder and produce additional cash crops. The problem is that the rewards are not believed to be worth the effort. After all, if a family has food, a house, and perhaps access to a radio and bicycle, what more could they want – or realistically aspire to?

In the late '70s Nepal actually exported large quantities of rice. The development of the Terai opened up new land, temporarily relieving some of the population pressure in the hills, and the so-called green revolution (utilising improved seeds, artificial fertilisers and pesticides) led to increased productivity. The population, however, has again begun to grow more rapidly than production and Nepal will soon be forced to import rice to meet its needs. It is already a net importer of food.

The average size of land holdings has continued to drop; it now stands at around half a hectare in the hills and a little over 1½ hectares in the Terai. In a good year half a hectare in the hills around Kathmandu might produce around 1000 kg of rice and about 500 kg of mixed vegetables, but if the farmer does not own the land up to 50% of this production will go to the owner as rent. Although there are theoretical limits on the amount of land an individual may own,

tenant farmers are still common and many are in debt to money lenders.

Where possible, crops are supplemented with livestock (especially in the mountain areas), but the animals are often of poor quality, partly because there is a serious shortage of fodder, especially in winter. One of the important uses for Nepal's remaining forests is as a source for animal fodder; unfortunately this can also lead to unsustainable damage.

Manufacturing & Services

Obviously, for many people there's not much food to spare, especially if the rains fail. Although outright starvation is rare, undernourishment is common, particularly in the undeveloped west of the country. A growing number of people are forced to seek seasonal work, or rely on money that is repatriated by other family members, to supplement what they can produce from their land.

Unfortunately, Nepal's embryonic manufacturing industries (mainly on the Terai) and service sector are unable to meet the demand for work, so there is significant underemployment. Only 6% of the GDP is accounted for by manufacturing industry, 34% by service industries. There is a desperate shortage of employment opportunities.

For many people the only accessible source of income is the tourist trade – either as a market for handicrafts and other small-scale businesses (lodges, shops, travel agents and so on) or as an employee (hotel staff, porters and so on). Others work as day labourers for wealthy peasants, or try to pick up menial work in Kathmandu.

Foreign Exchange & Trade

Tourism accounts for 17% of foreign exchange earnings, although there is some controversy over how much of this leaks out of the country again in paying for the goods and services that Westerners require. Remittances, primarily from Gurkha soldiers in the Indian, British and Sultan of Brunei's armies, account for another 7%.

Some cynics claim that the two mainstays of the Nepalese economy are really smuggling and foreign aid – there are no official figures for the smuggling, but foreign aid accounts for 35% of hard currency receipts! Almost half the government's revenue depends on foreign aid and borrowing.

The country has always been an intermediary between India and China. More recently, it has become a transit point for goods from Japan, Singapore and Hong Kong. One recent rumour alleged that in 1 year Nepal imported seven million zips – where are they now? Many other goods, it is claimed, travel in a circuit from India to Nepal and back to India. For instance, it's said that much of the subsidised salt which India supplies to Nepal eventually ends up back in India, after a profit has been skimmed off in Nepal.

Nepal's trade is dominated by India in almost every respect, and many activities within the country are Indian-owned or controlled. Jute, mustard and linseed are the major commodities exported to India, which is the recipient of over 60% of Nepal's exports. Unfortunately these do not earn hard currency and, in fact, in the 1987-88 financial year India had a trade surplus with Nepal that amounted to over Rs 3000 million.

On 23 March 1989, however, a serious dispute erupted between the two countries over the terms of a new trade and transit agreement. Amongst other things, the Indians sought concessions for Indian goods. In response to Nepal's refusal, the Indian government under Rajiv Gandhi mounted an unprecedented blockade. Because Nepal is a landlocked country international law obliged the Indians to keep several border crossings open and to allow the passage of goods from third countries, but virtually all official Indo-Nepalese trade came to a dead halt. Nepal, usually almost completely dependent on India for raw materials and manufactured goods (from petrol and kerosene to spare parts and pig iron), was forced to rely on imports shipped to the unreliable port of Calcutta from places like Singapore.

The result for Nepal was catastrophic. Manufacturing industry came to a standstill. Long queues formed for petrol, kerosene, firewood, sugar and salt. Rationing was established and the government-controlled prices for these items jumped sharply, but not to the heights that were reached by the black market. Despite the hardship facing many ordinary people, the government gave the tourism sector priority, so apart from the increased cost of hiring cars and the increased crowds on buses, tourists were unaffected.

Fortunately, in June 1990, the new Nepalese and Indian governments negotiated a return to the status quo prevailing before the conflict. India re-opened the border and lifted its trade embargo. The long-term impact of the dispute on Nepal, particularly its struggling manufacturing sector, cannot yet be fully assessed and the potential remains for further trouble.

Development

It is hard to be optimistic when looking at the prospects for Nepal, despite the ingenuity and decency of the Nepalese people. The growing population threatens to overwhelm the developments that have already taken place – and future developments will always be hampered by the impossible terrain. Whether the country can continue to carry the population it already has – given that soils and forests are already being exploited at unsustainable levels – might even be questioned. For a very large number of peasant families, existence appears set to become increasingly perilous. This is likely to lead to increased migration, to the Kathmandu Valley where resources are already strained, to the Terai and to India.

In Kathmandu, the gulf between the rich and the poor is already extreme. The aristocracy still wields considerable power and influence and many of its members lead lives that are extraordinarily pampered and unrealistic. These feudal survivors have been joined by a new business elite, whose strikingly ugly houses now dot the outskirts of Kathmandu. Corruption is endemic by any standards. It is only possible to negotiate government bureaucracies and regulations if you have a very large wad of rupees.

In the meantime, poverty and expectations are increasing. It is now possible to find shanty towns in forgotten corners of Kathmandu. Discontent is rising among students, the underemployed and many members of the small middle class.

The challenges facing Nepal are clearly immense. A large and growing proportion of the population lives in poverty and over 75% is illiterate. Health services, especially outside the Kathmandu Valley, are minimal – the ratio of doctors to people was 1:20,000 in 1987-88, and there were only 4000 hospital beds. Infant mortality is 129 for every 1000 live births – nearly four times that of China – and the average life expectancy is still only around 50 years.

Family planning is of primary importance, but most people are more likely to continue to regard children as a blessing – a vital and fulfilling part of their lives, an extra pair of hands and insurance for old age – not just an extra stomach. On the positive side of the ledger, education is spreading into distant valleys, and trekkers are likely to come across thriving primary schools in the most remote areas.

Since most people are dependent on agriculture, this is the most important area for development. Much can be done to increase and sustain productivity, but here as elsewhere, the topography means there is an amazing diversity of problems and tremendous difficulties in reaching the isolated valleys and ridges where the people live.

Communications are one area where improvements are highly visible. The telephone system certainly works much better than it used to and roads continue to extend further and further into remote parts of the country. It's strange to contemplate that Pokhara had no road connections with the rest of the country or with India until the 1970s and that in Kathmandu itself the first cars were carried in by hand, as the first road from India was only built in the 1950s. Often, however, new roads bring undesirable social changes and some question whether the huge sums of money involved in their construction and maintenance might not be better allocated to expanding and improving the existing network of walking tracks and bridges. What will trekking be like when you can drive everywhere?

Nepal's physical resources are extremely limited. There are few accessible minerals, and there is little unexploited arable land. There are, however, great hydroelectric power resources although the market for them is likely to be found in India and the capital and ecological costs involved in construction are huge. Perhaps one of the most optimistic trade delegations in recent times was one from Bangladesh that suggested a number of ways trade could be expanded between the two countries. Amongst other things, they were interested in importing Nepalese boulders!

Foreign Aid

Foreign aid sounds as if it should be a wonderful industry – on the surface, totally nonpolluting and ecologically sound. Nepal has lots of it and the end result is a highly questionable one. If you're interested in the impact of foreign aid on a country like Nepal the magazine *Himal* regularly has articles which will provide food for thought. Two recent books, ostensibly accounts of travels in Nepal, will also prove enlightening.

Peter Somerville-Large's *To the Navel of the World* (Hamish Hamilton, London, 1987) contrasts the successful, heavily touristed and heavily aided Solu Khumbu region of the Sherpas in eastern Nepal with the neglected regions of the far north-west. While critics debate the damage caused by tourism it seems hardly likely that the people living in the areas where trekkers are plentiful and aid projects abound would willingly switch to the areas of Nepal which are still 'off limits'.

Charlie Pye-Smith's *Travels in Nepal* (Aurum Press, London, 1988) were essentially a trek from one aid project to another and what he saw was not always a pretty sight. Too often the projects were pointless, imposed without consulting the people they were aimed at and without adequately understanding the local physical and cultural environment. Often the only people who benefited were the foreign companies who supplied equipment and expertise and the affluent Nepalese who skimmed off a profit as the project passed by them.

The author contends that most aid donors look for big projects (they like to have something visible to show off) and that government officials like the big ones too (there's more likely to be something in it for them). The projects that actually work, however, are much closer to ground level. He comes across disastrous Japanese irrigation projects, ill-planned Austrian hydroelectric power projects and well-meaning but inept US ecological projects, but also finds a British agricultural project near Dhankuta in the east which really seemed to work and an Australian forestry project which operated on a shoestring and seemed to work much better because of that.

He concludes, however, with questioning the whole basis of foreign aid in Nepal, and by extension in other countries like Nepal. Along the way he turns up numerous interesting thoughts. Hydroelectric power,

for example, is touted as an enormous energy saver but its main use is for electric lighting. Lighting with hydroelectric power generated electricity is much cheaper than with kerosene and a great deal of expensive kerosene can be saved. But with cheap lighting people stay up later and when they stay up they burn firewood. The end result of providing hydroelectric power can actually be an increase in the consumption of scarce timber!

One of the aid project disasters he observed was a tree planting exercise where the trees were not only badly planted but also planted in an area where the first monsoon deluge washed them away. This totally wasted plantation was fenced in by cutting down healthy trees! Even the whole horror story of Himalayan deforestation is brought into question. 'The only number which has any scientific validity at all in the Himalaya is sixty-seven', he writes. This is the factor by which estimates of per capita firewood consumption vary.

PEOPLE & POPULATION

Nepal's population is estimated to be about 18.5 million. The largest city is Kathmandu, the capital, with over 300,000 people.

The rate of population growth in this small and mountainous country is terrifying. Every year the population increases by nearly half a million. In the mountains the rate of increase is about 1.8% a year, but many people are moving down from the mountains to the lowland Terai in search of work, and in that part of the country the annual population growth is over 4%. The overall rate of increase is 2.6%. In addition many Nepalese are being forced to leave the country permanently. It has been estimated that nearly 10% of Nepal's total population has now moved to India, hardly a country of wide open spaces and low population density. This dramatic population growth continues in spite of extremely high rates of infant mortality and a low life expectancy.

The rapidly growing human population is putting enormous pressures on Nepal's fragile ecology. The devastation of the Himalayan forests is of enormous concern but Nepal has few natural resources and, since almost all fuel must be imported, much wood is still burnt for heating and cooking. At the present rate there will soon be no trees left to burn.

Like the geography the population of the country is extremely diverse as Nepal is the meeting point of the Indo-Aryan people of the plains of India with the Tibeto-Burman people from north of the Himalaya. In the south the Nepalese of the Terai are closely related culturally and linguistically to the people of the north Indian states of Uttar Pradesh and Bihar. At the other extreme the Sherpa people of the high Himalaya, close to the border with the Tibetan region of China, are essentially of Tibetan stock and speak a language closely related to Tibetan. In between there are numerous groups of people who are a blend of these racial types, some of them found in very small and often isolated pockets.

The close cultural ties with India extend both ways so that while the Nepalese of the southern Terai are closely related to the Indians just across the border, in the east of the country there is strong Nepalese influence in the neighbouring Indian state of Sikkim and around Darjeeling where the Nepali language is widely spoken.

Many people of the Nepalese hills are loosely known as Gurkhas, the courageous mercenaries who have been associated with the British army for over a century. In actual fact, however, there is no Gurkha group in Nepal. The name came from the principality of Gorkha which first unified Nepal under King Prithvi Narayan Shah. Gurkha soldiers may be from any of a number of Nepalese ethnic groups. The Hindu people of Nepal have four main castes: see the Religion section later for more information.

The peoples of Nepal include:

Newaris

The Newaris of the Kathmandu Valley are a good example of the result of this Himalayan melting pot. They number about 600,000 and speak Newari, a language distinct from Tibetan or Hindi; and while they follow the Hindu religion theirs is a variant of it with many Tibetan Buddhist overtones.

Sherpa woman weaving

Sherpas

Living high in the mountains of eastern and central Nepal, in particular in the Solu Khumbu region at the foot of Mt Everest, the Sherpas are probably the best known Nepalese ethnic group. The Sherpas are Buddhists and their name has become synonymous with mountaineering and trekking. Not all sherpas – the small 's' word describing a trek guide or mountaineer – are Sherpas but many of them are and they've won worldwide fame for their hardiness and loyalty. There are about 20,000 Sherpas.

Thakalis

Originating along the Kali Gandaki Valley in central Nepal, the Thakalis are a people of mixed Hindu and Buddhist influence who have become the entrepreneurs of Nepal. They honed these skills from the days when they played an important part in the salt trade between the subcontinent and Tibet but now they are found in many areas of modern commercial life. Most Thakalis are small farmers, but travellers will regularly meet them in their adopted role of hotelier. Many small hotels in Nepal are run by Thakalis; the Pokhara to Jomsom trek along the Kali Gandaki Valley is the best 'village inn' trek in Nepal, because of the numerous Thakali lodges along this route through their homeland. The actual number of Thakalis is very small, less than 10,000.

Tamangs

As you move out from the Kathmandu Valley and leave the Newari-Hindu people you start to meet the Tamang people who are Buddhists. There are about 800,000 Tamangs and despite their name, which is Tibetan for 'horse trader', most Tamangs are subsistence farmers. You will often see Tamangs in Kathmandu, down in the valley on shopping trips or as porters carrying goods down from the hills in their large *dokos* (baskets).

Magars

A numerically large group, the Magars are subsistence farmers found in many parts of the hill country of western and central Nepal.

Tamang people

Magars are found from the high Himalaya right down to the Terai and are renowned for their martial bravery as many Gurkha soldiers are Magars. Although they are essentially Tibeto-Burman they speak a variety of languages and adopt a variety of cultural styles, depending on where they live.

Gurungs

The Gurungs tend to live in higher country and generally further to the east than the Magars, but otherwise are similar to them in many respects. They number about 300,000 and are often shepherds with numerous families in a village contributing a handful of sheep to a larger village flock. During the summer months they move their sheep to higher pastures, then bring them down to the villages with the end of the monsoon and then even further south for the winter. Like the Magars the Gurungs also often work as Gurkha soldiers.

People of the Terai

In the south of the country where Indian influence is greatest the people can be roughly divided into caste and non-caste groups. The influence of caste is not as pervasive as in India but the Brahmins and Chhetris, the two upper castes, are by far the most important even though most members of these castes will still be subsistence farmers, just like the vast majority of Nepalese. Nevertheless the Brahmins – due in large part to their literate traditions – play a major role in the government and in business. The ruling class, however, is mainly Chhetri, as were the Rana prime ministers who controlled Nepal until the 1950s.

There are numerous non-caste groups in the Terai including the Tharus, Danuwars, Majhis and Darais across the length of the Terai or the Bodos, Dhimals, Rajbansis and Satars in the far east. The Tharus number about 600,000, making them one of the largest ethnic groups in Nepal. Although the people of the Terai are predominantly Hindu, while further north the religion is a Hindu-Buddhist blend with Tantric overtones or else exclusively Buddhist, there are also pockets of Muslims numbering perhaps 400,000 in total.

Other Nepalese Groups

Other people of the intermediate hill country, any of whom may be found soldiering as Gurkhas, include Rais, Limbus, Yakhas and Sanuwars. The Rais and Limbus together are descended from the Kiratis, one of the most ancient people of Nepal. There are estimated to be about 400,000 Rais and 250,000 Limbus. Smaller hill country groups include the Chepangs, Jirels and Panchgauns.

High in the Himalaya are other small groups with close ties to Tibet, like the Sherpas. The small hidden kingdom of Mustang, nestled up against the Tibetan border, north of the Himalayan watershed, is a good example although there are only a few hundred Lopas, the people of Mustang. The Dolpo people from north of Jomsom also number only a few hundred. The Tibetan-related people of the high Himalaya are sometimes referred to as Bhotias from the word *bhot*, which means 'Tibet'. There are about 6000 Tibetans in Nepal, mainly refugees from the Chinese takeover of their country.

CULTURE & CUSTOMS

Nepal has always been a dividing line between civilisations and cultures and a crossroads for the flow of commerce and culture between them. Here the plains of the subcontinent climb up to the high plateau of Tibet, the languages and people of India give way to those of China, and the Hindu religion blends into Buddhism. Nepal, the land at the margin, is often a complex blend of the two influences and this variation is further complicated by the diversity of ethnic groups within the country.

Some Cultural Considerations

In an often totally different culture it's inevitable that the visitor will make some gaffe at some point. A miscellaneous collection of simple suggestions that will help avoid mistakes include:

• Always remove your shoes before entering a Nepalese home.
• Dress appropriately – shorts or revealing clothes are never suitable for women. Shorts are acceptable for men when trekking but going without a shirt is not. Nudity is not acceptable anywhere.
• Public displays of affection are frowned upon. Nepalese men often walk around hand in hand, but this does not have the same implications it does in San Francisco!
• Always walk clockwise around Buddhist stupas, chortens or mani walls. Always remove your shoes before entering a Buddhist or Hindu temple or sanctuary. You may also have to remove any items made from leather such as belts and bags. Many Hindu temples do not permit Westerners to enter.
• It is the custom to give a white scarf or *khata* to a Buddhist abbot or *rimpoche* when you are introduced. The scarves can easily be found at Tibetan shops.
• Raising your voice or shouting shows extreme bad manners and will not solve your problem, whatever it might be. Always try to remain cool, calm and collected.

• Fire is sacred so do not throw rubbish into it. This particularly applies to a kitchen fire in a Nepalese home and theoretically should apply to a camping site fire when trekking as well. In practice burning the garbage before leaving camp is accepted, but it's probably best to wait until just before leaving camp before doing it, certainly not before cooking. In a Nepalese home the kitchen is off limits to strangers.

• Bodily contact is rarely made, even for shaking hands, although amongst Nepalese men with frequent Western connections it is becoming more accepted. Never touch anything or point at anything with your feet, the 'lowest' part of the body. In contrast the head is spiritually the 'highest' part of the body, so don't pat children on the head.

• Don't make inquiries about a person's caste.

• The Nepalese do not like to give negative answers or no answer at all: if you are given a wrong direction or told a place is much nearer than it turns out to be, it may be through fear of disappointing you!

• Avoid 'polluting' food by inadvertently touching it or bringing it into contact with a used plate or utensil. Using your own fork or spoon to serve out more food will do this. Putting your used plate on a buffet table risks making the food still on the table *jutho* or polluted. Notice how the Nepalese drink from a cup or water vessel without letting it touch their lips.

• Don't encourage begging children. The 'give me one rupee, school pen, bonbons' requests become very tedious in some places and acceding to them will only make them worse. If you want to help there are lots of excellent aid organisations which will make good use of your contribution. Local schools will be only too happy with a gift of ballpoint pens.

• Do not intrude with a camera, unless it is clearly OK with the people you are photographing. Ask before entering a temple compound whether it is permissible to enter and take photographs. Do not exchange addresses or offer copies of photos unless you definitely intend to follow it up later.

• Your very presence will have an effect; the challenge is not to impinge upon the rights of the local people. Remember Nepal is not a Disneyland or museum established for your convenience, but home to a vital, changing culture. Life for many is extremely hard but, despite an absence of material possessions – sometimes even food – there are many qualities that shame the so-called 'developed' world.

ARTS & CRAFTS

The whole Kathmandu Valley is really one enormous art gallery and museum, but the arts and architecture in Nepal are inextricably intermingled. The finest woodcarving and the best sculpture are often part of a building – a temple is simply not a temple without its finely carved roof struts. The crafts also reflect the uniquely Nepalese melting pot where Hindu art has Tantric Buddhist overtones and the dividing line between one religion and another is hard to discern.

Lydia Aran's *The Art of Nepal* (Sahayogi Prakashan, Kathmandu, 1978) is a handy and interesting introduction to Nepalese art and its religious background. There are detailed

descriptions of the many Hindu, Buddhist and Hindu-Buddhist deities and their associated religious terminology. This book is particularly interesting because it concentrates on the art actually in Nepal, as opposed to objects in overseas museums and private collections.

Architecture & Sculpture

The earliest architecture in the valley has faded with history. The four Ashoka stupas of Patan are simply grassy mounds today and the great stupas of Swayambhunath and Bodhnath have undoubtedly changed many times over the centuries. Nevertheless these simple hemispherical Buddhist structures are essentially unchanged from their earliest appearance – they're simply a solid mound rising from the ground and topped with a spire. You can find similar Buddhist stupas in Sri Lanka, Burma and Thailand.

The Licchavi period from the 4th to 9th centuries AD was a golden age for Nepal and while the temples may have disappeared the superb stone sculptures can still be found. Many temples around the valley have beautiful pieces of Licchavi craftwork in their courtyards, the temple of Changu Narayan at the eastern end of the valley in particular. The great reclining Vishnu image at Budhanilkantha is another wonderful example of Licchavi stonework.

The Licchavis undoubtedly worked in wood as well but wood is a perishable substance and no wooden buildings or carvings survive from that era. It was in the Malla period that the Nepalese artistry with wood really came into its own. The earliest woodcarving in the valley dates from the 12th and 13th centuries and includes the roof struts of the great Basantapur Tower in the old royal palace in Kathmandu's Durbar Square and the Kasthamandap building, also in the square, from which the town takes its name. The Uku Bahal monastery in Patan also dates from this period but you have to go out of the valley to Panauti, near Banepa, to find one of the oldest and finest survivors in the shape of the Indreshwar Mahadev Temple.

The artistic skills of the Newari people of the valley flourished under the Mallas and not only woodcarving but metalwork, terracotta, brickwork, stone sculptures and other crafts all enjoyed a long golden age. The finest metalwork includes the images of the two Tara goddesses at Swayambhunath and the river goddesses Ganga and Jamuna, standing guard in the palace of Patan.

The spread of the multiroofed Nepalese pagoda design to China and eastern Asia is credited to the architect Arniko, who with 24 assistants visited Tibet in the late 13th century and later also worked for the Ming emperor. The road to the Tibetan border is named the Arniko Highway in his honour. The contact with Tibet also began to make its way back to Nepal and the vivid Tibetan colours and fantastic Tibetan creatures also started to appear in Nepalese art and architecture.

The last centuries of the Malla period saw temple after temple rise over the Kathmandu Valley skyline. The squabbling city-states of Kathmandu, Patan and Bhaktapur vied with each other to raise yet more glorious temples and palaces. Much of the construction was still in the traditional multiroofed Nepalese pagoda style but there was also a great deal of Indian influence – such as the stone Krishna Mandir of Patan's Durbar Square or the shikara-style spires of the Mahabouddha Temple in Patan and the two temples at the top of the stairway to Swayambhunath.

With the invasion of the valley by King Prithvi Narayan Shah from Gorkha the great age of Nepalese architecture came to a dramatic end. The great woodcarved temples and palaces you marvel at in the valley today mainly date from that brilliant period prior to 1767. Although the skills used to build them have lain dormant in the centuries since then, there is no doubt that they are still alive. When the Hanuman Dhoka Palace in Kathmandu and the Tachupal Tole buildings in Bhaktapur were restored in the 1970s the work was performed by purely traditional means and with craftwork every bit as good as in the past. More recently the Chyasilin Mandapa in Bhaktapur, completely destroyed in the great earthquake of 1934, was totally

rebuilt in 1989-90, again using traditional skills.

Painting

Today Tibetan inspired *thangkas* are churned out for the tourist market but Nepal has a long history of painting and some high-quality traditional work is still being done today. The earliest Newari paintings were illuminated manuscripts dating from the 11th century and these were followed by miniature paintings, influenced by the miniature styles of north India, and then by scrolls and murals. By this time the Tibetan influence was starting to make itself felt on Newari painting, although from the 14th to 16th centuries the Newaris also had a great influence on Tibetan art.

Today some of the best examples of old Newari painting are hung in temples where they are rarely seen but the Art Gallery in Bhaktapur has a fine collection and is an excellent introduction to the development of art in Nepal. Newari artists have their own special caste of *chitrakar*. For more information on painting in Nepal today see the Things to Buy section in the Facts for the Visitor chapter.

Music & Dance

Despite the pervasiveness of Western music Nepalese music hangs constantly in the air, whether it is the plaintive notes of a flute or the gentle twang of the four stringed *saringhi*. Although the *gaines*, traditional professional musicians, are a dying breed they can still be heard. The folk music of rural Nepal still has a strong following and the gaines are often as much storytellers as musicians.

The *damais* are modern professional musicians, all drawn from the tailor caste, who form the backbone of wedding bands. This music can definitely be hard on Western ears, falling uncomfortably close to the painful standards of Indian video bus music. The blaring wail of long Tibetan horns at Buddhist religious sites also qualifies for the unlistenable category.

Dance also has a long and strong history in Nepal both in cheerfully performed folk dances and in the more formal classical dances. The Newaris of the Kathmandu Valley are the chief exponents of classical dancing, but there are also masked dances with a Tantric background and the colourful masked dances of Bhaktapur which are performed during the Indra Jatra festival each year.

RELIGION

In Nepal Hinduism and Buddhism are mingled into a complex blend which is often impossible to separate. The Buddha was actually born in Nepal but the Buddhist religion first arrived in the country around 250 BC, introduced, so it is said, by the great Indian Buddhist emperor Ashoka himself. Later, Buddhism gave way to Hinduism but from around the 8th century AD the Tantric form of Buddhism practised in Tibet also began to make its way across the Himalaya into Nepal. Today Buddhism is mainly practised by the people of the high Himalaya, like the Sherpas, Gurungs and Tamangs, and by the Tibetan refugees who have settled in Nepal.

Officially Nepal is a Hindu country but in practice the religion is a strange blend of Hindu and Tantric Buddhist beliefs with a pantheon of Tantric deities tagged onto the list of Hindu gods or, in many cases, inextricably blended with them. Thus Avalokitesvara, the prime Bodhisattva of this Buddhist era, becomes Lokesvara, a manifestation of the Hindu god Shiva, and then appears as Machhendranath, one of the most popular gods of the Kathmandu Valley. Is he Hindu or Buddhist? Nobody can tell.

Although the vast majority of the population is Hindu or Buddhist there are also small groups of Muslims and Christians. The Muslims are mainly found close to the border with India and in the odd isolated village.

Hinduism

India, the Indonesian island of Bali, the Indian Ocean island of Mauritius and possibly Fiji are the only places apart from Nepal where Hindus predominate, but it is the largest religion in Asia in terms of the number of adherents. Hinduism is one of the oldest extant religions with firm roots extending back to beyond 1000 BC.

The Indus Valley civilisation developed a religion which shows a close relationship to Hinduism in many ways. Later, it further developed on the subcontinent through the combined religious practices of the Dravidians and the Aryan invaders who arrived in the north of India around 1500 BC. Around 1000 BC, the Vedic scriptures were introduced and gave the first loose framework to the religion.

Hinduism today has a number of holy books, the most important being the four *Vedas*, or 'Divine Knowledge', which are the foundation of Hindu philosophy. The *Upanishads* are contained within the *Vedas* and delve into the metaphysical nature of the universe and soul. The *Mahabharata* is an epic poem describing in over 220,000 lines the battles between the Kauravas and Pandavas. It contains the story of Rama, and it is probable that the most famous Hindu epic, the *Ramayana*, was based on this. The *Bhagavad Gita* is a famous episode of the *Mahabharata* where Krishna relates his philosophies to Arjuna.

Hinduism postulates that we will all go through a series of rebirths or reincarnations that eventually lead to *moksha*, the spiritual salvation which frees one from the cycle of rebirths. With each rebirth you can move closer to or further from eventual moksha; the deciding factor is your karma, which is literally a law of cause and effect. Bad actions during your life result in bad karma, which ends in a lower reincarnation. Conversely, if your deeds and actions have been good you will reincarnate on a higher level and be a step closer to eventual freedom from rebirth.

Dharma is the natural law which defines the total social, ethical and spiritual harmony of your life. There are three categories of dharma, the first being the eternal harmony which involves the whole universe. The second category is the dharma that controls castes and the relations between castes. The third dharma is the moral code which an individual should follow.

The Hindu religion has three basic practices. They are *puja* or worship, the cremation of the dead, and the rules and regulations of the caste system. There are four main castes: the Brahmin, or priest caste; the Chhetris, or soldiers and governors; the Vaisyas, or tradespeople and farmers; and the Sudras or menial workers and craftspeople. These basic castes are then subdivided, although this is not taken to the same extent in Nepal as in India. Beneath all the castes are the Harijans, or untouchables, the lowest, casteless class for whom all the most menial and degrading tasks are reserved.

Westerners have trouble understanding Hinduism principally because of its vast pantheon of gods. In fact you can look upon all these different gods simply as pictorial representations of the many attributes of a god. The one omnipresent god usually has three physical representations. Brahma is the creator, Vishnu is the preserver and Shiva is the destroyer and reproducer. All three gods are usually shown with four arms, but Brahma has the added advantage of four heads.

Each god has an associated animal known as the 'vehicle' on which they ride, as well as a consort with certain attributes and abilities. Generally each god also holds symbols; you can often pick out which god is represented by the vehicle or symbols. Most temples are dedicated to one or other of the gods, but most Hindus profess to be either Vaishnavites (followers of Vishnu) or Shaivites (followers of Shiva). A variety of lesser gods and goddesses also crowd the scene. The cow is, of course, the holy animal of Hinduism.

Hinduism is not a proselytising religion since you cannot be converted. You're either born a Hindu or you are not; you can never become one. Similarly, once you are a Hindu you cannot change your caste – you're born into it and are stuck with it for the rest of that lifetime. Nevertheless Hinduism has a great attraction for many Westerners and India's 'export gurus' are numerous and successful.

A guru is not so much a teacher as a spiritual guide, somebody who by example or simply by their presence indicates what path you should follow. In a spiritual search one always needs a guru. A sadhu is an individual on a spiritual search. They're an easily recognised group, usually wandering around half-naked, smeared in dust with their hair and beard matted. Sadhus most often follow Shiva and generally carry his symbol, the trident.

Sadhus are often people who have decided that their business and family life have reached their natural conclusions and that it is time to throw everything aside and go out on a spiritual search. They may previously have been the village postal worker, or a business person. Sadhus perform various feats of self-mortification and wander all over the subcontinent, occasionally coming together in great pilgrimages and other religious gatherings. Many sadhus are, of course, simply beggars following a more sophisticated approach to gathering in the paisa, but others are completely genuine in their search.

Buddhism

Strictly speaking Buddhism is not a religion, since it is not centred on a god, but a system of philosophy and a code of morality. Buddhism was founded in northern India about 500 BC when Siddhartha Gautama, born a prince, achieved enlightenment. Gautama Buddha was not the first Buddha but the fourth, and is not expected to be the last 'enlightened one'. Buddhists believe that the achievement of enlightenment is the goal of every being so eventually we will all reach Buddhahood.

The Buddha never wrote down his dharma or teachings, and a schism later developed so that today there are two major Buddhist schools. The Theravada or Hinayana, 'doctrine of the elders' or 'small vehicle' holds that the path to nirvana, the eventual aim of all Buddhists, is an individual pursuit. In contrast, the Mahayana or 'large vehicle' school holds that the combined belief of its followers will eventually be great enough to encompass all of humanity and bear it to salvation. To some the less austere and ascetic Mahayana school is a 'soft option'. Today it is chiefly practised in Vietnam, Japan and China, while the Hinayana school is followed in Sri Lanka, Burma (Myanmar) and Thailand. There are other, sometimes more esoteric, divisions of Buddhism including the Hindu-Tantric Buddhism of Tibet which is the version found in Nepal.

The Buddha renounced his material life to search for enlightenment but, unlike other prophets, found that starvation did not lead to discovery. Therefore he developed his rule of the 'middle way', moderation in everything. The Buddha taught that all life is suffering, but that suffering comes from our sensual desires and the illusion that they are important. By following the 'eight-fold path' these desires will be extinguished and a state of nirvana, where they are extinct and we are free from their delusions, will be reached. Following this process requires going through a series of rebirths until the goal is eventually reached and no more rebirths into

the world of suffering are necessary. The path that takes you through this cycle of births is karma, but this is not simply fate. Karma is a law of cause and effect; your actions in one life determine the role you will play and what you will have to go through in your next life.

In India Buddhism developed rapidly when it was embraced by the great emperor Ashoka. As his empire extended over much of the subcontinent, so Buddhism was carried forth. Later, however, Buddhism began to contract in India because it had never really taken a hold on the great mass of people. As Hinduism revived, Buddhism in India was gradually reabsorbed into the older religion.

THE GODS OF NEPAL

There are so many gods, and related auspicious beings, in Nepal that being able to identify some of them makes understanding and enjoying Nepalese culture much easier. The definitions that follow include the most interesting and most frequently encountered 'big names' plus associated creatures, consorts, vehicles and religous terminology.

Incarnations, Manifestations & Aspects

There's a subtle difference between these three possibilities, something not easily grasped by the Western mind! Vishnu has incarnations, 10 of them in all. They include Narsingha, the man-lion, Krishna the cowherd and Buddha the teacher. Shiva, on the other hand, may be the god of 1000 names but these are manifestations – what he shows himself as – not incarnations. He is a god of many manifestations but few incarnations. And when you start to look at the Buddhist 'gods', which is all wrong because Buddhism is not supposed to have any gods, their various appearances are aspects rather than incarnations or manifestations!

Shiva

Shiva is probably the most important god in Nepal – as creator and destroyer – so it's important to keep on his good side! Shiva is often represented by the phallic *lingam*,

Shiva, Parvati & Ganesh

symbolic of his creative role. His vehicle is the bull Nandi and you'll often see this figure outside Shiva temples; there's a huge Nandi guarding the entrance to Pashupatinath. The symbol most often seen in Shiva's hand is the trident or *trisul*. Sadhus, the wandering pilgrims who are usually followers of Shiva, often carry a trident.

Shiva is also known as Nataraja, the cosmic dancer whose dance shook the cosmos and created the world. Shiva's home is Mt Kailash in the Himalaya, but across the border in Tibet, and he's also supposed to be keen on smoking hashish. He takes various forms including peaceful Pashupati and destructive Bhairab. Usually his fearsome side is handled by his *shakti* or consort (see the later Shakti section); sacrifices are usually made not to the male but to the female and must be of male animals.

Bhairab

In Nepal Shiva appears as Bhairab when he is in his fearful or 'terrific' form. Bhairab can appear in 64 different ways but none of them is pretty. Typically he has multiple arms, each clutching a weapon, he dances on a body and wears a headdress of skulls. More skulls dangle from his belt, and his staring eyes and bared fangs complete the picture. Bhairab is usually black, carries a cup made from a human skull and is attended by a dog. The gruesome figure of Bhairab near the Hanuman Dhoka Palace entrance in Kathmandu is a good example of this fearsome god at his worst.

Pashupati

In the Kathmandu Valley Shiva is most popularly worshipped as Pashupati, the lord of the beasts. As the keeper of all living things Pashupati is Shiva in a good mood and the temple of Pashupatinath is the most important Hindu temple in the country.

Machhendranath

Machhendranath is a strictly Nepalese Hindu god who has power over the rains and the monsoon. It's typical of the intermingling of Hindu and Buddhist beliefs in Nepal that, in the Kathmandu Valley at least, Machhendranath has come to be thought of as an incarnation of Avalokitesvara, the Bodhisattva of our era. In actual fact the connection from Avalokitesvara to Machhendranath is not quite so direct. Purely Buddhist Avalokitesvara is linked with Shiva through Lokesvara, the lord of the world. Machhendranath is then a manifestation of Lokesvara.

Brahma

Brahma, despite his supreme position, appears much less often than Shiva or Vishnu. Like those gods he has four arms but Brahma also has four heads, to represent his all-seeing presence. The four *Vedas* are supposed to have emanated from his mouths.

Ganesh

With his elephant head Ganesh is probably the most easily recognised of the gods and also the most popular. Ganesh is the god of prosperity and wisdom and there are many Ganesh shrines and temples in Nepal. Ganesh's parents are Shiva and Parvati and he obtained his elephant head due to his father's notorious temper. Coming back from a long trip, Shiva discovered Parvati in bed with a young man. Not pausing to think that their son might have grown up a little during his absence, Shiva lopped his head off! He was then forced by Parvati to bring his son back to life but could only do so by giving him the head of the first living thing he saw – which happened to be an elephant.

Shiva and Parvati's other son is Kumar, the god of war. He is also known as Kartikkaya.

Hanuman

Hanuman is the monkey god, the important character from the *Ramayana* who came to the aid of Rama and helped to defeat the evil Rawana and release Sita from his grasp. Hanuman's trustworthy and alert nature is commemorated by the many statues of

---

Hanuman & Medicine

Hanuman the monkey god has an important medicinal connection in Nepal and other Hindu countries. The *Ramayana* recounts how Rama desperately needed a rare herb grown only in the Himalaya and sent Hanuman to procure it for him. Unfortunately by the time he arrived in the mountains Hanuman had forgotten specifically which herb he had been requested to bring back, but got around the problem by simply grabbing a whole mountain, confident that somewhere on the mountain would be the required plant. On the walls of the Bir Hospital in Kathmandu you can see a large illustration of Hanuman flying through the air, tightly clasping a whole mountain. It's said that he paused for a rest on the banks of the Hanumante River in Bhaktapur and another picture of this event can be seen there. ■

Ganesh

Hanuman seen guarding palace entrances. The best known in Nepal is the image of Hanuman which stands beside the Old Royal Palace entrance in Kathmandu, and indeed gives the old palace its name of Hanuman Dhoka.

Vishnu

Vishnu is the preserver, although in Nepal, where he often appears as Narayan, he also plays a role in the original creation of the universe. Narayan is the reclining Vishnu, sleeping on the cosmic ocean, and from his navel appears Brahma, who creates the universe.

Vishnu has four arms and can often be identified by the symbols he holds – the conch shell or *sankha*, the disc-like weapon known as a *chakra*, the stick-like weapon known as a *gada* and a lotus flower or *padma*. Vishnu's vehicle is the man-bird Garuda and the figure of a Garuda will often be seen kneeling reverently in front of a Vishnu temple. Vishnu's shakti is Lakshmi, the goddess of wealth and prosperity.

Vishnu has 10 incarnations starting with Matsya, the fish. Then he appeared as Kurma, the tortoise on which the universe is built. Number three was his boar incarnation as Varaha, who destroyed a demon who would have drowned the world. Vishnu was again in a demon-destroying mood in incarnation four as Narsingha (or Narsimha), half man and half lion. See the Changunarayan section in the Around the Valley chapter for the legend behind this appearance. Nar-

singha statues often show a man with a lion's head and four arms holding the traditional Vishnu symbols. On the man-lion's lap will be the demon which Narsingha is about to disembowel.

Still facing difficulties from demons Vishnu's next incarnation was Vamana, the dwarf who reclaimed the world from the demon-king Bali. The dwarf politely asked the demon for a patch of ground upon which to meditate, saying that the patch need only be big enough that he, the dwarf, could walk across it in three paces. The demon agreed, only to see the dwarf swell into a giant who strode across the universe in three gigantic steps. Vishnu as the 'long strider' is often seen with his left leg raised, just about to take a mighty step.

In incarnation six Vishnu appeared as Parasurama, a warlike Brahmin who proceeded to put the warrior caste Chhetris in their place. The noble Rajputs of India's state of Rajasthan claim they are descended from the survivors of this clash with a god. Incarnation seven was as Rama, the hero of the *Ramayana* who, with help from Hanuman the monkey god, rescued his beautiful wife Sita from the clutches of Rawana, evil king of Lanka.

Incarnation eight was a gentle and much-loved one when Vishnu appeared as Krishna,

Vishnu reincarnated as Vamana

the fun-loving cowherd, who dallied with the *gopis* or milkmaids, danced, played his flute and still managed to remain devoted to his wife Radha. The Bhakti cult follow this passionate and happy incarnation.

For number nine Vishnu appeared as the teacher, the Buddha. Of course the Buddhists don't accept that Buddha was just an incarnation of some other religion's god but perhaps it was just a ploy to bring Hindu converts back into the fold? Incarnation 10? Well we haven't seen that one yet but it will be as Kalki the destroyer, when Vishnu wields the sword which will destroy the world at the end of the Kaliyuga, the age which we are currently in.

Garuda

The Garuda is the faithful man-bird vehicle of Vishnu and a winged Garuda statue will often be found kneeling reverentially in front of a Vishnu temple. Garuda has an intense hatred of snakes and is often seen destroying them.

Shakti

A Hindu god's consort is also known as his *shakti* as she is far more than just a companion. A shakti often symbolises certain parts of a god's personality, so while Shiva is the god of both creation and destruction it is often his shakti Parvati as Kali or Durga who handles the destructive business and demands the blood sacrifices. She is also the energetic and dominant partner in their sexual relationship, and shakti has come to mean any goddess in her energetic and dynamic mode.

The Kathmandu Valley has numerous shrines and temples dedicated to the great goddesses including four shrines dedicated to the Joginis, the mystical goddesses who are the female counterpart to the Bhairabs. These shrines are found near Sankhu at the eastern end of the valley, at Guhyeshwari near Pashupatinath, at Pharping and at Vijeshwari. Another group of four temples are known as *varahis* and are dedicated to shaktis as she-boars. Other shrines to goddesses are dedicated to the Ashta Matrikas, mother goddesses.

Garuda

Parvati

Shiva's shakti is Parvati the beautiful and she is the dynamic element in their relationship. Just as Shiva is also known as Mahadev, the great god, so she is Mahadevi, the great goddess. Just as Shiva is often symbolised by the phallic lingam so his shakti's symbol is the *yoni*, representing the female sex organ. Their relationship is a sexual one and it is often Parvati who is the energetic and dominant partner.

Shiva's shakti has as many forms as the great god himself. She may be peaceful Parvati but she may also be fearsome Kali, the black goddess, or Durga, the terrible. In these terrific forms she holds a variety of weapons in her 10 hands, struggles with demons and rides a lion. As Kali, the fiercest of the gods and goddesses, she demands sacrifices and wears a garland of skulls. The festival of Dasain, celebrated in her honour, is characterised by the sacrifice of animals.

Saraswati

The goddess of learning and consort of Brahma. She rides upon a white swan and holds the stringed musical instrument known as a *veena*.

Tara

Another deity who appears in both the Hindu and the Buddhist pantheon are the Tara goddesses. There are actually two Taras, Green Tara and White Tara. They are sometimes bilieved to be the two wives of King Songtsen Gompo who was the first royal patron of Buddhism in Tibet. The Taras are two of the female consorts to the Dhyani Buddhas. See the Swayambhunath section of the Kathmandu Valley chapter for details of the Dhyani Buddhas and their shaktis.

Vehicles

Each of the gods is associated with a particular animal which can either be simply an attendant or a vehicle on which the god may ride. These creatures are a clue to identifying a god. Vishnu's vehicle, for example, is the man-bird Garuda and the winged kneeling figure of Garuda in front of a temple usually indicates that it is a Vishnu temple. Similarly elephant-headed Ganesh's creature is the rat or shrew and a statue of a rat will indicate that you are in a Ganesh shrine.

Other vehicles include the great bull known as Nandi which is the vehicle of Lord Shiva. Indra, the king of the Vedic gods, has an elephant. Agni, the Vedic god of fire, has a chariot drawn by parrots while Vasudhara, the wife of Jambhala the god of wealth, has a chariot drawn by a pig! Fearsome Bhairab is accompanied by a dog, Yama the god of death by a crow. Ganesh's brother Kartikkaya, the god of war, has a cock. Brahma's creature is a swan or goose, his consort Saraswati has a swan.

Snakes

Snakes make lots of appearances in Hindu and Buddhist mythology in Nepal. Vishnu images usually have a snake somewhere in the picture and the sleeping Vishnu reclines upon a bed made from the coils of a snake. Vishu's consort Lakshmi often carries a snake but Garuda, Vishnu's man-bird attendant, has a passionate hatred of snakes and often kills them. Snakes are thought to have power over water so they're important for ensuring a good monsoon. They also appear guarding doorways to prevent evil entering, but if you get bitten by one you can turn to Janguli, the goddess who cures snake bites. Amoghasiddhi, the Dhyani Buddha of the north, sits under a canopy of seven hooded snakes and Vishnu's snake bed also has seven heads which form a canopy for him. The eight snake deities are known as the *nagas* and Anantnag is their king.

HOLIDAYS & FESTIVALS

Nepal's colourful holidays and festivals occur virtually year round and a visit to Nepal is almost certain to coincide with at least one, particularly in the Kathmandu Valley. Certain times of year, particularly August-September towards the end of the monsoon, are packed with festivals. They go a long way towards compensating for the less than ideal weather at that time of year.

For interesting accounts of many of the festivals and the legends behind them read Mary M Anderson's *The Festivals of Nepal* (first published by Unwin Hyman, London, 1971; republished by Rupa & Co, Calcutta, 1988).

Nepalese holidays and festivals are principally dated by the lunar calendar, falling on days relating to new or full moons. The Nepalese new year starts on 13 April and is 57 years ahead of the Gregorian calendar used in the West. The year 1991 in the West is 2048 in Nepal. The Newaris, on the other hand, start their new year from the day after Deepavali, which falls on the night of the new moon in late October or early November. Their calendar is 880 years behind the Gregorian calendar so 1991 in the West is 1111 to the Newaris of the Kathmandu Valley.

Predicting the exact dates for Nepalese holidays and festivals is not always easy. In Nepal the lunar calendar is divided into bright and dark fortnights. The bright fortnight is the 2 weeks of the waxing moon, as

Festival Calendar

Festival	Place	1990/91	1991/92	1992/93
Dasain				
(Fulpati)	all over Nepal	28 Sept	17 Oct	3 Oct
(Vijaya Dashami)	all over Nepal	1 Oct	18 Oct	6 Oct
(Kartika Purnima)	all over Nepal	4 Oct	21 Oct	9 Oct
Tihar				
(Deepavali)	all over Nepal	18 Oct	5 Nov	25 Oct
(Bhai Tika)	all over Nepal	20 Oct	8 Nov	27 Oct
Haribodhini Ekadashi	Pashupatinath	29 Oct	18 Nov	1 Nov
Bala Chaturdashi	Pashupatinath	17 Nov	6 Dec	19 Nov
Mani Rimdu	Solu Khumbu	Nov	Nov	Nov
Magh Sankranti	Narayanghat	mid-Jan	mid-Jan	mid-Jan
Basant Panchami	Swayambhunath	31 Jan	21 Jan	9 Feb
Shivaratri	Pashupatinath	25 Feb	13 Feb	27 Feb
Holi	all over Nepal	11 Mar	28 Feb	18 Mar
Chaitra Dasain	all over Nepal	2 Apr	23 Mar	10 Apr
Bisket Jatra	Bhaktapur	13 Apr	13 Apr	13 Apr
Buddha Jayanti	Kathmandu	9 May	28 Apr	16 May
Gai Jatra	Kathmandu	7 Aug	26 Aug	14 Aug
Krishna Jayanti	Patan	12 Sep	2 Sept	21 Aug
Teej	Pashupatinath	23 Aug	11 Sept	30 Aug
Indra Jatra	Kathmandu	4 Sept	22 Sept	10 Sept

it grows to become the full moon (*purnima*). The dark fortnight is the 2 weeks of the waning moon, as the full moon shrinks to become the new moon (*aunsi*). Therefore a festival might fall 'on the 11th day of the bright fortnight of Falgun'.

What sometimes seems like a cavalier attitude towards numbering days actually has a logical explanation. The sun rises every 24 hours but the period between successive moonrises can vary from 22 to 27 hours. Thus several times each year there can be a 'moon day' (the period from one moonrise to the next) which has no sunrise within it, and several others that have two sunrises. Thus the lunar calendar will sometimes jump a day, and on other occasions it will hiccup and repeat a day. Predicting a date far in advance is additionally complicated by the periodic adjustments which have to be made to bring the shorter lunar year back into line with the solar year which the Gregorian calendar follows.

The Nepalese months are:

October-November	*Kartik*
November-December	*Mangsir*
December-January	*Pus*
January-February	*Magh*
February-March	*Falgun*
March-April	*Chaitra*
April-May	*Baisakh*
May-June	*Jeth*
June-July	*Asaar*
July-August	*Saaun*
August-September	*Bhadra*
September-October	*Ashwin*

The festival calendar covers dates through to November 1992, hopefully with reasonable accuracy. Check the dates when you're in Kathmandu.

October-November

Dasain The pleasant post-monsoon period when the sky is clearest, the air is cleanest and the rice is ready for harvesting is also the time for Nepal's biggest annual festival. Dasain lasts for 15 days, finishing on the full moon day of late September or early October, and there are a number of important days right through the festival. Although much of Dasain is a quiet family affair there are colourful events for visitors to see both in Kathmandu and in the country. Dasain is also known as Durga Puja since the festival celebrates the victory of the goddess Durga over the forces of evil in the guise of the buffalo demon Mahisasura. Since Durga is a bloodthirsty goddess the festival is marked by wholesale bloodletting and features the biggest animal sacrifice of the year.

Even before Dasain commences the Nepalese spring-clean their houses, and in the country swings and primitive hand-powered ferris wheels are erected at the entrance to villages or in their main square. For trekkers Dasain is very much 'the festival of swings'! On day 1 of the festival a sacred jar of water is prepared in each house and barley seeds are planted in carefully prepared soil. Getting the seeds to sprout a few cm during Dasain ensures a good harvest.

Fulpati is the first really important day of Dasain and is called 'the seventh day' although it may not actually fall on the seventh day. *Fulpati* means 'the day of flowers' and a jar containing flowers is carried from Gorkha to Kathmandu and presented to the king at the Tundikhel parade ground. The flowers symbolise the goddess Taleju, the 'family' goddess of the royal family whose most important image is in the Gorkha Palace. From the parade ground the flowers are transported on a palanquin to the old royal palace on Durbar Square where they are inspected again by the king and his entourage.

Maha Astami (the 'Great Eighth Day') and Kala Ratri (the 'Black Night') follow Fulpati and this is the start of the sacrifices and offerings to Durga. The hundreds of goats you may see contentedly grazing on the Tundikhel on the days prior to Maha Astami are destined to die for the goddess. At midnight, in a temple courtyard near Durbar Square, eight buffaloes and 108 goats are beheaded and their executioners must perform the deed with a single stroke of the sword or knife.

The next day is Navami and the Kot Square near Durbar Square, scene of the great massacre of noblemen which led to the Rana period of Nepalese history, is the scene for another great massacre. Visitors can witness the bloodshed but you need to arrive early to secure a place on the foreigners' balcony. Sacrifices continue through the day and blood is sprinkled on the wheels of cars and other vehicles to ensure a safe year on the road. At the airport each Royal Nepal Airlines aircraft will have a goat sacrificed to it! The average Nepalese does not eat much meat, but on this day almost everybody in the country will find that goat is on the menu for dinner.

The 10th day of the festival, Vijaya Dashami, is again a family affair as cards and greetings are exchanged, family visits are made and parents place a red *tika* mark on their children's foreheads. In the evening the conclusion of the Dasain activities is marked by processions and masked dances in the towns of the Kathmandu Valley. The Kharga Jatra or sword processions feature priests dressed up as the various gods and carrying wooden swords, symbolic of the weapon with which Durga slew the buffalo demon. This day also celebrates the victory of Lord Rama over the evil King Rawana in the *Ramayana*. The barley sprouts which were planted on the first day are picked and worn as small bouquets in the hair.

Kartika Purnima, the full moon day which marks the end of the festival, is celebrated with gambling in many households and you will see even small children avidly putting a few coins down on various local games of chance. Women fast and many of them make a pilgrimage to Pashupatinath near Kathmandu. Although Dasain is principally a Hindu festival it has also been adopted by Buddhists, and special activities also take place at Buddhist shrines in Patan and Bhaktapur. In the country the swings and ferris wheels will be busier than ever, before finally being dismantled for another year.

Tihar With its colourful Festival of Lights or Deepavali, Tihar is the most important Hindu festival in India and in Nepal it ranks second only to Dasain. The 5 days of activities take place in late October or early November.

The festival honours certain animals on successive days, starting with offerings of rice to the crows which are sent by Yama, the god of death, as his 'messengers of death'. On day 2 dogs are honoured with garlands of flowers and tikas. This must be a considerable surprise to most Nepalese dogs, who are usually honoured with no more than the occasional kick, but the fact that in the afterworld it is dogs who guide departed souls across the river of dead must not be forgotten. Bhairab's vehicle also happens to be a dog. On day 3 it is cows who are remembered and on this day you will often see cows with one horn painted silver, one gold. On day 4 bullocks are honoured.

Day 3, Deepavali, is the most important day of the festival when Lakshmi comes to visit every home which has been suitably lit for her presence. Since one can hardly turn down a surprise visit from the goddess of wealth, homes throughout the country will be brightly lit with candles and lamps for the Festival of Lights. The effect is highlighted because Deepavali falls on the new moon day.

Day 4 is also the start of the Newari new year for the Newari people of the Kathmandu Valley. Day 5 is known as Bhai Tika and on this day brothers and sisters are supposed to meet and place tikas on each other's foreheads. Sisters offers small gifts of fruit and sweets to their brothers while the brothers give their sisters money in return. The markets and bazaars of Kathmandu will be busy supplying the appropriate gifts.

Haribodhini Ekadashi Ekadashi falls twice in each lunar month, on the 11th day after each new and full moon. Each Ekadashi is celebrated with ceremonies and activities but the Haribodhini Ekadashi, falling in late October or early November on the 11th day after the new moon, is the most important of them. On this day Vishnu awakens from his 4 month monsoonal slumbers and the best place to see the associated festivities is at Budhanilkantha, the temple of the sleeping Vishnu. Activities also take place at other Vishnu temples and many Vishnu devotees make a circuit of the important ones from Ichangu Narayan to Changu Naryan, Bishanku Narayan and Sekh Narayan.

Mahalakshmi Puja Lakshmi is the goddess of wealth, but to farmers wealth is rice so this harvest festival, following immediately after Haribodhini Ekadashi, honours the goddess with sacrifices and colourful dances.

November-December
Bala Chaturdashi Like Ekadashi there are two Chaturdashis each month and Bala Chaturdashi falls on the new moon day in late November or early December. Pilgrims flock to Pashupatinath for this festival, burning oil lamps at night and bathing in the holy river on the following morning. A pilgrimage is then made along a traditional route through the woods overlooking Pashupatinath, and as they walk the devotees scatter sweets and seeds for their deceased relatives to enjoy in the afterlife. The festival is at its most colourful during the first evening and is best observed from the other side of the Bagmati River, looking down towards the temple with its singing, dancing, lamplit pilgrims.

Bala, incidentally, once worked at Pashupatinath where he cremated corpses until an unfortunate incident transformed him into a demon. He then haunted the area around the temple until a means was found to dispose of him. Various legends relate how the demon was killed by one of poor Bala's ex-friends and the festival of Bala Chaturdashi was then instituted.

Sita Bibaha Panchami On the fifth day of the bright fortnight in late November or early December pilgrims from all over Nepal and

India flock to Janakpur to celebrate the marriage of Sita to Rama. It was in Janakpur that Sita was born and she and Rama both have temples in the town. The wedding is re-enacted with a procession carrying Rama's image to Sita's temple by elephant. Rama's birthday is celebrated in March in Janakpur and Kathmandu.

Mani Rimdu The Sherpa festival of Mani Rimdu takes place at the monastery of Thyangboche in the Solu Khumbu region. The 3 day festival features masked dances and dramas performed by the monastery's monks and celebrates the victory of Buddhism over the older Bon religion. Another Mani Rimdu festival takes place 6 months later in May-June at the Thami monastery a day's walk west of Namche Bazaar.

January-February
Magh Sankranti The end of the coldest winter months is marked by this festival with ritual bathing, despite the cold, during the Nepalese month of Magh. The festival is dated by the movement north of the winter sun and is one of the few festivals not timed by the lunar calendar. Soon after, on the new moon day the Tribeni Mela (a *mela* is a fair) is held at various places including Deoghat, on the banks of the Narayani River near the town of Narayanghat in the Terai.

Basant Panchami The beginning of spring is celebrated by honouring Saraswati and since she is the goddess of learning this festival has special importance for students and scholars. The shrine to Saraswati, just below the platform at the top of Swayambhunath, is the most popular locale for the festivities. This is also a particularly auspicious occasion for weddings.

February
Tibetan New Year The new year in Tibet commences with the new moon in February and is welcomed with particular fervour at the great Bodhnath Stupa. The colourfully dressed lamas parade around the stupa carrying banners and portraits of the Dalai Lama. Ceremonies are also performed at Swayambhunath and in the Tibetan community at Jawlakhel near Patan. Crowds of Tibetans, dressed in their most traditional costumes and furiously twirling their prayer wheels, watch the proceedings.

February-March
Maha Shivaratri Lord Shiva's birthday falls on the new moon day of the month of Falgun. Festivities take place at all Shiva temples but most particularly at the great Pashupatinath Temple, and devotees flock there not only from all over Nepal but also from all over India. Many sadhus make the long trek to Nepal for this festival and the King of Nepal will also appear late in the day since Shiva, as Lord Pashupati, is asked to protect Nepal at the conclusion of any official message. The crowds bathing in the Bagmati's holy waters at this time are a colourful and wonderful sight. The sadhus, meanwhile, will be up to all their usual fun and games whether it's rolling in the ashes, performing impossible feats of yoga or sticking thorns through their tongues. Overall, however, Maha Shivaratri is a serene and peaceful festival, reflecting the deep devotion which Hindus hold for their religion.

Holi or Fagu This exciting festival is closely related to the water festivals of Thailand and Burma and takes place on the full moon day in the month of Falgun. By this time, late in the dry season, it is beginning to get rather hot and the water which is sprayed around so liberally during the festival is a reminder of the cooling monsoon days to come. Holi is also known as the Festival of Colours and as well as spraying water on everything and everyone, coloured powder (particularly red) and coloured water is also dispensed. Foreigners get special attention, so if you venture out on Holi leave your camera behind (or keep it well protected) and wear old clothes which you don't mind getting colour-stained. At one time Holi used to take place on the 8 days leading up to the full moon; these days (perhaps fortunately) the full onslaught of activities is usually restricted to 1 day.

The festival is said to be inspired by the exploits of Krishna, particularly an incident when he caught his favourite milkmaids sporting in the Jamuna River. A pole supporting a three tiered umbrella is set up in front of the Basantapur Tower in the centre of Kathmandu and on the final day the umbrella is taken down and burnt.

Other activities also take place during Holi. Guru Mapa, the demon of the Yitum Bahal in Kathmandu (see Walking Tour 2 in the Kathmandu section), has his annual feed on Holi night. The inhabitants of Yitum Bahal sacrifice a buffalo on the banks of the Vishnumati River, cook it in the afternoon in their great courtyard and in the middle of the night carry it in huge cauldrons to the Tundikhel where the demon is said to live to this day. More peacefully, singing and dancing continues until late at night during another cheerful festival in the village of Tarkeghyang on the Helambu trek.

March-April

Chaitra Dasain Also known as 'small' Dasain, in contrast with the 'big' Dasain in the month of Kartik, this one takes place exactly 6 months prior to the more important festival. Like the other Dasain it's dedicated to Durga and once again it's a bad day for goats and buffaloes who do their unwilling bit for the goddess early in the morning in Kot Square.

Sweta Machhendranath The Chaitra Dasain sacrifices also signal the start of the Sweta or White Machhendranath festival, a month prior to the much larger and more important Rato Machhendranath festival in Patan. The festival starts with the removal of the image of Sweta Machhendranath from the temple at Kel Tole and placing it on a towering and creaky wooden temple chariot or *rath*. For the next 4 evenings the chariot proceeds from one historic location to another eventually arriving at Lagankhel in the south of Kathmandu. There the image is taken down from the chariot and carried back

to its starting point in a palanquin while the chariot is disassembled and put away until next year.

April

Bisket Jatra The Nepalese new year starts in mid-April, at the beginning of the month of Baisakh, and the Bisket Jatra festival in Bhaktapur is the most spectacular welcome for the new year and one of the most exciting annual events in the valley. Magh Sankranti is the only other important religious festival set by the solar rather than the lunar calendar.

Bisket is Bhaktapur's great chariot festival but whereas in Kathmandu and Patan it is Machhendranath who gets taken for a ride here it is Bhairab, accompanied by Betal and, in a second chariot, the goddess Bhadrakali. The ponderous chariots of the gods always appear shaky and unsafe and moving them requires enormous amounts of energy.

From Taumadhi Tole, outside Bhairab's temple, the huge temple chariot proceeds around the town, pausing for a huge tug of war between the eastern and western sides of town. The winning side is charged with looking after the images of the gods during their week-long riverside sojourn. After the battle the chariots slither down the steep road leading to the river. Here a huge 25 metre high lingam is erected and in the evening of the following day, new year's day, the pole is pulled down, again in an often violent tug of war. As the pole crashes to the ground the new year officially commences.

As is usual in Nepal, legend is piled upon legend and far in the past there's a tale of a beautiful princess and a valiant prince behind the Bisket festival. The king of Bhaktapur had an insatiable daughter who not only required a new lover each night but left them dead each morning! Finally a brave prince showed up and despite an exhausting session with the princess forced himself to stay awake afterwards. Late that night two thread-like whisps emerged from the beautiful princess's nostrils, and grew into venomous snakes in the night air. Before they could strike and consign the prince to the scrapheap of discarded lovers he drew his sword and killed them both. Of course the prince and princess married and lived happily ever after and from the top of the towering Bisket lingam stream two banners, symbolic of those two deadly snakes.

Other festivals and events also take place around Bhaktapur for a week preceding the new year and for some days thereafter. The potters' caste put up and haul down their own lingam, and processions also carry images of Ganesh, Lakshmi and Mahakali around the town. The new year is also an important time in the valley for ritual bathing and crowds of hill people come down to visit the Buddhist stupas of Swayambhunath and Bodhnath.

Balkumari Jatra Thimi, the smaller town near Bhaktapur, also welcomes the new year with an exciting festival. This event was also instituted by King Jagat Jyoti Malla in the early 1600s but here it is Balkumari, another of Bhairab's consorts, who is honoured.

All through new year's day devotees crowd around her temple in Thimi and as dusk falls hundreds of the ceremonial oil lamps known as *chirags* are lit. Some devotees lie motionless around the temple all night with burning oil lamps balanced on their legs, arms, chests and foreheads.

The next morning men come from the various *toles* or quarters of Thimi and from surrounding villages, each team carrying a palanquin known as a *khat* with images of different gods. As the 32 khats whirl around the temple red powder is hurled at them and the ceremony reaches fever pitch as the khat bearing Ganesh arrives from the village of Nagadish. The crowds parade up and down the main street until late in the morning when Ganesh, borne by hundreds of men, makes a break for home, pursued by the other khats. If they can catch Ganesh the activities are prolonged but eventually Ganesh departs and the festival moves on to the Taleju Temple and this part then ends.

Sacrifices are now made to Balkumari and in the small village of Bode another khat festival, with just seven of them rather than 32, now takes place. Here a volunteer spends the whole day with an iron spike piercing his tongue. Successful completion of this painful rite brings merit to the whole village as well as the devotee.

April-May
Rato Machhendranath Although Sweta and Rato Machhendranath may well be the same deity, the Rato or Red Machhendranath festival of Patan is a much more important occasion than the Kathmandu event. Machhendranath is considered to have great powers over rain and since the monsoon is approaching this festival is a plea for good rain. As in Kathmandu the festival consists of a day-by-day temple chariot procession through the streets of the town, but here it takes a full month to move from the Pulchowk area, where the image is installed in the chariot, to Jawlakhel where the chariot is dismantled.

Along the way the main chariot is accompanied for most of the way by a second smaller chariot containing the image of Rato Machhendranath's Bodhisattva companion from the Minanath Temple, near the Rato Machhendranath Temple south of Patan's Durbar Square. From Jawlakhel Rato Machhendranath does not return to his Patan temple, however. He has a second home in the village of Bungamati and he spends 6 months of each year at this temple, to where he is now conveyed on a khat. Every 12 years, however, the Rato Machhendranath festival becomes an even more important, and time-consuming, event when the chariot continues on all the way to Bungamati. The next enactment of the complete Patan to Bungamati procession will be in 1991.

The temple chariots or raths used in these processions are immense wooden affairs with wheels metres in diameter and a towering but often rather ramshackle edifice constructed on top. It takes hundreds of devotees to tow this creation and the Nepalese army is often called in to help in the Patan Rato Machhendranath festival, despite the intense local enthusiasm to take part in pulling the chariot. The long procession is often halted to await an auspicious occasion for the next leg, or to make important roadside repairs to the chariot. Similar temple chariot processions take place in India including the largest of them all, the great Jagannath procession in the state of Orissa.

Buddha Jayanti (Buddha's Birthday) The Buddha was born at Lumbini in Nepal, so it is fitting that his birthday should be celebrated on the full moon day of the month of Baisakh. Swayambhunath is the centre for the celebrations although events also take place at Bodhnath and in Patan.

A constant procession of pilgrims makes its way around the stupa at Swayambhunath. The stupa's collection of rare thangkas and mandalas are shown on the southern wall of the stupa courtyard on this single day each year. The stupa's lamas dress in colourful silk robes and dance around the stupa with accompaniment provided by musicians.

Mata Tirtha Puja The last day of the dark fortnight of Baisakh is Mata Tirtha Puja. It's the Nepalese equivalent of Mother's Day and every Nepalese should go to 'look upon their mother's face'. Those whose mothers have died in the past year are supposed to bathe at the Mata Tirtha pond, about 10 km south-west of Kathmandu and near the Thankot road.

May-June
Kumar Sasthi The birthday of Kumar or Kartikkaya, the god of war and brother of Ganesh, is also known as Sithinakha. The festival also marks the start of the rice planting season and an annual occasion for cleaning wells. Once upon a time the god of war's birthday was commemorated by stone-throwing contests. Since these often turned into strictly local, but often decidedly real, wars they're now mainly confined to young boys.

July-August
Naga Panchami On the fifth day after the new moon in the month of Saaun snakes or *nagas* are honoured in this festival. Numerous legends are told about snakes and they

are said to have all sorts of magical powers including special powers over the monsoon rains. Pictures of the nagas are hung over the doorway into houses and this not only propitiates the snakes but also keeps harm from the household. Various foods are put out for the snakes and there are interesting legends behind the offerings of milk and boiled rice.

A farmer inadvertently killed three baby snakes with his plough and the enraged mother snake chased the farmer back to his house and killed the farmer, his wife and his two sons. The daughter was about to get the same treatment when she offered the serpent a bowl of milk. The snake was so taken by this act of kindness that it spared the daughter and offered her any wish. Bring my parents and brothers back to life, replied the daughter and the snake duly did so. Ever since then snakes are offered a bowl of milk on Naga Panchami.

The bowl of rice is offered because of an incident at the Siddha Pokhari pond just outside Bhaktapur which, the legend relates, was once inhabited by an evil naga. A holy man determined to kill the naga by himself by taking the form of a snake, and told his companion to be ready with a bowl of magic rice. If, after he entered the pond, the water turned white then the naga had won and it was all over. If, on the other hand, the water turned red then he had defeated the naga and although he would emerge from the pond in the form of a snake the magical rice would restore his original form.

Sure enough the water turned red but when the holy man in the form of a hideous serpent emerged from the water his horrified companion simply turned tail and ran, taking the rice with him. The holy man tried to catch him but failed and eventually decided to return to the pond and remain there. To this day the inhabitants of Bhaktapur keep well clear of the Siddha Pokhari pond and on the day of Naga Panchami a bowl of rice is put out – just in case the holy man/snake turns up.

Janai Purnima On the day prior to and on

the day of the full moon in the month of Saaun all high caste, that is to say Chhetri and Brahmin, men must change the *janai* or sacred thread which they wear looped over their left shoulder and tied under their right arm. The three cords of the sacred thread symbolise body, speech and mind, and young men first put on the thread in an important ritual that officially welcomes them into their religion. From that date they wear the sacred thread for the rest of their lives, changing it on this one occasion each year as well as any time it has been damaged or defiled. One way of defiling the sacred thread is to come into contact with a woman while she is menstruating.

Although only men wear the thread, anybody, including curious foreigners, can wear a yellow thread or *raksha bandhan* around their wrist – right for men, left for women. Wearing this thread on your wrist is said to bring good fortune and on this day priests tie the threads on all comers. You are supposed to wear it for at least a week, but preferably for 3 months until the festival of lights in October-November.

Janai Purnima also brings crowds of pilgrims to the sacred Gosainkund Lake, across the mountains to the north of Kathmandu. There they garland a statue of Shiva and throw coins at the sacred lingam which rises up from the lake. A direct channel is said to lead from the lake to the pond in the Khumbeshwar Temple in Patan and a silver lingam is installed in the pond for the occasion. The rituals at the temple attract *jhankris*, faith healers who perform in a trance while beating drums.

Gai Jatra The Gai Jatra or Cow Festival takes place immediately after Janai Purnima on the day after the Saaun full moon, and is dedicated to those who died during the preceding year. Hindus believe that after death cows will guide them to Yama, the god of the underworld, and finding your way on this important journey will be much easier if by chance you should be holding on to a cow's tail at the moment of death! Therefore on this day cows are lead through the streets of the valley's towns or, if a cow is not available, small boys dress up as cows.

The festival also celebrates an event during the reign of King Pratap Malla (1641-1674). The king's youngest son died and the queen was utterly grief-stricken. Nothing could cheer her up and eventually the king offered rewards to anybody who could bring a smile to her face. The next day crowds of people appeared before the royal palace and danced and clowned, dressed in outlandish costumes. The queen could not help laughing at this mass outbreak of merry madness and the king proclaimed that henceforward Gai Jatra would be a day for costumes and games. So it is that many other peculiar outfits appear on the streets, apart from boys dressed up as cows, and the festival is celebrated with maximum energy on the streets of Bhaktapur.

Ghanta Karna Ghanta Karna, the Night of the Devil, falls on the 14th day of the dark

---

The Ages of Brahma
Each universe has a Brahma who lives for 100 years, Brahma years that is - they are much longer than our earth years. Each day in a Brahma year is a Kalpa and each Kalpa or Brahma day is in turn divided into 1000 Mahayugas or Great Ages.

In a single Great Age there are four Yugas which follow a prescribed pattern. In the first Yuga everything is fine, but in the second Yuga evil makes its appearance and the eternal struggle between good and evil commences. In the third Yuga good is in serious trouble and in the fourth Yuga, the Kaliyuga, evil comes out on top and it's time for Vishnu to take on his 10th incarnation as Kalki the destroyer and bring the whole mess to a quick end. And where are we currently in this cycle of existence? About half way through the fourth Yuga. ■

fortnight of Saaun. Ghanta Karna, which means 'Bell Ears', was a horrible demon who was so named because he wore bell earrings to drown out the name of Lord Vishnu, his sworn enemy. The festival celebrates his destruction when a god, disguised as a frog, lured him into a deep well where the people stoned and clubbed him to death. Ghanta Karna is burnt in effigy on this night and evil is cleansed from the land for another year.

August-September
Krishna Jayanti The seventh day after the full moon in the month of Bhadra is celebrated as Lord Krishna's birthday, sometimes known as Krishnasthami. Krishna is an incarnation of Vishnu and his daring exploits, good nature and general love of a good time endear him to many people. The Krishna Mandir in Patan is the centre for the celebrations and an all-night vigil is kept at the temple on the night before his birthday. Oil lamps light the temple and singing continues through the night.

Teej The festival of women lasts for 3 days, from the second to the fifth day following the new moon in the month of Bhadra. It is centred on Pashupatinath and women celebrate the festival in honour of their husbands and in hope of a long and happy married life.

The festival starts with a sumptuous meal and the women gather together and spend the rest of the day feasting and talking, right through until midnight when they must commence 24 hours of fasting. During the day of the fast women from all over the valley converge on Pashupatinath, traditionally dressed in red and gold saris, usually the ones in which they were married. In Nepal red is the colour of happiness and weddings, white is the colour of death and funerals. At Pashupatinath the women take ritual dips in the river and call on the gods to protect their husbands.

The following morning the women must offer their husbands small items of food which had previously been offered to the gods. The day-long fast can then be broken although in some years the festival continues for an extra day in which case this is a day of partial fasting. Another ritual bathing ceremony takes place on this day, preferably at the confluence of rivers, such as where the Bagmati River joins the Vishnumati River, just south of Kathmandu. Completion of these ceremonies washes away all female sin, including the sin of a woman touching her husband during her period!

Gunla The 15 days before and after the full moon in August or early September is celebrated as a full month of Buddhist ceremonies, penance and fasting. Activities are centred on Swayambhunath. Pancha Dan, the Festival of Five Offerings, is held in Patan during Gunla but there are various other festivals and ceremonies during the month.

Gokarna Aunsi The Nepalese equivalent of Father's Day is celebrated at Gokarna where deceased fathers are honoured and by visiting living fathers at their homes.

September
Indra Jatra The most important festival of the year runs from the end of the month of Bhadra into the beginning of Ashwin. Indra Jatra is a colourful and exciting festival which manages to combine homage to Indra with an important annual appearance by the Kumari (the living goddess), respects to Bhairab and commemoration of the conquest of the valley by Prithvi Narayan Shah. The festival also marks the end of the monsoon and the start of the fine months which follow.

Indra is the ancient Aryan god of rain and he once paid a visit to the Kathmandu Valley to pick a certain flower which his mother Dagini needed for the Teej puja. Unfortunately for Indra he was captured in the act of stealing the flowers and imprisoned until his mother came down to rescue him. When she revealed whom they had imprisoned his captors gladly released him but the festival continues to celebrate this remarkable achievement – villagers don't capture a real god every day of the week! In return for his release Dagini promised to spread morning moisture and dew over the crops for the coming months and to take back with her to heaven all those who had died in the past year.

Therefore the festival honours the recently deceased and pays homage to Indra and Dagini for the coming harvests. It starts with the erection of a huge pole outside the Hanumań Dhoka Palace. The carefully selected pole has first been brought to the Tundikhel and then carried to the square. The pole is set up while images and representations of Indra, usually as a captive, are displayed and sacrifices of goats and roosters are made. At the same time the screened doors obscuring the horrific face of White Bhairab are opened and for the next 3 days his gruesome visage will stare out at the proceedings.

The day before all this activity three golden temple chariots have been assembled in Basantapur Square, outside the home of the Kumari, the living goddess. In the afternoon, with the Durbar Square packed with colourful and cheerful crowds, two boys emerge from the Kumari's house. They play the roles of Ganesh and Bhairab and will each ride in a chariot as attendant to the goddess. Finally the Kumari herself appears either walking on a rolled-out carpet or carried by attendants so that her feet do not touch the ground.

The chariots move off and the Kumari is greeted from the balcony of the old palace by the king. The procession then continues out of Durbar Square towards Hanuman Dhoka Palace where it stops in front of the huge White Bhairab mask. The Kumari greets the image of Bhairab and then, with loud musical accompaniment, beer starts to pour from Bhairab's mouth! Grabbing a sip of this beer is guaranteed to bring good fortune, but one lucky individual will also get the small fish which has been put to swim in the beer – this brings especially good luck!

The procession moves off again and for the following days of the festival moves from place to place around the town, to the accompaniment of ceremonies, dances and other activities. Numerous other processions also take place around the town until the final day when the great pole is lowered and carried down to the river. It was during the Indra Jatra festival back in 1768 that Prithvi Narayan Shah conquered the valley and unified Nepal so this important event is also commemorated in this most spectacular of Kathmandu occasions.

Ganesh Chata On Ganesh Chata, the fourth day of the bright fortnight in September, offerings are made to Ganesh. The festival celebrates a bitter dispute between Ganesh and the moon goddess, and the Nepalese try to stay indoors on this night and shut out all signs of moonlight.

September-October
Pachali Bhairab Jatra The fearsome form of Bhairab, as Pachali Bhairab, is honoured on the fourth day of the bright fortnight in September or early October. The festivities are in line with Bhairab's bloodthirsty nature as there are numerous sacrifices.

Other Festivals & Ceremonies
Public Holidays Many of the holidays and festivals affect the working hours of government offices and banks.

They will be closed for, amongst others, Shivaratri, the Nepalese New Year, Teej, Indra Jatra, Dasain, Tihar, the queen's birthday on 7 November and the king's birthday on 29 December.

Ekadashi Ekadashi falls twice in each lunar month, 11 days after the full moon and the new moon. The annual Haribodhini Ekadashi is a major festival but the other Ekadashis are also celebrated, often with music and singing.

Marriage Ceremonies It is important that weddings take place on an auspicious date and some months of the year, Pus in particular, are extremely ill-starred for marriages. Only 5 months of the year – Magh, Falgun, Baisakh, Jeth and Mangsir – are ideal, although if pressed a talented astrologer can find an auspicious date at even the most inconvenient time. Spring is the favourite time of year and on ideal days in Baisakh there will be numerous wedding bands marching around town at the same time.

A traditional Newari wedding is a complicated affair lasting up to a week. The various stages of the ceremony move back and forth between the bride and groom's homes and include a procession led by a band. The religious ceremony, where a fire 'witnesses' the marriage, is held at the bride's house and the festivities conclude with a wedding banquet. Although more couples are making their own choice of partners many marriages are still arranged.

Very different forms of marriage take place in the hills and in parts of the Sherpa country polyandry, where a women takes more than one husband, is still practised.

In Nepal, as in a number of other Asian countries, the bride never wears white. White is the colour of death and funerals, red is a much happier and more auspicious colour. Married women wear vermilion in the parting of their hair.

LANGUAGE

It's quite easy to get by with English in Nepal; most people the average visitor will have to deal with in the Kathmandu Valley and in Pokhara will speak some English. Along the main trekking trails, particularly the Annapurna Circuit, English is widely understood.

However, it's interesting to learn at least a little Nepali and it's quite an easy language to pick up. Nepali is closely related to Hindi and, like Hindi, is a member of the Indo-European group of languages. If you want to know a bit more Nepali than the phrases and vocabulary that follow, the Lonely Planet *Nepal Phrasebook* is a handy introduction to the language.

Although Nepali is the national language of Nepal and is the linking language between all the country's ethnic groups there are many other languages spoken. The Newaris of the Kathmandu Valley, for example, speak Newari and there are other languages spoken by the Tamangs, Sherpas, Rais, Limbus, Magars, Gurungs and other groups. In the Terai, bordering India, Hindi and Maithili, another Indian language of this region, are often spoken.

Even if you learn no other Nepali, there is one word every visitor soon picks up – *namaste*. Strictly translated it means 'I salute the god in you', but it is used as an everyday greeting encompassing everything from 'hello' to 'how are you?' and even 'see you again soon'. Properly used it should be accompanied with the hands held in a prayer-like position, the Nepalese gesture which is the equivalent of Westerners shaking hands.

Studying Nepali

It is not too difficult to learn basic Nepali and with a few exceptions the pronunciation is straightforward. Peace Corps and other aid workers pick up a working knowledge of the language very quickly and there are language courses available which will enable you to get by with just 4 to 8 weeks of intensive study.

You will often see signs and notices around Kathmandu advertising language courses, many of them conducted by ex-Peace Corps workers. Places to try include the Global Language Institute (tel 4-16116) or the School of International Languages (tel 2-11713) at the university. At Rs 75 to Rs 150 an hour the Global Language Institute is expensive, but other places are cheaper.

Pronunciation

Vowels These are pronounced according to the following guide:

a	as the 'u' in 'hut'
aa	as the 'a' in 'garden'
e	as the 'e' in 'best' (only longer)
i	as the 'i' in 'sister'(only longer)
o	as the 'o' in 'more'
u	as the 'u' in 'put'
ai	as the 'i' in 'mine'
au	as the 'ow' in 'cow'

Consonants Most of the consonants are quite similar to their English equivalents. The exceptions are the so-called retroflex consonants and the aspirated consonants. Retroflex sounds are made by touching the back of the roof of the mouth with your tongue as you make the consonant; they are indicated by doubling the consonant:

tt   *Katthmanddu*

Aspirated consonants are sounded more forcefully than they would be in English and are made with a short puff of air; they are indicated by the consonant followed by an 'h':

bh   *bhatmaas*

Both retroflex and aspirated consonants are best learned by having a Nepalese demonstrate them for you. You could start with the word *Katthmanddu*, which contains both retroflex and aspirated consonants.

Some Useful Words

I
  ma
where?
  kata?
here
  yaha
there
  tyaha
OK
  theek
yes (I have)
  chaa
no (I don't have)
  chhaina
good, pretty
  ramro
stamp
  tikat
envelope
  kham
post office
  post afis
tourist office
  turist afis
bank
  baink

Greetings & Civilities

hello, goodbye
  namaste
How are you?
  Tapaailai kasto chha?
excuse me
  hajur
please (give me)
  dinuhos
please (you have)
  khaanuhos
thank you
  dhanyabad

People are not thanked as often as in the West. A thank you is rarely necessary in a simple commercial transaction and saying *dhanyabad* too often will sound distinctly odd.

I only speak a little Nepali.
  Ma ali Nepaali bolchhu.
I don't understand.
  Maile bujhina.
Please say it again.
  Pheri bhannuhos.
Please speak more slowly.
  Tapai bistaarai bolnuhos.
I do not need it.
  Malai chahinna.
I do not have it.
  Ma sanga chhaina.
Wait a minute.
  Ek chhin parkhanos.

Accommodation

room
  kothaa
cheap
  sasto
expensive
  mahango
clean
  safaa
dirty
  mailo
fan
  pankhaa
breakfast
  bihaanako khaana

Can I get a place to stay here?
Yahaa baas paunchha?
May I take a look at the room?
Kothaa herna sakchhu?

Getting Around
autorickshaw
tempo
bus
bus
taxi
taxi
boat
naau
ticket
tikat
Where does this bus go to?
Yo bus kahaa jaanchha?
How much does it cost to go to...?
...jaana kati parchha?
Does your taxi have a meter?
Tapaai ko taxi maa meter chha?

Trekking
way, trail
bato
bridge
pool
descent
oralo
ascent
ukao
left
baya
right
daya
cold
jado
Please give me ...
Malai ... dinuhos.
Which is the way to...?
...jaane bato kata parchha?
Is there a village nearby?
Najikai gaun parchha?
Where is the porter?
Bhariya kata gayo?
Please give me water.
Malai pani dinuhos.
I want to sleep.
Malai sutna man lagyo.

I feel cold.
Malai jado lagyo.
The food is cold.
Khaana cheeso chha.

Food & Drink
food/meal
khaana
bread
pauroti
rice
chamal
rice (cooked)
bhat
meat
masu
chicken
kukhura
boiled
umaleko
green, leafy vegetable
saag
vegetable (cooked)
tarkari
lentils
dahl
egg
phool

fruit
  phala
sugar
  chini
spicy
  peero
salt
  noon
pepper
  marich
curd
  dahi
milk
  doodh
tea
  chiya
water
  pani

Shopping
money
  paisa
cheap
  sasto
expensive
  mahango
less
  kam
more
  badhi
little bit
  alikati
That's enough.
  Pugyo.
How much?
  Kati?
I like this.
  Malai yo ramro lagyo.
I do not like this.
  Malai yo ramro lagena.
Where is the market?
  Bazar kata parchha?

Emergencies
medicine
  ausadhi
pharmacy
  ausadhi pasal
Where is the nearest hospital?
  Yahaa aspataal kahaa chha?

Please call a doctor for me.
  Daktar bolaidinus.
I do not feel well.
  Malai sancho chhaina.
I have diarrhoea.
  Dishaa laagyo.
I have altitude sickness.
  Lekh laagyo.
I have a fever.
  Joro aayo.

Times & Dates
minute
  minet
hour
  ghantaa
day
  din
today
  aaja
yesterday
  hijo
tomorrow
  bholi
now
  aile
week
  haptaa
month
  mahinaa
What time is it?
  Kati bajyo?
It's one o'clock.
  Ek bajyo.
What day is it today?
  Aaja ke baar?
Today is Thursday.
  Aaja bihibaar ho.

Numbers
1	*ek*
2	*dui*
3	*teen*
4	*char*
5	*panch*
6	*chha*
7	*saat*
8	*aath*
9	*nau*
10	*das*

20	*bees*	100	*saya*
30	*tees*	200	*dui saya*
40	*chaalis*	500	*panch saya*
50	*pachas*	1000	*hazar*
60	*saathi*	100,000	*lakh*
70	*sattari*	1,000,000	*das lakh*
80	*assi*	10,000,000	*crore*
90	*nabbe*		

Nepalese Numerals

Facts for the Visitor

VISAS

Visas are required by most nationalities (Indians are an exception) and they are available from embassies and consulates abroad, at the border with India or on arrival at Kathmandu Airport. The cost of a visa varies from country to country – in the UK it is £10 while in Australia it is A$25 – and it is valid for 30 days. A visa issued on arrival costs US$10 but is only initially valid for 15 days. It can be extended for another 15 days in Kathmandu or Pokhara at no additional cost, but you must provide proof that you have officially exchanged US$10 for each day of the extension (ie US$150 for the full 15 days). Obtaining visa extensions can be time-consuming as you have to queue up, fill in forms, stand around and generally waste a lot of time. It's worth getting your visa in advance if possible.

If you intend to get a visa before arrival but not in your home country they are most conveniently obtained in Bangkok (Thailand) or Calcutta (India) if you are travelling west, and in New Delhi (India) if you are travelling east.

Embassies

Nepalese diplomatic offices overseas include:

Australia
    3rd Level, 377 Sussex St, Sydney, NSW 2000 (tel (02) 264 7197)
    66 High St, Toowong, Qld 4066 (tel (07) 378 0124)
    Suite 23, 18-20 Bank Place, Melbourne, Vic 3000 (tel (03) 602 1271)
    4th Floor, Airways House, 195 Adelaide Terrace, Perth, WA 6000 (tel (09) 221 1207)
Bangladesh
    Lake Rd, Road No 2, Baridhara Diplomatic Enclave, Dhaka
Belgium
    M25 Ballegeer, RNCG Office, 20/8 Antwerp
Burma (Myanmar)
    16 Natmauk Yeiktha (Park Ave), PO Box 84, Rangoon

China
    No 1 San Li Tunxiliujie, Beijing
    Norbulingka Rd 13, Lhasa, Tibet Autonomous Region
Denmark
    36 Kronprinsessegade, DK 1006, Copenhagen K (tel 01-143175)
France
    7 Rue de Washington, Paris 75008
India
    1 Barakhamba Rd, New Delhi 110001 (tel 38 1484)
    19 Woodlands, Sterndale Rd, Alipore, Calcutta 700027 (tel 45 2024)
Italy
    Piazza Medaglie d'Orro 20, Rome (tel 348 176)
Japan
    16-23 Highashi-Gotanda, 3 chome, Shinagawa-ku, Tokyo 141
Netherlands
    Prinsengracht 687, Gelderland Building, Nl 1017 J V Amsterdam (tel 020 25 0388)
Norway
    Haakor, Vlls gt-5, 0116 Oslo (tel 2 414743)
Pakistan
    506 84th St, Attaturk Ave, Ramna 6/4, Islamabad 23
    Karachi Memon Cooperative Housing Society, Block 7-8 Modem Club Rd, Karachi 29 (tel 201908)
Philippines
    1136-38 United Nations Ave, Paco 2803, Manila (tel 58-93-93)

Sri Lanka
   290 R A de Mel Mawatha, Colombo 7
Sweden
   Birger Jarlsgatan 64, Karlavagen 97 S-115 22, Stockholm
Switzerland
   Schanzeigasse 22, CH-8044 Zurich (tel 816023)
Thailand
   189 Soi 71, Sukhumvit Rd, Bangkok (tel 391 7240)
UK
   12A Kensington Palace Gardens, London W8 4QU (tel 229 6231)
USA
   1500 Lake Shore Drive, Chicago, IL 60610
   Heideberg College, Tiffin, OH 44883 (tel (419) 448-2202)
   473 Jackson St, San Francisco, CA 94111 (tel (415) 434-1111)
   16250 Dallas Parkway, Suite 110, Dallas, TX 75248 (tel (214) 931-1212)
   212 15th St NE, Atlanta, GA 30309 (tel (404) 892-8152)
   2131 Leroy Place NW, Washington, DC 20008 (tel (202) 667 4550)
   Nepalese UN Mission, 820 Second Ave, Room 1200, New York, NY 10017 (tel (212) 370 4188)
West Germany
   Im Hag 15, 5300 Bonn, Bad Godesberg 2 (tel 34 3097)
   Flinschstrasse 63, 6000 Frankfurt am Main (tel 06 114 0871)
   Landsbergerstrasse 191, 8000 Munchen 21 (tel 089 570 4406)
   Handwerkstrasse 5-7, 7000 Stuttgart 80 (tel 0711 7864 614 617)

To extend your visa beyond 1 month costs Rs 75 per week (Rs 300 per month) for the second month and Rs 150 per week (Rs 600 per month) for the third month. In addition you must provide bank receipts or other official proof of exchange to show that you have changed US$10 for every day you wish to extend. Therefore for a 30 day extension you must have officially exchanged US$300. Obtaining a trekking permit automatically extends your visa without extra charge.

The Kathmandu Immigration Office (tel 4-12337) is only a short stroll from Thamel, on Tridevi Marg directly across from the modern shopping centre and the SAARC secretariat. See the Government Offices section in the Kathmandu, Patan & Bhaktapur chapter for details of operating hours.

In Pokhara the office is near the lake. Apart from extending visas the immigration offices also issue trekking permits. In an emergency local police stations can extend visas or trekking permits for up to 7 days.

Visa Extensions

Usually visas cannot be extended beyond 3 months although studying, teaching or involvement in a research project at the university or some other government-recognised institute may provide grounds for an application. Even waiting for money to arrive or a desperate desire to catch an upcoming festival can be enough to extend your visa beyond 3 months if you ask very nicely. In these situations you will have to obtain a recommendation from the Ministry of Home Affairs to present to the immigration office.

For most visitors it's much easier to take a 1 month vacation (the minimum necessary period outside the country) in India, then come back to start another 3 month cycle.

Trekking Permits

A Nepalese visa is officially only valid for the Kathmandu and Pokhara valleys and the Royal Chitwan National Park, although in practice this includes all the major motor roads through the country and the area around the Kathmandu and Pokhara valleys. If you intend to strike out from the main roads on the hill country trekking routes then you must first apply for a trekking permit.

Trekking permits are only issued in Kathmandu and Pokhara but they can be extended in those cities or, for a maximum of 7 days at a time, by any police office. Trekking permits are issued in Kathmandu by the immigration office. Applications must be made between 10 am and 1 pm from Sunday to Thursday, between 10 am and noon on Friday.

Trekking permits cost Rs 90 per week (or Rs 360 per month) for the first month, and Rs 112.50 per week (or Rs 450 per month) for the second and third months. The trekking permit fee automatically extends your visa so if you stay for 3 months in Nepal, the third month will cost Rs 150 per week to simply extend your visa, but only Rs 112.50 per week to get a trekking permit which includes the visa extension.

There are regular trekking permit inspection points along most trails and you wouldn't get far out of Kathmandu or Pokhara before being stopped and turned back if you didn't have a permit. Attempts to trek in the restricted areas, which still encompass large tracts of northern and western Nepal, without a permit could result in deportation. Peter Somerville-Large's amusing *To the Navel of the World* recounts his adventures of arriving in western Nepal from Tibet without a permit. He got away with it.

Working in Nepal

For a Western visitor, working in Nepal is very difficult although it is not impossible. The easiest work to find is teaching English as there are many private schools and a great demand for English language lessons. At less than US$100 a month the pay is very low. Other possibilities include work with airline offices, travel and trekking agencies, consultants or aid groups but the prospects are remote.

Officially you need a work permit if you intend to find employment in Nepal and you are supposed to have this before you arrive in the country. Changing from a tourist visa once you are in the country is rarely permissible. The work permit has to be applied for by your employer and you are supposed to leave the country while the paperwork is negotiated. The process can take months.

Onward Travel

Travellers continuing beyond Nepal are likely to require visas for China, India, Burma or Thailand.

The visa section of the Chinese Embassy in Kathmandu is open on Monday and Wednesday mornings from 10 am till noon. It takes 4 or 5 days to issue a visa which officially costs US$20, although that cost can be bumped up by another US$20 if the embassy decides they have to telex Beijing.

Visas for India are required of virtually every nationality these days and obtaining them can be time-consuming and annoying. This particularly applies to British citizens who also have to pay a much higher visa price than other nationalities.

Visas for Burma (Myanmar, Myanma or whatever else they're calling it this week) are currently only being issued for group tourists, although they do claim to issue visas for longer than the old 7 days maximum. Visas for Thailand are issued without any complication; they can be issued at Bangkok Airport for stays of 14 days or less.

See the Foreign Embassies section under Kathmandu for embassy addresses.

Other Paperwork

If it is possible you might drive a car or ride a motorcycle while in Nepal then it is worth having an international driving permit. An International Student Identity Card (ISIC) can be very useful if you're travelling on a tight budget. There's only one youth hostel in Nepal and it's neither conveniently located or good value, but there are many other hostels in Asia so a Youth Hostel Association (YHA) card may be worth having.

When travelling in Asia it's a good idea to have a number of passport photos for trekking permits, visa applications and other official documents. Passport photos are easily and cheaply obtained in Kathmandu these days.

CUSTOMS

You may be searched very thoroughly when you depart.

Antiques

Customs' main concern is preventing the export of antique works of art – with good reason since Nepal has a great many treasures, many kept under conditions of very light security. It would be a great shame if international art thieves and 'collectors' forced more of it to be kept under lock and key.

It is very unlikely that souvenirs sold to travellers will be antique (despite the claims of the vendors!), but if there is any doubt they should be cleared and a certificate obtained from the Department of Archaeology (tel 2-15358) in the National Archives building on Ram Shah Path. These controls also apply to the export of precious and semiprecious stones.

Animal Furs & Trophies
Unfortunately, there is still a thriving trade in animal furs and trophies, despite the fact that this is also officially prohibited. Many seriously endangered species, including the beautiful snow leopard, are still being hunted for valuable parts of their corpses.

While there is a market this will no doubt continue – the argument that because the animal is already dead there is no further harm caused by having its skin made into a coat is entirely spurious. If there is any cosmic justice, those that encourage the trade will be reincarnated as rabbits on fur farms in Siberia!

MONEY
The Nepalese rupee (Rs) is divided into 100 paisa (p). Major international currencies including the US dollar and pounds sterling are readily accepted, and in Nepal the Indian rupee is also like a hard currency. Official exchange rates are:

A$1	=	Rs 21
US$1	=	Rs 27
UK£1	=	Rs 45
DM1	=	Rs 14
I Rs 100	=	Rs 168

There are coins of 5, 10, 25 and 50 paisa and of 1 rupee. Banknotes are of 1, 2, 5, 10, 20, 50, 100, 500 and 1000 rupees. Away from major centres changing a 500 or 1000 rupee note could be very difficult, so it is always wise to get some of your money in small rupee denominations. The Nepal Bank is the main bank in the country but there are a number of other banks, particularly in Kathmandu. The usual banking hours are 10 am to 2 pm from Sunday to Thursday and from 10 am till noon on Friday. Larger hotels will also change travellers' cheques but usually only for their guests. The exchange rate in hotels is identical to the banks. Your passport is needed when making any official currency exchange.

Visitors are issued with a currency exchange form on arrival in Nepal and official exchanges should be entered on this form. If you later wish to extend your visa you will need the form to prove you have changed the required US$10 per day of the extension requested. Officially the form also allows you to change rupees back into hard currency on departure but don't count on it. There's an official limit on re-exchange of 10% of your total exchange or the last amount changed, whichever is greater. In practice it's much simpler just to run out of money at the end!

When you first arrive in Nepal you'll find exchange counters at the international terminal at Kathmandu Airport and moneychangers at the various border crossing points. Pokhara also has banking facilities but changing travellers' cheques could be difficult elsewhere in the country, even in quite large towns. Cash, preferably US dollars, would be easier.

If you're trekking take enough money with you to last the whole trek. Like many Third World countries suffering from relatively rapid inflation, Nepal's money often seems to be all paper. At one time though, once you were away from the Kathmandu Valley, it was rare to see anything apart from coins. Mountaineering books from the '50s often commented on the porters whose sole duty was to carry the expedition's money – in cold, hard and heavy cash!

Money Transfers from Overseas

If you do not follow the right steps money transfers from overseas can be very time-consuming. Make any transfer by telex as transfers by mail can take forever. Pin down every possible detail, ensure that you know which bank the money is going to, make sure they have your name exactly right and if possible ensure that you are notified at the same time as the bank. It's important to choose the right bank as well – check that your bank has links with a bank in Nepal and does not have to operate through an intermediary.

International banks operating in Kathmandu include Grindlays (tel 2-25181, Box 3990) which is owned by Australia's ANZ, Citibank (tel 4-28884, Box 3729) with offices in the Yak & Yeti Hotel, Indo-Suez (tel 4-11228, Box 3412) and Standard Chartered (tel 2-20129).

American Express has an office off the forecourt of the Hotel Mayalu on Jamal Tol just around the corner from Durbar Marg. It will make cash advances between 10 am and 1 pm. Grindlay's will make cash advances on Visa and MasterCard in Nepalese rupees. Note that you cannot make payments to these offices – you should make arrangements before you leave home.

Black Market

Nepal has an active and remarkably open black market although it's principally found around Kathmandu and to a lesser extent in Pokhara. It's so widely accepted that letters appear in the *Rising Nepal* complaining about the difficulty of walking through the streets of Thamel without being harassed by the 'want to change money' people and a popular T-shirt proclaims the owner is not interested in changing money!

If you do want to change money expect to get about 20% more than the official rate if you have US dollars cash in larger denominations. The US$50 or US$100 bills are preferred, US$1 bills are not wanted. Travellers' cheques are worth somewhat less but can also be exchanged. The young men in the street lead you to a shop where the transaction is actually completed. Once you know which shop to go to you don't have to deal with the people in the street at all, and you will also get a slightly better rate.

Apart from the better exchange rate changing money with these dealers is much more convenient – you can change money or travellers' cheques at any time and there's no paperwork and waiting around. Of course it is illegal! For most travellers there are some occasions when you must change money legally, however. If you want to extend your visa you must provide proof of official exchange of US$10 for each day you extend.

If you want to buy airline tickets they must also be paid for in foreign currency or with proof of official exchange.

Most hotels apart from the really rock bottom places will also require you to pay with 'official' money. This can either be by paying in foreign currency or travellers' cheques or by providing a currency exchange form to show you have changed sufficient official money to cover the bill. The establishment then marks on the form how much you have 'used up'.

COSTS

If you changed money on the black market, stayed in rock bottom accommodation and survived on a predominantly Nepalese diet you could live in Nepal for less than US$5 a day. On a 'village inn' trek your living costs are likely to be around that level.

On the other hand if you stayed in comfortable middle range hotels (say US$10 to US$20 a double), ate in popular tourist-oriented restaurants, rented bicycles and took taxis from time to time your living costs could be around US$20 to US$30 a day.

At the top end it is possible to spend US$100 a night for a 5 star double room in Kathmandu; a meal for two in one of Nepal's very best restaurants can cost US$30 to US$40; and a deluxe trek booked from overseas can cost US$100 a day.

TIPPING

Tipping is becoming more prevalent in Kathmandu. In expensive establishments you should tip up to 10% whereas in smaller places the loose change or Rs 10 will be appreciated. Don't worry about it in the really cheap restaurants. Taxi drivers don't expect to be tipped.

TOURIST INFORMATION
Tourist Office

There is a counter at the airport but the main tourist office (tel 2-11203) is near the corner of Basantapur Square, on Ganga Path close to Freak St in Kathmandu. It has a limited range of brochures and maps.

The Department of Tourism is behind the

National Stadium in Kathmandu. If you're writing from overseas the address is Department of Tourism, Tripureshwar, Kathmandu, Nepal.

GENERAL INFORMATION
Postal Services
Poste restante services in Nepal are quite efficient, but as with any other Asian country you should ask people writing to you to print your surname clearly and underline it. Misfiled mail often results from confusion between surnames and given names. In Kathmandu the poste restante section is in the main post office and consists of a room with boxes arranged alphabetically lined up on a long table. You can sit down at the bench and sort through the letters yourself. The Pokhara post office is inconveniently far from the lakeside where most visitors stay.

Postal rates from Nepal are:

	Africa Europe	Australia USA
Aerogrammes	Rs 4	Rs 4
Postcards	Rs 3	Rs 3
Letter to 20 gm	Rs 7	Rs 8

Telephones
Although internal phone communications can still be difficult it's easy to make international calls from Nepal. From the phone office at the Kathmandu Guest House you can make calls to Australia, the UK or USA for Rs 240 for 3 minutes.

Electricity
Electricity is only found in major towns and some odd outposts like Namche Bazaar in the Solu Khumbu. When available it is 220 volts/50 cycles and US 120 volt appliances need a transformer. Sockets usually take three round pin plugs, sometimes the small variety, sometimes the large. Some sockets take plugs with two round pins. Blackouts are not unknown.

Time
Nepal is 5 hours 45 minutes ahead of GMT; this curious time differential is intended to make it very clear that Nepal is a separate place to India, where the time is 5 hours 30 minutes ahead of GMT! When it's noon in Nepal it's 6.15 am in London, 1.15 am in New York, 10.15 pm the previous day in Los Angeles or San Francisco, and 4.15 pm in Sydney or Melbourne, not allowing for daylight saving time or other variations.

Business Hours
Most government offices in Kathmandu are open from 10 am to 5 pm from Sunday to Thursday during summer and from 9 am to 4 pm during the three winter months (roughly mid-November to mid-February since the winter starting date for the change of hours varies with the Nepalese calendar). Offices close at 3 pm on Fridays. Saturday is the weekly holiday and most shops and all offices and banks will be closed but Sunday is a regular working day. See the Festivals & Holidays section of the Facts for the Country chapter for information on Nepal's many and varied holidays.

MEDIA
Newspapers & Magazines
Nepal's English-language daily paper, the *Rising Nepal*, is often very hard to find. If you want a copy get one early in the day. The paper covers most important international news while events in Nepal are reported in a very individual style! This is basically a government mouthpiece; you're going to have to read papers from abroad if you want to find both sides of the story in Nepal.

The *International Herald Tribune* is widely available in Kathmandu; it's usually much easier to find than the *Rising Nepal*. *Time* and *Newsweek* are readily available and Indian dailies like the *Statesman* or the *Times of India* can also be found.

Nepal Traveller is an excellent free monthly tourist magazine distributed at many hotels including the Kathmandu Guest House. It often has very interesting articles about sightseeing, festivals, trekking and other activities in Nepal. *Himal* is a six-times-yearly magazine published in Nepal and devoted to development

Social Service Is The Epitome Of Humanity	**THE RISING NEPAL**	Let Us Keep Our City Clean

KATHMANDU — SEPTEMBER 24, 1989 (ASWEEN 8, 2046) SUNDAY — RUPEES TWO

G5 Ministers Discuss Dollar, Stability

Washington, Sept 23 (AFP): Finance ministers of five leading economic powers met for separate talks here Saturday and were expected to reaffirm their determination to maintain exchange rate stability and promote orderly unwinding of external imbalances, mainly between the United States and its key partners.

Japanese Finance Minister Ryutaro Hashimoto arrived at the U.S. treasury ahead of ministers from France, Britain and West Germany and was understood to have

Lebanese Factions Agree To Immediate Truce

Beirut, Sept. 23 (AFP): Lebanon's warring factions have agreed to an immediate ceasefire and to reopen Beirut airport after a five-month closure, an Arab League envoy said Saturday.

Algerian diplomat Lakhdar Ibrahimi, making the announcement after the first meeting here of a new security commission set up under the league's plan to end the vicious warfare, also said that

Lebanese Transport Minister Walid Jumblatt said measures' had been taken to reopen the airport, in Moslem

'necessary The airport director, Khaled Saab, appealed to international auth

Nine Killed In Solukhumbu Landslides

Kathmandu, Sept. 23 (RSS): The continuous rain of last Thursday claimed 9 lives in Kaku village panchayat, Ward no. 7 of Solukhumbu district when seven houses were swept away by landslides, it is learnt from the Home Ministry.

A relief team composed of local panchas, administration, police and social workers has already — for the area

---

and environment issues throughout the Himalaya.

Radio & Television

Radio Nepal has news bulletins in English at 8 am and 8.30 pm daily. Television arrived in Nepal in the mid-80s.

HEALTH

Travel health depends on your pre-departure preparations, your day-to-day health care while travelling and how you handle any medical problem or emergency that does develop. While the list of potential dangers can seem quite frightening, with a little luck, some basic precautions and adequate information, few travellers experience more than upset stomachs.

Travel Health Guides

There are a number of books on travel health:

Staying Healthy in Asia, Africa & Latin America (Volunteers in Asia, Stanford California, 1988). Probably the best all round guide to carry as it's compact but very detailed and well organised.

Travellers' Health, Dr Richard Dawood, (Oxford University Press, 1986). Easy to read, comprehensive, authoritative and highly recommended although it's rather large to lug around.

Where There is No Doctor, David Werner (Hesperian Foundation, Palo Alto, California, 1977). A very detailed guide intended for someone, like a Peace Corps

worker, going to work in an undeveloped country, rather than for the average traveller. *Travel with Children*, Maureen Wheeler, (Lonely Planet Publications, Hawthorn, 1990). Including basic advice on travel health for younger children.

Pre-Departure Preparations

Health Insurance A travel insurance policy which covers theft, loss and medical problems is a wise idea. There is a wide variety of policies and your travel agent will have recommendations. The international student travel policies handled by STA or other student travel organisations are usually good value. Some policies offer lower and higher medical expenses options but the higher one is mainly for countries like the US where medical costs are extremely expensive. Check the small print:

• Some policies specifically exclude 'dangerous activities' which can even include trekking. You probably don't want that sort of policy.
• You may prefer a policy which pays doctors or hospitals direct rather than you having to pay now and claim later. If you have to claim later make sure you keep all documentation. Some policies ask you to call back (reverse charges) to a centre in your home country where an immediate assess- ment of your problem is made.
• Check if the policy covers ambulances or an emergency flight home. If you have to stretch out you will need two seats and somebody has to pay for it! If you take out

trekking insurance make sure it covers a helicopter rescue service as well. Being flown out by helicopter costs US$1500 to US$2000 and they operate on a pay first, fly afterwards basis.

Medical Kit It's wise to carry a small, straightforward medical kit. In many countries if a medicine is available at all it will generally be available over the counter. Medicine is generally cheaper in Nepal than in the West. A possible medical kit includes:

• Aspirin or panadol – for pain or fever.
• Antihistamine (such as Benadryl) – useful as a decongestant for colds, allergies, to ease the itch from insect bites or stings or to help prevent motion sickness.
• Antibiotics – useful if you're travelling well off the beaten track but they must be prescribed and you should carry the prescription with you.
• Kaolin preparation (Pepto-Bismol), Imodium or Lomotil – for stomach upsets.
• Rehydration mixture – for treatment of severe diarrhoea, this is particularly important if travelling with children.
• Antiseptic, mercurochrome and antibiotic powder or similar 'dry' spray – for cuts and grazes.
• Calamine lotion – to ease irritation from bites or stings.
• Bandages and band-aids – for minor injuries.
• Scissors, tweezers and a thermometer – mercury thermometers are prohibited by airlines.
• Insect repellent, sun block, suntan lotion, chap stick and water purification tablets.

Ideally antibiotics should be administered only under medical supervision and should never be taken indiscriminately. Overuse of antibiotics can weaken your body's ability to deal with infections naturally and can reduce the drug's efficacy on a future occasion. Take only the recommended dose at the prescribed intervals and continue using the antibiotic for the prescribed period, even if the illness seems to be cured earlier. Antibiotics are quite specific to the infections they can treat – stop immediately if there are any serious reactions and don't use an antibiotic at all if you are unsure whether you have the correct one or not.

When buying drugs always check the expiry date and if possible buy from places where correct storage conditions have been followed. In many Third World countries drugs may be dispensed which are no longer recommended, or have even been banned in the West. Nepalese pharmacies stock a reasonable range of Western pharmaceuticals including aspirin (useful for high altitude headaches when trekking) and cough syrup (often necessary in the cold dry winter air).

Health Preparations Make sure you're healthy before you start travelling and that your teeth are OK – a visit to a Kathmandu dentist probably would not be your idea of fun. If you wear glasses bring a spare pair and your prescription. Losing your glasses can be a real problem although new spectacles can be made quickly, cheaply and competently.

If you require a particular medication take an adequate supply as it may not be available locally. Take the prescription, with the generic rather than the brand name, as it will make getting replacements easier. It's a good idea to have the prescription with you to show that you legally use the medication. It's surprising how often over-the-counter drugs from one place are illegal without a prescription or even banned in another.

Immunisations Vaccinations are able to provide protection against diseases you might be unfortunate enough to come into contact with. No specific immunisations are required for Nepal, but a number are certainly advisable and the further off the beaten track you go the more necessary it is to take precautions. All vaccinations should be recorded on an International Health Certificate which is available from your physician or health department.

Plan ahead for getting your vaccinations since some of them require an initial shot

followed by a booster while some vaccinations should not be given together. Most travellers from Western countries will have been immunised against various diseases during childhood but your doctor may still recommend booster shots against measles or polio, diseases still prevalent in many developing countries. The period of protection offered by vaccinations differs widely and some are contraindicated if you are pregnant.

In some countries immunisations are available from airport or government health centres. Travel agents or airline offices will tell you where. A list of possible vaccinations includes:

Cholera Cholera vaccination may be required if you are coming from an infected area but protection is not very effective, only lasts 6 months and is contraindicated for pregnancy.

Meningitis Immunisation is important as there have been recent outbreaks in Nepal. The vaccination offers good protection for over 1 year. In Kathmandu you can get the vaccination free of charge from the Infectious Diseases Clinic (tel 2-15550) in Teku or for US$15 from the CIWEC Clinic (tel 4-10983).

Tetanus & Diptheria Boosters are necessary every 10 years and protection is highly recommended.

Typhoid Protection lasts for 3 years and is useful if you are travelling for long in rural, tropical areas. You may have some side effects such as pain at the injection site, fever, headache and a general unwell feeling. In Kathmandu a typhoid vaccination at the CIWEC clinic costs US$25.

Infectious Hepatitis Gamma globulin is not a vaccination but a ready-made antibody which has proven very successful in reducing the chances of hepatitis infection. Because it may interfere with the development of immunity, gamma globulin should not be given until at least 10 days after administration of the last vaccine needed and as close as possible to departure because of its relatively short-lived protection period of 6 months. Gamma globulin injections at the CIWEC clinic in Kathmandu cost US$13 to US$25. They are cheaper at the Kalimati Clinic (tel 2-14743).

Smallpox Smallpox has now been wiped out worldwide so immunisation is no longer necessary.

Basic Rules

Care in what you eat and drink is the most important health rule; stomach upsets are the most likely travel health problem but the majority of these upsets will be relatively minor. Don't become paranoid: trying the local food is part of the experience of travel after all.

The number one rule is *don't* drink the water and that includes ice. If you don't know for certain that the water is safe always assume the worst. Reputable brands of bottled water or soft drinks are generally fine although in some places refilled bottles are not unknown. Take care with fruit juice, particularly if water may have been added. Milk should be treated with suspicion as it is often unpasteurised. Boiled milk is fine if it is kept hygienically, and yoghurt is always good. Tea or coffee should also be OK since the water would have been boiled.

Salads and fruit should be washed with purified water or peeled where possible. Ice cream is usually OK if it is a reputable brand name, but beware of ice cream that has melted and been refrozen. Thoroughly cooked food is the safest but not if it has been left to cool or if it has been reheated. Avoid undercooked meat. In general, places that are packed with travellers or locals will be fine, empty restaurants are questionable.

Nutrition Make sure your diet is well balanced. Eggs, tofu, beans, lentils (dhal) and nuts are all safe ways to obtain protein. Fruit you can peel (bananas, oranges or mandarins for example) are always safe and a good source of vitamins. Try to eat plenty of grains (rice) and bread. Remember that although food is generally safer if it is cooked well, overcooked food loses much of its nutritional value. If the food is insufficient in terms of nutrition it's a good idea to take vitamin and iron pills.

When the weather is hot make sure you drink enough; don't rely on feeling thirsty to indicate when you should have a drink. Not needing to urinate or very dark yellow urine is a danger sign. On long trips always carry a water bottle with you. Excessive sweating can lead to loss of salt and therefore muscle cramps. Salt tablets are not a good idea as a preventative but in places where not much salt is used, adding additional salt to food can help.

Water Purification The simplest way of purifying water is to boil it thoroughly. Technically this means for 10 minutes, something which happens very rarely! Remember that at high altitude water boils at lower temperature so germs are less likely to be killed.

Simple filtering will not remove all dangerous organisms so if you cannot boil water it should be treated chemically. Chlorine tablets (Puritabs, Steritabs or other brand names) will kill many but not all pathogens. Iodine is very effective in purifying water and is available in tablet form (such as Potable Aqua) but follow the directions carefully and remember that too much iodine can be harmful.

If you can't find tablets, tincture of iodine (2%) or iodine crystals can be used. Two drops of tincture of iodine per litre or quart of clear water is the recommended dosage; the treated water should then be left to stand for 30 minutes. Iodine crystals can also be used to purify water but this is a more complicated process as you have to first prepare a saturated iodine solution. Iodine loses its effectiveness if it is exposed to air or damp so keep it in a tightly sealed container. Flavoured powder will disguise the taste of treated water and is a good idea if you are travelling with children.

Health A normal body temperature is 37°C or 98.6°F; more than 2°C higher is a 'high' fever. A normal adult pulse rate is 60 to 80 per minute (children 80 to 100, babies 100 to 140). You should know how to take a temperature and a pulse rate. As a general rule the pulse increases about 20 beats per minute for each °C rise in fever.

Respiration rate (breathing) is also an indicator of illness. Count the number of breaths per minute: between 12 and 20 is normal for adults and older children (up to 30 for younger children, 40 for babies). People with a high fever or serious respiratory illness (like pneumonia) breathe more quickly than normal. More than 40 shallow breaths a minute usually means pneumonia.

Many health problems can be avoided by taking care of yourself. Wash your hands frequently, as it's quite easy to contaminate your own food. You should clean your teeth with purified water rather than straight from the tap. Avoid climatic extremes: keep out of the sun when it's hot, dress warmly when it's cold. Avoid potential diseases by dressing sensibly. You can get worm infections through bare feet. Try to avoid insect bites by covering bare skin when insects are around, screening windows or beds or using insect repellents.

Medical Problems & Treatment
Potential medical problems can be broken down into several areas. First there are the climatic and geographical considerations – problems which are caused by extremes of temperature, altitude or motion. Then there are diseases and illnesses caused by insanitation, insect bites or stings, animal or human contact. Simple cuts, bites or scratches can also cause problems.

Medical Facilities in Kathmandu The centrally located, government-operated Bir Hospital (tel 2-21119) has reasonable facilities. Inexpensive vaccinations are available at the Central Health Laboratory from 10 am to 1 pm. The Patan Hospital (tel 5-22278) is partially funded by Western missionaries and is in the Lagankhel district of Patan, close to the last stop of the Lagankhel bus.

The CIWEC clinic (tel 4-10983) is opposite the Soviet Embassy in Baluwatar and is used by many foreign residents of Kathmandu. It's open from 9 am to 1 pm and 2 to 4 pm, is staffed by Westerners and with a single visit costing US$25 the clientele is almost exclusively Westerners as well. The new Nepal International Clinic (tel 4-12842) is near Durbar Marg and the Jaya Nepal cinema and is rather less expensive than the CIWEC clinic although it also has a lab and vaccination facilities.

For simple complaints the Friends of Shanta Bhawan (tel 4-14106) at Jorpati near Bodhnath is open from 9 am to 3 pm Monday to Friday. This American-operated local health care programme is very inexpensive. A Japanese aid project finances a modern and well-equipped teaching hospital (tel 4-12303) at Maharajganj.

Doctors in Kathmandu who have been recommended include:

I Acharya – general practitioner
    Tripureshwar (tel 2-16532)
H Dixit – paediatrician
    Dilli Bazaar (tel 4-10604)
S K Pahari – general practitioner
    Jamal (tel 4-12521)
R P Pokhrel – opthalmologist
    New Rd Gate (tel 2-20101)
N C Rai – opthalmologist
    Blue Star Building (tel 5-22128)
M B Shrestha – dentist
    New Rd near Fire Brigade (tel 2-22282)

In Pokhara the Shining Hospital, formerly run by missionaries, has now been merged with the Gandaki Zonal Hospital and has fairly basic facilities.

Climatic & Geographical Considerations

Sunburn At high altitude you can get sunburnt surprisingly quickly even through cloud. You should use a sun block, and wearing a hat provides added protection. Use zinc cream or some other barrier cream for your nose and lips. Calamine lotion is good relief for mild sunburn.

Cold Too much cold is just as dangerous as too much heat, particularly if it leads to hypothermia. If you are trekking you should always be prepared for cold, wet or windy conditions.

Hypothermia occurs when the body loses heat faster than it can produce it and the core temperature of the body falls. It is surprisingly easy to progress from very cold to dangerously cold due to a combination of wind, wet clothing, fatigue and hunger, even if the air temperature is above freezing point. It is best to dress in layers: silk, wool and some of the new synthetic fibres are all good insulating materials. A hat is important as a lot of heat is lost through the head. A strong, waterproof outer layer is essential as keeping dry is vital. Carry basic supplies including food which contains simple sugars to generate heat quickly and lots of fluid to drink.

Symptoms of hypothermia are exhaustion, numb skin (particularly toes and fingers), shivering, slurred speech, irrational or violent behaviour, lethargy, stumbling, dizzy spells, muscle cramps and violent bursts of energy. Irrationality may take the form of sufferers claiming they are warm and trying to take off their clothes.

To treat hypothermia first get out of the wind and/or rain, remove wet clothing and replace with dry, warm clothing. Drink hot liquids, not alcohol, and eat high calorie, easily digestible food. This should be enough for the early stages of hypothermia, but if it has gone further it may be necessary to place the victim in a warm sleeping bag and get in with them. Do not rub the patient, place them near a fire or remove wet clothes in the wind. If possible place them in a warm (not hot) bath.

Altitude Sickness Called Acute Mountain Sickness or AMS this occurs at high altitude and can be fatal. The lack of oxygen at high altitudes affects most people to some extent. It's important to allow for acclimatisation: take it easy at first, increase your intake of liquid and eat well. However, even with acclimatisation you may still have trouble adjusting – headaches, nausea, dizziness, a dry cough, insomnia, breathlessness, loss of appetite are all signs to heed. If you reach a high altitude by trekking, acclimatisation takes place gradually and you are less likely to be affected than if you fly straight there.

Mild altitude problems will generally abate after a day or so but if the symptoms persist or become worse the only treatment is to descend – even a few hundred metres can help. Breathlessness, a dry, irritative cough – which may progress to the production of pink, frothy sputum – severe headache, loss of appetite, nausea and sometimes vomiting are all danger signs. Increasing tiredness, confusion and lack of coordination and balance are real danger signs. Any of these symptoms individually, even just a persistent headache, can be a warning.

There is no hard and fast rule as to how high is too high: AMS has been fatal at altitudes of 3000 metres, although 3500 to 4500 metres is the usual range. It is wise to always sleep at a lower altitude than the greatest height reached during the day and remember those three basic rules for the treatment of AMS – descend, descend, descend.

The voluntary Himalayan Rescue Association publishes a pamphlet on AMS which is available from the immigration office and from all trekking agencies. They have an office in the Kathmandu Guest House compound in Thamel.

Motion Sickness Eating lightly before and during a trip will reduce the chances of motion sickness. If you are prone to motion sickness try to find a place that minimises disturbance – near the wing on aircraft, near the centre on buses. Fresh air usually helps, reading or cigarette smoke doesn't. There are commercial preparations to prevent motion sickness, but they may cause drowsiness. Preparations have to be taken before the trip commences: when you're feeling sick it's too late. Ginger is a natural preventative and is available in capsule form.

Diseases of Insanitation

Diarrhoea A change of water, food or climate can all cause the runs but more serious is diarrhoea due to contaminated food or water.

Despite all your precautions you may still have a bout of mild travellers' diarrhoea but a few rushed toilet trips with no other symptoms is not indicative of a serious problem. Moderate diarrhoea, involving half a dozen loose movements in a day, is more of a nuisance. Dehydration is the main danger with any diarrhoea, particularly for children, so fluid replenishment is the number one treatment. Weak black tea with a little sugar, soft drinks left to go flat and diluted with water or soda water are all good. With severe diarrhoea a rehydrating solution is necessary to replace minerals and salts. You should stick to a bland diet as you recover.

Lomotil or Imodium can be used to bring relief from the symptoms although they do not actually cure it. Only use these drugs if absolutely necessary – if you *must* travel for example. For children Imodium is preferred. Do not use these drugs if the sufferer has a high fever or if he/she is severely dehydrated. Antibiotics can be very useful in treating severe diarrhoea especially if the illness is accompanied by nausea, vomiting, stomach cramps or mild fever.

Giardia This intestinal parasite is present in contaminated water and the symptoms are stomach cramps, nausea, bloated stomach, watery foul-smelling diarrhoea and frequent gas. Giardia can appear several weeks after exposure to the parasite, and the symptoms may disappear for a few days and then return; this might go on for a number of weeks. Metronidazole known as Flagyl is the recommended drug but should only be taken under medical supervision; antibiotics are no use.

Dysentery This serious illness is caused by contaminated food or water and is characterised by severe diarrhoea, often with blood or mucus in the stool. There are two kinds of dysentery. Bacillary dysentery is characterised by a high fever and rapid development; headache, vomiting and stomach pains are also symptoms. It generally does not last longer than a week, but it is highly contagious.

Amoebic dysentery is more gradual in developing, causes no fever or vomiting but is a more serious illness. It's not a disease that is self-limiting: it will persist until treated and can recur and cause long-term damage.

A stool test is necessary with dysentery but if no medical care is available tetracycline is the prescribed treatment for bacillary dysentery, metronidazole for amoebic dysentery.

Cholera The cholera vaccination is not very effective. Cholera outbreaks are generally widely reported so you can avoid these areas. The disease is characterised by a sudden onset of acute diarrhoea with 'rice water' stools, vomiting, muscular cramps, and extreme weakness. Medical help is required, but you should treat for dehydration which can be extreme. If there is an appreciable delay in reaching a hospital begin taking tetracycline. This drug should not be given to young children or pregnant women and it should not be used past its expiry date.

Viral Gastroenteritis This is not caused by bacteria but, as the name suggests, by a virus and is characterised by stomach cramps, diarrhoea, sometimes vomiting, and sometimes a slight fever. All you can do is rest and drink lots of fluids.

Hepatitis Hepatitis A is the most common form of this disease and is spread by contaminated food or water. The symptoms are fever, chills, headache, fatigue, feelings of weakness and aches and pains. This is followed by loss of appetite, nausea, vomiting, abdominal pain, dark urine, light coloured faeces and jaundiced skin. The whites of the eyes may turn yellow. In some case there may just be a feeling of being unwell, tired, no appetite, aches and pains and the jaundiced effect. You should seek medical advice, but in general there is not much you can do apart from resting, drinking lots of fluids, eating lightly and avoiding fatty foods. People who have had hepatitis must forego alcohol for 6 months after the

illness as hepatitis attacks the liver and it needs that amount of time to recover.

Hepatitis B, which used to be called serum hepatitis, is spread through sexual contact, through skin penetration, for example dirty needles, and blood transfusions. Avoid having your ears pierced, tattoos done or injections where you have doubts about the sanitary conditions. The symptoms and treatment of type B are much the same as type A but gamma globulin as a prophylaxis is only effective against type A.

Typhoid Typhoid Fever is another intestinal infection that travels the faecal-oral route, ie contaminated water and food are responsible. Vaccination against typhoid is not totally effective and it is one of the most dangerous infections so medical help must be sought.

The early symptoms are like so many others: you may feel like you have a bad cold or flu on the way, headache, sore throat and a fever which rises a little each day until it is around 40°C or more. The pulse is often slow for the amount of fever present and gets slower as the fever rises, unlike a normal fever where the pulse increases. There may also be vomiting, diarrhoea or constipation.

In the second week the high fever and slow pulse continue and a few pink spots may appear on the body along with trembling, delirium, weakness, weight loss and dehydration. If there are no further complications, the fever and symptoms will slowly go during the third week. However, you must get medical help before this as common complications are pneumonia (acute infection of the lungs) or peritonitis (burst appendix). Typhoid is very infectious.

The victim's fever should be treated by keeping them cool and watching that they don't become dehydrated. Chloramphenicol is the recommended antibiotic but there are fewer side affects with ampicillin.

Worms These parasites are most common in rural, tropical areas and a stool test when you return home is not a bad idea. They can be present on unwashed vegetables or in undercooked meat and you can pick them up through your skin by walking in bare feet. Infestations may not show up for some time, and although they are generally not serious, if left untreated they can cause severe health problems. A stool test is necessary to pinpoint the problem and medication is often available over the counter.

Diseases Spread by People & Animals

Tetanus This potentially fatal disease is found in undeveloped tropical areas and is difficult to treat but is preventable with immunisation. Tetanus occurs when a wound becomes infected by a germ which lives in the faeces of animals or people so clean all cuts, punctures or animal bites. Tetanus is known as lockjaw and the first symptom may be discomfort in swallowing, followed by stiffening of the jaw and neck, and then painful convulsions of the jaw and whole body.

Rabies Rabies is found in many countries and is caused by a bite or scratch by an infected animal. Dogs are a noted carrier. Any bite, scratch or even lick from a mammal should be cleaned immediately and thoroughly. Scrub with soap and running water then clean with an alcohol solution. If there is any possibility that the animal is infected medical help should be sought immediately. Even if the animal is not rabid, all bites should be treated seriously as they can become infected or can result in tetanus. A rabies vaccination is now available and should be considered if you are in a high risk category, eg people working with animals. The pre-exposure vaccination is available at the CIWEC clinic for US$25.

Meningococcal Meningitis There have been outbreaks of meningitis in Nepal. Trekkers should be particularly careful as the disease is spread by close contact with people who are carrying it in their throats and noses, and it is spread by coughing and sneezing. These people may not be aware that they are carriers. Lodges in the hills where travellers spend the night are prime spots for the spread of infection.

This very serious disease attacks the brain and can be fatal. The first symptoms are a scattered blotchy rash, fever, severe headache, sensitivity to light and neck stiffness which prevents forward bending of the head. Death can occur within a few hours so it is important to get immediate treatment.

The treatment is large doses of penicillin given intravenously, or, if that is not possible, intramuscularly, ie in the buttocks.

Tuberculosis Although this disease is widespread in many undeveloped countries it is not a serious risk to travellers. Young children are more susceptible than adults and vaccination is a sensible precaution for children under 12 travelling in endemic areas. TB is commonly spread by coughing or by unpasteurised dairy products from infected cows. Milk that has been boiled is safe to drink and the souring of milk to make yoghurt or cheese kills the bacilli.

Diptheria Diptheria can be a skin infection or a more dangerous throat infection. It is spread by contaminated dust contacting the skin or by the inhalation of infected cough or sneeze droplets. Frequent washing and keeping the skin dry will help prevent skin infection. A vaccination is available to prevent the throat infection.

Sexually Transmitted Diseases The most common of these diseases are gonorrhoea and syphilis. Note that AIDS can be spread through infected blood transfusions or by dirty needles – vaccinations, acupuncture and tattooing can potentially be as dangerous as intravenous drug use if the equipment is not clean.

Insect-Borne Diseases

Malaria This serious disease is spread by mosquito bites. Symptoms include headaches, fever, chills and sweating which may subside and recur. Without treatment malaria can develop more serious, potentially fatal effects. Malaria has been virtually eradicated from the Terai but malarial phrophylactics are still advisable, especially if you are travelling during the wet season. If your visit to Nepal is restricted to the high country – Kathmandu, Pokhara and the trekking routes – malaria protection is not necessary.

Antimalarial drugs do not actually prevent the disease but suppress its symptoms. Chloroquine is the usual malarial prophylactic and treatment consists of a tablet taken once a week for 2 weeks prior to arrival in the infected area until 6 weeks after you depart. Chloroquine resistant malaria is not a problem in Nepal.

Chloroquine is quite safe for general use, the side effects are minimal and it can be taken by pregnant women. Maloprim, generally recommended for areas where chloroquine resistance has been reported, can have rare but serious side effects. Fansidar, once used as a chloroquine alternative, is no longer recommended because of dangerous side effects but it may still be recommended as a treatment for malaria. Chloroquine is also used for malaria treatment but in larger doses than normal prophylaxis.

Mosquitoes appear after dusk and making an effort to avoid being bitten by covering bare skin and using an insect repellent will further reduce the risk. Insect screens on windows and mosquito nets on beds offer protection, as does burning a mosquito coil. Mosquitoes may be attracted by perfume, aftershave or certain colours.

Dengue Fever There is no prophylactic available for this mosquito-spread disease and the main preventative measure is to avoid mosquito bites. A sudden onset of fever, headaches and severe joint and muscle pains are the first signs before a rash starts on the trunk and spreads to the limbs and face. After a few more days, the fever subsides and recovery will begin. Serious complications are not common.

Cuts, Bites & Stings
Cuts & Scratches Skin punctures can easily become infected in hot climates and may be difficult to heal. Treat any cut with an antiseptic solution and mercurochrome.

Where possible avoid bandages and band-aids which can keep wounds wet.

Snake Bite The chances of being bitten by a snake in Nepal are remote. Snake bites do not cause instantaneous death and antivenins are usually available. Keep the victim calm and still, wrap the bitten limb tightly, as you would for a sprained ankle, and attach a splint to immobilise it. Then seek medical help, if possible with the dead snake for identification. Don't attempt to catch the snake if there is any remote possibility of being bitten again. Tourniquets and sucking out the poison are now comprehensively discredited.

Insect & Spider Bites & Stings Bee and wasp stings are usually painful rather than dangerous. Calamine lotion will give relief or ice packs will reduce the pain and swelling. There are some spiders with dangerous bites but antivenins are usually available.

Bedbugs & Lice Bedbugs live in various places, particularly dirty mattresses and bedding. Spots of blood on bedclothes or on the wall around the bed can be read as a suggestion to find another hotel. Bedbugs leave itchy bites in neat rows. Calamine lotion may help.

All lice cause itching and discomfort and make themselves at home in your hair (head lice), your clothing (body lice) or in your

pubic hair (crabs). They get to you by direct contact with infected people or sharing combs, clothing and the like. Powder or shampoo treatment will kill the lice and infected clothing should be washed in very hot water.

Leeches Leeches (*jukha*) are common along trekking trails or in the Royal Chitwan National Park during the monsoon. They attach themselves to your skin to suck your blood. For some time after the monsoon finishes they can still be found in damp areas. Walkers often get them on their legs or in their boots. Salt or a lighted cigarette end will make them fall off. Do not pull them off as the bite is then more likely to become infected. An insect repellent may keep them away so if they're a real nuisance it's worth soaking your socks in repellent.

Women's Health
Gynaecological Problems A poor diet, lowered resistance due to the use of antibiotics for stomach upsets and even contraceptive pills can lead to vaginal infections when travelling in hot climates. Keeping the genital area clean, wearing cotton underwear and skirts or loose-fitting trousers will help to prevent infections.

Yeast infections, characterised by a rash, itch and discharge can be treated with a vinegar or even lemon juice douche or with yoghurt. Nystatin suppositories are the usual medical prescription. Trichomonas is a more serious infection with a discharge and a burning sensation when urinating. Male sexual partners must also be treated and if a vinegar-water douche is not effective medical attention should be sought. Flagyl is the prescribed drug.

Pregnancy Most miscarriages occur during the first 3 months of pregnancy so this is the most risky time to travel. The last 3 months should also be spent within reasonable distance of good medical care as quite serious problems can develop at this time. Pregnant women should avoid all unnecessary medication, but vaccinations and malarial prophylactics should still be taken where possible. Additional care should be taken to prevent illness and particular attention should be paid to diet and nutrition.

DANGERS & ANNOYANCES
Theft
Things do get stolen in Nepal, just like anywhere else in Asia. There are pickpockets in crowded areas of old Kathmandu, and backpacks disappearing off the top of buses is another good way to lose things. One traveller wrote of having his backpack stolen from a Kathmandu to Barabise bus. There's little chance of getting it back in that circumstance but even getting a police report, a necessity for an insurance claim, can be difficult. If this happens the best bet is to avoid the local police stations and go straight to the Interpol Section, Police Headquarters, Laxal, Kathmandu. The telephone numbers are 4-11210, 4-10088, 4-11705 and 4-11059, and the postal address is PO Box 407. There is a local Interpol office near Durbar Square but it will only handle your case if the theft actually took place in Kathmandu.

FILM & PHOTOGRAPHY
A few years ago running out of film in Nepal could be a real problem but now there are numerous camera and film shops and good quality film is usually readily available. Don't count on finding exactly what you want, but if you're flexible, running out should not be a problem. Kodachrome 64 36-exposure slide film costs about Rs 290 including processing, Fujichrome 100 36-exposure slide film is about Rs 170, Fujicolor 100 print film is about Rs 90. Film can be readily developed in Kathmandu where a same-day service is offered. See the Kathmandu section for more details.

Nepal is an exceptionally photogenic country so bring plenty of film. It can also provide you with some challenging opportunities. For great shots you need a variety of lenses, from a wide angle lens if you're shooting inside compact temple compounds to long telephotos if you're after perfect mountain shots or close-ups of wildlife.

Remember also to allow for the exceptional intensity of mountain light when setting exposures at high altitude. A polarising filter can often be useful to provide contrast against the sky. At the other extreme it's surprising how often in Nepal you find the light is insufficient! Early in the morning, in dense jungle in the Royal Chitwan National Park, or in gloomy temples you may often find yourself wishing you had high speed film. A flash is often necessary for shots inside temples or to fill in shots of sculptures and reliefs.

Most Nepalese are content to have their photograph taken but you should ask first. Sherpa people are an exception and can be very camera shy. Those Nepalese who pose for you may insist on being given some baksheesh for doing so. Good manners are as important in Nepal as any other country. If people do not want to be photographed then don't do it. Respect people's privacy: just because somebody is bathing in a river doesn't mean they think they're out in the open for anyone to watch or photograph. To them the river may be just as private a place as your bathroom is to you. They don't expect other local people to stare and nor should you. Religious ceremonies can also be private affairs, so first make sure that photography is acceptable.

Don't make all your contact with local people a one-way vision through a camera lens. Your camera can even be a way of breaking the ice – children always love to look through the lens.

ACCOMMODATION

In Kathmandu there is a very wide variety of hotels from rock bottom flea pits to five star international places. The intense competition between the many cheaper places keeps prices down and standards up – Kathmandu has many fine places with pleasant gardens and rooms for less than US$10 a night including attached bathroom and hot water. At peak times, on the other hand, rooms in the four and five star places can be in short supply.

Pokhara also has a variety of places although the choice is concentrated more at the bottom end of the market. There's only one real luxury hotel in Pokhara. Elsewhere in the country the choice of hotels can be very limited but there are now places to stay along most of the major trekking trails. These days it's quite possible to trek from lodge to lodge rather than camping site to camping site. On some trails the standards may be spartan – the accommodation may be dormitory-style or simply an open room to unroll your sleeping bag. Smoke can be a real problem in places where the chimney has yet to make an appearance. At the other extreme some trails, like the popular Pokhara to Jomsom route, have excellent lodges and guest houses at every stopping place.

FOOD & DRINK

Real Nepalese food is distinctly dull. Most of the time it consists of a dish called *dhal bhat tarkari* which is made up of lentil soup, rice and curried vegetables. The occasional dhal bhat tarkari, prepared to tourist tastes in Kathmandu restaurants, can be just fine. Strictly local versions, eaten day in and day out while trekking, can get very boring indeed. Of course Indian cuisine has had a major influence on Nepal and many Tibetan dishes have come over the border, along with Nepal's many Tibetan refugees. Other popular local food and drink includes:

Beer – the locally produced beer is quite good, especially after a hard day's walking or bicycling around the valley. Beer is sometimes found in the hills as well, carried there by porters especially for thirsty trekkers. It's unlikely to be very cold, however. Iceberg is regarded as the best local brand but it's also the most expensive. Leo and Star beers are good.

Buff – water buffalo, casually abbreviated to buff, is the usual substitute for beef since cows are sacred and (officially at least) cannot be eaten. You may come across anything from buffburgers to buff steaks but in actual fact there are probably some real steaks around as well.

Chang – the home brew of the Himalaya is a mildly alcoholic concoction made from barley.

Curd – yoghurt is known throughout the subcontinent as curd and the buffalo milk curd of Nepal can be very good.

Gundruk – dried vegetables are used in this traditional Nepalese soup.

Gurr – potatoes are the staple food of the Sherpas and although they are a relatively recent introduction potatoes have come to assume the same importance in the Solu Khumbu as they do in Ireland. Gurr is made from raw potatoes ground and mixed with spices and then grilled like a large pancake and eaten with cheese.

Lassi – a very refreshing drink of curd mixed with water. Make sure the water is safe.

Momo or *Kothe* – these typical Tibetan dishes are made by steaming or frying meat or vegetables wrapped in dough. They are very much like dim sum or ravioli.

Sikarni – a sweet curd dessert.

Tama – another traditional Nepalese soup, this one is made from dried bamboo shoots.

Thupka – a traditional Tibetan meat soup.

Tsampa – the staple dish in the hill country, tsampa is ground grain mixed with tea, water or milk and eaten dry either instead of rice or mixed with it.

Although the real local food may be limited in its scope and heavily influenced by Indian cuisine, Kathmandu's restaurants offer an amazing variety of dishes. In the days of 'Asia overlanding', when many travellers arrived in Kathmandu having made a long and often wearisome trip through Asia from Europe, Kathmandu's restaurants had a near mythical appeal. Ecstatic reports filtered back along the trail of superb restaurants and fine cuisine.

These days, when most travellers jet straight in from abroad, the food doesn't seem quite so amazing but Kathmandu's many restaurants still do give international cuisine a damn good try and they will attempt

almost anything. There's a special appeal to being high in the Himalaya and being able to choose between not just European and Asian dishes but also almost anything else from Mexican tacos to Japanese sukiyaki. Of course Nepalese interpretations of foreign dishes often arrive a little off target but Nepal is a great place to try Tibetan dishes and the Indian food can also be very good.

This amazing variety of restaurants is particularly amazing when you consider that in 1955 Kathmandu (which really means all of Nepal) had just one restaurant. Leave Kathmandu behind, however, and apart from a few places in Pokhara and other scattered centres you're soon back to dhal bhat tarkari.

Eating & Drinking Customs

There are a number of 'rules' and customs relating to eating and drinking in Nepal and a number of ways in which you can make life much easier for yourself. For a start the Nepalese eating schedule is quite different from that in the West. The morning usually begins with little more than a cup of tea. Not until late morning is a substantial 'brunch' taken. In areas where Western visitors are not often seen and even more rarely catered for, finding food will be much simpler if you go along with this schedule.

You can also save yourself a lot of time and frustration if you pay attention to what you order as well as when you order it. In small local restaurants the cooking equipment and facilities are often very primitive. Places with some experience of catering to Western tastes will often offer amazingly varied menus, but just because they offer 20 different dishes doesn't mean they can fix two of them at the same time. If you and your five friends turn up at some small and remote cafe and order six different dishes you can expect to be waiting for dinner when breakfast time rolls around next day. In that situation it makes a lot of sense to order the same dish six times!

There are a number of religious restrictions you should observe. The kitchen of a home is a holy of holies where few, and certainly no non-Hindus, may venture.

Touching somebody else's food is a major faux pas – in Nepal you do not taste the soup from the pot! Notice how the Nepalese, when drinking from a jug or bottle, do so by pouring the liquid into their mouth without ever touching the container with their mouth.

Caste rules also play a part in Nepalese eating habits. A high caste Brahmin simply cannot eat food prepared by a lower caste individual, which effectively bans practising Brahmins from restaurants since they cannot know what is going on behind the kitchen door. If you are invited out to a meal at a Nepalese home you may find the women of the household remain totally in the background and do not eat with the men or with guests. As in India even at quite Westernised homes socialising goes on before the meal rather than afterwards. As the last mouthful is consumed the guests head out the door – nobody hangs around for conversation over the coffee!

Of course some foods are strictly taboo in Nepal. High caste Hindus and all Brahmins are, ostensibly at least, vegetarian, but carnivore or not, beef is strictly banned from the menu since the cow is a holy animal. The number one eating rule in Nepal, as in much of Asia, is always to use your right hand. The left hand, used for washing yourself after defecating, is never used to eat food and certainly should not be used to pass food to someone else.

Care in Eating & Drinking

Don't drink the water is the prime health rule on the subcontinent and it certainly applies to Nepal. Diarrhoea, dysentery or even hepatitis can all result from indulging in contaminated drinking water. It is much easier nowadays to keep clear of unhealthy water as bottled mineral water is readily available.

In actual fact the relative safety of the water varies with the season. Drinking tap water is never a good idea, but during the dry season from around November to April you would probably get away with it, in Kathmandu at least. During the monsoon, however, when the heavy rains wash all sorts of stuff into the water supply, don't even consider it. Drinking boiled and filtered water is a better idea at any time of year and absolutely imperative in the wet season.

Most good restaurants do boil and filter their water, although it's worth remembering that completely wiping out every potential pathogen requires keeping the water on the boil for a full 10 minutes. You can be certain that rarely happens. Furthermore at higher altitudes the boiling point of water drops, so again boiling becomes a less effective way of killing off the nasties. There's no way of telling if water has been boiled or not but you cannot make tea without boiling it so tea should generally be safe.

At higher altitudes the water is generally safer than lower down and in more densely populated areas. Nevertheless, trekkers should never drink water from springs or streams unless they are absolutely positive they are at a higher level than any villages or cattle. In Nepal that is a very hard thing to guarantee and it is always wiser to prepare your drinking water carefully. As an alternative to boiling water iodine treatment is also safe and has the added benefit of not requiring a fire. See the Health section for information on iodine treatment. Chang, the popular Tibetan beer, is generally safe and is found along many trekking routes.

Food stalls on the street should be approached with extreme caution and ice cream from street vendors should be completely avoided. In good restaurants the ice cream in Nepal is usually fine. Meat is more likely to be unhealthy than vegetable or egg dishes; a glance at most Nepalese butchers will soon show you why! If you're in doubt about the quality of meat dishes stick to vegetarian dishes.

Beware of salads except in places you know take special care with their food preparation. Salads rinsed in untreated water are notorious for causing stomach problems. Sandwiches can also be risky.

Health Problems Many travellers do develop some sort of stomach upset while in Nepal although fortunately it's usually just travellers' diarrhoea. In that case a little fasting, hot tea and fighting it off naturally is the best cure. That way you develop some resistance against further attacks. See the Health section for more details.

BOOKS & BOOKSHOPS

There is no shortage of books about Nepal – the Himalaya and heroic mountaineers, the colourful religions and exotic temples, the reclusive history and brave Gurkhas, have all inspired writers and photographers and the results are piled high in numerous bookshops in Nepal. Nepal has a surprisingly

---

Chang Recipe
If you develop a taste for chang and would like to brew some at home here's the recipe. Get a 25 or 50 litre fermenting vessel from a brewery supply shop. For the smaller vessel boil about 2 kg of millet for several hours. Millet swells considerably so make sure there is plenty of water and it doesn't stick. When it cools add water to liquefy it; you can also pass it through a blender to smooth it out. Then add burgundy yeast and the juice of a lemon and leave to ferment. This can take several weeks or a couple of months depending on taste. If you like a little extra kick to your chang add sugar, several kg, to the fermenting brew – this is really cheating since in Nepal sugar would be too expensive to be used in this way.

The final product will have to be strained through a cloth and racked to remove the yeasty taste. This should not be taken as the only way to produce chang – experiment with it; in Bhutan for example they drink a chang made from half millet and half rice.

Karel Tiller, Australia ■

good selection of bookshops, mostly in Kathmandu, although there are a number in Pokhara. The books that follow are only some of the more interesting titles and include books that are long out of print and others which may only be available in Nepal.

General

Although *Nepal – the Kingdom in the Himalayas* by Toni Hagen (Kummerley & Frey, Berne, 1980) is now rather out of date it is still one of the most complete studies of Nepal's peoples, geography and geology. Toni Hagen travelled extensively through Nepal in the '50s and the book reflects his intimate knowledge of the country and also has fine colour plates.

Another now rather dated account of Nepal is Jeremy Bernstein's *The Wildest Dreams of Kew* (Simon & Schuster, New York, 1970) which covers the country's history in a very readable style and includes an interesting trek to the Everest Base Camp.

Michel Peissel takes a trip to the fabled region of Mustang, close to the border with Tibet and to the north of Jomsom, in *Mustang – a Lost Tibetan Kingdom* (Collins & Harvill Press, London, 1968). A more recent saunter around Nepal and Tibet is recounted in the amusingly written *To the Navel of the World* by Peter Somerville-Large (Hamish Hamilton, London, 1987; paperback by Sceptre, London, 1988). The author also does some deep-winter trekking, using yaks, in the Solu Khumbu and up to the Everest Base Camp. His encounters with tourism in remote locations are very funny.

Pico Iyer's recent best seller *Video Night in Kathmandu* (Vintage Books, New York, 1989) gallivants all around Asia but in the chapter on Nepal his observations of the collision between Nepalese traditions and Western culture, video culture in particular, are astute and amusing.

The Waiting Land: A Spell in Nepal by Dervla Murphy (John Murray, London, 1967; and in paperback by Century Hutchinson) is an interesting account of a visit to Nepal at a time when great changes were in hand.

In *Mister Raja's Neighbourhood* (John Daniel, Santa Barbara, California, 1986) and *Shopping for Buddhas* (Harper & Row, San Francisco, 1990) Jeff Greenwald gives amusing accounts of his travels in Nepal.

Han Suyin's *The Mountain is Young* (Jonathan Cape, London, 1971; and various paperback editions) is a rather over-romantic novel set in Nepal in the mid-50s. It is surprising more novelists haven't used Nepal's colourful background for their writing.

History & Economics

Although browsing through a good Kathmandu bookshop will reveal plenty of histories of Nepal there is no definitive book which tells it all in a readable fashion. In particular there has been little accounting of recent events in Nepal, especially the push for great democracy and the underlying political unrest.

The Political History of Nepal by Margaret W Fisher (Institute of International Studies, University of California, Berkeley, 1960) is now 30 years old and even *Nepal in Crisis* by Blaikie, Cameron & Seddon (Oxford University Press, Oxford, 1978) is rather dated.

Travels in Nepal by Charlie Pye-Smith (Aurum Press, London, 1988) is a travel account on one level, but the author's travels around the country are highly directed: he was there to study the impacts and benefits of foreign aid to Nepal and his conclusions are incisive and interesting. In between the aid projects he chain-smokes his way around quite a few interesting places and appears to finish up as much in love with the country as many less single-minded visitors! See the Foreign Aid section in the Facts about the Country chapter for more about this book.

Culture, People & Festivals

Festivals of Nepal by Mary Anderson (Unwin Hyman, London, 1971 and Rupa & Co, Calcutta, 1988) is an excellent rundown on Nepal's many festivals and includes interesting accounts of many of the legends and tales behind them. There is also a great deal of background information about the Hindu religion. *The Gods of Nepal* Mary Rubel (Bhim Ratna Harsha Ratna, Kathmandu, 1968) is a detailed description of the Hindu and Buddhist deities of Nepal.

People of Nepal by Dor Bahadur Bista (Ratna Pustak Bhandar, Kathmandu, 1974) is written by a Nepalese anthropologist and describes the many and diverse ethnic groupings found in the country. The recently published *Ethnic Groups of Nepal* by D B Shrestha & C B Singh (Himalayan Booksellers, Kathmandu, 1987) is a readily available account of the many peoples of Nepal.

Sherpas of Nepal by C Von Furer Haimendorf (John Murray, London 1964) describes the Sherpas of the Everest region in a rather dry and academic manner. From the same author *Himalayan Traders* (John Murray, London, 1975) is a rather more readable follow up, concentrating on the changes in trading patterns and cultures among the Himalayan people of Nepal.

Tiger for Breakfast by Michel Peissel (Hodder & Stoughton, London, 1966; and in paperback by Allied Publishers) is a biography of the colourful gentleman who was probably the best known resident expatriate in the kingdom – Boris Lissanevitch of the Royal Hotel and Yak & Yeti Restaurant.

Natural History

The Royal Chitwan National Park's wildlife is detailed in *The Heart of the Jungle* by K K Gurung (Andre Deutsch, London, 1983). *Indian Wildlife* (Apa Productions, Singapore, 1987) covers all the national parks of the subcontinent including Chitwan and Bardia in Nepal, together with descriptions of the wildlife and with this publisher's usual high standards of photography.

Birds of Nepal by Robert Fleming Sr, Robert Fleming Jr & Lain Singh Bangdel (Nature Himalayas, Kathmandu, 1984) is a field guide to Nepal's hundreds of different birds. *Himalayan Flowers & Trees* by Dorothy Mierow & Tirtha Bahadur Shrestha (Sahayogi Press, Kathmandu, 1978) is the best available field guide to the plants of Nepal.

Art & Architecture

Lydia Aran's *The Art of Nepal* (Sahayogi Prakashan, Kathmandu, 1978) is both readily available in Nepal and concentrates on the art that can actually be seen in the country, not in overseas museums. See the Arts & Crafts section of the Facts about the Country chapter for more on this book.

The Austrian publisher Anton Schroll published two exhaustive studies of the architecture of the Kathmandu Valley. *Kathmandu Valley I* (Vienna, 1975) covers the most important temples and buildings in great detail while *Kathmandu Valley II* has individual plans of a great many temples and buildings. This is strictly for the academics but it's amusing to see how many other guidebooks have used these titles in their research. Often they've even copied the mistakes!

Mary Shepherd Sluiser's *Nepal Mandala – A Cultural Study of the Kathmandu Valley* (Princeton University Press, Princeton, 1982) is another two-volume academic study of the valley.

Nepal – Art Treasures from the Himalayas by Waldschmidt (Oxford & IBH, London, 1969) describes and illustrates many Nepalese works of art. The art of the whole Himalayan region is covered in *Himalayan Art* by Madanjeet Singh (Macmillan,

London, 1968), again with excellent photographs.

In *Kathmandu Valley Towns* (Weatherhill, New York, 1974) Fran Hosken writes about the temples, people, history and festivals of the towns of the Kathmandu Valley. The book is illustrated with a great many photographs both colour and half tone.

Erotic Themes of Nepal by Trilok Chandra Majupuria & Indra Majupuria (S Devi, Kirtipur, Kathmandu, 1981) is an interesting locally produced book on the erotic art seen on some temples, although it has to work hard to make a book-length study of the subject!

If you develop an interest in Tibetan rugs Hallvard Kåre Kuløy's *Tibetan Rugs* (White Orchid Books, Bangkok, 1982) is a fascinating and well-illustrated introduction to the subject. If you enjoy the Tibetan rugs made in Nepal you may be disappointed to find that the author summarily dismisses modern rugs as doing 'very little justice to a very splendid tradition'.

Travel Guides

Other guidebooks to Nepal include *Insight Nepal* (Apa Productions, Singapore, 1988) in the Insight series of photographic coffee table guides. *Nepal Namaste* by Robert Rieffel (Sahayogi Press, Kathmandu, 1987) is an excellent locally produced book with all sorts of odd titbits of information.

The Himalaya Experience by Jonathan Chester (Simon & Schuster Australia, Gladesville, 1989) is an interesting, colourful appetite-whetter for the entire Himalayan region. It has a great deal of interesting information about trekking and climbing and some wonderful photographs.

An Introduction to the Hanuman Dhoka (Institute of Nepal & Asian Studies, Kirtipur, 1975) is no longer readily available, but it gives a good short description of the buildings around the Durbar Square area of Kathmandu.

Trekking Guides

Lonely Planet's *Trekking in the Nepal Himalaya* by Stan Armington covers everything you need to know before setting out for a trek in Nepal, plus day-by-day coverage of all the main trekking routes. Stan's book has an excellent medical section covering the problems likely to be encountered in the mountains. *A Guide to Trekking in Nepal* by Stephen Bezruchka (The Mountaineers, Seattle, 1981) also covers all the main trekking routes with detailed descriptions.

If you're interested in treks close to Kathmandu, *Treks on the Kathmandu Valley Rim* by Alton C Byers III (Sahayogi Press, Kathmandu, 1987) details a number of 1 day and overnight treks near Kathmandu.

Trekking Accounts

John Morris' *A Winter in Nepal* (Rupert Hart-Davis, London, 1964) recounts in a very readable fashion a trek from Kathmandu to Pokhara. Like other accounts of the time it's interesting to compare it with the situation today – there was no Kathmandu to Pokhara road in those days. Morris was a retired British army Gurkha officer and his ability to speak Nepali gives him an excellent insight into Nepalese life.

Peter Matthiessen's *The Snow Leopard* (Chatto & Windus, London, 1979; also available in paperback) is, on one level, an account of a trek from Pokhara up to Dolpo in the west of Nepal, keeping an eye open for snow leopards on the way. On other levels,

however, it's clear the author is searching for much more than rare wildlife and this widely acclaimed book doggedly pursues the big questions with the Himalaya as a background.

George Schaller, Matthiessen's companion on this trek, includes this same journey in *Stones of Silence* (Viking, New York, 1979), an account of various journeys in the Himalaya.

Mountains & Mountaineering

There can be few activities that so inspire people to write about them as that of mountaineering. Every first ascent of a Himalayan peak – and a good many first routes, first this and first that – seems to have resulted in a book about it together with numerous other books written simply because it seemed a good idea. *The Ascent of Rum Doodle* by W E Bowman (paperback by Dark Peak, Sheffield, 1979) is a classic spoof of these often all-too-serious tomes.

Some mountaineering books are excellent reads. If you can find *Nepal Himalaya* by H W Tilman (Cambridge University Press, London, 1952) in a library it gives an often amusing account of some early trekking expeditions together with the odd mountain assault with, by today's standards, an amazing lack of advance planning. Although Tilman was a Himalayan mountaineering pioneer he probably contributed even more to the current popularity of trekking. His book has recently been republished together with other Tilman classics in *The Seven Mountain-Travel Books* (The Mountaineers, Seattle). Tilman's dry wit is quite delightful.

Annapurna by Maurice Herzog (Jonathan Cape, London, 1952) is a mountaineering classic. Herzog led the first group to reach the top of an 8000 metre peak, but the descent turned into a frostbitten nightmare taking them to the very outer edges of human endurance.

Naturally there have been numerous books about climbing Everest, including *Forerunners to Everest* by Rene Dittert, Gabriel Chevalley & Raymond Lambert (Harper & Row, New York, 1954). It describes the two Swiss expeditions to Everest in 1952 and includes a good description of the old expedition route march. *The Conquest of Everest* by Sir John Hunt (Hodder & Stoughton, London, 1953) is the official account of the first successful climb of the world's highest mountain. *Everest* by Walt Unsworth (Allen Lane, London, 1981) is probably the best history of Everest mountaineering.

In the 1970s unconquered peaks were few and far between so mountaineers' attention turned to climbing by more difficult or spectacular routes. This was technical climbing of a high order and Englishman Chris Bonnington's various expeditions were the best known examples of the craft. His book *Annapurna South Face* (Cassell, London, 1971) describes in detail the planning that goes into making a major expedition and the complicated logistics of the actual climb, and makes an authoritative account of a highly technical assault on a difficult face.

Bonnington also wrote *Everest the Hard Way* (Hodder & Stoughton, London, 1976; also available in paperback) describing his expedition's first ascent of the south-western face in 1975. This climb was a perfectly planned and executed race to the top, and the book is illustrated with superb mountain photography. Despite his record of leading some of the most acclaimed mountaineering expeditions of the time Bonnington did not reach the top of Everest until 1985, when he set a record as the oldest-ever Everest summiteer. He was 50 years old at the time but just 9 days later his record fell to 55 year old American climber Dick Bass!

Galen Rowell, the renowned mountain photographer, has written *Many people come, looking, looking* (The Mountaineers, Seattle, 1981). It is a thought-provoking study of the impact of trekking and mountaineering on the Himalayan region. There's a good description of the Annapurna Circuit Trek and a quick sidetrip to knock off a little 6000 metre peak!

Other mountaineering books include *Annapurna to Dhaulagiri* by Harka Gurung (Department of Information, HMG, Kath-

Top: Children at Kathmandu market (SB)
Left: All-seeing eyes watch over novice monks at Bodhnath, Kathmandu (RE)
Right: Fruit vendor, Kathmandu (SB)

mandu) which covers the period between 1950 and 1960 when most of Nepal's major peaks 'fell' to mountaineering expeditions. Herbert Tichy's *Himalaya* (Robert Hale, London, 1970) describes the author's journeys in the region from the 1930s including his ascent of Cho Oyu, the third highest peak climbed at that time.

Finally for keen do-it-yourself mountaineers Bill O'Connor's *The Trekking Peaks of Nepal* (Crowood Press, Marlborough, UK, 1989) is a complete description of the climbing routes up Nepal's 18 'trekking peaks'.

MAPS

An interesting account of the history of mapping in Nepal is found in *Maps of Nepal* by Harka Gurung (White Orchid Books, Bangkok, 1983) which covers historic maps right up to the latest (in the early '80s at least) trekking maps.

The Nelles Verlag *Nepal* map (possibly available as an Apa Map) is an excellent map for general tourism in Nepal although it only covers the eastern half of the country. There are enlargements for the Kathmandu Valley and Kathmandu city. The Schneider Map series includes excellent maps of the Kathmandu Valley, Kathmandu and Patan.

The Research Scheme Nepal Himalaya maps are better known as Schneider Maps, after their cartographer. These are the best trekking maps available although their price is as high as their quality. The series covers the routes into the Everest region in six separate maps.

There are many locally produced maps available in Nepal which are much cheaper and for most trekkers prove quite adequate. Most of these are produced by Mandala Trekking Maps, and although they are generally only in blueprint form they have recently produced coloured versions of the Helambu/Langtang map and the Annapurna Circuit map.

The problem with all the detailed maps of Nepal is that villages often have widely diverse names and their actual position is often equally open to question. Reality, when you're there on foot, is often very different from what the map says. Even the Schneider Maps often have highly original versions of common place names.

THINGS TO BUY

Nepal is a shopper's paradise whether you are looking for a cheap souvenir or a real work of art. Although you can find almost anything in the tourist areas of Kathmandu there are specific specialities in different parts of the valley. Wherever you shop remember to bargain, although with the increasing number of totally tourist-oriented shops more fixed-price establishments are beginning to appear.

Antiquities cannot be taken out of the country, and baggage is inspected by the Nepalese customs with greater thoroughness on departure than on arrival. If you've bought something which could have a question mark hanging over it you should get a receipt and a description of the object from the shop where you bought it. Art theft is a real problem in Nepal and it would be a great shame if some of the superb museum pieces which currently stand in the open, where they may have been for over 1000 years, have to be moved into protected museums.

A permit is required from the Department of Archaeology in order to take any object which looks as if it could be more than 100 years old out of the country. The office (tel

Flute sellers

2-15358) is in the National Archives building on Ram Shah Path and if you visit the office between 10 am and 1 pm you should be able to pick up a permit by 5 pm the same day. The customs office (tel 2-15525) at Tripureshwar can also provide information.

Thangkas

Thangkas are the traditional Tibetan paintings of religious and ceremonial subjects. They illustrate various gods, associated deities, mandalas, the wheel of life and other such subjects. The figures may be of the various Buddhas, of Bodhisattvas or of the Taras although often they are of the fierce and angry Tantric gods. Thangkas are usually colourful and packed with detail to every corner of the painting.

Although there are genuine antique thangkas to be found it's highly unlikely that anything offered to the average visitor will date from much beyond last week. Judicious use of a smoky fire can add the odd century in no time at all. Thangkas do vary considerably in quality but buy one because you like it, not as a valuable investment.

Thangkas are available in many locations including the Tibetan shops around Bodhnath. There are some good thangka shops in Thamel in Kathmandu and in the Durbar Square shops in Bhaktapur. There is also an outlet near the Pujari Math monastery. Thangkas can cost anything from Rs 200 to Rs 2000 and beyond, and like many other crafts the more you look at the more you will appreciate the difference between average and superior quality. Size also plays a part in the final price of course. Traditionally thangkas are framed in silk brocade.

Block Prints

Locally produced rice paper is used for the block prints of Nepalese, Tibetan and Chinese deities. They are sold as straightforward pictures or for calendars, cards, lanterns and many other uses. A print would typically cost from Rs 25 to Rs 50. In Thamel near the Kathmandu Guest House there is a particularly good selection in The Print Shop.

Other Paintings

Patan has some very interesting small shops selling paintings just north of Durbar Square. The two interesting specialities here are paintings of Nepalese birds and a naive art style clearly influenced by the Sherpa paintings of the Solu Khumbu region. See the Things to Buy section of Patan for more details.

Tibetan Carpets

Carpet weaving is a major trade in Nepal, brought from Tibet by the refugees who now carry on the craft with great success in their new homes. There are carpet-weavers

Antiques

Treat the word 'antique' with great caution in Nepal. Maureen and I were sitting on the top platform of the Shiva Temple in Kathmandu's Durbar Square watching life pass by one afternoon when one of Kathmandu's numerous young wheelers and dealers came by to practise his English with us. We talked about this and that, and then noticed another young man several steps below us busily working away on something with a variety of tools and a small blowtorch.

'Do you know what he's making?' said our companion.

'No,' we replied, 'what is he making?'

'He's making it very old,' was the reply.

Tony Wheeler ■

around the Kathmandu Valley and also in Pokhara. Some of their output is now exported to Tibet, where the Chinese have managed to totally stamp out the archaic craft! A genuine Tibetan carpet purchased in Tibet is probably indeed made by genuine Tibetans, but in Nepal the Tamang people also make carpets.

Jawlakhel, on the southern outskirts of Patan, is the carpet-weaving centre in the valley and there are numerous carpet shops as you enter the area. You can see carpets being woven here but also in other places around the valley, including around the Bodhnath stupa. There are larger and smaller sizes available, but the traditional size for a Tibetan carpet is 1.8 metres by 90 cm. They're sturdily woven with colourful designs featuring Tibetan Buddhist symbols and dragons. These days it is more difficult to find the brilliant reds and blues produced by chemical dyes: more often carpets will be in the pale pastel shades which come from vegetable dyes. Small square carpets are often used to make seat cushions.

Clothing & Embroidery

Tibetan and Nepalese clothes have always been a popular buy but recently Western fashions made strictly for the tourist market have also become an important industry. You can buy handmade shirts at outlets in Thamel and there are also shops in Kathmandu (see the Kathmandu Things to Buy section) selling superb handpainted silk dresses at a fraction of what they would cost in the West.

Despite the growing market for Western fashions there is still a demand for traditional styles such as the Tibetan wool jackets which are popularly known as *yakets*. Nepalese coats, crossing over at the front, closed with four ties and traditionally made in purple velvet material, are a popular buy.

Embroidery has always been popular in Nepal and there are lots of little tailor shops around Kathmandu where the sewing machines rattle on until late at night adding colourful dragons and Tibetan symbols to customers jackets and jeans. Mountaineering expeditions like to return from Nepal with jackets carrying the message that this was the Country X, Year Y expedition to Peak Z. You can take your own clothes to be embroidered or buy T-shirts and other items already embroidered. Badges embroidered with suitable messages are another good buy – you can add a badge to your backpack saying that you walked to the Everest Base Camp or completed the Annapurna Circuit.

Nepalese Caps

A Nepalese cap or *topi* is part of Nepalese formal wear for a man and they are traditionally made in Bhaktapur. There's a cap shop right beside the Bhairabnath Temple in Bhaktapur as well as a group of cap specialists between Indra Chowk and Asan Tole in the old part of Kathmandu. Caps typically cost from Rs 25 to Rs 150.

Pottery

Terracotta pottery is made in a number of sites but particularly in Thimi and Bhaktapur. The Potters' Square, just south of Durbar Square in Bhaktapur, is a wonderful sight with thousands of pots neatly lined up across the square while in the shelters around the sides of the square potters busily turn out more and more. In Thimi they specialise in making attractive little flowerpots, often in the shape of dragons, elephants or mythical beasts. You can buy them in Thimi or from stalls near Indra Chowk in Kathmandu or Taumadhi Tole in Bhaktapur.

Jewellery

Kathmandu's many small jewellery manufacturers turn out a wide variety of designs at an equally wide variety of quality standards. You can buy jewellery ready made; ask them to create a design for you or bring in something you would like copied. There are several good shops around Thamel, particularly down towards Chhetrapati.

These outlets mainly cater to Western tastes but there are also many shops for the local market as Nepalese women, like Indian women, traditionally wear their wealth in jewellery. Cheap ornaments can also be fun; you can buy an armful of plastic bangles for a few rupees or colourful beads by the handful.

Masks & Puppets

Papier-mâché masks and colourful puppets are sold at shops in Kathmandu, Patan and Bhaktapur. Thimi is the centre for manufacturing the masks which are used in the traditional masked dances in September and it's interesting to see them being made and painted there. Ganesh, Bhairab and the Kumari are the most popular subjects for the mask and they make good wall decorations. Prices typically range from around Rs 25 to Rs 100.

Puppets make good buys as gifts for children and are made in Bhaktapur as well as other centres. They're often of multiarmed deities, clutching little wooden weapons in each hand. The puppet heads may be made of easily broken clay or more durable papier-mâché. Smaller puppets cost from around Rs 80 to Rs 150 but you can also pay Rs 300 to Rs 400 for a larger figure. As usual quality does vary and the more puppets you inspect the more you will begin to appreciate the differences.

Metalwork

Patan is the valley centre for bronze casting and the best variety of metalwork will be found in the shops around Patan's Durbar Square. See the Patan Things to Buy section for more details. Often beautifully made figures featuring the full range of Tantric Buddhist deities can be bought at costs ranging from Rs 2000 to Rs 5000 for good-quality smaller figures. Of course cheaper and simpler work can be found much more cheaply. The metal gameboards and pieces for the traditional Nepalese game *bagh chal* make a good buy.

Tea

Tea is grown in the east of Nepal, close to the border with India near Darjeeling where the finest Indian tea is grown. Ilam and Mai Valley are the best Nepalese brands.

Other Nepalese Crafts

A khukri, the traditional knife of the Gurkhas, can cost from Rs 100 to Rs 1000. Bhaktapur is the centre for woodcarving and you can find good objects in and around Tachupal Tole. Cassettes of Nepalese, Indian and general Himalayan music are a fine souvenir of a visit to Nepal. There are lots of music shops in Kathmandu selling local music as well as bootlegged Western tapes. For all sorts of small souvenirs the huge market area in Basantapur Square in Kathmandu is a good place to browse. Wandering the crowded and bustling market street from Indra Chowk to Asan Tole is always likely to turn up some interesting bargain.

Other Tibetan Crafts

Tibetan crafts include a variety of religious items including the dorje symbols and the popular Tibetan prayer wheels. Tibetans are keen traders and prices at Bodhnath and Swayambhunath are often very high.

Tibetan using prayer wheel

Sending Purchases Home

By far the best way of getting something back home is to take it with you. Shipping or mailing objects is fraught with dangers and hidden expenses. For a start there's no guarantee that it will be sent at all. If you leave your purchase for a shop to mail to you and it never turns up what can you prove? They will say they mailed it and the post office has lost it somewhere along the line, and you have no idea whether they have or not.

If an object is shipped to you it's easy to find that customs charges, clearance and collection charges at your end can add up to more than the initial cost of sending it. Often it would have been worth paying extra to bring it with you in the first place.

If you absolutely cannot carry your purchase with you it could be mailed from the Foreign Post Office. The object must be inspected by officials before it is wrapped so do not take it to the post office already wrapped up. There are packers at the post office who will package it for a small fee.

Unless you are very sure about the reliability of the shop do not ask the shop where you made the purchase to send it for you. There are a number of packing companies in Kathmandu but some of them are no more reliable than a shop might be. Sharmasons Packers & Movers (tel 4-11474) and Atlas Packers & Movers (tel 2-21402) have been recommended. The international courier company DHL has an office on Durbar Marg.

WHAT TO BRING

Nepal's climatic variations due to altitude mean that at certain times of year you'll have to come prepared for almost anything. If you're in Nepal during the winter you'll find it's T-shirt weather if you're tracking wildlife in the Terai, but up at the Everest Base Camp you'll want the best down gear money can buy!

In the Kathmandu Valley the daytime weather is pleasant year round, but in winter the temperature drops as soon as the sun sets, or even goes behind a cloud. It never reaches freezing in the valley, however, so it's sweater or warm jacket weather, nothing worse. Climb higher to the valley edge at Nagarkot and you can find it much colder.

During the monsoon you'll need an umbrella or raincoat, particularly in Pokhara where the rainfall is much heavier than in Kathmandu. In the first month after the monsoon it can be pleasantly warm, even on treks so long as you're sticking to lower altitudes. Sunglasses, a hat and covering for unprotected skin are all necessary on high altitude treks or for prolonged exposure in the Terai. See the Trekking chapter for more details on clothing recommendations for trekking. Most clothing is easily and cheaply available in Nepal so if there's a question about a particular item leave it behind – you can always get one if you need it.

Most toiletries are readily available including toilet paper these days. Women should bring tampons if needed. If you're staying in cheap hotels a padlock can be useful as hotels in this category often lock the doors with a latch and padlock. If you're visiting the Royal Chitwan National Park or other places in the Terai a good insect repellent is a near necessity. Bring a torch (flashlight) for trekking and for power cuts.

AIR

Apart from Lufthansa's Frankfurt to Kathmandu service, or Royal Nepal Airlines' London, Frankfurt, Kathmandu service, flying to Nepal from Europe, North America or Australia usually requires a change of aircraft and/or airline en route.

Travellers arriving from Europe or from the east coast of North America usually transfer to Royal Nepal Airlines or Indian Airlines in New Delhi for the final short flight from New Delhi to Kathmandu.

From the west coast of North America or from Australasia, Bangkok is the usual departure point although there are also direct flights to Kathmandu from Hong Kong and Singapore. Thai International and Royal Nepal Airlines are the main operators on the Bangkok to Kathmandu route. The schedules are so designed that it is likely you will have to spend at least 1 night in Bangkok to make your connection. Fourteen-day visas to Thailand are issued at Bangkok Airport.

Discounts

If you're under 26 years of age and hold an International Student Identity Card you are eligible for a 25% reduction on Royal Nepal Airlines' domestic and international flights. Simply being under 30 years of age makes you eligible for a similar discount on certain Royal Nepal Airlines and Indian Airlines routes.

Where to Sit

If you want to see the mountains as you fly to Kathmandu you must sit on the correct side.

Flying from the east – Bangkok, Calcutta, Hong Kong, Rangoon or Singapore – you want the right side. Flying from the west – New Delhi or Varanasi – you want the left side.

Arrival

Customs at Kathmandu Airport is unlikely to cause difficulties, unless you're trying to import a dozen Walkmans and an armful of wristwatches. The new airport (opened in 1989) has a duty-free shop with a limited range of liquor and cigarettes available for sale in US dollars to arriving passengers. You are allowed to import 200 cigarettes and one bottle of alcohol (up to 1.15 litres).

If the banks in town will be closed, it's worth making a dash for the currency exchange counter (before you deal with entry documentation) as the queues can be long and frustrating. In most cases it will only be necessary to change a small amount.

See the Getting Around section in the Kathmandu, Patan & Bhaktapur chapter for information on transport from the airport.

From the UK

Check the travel page ads in the dailies, the weekly London 'what's on' magazines like *Time Out* or the London giveaway papers. Reliable specialists for cheap tickets in London include Trailfinders at 46 Earls Court Rd, London W8, and STA (Student Travel Australia) at 74 Old Brompton Rd, London SW7, or 117 Euston Rd, London, NW1. Count on around UK£500 return to Kathmandu.

From North America

Fares to Kathmandu will be about the same from the east or west coast of the USA – it's about as far away as you can get in either direction! Typical fares are around US$1200 to US$1500 return. Check the Sunday travel sections of papers like the *New York Times, San Francisco Chronicle-Examiner* or *Los Angeles Times* for cheap fares. Good budget travel agents include the student travel chains STA and CIEE (Council on International Educational Exchange).

Fares from Canada are similar to the USA, westbound from Vancouver or eastbound from Toronto or Montreal.

From Australia & New Zealand

Fares from Australia depend on the season and typically range from around A$1000 to A$1200 return. Bangkok is still the most popular transit point although you can also fly directly from Singapore or Hong Kong to Kathmandu.

From India

New Delhi is the main departure point for flights between India and Nepal. The regular 1 hour New Delhi to Kathmandu flight costs US$142. Other cities in India with direct air connections with Kathmandu are Calcutta US$96, Patna US$41 and Varanasi US$71. The flight from Varanasi is the last leg of the popular New Delhi, Agra, Khajuraho, Varanasi, Kathmandu tourist flight.

Impecunious travellers can save a few dollars by flying from New Delhi to Patna and Patna to Kathmandu. The combined fare is slightly less than a direct New Delhi to Kathmandu flight, but there are only two Patna to Kathmandu connections a week. For a total cost of less than US$50 it's possible to take the train from New Delhi to Patna and then fly from Patna to Kathmandu. You can complete the journey in less than 24 hours and avoid the long bus trip up from the Indian border to Kathmandu.

From Elsewhere in Asia

Other departure points for Kathmandu and approximate one-way fares include:

Bangkok, Thailand	US$225
Colombo, Sri Lanka	US$200
Dhaka, Bangladesh	US$110
Dubai, UAE	US$325
Hong Kong	US$375
Karachi, Pakistan	US$200
Lhasa, Tibet	US$200
Paro, Bhutan	US$150
Singapore	US$350

In some cases there are cheaper excursion fares available.

OVERLAND

Political and weather conditions permitting there are four main entry points into Nepal by land: three from India, one from Tibet.

The most popular crossing points with India are Bhairawa/Sunauli (south of Pokhara), Raxaul Bazaar/Birganj (south of Kathmandu) and Kakarbhitta (near Siliguri and Darjeeling). In 1989 a dispute over the terms of a new border treaty led India to close all but these three entry points, but the situation returned to normal in mid-1990. There are a number of other less popular options. During the monsoon, the road from Sunauli/Bhairawa to Pokhara may be closed for a few days by landslides. The eastern route from Kakarbhitta can be blocked by floods, in which case it would be necessary to travel by train from Siliguri to Patna before entering Nepal.

The route to Tibet, via Kodari and Khasa (Zhangmu), was also closed to individual travellers in 1989 because of political turmoil in Tibet. Organised groups of three or more were allowed to cross, but this option was expensive. In addition, the road is of poor quality and is regularly closed by landslides during the monsoons.

If you are travelling to or from New Delhi or elsewhere in western India then the route through Sunauli/Bhairawa is the most convenient. This entry point is now much more popular than the crossing at Birganj. Not only is it closer to Varanasi in India, but it's also a shorter trip from the border to Kathmandu or to Pokhara.

Coming from Calcutta or Patna in the east

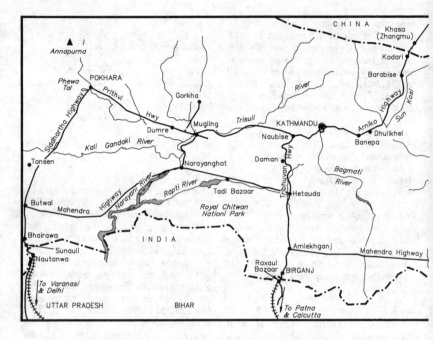

of India the Raxaul Bazaar/Birganj entry point is still more convenient. However, since the completion of the Narayanghat to Mugling road, buses now follow that route from Birganj to Kathmandu rather than the slower, though more scenic, Tribhuvan Highway through Hetauda and Naubise. This option also makes sense if you want to go to the Royal Chitwan National Park en route. From Darjeeling Kakarbhitta is the obvious choice.

From India, people usually take an Indian bus to the border, then a Nepalese bus from the border to Kathmandu or Pokhara. Raxaul Bazaar/Birganj and Bhairawa/Sunauli can be reached on the Indian side by train or bus, but it's usually preferable to opt for the bus. The trains in question travel on the narrow metre gauge rather than the much faster broad gauge so rail services tend to be tediously slow. It is faster and more convenient to take a bus from Patna, Muzaffarpur or Gorakhpur to the border.

At times direct buses run from the Tourist Camp in Delhi, and Varanasi, to Kathmandu.

Travel agents can handle all these bookings, but it's easy enough to organise it yourself as you go. An agent will of course charge a fee, and you will need to book at least a week in advance. Through an agent, Kathmandu/Pokhara to Delhi will cost around Rs 450, to Agra Rs 400, to Varanasi Rs 240, to Darjeeling Rs 450.

It is also possible to cross the border at Jogbani (near Biratnagar), Jaleshwar (near Janakpur), Koilabas (west of Pokhara), Nepalganj, Dhangadi and Mahendranagar (in the far west). It would be worth considering the crossings at Jogbani, and Jaleshwar, if you were coming from West Bengal, and at Nepalganj and Mahendranagar, if you were coming from Uttar Pradesh.

Varanasi to Sunauli/Bhairawa

Buses are the quickest and easiest way of

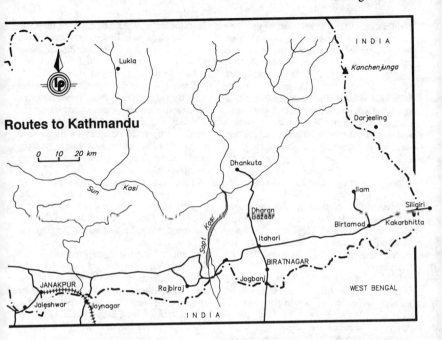

Routes to Kathmandu

getting from Varanasi to the Nepalese border. The Varanasi bus station is next to the main railway station. Buses leave almost hourly to Gorakhpur, 5 hours away. A tourist bus operates from there to Sunauli on the Nepal border; it takes 3 hours. There are also direct buses between Varanasi and Sunauli for about Indian Rs 40 or deluxe buses for Indian Rs 60.

Prior to the 1989 border dispute, private companies operated direct services to Kathmandu for around Indian Rs 200, and these may start up again. This was always of dubious value as there is no problem catching a bus to Sunauli, staying overnight on the Nepalese side of the border, then catching a Nepalese bus the next morning. There are several reasonable hotels in Sunauli and Bhairawa and the border is open 24 hours every day. This is not only cheaper but you get a much better choice of bus within Nepal. There are plenty of day and night buses to Kathmandu and Pokhara.

Sunauli/Bhairawa to Kathmandu or Pokhara

See the Terai chapter for details on the Nepalese towns that are mentioned in this section (Lumbini, the birthplace of Buddha, is 22 km from Bhairawa). Buses to Kathmandu travel east to Narayanghat and then north to Mugling before joining the Kathmandu-Pokhara (Prithvi) Highway. Buses to Pokhara travel north along the Siddhartha Highway.

Mahendra Highway to Kathmandu Day buses to Kathmandu from Sunauli cost around Rs 65 and take 9 hours – they are quicker and cheaper than the night buses. The blue, government-owned Saja Sewa buses are the best – they are faster and less crowded than most of the privately run buses. In Kathmandu they leave from the Bhimsen Tower, near the GPO.

From Bhairawa, a few km north of Sunauli, the buses travel north along the

Siddhartha Highway until Butwal, where they turn east. After 45 km you cross the low Someshwar Range and enter the Inner Terai, an area that has developed very rapidly since the late 1950s when malaria was eradicated. It's then another 70 flat, hot km until you get to Narayanghat on the Narayani River. Narayanghat is the main town and administrative centre for the Inner Terai; another modern, fast-growing city with little charm. You then turn north, following the river through the hills until you get to Mugling. See the Pokhara chapter for more information on the Kathmandu-Pokhara (Prithvi) Highway.

Siddhartha Highway to Pokhara Day buses between Pokhara and Sunauli take 9 hours and cost Rs 50. They use the beautiful Siddhartha Highway, which takes you through a cross-section of classic Nepalese landscapes.

From Bhairawa it's 24 km across the Terai until you reach the unattractive city of Butwal, which marks a sudden transition from the plains to the hills. One minute you're on the plains, surrounded by dust and people, the next you're in a narrow mountain gorge. For the next 40 km you drive through beautiful subtropical forest with some great views over the Tinau River. Tansen, an interesting, little-visited town, lies 5 km off the main road and is a good possibility if you want to break the journey. After the turn-off to Tansen you travel alongside, then cross, the distinctive Kali Gandaki River, one of the biggest in Nepal.

From the Kali Gandaki you climb a ridge and then descend into the valley of the Andhi River. As you wind closer to Pokhara there are superb views of the Annapurna Range, and particularly of Machhapuchhare, the famous fishtail mountain with its distinctive twin peaks.

Patna to Raxaul Bazaar/Birganj

It makes little sense to take a train to the Nepal border – the buses are much faster. The main bus station in Patna (for buses to Muzaffarpur and Raxaul Bazaar just before the Nepalese border) is just west of the Patna

Junction railway station, opposite the GPO and Hardinge Park. Buses cost Indian Rs 30 for the 3 hour trip to Raxaul Bazaar. From there, it costs about Rs 10 for a rickshaw across the border to Birganj.

Raxaul Bazaar is virtually a twin town with Birganj in Nepal. Both towns are dirty, unattractive transit points strung along the highway and are full of heavy traffic. The border is open 24 hours every day, and it takes about 30 minutes and Rs 10 to get from the border itself to the bus station in Birganj by cycle-rickshaw.

Single rooms at the *Hotel Kaveri* in Raxaul Bazaar cost Indian Rs 20. The slightly more expensive *Hotel Taj* is also a reasonable place to stay. Alternatively, you can cross the border and stay in Birganj.

Birganj to Kathmandu or Pokhara

See the Terai chapter for details on the Nepalese towns that are mentioned in this section. All direct buses go via the Mahendra Highway, because the road is easier, but it is still possible, with a little trouble, to go via the beautiful Tribhuvan Highway.

Mahendra Highway All direct buses between Birganj and Kathmandu or Pokhara turn west at Hetauda, then at Narayanghat turn north to Mugling which is on the Kathmandu-Pokhara (Prithvi) Highway. Although it is not as spectacular as the Tribhuvan Highway, this is nonetheless an interesting route with some beautiful views.

Between Birganj and Kathmandu direct buses take around 11 hours and cost Rs 75; between Birganj and Pokhara they cost Rs 70 and are marginally quicker. There are numerous night and day buses. It is worth catching a day bus, even though they no longer take you over the Tribhuvan Highway, since there is a lot of interesting country to see and some great views even if you go via Narayanghat. The best buses are the blue, government-owned Saja Sewa buses – they are faster and less crowded than most of the privately run buses. In Kathmandu they leave from the Bhimsen Tower, near the GPO.

From Birganj you travel past a depressing

line-up of Dickensian factories until you climb into the Siwalik Range. Here the country becomes more attractive – and the road falls apart. Fifty bone-jarring km from the border, Hetauda lies at the north-western edge of a wide valley known as the Inner Terai. It's not a particularly interesting town, although it is the starting point for a cableway that carries bulk goods from the Terai to Kathmandu.

From Hetauda, the road runs along the edge of the Mahabharat Range and the Rapti River. There are some rich, cultivated fields, but a great deal of forest remains. On the other side of the Rapti lies the Royal Chitwan National Park, famous for its tigers and rhinoceroses.

After Belva, the valley begins to broaden and the reason it is called the Inner Terai, becomes clear – it's flat, fertile and heavily populated. About 75 km after Hetauda, you come to the small roadside town of Tadi Bazaar, the departure point for Royal Chitwan National Park. Buses to this point from Birganj cost around Rs 30 and take 4 hours. From Tadi Bazaar it takes around 7 hours and costs Rs 35, to reach Pokhara or Kathmandu. Buses travel west to Narayanghat then turn north, following the Narayani River through the hills to Mugling. See the Pokhara chapter for more information on the Kathmandu-Pokhara (Prithvi) Highway.

Tribhuvan Highway If you have time and feel energetic, consider catching a bus to Hetauda (where direct buses turn west to Narayanghat), then a Saja Sewa bus over the mountains to Kathmandu. There are numerous buses to Hetauda for Rs 8, but only a couple per day that run from Hetauda to Kathmandu via Daman and the Tribhuvan Highway for Rs 35.

It's actually easier to undertake this route coming from Kathmandu, as you'll have no problems finding a bus from Hetauda to Birganj, whatever time you arrive. The Saja Sewa bus leaves from near the Bhimsen Tower in Kathmandu at 6.30 am (Rs 35, 8 hours). The privately run company Bhagmati

Sewa also runs buses on this route; they leave from Ratna Park.

If you are travelling in a group or have the funds, consider hiring a car. It won't be cheap, partly because you'll have to pay for the driver's return trip whether you go along or not. Think in terms of US$150. It's worth checking with the tourist office in Birganj to see if there is a car looking for passengers for this return trip (and extra profits).

You begin to climb into the Mahabharat Range the moment you leave Hetauda. The road is in good condition, in fact it's a magnificent engineering feat, but it's very narrow. It's a case of drivers leaning almost constantly on their horns and hoping they won't meet an out-of-control Tata truck around the next blind corner.

The change from the Terai is remarkably sudden; you're soon amongst forested hills and it is almost impossible to believe the plains are so close. As you gain altitude you enter magnificent rhododendron forests. The highest point on the road is 2400 metres, just before you reach Daman. Daman is famous for being a viewpoint with one of the most complete panoramas of the Himalaya that you can find. The view – from Dhaulagiri to Everest – is simply awe-inspiring.

After Daman you travel through the intensely cultivated Palung Valley. From here to Kathmandu, every possible inch of the hills is farmed. There are more good views of the Himalaya before you reach Naubise on the Kathmandu-Pokhara (Prithvi) Highway. Daman is about 3 hours from Kathmandu and Hetauda by car, 4 hours by bus.

Darjeeling to Kathmandu
There are a number of companies which handle bookings between Darjeeling and Kathmandu – although with all of them you have to change buses at the border and Siliguri.

In Darjeeling the main ones are Assam Valley Tours & Travels, opposite the post office, and Mahendra Tours on Laden La Rd above the main block of budget restaurants. From Darjeeling, you arrive at the border around 3 pm, leave again around 4 pm and arrive in Kathmandu around 9 or 10 am the next day. There is no Nepalese consulate in Darjeeling; the nearest one is in Calcutta, but 7-day visas are available at the border, and these can be extended in Kathmandu. In Kathmandu try Student Travels &. Tours in Thamel; they charge Rs 450 for a similar service. Don't forget that if you are intending to enter India by this route you will need a permit to visit Darjeeling as well as a visa for India.

It's almost as easy to get from Darjeeling to Kathmandu on your own though it involves four changes – a bus from Darjeeling to Siliguri (Indian Rs 16), then a bus from Siliguri to the border (Indian Rs 3), a rickshaw across the border to Kakarbhitta (Rs 2) and a bus from Kakarbhitta to Kathmandu (Rs 170). This is cheaper than the package deal, you have a choice of buses from the border, plus you have the option of travelling during the day and overnighting along the way.

Mahendra Highway See the Terai chapter for details on the Nepalese towns that are mentioned in this section. Buses to Kathmandu travel west along the Mahendra Highway to the Tribhuvan Highway between Birganj and Hetauda, then briefly north to Hetauda. They then travel west again until Narayanghat where they turn north to Mugling, on the Kathmandu-Pokhara (Prithvi) Highway. During the monsoon, floods can sometimes close the road between Hetauda and Kakarbhitta.

It's over 600 km between Kakarbhitta and Kathmandu, which means direct buses can take an exhausting 17 hours to complete the trip. The direct buses all travel at night; from Kakarbhitta they leave between 3 and 4 pm, from Kathmandu between 4 and 5 pm. Buses leave Kathmandu from Ratna Park and cost Rs 170 – it's worth booking in advance. Chandeshwari and National Deluxe are companies that have been recommended.

If you have time it is worth considering breaking your journey at Janakpur, which is roughly halfway, and an interesting place in

its own right. This will enable you to travel during the day – the flood plain of the Sapt Kosi is particularly interesting – and get a feel for the Terai. There are day buses from Kakarbhitta that go to a number of towns on the Terai including Janakpur (Rs 60), and night buses direct to Pokhara (Rs 170). Fifteen minutes from Kakarbhitta, past several tea plantations, is the town of Birtamod. A dirt road from here goes to Ilam, a starting point for treks in the Kanchenjunga region. The road is very poor, so the three buses a day that make the journey cost Rs 57 and take 6 or 7 hours.

The first town of real consequence that you come to is Itahari, 100 km from Kakarbhitta. There's nothing much to be said for it, however, apart from the fact that it is at the intersection of the road that runs south to Biratnagar, Nepal's second largest city, and north to Dharan Bazaar and Dhankuta.

After Itahari the road enters the flood plain of the Sapt Kosi, one of the largest tributaries to the Ganges. This mighty river is now partially controlled by the impressive Kosi Barrage and its surrounding earthworks. Even so, this low-lying region seems at times to be more water than land. Metres of silt have obviously made the fields extremely fertile and the population is growing rapidly.

Mud and thatch villages are built on small areas of high ground, and the people are closely related to their Indian neighbours. Emerald green paddies stretch to the horizon and the villages are surrounded by water lilies and hyacinths. Often, the houses are overgrown with pumpkin plants, which are trained onto the roofs. Fish are a vital part of the local diet, and wherever you look you'll see children and women fishing for the tiny fish that live in the canals and ponds. The bird life is prolific, with Brahmani kites, greater and lesser egrets, and cranes and ducks of every description.

On either side of the barrage the road is built on a raised levy, but it is in extremely poor condition. By the time you get to Mohanpur, you'll be lucky to have your teeth fillings still in place. After Mohanpur you begin a long stretch of the Terai proper, skirting the Churia Range, foothills of the Himalaya, which seem to jump from the plains.

Much of this land has been settled relatively recently, since the eradication of malaria in the 1950s. Many of the settlers have come from the hills, but they have swiftly adapted to their new environment and many have prospered. Frequently houses have been built on stilts to cope with the annual floods. Some of the towns look as if they could have been transplanted from northern New South Wales, Australia – stilts, verandahs and corrugated iron roofs contribute to the illusion.

Nearly 110 km past the Kosi Barrage you reach Lalbiti, the turn-off to Janakpur (25 km from the highway), one of the most attractive cities in Nepal. The countryside is intensively cultivated and densely populated. As you travel further east, however, there are fewer people, fewer of the bright Indian saris and more trees. Between Dalkebar and Amlekhganj (on the Tribhuvan Highway) there is an almost unbroken stretch of magnificent sal forest.

At Amlekhganj the Mahendra Highway briefly joins the Tribhuvan Highway to Hetauda. See the Birganj to Kathmandu or Pokhara section in this chapter for the rest of the route.

Lhasa to Kathmandu

Travel between Kathmandu and Lhasa in Tibet can be complicated by natural and political considerations. The natural problem is that the road is frequently cut by earthquakes, floods, landslides and other disasters.

Political disasters are even more likely than natural ones. Tibet is a volatile region with regular violent protests against Chinese rule and these upheavals are often followed by restrictions on visitors to the region. Usually these restrictions are applied more stringently to independent visitors than to people on organised tours. In 1989 not only were there particularly violent protests in Tibet, but there was also confusion following the massacre of students in Beijing. The baseline is that if you intend to enter or leave Nepal via Tibet you should come prepared with alternative plans should travel along this route prove impossible.

Organised Tours Organised tours (with a minimum of three people) were only briefly interrupted in 1989, but they are expensive. A number of agencies in Kathmandu organise fully inclusive round trips to Lhasa, with prices that vary from US$800 to US$1200 for 10 to 12 days.

Nepal Travels (tel 4-12899) was a pioneer of travel on this route and has trips departing on Tuesdays. Three day tours covering the northern side of Everest cost US$275. Eventually circuit of Everest treks could become just as feasible as the popular circuit of Annapurna is today.

Other tours to Lhasa go by land in one direction then fly in the other or continue on from Lhasa to Hong Kong. China International Travel Service (CITS), the state travel agency, operate the tours within China.

Other travel agencies in Nepal specialising in Tibet include:

Kathmandu Travels & Tours
    PO Box 459, Ganga Path, Kathmandu (tel 2-22511)
Natraj Tours & Travels
    PO Box 495, Durbar Marg, Kathmandu (tel 2-22014)
Yeti Travels
    PO Box 76, Durbar Marg, Kathmandu (tel 2-21234)

Independent Travel If independent travel into Tibet is permitted you must first get a Chinese visa (see the Embassy section in the Kathmandu Valley chapter for more details).

From Khasa (Zhangmu), the Tibetan town just over the border, there are just two buses a week to Lhasa at a cost of Y84 so you must plan carefully or you may be stranded for several days. Take food and drink on this trip, as there's not much available along the way. Minibuses and Toyota Landcruisers can be hired for the return trip to Lhasa. A Landcruiser should cost about Y450 per person (maximum seven passengers), a minibus about Y380 (maximum 10), but these figures are always open to bargaining and some travellers have done it for less. It's also possible to get rides on trucks to Shigatse for as little as Y30 but the 15 hour trip in the back of a truck is strictly for the hardy. From Shigatse there are local buses to Gyantse and from there to Lhasa.

Transport is the major expense on this trip, but you must be prepared to vary your itinerary where necessary and this is not an easy trip by any means. Altitude sickness is a real danger as the maximum altitude along the road is 5140 metres and there have been reports of deaths.

Arniko Highway Regardless of the situation with the border, the road to Kodari, the small town on the Nepalese side of the border, is an interesting trip from Kathmandu – if you have access to a car. There are some interesting towns on the highway and there are several points where you can get access to the Sun Kosi. If you have the use of a car it would be an enjoyable expedition; it's nearly 4 hours to Kodari from Kathmandu. Expect to pay between US$60 and US$80 for a day's hire.

It is not possible to catch a bus direct to Kodari, but eight buses a day do run to Barabise from Ratna Park in Kathmandu for Rs 22. They take around 5 agonising hours. From Barabise there are trucks/jeeps for Rs 15/20 that leave when full and take 2 hours to get to Kodari. Since there's nothing much to see from Kodari, travelling out here by bus is a little pointless unless you are actually going on to Tibet.

Many people who make the trek into the Solo Khumbu region and the Everest Base Camp travel out along the highway, taking the turn-off to Jiri, which is the last stop before you have to start walking. Buses to Jiri leave from the Central Bus Station between 6 and 7 am, cost Rs 80 and take 12 to 13 hours.

Past Barabise the road is particularly vulnerable to landslides and every monsoon large sections are swept away; it's very unlikely to be open between May and August. Even when the highway is passable it is of limited use in breaking India's stranglehold on Nepal. It is

an enormous distance from Lhasa to the industrial centres of China, so it is, in most cases, still cheaper to ship Chinese goods via Calcutta than to truck them over the mountains.

When roadbuilders first tackled the Himalaya, they decided to follow the rivers, which had already done the hard work of cutting through the mountains. They have now realised that the zone just above the rivers is particularly vulnerable to erosion from below and landslides from above – which is why Nepalese houses and traditional trails are often built along the top of ridges. As a result, many of the roads that have been developed by foreign countries' agencies have turned out to be serious liabilities for the Nepalese government, who must fund their ongoing maintenance.

The Arniko Highway skirts Bhaktapur and leaves the valley at its eastern end. It passes through Dhulikhel (see the Around the Valley chapter) – the only point on the road where there are good views of the Himalaya. After Dhulikhel the road descends into the beautiful Panchkal Valley, reaching the town of Panchkal after about 20 minutes. About 5 minutes beyond Panchkal a dirt road takes off to the left, giving road access to the Helambu region.

Eight km later you arrive at Dolalghat, a thriving town at the confluence of the Indrawati River and Sun Kosi. The turn-off to Jiri is another 14 km away on the right of the highway. Lamosangu is a few km after the intersection, and is an interesting Sherpa town with some decent trade stores. Next you pass a magnesite mine, one of the few mines in the country – the fact that it is beside a sealed road allowed its development.

Barabise is the next bustling bazaar town, and the final stop for buses from Kathmandu. There are several cheap and basic hotels in the main street: the *Barabise Guest House* has beds for Rs 10, the *Koshi Lodge* has doubles for Rs 30.

After Barabise the road follows a steep gorge along the Chaku River and soon deteriorates. The next point of interest is Tatopani, a small village with a string of small guest houses which survive by housing visitors to the hot springs. The springs are below the road at the eastern edge of the village. The guest houses have beds for Rs 15. The best is the *Tibetan Lodge & Restaurant*.

Kodari is nothing more than a collection of shanties perched perilously on the edge of the gorge on the Nepalese side of the Friendship Bridge. At one time this was the only accessible place where you could glimpse Tibet, but a glimpse is all you get. In the distance you can see Khasa (Zhangmu), a large Tibetan town. There are a couple of very ordinary lodges – you can do better in Tatopani. The *Everest Hotel* and the *Miteri Lodge* have beds for Rs 15.

LEAVING NEPAL

The departure tax for international flights is Rs 300, for domestic flights Rs 30. On departure, it is possible to re-exchange up to 15% of the Nepalese rupees you have officially changed, but you must be able to show bank receipts.

The airport duty-free shop has a limited range of liquor and cigarettes available for purchase with US dollars. Shoestring travellers often take their duty-free allowances with the intention of selling them at their next halt. Burma is a particularly popular country for selling duty-free items.

WARNING

This chapter is particularly vulnerable to change – prices for international travel are volatile, routes are introduced and cancelled, schedules change, rules are amended and special deals come and go. Airlines and governments seem to take a perverse pleasure in making price structures and regulations as complicated as possible and you should check directly with the airline or a travel agent to make sure you understand how a fare (and ticket you may buy) works. In addition, the travel industry is highly competitive and there are many lurks and perks. The upshot of this is that you should get opinions, quotes and advice from as many airlines and travel agents as possible before you part with your hard-earned cash.

The details given in this chapter should be regarded as pointers and are not a substitute for your own careful, up-to-the-minute research.

Getting Around

AIR

Royal Nepal Airlines operates a number of scheduled and charter flights around the country. The aircraft used are Hawker Siddeley 748s on the major routes and short take-off and landing (STOL) Twin Otters and Pilatus Porters to the smaller places. Some of these flights, such as the Kathmandu to Lukla services, are used mainly by trekkers. These trekking flights are frequent during the trekking season but the schedules can be extremely variable. Kathmandu to Jomsom flights, for example, are plagued by bad weather at both ends. Early morning departures from Kathmandu are often delayed by morning fog but if they don't arrive in Jomsom by around 11 am landing may be impossible due to high winds! The end result is regular cancellations. Flights out of Lukla are equally unreliable and there are often backlogs of frustrated trekkers waiting for flights back to Kathmandu.

It is advisable to book domestic flights 7 to 10 days in advance. Just as for flights out of Nepal the most important rule is to reconfirm and reconfirm again. Names can easily 'fall off' the passenger list, particularly where there is pressure for seats.

Air Fares Chart

Following is a list of air fares from Kathmandu to:

Bharatpur	US$45
Lukla	US$75
Meghauli	US$65
Pokhara	US$55
Phaplu	US$75
Jumla	US$120
Simara	US$40
Tumlingtar	US$40
Jiri	US$20
Manang	US$75
Nepalganj	US$100
Jomsom	US$75
Pokhara to Jomsom	US$45

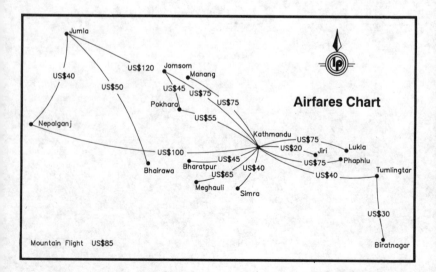

Airfares Chart

Biratnagar to Tumlingtar	US$30
Bhairawa to Jumla	US$50
Nepalganj to Jumla	US$40

Royal Nepal Airlines also has a mountain flight which costs US$85. See the Himalaya & Mountaineering chapter for details.

BUS & MINIBUS

Buses are the main form of public transport in Nepal. There are numerous services with buses and smaller minibuses around the Kathmandu Valley, out from Kathmandu towards the Tibetan border, down to the Indian border or to Pokhara. Buses also run from Pokhara down to the Indian border as well as along the length of the country from near Darjeeling in the east. This road runs through the lowland Terai, parallel to the Indian border. As well as the regular public buses between Kathmandu and Pokhara there are also a number of services aimed particularly at the Western tourist market.

DRIVING
Car Rental

There are no drive-yourself rental cars available in Nepal but you can easily hire cars with drivers. Due to the ongoing border dispute with India which has restricted imports of fuel, a rented car with driver can cost between US$60 and US$90 a day. The price is likely to drop when fuel does not have to be bought on the black market. For more details see the Getting Around section in the Kathmandu chapter .

Motorcycle Rental

Motorcycles can be rented in Kathmandu. See the Getting Around section in the Kathmandu chapter for details.

LOCAL TRANSPORT

See the appropriate town sections for more information on local transport.

Bus & Minibus

There is a wide variety of public and private bus and minibus services around the Kathmandu Valley. The public bus service around Pokhara has also expanded in recent years.

Taxi

Larger towns like Kathmandu and Pokhara have taxis and between a group of people a taxi can be a good way to explore the Kathmandu Valley. Metered taxis have black licence plates while private cars, which often operate as taxis particularly on long distance routes or for extended periods, have red plates.

Autorickshaw & Cycle Rickshaw

Metered autorickshaws, those curious and noxious three-wheeled motorcycle-engined devices, are also found in Kathmandu. Cycle rickshaws are common in the old part of Kathmandu and can be a good way of making short trips through the crowded and narrow streets.

Bicycle

In Kathmandu and Pokhara there are many bicycle rental outlets and this is a cheap and convenient way of getting around. A regular bicycle only costs Rs 15 to Rs 20 per day and you can take a day trip to almost anywhere in the Kathmandu Valley by bicycle. In Kathmandu you can also hire mountain bikes with 12 or more speeds, but they cost Rs 60 to Rs 90 a day. Children's bicycles can also be hired.

TOURS

Travel agencies in Kathmandu organise scheduled conducted tours and private tours by car or bus to places of interest around the valley and further afield. If your stay in Nepal is too short to permit exploration on your own, then it is best to join a conducted or private tour.

Kathmandu, Patan & Bhaktapur

For most visitors to Nepal, the Kathmandu Valley is their arrival point and focus of their visit. This small mountain-sheltered valley is the historical centre of Nepal and the place where kingdoms rose and fell, palaces and temples were built and rebuilt, and Nepalese art and culture were developed and refined.

The three major towns – Kathmandu, Patan and Bhaktapur – each has an artistic and architectural tradition that rivals anything you might find in the great cities of Europe. Kathmandu is the capital and the largest city in the country; it also has the international airport and is where most visitors stay. Patan, the second largest, is separated from Kathmandu by a river but in other respects the two cities are virtually continuous. Bhaktapur, the third largest, is towards the eastern end of the valley and its relative isolation is reflected in its slower pace and more distinctly mediaeval atmosphere.

Beyond the cities lie hundreds of temples and shrines, traditional villages and agricultural scenes of timeless beauty (see the Around the Valley chapter for more details). A great deal is easily accessible by foot, bicycle, bus or taxi, but the more time you have the better. You will be hard pushed to do any justice to the place in less than a week – double that and you stand a better chance.

HISTORY
The Newaris are regarded as the original inhabitants of the valley, but their origins are shrouded in mystery. They speak a Tibeto-Burmese language, which indicates they originated in the east, but their physical features range from distinctively Mongoloid, again suggesting the east, to Indo-Aryan, which of course points to India.

In balance, it seems most likely that the Kathmandu Valley has long been a cultural and racial melting pot with people coming from both east and west. This fusion has resulted in the unique Newari culture that is responsible for the valley's superb art and architecture.

The Newari golden age peaked in the 17th century when the valley consisted of small city-states, and Nepal was a vitally important trading link between Tibet and the north Indian plains. The valley's visible history is inextricably entangled with the Malla kings. It was during their reign, particularly in the 1600s and 1700s, that many of the valley's finest temples and palaces were built. Competition between the cities was intense and an architectural innovation in one place, such as the erection of a column bearing a statue of the ruling king, would inevitably be copied in the other cities.

Sorting out who built what and when is considerably complicated by the fact that at any one time there was not just one Malla king. Each of the three city-states in the valley – Kathmandu, Patan and Bhaktapur – had its own. Some of the most important individuals are listed in the introduction to the relevant cities.

The unification of Nepal in 1768 by Gorkha's King Prithvi Narayan Shah signalled the end of the Kathmandu Valley's fragmentation. Nepali, an Indo-European language, replaced Newari as the country's language of administration.

GEOGRAPHY
The bowl-like valley is about 25 km from east to west, perhaps 20 km from north to south. Kathmandu lies at a height of around 1300 metres, which gives it a temperate climate, while the surrounding hills range from 1500 metres to 2800 metres in height. If you fly in, you are made forcibly aware how isolated and unusual the valley is – embedded like a jewel in endless ranges of rugged mountains.

A large human population in the valley is posing numerous problems. Although it's not yet critical, Kathmandu is particularly vulnerable to air and water pollution. The surrounding mountains also make transport extremely difficult: the valley has only three fragile overland lifelines. There's one two-lane road and a cableway to India, and another road to Tibet that washes away every year.

The valley is phenomenally fertile, capable of growing grains (rice, corn, wheat) and a wide range of fruits (from bananas to oranges) and vegetables. The population is continuing to grow, however, and urban development is rapidly encroaching on valuable agricultural land, so the valley is increasingly dependent on imported food and fossil fuels.

A number of rivers drain towards the centre of the valley and join the holy Bagmati River, which then flows south through the Chobar Gorge to finally reach the Ganges River. Geologists have confirmed ancient myths that claim the valley once lay under water.

CLIMATE & WHEN TO GO

The Kathmandu Valley has a temperate climate that is pleasant most of the year. Snow is almost unheard of, although there are frosts, and the monsoons are nowhere near as debilitating as they are on the plains.

The best time to visit is between October and March. It can get quite cold at night (0°C) and the days become short, although it's sunny and warm between mid-morning and mid-afternoon (say 20°C). Visibility is particularly good from October to early February.

By April things start to heat up and there are often storms in the afternoon. The real heat and humidity coincide with the monsoon proper, which usually commences in mid-June. Expect daytime temperatures around the low to mid-30°Cs, night-time between 15°C and 20°C. Fortunately, much of the rain falls during the night or on the surrounding hills, so a visit is still feasible. This would be worth considering for a number of reasons: there are several important festivals, there are fewer tourists and prices are lower.

FLORA & FAUNA

Most of the valley has been converted to highly productive farmland, but several pockets of uncleared land remain: Gokarna, just past Bodhnath, Nagarjun, just past Balaju, and others on several of the surrounding hills, notably Pulchowki.

The native forests consisted of oak and other broad-leafed trees, pines, and magnificent rhododendrons (*laliguras*) that grow over 15 metres high. Pulchowki, the highest point overlooking the valley, has a magnificent rhododendron forest and should not be missed if you are in the valley in spring

(February to April). Australians will recognise plantings of eucalyptus, grevillea and bottlebrush that line many of the valley's roads.

Once upon a time the valley probably had populations of leopards, jungle cats, wolves, black bears, sloth bears, otters and jackals. These are long gone. If you visit Gokarna you will definitely see wild spotted deer (*chital*) and hog deer (*laghuna*), and you might see squirrels, porcupines or langur monkeys (with grey hair and black faces). There are also a number of domesticated Asian elephants.

No visitor to Swayambhunath will avoid the rhesus monkeys that infest the hillside. Nor, if you stay near the Old Royal Palace or Durbar, will you miss the colonies of fruit bats that spend their days chattering in the trees before they take to the sky every evening.

ECONOMY

Today the valley is the most developed part of Nepal with a network of roads and electricity linking most of the villages. Despite rapid development, however, much of the valley is still devoted to small scale farming. The availability of improved seeds, fertilisers and extensive irrigation has increased productivity and made it possible to grow wheat as well as the traditional rice.

Nepal's small industrial base is mainly concentrated in the lowland towns of the Terai, although the factories in the valley (including cement, brick, light engineering, food and beverage) contribute nearly 20% of the country's industrial output.

The Kathmandu Valley is the centre for many traditional crafts. Newari craftspeople have long exported pottery, brass ware and bronze religious artefacts. The tradition continues, only these days the buyer is often a tourist. The 'Tibetan' carpet industry is the valley's largest private employer and carpets are now a major export earner.

Kathmandu is the administrative and educational centre for the kingdom. Many of the Rana's grand palaces are now home to bureaucracies that are, arguably, of greater benefit to the general populace. Kathmandu is also the main focus for visiting tourists, so there has been a large investment in the necessary infrastructure and many people are dependent on the tourist dollar.

POPULATION & PEOPLE

Today the Newaris still form the largest single group in the valley and there are some smaller towns and villages, such as Thimi, Chapagaon or Sankhu, which remain Newari strongholds. Many of the people living on the surrounding hills are Tamangs, Brahmins and Chhetris, who can generally be distinguished from the Newaris by their solitary households.

In recent years, however, many immigrants – the ambitious and/or the destitute – from throughout the country have come to the valley in search of jobs and education. There are, therefore, significant minorities of almost every Nepalese ethnic group. Since the Chinese invasion of Tibet, thousands of Tibetan refugees have settled in the valley; there is also a large community of Indian traders and business people and significant communities of other foreigners.

It's difficult to estimate the population of the valley and the respective cities, partly because the last official census was taken in 1981 and there is a blurred line between country and city. In 1981 the city of Kathmandu had a population of 235,000, but it is now likely to exceed 300,000; Patan and Bhaktapur are estimated to have around 110,000 and 60,000 people respectively.

The population of the districts of Kathmandu, Lalitpur (Patan) and Bhaktapur (which encompass the Kathmandu Valley) totalled 617,000 in 1981 and may now be approaching 900,000. This would mean the valley is home to nearly 5% of Nepal's people and that the population density is about 1000 per sq km.

Newaris

It is not surprising that the Newari people were influenced by Tibet and India. What is surprising is their creative response to this stimulus, which actually led to a genuine exchange with their giant neighbours. Mediaeval Newari society has left a religious, architectural and artistic legacy that is uniquely its own and spectacular by any standard.

Although most Newaris have Mongoloid physical characteristics, many don't, so their origins are shrouded in mystery. It is now generally accepted that they are a mixture of many different peoples who were attracted to the valley.

Perhaps the Newaris' most striking characteristic is their love of communal life. Newari houses were invariably clustered together, usually around sites of religious significance. Although their economy was centred around agriculture and trade, they created sophisticated urban communities which catered to a breadth of human needs in an integrated way that has rarely been matched.

Today, there are around 600,000 Newaris, largely centred on the Kathmandu Valley. They have always been traders and merchants and continue to fill this role throughout the kingdom. Their proximity to the centre of power has also led to them having a disproportionate influence in the bureaucracies of Kathmandu. Many now live in heartbreakingly ugly bungalows on the outskirts of the city proper, and many of their traditions are on the wane.

Architecture The most important social unit was the family and the family house was the starting point for urban planning. Rich Newaris built handsomely proportioned brick houses with tiled roofs that were up to five storeys high. In the country, the ground floor was often used for stabling animals, in the city, for commerce.

A community developed when a series of houses was built in a rectangle around a courtyard/square or *chowk*. The *chowk*, often with running water and a temple or shrine, would be the centre of day-to-day life, and still is today. Virtually everything happens here: there are markets, children play, women work (weaving, washing, drying grain, etc) and chat, old people doze in the sun, men talk over the community's business and religious ceremonies take place.

The cities and towns of the valley were made up of a compact network of these interlocking squares, courtyards, twisting alleyways, ponds and temples often centred around a main square. Fortunately, much of this tradition remains. Decorated with woodcarved windows and doorways, statues and shrines, and humming with gregarious people, a Nepalese town is a remarkable synthesis of art and life.

Religion The vast majority of Newaris are Hindu and fall under a caste system, although there is still a significant minority of Buddhists. This simplistic description, however, masks an incredibly diverse and complex system of beliefs.

These two great religions competed, not through bloody wars, but through integration and assimilation. Since the 5th century, however, kings and aristocrats have been Hindu and their influence gradually led to Buddhists adopting castes and a hereditary priesthood (the *Banrhas*). There are many collapsing *bahals* (monasteries) that testify to a long-gone Buddhist golden age.

The end result is that a purist from either religion would not recognise many of the Newari gods or the practices that go into their worship. For not only have aspects of both religions combined, they have been added to by a Tantric tradition, Lamaism and even older local deities and beliefs.

This has led to a confusing proliferation of gods who are often hybrids unashamedly shuffled from one pantheon to another. There are literally hundreds of these divinities, and over 150 days of festivals a year to celebrate them. From a functional point of view, most people are free to follow whatever gods and goddesses particularly appeal to them, so theological consistency (including the distinction between Hinduism and Buddhism) is irrelevant, certainly to the people themselves. See the Religion section in the Facts about the Country chapter for more details.

Customs The Newaris are divided into castes, whether they nominally consider themselves Hindu or Buddhist, and these include untouchables (tinkers, butchers and some others). Caste rules are not quite as rigid as in some parts of India, but inter-marriage is still rare and untouchables are still grossly disadvantaged.

The usual dress for a Newari woman is a sari and blouse, often with a shawl. The men wear trousers with a baggy seat that are tighter around the calves (like jodhpurs), a long untucked double-breasted shirt, a vest (waistcoat) or coat and the traditional Nepalese cap (*topi*). The most distinctive caste is the *Jyapu*, or farmer, and many of them still lead highly traditional lives. Jyapu women wear black saris with a red border, while the men often wear the traditional trousers and shirt with a long piece of cotton wrapped around the waist. They prefer to carry goods and vegetables on a shoulder pole.

Newari children are welcomed into their community and caste at the age of seven when boys' heads are shaved leaving only a topknot, and girls are symbolically married to the soul of their future husband. Most Newaris have arranged marriages and on auspicious dates wedding processions are a common sight. The procession starts at nightfall, and is led by a band, often in ragtag uniforms making a cacophony with clarinets, trumpets and drums.

Traditionally, men were members of a unique cooperative institution known as a *guthi*. This is a religious and social group that may be based on family and other local links. Guthis may own land and are often responsible for the upkeep of particular temples and financing particular rites, as well as the welfare of their members.

Tamangs

The Tamangs are closely related to the Tibetans. Their name apparently means 'horse trader', although most are now sedentary farmers, soldiers or labourers. Their appearance, language and Lamaist Buddhist beliefs all bear testimony to their origins. Indeed, many of the 'Tibetan' souvenirs for sale in Kathmandu are actually made by Tamangs. They can be found throughout the middle hills, especially

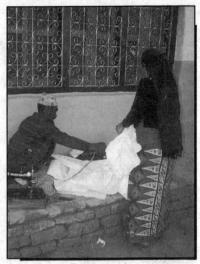
Tamang people

around the rim of the Kathmandu Valley and Trisuli.

Unlike the Newaris, their homesteads are often solitary. Houses may be constructed out of brick or stone, but in the Kathmandu Valley they are often modest in size with a porch and courtyard, a mud finish and a thatched roof.

Many Tamangs have been influenced in their dress by both Western and Newari styles. Traditionally, women wear a colourful wraparound skirt, a blouse, jacket and scarf. On important occasions they wear chunky gold or brass ear and nose rings set with semiprecious stones. Men wear loin-cloths or the traditional Newari pants, short-sleeved jackets and topis. Both men and women wear several metres of cloth wrapped around the waist.

Their religion is closely associated with Tibetan Lamaism (see the Religion section in the Facts about the Country chapter). Some Tamang follow Bon, the pre-Buddhist religion of Tibet, but the differences are not great. In Tamang areas you are certain to come across *chortens* (Buddhist shrines with a square base, topped with an onion-shaped dome) and *mani* stones (prayer stones engraved with mantras).

Today, there are around 600,000 Tamangs making them one of the largest groups in Nepal. They are disproportionately represented in the army and often work as day labourers in Kathmandu.

Brahmins & Chhetris

The Brahmins (sometimes called Bahuns in Nepal) are the priest caste while the Chhetris are the warrior caste. Because they are Hindu castes rather than a different religion or race, there is some overlap with other Hindu groups and no separate record of their numbers. Most are Indo-Aryans who migrated to Nepal over the centuries, perhaps as refugees from the Muslim invasions of India.

Despite their caste status the majority of Brahmins and Chhetris will be simple peasant farmers, but traditionally they have also formed the elite of society, and many occupy high positions in Kathmandu. They therefore tend to be more caste-conscious and orthodox than other Nepalese Hindus and this sometimes creates difficulties in their relationship with 'untouchable' Westerners. Many are vegetarians and do not drink alcohol; marriages are arranged within the caste.

There is no particular dress by which they can be recognised but men in both castes wear a sacred thread – the janai (see Janai Purnima in the Holidays & Festivals section of the Facts about the Country chapter).

Kathmandu

Kathmandu is the capital of Nepal, the largest city in the country and the main centre for hotels and restaurants. It's an amazing city that, in places, can seem to be one huge, intricate sculpture unchanged since the Middle Ages. At other times it seems to be rushing carelessly into the 20th century.

For many people, arriving in Kathmandu is as shocking as stepping out of a time machine – the sights, sounds and smells can lead to sensory overload. There are narrow streets and lanes with carved wooden balconies leaning over tiny shops, squares packed with extraordinary temples and monuments, markets bright with fruit and vegetables and a constant throng of humanity. Then there's choking dust and fumes, stinking gutters, concrete monstrosities, touts, Coca-Cola billboards and maimed beggars.

The gap between rich and poor is a chasm, but despite the pressures of extreme overcrowding and poverty, people retain a good-humoured self respect and integrity. It is probably safer to walk the streets here than it is in your home town – and certainly much more interesting.

Like Patan and Bhaktapur, the other major towns of the valley, Kathmandu's historic centre is concentrated around the Durbar (Palace) Square. There's a distinct difference between the tightly packed old city area and the more spacious newer parts of town.

Malla Kings

Malla kings of particular importance in Kathmandu included:

Ratna Malla	1482-1528
Mahendra Malla	1560-1574
Sadasiva Malla	1574-1583
Shiva Singh Malla	1578-1620
Pratap Malla	1641-1674
Prithvibendra Malla	1680-1687
Bhaskara Malla	1687-1714
Jagat Jaya Malla	1722-1736
Jaya Prakash Malla	1736-1768

ORIENTATION

Most of the interesting things to see in Kathmandu are clustered in the old part of town from Kantipath west towards the Vishnumati River. New Rd, constructed after the great earthquake of 1934, starts from the ornamental entranceway by Kantipath and goes straight into the heart of old Kathmandu, changing its name to Ganga Path before it comes to Durbar Square.

The international office of Royal Nepal Airlines (RNAC) is at the Kantipath end of

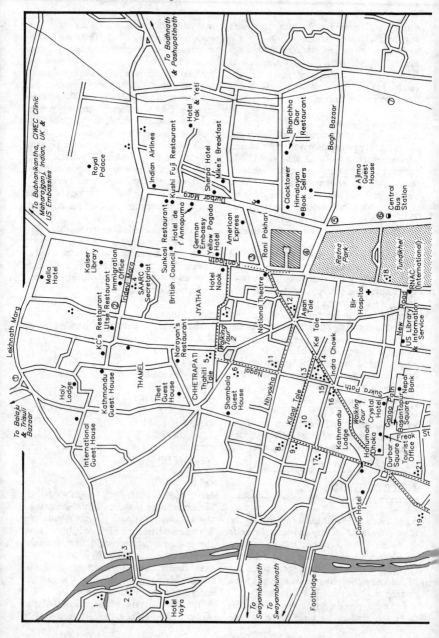

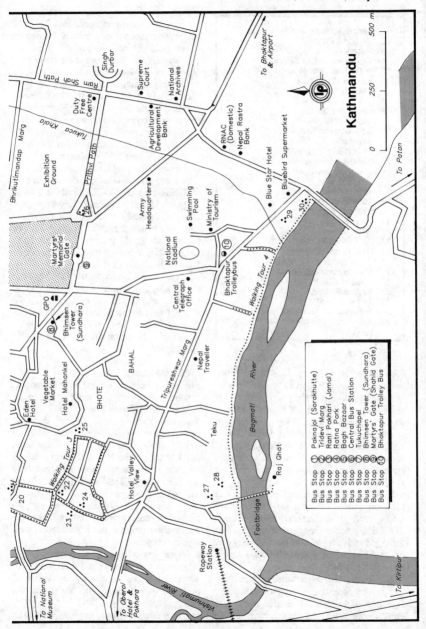

1	Shobabaghwati Temple
2	Bijeshwari Temple
3	Indrani Temple
4	Three Goddesses Temples
5	Nateshwar Temple
6	Kathesimbhu Stupa
7	Chusya Bahal
8	Nara Devi Temple
9	Narsingha Temple
10	Yitum Bahal
11	Ikha Narayan Temple
12	Annapurna Temple
13	Jana Bahal Temple
14	Sweta Machhendranath Temple
15	Shiva Temple
16	Akash Bhairab Temple
17	Yatkha Bahal
18	Mahakala Temple
19	Bhimsen Temple
20	Hari Shankar Temple
21	Adko Narayan Temple
22	Jaisi Deval Temple
23	Ram Chandra Temple
24	Takan Bahal
25	Machhendranath Temple
26	Bhadrakali Temple
27	Pachali Bhairab Temple
28	Tindeval Temple
29	Tripureshwar Mahadev Temple
30	Kalmochan Temple

Tower (also known as Sundhara). This is a major bus station area and is known as Khichapokhari, the 'pond of the dogs'. On the other side of Kantipath is the large open field known as Tundikhel.

Continuing north along Kantipath from New Rd takes you past the Bir (Government) Hospital on the left – look for Hanuman on the wall carrying a Himalayan mountain complete with medicinal herbs. On the right is Ratna Park and then Rani Pokhari. Kantipath crosses Tridevi Marg at the corner of the new Royal Palace compound and continues into Maharajganj, the embassy sector.

Running parallel to Kantipath is Durbar Marg, a wide street flanked by travel agencies, airline offices and a number of restaurants and expensive hotels. It ends at the main entrance to the new Royal Palace. Turn left from Durbar Marg in front of the palace, then cross Kantipath and Tridevi Marg will take you past the SAARC secretariat (the regional South Asian government organisation) and in a couple of blocks will bring you into the Thamel area, the popular cheaper accommodation centre of the city. Thamel is 15 to 20 minutes walk north from the centre of Kathmandu.

New Rd and along the road are banks, shops and the modern shopping centre where Indian visitors come to buy consumer goods not readily available back home. Continue further along New Rd to Ganga Path and you reach the large Basantapur Square, then Durbar Square where the old Royal Palace is located. Freak St, Kathmandu's famous street from the hippy/overland era, runs off Basantapur Square.

Running north-east from Durbar Square is the road which was once the main trading artery of the city and is still the busiest street in old Kathmandu. This narrow road, usually thronged with people, cuts through the heart of old Kathmandu from Indra Chowk through Kel Tole to Asan Tole.

Kantipath forms the north-south boundary between the older and newer parts of the city. Just south of the New Rd junction is the main GPO, easily located by the nearby Bhimsen

INFORMATION

There are a number of good notice boards in Thamel that are worth consulting if you are looking for information on such diverse things as apartments, Yoga and Buddhist courses, language courses and cultural events. The Kathmandu Guest House has a good board (to the left of the entrance), as does the Rum Doodle Restaurant, but there are others about. Trekkers who are looking for trekking partners should also consult these boards; in addition, there's a particularly useful one at the Himalayan Rescue Association office in the Kathmandu Guest House compound.

Nepal Traveller is a good-quality, free magazine that covers a broad range of interesting topics and has a good section of practical information, with addresses and phone numbers. If you can't find a copy or are interested in back copies, visit their offices on the south side of Tripureshwar Marg about 400 metres from the roundabout with Kantipath.

Tourist Office

The government tourist office (tel 2-20818) is on Ganga Path diagonally opposite Basantapur Square, and it may or may not have some brochures and maps. If it doesn't (and it should have a useful Visitors' Guide) try the Ministry of Tourism (tel 2-14519, Tripureshwar, Kathmandu) behind the National Stadium. There is also a tourist office at the airport.

Post

The Kathmandu GPO is on the corner of Kantipath and Khichapokhari, close to Bhimsen Tower. The stamp counter is open from 8 am to 7 pm, Sunday to Thursday, and from 11 am to 3 pm on Saturdays; however, many hotels and bookshops sell stamps and will also post letters for you. In Thamel, Tiwari's Pilgrims Book House will do this for no extra charge. An airmail postcard beyond the subcontinent will cost Rs 4.

The poste restante section is quite efficient:

the staff sorts letters into alphabetically arranged boxes and you simply sit down and go through them yourself. You are required to show your passport before you take anything away. Make sure your correspondents print and underline your surname; if in doubt check under your first name as well. The poste restante is not signposted very clearly, but it's to the left of the main doors, behind the counter. It's open from 10.15 am to 5 pm Sunday to Thursday (closing 1 hour earlier from mid-November to mid-February), from 10.15 am to 2 pm on Fridays, closed on Saturdays.

Parcels may be sent from the separate Foreign Post Office just north of the GPO. It's open from 10 am to 5 pm Sunday to Thursday and from 10 am to noon on Fridays. Parcels have to be examined and sealed by a customs officer and then packed in an approved manner. It's something of a procedure, so if you're short of time you're best off using one of the many cargo agencies.

American Express has a clients' mail service at their offices off the forecourt of the Hotel Mayalu in Jamal Tol. Address letters to American Express, Yeti Travels Pty Ltd, Hotel Mayalu, Jamal Tol, PO Box 76, Durbar Marg, Kathmandu.

Telephone

Nepal is linked to the rest of the world by satellite and there is international direct dialling. International phone calls can be made and faxes can be sent from the Central Telegraph Office about 200 metres south of the GPO. The International Telephone Service Counter here is open 24 hours. For the UK, Europe and Australia the first 3 minutes will cost Rs 225 and subsequent minutes, Rs 85. For the USA the first 3 minutes will cost Rs 255.

Hotels will also book phone calls; they usually charge by the minute and add a service charge. For international calls phone 186, for domestic information, 197, and for domestic trunk calls, 180.

Banks

The main Nepal Bank in New Rd is open from 10 am to 2 pm, Sundays to Thursdays and from 10 am to noon on Fridays. There is also a branch of the Rastriya Banijya Bank just off New Rd that stays open from 10 am to 5 pm. Coming from Kantipath there's a small road just to the left after the arch and the branch is on the right.

There are several banks on Durbar Marg where you can change money. The Nepal Indo-Suez Bank is convenient and efficient. The only place where you can *officially* change money in Thamel is at the immigration office – there's an exchange counter inside. However, once you've seen the queues in this place you're unlikely to want to return.

Kathmandu also has a Nepal Grindlay's Bank (tel 2-12882), GPO Box 3990, New Baneshwar (continue out along Bagh Bazaar until you cross the Dhobi River); Citibank (tel 2-28843), GPO Box 2865, a representative office in the Hotel Yak & Yeti; Standard Chartered (tel 2-20129), GPO Box 1526, Durbar Marg; and the Nepal Arab Bank (tel 2-11785), GPO Box 3729, Kantipath. Most travellers' cheques can be exchanged at these offices or, usually for resident guests only, at the main hotels. Unlike many countries, the exchange rate in hotels is identical to the banks.

American Express has an office off the forecourt of the Hotel Mayalu on Jamal Tol, just around the corner from Durbar Marg. It will make cash advances between 10 am and 1 pm. Grindlay's will make cash advances on Visa and MasterCard in Nepalese rupees. Note that you cannot make payments to these offices – arrangements should be made before you leave home. Kathmandu also has a great number of 'change money' men and although this black market is officially illegal it is so widely accepted that letters are regularly written to the *Rising Nepal* complaining about the constant importuning by money-changers. A popular T-shirt worn by many visitors announces that they don't want to change money! See the Money section in the Facts for the Visitor chapter for more on changing money in Nepal.

Government Offices

Most government offices in Kathmandu are open from 10 am to 5 pm from Sunday to Thursday and from 10 am to 4 pm during the three winter months (mid-November to mid-February). Offices close at 3 pm on Fridays.

The immigration office, where trekking permits are also issued, has moved to Tridevi Marg, close to Thamel. It's open from 10 am to 2 pm Sunday to Thursday and 10 am to noon on Fridays for applications, although you have to go back later to retrieve your passport. It's wise to start the process early as renewing a visa or obtaining a trekking permit can be very time consuming.

Foreign Embassies

Embassies in Kathmandu include:

Australia
  Bhatbhateni (tel 4-11578, 4-11304)
Bangladesh
  Naxal (tel 4-14943)
China
  Baluwatar (tel 4-11740)
India
  Lainchaur (tel 4-10900, 4-14990)
Japan
  Panipokhari (tel 4-14083, 4-10397)
Myanmar (formerly Burma)
  Chakupat, Patan (tel 5-21788)
Pakistan
  Panipokhari (tel 4-10565)
Thailand
  Thapathali (tel 2-13910, 2-13912)
UNDP
  Pulchowk (tel 5-21987)
UK
  Lainchaur (tel 4-11789, 4-14588)
USA
  Panipokhari (tel 4-11179, 4-12718)
West Germany
  Kantipath (tel 2-21763, 2-22902)

Travel Agencies

Kathmandu has a great number of travel agencies, particularly along Durbar Marg, Kantipath and in Thamel. See the Trekking chapter for information on trekking agencies.

Film & Photography

Colour print film can now be processed, rapidly, competently and economically in Kathmandu and there are numerous places offering a same day service for print film. The developing charge is typically Rs 25 plus around Rs 3.50 for each print. Even colour slides can now be developed in Kathmandu although pre-paid Kodachrome and Fujichrome still has to go overseas.

Although buying film in a country like Nepal can still be a little fraught it is now much more readily available and at better prices. There are many travellers' tales on the dangers of buying out of date or spoilt film and even film which turns out to have been stolen and already exposed. These days if you stick to the reputable photo processors you should have no problems. Typically a Fujicolor 100 print film costs about Rs 100, Fujichrome 36-exposure slide film about Rs 170 or Kodachrome 64 36-exposure slide film about Rs 290 including processing.

Libraries

There are a number of libraries and cultural centres in Kathmandu. The British Council Library (tel 2-21305) on Kantipath has a good selection of books on Nepal as well as British newspapers and magazines. It's open from 11 am to 6 pm, Sunday to Friday.

Unfortunately only Nepalese and foreign residents in Nepal are allowed to use the US Library & Information Service (tel 2-21250) on New Rd. If you qualify it's open from 11 am to 7 pm, Monday to Friday.

The French Cultural Centre (tel 2-24326) in Bagh Bazaar opposite the Bhaktapur bus stand has French publications and organises French film nights for which there is a small admission charge. The German Goethe Institute (tel 2-20528) is near the GPO and the Bhimsen Tower and also has film nights as well as library facilities.

Rastriya Pustakalaya, the Nepal National Library, is at Pulchowk in Patan and has books in English and Indian languages. The Tribhuvan University Library of Kirtipur has a good collection and is open Sunday to Friday from 9 am to 6 pm.

The Kaiser or Kesar Library is worth a visit just to see the building. It's on Kantipath opposite the new Royal Palace and has an incredible collection of books on Buddhism, Tibet and Nepal. Kaiser Shamsher Jung Bahadur Rana was a Rana aristocrat, scholar, scientist and gourmet. He built up a superb collection of books all of which, it is said, he read in their original language. Most of his palace is now used for government offices, but his library is kept as he left it and can be visited.

Bookshops

Recent years have seen new bookshops appear like weeds in Kathmandu and there is now a variety of good bookshops. Many have particularly interesting selections of books on Nepal including books which are not usually available outside the country.

TIWARI'S
PILGRIMS
BOOK HOUSE
THAMEL, P. Box 3872,
KATHMANDU (NEPAL)
TEL. 4-16744

PUBLISHERS

DISTRIBUTORS

FEATURING—
· WORLDWIDE BOOK SHIPPING
· MAIL AND TELEGRAM SERVICE
· FILM SALES AND PROCESSING
· QUALITY STATIONERY
· EXCLUSIVE JEWELLERY
· CERTIFIED GEMSTONES
· CLASSICAL CASSETTES
· AND MUCH MORE

SPECIALISING IN:—
· HIMALAYAN SUBJECTS
· OLD AND RARE BOOKS
· MAPS

BROWSING
WELCOME

Prices for British and American books are surprisingly competitive with their home market prices. As well as shops with new books there are many shops with second-hand books for sale and trade.

Thamel has a good selection including what is probably the best known and most popular bookshop in town, for visitors at least. Tiwari's Pilgrims Book House is a couple of doors north of the Kathmandu Guest House and has a stunning collection of books on Nepal and other Himalayan regions. It also has books on Buddhism, Hinduism, Tantrism, yoga, mountain climbing and trekking plus general books, maps, games, envelopes and a superb postcard selection. There's a second Tiwari's Pilgrims Book House about 100 metres south and this smaller shop has an antiquarian section. Tiwari's Pilgrims Book House is a bookshop which would not be out of place in any book conscious big Western city.

There are many other good bookshops around Thamel, such as Bookland on Tridevi Marg opposite the immigration office. Kantipath or near the clocktower are other good bookshop locations. Himalayan Book Sellers at Ghantaghar by the clocktower is a long-term survivor in the Kathmandu book business with an excellent selection of books on Nepal and the Himalaya. Everest Book Service and Asia Book House are good bookshops just round the corner from Durbar Marg towards the National Theatre.

Ratna Book Distributors at Bagh Bazaar near the French Cultural Centre is worth a visit, or Educational Enterprises beside the Mahakal Temple on Kantipath near New Rd Gate. The Himalaya Book Store is at Bagh Bazaar near the Bhaktapur bus stand.

Yoga & Buddhist Courses

Check the bulletin boards in Thamel for up-to-date information and shop around before you commit yourself. A number of courses are regularly advertised.

The Hotel Asia (tel 2-20441) in the centre of Thamel is home to the Kathmandu Western Buddhist Centre and there are regular courses and talks. Arogya Ashram

(tel 2-22305) near the Pashupatinath Temple teaches yoga.

The Himalayan Yogic Institute & Buddhist Meditation Centre (tel 4-13094) has talks, retreats and courses. To find the centre head away from Thamel on Lazimpat until you get to the Hotel Kathmandu; turn right after the hotel and the centre is on the right after about 200 metres. This centre is affiliated with the monastery at Kopan (see the Around the Valley chapter), north of Bodhnath. For more information on Kopan call 2-26717 in Kathmandu or write to the Nepal Mahayana Centre, PO Box 817, Kathmandu, Nepal.

Swimming Pools & Sauna

Pools in the major hotels can usually be used by friends of hotel guests or, at some hotels, by outsiders for a US$2 to US$3 charge.

There are public pools at Balaju and at the National Stadium although they close during the October to February winter months. The National Stadium pool in the south of Kathmandu costs Rs 15 and is open from 10 am to 5 pm; Monday is reserved for women. The Balaju pool costs Rs 10 but it can get very crowded.

In addition to having a masseur, fully equipped gym and aerobic classes the Kathmandu Physical Fitness Centre (tel 4-12473), near the Hotel Shankar on Lazimpat, has a sauna and jacuzzi. Its day rate is Rs 60. The Yak & Yeti also has a health club.

DURBAR SQUARE

Durbar in Nepali means 'palace' and in Patan and Bhaktapur, as well as Kathmandu, there are Durbar squares in front of their old palaces. The king no longer lives in the old town centre palace in Kathmandu: the Royal Palace was moved north to Narayanhiti about a century ago. At that time it was on the edge of the city, now it's close to the popular tourist area of Thamel.

Around the central Durbar Square are the old Royal Palace known as the Hanuman Dhoka, numerous interesting temples, the Kumari Chowk or Kumari Bahal (the resi-

Saddhu, Durbar Square

open area Makhan Tole, at one time the main road in Kathmandu and still the most interesting street to walk down, continues north-east.

A good place to start an exploration of the square is with what may well be the oldest building in the valley, the unprepossessing Kasthamandap.

Kasthamandap (2)

In the south-western corner of the square the Kasthamandap or House of Wood is the building which gave Kathmandu its name. Although its history is uncertain it is possible that it was originally constructed around the 12th century. A legend relates that the whole building was made with the wood from a single sal tree. At first it was a community centre where visitors gathered before major ceremonies, but later it was converted to a temple to Gorakhnath.

A small wooden enclosure in the centre of the building houses the image of the god. Images of Ganesh can be found at each corner of the building and there are also shrines to a number of other gods. Bronze lions guard the entrance, and Hindu epics are illustrated around the 1st floor cornices of the three storey building.

The squat, mediaeval-looking building is busy in the early morning hours when porters

dence of the living goddess) and the Kasthamandap.

It's easy to spend hours wandering around the colourful and busy area of Durbar Square and the adjoining Basantapur Square. This is very much the centre of old Kathmandu and watching the world go by from the terraced platforms of the towering Maju Deval is a wonderful way to get the feel for the city. Although many of the buildings around the square are very old, a great deal of damage was caused by the great earthquake of 1934 and many buildings were subsequently rebuilt, not always in their original form.

The Durbar Square area is actually made up of three loosely linked squares. To the east is the open Basantapur Square area, off which runs Freak St. The main Durbar Square area, with its popular watch-the-world-go-by temples, is to the west. Running off north-east is a second part of Durbar Square, dotted with temples and with the entrance to the Old Royal Palace. From this

Kasthamandap Temple

sit here, waiting for customers who need to have loads carried.

Ashok Binayak (4)

On the northern side of the Kasthamandap, at the top of Maru Tole, the laneway down to the river, stands the tiny Ashok Binayak or Maru Ganesh Shrine. The small size of this shrine belies its importance as this is one of the four most important Ganesh shrines in the valley. Ganesh is a much-loved god and there is a constant stream of visitors here. A visit to this shrine is highly recommended by Hindus to ensure safety on a forthcoming journey. It's uncertain how old the temple is although its gilded roof was added in the 19th century.

Shiva Temple (3)

The Shiva Temple near the Kasthamandap and the Ashok Binayak is used by barbers who can generally be seen squatting on the temple platform, administering short back and sides.

Maru Tole

Maru Tole leads down to the Vishnumati River where a footbridge crosses to the pathway to Swayambhunath on the other side. This was a busy street in the days of hippy flower power, but today there's little sign of why it should have been called either Pie or Pig Alley – not only are the pie shops gone it's also much cleaner. One thing Maru Tole does have is Maru Hiti, one of the finest sunken water conduits in the city.

Maju Deval (12)

A pleasant hour can easily be spent sitting on the platform steps of the Shiva temple known as the Maju Deval. From here you can watch the constant activity of fruit and vegetable hawkers, the coming and goings of taxis and trishaws and the flute and other souvenir sellers importuning tourists. The nine stage platform of the Maju Deval is probably the most popular meeting place in the city. The large, triple roofed temple has erotic carvings on its roof struts and offers great views over the square and across the roofs of the town.

The temple dates from 1690 and was built by Bhaktapur King Bhupatindra Malla's mother. Although the temple has a well known Shiva lingam inside, the roof is topped by a pinnacle shaped like a Buddhist stupa. At the bottom of the temple stairway is a small *shikhara* (see the Glossary) style temple to Kam Dev, a 'companion' of Lord Shiva.

Maju Deval

Trailokya Mohan Narayan Temple (8)

The other temple standing out in the open area of the square is the smaller five tiered, three roofed Trailokya Mohan Narayan. The

Top: Vegetable stalls, Kathmandu (CG)
Bottom: Under a temple's eves, market stalls in Asan Tole, Kathmandu (RE)

Top: The bounty of the land, Bungamati, Kathmandu Valley (RE)
Left: Swayambhunath and monk (SB)
Right: Classic Newari architecture, Bungamati, Kathmandu Valley (RE)

Trailokya Mohan Temple

temple was built by Prithvibendra Malla in 1680 and is easily identified as a temple to Narayan or Vishnu by the fine Garuda kneeling before it. The Garuda figure was a later addition, erected by the king's widow soon

after his death. Look for the Vaishnavite images on the carved roof struts and the window screens with their decoratively carved medallions.

Shiva-Parvati Temple (14)

From the steps of the Maju Deval you can look across the square to the Shiva-Parvati Temple, where images of Lord Shiva and his consort look out from the upstairs window on the comings and goings below them. The temple was built in the late 1700s by Bahadur Shah, son of Prithvi Narayan Shah. Although the temple is, by Kathmandu's standards, not very old it stands on a two stage platform which may have been an open dancing stage hundreds of years earlier. A Vishnu Temple stands to one side of it.

Shiva Parvati Temple

Kumari Bahal (10)

At the junction of Durbar and Basantapur squares is a white three storey building with intricately carved windows. The House of the Living Goddess – the Kumari Bahal – faces Durbar Square, its door guarded by stone lions. The building, in the style of the courtyarded Buddhist viharas of the valley, was built in 1757 by Jaya Prakash Malla. Inside lives the young girl who is selected to be the town's living goddess, until she reaches puberty and reverts to being a normal mortal!

Inside the building the three storey courtyard, or Kumari Chowk, is enclosed by magnificently carved wooden balconies and windows. A little baksheesh to a waiting attendant may well prompt a brief appear-

Kumari Devi

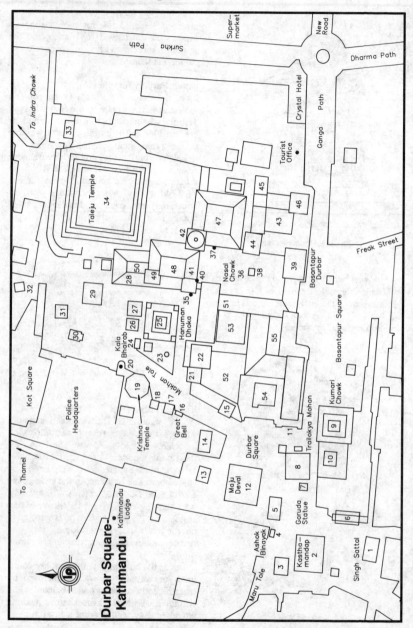

Durbar Square - Kathmandu

1	Singh Sattal	28	Stone Inscription
2	Kasthamandap Temple	29	Kakeshwar Shiva Temple
3	Shiva Temple	30	Kotilingeshwar Mahadev Temple
4	Ashok Binayak (Maru Ganesh Shrine)	31	Mahavishnu Temple
5	Lakshmi Narayan Temple	32	Mahendreshwar Temple
6	Kabindrapur Temple	33	Tana Deval Temple
7	Garuda Statue	34	Taleju Temple
8	Trailokya Mohan Narayan (Vishnu) Temple	35	Hanuman Statue
9	Kumari Chowk	36	Nasal Chowk
10	Kumari Bahal	37	Dancing Shiva Temple
11	Gaddi Baithak	38	Coronation Platform
12	Maju Deval	39	Basantapur Tower
13	Narayan Temple	40	Narsingha Statue
14	Shiva-Parvati Temple	41	Gaddi Baithak (Audience Chamber)
15	Bhagwati Temple	42	Panch Mukhi Hanuman
16	Great Bell	43	Lohan Chowk
17	Stone Vishnu Temple	44	Kirtipur Tower
18	Saraswati Temple	45	Bhaktapur Tower (Lakshmi Bilas)
19	Krishna Temple	46	Patan Tower (Lalitpur Tower)
20	Great Drums	47	Mul Chowk
21	Sweta (White) Bhairab	48	Mohan Chowk
22	Degutaleju Temple	49	Mohan Tower
23	King Pratap Malla's Column	50	Sundari Chowk
24	Kala (Black) Bhairab	51	Tribhuvan Museum
25	Jagannath Temple	52	Masan Chowk
26	Indrapur Temple	53	Dahk Chowk
27	Vishnu Temple	54	Hnuluche Chowk
		55	Lam Chowk

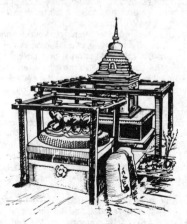

Kumari Bahal

ance – he calls out 'Hey goddess' in Newari! Photographing the goddess is forbidden, but you are quite free to photograph the court-yard when she is not present. Westerners are not allowed to go beyond this area. The courtyard contains a miniature stupa carrying the symbols of Saraswati, the goddess of learning.

The big gate beside the Kumari Bahal conceals the huge chariot which takes the Kumari around the city of Kathmandu once a year. This festival also commenced under Jaya Prakash Malla.

Gaddi Baithak (11)
The eastern side of Durbar Square is closed off by this white neoclassical building. The Gaddi Baithak with its imported European style was built as a part of the palace during the Rana period and makes a strange contrast to the traditional Nepalese architecture that dominates the square.

Bhagwati Temple (15)
Next to the Gaddi Baithak, this triple storey, triple roofed temple is easily missed since it

surmounts the building below it. The best view of the temple with its golden roofs is probably from the Maju Deval across the square. The temple was built by Jagat Jaya Malla and originally had an image of Narayan. This image was stolen in 1766 so when

The Kumari Devi

Not only does Nepal have countless gods, goddesses, deities, Boddhisattvas, avatars, incarnations and manifestations, which are worshipped and revered as statues, images, paintings and symbols, the country also has a real living goddess. The Kumari Devi is a young girl who lives in the building known as the Kumari Bahal, right beside Kathmandu's Durbar Square.

The practice of having a living goddess probably came about during the reign of Jaya Prakash Malla, the last of the Malla kings of Kathmandu whose reign abruptly ended with the conquest of the valley by Prithvi Narayan Shah in 1768. As usual in Nepal, where there is never one simple answer to any question, there are a number of legends about the Kumari.

One is that the Malla king had intercourse with a pre-pubescent girl, that she died as a result and that he started the practice of venerating a young girl as a living goddess in penance. Another tells of a Malla king who regularly played dice with the goddess Taleju, the protective deity of the valley. When he made an unseemly advance she threatened to withdraw her protection but relented and promised to return in the form of a young girl. Still another tells of a young girl possessed by the goddess Durga and banished from the kingdom. When the furious queen heard of this she ordered her husband to bring the young girl back and keep her as a real goddess.

Whatever the background the reality is that there are a number of living goddesses around the Kathmandu Valley but it is the Kumari Devi or Royal Kumari who is the most important. The Kumari is selected from a particular caste of Newari gold and silversmiths. She is customarily somewhere between 4 or 5 years of age and puberty and must meet 32 strict physical requirements ranging from the colour of her eyes and the shape of her teeth to the sound of her voice. Her horoscope must also be appropriate of course.

Once suitable candidates have been found they are gathered together in a darkened room where terrifying noises are made, men dance by in horrific masks and gruesome buffalo heads are on display. Naturally these goings-on are unlikely to frighten a real goddess, particularly one who is an incarnation of Durga, so the young girl who remains calm and collected through this ordeal is clearly the new Kumari. In a process similar to the selection of the Dalai Lama the Kumari then chooses items of clothing and decoration worn by her predecessor as a final test.

Once chosen as the Kumari the young girl moves in to the Kumari Bahal with her family and lives there apart from a half-dozen ceremonial forays into the outside world each year. The most spectacular of these occasions is the August-September Indra Jatra festival, when she travels through the city on a huge temple chariot over a 3 day period. During this festival the Kumari customarily blesses the king of Nepal and it is curious that Prithvi Narayan Shah's defeat of the Malla kingdoms took place at this time, just as if the goddess Taleju had indeed withdrawn her protection over the valley. The new king was blessed by the Kumari and the custom continued without skipping a beat!

The Kumari's reign ends with her first period, or any serious accidental loss of blood. Once this first sign of puberty is reached she reverts to being a normal mortal, and the search must start for a new Kumari. During her time as a goddess the Kumari is supported by the temple income and on retirement she is paid a handsome dowry. It is said that marrying an ex-Kumari is unlucky, but it's more likely a natural belief that taking on a spoilt ex-goddess is likely to be hard work! ■

Prithvi Narayan Shah conquered the valley only a year later he simply substituted it with an image of the goddess Bhagwati, which he just happened to be toting around with him. In April each year the image of the goddess is conveyed to the village of Nuwakot, 65 km to the north, then returned a few days later.

A succession of interesting buildings and statues stand to the north-east of the Bhagwati Temple.

Bhagwati Temple

The Great Bell (16)

On your left as you leave the main square along Makhan Tole is the Great Bell erected by Bahadur Shah in 1797. During the Malla era a novel addition to one of the valley town's Durbar squares would almost immediately be imitated in another's. Curiously, Patan and Bhaktapur got their bells in 1736, while the Kathmandu version did not follow until long after the fall of the Mallas. The bell's ring will drive off evil spirits, but it is only rung

when puja is being offered at the Degutaleju Temple.

Vishnu Temple (17)

Next to the bell is a small stone Vishnu Temple about which very little is known. It was badly damaged by the earthquake of 1934 and has only recently been restored.

Saraswati Temple (18)

Next is the Saraswati Temple which also suffered badly from the great earthquake. Prior to the quake it was over 14 metres high, now it is only half that height. Like the adjoining Vishnu Temple little is known about its history.

Krishna Temple (19)

The history of the octagonal Krishna Temple is well documented. It was built in 1648 by Pratap Malla, perhaps as a reply to Siddhinarsingh's magnificent Krishna Mandir in Patan. Inside there are images of Krishna and two goddesses which, according to a Sanskrit inscription, are modelled from the king and his two wives! The temple also has a Newari inscription but this neglects to mention the king's little act of vanity. The triple roofed temple has lower roofs of tile topped by a copper roof.

Krishna Temple

Just beyond the temple are the Great Drums (20) to which a goat and a buffalo must be sacrificed twice a year. Then there is the police headquarters building beyond which is Kot Square. It was here where Jung Bahadur Rana perpetrated the famous 1846 massacre which led to the 100 year period of Rana rule. *Kot* means 'armoury' or 'fort'. During the Durga Puja festival each year blood again flows in Kot Square as hundreds of buffaloes and goats are sacrificed. Young soldiers are supposed to lop each head off with a single blow.

King Pratap Malla's Column (23)
Across the road from the Krishna Temple there are a host of smaller temples and other structures, all standing on a huge raised platform in front of the old Royal Palace and the towering Taleju Temple (34). The square, stone pillar known as the Pratap Dhvaja is topped by a statue of the famous King Pratap Malla, seated with folded hands and surrounded by his two wives, his four sons and his infant son. He looks towards his private prayer room on the 3rd floor of the Degutaleju Temple. The column was erected in 1670 by Pratap Malla and preceded the similar columns in Patan and Bhaktapur.

Sweta Bhairab (21)
Sweta (White) Bhairab's horrible face is hidden away behind a grille opposite the

Pratap Malla column. The huge mask dates from 1794 during the reign of Rana Bahadur Shah, the third Shah dynasty king. Each September during the Indra Jatra festival the gates are swung back to reveal the mask for a few days. At that time the face is covered in flowers and rice and at the start of the festivities beer is poured through the horrific mouth. Crowds of men fight to get a drink of this blessed beer! At other times of year you can peek through the lattice to see the mask which is used as the symbol of Royal Nepal Airlines.

Jagannath Temple (25)
This temple, noted for the erotic carvings on its roof struts, is the oldest structure in this part of the square. Pratap Malla claimed to have constructed the temple during his reign but it may actually be far older, dating back to 1563 during the rule of Mahendra Malla. The temple has a three tier platform and two storeys. There are three doors on each side of the temple but only the centre door opens.

Jagganath Temple

Kala Bhairab (24)
Behind the Jagannath Temple is the large figure of Kala (Black) Bhairab. Bhairab is Shiva in his most fearsome aspect and this huge stone image of the terrifying Kala

Sweta Bhairab

Bhairab has six arms, wears a garland of skulls and tramples a corpse, symbolic of mankind's ignorance. The figure was said to have been brought here by Pratap Malla, having been found in a field to the north of the city. The image was originally cut from a single stone although the upper right-hand side has been repaired with another stone and the sun and moon to the left and the lions at the top are later additions. It is said that telling a lie while standing before Kala Bhairab will bring instant death and it was once used as a form of trial by ordeal!

that the temple is to Vishnu. And to compound the puzzle the temple's name clearly indicates it is dedicated to Indra! The temple's simple design and plain roof struts together with the lack of an identifying *torana* (the space above temple doors indicating the deity to which the temple is dedicated) give no further clues.

Indrapur Temple

Vishnu Temple (27)

Little is known about the adjoining Vishnu Temple either. The triple roofed temple stands on a four level base. The roof strut carvings and the golden image of Vishnu inside show that it is a Vishnu temple, but it is not known how old the temple is, although it was in existence during Pratap Malla's reign.

Kala Bhairab

Indrapur Temple (26)

Immediately to the east of horrific Bhairab stands the mysterious Indrapur Temple. This curious temple may be of great antiquity but little is known of its history. Even the god to which it is dedicated is controversial – inside there is a lingam indicating that it is a Shiva temple. But half buried on the southern side of the temple is a Garuda image, indicating

Kakeshwar Temple (29)

North of the Vishnu Temple this temple was originally built in 1681 but rebuilt after it was badly damaged in the 1934 earthquake. It may have been considerably altered at that time as the temple is a strange combination of styles, starting with a two level base from which rises a lower floor in typical Nepalese style. Above the 1st floor, however, the temple is in Indian shikhara style, topped by

Vishnu Temple

a spire shaped like a water vase or *kalasa*, indicative of a female deity.

Stone Inscription (28)

On the outside of the palace wall, opposite the Vishnu Temple (27) is a stone inscription to the goddess Kalika written in 15 languages, including English and French. King Pratap Malla, renowned for his scholastic abilities, set up this inscription in 1664 and a Nepalese

legend relates that milk will flow from the spout in the middle if somebody is able to read all the languages!

Kotilingeshwar Mahadev Temple (30)

This early Malla temple dates from the reign of Mahendra Malla in the 1500s. The three stage plinth is topped by a temple in the *gumbhaj* style, which basically means a square structure topped by a dome. The bull facing the temple indicates that it is a Shiva temple.

Kotilingeshwar Temple

Mahavishnu Temple (31)

Built by Jagat Jaya Malla, this double roofed temple on a four level plinth was badly damaged in the 1934 earthquake and was not restored to its former magnificence. Only the golden spire on the roof, topped by a golden umbrella, hints at its appearance prior to the tremblor.

Mahendreshwar Temple (32)

At the extreme northern end of the square this temple dates from 1561, during Mahendra Malla's reign. The temple was restored in 1963 and is dedicated to Shiva. Inside there is a lingam, a small image of Shiva's bull Nandi fronts the temple and at the north-eastern corner of the temple there is an image of Kam Dev. The temple has a wide, two level plinth and a spire topped by a golden umbrella.

Kakeshwar Temple

Taleju Temple (34)

The square's most magnificent temple stands at the north-eastern extremity of the square but is not open to the public. Even the Nepalese can only visit the temple during the annual Durga Puja festival. You will have to be content with the view of the beautiful three storey golden temple from the outside.

The Taleju Temple was built in 1564 by Mahendra Malla. Taleju Bhawani was originally a goddess from the south of India, but she became the titular deity or royal goddess of the Malla kings in the 14th century. Taleju temples were erected in her honour in Patan and Bhaktapur as well as in Kathmandu.

The temple stands on a 12 stage plinth and reaches over 35 metres high, dominating the Durbar Square area. The eighth stage of the plinth has a wall around the temple, in front of which are 12 miniature temples, four more miniature temples stand inside the wall which has four wide and beautifully carved gates. If entry to the temple were permitted it could be reached from within the palace or from the Singh Dhoka or Lion Gate from the square.

Taleju Temple

OLD ROYAL PALACE OR HANUMAN DHOKA

Hanuman's brave assistance to noble Rama during the exciting events of the *Ramayana* has led to the monkey god's appearance guarding many important entrances. Here Hanuman's statue (35), cloaked in red and sheltered by an umbrella, marks the entrance, or *dhoka*, to Kathmandu's Old Royal Palace and has even given the palace its name. The statue dates from 1672, but the face has disappeared under a coating of red paste applied by faithful visitors.

Standards bearing Nepal's double-triangle flag flank the statue while on each side of the palace gate are stone lions, one ridden by Shiva, the other by his wife Parvati. Above the gate a brightly painted niche is illustrated with a figure of a ferocious Tantric version of Krishna in the centre. On one side is the gentler Hindu Krishna in his traditional blue colour accompanied by two of his comely *gopis*, or milkmaids. On the other side is King Pratap Malla and his queen. Entrance to the palace costs Rs 10 and it is open from 10.30 am to 4 pm daily.

The palace was originally founded during the Licchavi period, but as it stands today most of it was constructed by King Pratap Malla in the 17th century. The palace was renovated many times in later years and the Shah kings continued to live here until the end of the 19th century. The oldest parts are the smaller Sundari Chowk (50) and Mohan Chowk (48) at the northern part of the palace. From here construction moved south and in all there are 10 courtyards, or *chowks*, in the palace. The largest is the Nasal Chowk (36), immediately inside the palace entrance.

Nasal Chowk (36)

Inside the palace there are many *chowks* and from the entrance gate you immediately enter the most famous one. *Nasal* means 'dancing one' and the courtyard takes its name from a small figure of the Dancing Shiva (37) on the eastern side of the square. Although the courtyard was constructed in the Malla period many of the buildings around the square were Rana constructions.

During that time the Nasal Chowk became the square used for coronations, a practice which continues to this day. King Birendra was crowned in the 1975 ceremony on the platform (38) in the centre of the courtyard.

The rectangular courtyard is aligned north-south and the entrance is at the north-eastern corner. The nine storey Basantapur Tower (39) looms over the southern end of the courtyard. Proceeding around the courtyard in a clockwise direction there is a surprisingly small but beautifully carved doorway which once led to the Malla kings' private quarters. The panels have images of four gods.

Beyond the door is a large statue of Narsingha (40), Vishnu in his man-lion incarnation in the act of killing a demon. The stone image was erected by Pratap Malla in 1673 and the inscription on the pedestal explains that he placed it here in fear that he had offended Vishnu by dancing in a Narsingha costume!

The Kabindrapur Temple (6) in the main square was built for the same reason.

Next there is the Gaddi Baithak (41), or Audience Chamber, of the Malla kings. The open verandah houses the Malla throne and portraits of the Shah kings. The small Dancing Shiva Temple (37) which gave the courtyard its name is on the eastern wall, the Malla kings probably used the courtyard for dance performances. A golden image of Mahavishnu is set into an open verandah on the eastern wall. This image was originally in the Mahavishnu Temple (31) in the square, but was moved here after the 1934 earthquake.

Panch Mukhi Hanuman Temple (42)

At the north-eastern corner of the Nasal Chowk stands the Panch Mukhi Hanuman with its five circular roofs. Each of the valley towns has one five storey temple although it is the great Nyatapola Temple of Bhaktapur which is by far the best known. Hanuman is

Erotic Art

The most interesting woodcarving on Nepalese temples is on the roof struts, and on many temples these carvings include erotic scenes. The erotic scenes are rarely the central carving on the strut, usually they're the smaller carving at the bottom of the strut, like a footnote to the larger image. Nor are they the sensuous, finely sculptured erotic figures like those at Khajuraho and Konarak in India. In Nepal the figures are often smaller, cruder, even quite cartoon like.

The themes have a Tantric element, a clear connection to the intermingling of Tibetan Buddhist and Hindu beliefs in Nepal since both have Tantric elements, but their real purpose is unclear. Are they simply a celebration of an important part of the cycle of life? A more explicit reference to Shiva's creative role than the enigmatic lingams and yonis scattered around so many temples? Or are they supposed to play some sort of protective role for the temple? It's popularly rumoured that the goddess of lightning is a shy virgin who wouldn't dream of striking a temple with such goings-on, although that's probably more a tourist guide tale than anything else.

Whatever the reason for their existence the Tantric elements can be found on temples in all three of the major towns of the valley. On some temples it may just be the odd depiction here and there while on others something will be happening on every roof strut. The activities range from straightforward exhibitionism to the *mithuna* scenes of couples engaged in often quite athletic acts of intercourse. More exotic carvings include ménages à trois scenes of oral or anal intercourse or couplings with demons or animals.

Temples with some of the more interesting erotic carvings include:

Kathmandu In Durbar Square there are carvings on many of the roof struts of the Jagannath Temple just outside the Hanuman Dhoka palace entrance. The lofty Basantapur Tower of the old palace, overlooking Basantapur Square, has some of the finest erotic carvings on its roof struts. The large Shiva Temple in the middle of the square, also known as the Mahadev

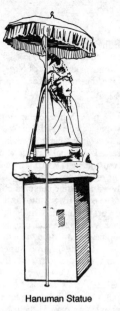

Hanuman Statue

worshipped in the temple in Kathmandu but only the priests of the temple may enter it.

Basantapur Tower (39)

King Prithvi Narayan Shah, first of the Shah dynasty kings, was involved in the construction of the four red-coloured towers around the Lohan Chowk (43). The towers represent the four ancient cities of the valley: the Kathmandu or Basantapur, Tower, the Kirtipur Tower (44), the Bhaktapur Tower (45) and the Patan or Lalitpur Tower (46).

The dominant nine storey Basantapur Tower was extensively restored prior to King Birendra's coronation in 1975. A series of steep stairways climbs to the top from where there are superb views over the palace and the city. The struts along the facade of the Basantapur Tower, particularly those facing out to Basantapur Square, are decorated with erotic carvings.

Temple or the Maju Deval Temple, is a popular place to watch the activity in the square and also has some erotic struts.

North of the centre, near the restaurant and guest house centre of Thamel, the Three Goddesses Temples - dedicated to Dakshinkali, Mankamna and Jawalamai - have a number of interesting roof struts. The Indrani Temple, on the east bank of the Vishnumati River where you cross it going from Thamel to Swayambhunath, is another temple with interesting scenes. South of Durbar Square the small Ram Chandra Temple has some tiny carvings on each of its roof struts.

Patan In Patan's Durbar Square the Jaganarayan or Charnarayan Temple is the most interesting temple in the town for erotic carvings.

Bhaktapur Several temples in Bhaktapur have erotic scenes including the Pashupatinath Temple in Durbar Square. There are also some carvings in the Cafe Nyatapola in Taumadhi Tole where the soaring five storey Nyatapola Temple is located. The Dattatraya Temple near the Pujari Math monastery in the eastern part of town also has low relief figures around its base.

Elsewhere in the Valley There are many other temples with erotic artwork around the valley. The Jal Binayak Temple dedicated to Ganesh at Chobar Gorge, just south of Patan, has many interesting roof struts as does the Mahadev Temple at Gokarna, east of Bodhnath. Other temples worth inspecting include the small Ajima or Shitla Devi Temple in the Balaju park, near the sleeping Vishnu figure, and the Bagh Bhairab Temple in Kirtipur.

Several temples in and around Pashupatinath have erotic scenes but non-Hindus aren't permitted to enter the temple courtyards to see them. En route to Pashupatinath, however, you can visit the Mahadev Gyaneshwar in Deopatan, the village by Pashupatinath. ■

Mul Chowk (47)

This courtyard was completely dedicated to religious functions within the palace and is configured like a vihara (a dwelling place for Buddhist monks) with a two storey building surrounding the courtyard. Mul Chowk is dedicated to Taleju Bhawani, the royal goddess of the Mallas, and sacrifices are made to her in the centre of the courtyard during the Dasain festivals. A smaller Taleju Temple stands in the southern wing of the square and the image of the goddess is moved here from the main Taleju Temple during the Dasain festival. Images of the goddesses Ganga and Jamuna guard the golden temple doorway which is topped by a golden torana. Unfortunately, from the Bhaktapur Tower or Lakshmi Bilas (45), where visitors normally observe the courtyard, the view is less than inspiring and the temple itself cannot be seen at all.

Degutaleju Temple (22)

Degutaleju is another manifestation of the Malla's personal goddess Taleju and this temple was built by Shiva Singh Malla and is integrated into the palace structure itself, like the Bhagwati Temple just round the corner. The triple roofed temple actually starts from above the common buildings it surmounts.

Mohan Chowk (48)

North of the Nasal Chowk is the residential courtyard of the Malla kings. It dates from 1649 and at one time a Malla king had to be born here to be eligible to wear the crown. The last Malla king, Jaya Prakash Malla, had great difficulties during his reign even though he was the legitimate heir because he was born elsewhere. The golden water spout, known as Sun Dhara, in the centre of the courtyard delivers water from Budhanilkantha in the north of the valley. The richly sculptured spout is actually several metres below the courtyard level. The Malla kings would ritually bathe here each morning.

The courtyard is surrounded by towers at its four corners and north of the Mohan Chowk is the small Sundari Chowk (50).

Rana Additions & Tribhuvan Museum (51)

The part of the palace west of Nasal Chowk, overlooking the main Durbar Square area, was principally constructed by the Ranas in the mid to late part of the last century. Ironically, it is now home to an interesting museum that celebrates King Tribhuvan's successful revolt against their regime. If you are interested in Nepal's modern history a visit is a must; it costs Rs 10. There are some fascinating recreations of the king's bedroom and study with genuine personal effects that give quite an eerie insight into his life. There are also lots of photos and newspaper clippings that catch the drama of his escape and triumphant return. And there are several magnificent thrones, some superb stone carvings and, oddly, a coin collection.

FREAK ST

Kathmandu's most famous street from the old hippy overland days of the late '60s and early '70s runs south from Basantapur Square. Its real name is still Jochne but since the early '70s it has been far better known as

Freak St. In its hippy prime this was the place for cheap hotels, colourful restaurants, hashish shops, moneychangers and, of course, the weird and wonderful 'freaks' who gave the street its name. In those days Freak St was one of the great gathering places on the road east.

Times change and Freak St today is a pale shadow of its former colourful self and, while there are still cheap hotels and restaurants, it's now the Thamel area in the north of the town which is the main gathering place. Some shoestring travellers still stay here. Its recent historical connections are interesting and you are right in the heart of old Kathmandu whereas Thamel is about 20 minutes walk away. Some say it is beginning to pick up again.

FOUR WALKING TOURS

A stroll around Kathmandu will lead the casual wanderer to many intriguing sights, especially in the crowded maze of streets, courtyards and alleys in the market area north of Durbar Square. There are temples, shrines and many individual statues and sculptures hidden away in the most unlikely places. You really appreciate Kathmandu's museum-like quality when you stumble upon a 1000 year old statue, something which would be a prize possession in many Western museums, used as a children's plaything or something to hang washing on. The walks that follow can be made anytime you have an hour or two to spare. Walking Tours 1 and 2 can be used as a route from the accommodation centre of Thamel to the central Durbar Square area.

All the walks take you to a number of markets, temples and *chowks*, which are the centre of Nepalese life. A number of *chowks* are surrounded by *bahals* or *bahils*, dwellings for monastic Buddhist communities, although very few are used for that purpose today – they have been taken over by families and sometimes schools.

The courtyards may be large and open, dotted with chaityas and shrines, or they may be tightly enclosed within a single building. A bahil is distinguished from a bahal because it also included accommodation for non-monastic visitors, is generally simpler, and the main shrine may not necessarily be in the centre of the courtyard.

The first three walks can be made as individual strolls or linked together into one longer walk. The first walk gives you a taste of the crowded and fascinating shopping streets in the oldest part of Kathmandu and also takes you to some of the city's most important temples. The second walk visits some very old bahals, an important Buddhist stupa, passes by a number of ancient and important stoneworks and introduces you to a toothache god. The third walk takes you to a less well known section of Kathmandu, without spectacular attractions but where the normal life of the city goes on and tourist

---

Marijuana
In Kathmandu's flower power era in the '60s and early '70s, the easy availability of marijuana and hashish was undoubtedly a major attraction. In its hippy heyday Kathmandu had hash shops and hash calendars, and hash cookies appeared on every hip restaurant menu. Many of the 'freaks' who congregated in Nepal in those days were high in other places than the Himalaya! The drug had always been easily available, but its users were mainly sadhus for whom it has religious importance. Then, in the run up to King Birendra's coronation, hashish was banned and, possibly in protest, the huge Singh Durbar building, a palace from the Rana period, burnt down the next night! Hashish is still banned but illegal or not it's readily available in Nepal, although potential potheads should keep the less than five star condition of Nepalese jails firmly in mind. Don't try taking any out of the country either – travellers have been arrested at the airport on departure. ∎

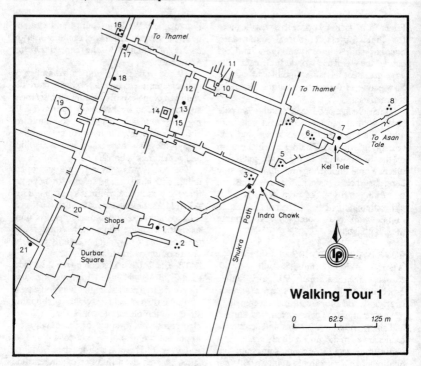

Walking Tour 1

0   62.5   125 m

intruders are fairly rare. The fourth and last walk runs along the peaceful banks of the Bagmati River past a number of little known, rarely visited temples.

Walking Tour 1
North from Durbar Square

The road angling across the town from Durbar Square to the artificial lake of Rani Pokhari is the most interesting street in old Kathmandu. Modern roads like Durbar Marg are no match for this narrow artery's varied and colourful shops, temples and people. The road, which starts from the north-eastern end of Durbar Square as Makhan Tole, was at one time the main street in Kathmandu and the start of the route to Tibet. It was not replaced as Kathmandu's most important street until the construction of New Rd, after the great

1   Garuda Statue
2   Tana Deval Temple
3   Akash Bhairab Temple
4   Ganesh Shrine
5   Shiva Temple
6   Sweta (White) Machhendranath Temple
7   Lunchun Lunbun Ajima
8   Krishna Temple
9   Jana Bahal Temple
10   Kilgal Tole
11   Pagoda Temple Platform
12   Yitum Bihal
13   Stupa
14   Kichandra Bahal
15   Chaitya
16   Nara Devi Temple
17   Platform
18   Wooden Window
19   Yatkha Bahal
20   Kot Square
21   Kathmandu Lodge

earthquake of 1934, and it was not paved until the '60s.

Makhan Tole The crowded street known as Makhan Tole (*makhan* is Nepali for 'butter') starts from the north-eastern corner of Durbar Square, by the Taleju Temple, towards the busy market place of Indra Chowk. Many shops along this stretch of the street sell thangkas, paintings and clothes.

Directly across from the Taleju Temple, at the start of the street, is a kneeling 10th century Garuda statue (1). It probably faced a now long lost Vishnu temple. To your right, just past the long row of stalls selling thangkas, artefacts and other tourist necessities, is the Tana Deval Temple (2) with three carved doorways and struts showing the multiarmed Ashta Matrikas mother goddesses.

Indra Chowk The busy shopping street of Makhan Tole soon spills into Indra Chowk, the 'courtyard of Indra', the ancient Vedic deity. On the left of the square is a building covered in brightly coloured modern ceramic tiles. From the balcony four metal lions rear out over the street. This is the temple of Akash Bhairab (3), the 'Bhairab of the sky', but the temple is actually upstairs, the ground floor is occupied by shop stalls.

To get to the temple you have to climb a flight of steps at the right-hand end of the building, guarded by two more metal lions. Halfway up a sign announces that non-Hindus may not enter and in any case there's not much to see. The silver image is visible through the open windows from out in the street and during important festivals, particularly Indra Jatra, the image is displayed in the square. A large lingam is also erected in the centre of the square at that time.

In a small niche just before the Akash Bhairab Temple is a very small but much visited brass Ganesh shrine (4). Indra Chowk is traditionally a centre for the sale of blankets and cloth and there are usually many sellers and buyers on the platforms of the Mahadev Temple. Carpets and woollen rugs are sold from the platform of the Shiva

Temple (5), which is a smaller and simplified version of Patan's Krishna Mandir.

The many flower sellers around Indra Chowk add a bright touch to the busy square. From the south of the square Shukra Path leads to New Rd; the shops along this road sell consumer goods imported from Hong Kong and Singapore; many of them end up in India. The road heading directly north from Indra Chowk leads to Thamel. Before you leave Indra Chowk look for the narrow alley to the right, crowded with stalls selling the bangles and beads which are so popular with Nepalese women.

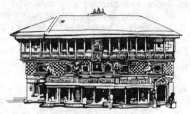

Akash Bhairab Temple

Kel Tole It's only a short stroll from Indra Chowk to the next square, Kel Tole, where you find the Sweta (White) Machhendranath Temple (6), one of the most important and ornate temples in Kathmandu. The arched entranceway to the temple is guarded by a small Buddha figure on a high stone pillar, facing two metal lions. The temple attracts both Buddhists and Hindus as the Buddhists consider him to be a form of Avalokitesvara while to the Hindus he is an incarnation of Shiva who can bring the rain. Although the temple's age is not known, it was restored during the 17th century.

In the courtyard there are numerous small shrines, chaityas and statues including a mysteriously European looking figure facing the temple. It may well have been an import from Europe, which has been simply accepted into the pantheon of gods. Facing the other way, just in front of the temple, are two graceful bronze figures of the Taras seated on top of tall pillars.

Inside the temple you can see the white-faced image of the god, sitting rather like a seated Buddha image. The image is taken out of the temple during the Sweta Machhendranath festival in March-April each year and is paraded around the city in a chariot. The procession finally ends at the Machhendranath Temple in the south of the city, visited on Walking Tour 3.

During the day the courtyard is busy with worshippers, playing children and the people whose homes surround it, but at night musicians come here to play in the entrance porch. You're quite welcome to drop by; the traditional music usually starts around 9 pm.

As you leave the temple to the right there are a number of stores which specialise in Nepalese caps. The small triple roofed Lunchun Lunbun Ajima (7) is a Tantric temple, white tiled around the lower level and with some erotic carvings on the struts at the back. The diagonal street continues to Asan Tole, the busiest of the junctions along the old street, but that is covered on Walking Tour 2. Walk partway towards Asan Tole to see the three, four and five storey houses, tightly squeezed together on this stretch of the street. On the left the polygonal Krishna Temple (8) is jammed between other buildings with the ground floor occupied by shops. The woodcarvings on this temple are very elaborate.

Return to Kel Tole and turn west. At the next junction the large Jana Bahal Temple (9) is on your left. The domed temple is of little interest, it was probably a hastily thrown up construction after an earlier temple was destroyed, perhaps by an earthquake.

Sweta Machhendranath

A Child-Eating Demon Continue across the junction and on your left you pass the small Kilgal Tole (10) beside the road. It's a grubby little square with a couple of decaying temples and, in the middle, a fine Shiva lingam with faces on each side. For some reason there is often a calf or two standing on the pagoda temple platform (11).

An opening leads into the long, rectangular Yitum Bahal courtyard (12). A small white painted stupa stands in the centre of the courtyard (13). Opposite it, on the western side of the courtyard, is one of the oldest bahals in the city, its entrance flanked by stone lions as usual. This is the Kichandra Bahal (14), dating from 1381. Above the entrance is a superb torana with the Buddha reaching down to touch the earth, asking it to witness his resistance to the temptations of Mara. A chaitya (15) in front of the entrance is completely shattered by a tree which has grown right up through its centre.

Inside the courtyard there is a pagoda-like sanctuary in the centre and to the south is a small chaitya decorated with Bodhisattvas in a standing, rather than usual sitting, position. On the northern side of the courtyard are four brass plaques mounted on the upper storey wall. The one on the extreme left shows a demon known as Guru Mapa taking a child from a woman and stuffing it greedily into his mouth. The demon had an appetite for bad children and the two central plaques show two more children, presumably lining up to be consumed! Eventually the demon was bought off with a promise of an annual feast of buffalo meat and the plaque to the right shows him sitting down and dipping into a pot of food. To this day Guru Mapa is said to live in a tree in the Tundikhel field and a buffalo is sacrificed to him every year. With such a clear warning on the end result of juvenile misbehaviour it's probably fitting that the courtyard houses a kindergarten, right under the Guru Mapa plaques!

Nara Devi Temple From Yitum Bahal go back into the large courtyard and exit again at the north and turn left. On your right at the next junction is the Nara Devi Temple (16) which gives the street its name. The temple is dedicated to Kali, Shiva's consort in her destructive incarnation, and is also known as the White or Sweta Kali Temple.

Although the temple, with its three tiers, glowing golden roof and red and white guardian lions, is quite old, some of the decorations (including the black and white chequerboard paint!) are clearly much later additions. Kali's powers protected the temple from the 1934 earthquake which destroyed so many temples in the valley. A Malla king once stipulated that a dancing ceremony should be held for the goddess every 12 years and dances are still performed on the small platform (17) across the road. Hidden away across the road is a three roofed Narsingha Temple to Vishnu as the demon destroying man-lion. You have to find your way to it through a maze of small courtyards.

A Postage Stamp Window At the Nara Devi corner turn left (south) and you soon come to a nondescript modern building on your left with an utterly magnificent wooden window (18). It's been called *deshay madu* in Nepali, which means 'there is not another one like it'. A Rs 0.50 stamp issued in 1978 showed the window. Next to the building is an unimportant triple roofed pagoda which serves as a locator.

A little further south and on your right is the entrance to the Yatkha Bahal (19), a huge open courtyard with an unremarkable stupa in the centre. Directly behind it is an old building which used to have its projecting upper storey supported by four superb carved wooden struts. Dating from the 14th century they were carved in the form of yakshis, or nymphs, one of them gracefully balancing a baby on her hip. Unfortunately in late '89 they had been removed, hopefully just for refurbishment and replacement.

Back on the road and heading south you soon pass Kot Square (20), scene of the great massacre that brought the Ranas to power in 1846. The Kathmandu Lodge (21) is on your right and you soon see Durbar Square ahead.

Walking Tour 2
South of Thamel

The second walk can be started from the southern end of Thamel or can easily be linked on to Walking Tour 1 to make a figure eight either from Thamel or Durbar Square. This walk can be started from Thahiti Tole or, if that's hard to find, from the Hotel Nook on Kantipath. To get to Thahiti Tole walk south from Thamel on the road from the main junction. Soon after La Cimbali Restaurant you enter the square.

Thahiti Tole In the stupa (1) in the centre of the square is a stone inscription indicating it was constructed in the 15th century. Legends relate that it was built over a pond which was plated with gold and the stupa served to keep thieves at bay. Or perhaps the pond was full of dangerous snakes and the stupa kept the snakes in their place, these legends vary!

The Nateshwar Temple (2), on the northern side of the square, is dedicated to Shiva and the metal plates on the doors show creatures busily playing a variety of musical instruments. Above the door are somewhat crudely painted pictures of Shiva's *ganas*, or companions, in this case a skeleton-like creature and what looks remarkably like a yeti!

Nateshwar Temple

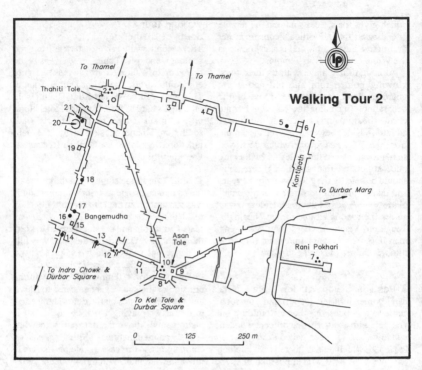

Walking Tour 2

1 Stupa
2 Nateshwar Temple
3 Musya Bahal
4 Chusya Bahal
5 Kabab Corner Restaurant
6 Hotel Nook
7 Shiva Temple
8 Annapurna Pagoda
9 Ganesh Pagoda
10 Narayan Temple
11 Haku Bahal
12 Ugratara Temple
13 Sunken Shrine
14 Wood With Nails
15 Ikha Narayan Shrine
16 Standing Saraswati Statue
17 Standing Buddha Statue
18 Stone Relief
19 Nag Bahal
20 Kathesimbhu Stupa
21 Standing Avalokitesvara Statue

Two Ancient Bahals Walk to the corner at the north-east of the square and take the narrow road running east. You soon come to the entrance of the Musya Bahal (3) on your right, guarded by white painted lions. The road continues east and then takes a right-left bend at the corner of which is a second, and much better preserved, old monastery, the Chusya Bahal (4).

This stretch of street is popular with potters and you often see them working in the road outside the bahals, or see their products piled up inside. Often it's just the simple little disposable cups used by chai sellers.

Beyond the second bahal there's a string of upper level budget hotels, the Kabab Corner Restaurant (5) and, right on the corner with Kantipath, the Hotel Nook (6). Turn south past the Air India office and cross the road to the Rani Pokhari.

Chusya Bahal

Rani Pokhari First cross the road to the large fenced lake called Rani Pokhari or the Queen's Pond. It was built by King Pratap Malla in 1667 to console his queen over the death of their son. Unfortunately the gate to the tank is kept locked except on one day each year during the festival of Diwali; you will have to be content with peering through the fence. A causeway leads across the tank to a small Shiva Temple (7) which was rebuilt after it collapsed in the 1934 earthquake. The elephant on the southern side of the tank carries three riders, supposedly Pratap Malla, his queen and their son. You can walk down that side of the tank, outside the fence, to inspect the elephant more closely. Interestingly, various legends and tales are connected with the tank and it's believed that it may actually have been built by Pratap Malla at an earlier date and only renamed for his queen after their son died: according to records he was trampled by an elephant.

Behind the tank you can see the clocktower, a very useful landmark dating from 1895. Across Kantipath from the tank is the long building originally known as the Durbar School which was the first school in Nepal. It has been renamed the Bhanubhakta School after the Nepalese poet of that name. Retrace your steps north to the junction at the north-western corner of the Rani Pokhari and cross Kantipath to Bhothahiti then walk south-west past the bicycle hire and repair shops to Asan Tole.

Asan Tole From dawn until late at night Asan Tole is jammed with buyers, sellers and passers-by. The six roads meeting at this busy crossroads make it the busiest junction in Kathmandu. Every day fresh fruit and vegetables are carried to this popular marketplace from all over the valley so it is fitting that the three storey pagoda (8) is that of the goddess Annapurna, the goddess of abundance. The smaller two storey pagoda (9) is dedicated to Ganesh. On the left-hand (western) side of the square are shops which sell dried fruit. Near the centre of the square is a third temple, a small Narayan or Vishnu Temple.

Annapurna Temple

Sore Eyes & a Toothache Take the road leading directly west out of Asan Tole and after a short distance, on your left, an anonymous entranceway leads into Haku Bahal (11). A blue sign in Nepali may offer a clue. This tiny bahal has a finely carved wooden window looking over the courtyard.

A few strides further you come to the triple roofed Ugratara Temple (12), directly across from a small lane which heads off north. Come here if your eyes are sore: a prayer at the shrine is said to work wonders for the eyes. A few steps further along is a small sunken shrine (13) and you then arrive at a crossroads with a large open square to the north. Turn left (south) and on your left you will see a lump of wood (14) into which thousands of nails have been hammered. A nail embedded in the wood is supposed to cure toothache, and the deity who looks after this ailment is represented by a tiny image in the ugly lump of wood. The square at the junction here is known as Bangemudha, which means 'twisted wood'.

An Ancient Buddha Turn north again to the open square where the small double roofed Ikha Narayan Temple (15) is easily identified by the kneeling Garuda figure in front of it. The temple is said to house a 10th or 11th century four armed Vishnu figure but the inside of the temple is so dark that you would need a powerful light to shine through the barred doors. The square also has a fine standing image of the goddess Saraswati (16) playing her lute.

The northern side of the square is closed by a modern building with shops shut by blue roller doors on the ground floor. In the middle of this nondescript frontage, directly beneath an upper-storey sign (if it's still there) announcing 'Urgent Ladies Tailor' is a standing Buddha figure (17), framed by modern blue and white tilework. The image is only about 60 cm high but it dates from the 5th or 6th century. A very similar Buddha figure stands on the riverbank near the temple of Pashupatinath.

If the toothache god hasn't done his duty you now pass a string of dentists' shops, proclaimed by the standard signs showing a smiling mouthful of teeth. On the right there's a small open area with a red-coloured Ganesh head and then a small but intricate

---

Asan's Fish

A few steps in front of the Annapurna Temple in Asan Tole is a paving stone with a foot-shaped depression which is said to be of a fish. Since the square is almost always crowded with fruit and vegetable sellers there's likely to be a pile of cauliflowers on top of it – but don't worry, it is there, and an interesting little legend relates how this 'fish' fell out of the sky one day.

Once upon a time a famous astrologer named Barami was about to become a father. A bell would be rung to announce the birth of his child so he waited expectantly in his study. At the instant that he heard the sound of the bell across the rooftops, he cast his newborn son's horoscope, and discovered to his horror that he was not the father. In anger and disgust he abandoned his wife and new child and fled from the kingdom. Not until many years later did he return to Kathmandu where he became the pupil of a younger but even more brilliant astrologer named Dak.

As a final test Dak asked Barami to foretell what miraculous event would shortly occur in Asan Tole. Barami correctly predicted that a fish would fall from the heavens, he correctly predicted the exact time this strange event would occur, but he missed by several steps the exact place where it would crash to earth. His teacher suggested that he had forgotten to take account of the wind. Sure enough this was found to be the case.

Barami realised he had forgotten to take account of the wind once before: on the occasion that the sound of a bell carried to his ears the news of his son's birth. Correcting for the wind factor Barami once again cast his son's horoscope. To his delight he discovered that it was indeed his own son, and to his amazement that the boy's name was Dak!

This left Dak and Barami with a peculiar problem: a son must revere his father and a pupil must revere his teacher yet here the son had been teaching the father. Eventually the decision was reached that father and son should jointly erect a monument to the event that had brought them together again. And there it is in Asan Tole, a small memorial to a fish that fell out of the sky. ■

stone relief (18) dating from the 9th century. It shows Shiva sitting with Parvati on Mt Kailash, his hand resting proprietorialy on her knee in the pose known as Uma Maheshwar. Various deities and creatures, including Shiva's bull Nandi, stand around them.

There's a good wooden balcony across the road which is said to have had the first glass windows in Kathmandu! Nearby is a rather worn-out, and bricked-in, stone trough. A little further on your left a single broken stone lion (his partner has disappeared) guards a passageway above which hangs a carved wooden torana. Inside is the small enclosed courtyard of the Nag Bahal (19) with painted murals above the shrine, which is flanked by banners with double-triangle flags.

A Mini-Swayambhunath Just a couple of steps beyond the Nag Bahal entranceway is a wider entrance to the Kathesimbhu Stupa (20), just south of Thahiti Tole. The entrance is flanked by stone lions which have been beheaded, and more recent metal lions atop tall pillars.

In the courtyard is a copy, dating from around 1650, of the great Swayambhunath complex just outside Kathmandu. If a devotee is unable to make the ascent to Swayambhunath then a circuit of this miniature replica is said to be a good substitute. Just as at Swayambhunath, there is a small pagoda to Harti, the goddess of smallpox, right behind the main stupa.

Various statues and smaller chaityas stand around the temple including, off the north-east of the stupa, a fine standing image of Avalokitesvara (21). He carries a lotus flower in his left hand; the face of the Dhyani Buddha Amitabha can be seen in the centre of his crown and his eyes are downcast.

From Kathesimbhu it's only a short walk north to the starting point of Walking Tour 2 at Thahiti Tole.

Walking Tour 3
South from Durbar Square
Starting from beside the Kasthamandap (1)

Kathesimbhu Stupa

in Durbar Square another circular walk can be made to the older parts in the south of the city. This area is not as packed with historical interest as the walks north of Durbar Square, but the streets are less crowded and you are far less likely to run into other tourists.

Bhimsen Temple Starting from the Kasthamandap in the south-western corner of Durbar Square the road out of the square forks almost immediately around the Singh Sattal (2), a squat building with small shop stalls around the ground floor and golden winged lions guarding each corner of the upper floor. Take the road running to the right of this building and you soon come to a square tank-like *hiti* (3), or water conduit, where people will usually be washing clothes.

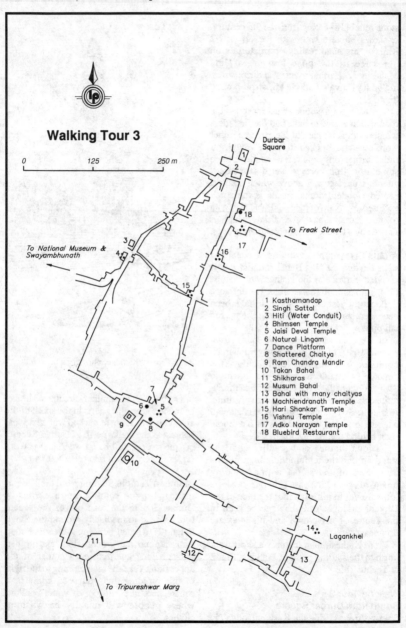

Walking Tour 3

0   125   250 m

To National Museum &
Swayambhunath

To Freak Street

Durbar
Square

To Tripureshwar Marg

Lagankhel

1   Kasthamandap
2   Singh Sattal
3   Hiti (Water Conduit)
4   Bhimsen Temple
5   Jaisi Deval Temple
6   Natural Lingam
7   Dance Platform
8   Shattered Chaitya
9   Ram Chandra Mandir
10 Takan Bahal
11 Shikharas
12 Musum Bahal
13 Bahal with many chaityas
14 Machhendranath Temple
15 Hari Shankar Temple
16 Vishnu Temple
17 Adko Narayan Temple
18 Bluebird Restaurant

Immediately beyond this is the brightly painted Bhimsen Temple (4) fronted by a brass lion on a pillar and with white painted lions guarding the two front corners. Bhimsen is supposed to watch over traders and artisans so it's quite appropriate that the ground floor of this well kept temple should be devoted to shop stalls. Immediately beyond the Bhimsen Temple a road branches off down to the river and across to the National Museum and Swayambhunath.

shattered chaitya (8), seemingly held together only by the roots of the tree that destroyed it.

Jaisi Deval Temple

Bhimsen Temple

Jaisi Deval Temple Continue south beyond the Bhimsen Temple then turn sharp left (uphill) where the road ends. At the top of the hill you'll come out by the tall, triple roofed, 17th century Jaisi Deval Temple (5), standing on a seven level base, its tiers painted a becoming shade of pink. This is a Shiva temple, as shown by the bull on the first few steps and the mildly erotic carvings on some of the temple struts. Right across the road from the temple is a natural (but quite realistic looking!) lingam (6) rising a good 2 metres from a yoni. This is definitely a god-sized phallic symbol and a prayer here is said to aid fertility.

In its procession around the town during the Indra Jatra festival the Kumari Devi's chariot pauses here. During its stop dances are held on the small platform (7) across the road from the temple. Next to the temple is a

Ram Chandra Mandir Cross the road from the broken chaitya and enter the courtyard of the Ram Chandra Mandir (9). This small temple is notable for the teensy little erotic scenes on its roof struts. This is straightforward sex and no funny business, it looks as if the carver set out to illustrate 16 different positions, starting with the missionary position, and just about made it before running out of ideas.

Bahals & Machhendranath Temple There are a series of bahals on the next stretch of the walk but most of them are of little interest. Cross the road from the Ram Chandra Mandir and enter the small courtyard of the Takan Bahal (10). The 14th century stupa in the centre is decidedly dilapidated as a tree has grown straight up through the precise centre of the stupa, lifting the crown a good 4 metres above the stupa top!

The road continues with a few slight bends then turns sharply back at a junction marked by several temples (11) including a taller shikhara-style one. If you took the downhill road leading off from this junction you'd merge on to Tripureshwar Marg, just beyond the Vishnumati River bridge. Across this busy road another road continues down to the river and the starting point of the ropeway used to transport goods over the foothills from the Terai. Ignoring this possible diversion the walk continues to the Musum Bahal (12) with four ancient Licchavi chaityas and a caged-in well. Turn sharp left (north) at the next junction and look in to a large, open bahal (13) packed with numerous chaityas.

The road opens into Lagankhel, an open square with a Machhendranath temple (14) standing about 10 metres high. During the annual Sweta Machhendranath festival the image of the god is transported here from the Sweta Machhendranath Temple in Kel Tole (see Walking Tour 1). The final stage of the procession is to pull the god's chariot three times around the temple, after which the image is taken back to its starting point on a palanquin while the chariot is dismantled here.

Turn left out of Lagankhel and walk back to the tall Jaisi Deval Temple, then turn right (north) back towards Durbar Square.

Shiva & Vishnu Temples At the next crossroads the small, spindly looking Hari Shankar Temple (15) stands to the left of the road. The narrow brick-paved laneway beside this combination Shiva and Vishnu temple runs down to the Bhimsen Temple passed earlier on. Continue north past a Vishnu temple (16) to a second Vishnu temple, the Adko Narayan (17). This temple may not look impressive but it is said to be one of the four most important Vishnu temples in Kathmandu. A Garuda figure fronts the temple, lions guard each corner, tiny ceramic tiles decorate the ground floor and there are mildly erotic scenes on some of the upper roof struts. It's also the temple of motorcycle repairs, and mechanics work away around the back of the building.

Immediately beyond the temple is the long-running Blue Bird Restaurant (18) and

then you pass the Singh Sattal building once again and arrive back at the starting point of this walk.

Adko Narayan Temple

Walking Tour 4
West from Patan Bridge

The Bagmati River is a tributary of the Ganges River and is doubly holy to some because of its association with Shiva, who is believed to have lived on its banks at Pashupatinath. Not surprisingly, there are many temples along its length.

Apart from the complex at Pashupatinath there is a string of temples west of Patan Bridge to the Bagmati River's junction with the Vishnumati River. This is a quiet and forgotten corner of Kathmandu. There is no traffic and, although it is only a short walk from Durbar Square, there are few visitors.

Nothing much seems to have happened here in the last 30 years and as a consequence you can see some of the best and worst of Kathmandu. Many of the temples are in a state of picturesque decline and the traffic, crowds and noise of the city seem a long way away. Their place is taken by water buffaloes, egrets, sadhus and children.

Unfortunately, the riverbanks are littered

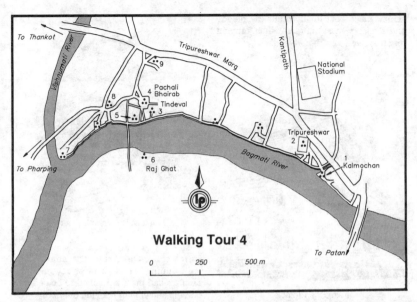

Walking Tour 4

0   250   500 m

with rubbish and the impressive ghats are no longer in serious use. There is also a great deal of poverty, with many families living in squalor in and amongst the decaying buildings. It is hard to imagine that this must once have been a thriving, vital part of Kathmandu and it is hard not to feel sadness at its decline.

It's possible to walk from Patan Bridge to the confluence of the rivers and back to Tripureshwar Marg in an hour or so, but you may choose to linger. Probably the best way to do it is to catch autorickshaws, or ride a bike to/from the starting and finishing points. The track is rough in places, too rough to ride, but not so rough that you can't just push a bike along. Watch where you put your feet: the pervasive smell of shit gives fair warning of another hazard.

Kalmochan Temple (1) On the Kathmandu side of the Bagmati River, 150 metres to the west of the Patan Bridge, you'll see a huge, square, whitewashed block, topped by a mosque-like onion dome with gilt beasts rearing up at each corner. This is the Kalmochan or Satya Narayan Temple. To get

to it and start the walk, descend the steps to the riverbank beside the bridge, turn right and walk downstream past a well kept army building. Enter through a carved doorway.

The Kalmochan Temple may have been commenced as early as 1852, but it was completed in 1873 by Jung Bahadur Rana. It is dedicated to Jagannath and was built to commemorate the Gurkha wars with Tibet and Britain. It is one of the most successful of the few Moghul (Muslim north Indian) influenced buildings in Nepal, but the decorations are pure Nepalese. The beasts once stood on a Vishnu temple in the Tundikhel and there is some very high quality woodcarving.

The temple's name (*kal* means 'death') indicates that it was built in connection with a person's funeral and it is said that the temple is actually built over the mass grave of the noblemen that Jung Bahadur Rana killed in the Kot Massacre which brought him to power. A statue of Mr Rana faces the temple from the courtyard and, whether or not he built it to appease his conscience, the inscription below his statue extols his many achievements, but totally omits the bloody and decisive mass murder which brought him to power!

Kalmochan Temple

Tripureshwar Mahadev Temple

Tripureshwar Mahadev Temple (2) After leaving the Kalmochan Temple, continue downstream and cross the grubby little Tukucha Khola stream. Veer right from the river towards the huge three roofed temple. The footpath goes through to Tripureshwar Marg, the main road, past the entry to the temple itself.

The temple was built in the 19th century by the wife of Jung Bahadur Rana but despite its impressive size attracts few tourists or worshippers. It's monumental but doesn't have the same pleasing proportions as the best examples of pagoda architecture. There are some fine gilded figures on columns, including one of Mrs Rana herself sitting under an umbrella.

Tindeval Temple (3) Return to the river and continue to the west on a rough path for about 1 km. After about 15 minutes you'll come to the unusual and beautiful Tindeval Temple. It is easily recognised by its three shikharas (spires reminiscent of a folded umbrella).

Enter the *chowk* from the south. The surrounding bahal is now occupied by families and there are bound to be children playing and clothes hanging out to dry.

The shikhara style began to develop under the Guptas in India (during the 5th and 6th centuries) until it became the most distinctive and common forms in north India (especially from the 9th to 11th centuries). There are a number of examples around the valley, and the style was also used in Buddhist countries throughout South Asia.

The intriguing aspect of the Tindeval Temple is the way the shikharas have been successfully integrated with a pagoda-style base and 1st floor. There are also clear examples of the coexistence of Hinduism and Buddhism: Shiva's trident alongside a *dorje* (a Tibetan word for 'thunderbolt'). Note the beautiful decorative brickwork forming nagas (snakes) around the base of the shikharas.

Pachali Bhairab (4) Leave the Tindeval Temple by the western door (to the left as you entered) and veer to the right towards the huge pipal tree 50 metres away. This ancient tree forms a sanctuary over the image of Pachali, which is surrounded by tridents. Nearby lies what some believe to be the brass body of Baital, another of Shiva's manifestations. Others believe it is Surya, the sun god. Worshippers gather here on Tuesdays and Saturdays.

Raj Ghat Return directly to the river past a very dilapidated temple on the right (5) that nonetheless has some fine carvings. If you're feeling energetic, cross the river on the old pedestrian footbridge to the Raj Ghat (6), where there is another group of Shaivite temples and shrines. There's an attractive view looking back to the city.

Teku Cross back to the northern side of the river and turn left towards the confluence of the Vishnumati and Bagmati rivers which is marked by another shikhara (7). River junctions are always regarded as significant in Nepal, and between the bridge and the Vishnumati there is a veritable art gallery densely packed with shrines and sculptures. There are lingams representing Shiva, Buddhist chaityas (most with the Dhyani Buddhas), and statues of elephant-headed Ganesh, Saraswati with her lute and many more.

Nava Durga From the river junction turn inland (north-east) and backtrack along a paved road past another dilapidated and unusual shikhara-style temple (8). In 10 minutes you come to what looks like a bomb site – in actual fact it is a roads department depot most inappropriately located – adjoining the Pachali Bhairab. When you intersect with the road that runs through to the pedestrian bridge on your right, turn left and keep heading north-east.

In about 5 minutes you reach a point where the road forks, about 50 metres before Tripureshwar Marg. Take the right fork and you pass Nava Durga (9), a small two storey temple. From Nava Durga you can turn right along Tripureshwar Marg to complete the loop.

OTHER TEMPLES & BUILDINGS
Three Goddesses Temples
Next to the modern shopping centre and across the road from the immigration office, near Thamel, are the temples of the three goddesses. The street here is named Tridevi Marg – *tri* means 'three' and *devi* means 'goddesses'. The goddesses are Dakshinkali, Mankamna and Jawalamai and the temples are chiefly interesting for the roof struts, some with erotic carvings illustrating some rather interesting positions.

Mahakala Temple
This temple, on the Tundikhel Park side of Kantipath just north of New Rd, was very badly damaged in the 1934 earthquake and is of little architectural merit following its reconstruction. If you can see inside the darkened shrine you may be able to make out the 1½ metre high figure of Mahakala, the Great Black One, a particularly ferocious form of Shiva. *Kal* means 'death' as well as 'black' in Nepali so it can also be described as the Temple of Great Death. The Tantric god has Buddhist as well as Hindu followers. You can climb to the top of one of the buildings around the courtyard to look over the Tundikhel.

Bhimsen Tower
This white, minaret-like watchtower, also known as Sundhara, is a useful landmark although it's of no importance. It stands near the GPO and was built by a Rana prime minister and rebuilt after being severely damaged by the 1934 earthquake.

NATIONAL MUSEUM & ART GALLERY
Not far from Swayambhunath, the National Museum is a bit disappointing and in late '89 the Art Gallery was closed. A visit can easily be combined with a trip to Swayambhunath, but unless the Art Gallery opens, or you're fascinated with old weapons and idealised portraits of Shahs and Ranas, don't make a special visit.

The museum is a rather eccentric collection that includes some moon rock, a number of moth-eaten stuffed animals, a vast number of uniforms and military decorations, swords and guns, and a mind-numbing portrait gallery. The most interesting exhibit is a *leather* Tibetan cannon.

When open, the Art Gallery displays a number of treasures. There's a superb collection of statues and carvings (stone, wood, bronze, terracotta) – some pieces date to the 1st century BC. If you have an interest in this area of art a visit is a must.

The museum is closed on Tuesdays and is open from 10.30 am to 2.30 pm on Fridays. The rest of the week it opens from 10.30 am to 4.30 pm in summer and until 3.30 pm in winter. Ticket sales stop an hour earlier than the closing time and the sign announcing the hours enigmatically adds that on Friday the museum opens at 10 am, but tickets won't go on sale until 10.30! The entry fee is Rs 5.

PLACES TO STAY

Kathmandu has an excellent range of places to stay, from expensive international-style hotels to cheap and comfortable lodges.

This section is divided by price into bottom end, middle and top end, then by location. A bottom end hotel or guest house is a place where you can get a room for less than Rs 350, say US$10. There are lots of places in Kathmandu where you can get a room for less than Rs 100 (say US$3) and some where you can pay less than Rs 50 (US$1.50). Middle means up to US$40 a night and the top end is from there up. A double room in the most expensive hotels in Kathmandu now costs over US$100 a night, getting close to the nation's average annual per capita income!

It is definitely worth looking around if you plan to stay for any length of time. It's difficult to recommend particular hotels, especially in the bottom end and middle brackets, because particular rooms in each hotel can vary widely. Many of these hotels have additions to additions, and while some rooms may be very gloomy and run-down others might be very pleasant! A friendly crowd of fellow travellers can also make all the difference.

For bottom end and lower middle places Thamel is the main locale – and something of a tourist ghetto. Its development has been rapid and uncontrolled, with ugly multi-storey hotels and signboards taking the place of beautiful Newari houses. This is where the largest number of independent travellers stay, and there are dozens and dozens of lodges, restaurants, travel agencies and shops, and a bustling cosmopolitan atmosphere. It's still a convenient and enjoyable area to stay, however, especially if you want to meet fellow travellers. It can be a welcome relief to find Western menus, people who speak English and hot showers at budget prices!

There is still a scattering of really rock bottom places along Freak St, close to the central Durbar Square, but its late '60s and early '70s heyday is long past. There are faint signs it might be beginning a bit of a comeback.

Middle range places are more widely scattered: you'll find them in and around Thamel and in many other areas. Kathmandu's limited number of international-standard hotels are also widely scattered, some of them quite a distance from the centre.

There's a hotel reservations counter as soon as you get out of customs & immigration at the airport. Most of the hotels it represents are reasonably expensive, but it has a few in the Rs 150 (US$5) to Rs 300 (US$10) bracket and the staff arrange for free transport. If you don't feel like tackling the touts and taxis outside the main doors, this can be very useful – especially considering a taxi can cost up to Rs 100. You can always change to another hotel the next day after you've had a chance to get your bearings.

Touts and agents for the cheaper hotels often cluster outside the terminal looking for customers. During the peak seasons (October-November and March-April in particular) rooms in the top class hotels can be in short supply. Otherwise, there are so many fiercely competitive middle range and bottom end places that only the really popular hotels are likely to be full.

All hotels charge a government tax which seems to vary between 10% and 14%. In most hotels above the rock bottom range you must pay your bills in convertible currency –

which means either with foreign cash or travellers' cheques, with rupees accompanied by proof of official exchange, or with a credit card. Middle range places almost all quote their prices in US dollars while the real bottom end places usually quote, and will let you pay in, rupees.

Places to Stay – bottom end

Intense competition between Kathmandu's enormous number of low-priced hostelries means that you can find hot showers in even the cheapest places, although the hot water may only be operating at certain hours.

Hotels in this category do not have heating and Kathmandu in winter is a rather chilly place. In winter you'll appreciate places with a garden as it's always pleasant to sit outside during the cool, but invariably sunny, autumn and winter days. A south facing room will mean you get some sunlight in your room. In general the top-floor rooms are the best, as you stand a chance of getting a view and having easy access to the roof (usually a nice place to relax).

Thamel & Chhetrapati Area The Thamel area, about 15 minutes walk from the centre of Kathmandu, is the main budget accommodation locale. From the city centre walk along Kantipath, the road north from New Rd gate towards the embassy area, and turn left when you come to the corner by the new Royal Palace. Two blocks further will bring you into Thamel, but you'll start to see the signs and general activity almost immediately. When you've been in Kathmandu for a while you'll discover shorter and much more interesting routes through the maze of narrow streets and alleys that wind between Thamel and the Durbar Square area.

Any mention of Thamel has to start with the *Kathmandu Guest House* (tel 4-13632) which is not only the most popular cheaper hotel in Kathmandu, and hence in Nepal, but also serves as the central landmark in Thamel. Everything is 'near to the Kathmandu Guest House', '5 minutes from the Kathmandu Guest House' or whatever. Its long-term popularity means this is one

cheaper hotel that is often booked out; it's also not the best value for money in town. The Kathmandu Guest House has made a distinct lurch up-market over the years and many places offer cheaper rooms or better rooms at the same cost.

Still, it's a great address and you definitely feel you're in the travellers' nerve centre with overland trucks and mountain bike expeditions coming and going, trekkers looking for partners and a constant hum of activity. There's parking space for cars out front, a very pleasant garden, a popular restaurant, a money change desk, a storage area for luggage and for valuables, a phone office where you can conveniently and quickly make overseas calls, a travel desk, even an art gallery upstairs – this is budget travel in the deluxe category! In the newer wing quite pleasant rooms with bathroom are US$14/17 for singles/doubles. Similarly equipped rooms in the old wing are US$7/9. Other rooms, with just a washbasin or without private facilities at all, cost from US$3 to US$8. There's a 12% tax on top of all these prices.

If this is too deluxe for your budget you don't have to go far for something cheaper – there are a dozen or more places within a stone's throw of the Kathmandu Guest House. Right next door is the *Tukche Peak Guest House* (tel 2-15739) where singles/ doubles are Rs 70/90 or Rs 90/120 with bathroom. It's another long-term survivor, and there's a garden, although the rooms are fairly simple and spartan. Continue north a few doors and you come to *Yeti Cottage* (tel 4-17089) with a nice garden and a popular restaurant. Singles/doubles here are Rs 60/100, plus 10% tax.

Continue round the double bend and turn left to the well kept *Holy Lodge*. It's just far enough from the very centre of Thamel to be reasonably quiet and offers neat and clean rooms for Rs 50 a single and Rs 80 to Rs 100 a double. Some of the upstairs rooms are bright and airy with good views, and there's an excellent deluxe room at the top which costs Rs 250 .

Turn the other way from the Kathmandu

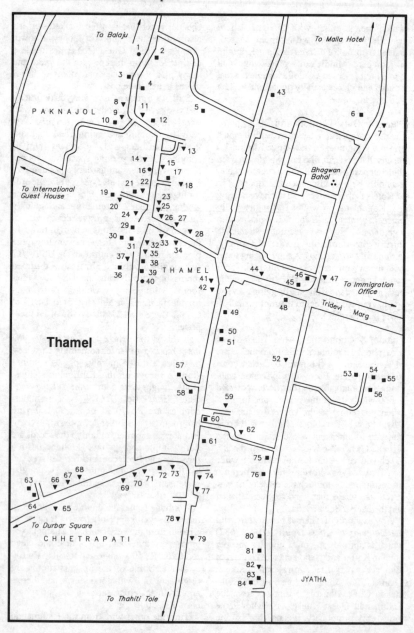

Thamel

To Balaju

To Malla Hotel

PAKNAJOL

To International
Guest House

Bhagwan
Bahal

THAMEL

To Immigration
Office

Tridevi Marg

To Durbar Square

CHHETRAPATI

JYATHA

To Thahiti Tole

Guest House and there's a cluster of hotels on its southern side. The *Hotel Star* (tel 4-12100), right next door, has long been a popular alternative and the service is friendly and helpful although the rooms are nothing to write home about. Rooms start at US$3, doubles with bathroom are US$8. Adjacent to the Hotel Star are the *Cosy Corner Lodge* and the *Pupil Lodge*, both simple, good value, base priced places. Rooms at the back of the Cosy Corner are quieter. The *Pheasant Lodge* (tel 4-17416), down a side street next to the Star Hotel, is very good value and friendly. Singles start at Rs 60.

Continue south a few more steps and you come to the *Earth House Lodge* (tel 4-10050), a simple, clean, bottom end place offering straightforward singles/doubles at Rs 60/120. Across the road is the dirt cheap *Himal Cottage* with rooms at just Rs 35/60. Next along is the *Lucky Rest House* (tel 4-17184) which is run by helpful people and has basic but clean rooms at Rs 60 to Rs 150, depending on whether you want a private bath. There are two pleasant rooms on the top floor that look across to Swayambhunath from this recommended hotel.

One block to the east the parallel street also has some popular cheapies including the *Om Guest House* (tel 2-21979) at Rs 120 for a room with shower and toilet, the adjacent *Hotel Asia* (tel 2-16541) and the *Stupa Guest House* (tel 2-220658) a bit further down the road.

If you're willing to pay more many other Thamel places offer better rooms, similar in standard to the more expensive rooms at the Kathmandu Guest House. The brand new *Hotel Garuda* (tel 4-16340, 4-16776) is about 100 metres north. It's very good: it's well run, clean, has hot water and is excellent value offering singles from US$7 to US$10 and doubles from US$9 to US$12, all with bathroom. There's a great view over the Thamel area from the top of this friendly hotel. Continue round the double bend to the clean and well kept *Hotel Iceland* (tel 4-16956) where singles/doubles cost US$6/8 with common bathroom, from US$8/12 to US$10/16 with private bathroom, all plus 10%.

Alternatively, head south from the Kathmandu Guest House. About 200 metres walk takes you from Thamel into the adjoining Chhetrapati area. Turn left at the junction (Narayan's Restaurant is a good landmark here) and you'll see the very popular *Potala Guest House* (tel 2-20467) where singles are US$5 to US$7, doubles from US$10 to US$13, all plus 10%. There's hot water and a small, quiet garden.

Turn left (east) only a short distance down the Jyatha road from Thamel and a couple of twists and turns will bring you to a neat little cluster of newer guest houses, directly behind the modern shopping centre on Tridevi Marg. This is a conveniently central but quieter location and the well managed *Shangrila Guest House* (tel 2-25930) has rooms at Rs 120 or Rs 150 with bathroom and has been recommended by a number of satisfied travellers. The *Imperial Guest House*, *White Lotus Guest House* and the *Tibet Holiday Inn* are in this same small group of places.

Closer to the centre of Thamel on Tridevi Marg the popular *Marco Polo Guest House* (tel 2-27914) is very much in the centre of things, but the rooms are set far enough back to avoid the worst of the noise. Doubles cost Rs 120; with bath they're Rs 180. Turn north from here and the more expensive *Hotel Shakti* (tel 4-10121) has a quiet garden setting and was undergoing renovations in 1989.

Instead of turning left towards the Kathmandu Guest House from the main Thamel intersection continue straight ahead (north). About 200 metres down an interesting street that is alive with shops that sell everything – except carpets, T-shirts, and carvings – there are a couple of decent places to stay. Old Kathmandu survives here.

The *Hotel Dreamland* has definitely seen better days, but the location is good and the people are pleasant, which may or may not make up for the fact that it is run-down! Doubles with bathrooms cost Rs 80. The *Hotel Bhrikuti* is down the first lane on the left. There are a variety of rooms ranging from Rs 60 to Rs 200, depending on their quality and whether they have a bathroom.

Around Thamel Thamel's main problem is simply that it is such a scene. There are a number of places on the periphery of Thamel that are close enough to be reasonably convenient but aren't absolutely in the centre of the maelstrom! Some of these, like the International Guest House in Paknajol-Kaldhara, are at the bottom of the middle range bracket but Jyatha has a number of good cheap places. Like Chhetrapati, it's really continuous with Thamel and there are many hotels along the road running south, parallel to Kantipath, and the road running east, meeting Kantipath by the Hotel Nook.

The *Tibet Rest House* (tel 2-14952, 2-25319) is run by the same people as the popular Tibet Guest House in Chhetrapati and has singles/doubles at Rs 70/150 or with a bathroom at Rs 170/200. The *Lhasa Guest House* is another cheaper place or there's the pricier *New Gajur* (tel 2-26623) with rooms from US$12.

The road meeting Kantipath beside the Hotel Nook has a number of possibilities including the *Garden Guest House* (tel 4-12987) with singles at Rs 90 and doubles at Rs 120 or Rs 130. The rooms have bathrooms and there's a very small garden. The *Hotel Kohinoor* (tel 2-13930, 2-11997) has rooms at Rs 175/225 or deluxe doubles at Rs 275, all plus 12%. The rooms all have bathrooms. At the *Hotel Himalayan View* (tel 2-14890, 2-16531) singles/doubles are Rs 100/125 with common bathroom or Rs 130/170 with private bathroom, plus 12%. It's not particularly inspiring, but the location is good, and this is one of the hotels offered by the reservations counter at the airport. The *Hotel Sunrise* (tel 2-16492) is another hotel in this same area.

Alternatively, go south to the Chhetrapati end of Thamel but continue past the Tibet Guest House to Chhetrapati Square. Turn south towards Durbar Square and on your left (to the east) you'll soon see the *Shambala Guest House* (tel 2-12524, 2-25986) where rooms start at US$5.50/7.50 with common bathrooms and go up to US$9 to US$10.50 for singles with bathroom or US$10.50 to US$18 for doubles with bathroom, all plus 12%. There is a 1st floor balcony garden and good views from the roof of this friendly, Tibetan-run hotel.

The *Hotel Paramount*, in the Thahiti area to the south of Thamel, has rooms for Rs 90. There is hot water and the staff is friendly.

Freak St & Around Durbar Square In the hippy overland days Freak St was the centre of the scene in Kathmandu but today there are just withered memories of the flower power '60s. Nevertheless, there are still a few

determined restaurants and lodges that have hung on. Staying here offers two big pluses – you won't find much cheaper anywhere in Kathmandu and you're right in the heart of the old city, close to the old Royal Palace, Durbar Square and other major attractions. Thamel is so crowded and hectic that Freak St seems to be making some tentative steps towards a comeback.

Freak St's real name is Jochne (although no-one uses it) and it runs south from Basantapur Square, the open square full of souvenir sellers adjoining Durbar Square. *Century Lodge* (2-15769) is one of Freak St's long-term survivors and remains a popular place offering excellent value for money. A double room here costs just Rs 45 or Rs 55 with bathroom. It's often full up. The *Pagoda Lodge* is reached from the same courtyard in the heart of Freak St.

Right across the road is the *Monumental Lodge* (tel 2-14864) with rooms at Rs 44 or Rs 90 with bathroom. They're as spartan and straightforward as the price would indicate, but if you're travelling on a very tight budget they offer all you can expect!

Take a few steps further down Freak St and turn left (east) to reach the popular *Saymi Lodge* where doubles are Rs 60. Its Lunch Box restaurant is still part of the Freak St 'scene' and is a great place to spend an afternoon. The food is good and cheap and the company is interesting.

Other minimum price Freak St hostelries include the *Annapurna Lodge* and the *Pokhara Lodge*. At the southern end of the Freak St area the *Eden Hotel* (tel 2-13363) is a more expensive hotel with rooms from Rs 250, but it's a gloomy run-down place.

Maru Tole, the road running down to the river from behind the Kasthamandap Temple, used to be known as Pig Alley or Pie Alley in the old hippy days. The pigs have disappeared since the street was cleaned up and the pie shops have almost all moved to Thamel but the *Camp Hotel* still remains, a flower power survivor from the mid-60s which still offers good rock bottom accommodation and which even had a renovation a few years back.

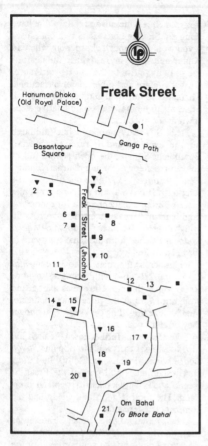

Freak Street

Hanuman Dhoka
(Old Royal Palace)

Basantapur
Square

Ganga Path

Freak Street (Jhochhe)

Om Bahal
To Bhote Bahal

Only a few steps north of Durbar Square, then to your right on Pyaphal Tole, the *Kathmandu Lodge* (tel 2-14893) is obviously doing something right as it's often full. Rooms cost Rs 50/60 for singles/doubles with common bathroom, Rs 100/120 with private bathroom.

Bhote Bahal South of the GPO and just north of Tripureshwar Marg, the Bhote Bahal district has developed as a new accommodation area, well away from the Thamel hype. There are a number of upper bottom end or lower middle range hotels here.

The clean and comfortable *Hotel Saya-patri* (tel 2-23398) has singles/doubles at Rs 200/275 including breakfast, plus 10% tax. It's run by Thakalis, those 'professional hoteliers' from the Pokhara-Jomsom area in the west of Nepal, and has a pleasant garden in the back and great views from the roof. The friendly *Hotel Janak* is excellent value with doubles at US$15 including breakfast; there are discounts for stays longer than 3 nights. It's very clean with big sunny rooms, hot water, a good restaurant and bicycle and car rental.

Other nearby places include the *Hotel New Ganesh, Hotel Laxman* and *Nirvana Guest House*. The *Hotel Red Pagoda*, just north of Tripureshwar Marg, is one of the cheaper ones here with simple double rooms at Rs 70.

If you take the narrow road from the south-western corner of the square around the Bhimsen Tower, you come to a large pipal tree and three cheap and basic guest houses mostly used by Nepalese: *Biju Guest House,*

Maha Laxmi Guest House and the *Irjana Guest House*. At Rs 50 a double there's not much to separate them.

Continue to the right away from Bhote Bahal proper and you come to two pleasant places that are well off the beaten track. The road is actually a continuation of Freak St, and you're not far from the centre of things. The *New Hotel Anand* is clean and well organised, with its own restaurant. Doubles with bathrooms are Rs 200. On the other side of the road, the *Hotel Mahankel* is a bargain. The rooms are sunny, comfortable and clean, though characterless. Singles/doubles with common bathrooms are Rs 65/100. A double with bathroom is Rs 165.

Further Afield A scattering of budget places can be found away from Thamel, Freak St or Bhote Bahal. Bagh Bazaar is east of Durbar Marg and there are a couple of places to stay here, right by the Bhaktapur bus stop. They don't come much cheaper than the *Ajima Guest House* (tel 2-26716), where singles/doubles are just Rs 25/50. A couple of doors away is the *Sony Guest House*.

For those who really want to get away from it all, take the road to Swayambhunath via the National Museum; just after you cross the bridge you come to the *Peace Lodge* where you can still get a room for as little as Rs 20. Other rooms cost up towards Rs 50 but it's as basic as the prices might indicate.

Continue towards the museum and Swayambhunath, then turn off (it's signposted) and follow the meandering route back towards the river to find the very quiet *Hotel Catnap* (tel 2-72392). It's well off the beaten track but if you don't mind the location it's good value at Rs 80 to Rs 130 for singles, Rs 90 to Rs 170 for doubles, all plus 10%.

In the Jawlakhel area of Patan, *Mahendra Yuvalaya* (tel 5-21003) is the only youth hostel in Nepal, with 72 dorm beds at Rs 25. It's a peaceful area but a long way from the bright lights and big city atmosphere of Thamel.

Renting a House For longer stays you can rent a house for as little as US$50 a month. Cheaper places are mainly around Freak St, Swayambhunath or Bodhnath, but there are many other areas where more expensive houses can be found. The Jawlakhel area of Patan is popular with many foreign residents as a number of the aid agencies are based there.

If you're looking for a place to rent check the notice boards around town or simply inquire in the appropriate areas. If you can take over a house from a departing visitor you will probably save having to find furniture and other essentials. As refrigerators are not readily available try to be near a market.

Real estate agents who can sometimes find appropriate places include Kantipur Real Estate Services (tel 2-20566) on Kantipath next to the British Council, or New Kathmandu Real Estate Service (tel 2-23019) near the clocktower.

Places to Stay – middle
Middle range in Kathmandu means from around US$10 to US$40 for a double. Of course the border line is a fuzzy one, these days the Kathmandu Guest House is really a middle range hotel as most of its rooms are over US$10, but it does offer cheaper ones as well. Some distinctly middle range hotel will still have some cheaper rooms, perhaps without bathrooms, which fall into the bottom end price category.

Thamel & Chhetrapati Area Hotels in this area are mainly bottom end or bottom to lower middle range but there are some distinctly mid-range places like the newish *Hotel Mandap* (tel 4-13321), just round the double bend north of the Kathmandu Guest House. Rooms in this pleasant looking hotel are US$17/21 for singles/doubles plus 12% tax.

Just north of Thamel the *Hotel Gauri Shanker* (tel 4-11605) has singles/doubles, all with bathroom, at US$14/19 plus 10%. Two popular new lower middle range hotels can be found in Chhetrapati. Coming from the Kathmandu Guest House in Thamel turn right at the junction by Narayan's Restaurant and you pass a string of restaurants, book-shops and guest houses on your way to Chhetrapati Square. The *Ngawal View Guest House* and the *Tibet Guest House* (tel 2-14383, 2-15893) are in adjoining new buildings, both in the upper bottom end to lower middle bracket. The Tibet Guest House has rooms at US$11.50 to US$15 with bathroom, a few dollars cheaper with common bathroom, all plus 10% tax. There's a restaurant, a pleasant garden and good views from the rooftop of this recommended hotel.

Around Thamel Go round the double bend north of the Kathmandu Guest House then turn left to the Holy Lodge but continue past several more sharp bends, following the signs for the *International Guest House* (tel 4-10533). It's in an area known as Paknajol Kaldhara and has singles/doubles for US$10/15 with common bathroom, US$16/19 with private bathroom, plus 10% tax. This area is quieter and less of a scene than Thamel but not too far to walk when you want to head for the restaurants.

On the southern side of Thamel in Jyatha the *Hotel Blue Diamond* (tel 2-26320, 2-26392, 2-26907) has rooms at US$12/15 or with air-con at US$16/19, plus 12%. It's a fairly new place, set well back from the street.

Still in the Jyatha area there is a number of middle range hotels in Kantipath and along the road running west from beside the Hotel Nook. The *Hotel Nook* (tel 2-13627) is certainly one of Kathmandu's long-term survivors. There are 24 rooms at US$13/20 plus 12% tax, for singles/doubles and a small restaurant at this rather busy location. A few doors down on Kantipath the *Hotel Tushita* (tel 2-16913) is in the building which at one time housed the US embassy. Rooms with bathroom are US$10/14 plus 10% tax; there is a pleasant small garden, good views from the roof terrace and the Palpasa Art Gallery is also here.

Turn the corner from the Hotel Nook to a small string of upper bottom end to lower middle range hotels, starting with *Hotel Gautam* (tel 2-15014, 2-15016) where singles/doubles are US$20/24 plus 12% tax. It's well equipped and the hotel's Kabab Corner Restaurant has an excellent reputation for its Indian food.

North of Thamel, in the southern part of

the embassy area, the *Hotel Ambassador* (tel 4-10432, 4-14432) is in Lazimpat and run by the same people as the Kathmandu Guest House. There's a good restaurant and a garden which has shrunk with recent extensions. The hotel's within walking distance of Thamel or Durbar Marg. Rooms cost from US$19 to US$24 for singles, US$22 to US$27 for doubles. In the same Lazimpat area the *Hotel Manaslu* (tel 4-13470) has recently been completely renovated and has rooms at US$18/24.

Central Kathmandu There are several older middle range hotels right in the centre of old Kathmandu. *Hotel Panorama* (tel 2-21502) is a larger hotel near New Rd with rooms from US$12. *Hotel Mt Makalu* (tel 2-23955, 2-24616) is also centrally located at 65 Dharmapath and singles/doubles are US$14/16.

Further Afield Across the river in the Bijeshwari area, on the way from Thamel to Swayambhunath, *Hotel Vajra* (tel 2-71545, 2-72719) is one of Kathmandu's most interesting hotels in any price category. For all the glories of the old Nepalese temples the less said about most modern Nepalese architecture the better. The Hotel Vajra (*vajra* means thunderbolt) is a pleasant exception with a distinct style and a superb location looking across the river to Kathmandu.

The Hotel Vajra has an art gallery, its own theatre where classical Nepalese dances are performed as well as its own unusual annual performances, a library with books on Tibet and Buddhism, a rooftop garden and the Explorer's Restaurant. Singles/doubles start at US$11/13 with common bathrooms although the rooms do have washbasins. With bathrooms singles are US$19 to US$23, doubles US$23 to US$25. In the new wing there are rooms from US$30 to US$50. There is an additional 12% tax on all prices. The one catch to staying at the Hotel Vajra is its location, great for the view, terrible for getting a taxi. If you're staying here it's wise to have a bicycle at the ready.

Patan has a popular middle range hotel if you'd like a complete break from Kathmandu although none of Patan's accommodation is that close to the centre of the old town. The *Aloha Inn* (tel 5-22796, 5-24177, 5-24571) is in the Jawlakhel area, not that far from the southern edge of the old city. Rooms here are US$18/24 plus 12% tax. The name is certainly a strange one for Nepal but it's friendly, clean, well kept, quiet and popular with people working at the aid agencies in the area. There's a very pleasant garden.

Finally there are two other medium price hotels near Bodhnath, the *Hotel Stupa* (tel 4-12400) and the *Taragaon Resort Hotel* (tel 4-10409). The Taragaon is part of a mini chain with hotels in Nagarkot and Kakani. Singles/doubles cost US$15.50/21, and there are also good value weekly and full board rates. The weekly rate for singles/doubles is US$80/115.

Places to Stay – top end
Top end hotels in Kathmandu cost from US$40 for a double room; the most expensive hotels are around US$100 for a double. Only a handful of these hotels are centrally located although the less conveniently positioned hotels do usually offer a free bus service into town.

Central Kathmandu *Hotel de l'Annapurna* (tel 2-21711) is one of Kathmandu's longest established 'new' hotels and its central location on Durbar Marg can't be beaten. There are 159 rooms, all with air-con, plus restaurants, a bar, a swimming pool and prices for singles/doubles of US$80/90 plus 15% tax. Also right on Durbar Marg and directly across from the Hotel de l'Annapurna, the new *Hotel Sherpa* (tel 2-22585, 2-28021, 2-28898) has a convenient location, rooms at US$75/85 plus 14% tax and a rooftop garden terrace.

Entered from Durbar Marg, but set well back from the road, the *Hotel Yak & Yeti* (tel 2-22635, 4-13999) boasts probably the best known hotel name in Nepal, due to its connections with the legendary Boris, its original owner. Its story may be a long one but the hotel itself is actually quite new and offers everything from restaurants (including the famous Chimney Room) and bars to a superb garden complete with lake, tennis courts, sauna and swimming pool. Prices match the standards, singles/doubles are US$95/105 plus 15% tax.

Just south of the Hotel de l'Annapurna on Durbar Marg is *Hotel Woodlands* (tel 2-22683 and many other numbers). Singles/doubles here are US$44/55 plus 14% and it has the popular Greenlands vegetarian restaurant. A block over from Durbar Marg on Kantipath the *Hotel Yellow Pagoda* (tel 2-20337, 2-20338, 2-20392) is a cheaper top end hotel with rooms at US$44/54 (plus 13% tax) including breakfast. There's a restaurant, snack bar, roof garden and the hotel has recently had some renovations.

Hotel Malla (tel 4-10320) is on the northern edge of Thamel or the southern border of the embassy area, near the new Royal Palace. The rooms are all well equipped, there's a restaurant and bar and a superb garden, complete with a mini-stupa topping a mini-hill in the centre. Rooms at the Malla cost from US$70 to US$90.

The long-running *Hotel Crystal* (tel 2-23636) is on the corner of New Rd and Shukra Path, the only top end hotel actually in the heart of old Kathmandu. There are fine views over the city from its upper terraces, Durbar Square is just a short stroll away and rooms cost US$45. *Hotel Blue Star* (tel 2-11470) is on the southern edge of the city, close to the bridge to Patan. It's another long-term survivor and has single/doubles at US$55/75.

Further Afield Kathmandu's original luxury hotel, the *Soaltee Oberoi* (tel 2-72550, 2-72551), is on the western edge of town but operates a bus service into town for its guests. It's one of the largest hotels in Nepal and apart from restaurants, bars, swimming pool and other facilities it also has a casino. Singles/doubles at the Soaltee Oberoi are US$100/110.

Hotel Everest International (tel 2-20567) is on the eastern edge of town, beside the main road to the airport and Bhaktapur. The hotel is in a modern building with fine views from the rooftop, a swimming pool and rooms at US$80 to US$90.

North of the city in the Lazimpat embassy area *Hotel Shanker* (tel 4-10151, 4-10152) is an atmospheric place in a converted old Rana palace. Rooms here are US$55 to US$75 and the palace has a fine lawn and gardens. *Hotel Shangrila* (tel 4-12999) is a newer hotel in this same area with singles/doubles at US55/75. Keep travelling out from the city, towards Budhanilkantha, and you'll come to *Hotel Kathmandu* (tel 4-10786, 4-13082), still in the embassy area in Maharajganj but a long, long way from the city centre. It's overrated and overpriced; rooms in this new hotel are US$75/95.

The *Dwarika's Village Hotel* (tel 4-14770) is near the airport and Pashupatinath Temple and is an interesting hotel making much use of traditional woodcarving and construction. It won a Heritage Award from PATA, the Pacific Asia Travel Association, and has just 31 rooms at US$60 to US$80.

Patan Patan now has a number of top end hotels although none of them are close enough to the interesting centre of the old city to be really convenient. Two hotels are found very close to the UN office in Kopundol.

The *Summit Hotel* (tel 5-21894, 5-24694) tops a hillock in the Kopundol area and has great views across the river to Kathmandu and of the mountains beyond. There's a very beautiful garden with a swimming pool, a real pleasure in hot weather. The Summit Hotel's inconvenient location is its only drawback, finding taxis can sometimes be difficult and taxi drivers can be reluctant to take you there without extra payment. Singles/doubles cost US$35/49 for the regular rooms, US$45/65 for the newer ones, all plus 12%. There's a pleasant bar and the Summit's Garden Restaurant turns out superb food so the fact that you're a long way from the restaurants of Kathmandu is no hardship.

Also topping the Kopundol hill is the

nearby *Hotel Greenwich Village* (tel 5-21780, 5-22399) with singles at US$32 and doubles at US$42 to US$50, which really puts it more in the middle price range. There's a top-floor restaurant to take advantage of the view.

Two other Patan hotels are more distinctly in the top end price bracket. The *Hotel Narayani* (tel 5-21711, 5-21442, 5-21408, 5-21712) has a garden, a swimming pool and singles/doubles at US$45/52, plus 14% tax. The new *Hotel Himalaya* (tel 5-23900) has terrific views, a swimming pool, tennis and badminton courts and is at the top of the Kathmandu price range with rooms from US$70/85 plus 14%.

PLACES TO EAT

Kathmandu's restaurants attempt an amazing variety of international cuisines with a reasonable degree of success. There are few places in south Asia where your choice of restaurants is so varied. After long months on the road in India or long weeks trekking in Nepal most travellers still find Kathmandu a great place to eat. Recent arrivals from the West may not be quite so impressed, but some places are great value by any standards.

If you are eating in the really rock bottom restaurants around Kathmandu it is wise to be cautious about hygiene. Few travellers spend long in Nepal without coming across something which disagrees with them even if they're very fastidious about where they eat. Eating 'street food' from stalls and pavement kitchens in Kathmandu is likely to wreak havoc on all but the strongest of stomachs. Health standards have definitely improved in Kathmandu over the years, however, and you're very unlikely to have serious problems if you eat in the popular tourist-oriented restaurants. In these places it's even safe to try a salad, drink a glass of water and eat the ice cream – although some would argue that this is living dangerously!

At the bottom end of the price range Kathmandu has numerous tea stalls and shops. Many may not even have a name but at these stalls dhal bhat tarkari – the lentil soup, rice and vegetable everyday meal of

most Nepalese – will be the main dish on offer. By up-country standards these places aren't cheap – dhal bhat tarkari will probably set you back Rs 20.

In Thamel, if you stay away from beer, you can eat until you burst for less than Rs 70. A bottle of the excellent Iceberg beer can cost anything from Rs 45 to Rs 70 and double your bill. Star beer is usually cheaper and it's just as good.

As you might expect, the top restaurants have prices to match but by Western standards they're still reasonable. More expensive restaurants slap a 10% to 15% government tax on top of their bill, but you'll still probably only pay between US$10 and US$20 per person.

Tipping is becoming more accepted (and appreciated) in Nepal but the loose change or 5% is fine in cheaper places; a bit more will be expected in the expensive restaurants.

This section is divided geographically, with a final section on expensive places.

Thamel & Chhetrapati

Thamel restaurants spill into Chhetrapati, just like Thamel hotels. The junction just outside the Kathmandu Guest House is the centre of Thamel dining and you can find numerous restaurants within a minute's walk in each direction. This is the restaurant centre of Kathmandu, particularly when it comes to budget priced travellers' restaurants. Many of these restaurants offer a virtually standard try-anything menu with Asian and Western dishes. Italian and Mexican food features on many of these menus and you can try some amazing interpretations of pizzas, pasta dishes, tacos and the like.

The central Thamel restaurants include the best known of the lot, *KC's Restaurant*. Kaysee himself may no longer preside over his restaurant (he's doing time) but he hit the magic travellers' restaurant formula spot on. It can be crowded from breakfast time to late at night and with good reason because the food here, pseudo-Western or not, can be genuinely delicious. At breakfast time there's muesli, porridge, cereals, toast and so on. Other meals include burgers from Rs 35, pizzas and pastas from Rs 50, cakes at Rs 20 to Rs 25 and KC's famous steaks (Kathmandu's sizzle plate mania started right here) from Rs 70 to Rs 80. KC's is closed on Wednesdays.

On this same stretch of Thamel's restaurant centre you can try the *Pumpernickel Bakery* for freshly baked bread. In the morning travellers crowd in here for croissants in the pleasant garden area at the back. The bakery counter up front offers brown bread, rolls, cinnamon rolls and other goodies. The *East West Restaurant* has good food, a good view of the bustling Thamel street scene and friendly service. As the name of the restaurant suggests, the menu is diverse. Momos are Rs 16, vegetable curry Rs 16, fillet steak Rs 45 and 'kentucky fried' Rs 40.

Also across the road from KC's is *Helena's Restaurant* with the standard Kathmandu menu ranging from vegetarian dishes and soups through pastas and burgers to steaks with a great selection of cakes and pies to follow at around Rs 20. There is a second branch, *Helena's Country Kitchen*, just round the corner and upstairs. This is pleasant and good value, with a good variety of vegetarian dishes. A huge serve of delicious eggplant (aubergine) lasagna costs Rs 45.

Down the road from the Lucky Rest House, *Skala* also serves good vegetarian food. Its buffet costs Rs 45. It has a pleasant garden and it's a nice quiet place for breakfast, with newspapers to read and a background of classical music. The set breakfast will set you up for the day for Rs 35.

The *Sungava Restaurant*, next to the Kathmandu Guest House, serves good food indoors or outdoors although the service can be very slow.

Nearly every Thamel restaurant has a go at some Italian dishes, but there are several places which claim to specialise. Near the Kathmandu Guest House corner the *Mona Lisa Restaurant* is very popular, so it has to be doing something right. For all that, it's not particularly cheap and the food is not particularly special – lasagna costs Rs 40, fried chicken Rs 50. On the corner is *La Dolce Vita*

Restaurant, right across from the Kathmandu Guest House's entrance.

Continue a little north and you come to Yeti Cottage where the *Rainbow Restaurant* has a particularly pleasant garden and a good reputation for pizza and pasta dishes. Avoid their gravy soaked hamburgers though. Turn the corner, passing *Pizza Hut* (no relation whatsoever!), and you come to *San Francisco Pizza House* which connoisseurs of Kathmandu pizzas claim does a pretty good job.

Across the road *Primo's*, in the courtyard of the Garuda Hotel, also follows the Italian route. On the other side of Thamel, towards Durbar Marg, the *Marco Polo Restaurant*, upstairs in the guest house of the same name, is another place which attempts Italian food with sometimes quite reasonable results. South of Thamel, towards Thahiti Tole, is *La Cimbali Restaurant* where the Italian food may not be the best but it does make cappuccino.

Several other popular restaurants cluster close to that landmark Kathmandu Guest House corner. The name may be French but it's the familiar international menu with lots of pasta dishes at *Le Bistro Restaurant*. A prime attraction here is the large open courtyard, ideal for pleasant outdoor dining, and it's particularly popular for breakfast. A minestrone soup will cost Rs 20, and its excellent vegetarian pizza (it's more like a flan) is Rs 35.

Right beside the Kathmandu Guest House entrance is the *Red Square Restaurant*. The original owner was once the chef for the famous Boris of the Yak & Yeti – which is where the name and the borsch came from. On the other side is the friendly, efficiently run *G's Terrace*. It's a good place for an evening drink – it has a good music selection – and the food is designed for the spiced-out palate and pockets with Rs 30 to Rs 50 to spend on a main course.

The Kathmandu Guest House's *Ashta Mangala Restaurant* serves up straightforward, well prepared food and is another popular breakfast spot. This is a good place to try traditional Tibetan dishes like momos.

Directly across the road and upstairs is *Hem's Bar & Restaurant*, a pleasant rooftop spot where you can overlook the Thamel activity below. Hem's does very good tandoori and curry dishes, but also offers all the Thamel specialities. The main courses range from Rs 30 to Rs 50.

Continue a few steps north of the Kathmandu Guest House entranceway and you'll see the alley to *Rum Doodle Restaurant* named, of course, after the world's highest mountain, the 40,000½ foot Mt Rum Doodle. The heroic conquest of Rum Doodle was dramatically described in that spoof on heroic mountaineering books *The Ascent of Rum Doodle* (Dark Peak, Sheffield, 1979). The restaurant specialises in steaks and pastas and is a favourite meeting place for mountaineering expeditions, particularly in the upstairs 40,000½ Foot Bar of course. The walls are liberally plastered with yeti footprints, autographed by expedition members.

Further north again is the *Nirmala Vegetarian Restaurant*, a pleasantly relaxed upstairs place with some interesting and well prepared vegetarian dishes including pizzas at Rs 45; skip the rather ordinary soups. A few doors beyond is the airy *Kasthamandap Restaurant* in the new Hotel Mandap.

Reverse direction and go the other way from KC's and you soon come to the *Mandala Restaurant*, which used to live on Pie Alley in a previous incarnation. Round the corner the *Utse Restaurant* is one of the longest running restaurants in Thamel and turns out Chinese and Tibetan dishes ranging from sweet & sours to Tibetan kothes and momos. The service is poor, but the food is good.

On the same side of the road, across from the Marco Polo, is the *Old Vienna Inn* with traditional heavy Bavarian cooking to make German speakers feel at home. If you're after Wiener schnitzel, goulash and other middle European dishes this is the place. Next door, *Coppers Restaurant* specialises in English-style food. If you prefer your food on the bland side this is a pleasant atmospheric spot with good service. A bit too atmospheric perhaps, because the fumes from the lamps

can be quite strong! A serving of shepherd's pie costs Rs 75, and if you want to fill up you'll probably spend over Rs 100.

Head south from Thamel into Chhetrapati to find more popular travellers' restaurants including *Narayan's Restaurant*, another of the long-term survivors in this area. It's very popular, competent and low priced with a wide range of breakfast dishes, pastas at Rs 30 to Rs 40, soups at Rs 15 to Rs 20 and main courses predominantly in the Rs 45 to Rs 55 bracket. Narayan's also produces good ice cream in a half dozen different flavours and offers a great selection of pies and cakes.

A couple of doors down *Namkha Dhing* specialises in Tibetan dishes. The decor might not look too impressive and the service can be slow, but the food is good and very cheap. A serving of momos is only Rs 15.

Cross the road to *Pizza Maya* for, that's right, pizzas and Mexican food! This a popular spot with a good range of vegetarian dishes. A pizza will cost around Rs 30 – so will tacos. Next is the *Nepalese Kitchen*, an interesting venture attempting something rather different from the ubiquitous pseudo-Western food. Traditional Nepalese food is definitely rather unusual in Kathmandu, but this restaurant offers a variety of dishes including a choice of set meals from Rs 55 to Rs 120.

On the street running south from Thamel to Jyatha the *Rose Restaurant*, near the Blue Diamond Hotel, does good Chinese/Tibetan food. Or head north from Thamel towards the Malla Hotel to find the pleasant *Romeo's Restaurant*.

Finally on the northern edge of Thamel, in the courtyard of the Malla Hotel, the *Mountain City Chinese Restaurant* concentrates on the hotter Sichuan and Shanghai dishes rather than the familiar Cantonese. It has a filling soup for Rs 32, and most other dishes are Rs 30 to Rs 60.

New Rd & Freak St

Despite its decline in popularity Freak St still has a number of restaurants where you can find good food at low prices. Even if you're staying in other areas of the city it's nice to know there are some good places for lunch if you're sightseeing around Durbar Square.

Just off Durbar Square beside the Great Bell, with slightly complicated access through a courtyard and upstairs, is the *Big Bell Restaurant*. This is a good place to relax if your feet are giving way and you want a calm, rooftop oasis overlooking the street.

On Freak St itself the *Oasis Garden Restaurant* has a pleasant little outdoor dining area at the front and the standard travellers' menu with which it does a good job. Most of its dishes are in the Rs 30 to Rs 40 bracket. Its sandwiches are fine, and vegetable curry and parathas at the Oasis makes a delicious and filling lunch. Across the road from the Oasis Garden the *Paradise Restaurant* is also good for vegetarian food.

The long-running *Lunch Box* is just off Freak St and is still very much a 'scene'! Come here for a faint reminder of those hippy overland days when Freak St really was the flower power centre. Most of the main meals are around Rs 30.

Up at the Basantapur Square end of Freak St the *Mona Lisa* is a pleasant place with friendly staff. Right next door and also overlooking the square is the *Cosmopolitan Restaurant*. Both places have newer offshoots in Thamel.

Other consistent Freak St places include *Kumari's Restaurant* in the same courtyard as the Century Lodge. Or there's the *Lost Horizon* near the Lunch Box and the *Bluebird*, just south of the Kasthamandap and Singh Sattal, near Durbar Square. The venerable *New Style Pie Shop* is all there is left to show where Pie Alley, running from Durbar Square down to the river, got its name. Kathmandu's famous pie shops used to turn out pies which knocked the socks off recently arrived travellers, crawling in from long months on the Asia overland trail. Lots of places still do bake a pretty good pie but Pie Alley certainly isn't the centre for them anymore.

New Rd restaurants are aimed at the local rather than the tourist market but try *Marwari Sewa Samiti*, near the cinema, or the nearby *Tripti Restaurant* for very economically priced all-you-can-eat south Indian vegetarian thalis.

Durbar Marg & Kantipath

The restaurants in the glossier Kantipath and Durbar Marg areas are generally more expensive than around Thamel although there are a few lower-priced exceptions. See the concluding Expensive Restaurants section for Kathmandu's real night-out possibilities.

You can start the day with one of the best and most popular breakfast places in the city. As the name suggests *Mike's Breakfast* specialises in breakfasts and they do them well. It's directly behind the Sherpa Hotel, a beautiful old house with an equally beautiful garden around a pond. Mike's Breakfast is open 7 days for breakfast and lunch and also does pizzas on Monday nights only. The breakfast menu includes excellent pancakes at Rs 35 to Rs 50; toast, eggs and tea will come to about Rs 50.

Several places on Durbar Marg have good food from the subcontinent. The *Bangalore Coffee House* serves good south Indian vegetarian dishes like masala dosa and is a popular local gathering place.

The *Sunkosi Restaurant* does traditional Nepalese and Tibetan dishes. It's popular with tour groups who are getting a taste of indigenous cuisine but, although the food is definitely good, shoestring trekkers will baulk at paying Rs 140 for a tricked-up dhal bhat tarkari. It has a number of set menus ranging from Rs 140 to Rs 200, and the staff prefers to push these options although the restaurant also has an interesting menu. If you won't have an opportunity to eat Nepalese food elsewhere, it's worth a visit.

Still on Durbar Marg the *Nanglo-Pub* has a popular rooftop dining area and an international menu. There's quite a lively atmosphere and the place is a favourite for people in the travel business. A large pizza will cost Rs 36, a steak Rs 48. In the Woodlands Hotel the *Greenlands Restaurant* is an Indian vegetarian restaurant.

Nirula's Restaurant, near the Hotel de l'Annapurna on Durbar Marg, is the closest

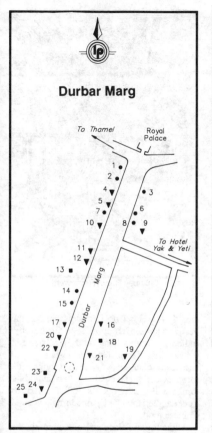

Durbar Marg

you'll find to a McDonald's in Nepal. Its menu features burgers at Rs 20 to Rs 40, pizzas at Rs 30 to Rs 45 and 21 flavours of ice cream at Rs 10 to Rs 15 for cones or cups. This is also the place to come if, while trekking, you've developed an uncontrollable urge for a chocolate milkshake (Rs 22)! Despite the fast-food atmosphere and service it still operates the traditional Indian method of deciding what you want, going back to the cashier and paying for it and then taking the receipt to the counter to collect it!

Beside the entrance to the Hotel de l'Annapurna the *Annapurna Coffee Shop* offers a standard 'big hotel' style menu with hot dogs at Rs 35, burgers at Rs 50, sandwiches at Rs 40 to Rs 50, milk shakes or lassi at Rs 30 and ice cream at Rs 15. It's popular but the food is only average. Across the road the Hotel Sherpa's *Cafe de la Paix* has a similar coffee shop menu.

Other Durbar Marg possibilities include the moderately priced *Koto Restaurant* for Japanese food. It has another branch in Thamel. The nearby *Kushi Fuji Restaurant* also does Japanese food although recent reports indicate that the standards have fallen of late.

Still on Durbar Marg the *Amber Restaurant* serves good quality Indian food (it also has a continental menu) and attracts a lively crowd of affluent young Nepalese, especially when the music is good. The crowd varies depending on who is playing, but this can be a fun night out. Without including beer, it's possible to eat well for less than Rs 100.

Just off Kantipath in the Gautam Hotel, round the corner from the Hotel Nook, the *Kabab Corner* is another restaurant which has survived the years. The menu features Western and Chinese dishes but Indian tandoori food is the speciality and they do it very well. It's a pleasant place with white tablecloths, definitely a bit fancier than the Thamel restaurants. Vegetable curry dishes are Rs 20 to Rs 30, biryanis and pulaos Rs 25 to Rs 55, tandoori dishes from Rs 60 to Rs 70, on up to Rs 90 to Rs 120 for larger dishes.

On the eastern side of Kantipath, overlooking Rani Pokhara, the *Aroma Restaurant* is a pleasant place to watch the sunset and rest your feet after a day of exploring Kathmandu. There's a pleasant rooftop garden and you can get reasonably priced snacks and drinks – for example crumbed onion rings for Rs 15.

Chimney Room Restaurant

Expensive Restaurants

Kathmandu's big hotels have some interesting restaurant possibilities and although the prices are sky high by Nepalese standards they're remarkably cheap compared to what similar restaurants would cost you in the West. One thing you will consistently find in these more expensive places is heating. Kathmandu can get very cold in winter and few of the cheaper places have any form of heating.

One of the most famous would have to be the Hotel Yak & Yeti's *Chimney Room*. Its history goes back to Russian-born Boris and the Royal Hotel, Kathmandu's original hotel for Western visitors. Later it moved to an old Rana palace off Durbar Marg and then the new Hotel Yak & Yeti was built beside it. The central open fireplace gives it plenty of atmosphere, but unfortunately apart from the borsch, which is still excellent, there are few reminders of the Russian flavour from Boris' days. Nevertheless the food is well prepared and served, if somewhat bland, and a complete meal for two including drinks will cost about Rs 900.

The *Ghar-e-Kebab*, on Durbar Marg

outside the Hotel de l'Annapurna, has the best Indian and tandoori food in the city. Indian miniatures hang on the walls and in the evenings classical Indian music is played and traditional Urdu *ghazals* (songs) are sung. A complete meal for two including drinks will cost about Rs 700. The *Arniko Room* at the Hotel de l'Annapurna has good Chinese food.

At the Royal Palace end of Kantipath, the *Fuji Restaurant* serves good value Japanese food. It's away from the road in an atmospheric pavilion that was built in 1905 in the grounds of the nearby Bahadur Bhawan Palace (now government offices). It has set lunches for only Rs 80 and Rs 90. It's quite a bit more expensive in the evenings with a sukiyaki set menu for Rs 150 and a tempura set menu for Rs 130. A full meal for two with drinks will probably come to around Rs 700.

The trek out to the Soaltee Oberoi Hotel, on the western side of town, may be worthwhile to try the excellent Indian and Nepalese dishes at the *Himalchuli Restaurant*. It features woodcarvings from Bhaktapur and traditional

Nepalese music plays in the background. The *Al Fresco Italian Restaurant* claims to serve the best Italian food in Nepal; count on about Rs 800 for two including drinks.

Also out of town at the Everest Hotel the *Far Pavilions Restaurant* offers great views over Kathmandu from its 7th floor vantage point and a popular chicken tandoori to go with it. Closer to the centre the Shanker Hotel's *Kailash Restaurant* does a variety of Indian, Nepalese and even Russian dishes.

Finally, *Bhanchha Ghar* is Nepali for Nepalese Kitchen and is in a traditional three storey Newari house, just east of Durbar Marg from the turn-off by the clocktower. It's worth eating here just to see the imaginative redevelopment of this beautiful old building. There's an upstairs loft where you can stretch out on handmade carpets and cushions for a drink, then take advantage of an excellent menu of traditional Nepalese dishes and delicacies. Downstairs, musicians stroll between the tables playing traditional Nepalese folk songs. It's not cheap (around Rs 600 for two, with drinks), but the food is delicious.

ENTERTAINMENT

Nepal is an early to bed country and even in Kathmandu you find few people on the streets after 10 pm. Few visitors come to Nepal for nightlife and Kathmandu's discos and other nightspots have had a remarkably low survival rate. Of course the crowded restaurants and bars are great places to meet and talk with people and the big hotels do offer some traditional nightlife for those who positively cannot live without it. Kathmandu also has cultural shows, cinemas and one of West Asia's very few casinos.

Casino

The *Soaltee Oberoi Casino* is the only casino on the subcontinent. If you turn up within a week of arrival with your inward airline ticket and your passport you can get Indian Rs 100 of free coupons. You can play in either Indian rupees (almost a hard currency in Nepalese terms) or US dollars, and winnings (in the same currency) can be taken out of the country when you leave.

The casino offers blackjack, poker and roulette, and slot machines which take only rupees. The casino is open 24 hours a day and there are free buses from all the leading hotels of Kathmandu from 8 to 11 pm. They return hourly from 11 pm to 4 am. Just why does Nepal need a casino? To make money of course but the casino's main attraction is probably to allow rich Indians to 'launder' their 'black money'.

Cultural Programmes

There are regular performances of Nepalese music and dancing in Kathmandu, including at the *National Theatre*, although these are usually in Nepali.

The *Everest Cultural Society* (tel 2-20676) performs Nepalese folk dances in the Hotel de l'Annapurna every evening from 7 pm. Entry to the 1 hour show is Rs 90 and it includes dances from the Sherpa highlands, from the Newaris of the valley and from other ethnic groups including the yak dance, peacock dance, mask dance and witch doctor dance. Dances are also performed at the Hotel Shankar by the *New Himalchuli Centre* (tel 4-10151). The entry fee is Rs 60 and its show also commences at 7 pm. At the Soaltee Oberoi Hotel traditional dances are also performed at the *Himalchuli Restaurant*.

The *Explorer's Restaurant* at the Hotel Vajra (tel 2-24545) is the venue for a Tibetan music performance at 6 pm each evening. At the Hotel de l'Annapurna's *Ghar-e-Kebab Restaurant* (tel 2-21711), Indian classical music is played to the accompaniment of traditional Urdu ghazals at 7 pm every evening except Thursdays.

A cultural programme and Indian classical music are also performed most nights of the week at the *Hotel Everest International* (tel 2-20567).

The Sweta Machhendranath Temple in Kel Tole has traditional Nepalese music around 9.30 pm each evening. 'The warming up of the musicians', reported one visitor, 'is done with a large chillum and the music begins when the coughing stops.'

Cinemas

Video Night in Kathmandu has certainly had an impact on the city – there are video shops everywhere and cinemas are having a hard time of it. Indian films, usually not subtitled, are the usual cinematic fare in the valley although there are occasional English language films. Admission charges range from Rs 8 to Rs 15 and catching a Hindi movie is well worthwhile since not understanding the language is not a real obstacle to enjoying these comedy-musical spectaculars. The Indians call them 'masala' movies as they have a little bit of everything in them.

In the small video parlours popular Western movies appear in pirated videos almost as soon as they hit the cinemas in the West. *Batman* was Kathmandu's most popular video movie within weeks of the film's original US release.

THINGS TO BUY

See the Things to Buy section in the Facts for the Visitor chapter for the full story on shopping possibilities in Nepal. Everything turned out in the various centres around the valley can be found in Kathmandu although you may often find a better choice or more unusual items in the real centres – head for Jawlakhel south of Patan for Tibetan carpets for example, to Patan for cast metal statues, to Bhaktapur for the finest woodcarvings and pottery, to Thimi for more pottery and masks.

There are countless shops around Thamel and around Durbar Square. The Bluebird Supermarket, near the Patan Bridge on the southern edge of Kathmandu, has a wide variety of Western supermarket goods.

Clothing

Kathmandu is the best place in the valley for clothes and many places now have good quality ready to wear Western fashions, particularly shirts. Amusing embroidered T-shirts are a popular speciality. There are lots of good tailors around Thamel and apart from wonderfully embroidered T-shirts they'll also embroider just about anything you want on your own jacket or jeans. Tara

Boutique, with shops on Tridevi Marg near Thamel and on Durbar Marg, makes wonderful hand-painted pure silk women's fashions. Dresses are certainly not cheap at US$50 to US$100 and up, but in the West they'd be many times that price.

GETTING THERE & AWAY

See the Getting There chapter for details of getting to Kathmandu by air or land.

Air

Kathmandu is the only international arrival point for flights to Nepal and is also the centre for most domestic flights. Offices of the airlines which fly to Nepal include:

Bangladesh Biman
    Durbar Marg (tel 2-22544)
CAAC
    Lal Durbar Camp, Kamaladi (tel 4-11302)
Dragon Air
    Durbar Marg (tel 2-23162)
Druk Air
    Durbar Marg (tel 2-25166)
Indian Airlines
    Durbar Marg (tel 2-23053)
Lufthansa
    Durbar Marg (tel 2-24341)
Myanmar (Burma) Airways
    Durbar Marg (tel 2-24893)
Pakistan International Airlines
    Durbar Marg (tel 2-23102)
Royal Nepal Airlines
    Ramshah Path – domestic (tel 2-20757)
    Kantipath – international (tel 2-14491)
Singapore Airlines
    Durbar Marg (tel 2-20759)
Thai International
    Durbar Marg (tel 2-23565)

Numerous other airlines are represented in Kathmandu although they do not fly there. There are three important rules with flights out of Kathmandu – reconfirm, reconfirm, reconfirm! This particularly applies to Royal Nepal Airlines, but at peak times of year when flights are heavily booked you should reconfirm when you first arrive in Nepal and reconfirm again towards the end of your stay. Even this may not guarantee you a seat – make sure you get to the airport very early as people at the end of the queue can still be left behind.

Bus

If you are travelling by land you may arrive/depart from a number of alternative bus stops. See the main Kathmandu map and the bus stop key to locate the correct arrival/departure point.

If you use public buses between Kathmandu and the Indian border or from Pokhara, the bus stop will either be at the foot of Bhimsen Tower near the GPO (Bus Stop 8) or the Central Bus Station (Bus Stop 6). From either of these points it's only a short walk to Freak St and Durbar Square or a quick taxi or rickshaw ride to the Thamel area.

Public buses for Pokhara depart from the foot of the Bhimsen Tower (Bus Stop 8) or from the Central Bus Station (Bus Stop 6) and cost Rs 45. The more expensive tourist buses (Rs 110 to Rs 120) which are heavily promoted in Thamel are more comfortable and usually pick up and drop off in Tridevi Marg in Thamel (Bus Stop 2). See the Getting Around and Pokhara chapters for more details.

GETTING AROUND

The best way to see Kathmandu and the valley is to walk or ride a bike. Most of the sights in Kathmandu can easily be covered on foot, and this is by far the best way to appreciate the city. When and if you run out of steam, there are plenty of reasonably priced taxis and autorickshaws. There are also limitless opportunities for short walks around the valley. A number are described in the Around the Valley chapter. The valley is the perfect size and shape for bicycling. Around the three main cities a single-speed bike is fine, but if you want to get into the countryside consider hiring a multigeared machine. Since the furthest point in the valley is never more than about 20 km from Kathmandu you can ride out (uphill) and return (downhill) easily within a day. Bike speed allows you to appreciate your surroundings and stop whenever you like.

Airport Transport

Kathmandu's international airport is named Tribhuvan Airport after the late king. It used to rejoice in the name Gaucher or Cow Pasture Airport!

There's a hotel reservations counter as soon as you get out of Customs & Immigration. See the earlier Places to Stay section for information on this service and free transport into town. When you leave the airport terminal you're immediately confronted by agents and touts for cheaper hotels. A free ride into town may be offered as an enticement to try their hotel. If not, it's only about 6 km into town but Kathmandu taxi drivers are very reluctant to use their meters to or from the airport. They'll probably ask at least Rs 100 but they can be beaten down to around Rs 70 or Rs 80.

Buses are sometimes available from Royal Nepal Airlines for Rs 15. There are public buses but they're only really usable if you have very little luggage.

Bus

Bus travel is very cheap although often unbelievably crowded. The primary disadvantage, apart from severe discomfort, is that you cannot see the views or stop when you want to. Still, if you're short of cash and want to get from point A to B *reasonably* quickly they'll do. Over a short distance – say from Thamel to Bodhnath – you'll probably be just as quick on a bicycle. Look for the blue, government-owned Saja Sewa buses if possible. The smaller minibuses and curious little three-wheel tempos are generally quicker than the full-sized buses and a bit more expensive.

The bus stations are hectic and hard to use – there are no signs. You may arrive/depart from a number of alternative bus stops depending on your destination/starting point. See the main Kathmandu map and the bus stop key to locate the correct place.

Kakani, Trisuli Bazaar & Dhunche Buses leave from the intersection of Lekhnath Marg and the road to Balaju (Bus Stop 1 – Paknajol). Buses to Trisuli and Dhunche (for the Langtang treks) leave around 6 am and cost Rs 55 and Rs 22 respectively. Look for the Saja Sewa bus. Kakani is about 3 km off the main road, so catch one of the buses going through, and get off at Kaulithana (approximately Rs 10).

Budhanilkantha There are regular mini-buses from Rani Pokhari (Bus Stop 3) for Rs 2.

Pashupatinath & Bodhnath There are regular minibuses from Rani Pokhari (Bus Stop 3) for Rs 1.50. The buses depart when full and go via Pashupatinath – the stop is Gosala.

Gokarna Buses leave from Ratna Park (Bus Stop 4) and cost Rs 2.50.

Sundarijal Buses leave from Tukuchapul (Bus Stop 7) near the Central Bus Station for Rs 7 and take half an hour.

Sankhu There are two or three buses a day to Sankhu, leaving near Martyrs' Memorial Gate (Bus Stop 9) – not far from the Bhadrakali Temple. They take 1½ hours and cost Rs 3. You may also find something at the Central Bus Station (Bus Stop 6).

Bhaktapur There are two alternatives. The easiest and most comfortable, although it does involve a walk at both ends of the trip, is the regular electric trolley buses that run along the Arniko Highway. They leave from the roundabout at the southern end of Kantipath near the National Stadium (Bus Stop 10), cost Rs 2 and drop you off a 10 minute walk from the centre of Bhaktapur.

Alternatively you can catch a normal bus from Bagh Bazaar (Bus Stop 5) for Rs 1.50.

Banepa, Dhulikhel & Panauti Regular buses leave from the Central Bus Station (Bus Stop 6). Buses to Banepa and Dhulikhel take about an hour and cost Rs 6 – it's a little more for Panauti.

Jiri This small town is the starting point for the Everest Trek and buses go there directly

from the Central Bus Station (Bus Stop 6) or you can take a bus to Lamosangu and change. They leave early and cost around Rs 70.

Patan The Lagankhel bus stop in Patan services those towns to the south of Kathmandu (Godavari, Lele and Chapagaon). See the Patan map. Regular buses and minibuses leave for the centre of Patan, Lagankhel and Jawlakhel (the Tibetan refugee centre) from Ratna Park (Bus Stop 4), take 15 minutes and cost Rs 1.50. Buses to Bungamati leave from Jawlakhel.

Godavari There are local minibuses and several Saja Sewa buses. They leave from Lagankhel in Patan and the 1 hour journey costs Rs 3.50.

Chapagaon There are local minibuses and a Saja Sewa bus. They leave from Lagankhel in Patan and the 1 to 1½ hour journey costs Rs 3.75.

Bungamati Buses leave from Jawlakhel (the road that runs past the zoo), take half an hour and cost Rs 2.

Pharping & Dakshinkali Buses are very crowded on Tuesdays and Saturdays – the most important days for sacrifices at Dakshinkali – even though there are plenty of them. After you pass the police checkpoint on the ring road you can sit on the roof and enjoy the spectacular views. Buses leave from Martyrs' Gate (Bus Stop 9). There are minibuses, although they only run in the mornings, normal buses (Rs 5, 1½ hours) and express buses (Rs 15, 45 minutes).

Kirtipur There are numerous buses and minibuses departing from Ratna Park (Bus Stop 4). They take around half an hour and cost Rs 2.

Taxi
Taxis are quite reasonably priced – shorter rides around town should come to less than Rs 30. Between several people longer trips

around the valley or even outside it are also reasonably priced.

By the day, count on about US$50 plus fuel although this may drop now the border problems with India are sorted out. Because of fuel rationing due to the border dispute, drivers were reluctant to use their meters as much as usual. Note that in Nepal real taxis have black licence plates while private cars (many of which operate as taxis but don't have meters) have red plates. If you need a taxi at night ring 2-24374.

Autorickshaw & Cycle Rickshaw

Metered autorickshaws have become quite common in Kathmandu and cost as little as half of what you would pay for a cab. They're still a bit of a lottery – some will blankly refuse to use the meter and if this is the case make sure you establish a price. Most rides around town should cost less than Rs 15. Bicycle rickshaws cost Rs 15 to Rs 25 for most rides around town, although in many cases they're more expensive than going by taxi. You must be certain to agree on a price before you start.

Driving

Car Rental Although you cannot rent cars on a drive-yourself basis they can readily be rented with a driver from a number of operators. Try Gorkha Travels (tel 2-24896) or American Express (tel 2-23596) in Kathmandu or just go to the alley by Mike's Breakfast, behind the Sherpa Hotel on Durbar Marg. This is the main hangout for drivers looking for hire by the day.

The rental cost is fairly high both in terms of initial hiring charge and fuel – about US$1 per litre. Full day charges were as high as US$100 a day during the fuel crisis, although usually they are considerably lower, especially if you are not covering a huge distance. Around the valley expect to pay about US$50 plus fuel.

Motorcycle

There are a number of motorcycle rental operators around Freak St or in Thamel.

Bicycle

Once you get away from the crowded streets of central Kathmandu, bicycle riding is a pleasure and if you're in good shape this is the ideal way to explore the valley. It costs from Rs 15 to Rs 20 a day for a regular single-speed Indian or Chinese-made bicycle. Check the brakes before taking it out and be certain to lock it whenever you leave it. The bikes have a simple claw type lock which stops the back wheel turning.

Multigeared mountain bikes have become the current rage in Kathmandu and a number of places around Thamel – at Chhetrapati Square and Thahiti Tole for example – rent them out. Count on Rs 80 to Rs 120 a day, which, if you are planning to really explore the valley, can be money well spent. It's a real pleasure to surge up the long hill into Patan, effortlessly sweeping by all the riders of regular bikes who have to get off and push.

Tours

There are numerous tour operators in Kathmandu with bus and car tours to all the established tourist sights. Typical costs for day tours are Rs 150 to Rs 250 and if your time is limited this can be a good way of seeing the valley's scattered attractions.

Grayline (tel 4-12899, 4-13188) has a wide variety of tours including Bhaktapur to Bodnath and Pashupatinath on Mondays, Wednesdays, Fridays and Saturdays; Patan to Swayambhunath on Sundays, Tuesdays and Thursdays; Chobar Gorge to Dakshinkali on Tuesdays and Saturdays; plus dawn trips to Nagarkot, Dhulikhel and Kakani for the Himalayan sunrise.

Kathmandu Travel (tel 2-24536), Everest Travel Service (tel 2-22217, 2-24661) and others also operate tours or will arrange them.

Patan

Patan is separated from Kathmandu only by the Bagmati River and is the second largest town in the valley. It is sometimes referred

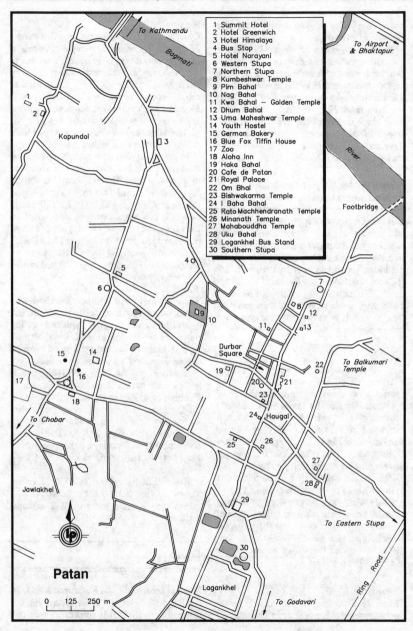

1 Summit Hotel
2 Hotel Greenwich
3 Hotel Himalaya
4 Bus Stop
5 Hotel Narayani
6 Western Stupa
7 Northern Stupa
8 Kumbeshwar Temple
9 Pim Bahal
10 Nag Bahal
11 Kwa Bahal – Golden Temple
12 Dhum Bahal
13 Uma Maheshwar Temple
14 Youth Hostel
15 German Bakery
16 Blue Fox Tiffin House
17 Zoo
18 Aloha Inn
19 Haka Bahal
20 Cafe de Patan
21 Royal Palace
22 Om Bhal
23 Bishwakarma Temple
24 I Baha Bahal
25 Rato Machhendranath Temple
26 Minanath Temple
27 Mahabouddha Temple
28 Uku Bahal
29 Lagankhel Bus Stand
30 Southern Stupa

Patan

0   125   250 m

to as Lalitpur, the city of beauty. Patan has a long Buddhist history and the four corners of the city are marked by stupas said to have been erected by the great Buddhist emperor Ashoka himself around 250 BC. Later inscriptions refer to palaces in the city in the 5th century AD although Patan's great building boom took place under the Mallas in the 16th, 17th and 18th centuries. Patan's central Durbar Square is absolutely packed with temples: it's an architectural feast with a far greater concentration of temples per square metre than in Kathmandu or Bhaktapur. Numerous other temples of widely diverse style as well as many bahals (Buddhist monasteries) are scattered around this fascinating town.

Malla Kings

The Malla kings of Patan were responsible for most of the city's great buildings. They included:

Jayasthiti Malla	1380-1395
Siddhinarsingh Malla	1620-1661
Srinivasa Malla	1661-1684
Yoganarendra Malla	1684-1705
Vishnu Malla	1729-1745
Rajya Prakash Malla	1745-1758
Visvajita Malla	1758-1760

INFORMATION & ORIENTATION

The Durbar, or Palace, Square is the centre of Patan to a greater extent than the equivalent Durbar squares are to Kathmandu or Bhaktapur. From the square four main roads lead to the four Ashoka stupas while the city radiates out in concentric circles from this important centrepoint.

It is possible to stay in Patan, although it's so close to Kathmandu that it scarcely seems worthwhile and the choice of accommodation and restaurants is far more limited than in the capital.

Jawlakhel, to the south of the city, has a major Tibetan population and is the centre for carpet weaving in the valley.

Buses from Kathmandu drop you at the Patan city gate, about 15 minutes walk from Durbar Square. There's another, larger bus halt directly south of Durbar Square, near the Southern or Lagan Stupa. Taxis normally drop you at the square. If you come to Patan by bicycle an interesting route is to take the

Washing area, Durbar Square

track down to the river from opposite the big Everest Hotel on the Bhaktapur road. A footbridge crosses the river here and you enter Patan by the Northern Stupa near the Kumbeshwar Temple.

DURBAR SQUARE

As in Kathmandu, the ancient royal palace of the city faces on to the square, but Patan's Durbar Square is a concentrated mass of temples, undoubtedly the most visually stunning display of Newari architecture to be seen in Nepal. The rectangular square has its longer axis running north-south and the palace forms the eastern side of the square while a continuous row of temples in widely diverse styles face it on the western side.

The square rose to its full glory during the Malla period, and particularly during the reign of King Siddhinarsingh Malla. Patan's major market, the Mangal Bazaar, is beside the square.

Bhimsen Temple (2)

At the northern end of Durbar Square the Bhimsen Temple is dedicated to the god of trade and business, which possibly explains its well kept and prosperous look. Bhimsen, a hero of the *Mahabharata*, was said to be extraordinarily strong. The three storey temple has had a chequered history. Although it is not known when it was first built, an inscription records that it was rebuilt in

1	Kwa Bahal, Hiranya Varna Mahavihar or Golden Temple
2	Bhimsen Temple
3	Ganesh Temple
4	Mani Mandap
5	Vishwanath Shiva Temple
6	Manga Hiti
7	Garuda Statue on Column
8	Krishna Mandir
9	Jagannarayan Temple
10	Golden Gate
11	Mani Keshar Chowk
12	Vishnu Temple
13	Narsingha Statue
14	King Yoganarendra Malla's Statue
15	Taleju Temple
16	Hari Shankar Temple
17	Degutalle Temple
18	Bhai Dega Shiva Temple
19	Taleju Bell
20	Mul Chowk
21	Statue of Ganga
22	Statue of Jamuna
23	Krishna Temple
24	Narsingha Statue
25	Ganesh Statue
26	Hanuman Statue
27	Sundari Chowk

1682 after a fire. Restorations also took place in 1934, after the great earthquake which did so much damage throughout the valley, and again in 1967. A lion tops a pillar in front of the temple, while the brick building has an artificial marble facade and a gilded facade on the 1st floor.

Manga Hiti (6)

Immediately north of the palace is the sunken Manga Hiti, one of the water conduits with which Patan, and even more so Bhaktapur, are so liberally endowed. This one has a lotus-shaped pool and three wonderfully carved stone crocodile-head waterspouts. Next to it is the Mani Mandap, a pavilion built in 1700 and used for royal crownings.

Vishwanath Temple (5)

Next to the Bhimsen Temple stands the Vishwanath, or Shiva, Temple. The elaborately decorated two storey temple was built in 1627 and has two large stone

Bhimsen Temple

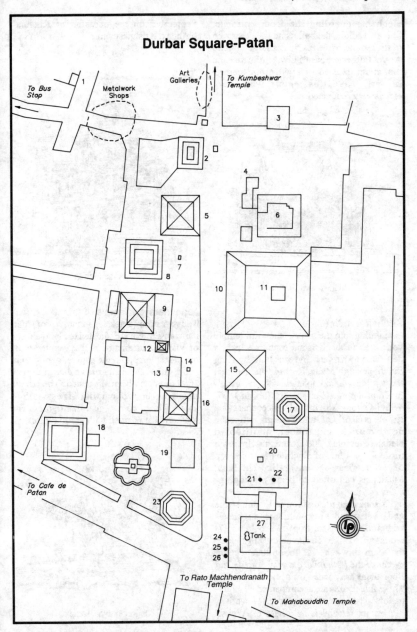

Durbar Square-Patan

To Bus Stop

1

Metalwork Shops

Art Galleries

To Kumbeshwar Temple

3

2

4

5

6

7

8

9

10

11

12

13

14

15

16

17

18

19

20

21 22

23

To Cafe de Patan

24
25
26

27

Tank

To Rato Machhendranath Temple

To Mahabouddha Temple

elephants guarding the front entrance. Shiva's vehicle, the bull, is on the other side of the temple while inside is a large lingam. As yet further proof of Shiva's influence the roof struts are decorated with erotic themes. In early 1990 this temple was being extensively renovated.

Vishwanath Temple

September on the occasion of Krishna's birthday, Krishnasthami.

Krishna Mandir

Krishna Mandir (8)

Continuing into the square, the third temple you reach is the Krishna Mandir which is dedicated to Krishna and was built by King Siddhinarsingh Malla. Records indicate that the temple was completed with the installation of the image on the 1st floor in 1637. With its strong Moghul influences this stone temple is clearly of Indian design, unlike the nearby brick and timber, multiroofed Nepalese temples. The 1st and 2nd floors are made up of a line of pavilions from the top of which rises a corncob-like shikhara. Musicians can often be heard playing upstairs.

Krishna is an incarnation of Vishnu so the god's vehicle, the man-bird Garuda, kneels with folded arms on top of a column (7) facing the temple. The stone carvings along the beam above the 1st floor pillars recount events of the *Mahabharata* while on the 2nd floor there are scenes from the *Ramayana*. These fine friezes are accompanied by explanations of the narrative scenes in Newari.

A major festival is held here in August/

Jagannarayan Temple (9)

The two storey brick Jagannarayan or Charnarayan Temple is dedicated to Narayan, one of Vishnu's incarnations. It is reputed to be the oldest temple in the square, dating from 1565, although an alternative date in the late 1600s has also been suggested. The temple stands on a brick plinth with large stone lions above which are two guardian figures. The roof struts are carved with erotic figures.

Jagannarayan Temple

King Yoganarendra Malla's Statue (14)

Immediately north of the Jagannarayan Temple, between it and the Krishna Temple, is a tall column topped by a figure of King Yoganarendra Malla. The golden figure of the kneeling king has been facing towards his palace, protected by the hood of a cobra, since the year 1700. On top of the cobra's head is the figure of a bird: legends say that as long as the bird remains there the king may still return to his palace. Accordingly a door and window of the palace is always kept open and a *hookah* (a water pipe used for smoking) is kept ready for the king should he return. A rider to the legend adds that when the bird flies off, the elephants in front of the Vishwanath Temple will stroll over to the Manga Hiti for a drink!

Assorted Vishnu Temples

Behind the statue of the king are three smaller Vishnu temples. The small plastered shikhara temple was built in 1590 and is dedicated to Narsingha, Vishnu's man-lion incarnation. To one side is a small Narayan Temple and behind it another Vishnu Temple.

Hari Shankar Temple (16)

This three storey temple to Hari Shankar, half Vishnu/half Shiva, has roof struts carved with scenes of the tortures of the damned, a strange change from the erotic scenes on the Jagannarayan. It was built in 1704-05 by the daughter of King Yoganarendra Malla.

Taleju Bell (19)

Diagonally opposite the Taleju Temple (15) in the palace complex, the large bell, hung between two stout pillars, was erected by King Vishnu Malla in 1736. An earlier bell, erected in 1703, was moved to the Rato Machhendranath Temple at that time. Petitioners could ring the bell to alert the king to their grievances. Shop stalls are in the building under the bell platform, and behind it is a lotus shaped pool with a bridge over it.

Krishna Temple (23)

An attractive octagonal stone Krishna Temple, also known as the Chyasim Deval, completes the 'front line' of temples in the square. The stairway to the temple, which faces the palace's Sundari Chowk, is guarded by two stone lions. The temple was built by King Vishnu Malla in 1723 and, like the square's Krishna Mandir mentioned earlier, makes a clear contrast with the usual Nepalese pagoda temple designs.

Hari Shankar Temple

Krishna Temple

Bhai Dega Temple (18)

Behind the Krishna Temple stands the squat Bhai Dega, or Biseshvar, Temple dedicated to Shiva. It's a singularly unattractive temple although it is said to contain an impressive lingam. A few steps back from the square there's another stone shikhara temple, clearly owing inspiration to the important Krishna Mandir of the square. This same design pops up in several other temples around Patan. The popular Cafe de Patan is just behind this temple.

Bhai Dega Temple

ROYAL PALACE

Forming the whole eastern side of the Durbar Square is the Royal Palace of Patan. Parts of the palace were built in the 14th century, but the main period of construction was during the 17th and 18th centuries by Siddhinarsingh Malla, Srinivasa Malla and Vishnu Malla. The Patan Durbar Square palace predates the palaces of Kathmandu and Bhaktapur. It was severely damaged during the conquest of the valley by Prithvi Narayan Shah in 1768 and also by the great earthquake of 1934, but it remains one of the architectural highlights of the valley with a series of connecting courtyards and three Taleju temples dedicated to the valley's main deity, the goddess Taleju.

Mul Chowk (20) & the Taleju Temples

The central courtyard is the largest and oldest of the palace's three main *chowks*. Two stone lions guard the entrance to the courtyard which was built by Siddhinarsingh Malla, destroyed in a fire in 1662 and rebuilt by Srinivasa Malla in 1665-66. At the centre of the courtyard stands the small gilded Bidya Temple.

The palace's three Taleju temples stand around the courtyard. The doorway to the Shrine of Taleju or Taleju Bhawani, on the southern side of the courtyard, is flanked by the river goddesses Ganga on a tortoise and Jamuna on a mythical crocodile or *makara*.

The five storey Degutalle Temple, topped by its circular triple roofed tower, is on the north-eastern corner. The larger square triple roofed Taleju Temple is directly north, looking out over Durbar Square. It was built by Siddhinarsingh Malla in 1640, rebuilt after a fire and totally rebuilt after the earthquake of 1934 which completely demolished it. The goddess Taleju was the personal deity of the Malla kings from the 14th century, and Tantric rites were performed to her in this temple.

Taleju Bhawani Temple

Sundari Chowk (27) & Tusha Hiti

South of the larger Mul Chowk is the Sundari Chowk with its sunken tank known as the

Tusha Hiti. The superbly carved stonework in the tank depicts the eight Ashta Matrikas, the eight Bhairabs and the eight Nagas. The tank was originally built in about 1670 and restored in 1960. Above the bath stands a toy-size replica of the Krishna Mandir out in the main square.

The courtyard is surrounded by a three storey building with finely carved struts and windows. The entrance to the courtyard from the main square is guarded by stone statues of Hanuman, Ganesh and Vishnu as Narsingha, the man-lion. The gilded metal window over the entrance from the square is flanked by windows of carved ivory. Behind the Sundari Chowk, but unfortunately not open to the public, is the Royal Garden with a water tank known as the Kamal Pokhari.

Mani Keshar Chowk (11)

The northern courtyard is entered from the square by the Golden Gate, or Sun Dhoka. This is the newest part of the palace, its construction was completed in 1734. The courtyard is entered through a magnificent gilded door topped by a golden torana showing Shiva, Parvati, Ganesh and Kumar. Directly above the golden door is a golden window, at which the king would make public appearances.

There is another courtyard reached by a passage between the Mani Keshar Chowk and the Taleju Temple but this is not open to the public. It was used for dance and drama performances during the Malla period and one wall is decorated with erotic figures.

GOLDEN TEMPLE

Also known as the Hiranya Varna Mahavihar, the Kwa Bahal, or the Suwarna Mahavihara (Golden Temple), this unique Buddhist monastery is only a few minutes walk north of Durbar Square. Legends relate that the monastery was founded in the 12th century although the earliest record of its existence is 1409. From the street a sign points to the monastery which is entered through a doorway flanked by painted guardian lion figures. The simple entrance gives no hint of the magnificent structure in the courtyard within.

The large rectangular building has three roofs and a copper-gilded facade. Inside the shrine are images of the Buddha and Avalokitesvara and a stairway leads to the 1st floor where monks will show you the various Buddha images and frescoes which illustrate the walls. The life of the Buddha is illustrated in a frieze in front of the main shrine.

The inner courtyard has a railed off walkway around three sides. Leather shoes and other leather articles must be removed if you leave the walkway and enter the actual inner courtyard. In the centre of the courtyard is a small but very richly decorated three storey temple crowned by a golden roof with an extremely ornate *gajur* (a bell-shaped top). Look for the sacred tortoises who potter around in the courtyard, they are temple guardians. The monastery was dedicated by a Patan merchant, grown rich from the important trade with Tibet.

KUMBESHWAR TEMPLE

Directly north of Durbar Square is one of the valley's three five-storey temples. The others are the towering Nyatapola Temple of Bhaktapur and the smaller Panch Mukhi Hanuman of the old Royal Palace in Kathmandu.

The Kumbeshwar Temple dominates the streets around it and is said to date from 1392, when it was completed by Jayasthiti Malla, making it the oldest extant temple in Patan. The temple is noted for its fine proportions and elegant woodcarvings and there are numerous statues and sculptures around the courtyard dating from a number of Nepalese dynasties from the Licchavis to the Mallas. They include a particularly fine Ganesh figure and others of Ganesh and other Hindu deities. The temple is, however, dedicated to Shiva, as the large Nandi, or bull, facing the temple inside the main entrance indicates.

The temple platform has two ponds whose water is said to come straight from the holy lake at Gosainkund, a long trek north of the valley (see the Gosainkund trekking section in the Trekking chapter). An annual ritual bath in the Kumbeshwar Temple's tank is claimed to be as meritorious as making the arduous walk to Gosainkund.

South of the courtyard is an important Bhairab Temple with a life-size wooden image of the god. Also on the southern side of the Kumbeshwar Temple is the single storey Baglamukhi Temple where the goddess is represented by the small temple's gilded archway with its canopy of snakes. On the western side of the Kumbeshwar Temple courtyard is the large Konti Hiti tank, a popular gathering place for local women.

Thousands of pilgrims visit the temple during the Janai Purnima festival in July and August each year and worship the silver and gold lingam which is set up in the tank. It's a colourful occasion with bathers immersing themselves in the tank while members of the Brahmin and Chhetri castes replace the sacred thread they wear looped across their left shoulder. Jhankris (sorcerers) beating drums and wearing colourful headdresses and skirts dance around the temple to complete the dramatic scene.

Kumbeshwar Temple

UMA MAHESHWAR TEMPLE
There are a number of other interesting temples and bahals in this northern area of Patan. Returning from the Kumbeshwar Temple to Durbar Square the small and inconspicuous double roofed Uma Maheshwar Temple is set back from the road on its eastern side. Peer inside the temple where you will see (a light will help) a very beautiful black stone relief of Shiva and Parvati in the pose known as Uma Maheshwar – the god sitting cross legged with his shakti leaning against him rather seductively.

BISHWAKARMA TEMPLE
Walk south from Durbar Square through the Hauga area with its many brassware shops and workshops. There is a small bahal almost immediately on your right (west) and then a laneway also leading west. A short distance down this lane is the brick Bishwakarma Temple, with its entire facade covered in sheets of embossed copper. Directly above the doorway is what looks like a Star of David. The temple is dedicated to carpenters and craftworkers and, as if in proof, you can hear the steady clump and clang from metalworkers' hammers in nearby workshops.

Returning to the main road running south from Durbar Square you soon come to a chaitya shrine of Lakshmi Narayan on the

Bishwakarma Temple

eastern side of the road and the I Baha Bahil monastery on the western side. The monastery dates from 1427 but is now rather run-down and decrepit; part of it is being used as a school. A little further south is the old but recently restored Chakba Lunhiti tank with three water spouts.

RATO MACHHENDRANATH TEMPLE

Continue south from Durbar Square for a few more minutes walk to the Rato, or Red, Machhendranath Temple, on the western side of the road. Rato Machhendranath, the god of rain and plenty, comes in a variety of incarnations. To Buddhists he is the Tantric edition of Avalokitesvara while to Hindus he is another version of Shiva.

Standing in a large, spacious courtyard the three storey temple dates from 1673 although an earlier temple may have existed on the site since 1408. The temple's four elaborately carved doorways are each guarded by lion figures and at ground level on the four corners of the temple plinth are reliefs of a curious yeti-like creature. A diverse collection of animals including peacocks, horses, bulls, lions, elephants and fish top pillars facing the northern side of the temple; they are the Tibetan symbols for the months of the year. The metal roof is supported by struts each showing Avalokitesvara standing above figures being tortured in hell. Prayer wheels are set into the base of the temple.

The Machhendranath image is just a crudely carved piece of red-painted wood, but each year it is paraded around the town on a temple chariot during the Red Machhendranath celebrations. The complex celebration moves the image from place to place over a period of several weeks in the month of Baisakh (April-May) finally ending at Jawlakhel where the chariot is disassembled.

Occurring on a 12 year cycle (the next time will be in 1991) the procession continues out of Patan to the village of Bungamati, 5 km to the south. Dragging the heavy chariot along this bumpy and often uphill track is no easy feat. In the village the god has another temple and since 1593 it has been the custom for the image to spend 6 months each year residing in this temple, returning to Patan for the other 6 months. Usually the image is transferred back and forth on a palanquin.

Rato Machhendranath Temple

MINANATH TEMPLE

To the eastern side of the main road from Durbar Square is a two storey temple dedicated to a Buddhist Bodhisattva who is considered to be the brother of Rato Machhendranath. The Minanath image is also towed around town during the Rato Machhendranath chariot festival, but in a much smaller chariot. The temple originally dates from the Licchavi period but has undergone several recent restorations and 'improvements' and has roof struts carved with figures of multiarmed goddesses, all extraordinarily brightly painted. A large prayer wheel stands in a cage beside the temple.

MAHABOUDDHA TEMPLE

Despite its height, the Temple of the Thousand Buddhas, or Mahabouddha Temple, is not immediately visible as it is tightly surrounded by other buildings. This

Minanath Temple

shikhara-style temple is modelled after the original Mahabouddha Temple at Bodhgaya in India, where the Buddha gained enlightenment. At Pagan in Myanmar (formerly Burma) there's another Mahabouddha Temple, which is also a copy of the Bodhgaya original.

The temple takes its name from the terracotta tiles with which it is covered, each bearing an image of the Buddha. The temple is believed to have originally been built in 1585 although some sources suggest an earlier date. Whatever its first construction, it suffered severe damage in the 1934 earthquake and was completely rebuilt. Unfortunately, without plans to work from, the rebuilders ended up with a rather different looking Mahabouddha Temple and there were enough bricks left over to construct a smaller shikhara shrine to Maya Devi, the Buddha's mother. It stands to the south-west of the main shikhara.

The Mahabouddha Temple is about 10 minutes walk south-west of Durbar Square. An arrow signpost points down a lane full of curio shops leading to the temple, but if you have trouble finding it simply ask directions. The roof terrace of the shops at the back of the courtyard gives you a good view of the temple.

Mahabouddha Temple

RUDRA VARNA MAHAVIHARA

Also known as Uku Bahal, this Buddhist monastery near the Mahabouddha Temple is one of the best known in Patan. A large rectangular structure with two storey gilded roofs encloses a courtyard absolutely packed with interesting bits and pieces. There are dorjes, bells, banners, peacocks, elephants, Garudas, rampant goats, kneeling devotees and a regal looking statue of a Rana general. The lions are particularly curious – apart from regular Nepalese ones, seated on pillars with one paw raised in salute, there are also a couple of decidedly British appearance, looking as if they should be guarding a statue of Queen Victoria in her 'not amused' incarnation rather than a colourful Nepalese monastery.

As you enter the courtyard look for the exceptionally finely carved wooden struts on the right. They are said to be amongst the oldest of this type in the valley and prior to a recent restoration they were actually behind the monastery but were moved to this safer location inside the courtyard. The monastery in its present form is probably 19th century but certain features and the actual site are much older.

HAKA BAHAL

Take the road west from the southern end of the Durbar Square, past the Cafe de Patan, and you soon come to the Haka Bahal, a typical rectangular building with internal courtyard. Traditionally Patan's living goddess, or kumari, is a daughter of one of the priests of this monastery.

ASHOKAN STUPAS

The four stupas marking the boundaries of Patan are said to have been built when the great Buddhist emperor Ashoka visited the valley 2500 years ago. Although remains of all four can still be seen today they probably bear little similarity to the original stupas. The Northern Stupa is just beyond the Kumbeshwar Temple, not far from the Durbar Square. It's well preserved and whitewashed. The other three are all grassed over. The Southern, or Lagan, Stupa is just south of the bus stand and is the largest of the four. The smaller Western, or Pulchok, Stupa is beside the main road from Kathmandu through to Jawlakhel and directly opposite the Narayani Hotel. Finally, and most remote, the small Eastern, or Teta, Stupa is well to the east of centre, across the Ring Rd and just beyond a small river.

ZOO

Nepal's only zoo is in the southern part of Patan, just north of Jawlakhel. Admission is only Rs 0.50 and it has rhinos, tigers and other varieties of Himalayan and Terai wildlife. This is, however, another depressing and miserable Third World zoo and the saddest thing you can say about it is that there are many others which are even worse.

JAWLAKHEL

The 'Tibetan refugee camp' is no longer really a camp at all. Today it's simply the area of Patan where the refugees from Tibet first settled. It is, however, a great place to see and buy carpets, rugs and other Tibetan crafts. If you go to Lhasa in Tibet the genuine Tibetan carpets on sale there may well have come from Jawlakhel, as the craft has pretty well disappeared in Tibet itself.

KOTESHWAR MAHADEV TEMPLE

Actually outside the Patan city limits, the important temple of Koteshwar Mahadev is just north of the confluence of the Manohara and Hanumante rivers, which in turn shortly joins the Bagmati River. Mahadev means 'great god', the usual term for Shiva, but Koteshwar can also be translated as 'millions of gods' so this is a temple of Shiva with many faces, a particularly powerful form of Lord Shiva. The shrine's Shiva lingam is said to date from the 8th century.

A little south of the temple is the Kuti Bahal where travellers bound for Tibet were customarily farewelled. The monastery has a 15th century chaitya.

PLACES TO STAY

Kathmandu and Patan are virtually continuous these days and the accommodation in Patan is covered in the main Kathmandu Places to Stay section on page 150. Apart from Nepal's only youth hostel the accommodation in Patan consists of middle range and top end places. It would be interesting to have some small guest houses close to the Durbar Square area, like those which have sprung up in Bhaktapur. Some overseas aid agencies are in Patan, particularly around Jawlakhel, and many long-term foreign residents of Nepal live here.

PLACES TO EAT

Patan could do with a few more good places to eat. Just a few steps from the south-western corner of Patan's Durbar Square the small *Cafe de Patan* has a pleasant little open air dining area and is a good place for a drink, snack or even a meal close to the centre of things in Patan. It turns out a superb lassi and the addition of a new 1st floor area may ease the lunch time crush. See the following

Things to Buy section about the music you hear with your meal.

Other than the Cafe de Patan there's really nowhere to eat in the centre. Near the zoo roundabout at Jawlakhel the *German Bakery* does cakes, pastries, cold drinks and sandwiches. Across the road is the rather basic *Blue Fox Tiffin Room*. At the city gate, by the Patan bus halt, the *RM Momo Restaurant*, the *Cake & Coffee Corner*, the *Dorje Restaurant* and the *Yeti Restaurant* are other rather basic possibilities.

THINGS TO BUY
Patan has many small handicraft shops and for certain crafts it is the best place in the valley.

Metalwork
Patan is the centre for bronze casting and other metalwork. The statues you see on sale in Kathmandu will most probably have been made in Patan and there are a number of excellent metalwork shops just north of Durbar Square. They have fine images of Buddha, the Green and White Taras and other figures from the Tantric Buddhist pantheon. Good quality gold plated and painted bronze figures will cost Rs 2000 to Rs 5000 for smaller ones, up beyond Rs 10,000 for large images.

Paintings
Immediately north of the square, just beyond the Bhimsen Temple, are a number of interesting shops selling paintings. The Arjun Art Gallery has Sherpa-style naive art paintings rather like the Balinese 'young artist' paintings from Indonesia. It's clearly something developed for the tourist trade but never mind, they're nicely done and you can have all of the Kathmandu Valley, or even all of Nepal, in one painting. Prices range from around Rs 1500 to Rs 3000.

A couple of doors down is the Madhu Chandra Art Gallery which has excellent paintings of Nepalese birds by C B Singh. The prices range from Rs 150 or Rs 200 and up. The B B Thapa Gallery in Jawlakhel also has interesting artwork.

Other Items
The Tibetan Jawlakhel area in the south of Patan is the place for Tibetan crafts and carpets. There is a string of carpet shops as you enter Jawlakhel.

A pleasant attraction at the popular Cafe de Patan near Durbar Square is the selection of Indian, Nepalese and Himalayan music played on cassette tapes while you eat. The tapes are sold by the adjoining shop and typically cost around Rs 125 so if you like the music you hear with your meal you can take it away with you.

GETTING THERE & AWAY
You can easily get to Patan from Kathmandu whether it be by bicycle, taxi, bus or tempo. It's an easy 5 km ride from Thamel to Patan's Durbar Square. The same trip will cost around Rs 30 if the taxi uses a meter.

Buses leave regularly from Ratna Park (Bus Stop 4) and cost Rs 1.50. They drop you at the Patan Gate, a short walk from the Durbar Square. There are also tempos operating from the main post office as soon as they have six passengers.

Bhaktapur

Bhaktapur, also known as Bhadgaon (pronounced bat-gown) or the City of Devotees, is the third major town of the valley and in many ways the most mediaeval. Since the major West German-funded Bhaktapur Development Project in the 1970s, it has been a much cleaner and tidier town, but there's still a distinctly timeless air to the place. The project not only restored buildings and paved dirt streets but also brought sewerage facilities.

The oldest part of the town is around the Tachupal Tole, or Dattatraya Square, to the east of the town. Bhaktapur was the capital of the whole valley during the 14th to 16th centuries and during that time the focus of the town shifted west, to the Durbar Square area. Much of the town's great architecture dates from the end of the 17th century during the rule of King Bhupatindra Malla.

Malla Kings

As in Kathmandu and Patan the town's important buildings date from the Malla period. Notable Malla kings of Bhaktapur include:

Yaksha Malla	1428-1482
Raya Malla	1482-1505
Eksha Mal Malla	1505-1568
Jagat Jyoti Malla	1613-1637
Jagat Prakash Malla	1644-1673
Jitamitra Malla	1673-1696
Bhupatindra Malla	1696-1722
Jaya Ranjit Malla	1722-1769

Ranjit Malla enjoyed a relationship with King Prithvi Narayan Shah which saved his city from destruction and also resulted in the deposed Malla kings of Kathmandu and Patan taking shelter here.

INFORMATION & ORIENTATION

Bhaktapur rises up on the northern bank of the Hanumante River. Although you can drive through Bhaktapur thankfully most cars don't. It's basically a pedestrian's city and much better for it. Minibuses and usually taxis as well stop at the Navpokhu Pokhari on the western edge of town. If you come to Bhaktapur by trolley bus the halt is on the main road bypassing Bhaktapur, a 10 to 15 minute walk south of Taumadhi Tole.

For the visitor Bhaktapur is really a town of one curving road, punctuated by squares. From the bus and taxi halt you come first to the Durbar Square, then Taumadhi Tole with the famous five storey Nyatapola Temple, then to Tachupal Tole, or Dattatraya Square. Keep walking in that direction and you'll eventually reach Nagarkot, high up on the edge of the valley.

Bhaktapur has several cheap guest houses around the centre of town and it's a fascinating place to stay overnight. There's a tourist information counter in Durbar Square.

NAVPOKHU POKHARI INTO TOWN

Approaching Bhaktapur the road skirts the open field known as the Tundikhel and the Siddha Pokhari tank. From the large Navpokhu Pokhari tank you simply follow the road a few hundred metres to the Durbar Square. If you're staying overnight in

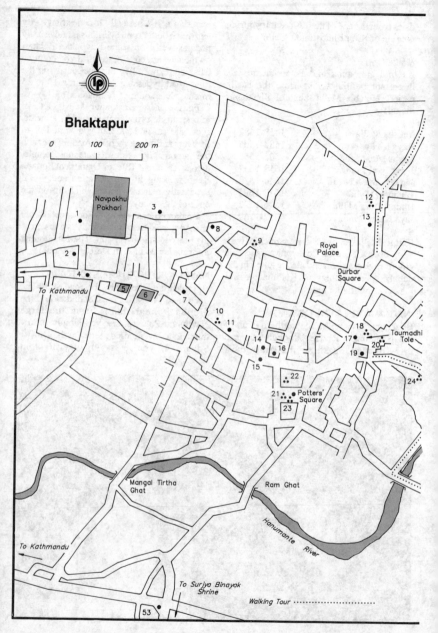

Bhaktapur

0   100   200 m

Navpokhu Pokhari

1
2
3
4
5
6
7
8
9
10
11
12
13
14
15
16
17
18
19
20
21
22
23
24

To Kathmandu

Royal Palace

Durbar Square

Taumadhi Tole

Potters' Square

Mangal Tirtha Ghat

Ram Ghat

Hanumante River

To Kathmandu

To Suriya Binayak Shrine

Walking Tour ·······················

53

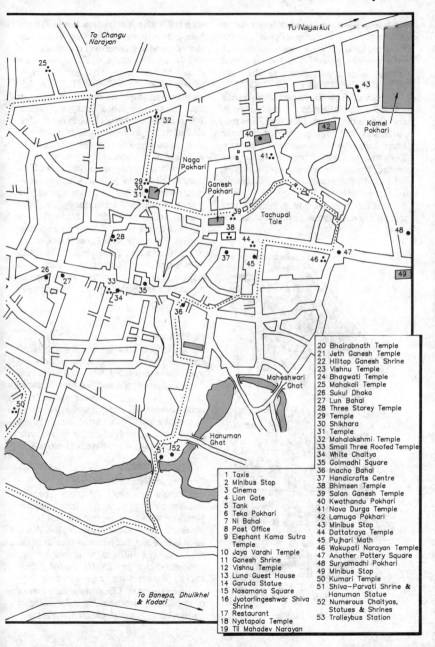

To Changu Narayan

To Nagarkot

Kamel Pokhari

Naga Pokhari

Ganesh Pokhari

Tachupal Tole

Maheshwari Ghat

Hanuman Ghat

To Banepa, Dhulikhel & Kodari

1 Taxis
2 Minibus Stop
3 Cinema
4 Lion Gate
5 Tank
6 Teka Pokhari
7 Ni Bahal
8 Post Office
9 Elephant Kama Sutra Temple
10 Jaya Varahi Temple
11 Ganesh Shrine
12 Vishnu Temple
13 Luna Guest House
14 Garuda Statue
15 Nasamana Square
16 Jyotorlingeshwar Shiva Shrine
17 Restaurant
18 Nyatapola Temple
19 Til Mahadev Narayan

20 Bhairabnath Temple
21 Jeth Ganesh Temple
22 Hilltop Ganesh Shrine
23 Vishnu Temple
24 Bhagwati Temple
25 Mahakali Temple
26 Sukul Dhoka
27 Lun Bahal
28 Three Storey Temple
29 Temple
30 Shikhara
31 Temple
32 Mahalakshmi Temple
33 Small Three Roofed Temple
34 White Chaitya
35 Golmadhi Square
36 Inacho Bahal
37 Handicrafts Centre
38 Bhimsen Temple
39 Salan Ganesh Temple
40 Kwathandu Pokhari
41 Nava Durga Temple
42 Lamuga Pokhari
43 Minibus Stop
44 Dattatraya Temple
45 Pujhari Math
46 Wakupati Narayan Temple
47 Another Pottery Square
48 Suryamadhi Pokhari
49 Minibus Stop
50 Kumari Temple
51 Shiva–Parvati Shrine & Hanuman Statue
52 Numerous Chaityas, Statues & Shrines
53 Trolleybus Station

Bhaktapur you'll want to get into town as quickly as possible to drop off your bags, but if not the southern route into town is much more interesting since it is the main road through Bhaktapur connecting Taumadhi Tole and Tachupal Tole.

Turn south from the corner of Navpokhu Pokhari and then left on the road, immediately before the town's Lion Gate. You pass a small tank on your right and then the much larger Teka Pokhari. Just before the next major road junction, to your left, is the constricted, tunnel-like entrance to the tiny Ni Bahal, dedicated to the Maitraya Buddha, the Buddha yet to come.

Cross the junction, where the road runs downhill to the Mangal Tirtha Ghat, and on

your left is the red brick Jaya Varahi Temple, jutting into the street. There are elaborately carved wooden toranas over the central door and the window above it. The upper torana shows Vishnu in his boar incarnation, to whom the temple is dedicated. At the right end of the temple is the entrance to the upper floor, flanked by stone lions and banners. The ornate windows include two, on either side of the upper torana, which at one time were coloured gold and some traces remain.

A few more steps brings you to a small Ganesh shrine jutting out into the street. Continue to Nasamana Square, which is somewhat decrepit but has a Garuda statue without a temple. Almost immediately there's a second square with the Jyotirlingeshwar Shiva shikhara which houses an important lingam. Behind the shrine is an attractive hiti, one of the sunken water conduits of which there are so many in Bhaktapur. A few more steps brings you to the turn-off to Potters' Square while a little further on you come to Taumadhi Tole.

DURBAR SQUARE

Bhaktapur's Durbar Square is much larger and more spacious than Kathmandu's and much less crowded with temples than Patan's. It wasn't planned that way: Victorian illustrations show the square packed with temples and buildings, but the disastrous earthquake of 1934 destroyed many of them and today empty plinths show where some of them once stood and have not been rebuilt.

The Erotic Elephants Temple (2)

Just before you enter the square, coming from the bus stop, pause for a little bit of wry Nepalese humour. On your left just before the entranceway to the square is a hiti. A few steps before that, but on the south side of the road, perhaps 100 metres before the entranceway, is a tiny double roofed Shiva-Parvati Temple with some erotic carvings on its temple struts. One of these shows a pair of copulating elephants. In the missionary position! It's a hathi (elephant) Kama Sutra.

Jaya Varahi Temple

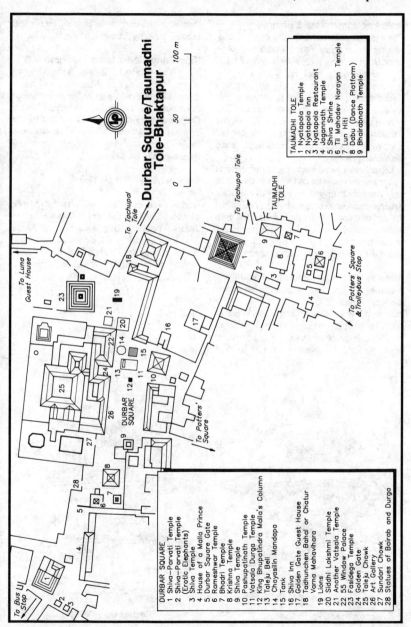

**Durbar Square/Taumadhi
Tole-Bhaktapur**

0   50   100 m

TAUMADHI TOLE
1 Nyatapola Temple
2 Nyatapola Inn
3 Nyatapola Restaurant
4 Jagannath Temple
5 Shiva Shrine
6 Til Mahadev Narayan Temple
7 Lun Hiti
8 Dabu (Dance Platform)
9 Bhairabnath Temple

DURBAR SQUARE
1 Shiva-Parvati Temple
2 Shiva-Parvati Temple
   (Erotic Elephants)
3 Shiva Temple
4 House of a Malla Prince
5 Durbar Square Gate
6 Rameshwar Temple
7 Bhadri Temple
8 Krishna Temple
9 Shiva Temple
10 Pashupatinath Temple
11 Vatsala Durga Temple
12 King Bhupatindra Malla's Column
13 Taleju Bell
14 Choyoslin Mandapa
15 Tank
16 Shiva Inn
17 Golden Gate Guest House
18 Tadhunchen Bahal or Chatur
   Varna Mahavihara
19 Lions
20 Siddhi Lakshmi Temple
21 Another Vatsala Temple
22 55 Window Palace
23 Fasidega Temple
24 Golden Gate
25 Taleju Chowk
26 Art Gallery
27 Sundari Chowk
28 Statues of Bairab and Durga

Statue of Ugrachandi & Bhairab

The square is entered from the western end, passing by an entry gate (5) with two large stone lions built by King Bhupatindra Malla. On the northern wall are statues of the terrible Bhairab and the equally terrible Ugrachandi, or Durga, the fearsome manifestation of Shiva's consort Parvati. The statues date from 1701 and it's said that the unfortunate sculptor had his hands cut off afterwards, to prevent him from duplicating his masterpieces.

Ugrachandi has 18 arms holding various weapons and symbols and she is in the act of very casually killing a demon with a trident. Bhairab has to make do with just 12 arms but the god and goddess are both garlanded with necklaces of human heads! The gates and courtyard which these powerful figures guard are of no particular importance.

Temples at Western End of the Square

A number of less significant temples crowd the western end of the Durbar Square. They include the Rameshwar Temple (6) to Shiva and the Bhadri Temple (7) to Vishnu as Narayan. In front of them is an impressive larger Krishna Temple (8) and just beyond that is a shikhara-style Shiva Temple (9) erected by King Jitamitra Malla in 1674.

King Bhupatindra Malla's Column (12)

King Bhupatindra Malla was the best known of the Malla kings of Bhaktapur and had a great influence on the art and architecture of the town. Like the similar column in Patan's Durbar Square this one was a copy of the original in Kathmandu. The king sits with folded arms, studying the magnificent entrance gate to his palace.

Vatsala Durga Temple (11) & Taleju Bell (13)

Beside the king's statue and directly in front of the palace is the stone Vatsala Durga Temple, built by King Jagat Prakash Malla in 1672. The shikhara-style temple has some similarities to the Krishna Mandir in Patan. In front of the temple is the large Taleju Bell

Krishna Temple

Vatsala Durga Temple

which was erected by King Ranjit Malla in 1737 to call the faithful to prayer at the Taleju Temple.

A second, smaller bell stands on the temple's base plinth and is popularly known as the 'barking bell'. It was erected by King Bhupatindra Malla in 1721, supposedly to counteract a vision he had in a dream, and to this day dogs are said to bark and whine if the bell is rung.

Chyasilin Mandapa (14)
Beside the Vatsala Durga Temple is an attractive tank (15) and in front of that will soon be the Chyasilin Mandapa. This octagonal temple was one of the finest in the square until it was destroyed by the 1934 earthquake. Using some of the temple's original components it is being totally rebuilt and should be completed by the time you read this.

Pashupatinath Temple

Siddhi Lakshmi Temple (20)
By the south-eastern corner of the palace stands the stone Siddhi Lakshmi Temple. The steps up to the temple are flanked by male and female attendants each leading a

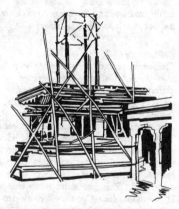

Chyasilin Mandapa

Pashupatinath Temple (10)
Behind the Vatsala Durga Temple is the Pashupatinath Temple, dedicated to Shiva as Pashupati. The temple dates from the 17th century and is a replica of the main shrine at Pashupatinath. It's notable for the erotic carvings on the roof struts which show some exhausting looking positions.

Siddhi Lakshmi Temple

rather reluctant child and a rather eager looking dog. On successive levels the stairs are flanked by horses, rhinos, man-lions and camels. The 17th century temple marks the dividing line between the main Durbar Square and its secondary part, at the eastern end of the Royal Palace. Behind the temple is another Vatsala Temple (21) while to one side of it are two rather lost looking large stone lions (19), standing by themselves out in the middle of the square.

Fasidega Temple (23)

The large, white, rather ugly Fasidega Temple is dedicated to Shiva and stands in the centre of the secondary part of the Durbar Square. There are various viewpoints around the valley – the Changunarayan Temple is one of them – from where you can study Bhaktapur at a distance. In each case the white bulk of the Fasidega is always an easy landmark to pick out. The temple sits on a six level plinth with elephant guardians at the bottom of the steps, lions and cows above them.

Fasidega Temple

Tadhunchen Bahal or
Chatur Varna Mahavihara (18)

The southern and eastern side of the secondary part of the square is made up of double storey *dharamsalas* (rest houses for pilgrims) now used as shops. As you enter the street leading east from the square the Tadhunchen Bahal is an ancient looking monastery on the southern side. In the inner courtyard the roof struts on the eastern side have some highly unusual carvings showing the tortures of the damned. In one a snake is wrapped around a man, another shows two rams butting an unfortunate's head from opposite sides while a third strut shows a nasty tooth extraction being performed with a large pair of pliers! The monastery dates from the 15th century.

ROYAL PALACE

Bhaktapur's Royal Palace was founded by Yaksha Malla and added to by successive kings, particularly Bhupatindra Malla. As with the old palaces of Kathmandu and Patan, you are very restricted as to how far you can go within the palace, but only seven courtyards remain of the 99 the palace was once claimed to have. Unfortunately the palace suffered great damage in the 1934 earthquake and its subsequent reconstruction did not match its original artistry.

Art Gallery (26)

The western end of the palace has been made into an Art Gallery. The entrance to the gallery is flanked by figures of Hanuman the monkey god and Vishnu as Narsingha, his man-lion incarnation. These guardian figures date from 1698 and Hanuman appears in Tantric form as the four armed Hanuman-Bhairab. The gallery has a fine collection of Hindu and Buddhist paintings, palm leaf manuscripts, thangkas and metal, stone and wood crafts. This part of the palace was once known as the Malati Chowk. Admission to the gallery is Rs 5 and it is open from 10.30 am to 4 pm daily except Tuesdays.

Golden Gate (24) &
55 Window Palace (22)

Adjoining the gallery the magnificent Golden Gate, or Sun Dhoka, is the entrance way to the 55 Window Palace. The Golden Gate is generally agreed to be the single most important piece of art in the whole valley. The gate and palace were built by King

Hanuman-Bhairab

TAUMADHI TOLE
A short street, lined with tourist shops, leads downhill from behind the Pashupatinath Temple in Durbar Square to the second great square of Bhaktapur, the Taumadhi Tole. Here you find the highest temple in the valley and also Cafe Nyatapola whose balconies provide a great view over the square. The building was renovated for its new purpose in 1977 and even has some finely carved roof struts with erotic themes.

Nyatapola Temple (1)
The five storey, 30 metre high Nyatapola Temple is not only the highest temple in the whole Kathmandu Valley, but also one of the best examples of traditional Nepalese temple architecture. The towering temple is visible from Durbar Square, but some of the finest views of the temple are from further away. If you take the road running out of the valley to Banepa and Dhulikhel or walk up towards the Surjya Binayak Temple south of Bhaktapur you can see the temple soaring up above the other buildings with the hills at the edge of the valley as a background behind.

The temple was built during the reign of King Bhupatindra Malla in 1702 and its design was so elegant and its construction so well done that the 1934 earthquake, which completely destroyed many buildings throughout the valley, only caused minor damage. The stairway leading up to the temple is flanked by guardian figures at each plinth level. The bottom plinth has the legendary wrestlers Jayamel and Phattu, said to have the strength of 10 normal men. On the plinths above are two elephants, then two lions, two griffins and finally two goddesses, Baghini in the form of a tiger and Singhini in the form of a lion. Each figure is said to be 10 times as strong as the figure on the level below and presiding over all of them, but hidden away inside the temple is the mysterious Tantric goddess Siddhi Lakshmi to whom the temple is dedicated.

Only the temple's priests can see the image of the goddess, but the temple's 108 carved and painted roof struts depict her in her various forms. Various legends and tales

Bhupatindra Malla but not completed until 1754 during the reign of Jaya Ranjit Malla.

A Garuda, the vehicle of Vishnu, tops the gate and is shown disposing of a number of serpents, the Garuda's sworn enemies. The four headed and 16 armed figure of the goddess Taleju Bhawani is below the Garuda and directly over the door. She is the family deity of the Malla dynasty and there are temples to her in the royal palaces in Kathmandu, Patan and Bhaktapur.

The Golden Gate opens to the inner courtyards of the palace. First you enter a small entrance courtyard then the larger Mul Chowk which leads round to the Taleju Chowk entrance. Unfortunately you cannot enter Taleju Chowk and a military guard ensures you don't try. The guard will, however, invite you to peer in from the doorway. Beyond Taleju Chowk is Kumari Chowk and Sundari Chowk (27) with its bathing tank, the Kamal Pokhari.

relate to the temple and its enigmatic inhabitant. One is that she maintains a balance with the powers of the terrifying Bhairab, comfortably ensconced in his own temple just across the square.

Bhairabnath Temple (9)

The triple roofed Bhairabnath Temple (also known as the Kasi Vishwanath or Akash Bhairab) has an unusual rectangular plan and has had a somewhat chequered history. It was originally built as a one storey temple in the early 17th century but rebuilt with two storeys by King Bhupatindra Malla in 1717. The 1934 earthquake caused great damage to the temple and it was completely rebuilt and the 3rd floor added.

Casually stacked beside the temple you can see the enormous wheels and other parts of the temple chariot on which the image of Bhairab is conveyed around town during the Bisket festival. Curiously, despite Bhairab's fearsome powers and his massive temple, his image is only about 30 cm high! A small hole in the central door is used to push offerings into the temple's interior, but the actual entrance to the Bhairabnath Temple is through the small Betal Temple, behind the main temple. The temple is guarded by two brass lions and there's a host of interesting details on the front.

Til Mahadev Narayan Temple (6)

It's easy to miss the square's third interesting temple. The Til Mahadev Narayan Temple is hidden away behind the buildings on the southern side of the square. You can enter the temple's courtyard through a narrow entrance through those buildings or through an arched entrance facing west, just to the south of the square.

This double roofed Vishnu temple has a Garuda kneeling on a high pillar in front, flanked by pillars bearing Vishnu's conch and chakra symbols. Some of the temple's struts also have Garudas. A lingam in a yoni stands in a wooden cage in front and to one side of the temple. Despite the temple's neglected setting it is actually an important place of pilgrimage and one of the oldest temple sites in the town: an inscription indicates that the site has been in use since 1080. Another inscription states that the image of Til Mahadev installed inside the temple dates from 1170.

Til Mahadev Narayan Temple

POTTERS' SQUARE

Potters' Square can be approached from Durbar Square, Taumadhi Tole or along the southern road into town from Siddha Pokhari and Navpokhu Pokhari. You also pass right by the square when walking into town from the trolley bus stop.

Bhairabnath Temple

On the northern side of the square a small hillock is topped by a Ganesh shrine and a shady pipal tree. There are fine views from here over the river to the hills south of Bhaktapur. The square itself has two small temples, a solid brick Vishnu Temple and the double roofed Jeth Ganesh Temple. The latter is an indicator how long the activity all around the square has been going on – the temple was donated by a wealthy potter in 1646 and to this day its priest is a potter. Pottery is very clearly what this square is all about. Under shady open verandahs or tin-roofed sheds all around the square potters' wheels spin and clay is thrown. In the square itself literally thousands of finished pots sit out in the sun to dry, and stalls around the square and between the square and Taumadhi Tole sell them.

TAUMADHI TOLE TO TACHUPAL TOLE

The curving main road through Bhaktapur runs from beside the Bhairabnath Temple in Taumadhi Tole to Tachupal Tole, the old centre of town. The first stretch of the street is a busy shopping thoroughfare with a constant hum of activity and everything from brass pots to video cassettes, from porters' tumplines (the leather or cloth strips across the forehead or chest used to support a load carried on the back) to tourists' mineral water, on sale.

As the road makes its first bend there are two interesting old buildings on the right-hand (southern) side. The Sukul Dhoka is a *math*, a priest's house, and has superb wood-carving both outside on its facade and inside in the courtyard. Almost next door is the Lun Bahal which was originally a Buddhist monastery, built in the 16th century, but with the addition of a stone statue of Bhimsen it was converted into a Hindu shrine. If you look into the sanctum, in the inner courtyard, you can see the statue, dating from 1592, complete with a ferocious-looking brass mask.

A little further along, the road opens into the Golmadhi Square with a deep hiti, the small triple roofed Golmadhi Ganesh Temple and adjacent to it a white chaitya. Another short stretch of road brings you to another small open area with a *path* or pilgrim's shelter on your right, behind it is a tank and the Inacho Bahal, described in the Circular Walk section. A few more steps brings you into Tachupal Tole.

TACHUPAL TOLE

It's only about 10 minutes walk from the temple of Nyatapola to the square containing the Dattatraya Temple and the Pujari Math monastery. Today you stroll down a well paved street, a result of the major 'renovation' Bhaktapur underwent in the late '70s. These new-looking brick-paved streets are a real contrast to some of the muddy, potholed alleys which you can still find in the back blocks of town. South from this square a maze of narrow laneways, passageways and courtyards run down to the ghats on the river. Tachupal Tole, also called Dattatraya Square, was probably the original central square of Bhaktapur so this is the oldest part of the town.

Dattatraya Temple

This tall, square temple was originally built in 1427 but alterations were made in 1458. Like some other important structures in the valley it was said to have been built using the timber from a single tree. The temple is dedicated to Dattatraya although the Garuda-topped pillar and the traditional weapons of

Dattatraya Temple

Vishnu indicate that Dattatraya is actually another of Vishnu's many incarnations. He is also said to have been Shiva's teacher and is even claimed to have been a cousin of the Buddha so the temple is important to Shaivites, Vishnaivites and Buddhists.

The three storey temple is raised well above the ground on its base, around which are carved some erotic scenes. The front section, which was a later addition to the temple, stands almost separate and the temple entrance is guarded by the same two Malla wrestlers who watch over the first plinth of the Nyatapola Temple.

Bhimsen Temple

At the other end of the square is the two storey Bhimsen Temple, variously dated as 1605, 1645 or 1655. The temple is squat, rectangular and open on the ground floor. It's fronted by a platform with a small double roofed Vishnu temple and a pillar topped by a brass lion. Behind it is the deeply sunken and rather pretty Bhimsen Pokhari.

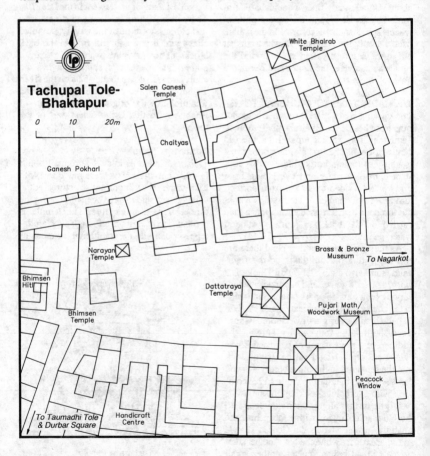

Tachupal Tole- Bhaktapur

Bhimsen Temple

Pujari Math & Museums

There are 10 buildings around the square which were originally used as *maths* or accommodation for monastic priests. The best known of these *maths* was the Pujari Math, which has been restored by the same West German aid project which has done so much work in Bhaktapur. The Pujari Math was originally constructed in the 15th century during the reign of King Yaksha Malla, but restored in 1763. Until this century an annual caravan brought tributes to the monastery from Tibet.

The Pujari Math is principally famed for the superb peacock window, in the small alley alongside the monastery, on its left-hand side if you face it from the square. The window is reputed to be the finest carved window in the valley and is the subject of countless postcards and photographs. There are some extraordinarily rich woodcarvings inside the building's courtyard.

The building now houses a Woodcarving Museum which is open from 10 am to 5 pm daily except Friday when it closes at 3 pm and Tuesday when it is closed all day. Admission is Rs 5 plus Rs 10 to use a camera. The museum has some fine examples of the woodcarving that Bhaktapur, and indeed the whole Kathmandu Valley, has long been famous for. Directly across the square from the Pujari Math is the Brass & Bronze Museum with fine examples of metalwork

from the valley. It's open for the same hours and days and at the same admission price. At the other end of the square, near the Bhimsen Temple, is a Handicrafts Centre selling woodcarvings and other examples of Bhaktapur crafts.

Salan Ganesh Temple

Just north of Tachupal Tole is another open area with the small Salan Ganesh Temple, dating from 1654. The open temple is ornately decorated, but the image is just a rock with only the vaguest elephant head shape. To one side of the temple is the Ganesh Pokhari, a large tank.

A CIRCULAR WALK

Bhaktapur is a fascinating town to wander in and the lack of traffic makes walking a real pleasure, particularly in comparison to Kathmandu where walking would be so much more enjoyable without motor vehicles to dodge. This circular walk takes you by a number of interesting temples and shrines, but in Bhaktapur it's simply observing the timeless and seemingly unchanging rituals of life which is most interesting. Look for grains laid out to dry in the sun, people collecting water or washing under the communal taps, dyed yarns hung out to dry, children's games, fascinating shops, potters at work or women pounding grain, there's plenty to see. Most of all it's Bhaktapur's mediaeval atmosphere which is so totally entrancing.

The North of Town

Starting from the north-eastern corner of Durbar Square walk to the east of the high Fasidega Temple, following the sign to the Luna Guest House, pass the guest house and a little further up the road a walled in Vishnu temple. Cross the junction and walk uphill past a large tank surrounded by fine old houses. Turn right towards Nagarkot and you soon come to the Mahakali Temple, where the shrine tops a small hill and is reached by a steep flight of steps.

Just beyond this temple turn right, walk downhill and then turn left and continue until you reach the tiny, open double roofed

Mahalakshmi Temple. Turn right (south) here and continue down to another large tank, the Snake or Naga Pokhari. Bhaktapur has an amazing number of water tanks (known as *pokhari*), none of them looking particularly appetising! Here the green water contrasts nicely with the dyed yarns hung out to dry alongside the tank. On the western side of the tank two temples flank a central white shikhara while a cobra rears up from a small island in the middle of the tank.

Nava Durga Temple

Turn left around the tank, continue to a second tank and then to the Salan Ganesh Temple, described in the Tachupal Tole section. A little further on take a short detour north to the Nava Durga Temple. This Tantric temple is said to be the site for strange sacrificial rites. The golden door is surmounted by a golden window and is guarded by metal lions. It all contrasts nicely with the red-painted brick frontage. There's another large tank, the Quathandau Pokhari, just north of the temple.

Nava Durga Temple

Wakupati Narayan Temple

Back on the route you soon come back to the main east-west road which runs through Taumadhi Tole and Tachupal Tole. Around this area there are more potters at work. Turn right (west) and immediately on your left is the entrance to the Wakupati Narayan Temple. The ornate, golden temple is double roofed and is fronted by a line-up of no less than four Garudas!

Wakupati Narayan Temple

The South of Town

Continue on to Tachupal Tole and turn left down the side of the Pujari Math; directions to its famous peacock window are well signposted. Jog right, left, right and left again then immediately on your left is the ornate little Inacho Bahal with prayer wheels, Buddha figures and a strange miniature pagoda roof rising up on a pillar above the courtyard.

The Riverside Ghats

From here the road drops down to the Hanumante River, leaving urban surroundings for rural ones and passing by a curious collection of shrines, chaityas, statues and lingams, including a bas-relief of a well endowed nude Lord Shiva. Just to the left of the bridge on the Hanuman Ghat is a shrine with a bas-relief of Rama and Sita, guarded by a statue of their faithful ally Hanuman. On the nearby building are four paintings including one showing Hanuman returning to Rama from his Himalayan medicinal herb foray, clutching a whole mountain in his hand. It's said that he paused here for a rest.

Cross the bridge and then take a hairpin turn back from the road onto a pleasant paved footpath. This rural stroll ends by another temple complex where you cross the river by the Chuping Ghat. Here, as at the Hanuman Ghat or the Ram Ghat by the bridge to the trolley bus stop, there are areas for ritual bathing and cremations.

The Bisket Festival

Above the river is the open area of Khalna Tole, the centre for the spectacular activities during the annual mid-April Bisket Festival. Bhairab's huge triple roofed chariot is assembled from the parts scattered beside the Bhairabnath Temple and behind the Nyatapola Temple in Taumadhi Tole. The chariot is hauled here with Betal, his sidekick from the tiny temple behind the Bhairabnath Temple, riding out front like a ship's figurehead while Bhadrakali, his consort, accompanies them in her own chariot. The images of the gods shelter in the octagonal *path* during the festival and a towering 25 metre high lingam is erected in the stone yoni base. Bisket ends and the Nepalese New Year starts when the lingam is taken down. Bhairab and Betal return to Taumadhi Tole while Bhadrakali goes back to her shrine by the river.

The circular walk ends with the gentle climb back into the town, emerging at the southern side of Taumadhi Tole.

SURJYA BINAYAK TEMPLE

About a km out of town this 17th century Ganesh temple is said to be a good place to visit if you're worried about your children being late speakers! It's also popular with Nepalese marriage parties. To get there take the road down past the Potters' Square to Ram Ghat, cross the river and continue to the main road by the trolley bus stop. The road continues across the other side and rises gently uphill with some fine views back over the rice paddies to Bhaktapur.

Where the road turns sharp right, a steep stairway climbs up to the temple, on a forested hilltop. As you step inside the temple enclosure the very realistic looking longtailed rat, sitting on top of a tall pillar, immediately indicates that this temple belongs to Ganesh. The image of the god sits in an enclosure in the bottom of a shikhara and there's a second golden image on the shikhara spire. Statues of kneeling devotees face the image and the shikhara is flanked by large bells.

PLACES TO STAY

A growing number of visitors to Bhaktapur stay overnight, there's plenty to see and one of the real pleasures of staying in Bhaktapur is that once evening falls all the day trippers from Kathmandu disappear, and don't return until after breakfast the next day. There are a number of small guest houses, all close to Durbar Square and all in the low price category. If you want private bathrooms and other mod cons you'd better stay in Kathmandu.

The pick of the bunch is the new *Golden Gate Guest House* (tel 6-10534), entered by a passageway from Durbar Square or from the laneway between Durbar Square and Taumadhi Tole. The owners are friendly, there are fine views from the roof and rooms cost Rs 45 for singles, Rs 75 for doubles or Rs 100 with toilet. The showers and washbasins are still downstairs, however. Some of the rooms have balconies and there's also a restaurant downstairs.

Across the laneway from the Golden Gate is the entrance to the *Nyatapola Inn* which is right on Taumadhi Tole, looking out to the temples. Rooms cost Rs 40, Rs 60 and Rs 80, the more expensive rooms with views over the square. This is a traditional old house with the traditional old drawbacks like no glass in the windows (which makes it easy for the mosquitoes to get in). Still if you really want to experience Bhaktapur it can be interesting! There are hot showers downstairs.

Entered from behind the Pashupatinath Temple on Durbar Square the *Shiva Inn* (tel 6-10740, 6-10227) has singles/doubles at Rs 40/70, again simple and spartan with shared restaurant on the top floor and rooftop. A few minutes walk north of Durbar Square brings you to the *Luna Guest House* with more rock bottom accommodation at Rs 25 for singles, Rs 40 to Rs 45 for doubles.

PLACES TO EAT

Bhaktapur is certainly no competition for Kathmandu when it comes to restaurants, but you won't starve. Right in Taumadhi Tole the *Nyatapola Restaurant* is in a building which was once a traditional pagoda temple, it even has erotic carvings on some of the roof struts! From upstairs there are wonderful views over the square although this is mainly a place for drinks, light snacks or lunch. It closes in the evening after the day visitors depart.

Right on the corner of the square, beside the Nyatapola Temple, there's another restaurant with good views over the square. The sign simply says *Restaurant*, or *1st Floor Restaurant*, and again it's mainly a lunch time place although it does open for breakfast. The menu is quite similar at both these places.

Otherwise there are restaurants attached to the *Golden Gate*, *Shiva Guest House* and *Luna Guest House* and these are open for all meals. The Golden Gate certainly has a pretty good go at turning out breakfast to Western tastes, its porridge and its muesli are rather good.

Don't forget to try Bhaktapur's famous speciality *jujudhau*, the 'king of curds', while you are here. You can have it at the *Nyatapola Restaurant* and there are several places selling curd near the Navpokhu Pokhari bus stand.

THINGS TO BUY

As in Patan there are a number of crafts for

Tigers & Goats

Nepal's national board game is *bagh chal*, which literally means 'move (chal) the tigers' (bagh). The game is played on a lined board with 25 intersecting points. One player has four tigers, the other has 20 goats and the aim is for the tiger player to 'eat' five goats by jumping over them before the goat player can enircle a single tiger and prevent it moving.

The game starts with the four tigers at the four corners of the board. Play alternates between the goats and the tigers and the goat player brings his goats on to the board one at a time. No goat can be moved from its initial position until every goat has been brought on to the board. By backing up one goat with another so that the tiger cannot jump them the goats can soon clutter up the board so effectively that the tigers cannot move. That is if the tigers haven't done a good job of eating goats!

All you need to play is a board scratched out on the dirt and 24 bottle caps or stones as markers, but you can also buy attractive brass bagh chal sets in Kathmandu and particularly in Patan where they are made. ■

which Bhaktapur is the centre. You'll find all the Kathmandu Valley crafts on sale in Kathmandu itself, but it's often fun to shop for them close to their point of origin and you may well find better examples or unusual pieces. There are plenty of shops and stalls catering to visitors around Durbar Square and Taumadhi Tole.

Pottery
Bhaktapur is the pottery centre of the valley and a visit to Potters' Square is a must. There are many stalls around the square or just below Taumadhi Tole selling pottery. Much of the work is in traditional pots for use in Nepalese households (nice but not very transportable), but they also make items obviously to tourist tastes such as attractive elephant or dragon planters.

Woodcarving & Puppets
Bhaktapur is renowned for its woodcarving and you'll see good examples in the Handicrafts Centre on Tachupal Tole. There are other shops around the squares and you will find unusual pieces in the alley beside the Pujari Math, right under the peacock window in fact. If you buy anything which looks like it might be old be certain to get a descriptive receipt for it as it's likely to be checked on departure from Kathmandu. If it really is very old you will not be allowed to take it out of the country. Some of the best puppets, on sale in their thousands in all the valley towns, come from Bhaktapur.

Thangkas & Caps
Bhaktapur is reputed to be a centre for painting thangkas although these days you find them everywhere. Nepalese caps are another Bhaktapur speciality. There's a cap shop right beside the Bhairabnath Temple.

GETTING THERE & AWAY
Travelling by bus or minibus to Bhaktapur you disembark at the walled water tank called Navpokhu Pokhari, just beyond the even larger Siddha Pokhari and a short walk from Durbar Square. If you travel on the Chinese-built trolley bus line you have a slightly longer walk to the river by Ram Ghat and up into the town by Potters' Square. The trolley bus is rarely uncomfortably crowded and leaves Kathmandu from Tripureshwar Marg (Bus Stop 10) and costs Rs 2. Normal buses leave from Bagh Bazaar (Bus Stop 5) and cost Rs 1.50. A taxi from Kathmandu will cost about Rs 225.

Around the Kathmandu Valley

Apart from the three major cities of the valley – Kathmandu, Patan and Bhaktapur – there are countless villages, temples and stupas around the valley and on the surrounding hills. The crowds, traffic and modern trappings of Kathmandu can quickly be left behind for quiet villages and lush, terraced hills.

The valley beyond the cities has certainly changed over the years though not always for the good, especially along the roads. Fortunately, however, aspects of customary life are maintained as the people of the valley coax their livelihood from the land, and thriving temples continue to provide a focal point for their lives. The seasons roll on, and the timeless demands of the fields, the family and the gods are still the major priorities.

You can even find good treks in the valley – ranging from day walks to more ambitious hikes. Some of the limitless possibilities are described in this chapter.

The ancient Buddhist stupa of Swayambhunath, a dramatic spot, within walking distance of central Kathmandu, is probably the best known site in Nepal and attracts a constant stream of worshippers. The hilltop site offers a fine view over the valley that is helpful for orienting yourself if you've just arrived.

The most important Hindu temple is Pashupatinath, on the eastern side of Kathmandu near the airport. It's a centre for pilgrims from all over the Indian subcontinent. A visit here can be combined with Bodhnath, another Buddhist stupa and the centre for a thriving Tibetan community.

If you will not have the opportunity to trek elsewhere, it is especially worth visiting one of the famous viewpoints on the rim of the valley, from where you can see the snow peaks of the Himalaya. There are numerous lodges and hotels at Nagarkot, Dhulikhel and Kakani.

If you have more time there are less well-known, although important, temples like Changunarayan (north of Bhaktapur – a treasure house of Nepalese art), Dakshinkali (in the south-western corner of the valley – the site for animal sacrifices to Kali), or Budhanilkantha (north of Kathmandu – a massive 1400 year old statue of Vishnu). There are many more.

The smaller towns and villages have tended to retain a more traditional Newari life style and if you found Bhaktapur interesting consider visiting Kirtipur (south-west of Kathmandu), Sankhu (north of Bhaktapur) or Panauti (outside the valley near Banepa). Again, there are many more alternatives.

There are two day-trips from Kathmandu that are not covered in this chapter, but are, nevertheless, worth considering: the Arniko Highway is a spectacular road that runs to the Tibetan border (see the Getting There chapter); and Daman, a viewpoint that overlooks the entire Himalaya from Dhaulagiri to Mt Everest (see the Terai chapter).

Some Cultural Considerations
You do not have to go far to escape the hordes of camera-clutching tourists, but you will

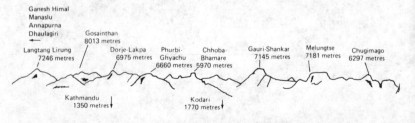

enter and photograph the temples described in this chapter.

See the Culture & Customs section in the Facts about the Country chapter for further details on cultural considerations.

GETTING AROUND

Swayambhunath and Pashupatinath can be reached on foot, but by far the easiest and most economical way of getting around the valley is by bicycle. If you are aiming for somewhere on the rim of the valley, make that a mountain bike! On a mountain bike it's possible for a reasonably fit person to go anywhere in the valley

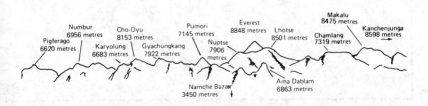

nonetheless be unable to escape their legacy: suspicious people and the cries of 'One rupee...one rupee?' from the children. If you do venture off the beaten track, your responsibility as a visitor is greater than ever.

Whatever the temptation do not give gifts to begging children. Do not intrude with a camera, unless it is clearly OK with the people you are photographing. Ask before entering a temple compound, although unless otherwise noted, it is permissible to

and return to Kathmandu within daylight.

Buses and minibuses service all of the roads, but although cheap, they are uncomfortable and limiting. If you are part of a group or if the budget allows, you could consider hiring a car or taxi for the day.

There are a number of companies that offer tours around the valley with prices ranging from Rs 160 to Rs 200 for half a day. If you have limited time or want a speedy introduction to the area, they're good value.

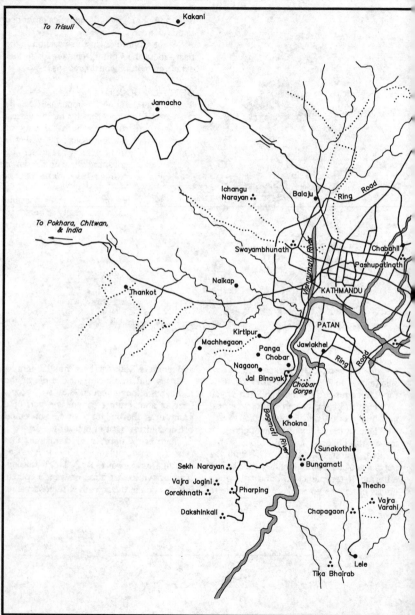

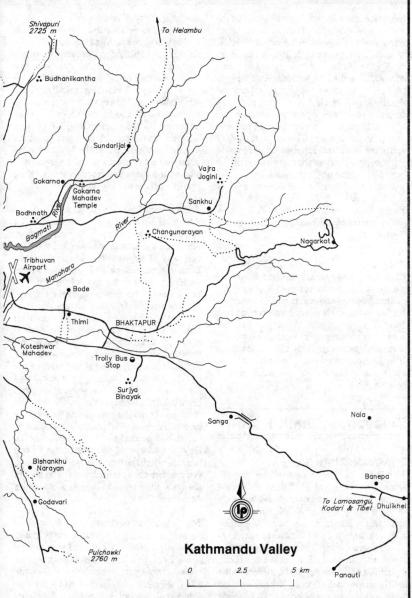

Kathmandu Valley

0   2.5   5 km

Valley Walks

There are many interesting walks around the valley and many of them make pleasant alternatives to powered transport or bicycles. You can, for example, follow a trail from Kirtipur to Chobar and from there into Patan, or walk from the Gokarna Mahadev Temple to Bodhnath. These walks, and others, are detailed in the Getting There & Away information for the appropriate sections.

In addition, there are a number of interesting walks down from Nagarkot on the valley rim to various points in the valley and outside it including a pleasant short stroll down to the beautiful temple of Changunarayan.

For more details on walks on the edge of the Kathmandu Valley, look for Alton C Byers' *Treks on the Kathmandu Valley Rim*, which is readily available in Kathmandu bookshops.

Routes

This chapter has been organised following the roads that radiate out from Kathmandu.

Distances quoted are from the centre of Kathmandu. Each route has been named for the most important sites along the route, which are given clockwise from the Swayambhunath route. In most cases there is no alternative to going and returning on the same route unless you walk across country.

Swayambhunath Route

SWAYAMBHUNATH (2 km)

The Buddhist temple of Swayambhunath, situated on the top of a hill west of the city, is one of the most popular and instantly recognisable symbols of Nepal. The temple is colloquially known as the 'monkey temple' after the large tribe of handsome monkeys which guard the hill and amuse visitors and devotees with their tricks including sliding gracefully down the double bannisters of the main stairway to the temple. The roving band quickly snatch up any offerings of food made by devotees and will just as quickly grab anything you may be carrying.

Geologists believe that the Kathmandu Valley was once a lake and legends relate that the hill on which Swayambhunath stands was an island in that lake. It is said that Emperor Ashoka paid a visit to the site over 2000 years ago. An inscription indicates that King Manadeva ordered work done on the site in 460 AD and by the 1200s it was an important Buddhist centre. In 1346 Muslim invaders from Bengal broke open the stupa to search for gold. Under the Mallas various improvements were made and the great stairway to the stupa was constructed by King Pratap Malla in the 17th century.

The Eastern Stairway

Although you can get to the temple by vehicle, and save yourself the long climb up the stairs, the eastern stairway is by far the best way of approaching Swayambhunath. Look for the yellow and red stone seated Buddha figures at the base of the hill. The bottom end of the steps is guarded by figures of Ganesh and Kumar on their animals. Near the start of the steps is a huge 'footprint' on a stone, said to be either that of the Buddha or of Manjushri. Halfway up the steps there's another small collection of stonework including a scene showing the birth of the Buddha, his mother holding a tree branch and the Buddha taking seven miraculous steps immediately after his birth.

As you climb the final stretch look for the pairs of animals – Garudas, lions, elephants, horses and peacocks – the 'vehicles' of the Dhyani Buddhas. If you tire on the ascent, pause to watch the monkeys' antics and when you reach the top remember that you should always walk around a stupa in a clockwise direction.

The Great Thunderbolt

As well as building the great stairway Pratap Malla also added a pair of shikharas and the stone lions and dorje which visitors see immediately upon reaching the top of the stairs. *Dorje* is the Tibetan word for this thunderbolt symbol, in Sanskrit it is called a

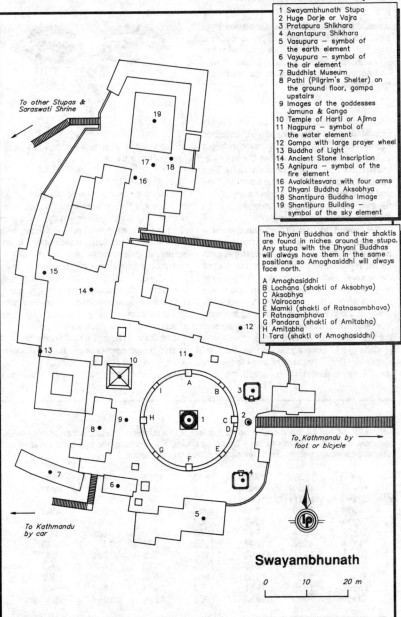

1 Swayambhunath Stupa
2 Huge Dorje or Vajra
3 Pratapura Shikhara
4 Anantapura Shikhara
5 Vasupura — symbol of
  the earth element
6 Vayupura — symbol of
  the air element
7 Buddhist Museum
8 Pathi (Pilgrim's Shelter) on
  the ground floor, gompa
  upstairs
9 Images of the goddesses
  Jamuna & Ganga
10 Temple of Harti or Ajima
11 Nagpura — symbol of
   the water element
12 Gompa with large prayer wheel
13 Buddha of Light
14 Ancient Stone Inscription
15 Agnipura — symbol of the
   fire element
16 Avalokitesvara with four arms
17 Dhyani Buddha Aksobhya
18 Shantipura Buddha Image
19 Shantipura Building —
   symbol of the sky element

The Dhyani Buddhas and their shaktis
are found in niches around the stupa.
Any stupa with the Dhyani Buddhas
will always have them in the same
positions so Amoghasiddhi will always
face north.

A Amoghasiddhi
B Lochana (shakti of Aksobhya)
C Aksobhya
D Vairocana
E Mamki (shakti of Ratnasambhava)
F Ratnasambhava
G Pandara (shakti of Amitabha)
H Amitabha
I Tara (shakti of Amoghasiddhi)

To other Stupas &
Saraswati Shrine

To Kathmandu by
foot or bicycle

To Kathmandu
by car

Swayambhunath

0   10   20 m

vajra. Dorjes are often accompanied by a bell, the thunderbolt symbolises male force and the bell symbolises female wisdom. Around the pedestal supporting Swayambhunath's mighty dorje are the animals of the Tibetan calendar.

The Stupa

From the flattened top of the hill, the soaring central stupa is topped by a gold-coloured square block from which the watchful eyes of the Buddha gaze out across the valley in each direction. The question mark-like 'nose' is actually the Nepali number *ek* or one and is a symbol of unity. Between and above the two eyes is a third eye, symbolising the Buddha's clairvoyant powers.

Set around the base of the central stupa is a continuous series of prayer wheels which pilgrims, circumambulating the stupa, spin as they pass by. Each carries the sacred mantra *om mani padme hum*. The prayer flags fluttering from the lines leading to the stupa's spire also carry mantras and each wave in the breeze carries the words away. The stupa's white-painted base represents the four elements – earth, fire, air and water – while the 13 concentric rings on the spire symbolise the 13 degrees of knowledge and the 13 steps that must be taken towards

nirvana, which in turn is represented by the umbrella at the top.

The Stupa Platform

The great stupa is only one of many points of interest at Swayambhunath. Starting from the massive dorje at the top of the stairs turn right to the monastery or *gompa* where, with a great deal of crashing, chanting and trumpeting, a service takes place every day at around 4 pm. Inside the gompa there's a huge prayer wheel and a 6 metre high figure of Avalokitesvara. Behind the stupa, adjacent to the International Buddhist Library, is a path or rest house for pilgrims with an open ground floor and a gompa above it.

The dorje at the top of the stairs is flanked by two white temples in the Indian shikhara style, both dating from 1646. The one to the right, in front of the gompa, is the Pratapura

The Tibetan Calendar

Around the base of the great dorje at the top of the stairway to Swayambhunath are the symbols of the 12 animals of the Tibetan calendar. The animals are similar to those of the Chinese calendar and through this century they fall as follows:

Snake	1929	1941	1953	1965	1977	1989
Horse	1930	1942	1954	1966	1978	1990
Sheep	1931	1943	1955	1967	1979	1991
Monkey	1932	1944	1956	1968	1980	1992
Goose	1933	1945	1957	1969	1981	1993
Dog	1934	1946	1958	1970	1982	1994
Pig	1935	1947	1959	1971	1983	1995
Rat	1936	1948	1960	1972	1984	1996
Bull	1937	1949	1961	1973	1985	1997
Tiger	1938	1950	1962	1974	1986	1998
Hare	1939	1951	1963	1975	1987	1999
Dragon	1940	1952	1964	1976	1988	2000 ∎

Shikara while to the left is the identical Anantapura Shikara. Behind the stupa is the Hariti Temple, a pagoda-style temple with a beautiful image of Hariti, the goddess of smallpox. This Hindu goddess (to the Newaris she is Ajima), who is also responsible for fertility, indicates again the constant interweaving of Hinduism and Buddhism in Nepal.

Near the Hariti Temple there are pillars on which figures of various gods and goddesses are seated. Look for the figure of Tara making the gesture of charity. There are actually two Taras, Green Tara and White Tara, who are sometimes believed to be the two wives of King Songtsen Gompo, the first royal patron of Buddhism in Tibet. The Taras are two of the female consorts to the Dhyani Buddhas.

Behind the stupa bronze images of the river goddesses Ganga and Jamuna guard an eternal flame in a cage.

The symbols for the five elements – earth, air, water, fire and sky – can be found around

The Dhyani Buddhas

There are five Dhyani Buddhas or 'Buddhas in Meditation' who represent various aspects of Buddhahood, unlike the mortal flesh-and-blood Buddhas like Gautama Buddha. Around many stupas the figures of the five Dhyani Buddhas in different meditative postures face out from the stupa in niches, four of them facing the four cardinal directions. Once you know the hand positions you can use a stupa like a compass! The Swayambhunath stupa is a good place to study the Dhyani Buddhas, and the description that follows is from that stupa.

Amoghasiddhi faces north and raises his right hand, palm out to shoulder height in what is known as a protective position. His animal or 'vehicle' is the Garuda. You can see the animals in niches below the Buddhas' shrines. As you move round the stupa clockwise you'll come to Aksobhya, the lord of the east; one of his hands touches the earth. This is known as the position of subduing the devil Mara. The Buddha reaches down to touch the earth, in order that it witness his resistance to temptation. His vehicle is the elephant.

Facing south is Ratnasambhava who rides a horse and turns his palm outwards. Amitabha faces the west and his hands rest on his lap, palm up in a meditative position. His vehicle is the peacock. The fifth of the Buddhas is Vairocana who usually appears in the centre of the stupa and therefore is not so easily seen. If he is shown he normally faces the south-east, and at Swayambhunath you can see his figure standing beside Aksobhya in the eastern niche. His animal is the lion; his hands are held up to his chest and he makes two circles with his fingers, rather like a scuba diver's 'OK' sign!

Each Dhyani Buddha is identifiable by his colour, his hand positions, his direction and his vehicle but each also has a shakti or female companion and a Bodhisattva or spiritual follower. Their shaktis are shown at the subcardinal points around the stupa. Amitabha is the Dhyani Buddha of our era and his Bodhisattva is none other than Avalokitesvara or, as he is often known in the valley, Manjushri or Machhendranath.■

A   Amoghasiddhi
B   Locana (shakti of Aksobhya)
C   Aksobhya
D   Vairocana
E   Mamki (shakti of Ratnasambhava)
F   Ratnasambhava
G   Pandara (shakti of Amitabha)
H   Amitabha
I   Tara (shakti of Amoghasiddhi)

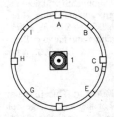

the hilltop. Behind the Anantapura Temple are Vasupura, the symbol for earth, and Vayupura, the symbol for air. Nagpura, the symbol for water, is just north of the stupa while Agnipura, the symbol for fire, is at the north-western corner of the platform. Shantipura, the symbol for sky, is at the extreme north of the platform, in front of the Shantipura building.

In this same northern area of the platform you will find an ancient stone inscription, dating from 1372, and a large image of the Buddha, next to the Agnipura symbol. There are numerous little shops and stalls around the stupa that sell jewellery and curios.

From its hilltop setting, Swayambhunath offers fine views over Kathmandu and the valley. It's particularly striking in the early evening when the city is illuminated and the site is also very attractive under the soft glow of moonlight.

Around Swayambhunath
There are many small buildings and shrines down the hillside behind Swayambhunath. A smaller stupa stands on a hillock, with an adjacent gompa and an important shrine to Saraswati, the goddess of learning. At exam time, many scholars come here to improve their chances and schoolchildren come here during Basant Panchami, the festival of knowledge.

There are various Tibetan settlements and gompas around the base of the Swayambhunath hill. Just to the north of the long eastern stairway, on the road round the hill, is a gompa with an immense prayer wheel standing a good 6 metres high. The 2 or 3 km walk beyond Swayambhunath will take you to Ichangu Narayan, an interesting Hindu temple. The National Museum & Art Gallery, described in the Kathmandu, Patan & Bhaktapur chapter, is on the road from Kathmandu to the stupa.

Natural History Museum This museum, west of Swayambhunath, has a large collection of butterflies, fish, reptiles, birds and animals. It is open every day from 10 am to 5 pm except Saturdays and government holidays and admission is free.

The Three Riverside Temples There are several routes to Swayambhunath from Kathmandu and if you take the route from Thamel, via the Chhetrapati Square and down to the Vishnumati River, there are three interesting temples to look at. The Indrani Temple is just beside the river on the Kathmandu side and is chiefly notable for the brightly coloured erotic scenes on its roof struts. There are cremation ghats beside the river; in 1989 the bridge here collapsed during the heavy monsoon. Across the river and just upstream is the Shobabaghwati Temple. A footpath runs from here up the steep hill to the Bijeshwari Temple, from where the road continues to the Swayambhunath hill.

Getting There & Away
You can approach Swayambhunath by taxi or under your own power – either on foot or by bicycle. The taxi will take you on the road via the National Museum & Art Gallery and deposit you at the southern entrance, from where it's just an easy climb to the top of the hill. Share taxis also operate from Bangemudha, the junction a block south of Thahiti Tole going from Thamel towards New Rd. The other routes end with the long steep climb up the eastern stairway to the stupa, but this is a far more interesting way to approach Swayambhunath and the easy stroll from Kathmandu is a pleasure in itself.

There are two popular foot or bicycle routes to Swayambhunath, using both makes the trip into a pleasant circuit. Starting from Durbar Square take Maru Tole (Pie Alley) down to the river where a footbridge crosses to the western side. Flat stone cremation ghats can be seen by the riverside. From there the path leads through houses and shops to the open green at the base of the hill. Along the way you'll see people working in vegetable gardens and preparing wool for Tibetan carpets. There's quite a Tibetan community in this area and also a small group of longer term Western visitors near the base of the hill.

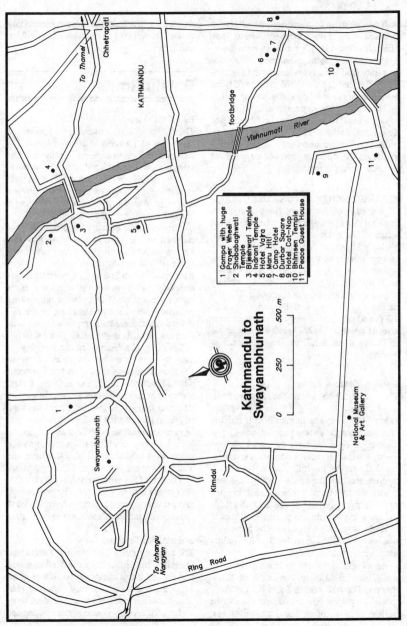

Kathmandu to Swayambhunath

1 Gompa with huge Prayer Wheel
2 Shobabaghwati Temple
3 Bijeshwari Temple
4 Indrani Temple
5 Hotel Vajra
6 Maru Hiti
7 Camp Hotel
8 Durbar Square
9 Hotel Cat-Nap
10 Bhimsen Temple
11 Peace Guest House

If you go there by bicycle you are likely to find a number of small boys offering to 'look after' your bicycle. It's probably wise to pay a rupee or two 'protection money', otherwise you may find your tyres have gone mysteriously flat and a pump will then have to be rented from one of the nearby shops!

The alternative route starts from Chhetrapati, near Thamel. From the Chhetrapati Tole junction the road descends to the river, with the Swayambhunath stupa clearly visible in the distance, and passes the three riverside temples mentioned.

ICHANGU NARAYAN TEMPLE (5 km)

At the edge of the valley floor, 2 or 3 km beyond Swayambhunath, the shrine of Ichangu Narayan is one of the Kathmandu Valley's important Vishnu shrines. The two storey 18th century temple is fronted by two square stone pillars bearing Vishnu's conch shell and chakra symbols. Various statuary can be found around the courtyard. The site of the temple was actually consecrated in 1200 and an earlier temple was built here after a famine in 1512. There's a small temple to Bhagwati on a hill overlooking Ichangu Narayan.

Getting There & Away

The road to Ichangu Narayan starts immediately beyond the Ring Rd, on the western side of the Swayambhunath hill. It quickly changes from a road to a track and as it climbs a steep hill (look back for the views over the valley), the track soon becomes a footpath. From the top of the hill, marked by a small temple, the trail descends slightly and then continues to climb gradually, leaving the valley proper. Finally at the end of a little village is the temple compound. Going back to Kathmandu, if you've come by bicycle, is one long downhill breeze but you'll certainly work up a sweat getting here.

An alternative route to Ichangu is a day walk from Balaju, to the north of Kathmandu. The trail climbs from Balaju to the top of Nagarjun Hill and skirts around the valley edge through the Jamacho forest

reserve and the Nagarjun forest, descending to the Ichangu trail to the west of the village and temple.

Balaju Route

BALAJU (3 km)

The industrial centre of Balaju is less than 2 km north of Thamel, just beyond the Ring Rd, and the expansion of the capital has virtually swallowed up this nearby suburb. Despite this the Balaju park is still a peaceful retreat and its image of the sleeping Vishnu makes an interesting contrast with the larger Vishnu image at Budhanilkantha.

The gardens at Balaju were originally constructed in the 18th century and are now known as Mahendra Park. They are something of a disappointment – there's lots of concrete, litter and numerous ineffectual gardeners. Apart from the Vishnu image, there are a couple of small temples, an interesting group of chortens and lingams (for the aficionado) and the 22 waterspouts from which the park takes its name, 'Bais dhara Balaju'.

Officially the Vishnu image at Balaju is said to be a copy of the older image at Budhanilkantha but there is no positive proof which is actually older. Certainly the Balaju image is in more pleasant surroundings than its better known relation. Although the king of Nepal cannot visit Budhanilkantha, since he is an incarnation of Vishnu and to gaze on his own image could be disastrous, no such injunction applies to Balaju, where the Vishnu image is just a copy of the real thing!

There's a Rs 1 admission fee, plus another Rs 1 if you take in a camera. The pool, which can get very crowded, is open from March to September and the admission fee is Rs 10.

Shitala Mai Temple

The double roofed 19th century Shitala Mai Temple stands in front of the Vishnu image and around it is a curious assembly of gods. They include a 16th century image of Hari Shankar – the half-Shiva, half-Vishnu deity – and 14th century figure of the multiarmed goddess of smallpox, Shitala Mai. Others include Bhagwati, Ganesh and, in the usual clash of Hindu and Buddhist imagery, a statue of the Buddha protected by the hood of a snake.

Getting There & Away
You can get to Balaju by tempo from the National Theatre corner of the Rani Pokhari or walk there from Thamel. It's an interesting day walk from Balaju to Ichangu Narayan, west of Swayambhunath, skirting round the edge of the valley.

NAGARJUN
On the hill behind Balaju is the walled Nagarjun forest reserve with pheasants, deer and other animals. This, along with the Gokarna Wildlife Reserve and Pulchowki, is one of the last significant areas of untouched forest in the valley. You can continue up the hill through to Jamacho, the Buddhist chaitya at the top of the hill. It's nearly 20 km all the way to the top but from there you have excellent views to the north stretching, on a clear day, all the way from the Annapurnas to Langtang Lirung, while the whole of the Kathmandu Valley is laid at your feet to the south.

Getting There & Away
A footpath takes off from behind the Balaju gardens, but the main entry and road are 1½ km past Balaju on the Dhunche road.

KAKANI (23 km)
Standing at 2073 metres on a ridge northwest of Kathmandu, Kakani is nowhere near as popular as Nagarkot but does offer magnificent views of Ganesh Himal and the central and western Himalaya.

Apart from looking at the view (one could argue this is enough) there's not much to do. There is a century old summer villa used by the British Embassy and a large army camp, although this does not seriously impinge on the peacefulness of the surroundings.

The road to Kakani also offers beautiful views. Once you're through the pass and out

of the valley Kathmandu seems light years away. Although the valley is terraced 1000 metres from top to bottom, many trees have been left behind and prosperous-looking houses dot the hillsides.

Place to Stay & Eat
The only option is the *Taragaon Kakani Hotel* (tel 2-28222). It's old-fashioned, has wonderful views and although it's small it's also quite comfortable. Singles/doubles are US$13/18 and it serves reasonably priced meals.

Although it's easy to get to Kakani on a day trip, if you want to see the view you stand a much better chance if you are there early in the morning before the clouds roll in. So it is worth staying overnight at this place.

Getting There & Away
It is an hour by car from Kathmandu, so it would be a long, though rewarding, bike trip. The road is sealed almost all the way and it is a fairly gentle climb – although consistent. It is all downhill on the way home! Kakani is 3 km from the main Dhunche road. The dirt road is just before the Kaulithana police checkpost (the first outside Kathmandu) and there is a signpost for a Telecom Repeater Station.

Buses leave Kathmandu from the intersection of Lekhnath Marg and the road to Balaju (Bus Stop 1 – Paknajol). Buses to Trisuli and Dhunche leave around 6 am, so catch one of them and get off at Kaulithana (about Rs 10). Look for the Saja Sewa bus.

Grayline (tel 4-12899) has 4-hour tours on Tuesday and Thursday for Rs 180.

Budhanilkantha Route

DHUM VARAHI (5 km)
Lying in an unprepossessing schoolyard just inside the Ring Rd to the north-east of the city proper, a huge pipal tree encloses a small shrine and a dramatic 5th century sculpture of Vishnu. Vishnu is shown reincarnated as

a wild boar with a stocky human body, holding Prithvi, the earth goddess, on his left elbow.

From a historical point of view, it is interesting because it is an original depiction of an animal/human, created before iconographic rules were established, which perhaps contributes to the unusual sense of movement and vitality that the statue possesses. The statue shows Vishnu rescuing Prithvi from the clutches of a demon.

Getting There & Away

A visit to Dhum Varahi could easily be combined with a visit to Budhanilkantha, especially if you are approaching the Budhanilkantha intersection on the Ring Rd from Chabahil and Pashupatinath. If you are coming from Chabahil take the first dirt road on your left after crossing the Dhobi River (see the map in the Pashupatinath section). The statue lies under a huge pipal tree in the grounds of the Shridhumrabarah Primary School.

If you are coming from the intersection of the Budhanilkantha road with the Ring Rd take the first right turn after the Panchayat Silver Jubilee Garden, which features a huge, square, black marble column topped with a conch shell. Continue until you see the pipal tree after about a km.

BUDHANILKANTHA (9 km)

Vishnu has many incarnations and in Nepal he often appears as Narayan, the creator of all life, the god who reclines on the cosmic sea. From his navel grew a lotus and from the lotus came Brahma, who in turn created the world. So in the end everything comes from Vishnu and at Budhanilkantha the legend is made real. Here, a stone image of Vishnu lies serenely in a pond, the most impressive, if not the most important, Vishnu shrine in the kingdom.

The 5 metre long image of Vishnu as Narayan is believed to have been created in the 7th or 8th century. It was sculptured during the Licchavi period, probably somewhere outside the valley and laboriously dragged here. Two other similar figures of the reclining Vishnu were also carved out of

stone and all three were subsequently lost for many centuries. The image here at Budhanilkantha was the first found and is also the largest but it remains a controversial issue as to whether it was also the original one, from which the others were copied.

Narayan lies peacefully back on a most unusual bed – the coils of the multiheaded snake, Ananta. The snake's 11 hooded heads rise protectively around Narayan's head. Narayan's four hands hold the four symbols of Vishnu – a chakra (representing the mind), a mace (primaeval knowledge), a conch shell (the five elements) and a lotus seed (the moving universe). A legend relates that the lost image was discovered when a horrified farmer saw blood coming from the ground when his plough struck the huge buried image.

During the early Malla period, Vishnuism had gone into decline as Shiva became more popular. King Jayasthiti Malla is credited with reviving the popularity of Vishnu, in part by claiming to be an incarnation of the multi-incarnated god.

To this day, the kings of Nepal make the same claim and because of this they are forbidden, on pain of death, from seeing the image at Budhanilkantha. They are allowed to look at the valley's other two reclining Vishnu images, which are said to be simply copies of the Budhanilkantha figure. One of these 'replicas' is at Balaju, the other, not on view to tourists, is in the Old Royal Palace in Kathmandu.

The sleeping Vishnu image attracts a constant stream of pilgrims and prayers take place every morning at 9 am. Vishnu is supposed to sleep through the four monsoon months, waking with the end of the monsoon. A great festival takes place at Budhanilkantha each November, on the day Vishnu is supposed to awaken from his long annual slumber.

Getting There & Away

Buses and tempos run somewhat irregularly to Budhanilkantha from the National Theatre building at the north-western corner of Rani Pokhari (Bus Stop 3) and cost Rs 2. Buses run more regularly to Bansbari, site of a shoe factory about half way from the centre of

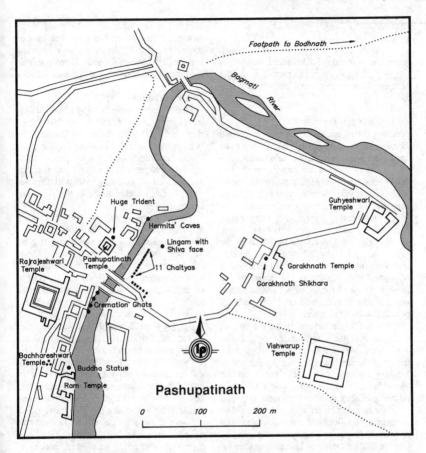

Pashupatinath

0   100   200 m

Kathmandu to Budhanilkantha. A taxi might cost Rs 80. By bicycle it's a long uphill haul all the way, hard sweaty work but a very pleasant return trip. You could pause at Dhum Varahi on one leg of your trip.

Pashupatinath & Bodhnath Route

PASHUPATINATH (5 km)
Nepal's most important Hindu temple stands on the banks of the Bagmati River, between Kathmandu and the airport and slightly south-west of Bodhnath. You can visit Pashupatinath en route to Bodhnath – they are an interesting short walk apart.

Festivals
Activities take place at Pashupatinath almost all the time but the best time to visit the temple is on Ekadashi – 11 days after the full and new moon each month. On those days there will be many pilgrims and in the evening the ringing of bells will indicate

that the *arati* (light) ceremony is to take place.

In the month of February or March each year the festival of Shivaratri celebrates Shiva's birthday with a great fair at the temple. Another fair takes place in November.

Pashupatinath Temple

Not only is Pashupatinath the most important Hindu temple in Nepal it's one of the most important Shiva temples on the subcontinent and draws numerous devotees from all over India each year, including many colourful sadhus, those wandering ascetic Hindu holy men. Shiva is the destroyer and creator of the Hindu pantheon and appears in many forms. His 'terrible' forms are probably best known, particularly his appearance in Nepal as the cruel and destructive Bhairabs, but he also has peaceful incarnations including those of Mahadev and Pashupati, the Lord of the Beasts. As the shepherd of both animals and humans Shiva as Pashupati shows his most pleasant and creative side.

Pashupati is considered to have a special concern for the kingdom of Nepal and accordingly he features in any message from the king. Before commencing any important journey the king will always pay a visit to Pashupatinath to seek the god's blessing. Although Shiva is often a bloodthirsty god he is not so in his incarnation as Pashupati so no animal sacrifices are made here although they are at the nearby Guhyeshwari Temple. Nor is leather (since it comes from cows) allowed inside the temple and you will see Hindus removing their shoes before entering.

Near the entrance to the temple there are people selling flowers, incense and other offerings. Although non-Hindus are not allowed inside the temple you may catch a glimpse of the mighty figure of Nandi, Shiva's bull, inside the temple. It dates from the last century but the small bull in front of the temple is about 300 years old. The black, four-headed image of Pashupati inside the temple is said to be even older and an even earlier image was destroyed by the Muslim

invaders in the 14th century. Although Westerners are not allowed to enter the temple, there is plenty to be seen along the riverbanks and you can look down into the temple from the terraced hillside on the opposite bank.

The Riverbanks

On the riverbanks are burning ghats for, like the Ganges in India, the Bagmati is a holy river and, as at Varanasi on the Ganges, this is a popular place to be cremated. The ghats immediately in front of the temple, north of the footbridges, are reserved for the cremation of royalty although you will often see ritual bathing taking place in the river just here.

The four square burning ghats just south of the bridges are for the common people and there is almost always a cremation going on. The log fires are laid, the shrouded body lifted on top and the fire lit with remarkably little ceremony and there's often a crowd of tourists – cameras and video cameras at the ready – watching from the opposite bank. Photography does appear to be permitted, and if you want to take photographs be more courteous and discreet than many of the tourist visitors seem to be.

Further south of these cremation ghats, but still on the western (Kathmandu) bank of the river, is the ancient 6th century Bachhareshwari Temple with Tantric figures and erotic scenes. It is said that at one time the Shivaratri activities would include human sacrifices at this temple. Just outside the temple entrance, right at the end of the western embankment, is a half buried, but quite beautiful, 7th century standing Buddha image.

Two footbridges cross the Bagmati River and facing the temple from across the river are 11 stone chaityas, each containing a lingam. From this embankment you can watch the activities on the other bank, in front of the temple. Offerings and flowers are on sale, devotees dip in the river and there's a constant coming and going. From the northern end of the embankment you can see the cave-like shelters where at one time hermits and sadhus used to shelter. These days the yogis and sadhus head for the Ram

Temple, further down the river, especially during the great festival of Shivaratri.

The Terraces

Climb up the steps from the western riverbank to the terrace where you can look down into the Pashupatinath Temple. It's not a very inspiring sight: the golden roof of the central triple roofed temple, which dates from 1696, is surrounded by ugly corrugated iron roofs, just like some worn-out, inner-city Australian suburb. Look for the enormous golden trident rising up on the right (northern) side of the temple and the golden figure of the king kneeling in prayer on the left side. Behind the temple, you can see a brightly coloured illustration of Shiva and his shakti looking out over his temple.

At the northen end of this terrace is a Shiva lingam on a circular pedestal. A finely featured face of the god has been sculptured on one side of the lingam. It's an indication of the richness of Nepal's artistic heritage that this piece of sculpture, so casually standing here on the grassy terrace, is a masterpiece dating from the 5th or 6th century!

Gorakhnath & Vishwarup Temples

The steps continue up the hill and, as with the stairway up to Swayambhunath, it's a popular playground for monkeys. The Gorakhnath complex is at the top of the hill. A shikhara fronted by a towering Shiva trident is the main structure but there's a positive jungle of temples, images, sculptures and chaityas with Shiva imagery everywhere. Images of the bull Nandi stand guard, tridents are dotted around and lingams rise up on every side.

You can turn right from the path to the Vishwarup Temple but there's no point since again Westerners are denied entry to the temple precinct and from outside there's nothing to see. Instead continue beyond the Gorakhnath shikhara where the pathway turns steeply downhill to the river.

Guhyeshwari Temple

The Guhyeshwari Temple is dedicated to Shiva's shakti in her terrible manifestation as Kali. Like the Pashupatinath Temple, entry is banned to all but Hindus and the high wall around the temple prevents you from seeing inside. Guhyeshwari was built by King Pratap Malla in the 17th century and the temple, standing in a paved courtyard surrounded by dharamsalas, is topped by an open roof with four gilded snakes arching up to support the roof finial. You can see the snakes from outside. The temple's main entrance gate by the river is an imposing and colourful affair. To the west of the main temple building are a series of white, stupa-like temples.

The temple's curious name comes from *guhya* (vagina) and *ishwari* (goddess) – it's the temple of the goddess' vagina! When Shiva was insulted by his father-in-law, Parvati was so incensed that she burst into flames and it was this act of self-immolation which gave rise to the practice of sati or suttee, where a widow was consigned to the same funeral pyre as her deceased husband. The grieving Shiva carried off his shakti's corpse but as he wandered aimlessly, the body disintegrated and this is where her yoni fell.

Getting There & Away

Buses to Bodhnath go via Pashupatinath. They leave from Rani Pokhari (Bus Stop 3) and the Pashupatinath stop is called Gosala. It's an easy bicycle ride from Kathmandu, simply ride east from Thamel along Tridevi Marg, passing in front of the new Royal Palace.

It's a pleasant short walk between Pashupatinath and Bodhnath. From the Guhyeshwari Temple, the dome of Bodhnath is clearly visible to the north but the footbridge shown on some maps right in front of Guhyeshwari does not exist! Walk west along the riverbank for a couple of hundred metres to the bridge by some ghats, cross the river and a footpath leads off north-east through pleasant rural scenery to Bodhnath. You eventually come out on the main road, right across from the main entrance to the stupa enclosure. Unfortunately the last 100 metres or so of the walk goes right through the Bodhnath village garbage dump!

CHABAHIL (6 km)

The Chabahil stupa is like a small replica of Bodhnath, about 1½ km west of Bodhnath, back towards Kathmandu. The small village of Chabahil has been virtually swallowed up by the expansion of Kathmandu but the site is very old and the original stupa was said to have been built by Ashoka's daughter Charumati. It certainly predates Bodhnath and around the main stupa are a number of small chaityas from the Licchavi period, dating back to the 5th to 8th centuries. The site includes a metre high 9th century statue of a Bodhisattva which is claimed to be one of the finest pieces of sculpture in the valley.

Nearby is the small Chandra Binayak Ganesh Temple with a double roof in brass. Ganesh's shrew stands on a pillar in front of the shrine, waiting for the tiny image of the god inside. A short distance south, but still on the Kathmandu side of the main road, is the well designed late 17th century Jayabageshwari Temple.

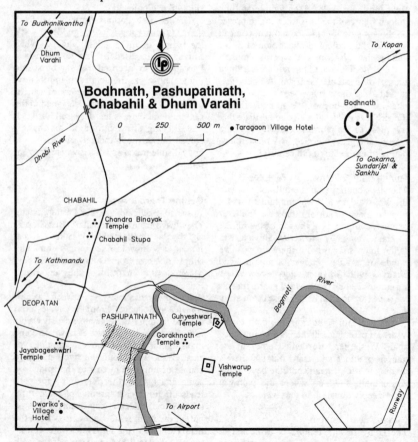

Top: Looking down from the Bodhnath stupa, Kathmandu Valley (TW)
Left: Shop-houses around the great circle at Bodhnath, Kathmandu Valley (TW)
Right: Turning prayer wheels around the Bodhnath stupa, Kathmandu Valley (TW)

Top: Corn is hung out to dry in front of houses in Chobar, Kathmandu Valley (TW)
Left: View of Kathmandu Valley on the walk from Kirtipur to Chobar (TW)
Right: A typical rural scene in Kathmandu Valley (TW)

BODHNATH (6 km)

On the eastern side of Kathmandu, just north of the airport and an interesting walk from Pashupatinath, is the huge stupa of Bodhnath, the largest stupa in Nepal and one of the largest in the world. It is the religious centre for Nepal's considerable population of Tibetans and there are a number of thriving monasteries and many small shops here selling Tibetan artefacts (beware, prices are high and bargaining is essential).

Many of these Tibetans are refugees who fled their country following the unsuccessful uprising against the Chinese invaders in 1959. They have been energetic and successful in the intervening years, as the large houses surrounding Bodhnath testify. While the political and religious oppression continues in Tibet, this is one of the few places in the world where Tibetan culture is both accessible and unhindered.

The late afternoon is a good time to visit when the group tours depart and the place returns to being a Tibetan town. Prayer services are held in the surrounding gompas and as the sun sets the community turns out to circumambulate the stupa. This seems to be a combination between religious observance (the very devout are very serious) and a social event (family groups laugh and chat). Do not forget to walk around the stupa in a clockwise direction.

Bodhnath has always been associated with Lhasa and Tibetan Buddhism. One of the major trade routes from Lhasa came through Sankhu, and Bodhnath therefore lies at the Tibetan traders' entry to Kathmandu. One can easily imagine the traders giving thanks for their successful journey across the Himalaya, or praying for a safe return. People still come here to pray before undertaking a journey in the Himalaya.

Festivals

The Tibetan new year in February is celebrated by large crowds of pilgrims, who come to watch the lamas perform their rites. Long copper horns are blown, a portrait of the Dalai Lama is paraded around and masked dances are performed.

The Stupa

There does not seem to be any agreement on how old the site is, but it is likely that the first stupa was built some time after 600 AD after the Tibetan king, Songtsen Gampo, was converted to Buddhism by his two wives: the Nepalese princess Bhrikuti (sometimes regarded as an incarnation of the Green Tara) and Wen Cheng Konjo from China (the White Tara). The current stupa was probably built after the depredations of the Moghul invaders in the 14th century.

Stupas were originally built to house holy relics, or to commemorate an event or place, with a structure that symbolises Buddhist beliefs. They are never hollow. It is not certain if there is anything interred at Bodhnath, but some believe that there is a piece of bone that once belonged to Gautama Buddha.

The base of the stupa takes the shape of a mandala (symbolising earth); on this four tiered base sits the dome (symbolising water); then comes the spire (symbolising fire); the umbrella (symbolising air); and the pinnacle (symbolising ether). The Buddha's ever watchful eyes glare out in four directions from the square base of the spire. There is a third eye between and above the two normal eyes and the 'nose' is not a nose at all but the number one, signifying the oneness of all life. The spire is made up of 13 steps, representing the 13 stages on the journey to nirvana.

Around the base of the stupa's circular mound are 108 small images of the Dhyani Buddha Amitabha. A brick wall around the stupa has 147 niches, each with four or five prayer wheels bearing that immortal mantra *om mani padme hum*. On the northern side of the stupa is a small shrine dedicated to Ajima, the goddess of smallpox.

Gompas

There are a number of gompas surrounding Bodhnath that can be visited so long as you are respectful and discreet. Do not forget to remove your shoes before you enter one and

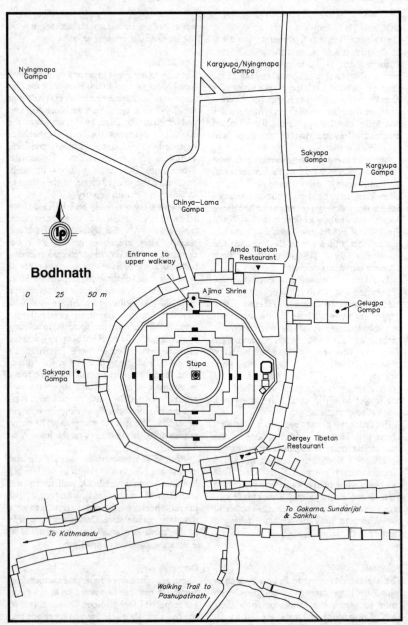

Nyingmapa
Gompa

Kargyupa/Nyingmapa
Gompa

Sakyapa
Gompa

Kargyupa
Gompa

Chinya–Lama
Gompa

Bodhnath

0   25   50 m

Entrance to
upper walkway

Amdo Tibetan
Restaurant

Ajima Shrine

Gelugpa
Gompa

Sakyapa
Gompa

Stupa

Dergey Tibetan
Restaurant

To Gokarna, Sundarijal
& Sankhu

To Kathmandu

Walking Trail to
Pashupatinath

ask before taking photos. Do not let loose with your flash in the middle of a service. It is appropriate to make an offering to the lama, especially if you do take photographs. A khata is traditional, but these days rupees are also appreciated! These monasteries depend for their existence on the donations of the faithful.

Decorations All the gompas are decorated with impressive mural paintings depicting mythological scenes, and sometimes thangkas (painted on cotton, framed in brocade and hung), although there is quite a range in quality. The subjects are usually gods, great lamas and ritual diagrams (mandalas which represent the forces of the universe and aid meditation) and the wheel of life. The wheel of life is represented in the porch of every gompa and represents Buddha's knowledge and the way humans can escape their conditioning and achieve nirvana. Extremely complex rules govern every detail of these traditional arts; all stress spirituality, order and symmetry, not originality!

You will also see huge statues of various Buddhas (the Tibetans believe Buddha has been reincarnated many times), prayer wheels, lamps filled with ghee (clarified butter) arranged strategically, and sometimes offerings of rice. To the Western eye, the gompas are riots of colour, but awesome nonetheless. Most religious rites involve the recitation of sacred texts and chanting, often punctuated by musical instruments. The instruments dramatise and underline particular passages – usually in a quite unmusical way. Drums and cymbals crash, and

trumpets and oboes moan repetitively. The result can be dramatic and moving.

Sects There are four major sects in Tibetan Buddhism and all of them are represented at Bodhnath: Nyingmapa, Kargyupa, Sakyapa (often, for obvious reasons, referred to as Red Hat sects), and Gelugpa (the Yellow Hat sect). The real differences are quite esoteric with their roots often in political rather than major theological disputes.

Sometimes the Nyingmapa sect is referred to as the Old One, because its teachings are based on Buddhist texts that were translated into Tibetan from the 7th to 11th centuries. The Kargyupa sect was founded by Marpa in the 11th century and has a strong Tantric influence. Marpa's most famous disciple was Milarepa, Tibet's most revered poet. The Sakyapa was also founded in the 11th century and it rose to a position where it ruled Tibet (with the support of the Mongols) until it ran into conflict with a strict 'reformed' sect, the Gelugpa which had been founded in the 14th century.

Unlike the Sakyapa, the Gelugpa (or Yellow Hats) was celibate and disciplined. It introduced the system of reincarnated spiritual leaders and ultimately came to power – again with the support of the Mongols – in the late 17th century. It was a Mongol ruler who conferred the title *Dalai Lama* (Ocean of Wisdom) on the leader of the sect. The Gelugpa completely isolated Tibet and maintained a strict theocratic state.

Sakyapa Gompa This is the only gompa that opens directly onto the stupa (on the western

Bodhnath
Swayambhunath
Kathesimbhu

side). There are some fine paintings and a magnificent Tara covered in beautiful embroideries. Don't miss the massive prayer wheel on the left of the entrance.

Chinya-Lama Gompa Named after a lama who had trained in China, this gompa is on the right of the path that leaves to the north of the stupa.

Nyingmapa Gompa This is one of the most recently completed (1984) and impressive gompas. It has a large and thriving community – there are lots of young novices. The gompa is a large, pale-yellow building (designed after a monastery in Tibet) surrounded by lower white buildings that form a courtyard. There are some very fine interior decorations that are the work of artists from Bhutan.

Kargyupa/Nyingmapa Gompa Equal to the Nyingmapa Gompa in size, this large white gompa has a richly decorated interior with some fine paintings and large thangkas. The entrance is to the left of the main metal gates and Westerners are welcome; the lama speaks English.

Sakyapa Gompa This gompa, to the north-east of the stupa, does not have the imposing architectural unity of the previous two – it has obviously been built in stages over a number of years – but it is no less interesting. There are some high quality frescoes (inside the vestibule) and the main room is richly gilded and atmospheric.

Gelugpa Gompa To the right of the lane that runs north-east from the stupa, the Gelugpa Gompa is the least imposing gompa in appearance, but it nonetheless attracts large crowds of worshippers and has many young monks.

Places to Eat
There are a number of small restaurants along the main road outside the stupa enclosure and a couple of Tibetan restaurants around the stupa itself. You can try the *Amdo*

Tibetan Restaurant or the *Dergey Restaurant*. There's quite good food at the latter although service is slow and the large cake selection can be rather stale.

Getting There & Away
Buses to Bodhnath run from Rani Pokhari (Bus Stop 3) for Rs 1.50, or you can get there by taxi or bicycle. It's an interesting short walk between Bodhnath and Pashupatinath (see the Pashupatinath section for details).

Most tour operators include Bodhnath on their itineraries, usually in combination with Pashupatinath, and sometimes with Swayambhunath. Expect to pay around Rs 140 for a 3 hour tour. Grayline (tel 4-13188) and Everest Travel Service (tel 2-22217) are two you could consider.

KOPAN (9 km)
The Kopan monastery, a popular centre for courses on Buddhism and other Tibetan related subjects, stands on a hilltop to the north of Bodhnath. You can visit Kopan on a walk between Bodhnath and the Gokarna Mahadev Temple.

The centre has short courses on Tibetan medicine, thangka painting and other subjects but the major attraction for Westerners interested in meditation and Buddhism is the course run in November-December each year. The cost is about US$200 including accommodation and food, but the participants must observe strict disciplinary rules.

In Maharajganj in Kathmandu, the Himalayan Yogic Institute (tel 4-13094) is associated with the monastery and also operates courses. Call 2-26717 in Kathmandu or write to the Nepal Mahayana Centre, PO Box 817, Kathmandu, Nepal for more information on Kopan.

GOKARNA MAHADEV TEMPLE (10 km)
Only a short distance beyond Bodhnath the Sundarijal road turns off from the Sankhu road and a couple of km of twists and turns takes you to the old Newari village of Gokarna, just north of the Gokarna Game Reserve. The village is surrounded on three

sides by the reserve and is notable for its fine riverside Shiva temple.

Built in 1582 the triple roofed Mahadev (Great God) or Gokarneshwar (Lord of Gokarna) Temple stands on the banks of the Bagmati River and its inner sanctum enshrines a particularly revered Shiva lingam. Over the temple entrance is a golden torana with Shiva and Parvati making an appearance in the centre in the Uma Maheshwar position and a figure of the Garuda above them.

For visitors, the temple's great interest is the surprisingly varied collection of sculp-

tures and reliefs all around the site. They even line the pathway down from the road to the temple courtyard, starting with a Buddha figure at the top, and feature a varied collection of gods and goddesses, some dating back to over a thousand years.

The sculptures include figures from Hindu mythology including Narad, Surya (Sun God), Chandra (Moon God) and Kamadeva (God of Love). There's a bearded image of Brahma, Ganesh makes his usual cheerful appearance and Vishnu appears as Narsingha, making a particularly thorough job

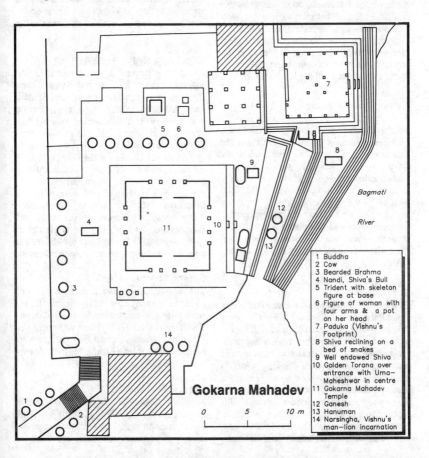

Gokarna Mahadev

0   5   10 m

1 Buddha
2 Cow
3 Bearded Brahma
4 Nandi, Shiva's Bull
5 Trident with skeleton figure at base
6 Figure of woman with four arms & a pot on her head
7 Paduka (Vishnu's Footprint)
8 Shiva reclining on a bed of snakes
9 Well endowed Shiva
10 Golden Torana over entrance with Uma–Maheshwar in centre
11 Gokarna Mahadev Temple
12 Ganesh
13 Hanuman
14 Narsingha, Vishnu's man–lion incarnation

Bagmati

River

of disembowelling a nasty demon. Shiva's bull Nandi stands beside the temple and apart from the inevitable lingams dotted around there's even a nude figure of Shiva, complete with erect lingam. Durga makes three appearances, one of them as Ajima, the goddess of smallpox. The finest of the Gokarna statuary is housed in the small shrine house in the north-western corner of the courtyard. This 8th century sculpture of the beautiful goddess Parvati shows her at her radiant best, you can see why Lord Shiva fancied her!

To one side of the main temple, just above the river, is the small, open, single storey Vishnu Paduka. This relatively recent addition shelters a metal plate bearing Vishnu's footprint. Outside, and set into the steps above the river, is an image of Shiva, reclining on a bed of cobras, just like the reclining Vishnu images at Budhanilkantha and Balaju.

Getting There & Away

You can walk, cycle or take a taxi to Gokarna but there's also an interesting walking route between Gokarna and Bodhnath via the monastery at Kopan. The clear trail starts from just beyond the bridge, on the Kathmandu side of Gokarna. It starts off steeply north-west and runs through fields and bamboo groves past teahouses to Kopan on top of a small hill. There are regular courses on meditation and Buddhism at the Kopan monastery and many Westerners take part. From Kopan it's an easy walk south-west to Bodhnath.

SUNDARIJAL (15 km)

At the edge of the valley, the streams which eventually join the Bagmati River flow over the waterfalls at Sundarijal into a 100 year old reservoir. This is also the starting point for the popular trek to Helambu, and the main reservoir which supplies drinking water to the valley is about a 2 hour walk uphill from here. A smaller trail forks off before the reservoir to a small rock cave, where a 13th century image of Mahadevi can be found. See the Nagarkot section for details of the long valley rim walk to Sundarijal from Nagarkot.

Getting There & Away

Buses leave from Tukuchapul (Bus Stop 7) near the Central Bus Station and cost Rs 7. It's a pleasant bicycle ride along the quiet roads past Gokarna.

Sankhu & Vajra Jogini Route

The route to Sankhu follows the old Tibetan trade route past Bodhnath. After Bodhnath the road to Sundarijal turns off to the north-east and the road to Sankhu continues to the east.

GOKARNA GAME RESERVE (10 km)

Continuing beyond Bodhnath from Kathmandu, the entrance to the Royal Game Reserve or King's Forest is off the Sankhu road. A deer park was created here late in the last century and the walled reserve has spotted deer (chital), hog deer (laghuna), monkeys and birds.

This is one of the few examples of woodland left on the valley floor, and it's a pleasant spot for a picnic. You can go wandering on foot, ride an elephant (Rs 175 per person per hour) or a horse (Rs 125 per person per hour). There's also a quite decent nine hole golf course (no, you can't use the elephants as golf buggies). Entrance costs Rs 25 and the park is open from 8 am to 6 pm in summer.

Getting There & Away

The reserve is about 2½ km from Bodhnath, so it can be easily reached by bicycle. Buses run quite frequently to Sundarijal from Tukuchapul (Bus Stop 7) and you could get off at the intersection; less frequent buses to Sankhu leave from near the Martyrs' Memorial Gate (Bus Stop 9).

SANKHU (20 km)

Sankhu was once an important post on the trading route between Kathmandu and Lhasa, and although the town's great days are over, you can still see many signs of its former prosperity. The town was first settled in the Licchavi era and there are many old homes decorated with fine woodcarving. Although many traditional aspects of Newari life continue in the town, the most persuasive reason to visit this place is the beautiful Vajra Jogini Temple, about 2 km north of town.

Getting There & Away

There are two or three buses a day to Sankhu, leaving from near Martyrs' Memorial Gate (Bus Stop 9) – not far from the Bhadrakali Temple. They take 1½ hours and cost Rs 3. You may also find something at the Central Bus Station (Bus Stop 6).

It's easy to reach Sankhu by bike. The road is sealed and since it basically follows the Manohara River it's flat (with a few minor exceptions). It's an attractive and interesting ride taking about 1½ hours beyond Bodhnath. Rather than backtrack all the way, in the dry season at least it is possible to cross the Manohara River and climb to the fascinating Changunarayan Temple (see the Changu-

narayan section for details). See the Nagarkot section for details of the interesting walk down to Sankhu.

VAJRA JOGINI (22 km)

Perched high above the valley, in a grove of huge, old trees, this complex of temples is well worth visiting. The main temple was built in 1655 by Pratap Malla of Kathmandu, but it seems likely the site has been used for much longer than that. The origins of the Tantric goddess who is worshipped in this bewitching spot are hard to determine.

The climb up the stone steps to the temple is steep and hot but there are a number of water spouts where you can cool off. About half way up there's a shelter and some carvings of Kali and Ganesh. A natural stone represents Than Bhairab and sacrifices are made at its foot.

As you enter the main temple compound you will see several fine bells (the Tantric female equivalent to the vajra or thunderbolt) on your right. There are two temples and the

Tantric Goddesses

The name Vajra Jogini suggests a close association with Tantric beliefs. A *vajra* (*dorje* in Tibetan) is the Buddhist thunderbolt symbol that looks a bit like a hollow dumb-bell and Vajrayana is the name for the Tantric form of Buddhism. Tantric beliefs developed as a synthesis of ancient pre-Hindu religions and new ideas that rejected many orthodox Hindu and Buddhist beliefs. Tantric believers hold that endless rebirths on the journey to nirvana can be avoided by incorporating magical rites with all the energies of existence – both good and bad – under the strict tutelage of a lama. Sex and sexual imagery play a central role.

Hinduism was initially a patriarchal religion introduced by the Aryan invaders of India, and overriding the existing earth goddesses. The development of *shaktis* or the female consorts of the new male gods allowed the resurgence of the female forces. These goddesses have enjoyed tremendous popularity in the Kathmandu Valley, sometimes completely overshadowing their male counterparts, especially in Tantric belief. A parallel development in Buddhism produced the female counterparts to the Dhyani Buddhas.

A Jogini is the female counterpart to a Bhairab, one of the wrathful forms of Shiva. In other words, a Jogini is the wrathful form of Shiva's partner Mahadevi (the Great Goddess), who in a more peaceful manifestation is Parvati. Amongst some of Mahadevi's fearsome manifestations are Kali, Durga, Annapurna and Taleju.

So who is Vajra Jogini you ask? A Tantric goddess is the simple answer – a unique Nepalese goddess possibly combining elements from Hinduism, Buddhism and perhaps even earlier religions. ∎

one nearest to the entrance is the Vajra Jogini temple, a pagoda with a three tiered roof of sheet copper. There is some beautiful repoussé work on the southern facade. The struts are carved with protective animals and gods from the Buddhist pantheon. The goddess' image cannot actually be made out through the door.

The two tiered temple furthest from the entrance enshrines a chaitya and commemorates Ugra Tara, or Blue (*Nilo*) Tara, a Buddhist goddess. The woodcarving around the doors is very fine. There are various chaityas around the platform and a gilt lion on a pillar. In the north-western corner of the courtyard (the far left when you enter) is the entrance to a cave, which is used for Tantric practices, and a Tibetan inscription. Behind the temples and up some stairs are buildings which were once used as pilgrim rest houses and priests' houses.

Getting There & Away

At Sankhu, turn left at the bus stop and walk north through the village (there is some beautiful woodcarving). Just after the road turns to the right take the road on the left which runs out of the village (under an ugly concrete archway). There are some fine stone carvings of Vishnu and Ganesh after the arch. The road then forks: the left fork is the traditional approach for pedestrians on foot and follows the small river; the right fork is driveable (though rough) and is OK for bikes.

There's a car park at the foot of the steps to the temple. If you get there by bicycle, it will be necessary to pay a few rupees to someone to look after it for you. It's quite a stiff climb to the temple.

Changunarayan Route

THIMI (10 km)

Thimi is the fourth largest town in the valley, outranked only by Kathmandu, Patan and Bhaktapur. It's a typical Newari town and its 'capable people' (the name of the town is derived from this Newari expression) operate thriving cottage industries producing pottery and papier mâché masks. They also grow vegetables for the markets of Kathmandu.

The main road of the town runs north-south between the old and new Bhaktapur roads which form the east-west top and bottom of the town. In the centre of the southern square is the 16th century Balkumari Temple. Balkumari was one of Bhairab's shaktis (a jogini) and a much less magnificent Bhairab Temple is found nearby (see the Vajra Jogini section for a brief discussion of Tantric goddesses). Thimi also has a 16th century Narayan Temple and a 15th century Mahadev Temple.

Just to the north of Thimi is Nade and from here a stone pathway leads up through an archway to the Ganesh Dyochen. Nearby is a locally popular triple roofed Ganesh Temple. Further north is Bode with an interesting 17th century Mahalakshmi Temple.

1	Garuda Image on Rs 10 Note
2	Krishna Shrine
3	Nriteshwar Shrine
4	Winged Lions
5	Vishnu Image
6	Mahavishnu
7	Mahadev Shiva Lingam
8	Images of Avalokitesvara & Vishnu
9	Changunarayan Temple
10	Griffins
11	Ganesh Shrine
12	Elephants
13	Mahadev Shiva Shrine
14	Reliefs of Narayan on the Serpent Ananta & Uma Maheshwar
15	Lakshmi Narayan Temple
16	Relief of Vishnu as Vikranth
17	Relief of Vishnu as Narsingha
18	Bhairab Shrine
19	Pashupatinath Shrine
20	Pillar with Conch Shell Symbol
21	Lions
22	Statue of King Bhupatindra Malla & His Queen
23	Garuda Statue
24	Pillar with Chakra Symbol

Festivals

In a Nepalese new year's day ceremony, 32 deities are carried to the Balkumari Temple in Thimi in palanquins. The arrival of the Ganesh image from Nade is the high point of the colourful (a great deal of bright red powder gets chucked around) festivities. A similar but smaller ceremony also takes place at the Mahalakshmi Temple in Bode.

CHANGUNARAYAN TEMPLE (22km)

The beautiful and historic temple of Changunarayan stands on a hilltop at the eastern end of the valley, about 4 km north of Bhaktapur. Although the temple dates from 1702, when it was rebuilt after a fire, its origins go right back to the 4th century and there are many important stone images and sculptures dating from the Licchavi period. Despite the temple's beauty and interest it attracts relatively few visitors because of its comparative inaccessibility. These days you can drive right to the temple via Bhaktapur or, much better, it makes a pleasant walk from that town or an interesting destination on the walk down from Nagarkot. The double

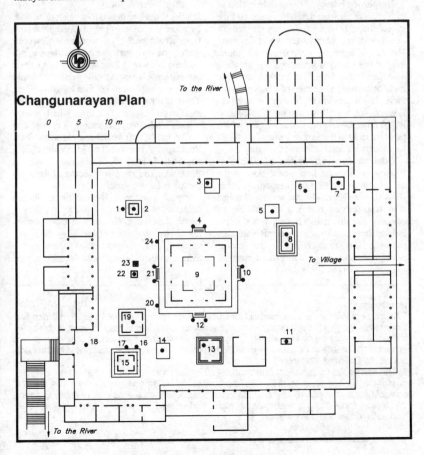

Changunarayan Plan

0   5   10 m

To the River

To Village

To the River

roofed temple is dedicated to Vishnu in his incarnation as Narayan and is exceptionally beautiful with quite amazingly intricate roof struts depicting multiarmed goddesses. The temple is fronted by a figure of Garuda said to date from the 5th century. The man-bird mount of Vishnu has a snake around his neck and kneels with folded hands facing the temple. Stone lions guard the wonderfully gilded door, flanked by equally detailed gilded windows. Two pillars at the front corners carry the traditional symbols of Vishnu, the conch shell and the chakra.

Despite the beauty of the temple itself it is, in Nepalese terms, relatively recent and the much older images found in the temple courtyard are of equally great interest. Various images of Vishnu can be found around the courtyard, carrying the symbols associated with the god in his four hands. In the north-western corner of the courtyard there is an image of Vishnu astride the Garuda which is illustrated on the Nepalese Rs 10 note. Beside the Garuda figure which faces the front of the temple is one of the oldest Licchavi stone inscriptions in the valley.

Other images include one of Vishnu as Narsingha, his man-lion incarnation, in the act of disembowelling a demon. Another shows him as Vikrantha, the six armed dwarf who transformed into a giant capable of covering the universe in three gigantic steps. Behind these two images is a small black slab showing Narayan reclining on the serpent Ananta at the bottom and Vishnu with 10 heads and 10 arms in the centre. This beautifully carved image dates from the 5th or 6th century.

Other points of interest include the statues of King Bhupatindra Malla and his queen, kneeling in a gilded cage in front of the temple. Look at the brick paving of the courtyard. In the centre, triangular bricks are used while out towards the edge there are older rounded-corner bricks. The village of Changu stands below the temple hill and has some Licchavi remains.

Getting There & Away

It takes about 2 hours on foot or about an hour by mountain bike to get to Changunarayan from Bhaktapur. It's a wonderful downhill run on the way back but quite a steep climb on the way there. A long spur runs down from the eastern edge of the valley and the temple tops the final bump of this lengthy ridge. There is now a sealed road from Bhaktapur right to the village of Changu, which is only a short stroll from the temple, and you can easily get a taxi to Changunarayan from Bhaktapur. A number of walking trails, clearly signposted, lead to Changunarayan from Bhaktapur and once you get out of the town the hill is clearly visible.

If you're on foot or bicycle it's possible to continue to Bodhnath, Sankhu, the Royal Game Reserve at Gokarna or other attractions in the north-east of the valley. From the northern and western entranceways to the temple a short, steep path descends to the

---

Narsingha

The image of Vishnu as Narsingha or Narsimha is a common one in the valley. In his man-lion incarnation the god is traditionally seen with a demon stretched across his legs, in the act of killing the creature by disembowelling it. You can find Narsingha at work at Changunarayan, in front of the palace in Patan, just inside the Hanuman Dhoka palace entrance in Kathmandu and at the Gokarna Mahadev Temple.

The demon was supposedly undefeatable as it could not be killed by man or beast, by day or night or by any weapon. Vishnu's appearance as Narsingha neatly overcame the first obstacle for a man-lion is neither a man or a beast. He then waited until evening to attack the demon, for evening is neither day or night. And instead of a weapon Narsingha used his own nails to tear the demon apart. ■

Manohara River, which can easily be waded across or crossed by a temporary bridge during the dry season (it won't be possible in the monsoon). This brings you out to the Sankhu road at the village of Bramhakhel about 3½ km east of the Gokarna Game Reserve.

If you approach Changunarayan from the Sankhu road you'll see a small sign for Changunarayan on a building wall on the south side at the entry to Bramhakhel. It's a 5 minute walk across the fields to the river and the temporary bridge. It's quite a steep and difficult scramble up the hill that will take at least 45 minutes (especially if you're carrying a bike). You might like to go slower as there are a couple of small Newari hamlets along the way, and great views.

There's quite a labyrinth of paths up the hill and it's not a bad idea to have a guide (and bicycle carrier). You will probably find small boys offering their services – establish a price in advance. If not, just keep going up! From Changunarayan it's an exhilarating half hour bike ride to Bhaktapur, which is another 45 minutes from Kathmandu.

A third way of reaching Changunarayan is by the pleasant downhill stroll from Nagarkot (see the following Nagarkot section). Walking down from Nagarkot to Changunarayan and then on to Bhaktapur is a much more interesting walk than the straightforward walk down to Bhaktapur.

Nagarkot Route

The route to Nagarkot goes by Thimi and Bhaktapur before climbing steeply up to the village on the valley rim.

NAGARKOT (30 km)
There are various places around the edge of the Kathmandu Valley which offer great mountain views but the village of Nagarkot is generally held to be the best viewpoint. Every day mountain watchers make their way up to the village, stay overnight in one of Nagarkot's many lodges, then rise at dawn to see the sun appear over the Himalaya.

Nagarkot is on a ridge on the north-eastern rim of the valley and the view extends all the way from Dhaulagiri in the west past Mt Everest (little more than a dot on the horizon) to Kanchenjunga in the east. An easy hour's walk north from the village will give an even better view from a lookout tower on a ridge.

The pilgrimage to Nagarkot will nearly always be rewarded with a clear view between October and April but you will be very lucky to catch more than a glimpse through the clouds of some snow-capped mountain in the June to September monsoon period. It can get very cold at Nagarkot in autumn or winter so if you're staying overnight come prepared with warm clothing.

The road to Nagarkot from Bhaktapur winds up the hillside to a cluster of shops and buildings, which is the real 'centre' of the village. From there it continues along the

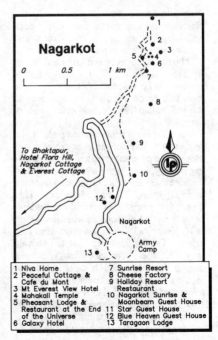

Nagarkot

0   0.5   1 km

To Bhaktapur,
Hotel Flora Hill,
Nagarkot Cottage
& Everest Cottage

Nagarkot

Army Camp

1 Niva Home	7 Sunrise Resort
2 Peaceful Cottage & Cafe du Mont	8 Cheese Factory
	9 Holiday Resort Restaurant
3 Mt Everest View Hotel	10 Nagarkot Sunrise & Moonbeam Guest House
4 Mahakali Temple	
5 Pheasant Lodge & Restaurant at the End of the Universe	11 Star Guest House
	12 Blue Heaven Guest House
6 Galaxy Hotel	13 Taragaon Lodge

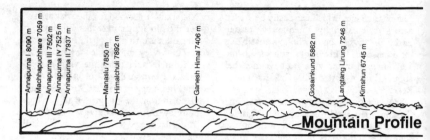

Annapurna I 8090 m
Machhapuchhare 7059 m
Annapurna III 7502 m
Annapurna IV 7525 m
Annapurna II 7937 m
Manaslu 7850 m
Himalchuli 7892 m
Ganesh Himal 7406 m
Gosainkund 5862 m
Langtang Lirung 7246 m
Kimshun 6745 m

Mountain Profile

ridge for another km or so, finally ending at an army camp.

There are a number of ways to get to or away from Nagarkot including fine walks down to Sundarijal, Sankhu, Changunarayan or Bhaktapur in the valley or to Banepa beyond the valley to the east. There is a cheese factory in Nagarkot where you can buy some food to eat on your way down.

Places to Stay & Eat

Nagarkot has a surprising number of lodges and guest houses, nearly all of them distinctly rock bottom in price and facilities.

The Nagarkot accommodation is found in three places – on the way up to the village, just beyond the village corner where there is a group of popular lodges around the Ma- hakali Temple, and near the army camp.

Nagarkot is very much a one night stand, few visitors stay longer although you can make some pleasant strolls in the surrounding country. Late in the afternoon each day there's a mass arrival and after breakfast each morning there's a mass departure. This means that every lodge around can simultaneously run out of rooms so when you get up to Nagarkot make finding a room your first priority. The best rooms go first, late arrivals may find the accommodation standards dropping precipitously. On the other hand, in the off season there are fewer visitors and so prices are highly negotiable.

Only two places at Nagarkot have electricity, not many have running water and hot water is also a rarely seen luxury. The nights can get very cold so warm clothing and even a sleeping bag can be worth having.

Below the Ridge Staying below the ridge means you have a long walk up to the top for the sunrise views. The places here are a couple of km before you reach the ridge top although they are right by the road. The *Everest Cottage* and *Nagarkot Cottage* are both basic cheapies while the *Hotel Flora Hill* (tel 2-26893) is one of the two places with electricity. At US$38 for a double, prices at the Flora Hill reflect its luxurious nature.

Around the Mahakali Temple The winding road takes a sharp turn at the cluster of shops which marks the 'centre' of Nagarkot. From here a dirt track turns off and after a couple of hundred metres comes to a hilltop group of hotels which are the most popular and best situated at Nagarkot. They cluster around the Mahakali Temple on the top of the hill and many rooms at these lodges offer Himalayan views straight from your bed. At the worst you'll just have to take a few steps outside to bring the whole sweep into view.

With one exception all these places are very much rock bottom in character. None of the lodges have electricity and at most of them the rooms vary widely in standard, if you arrive late you can find yourself in one of the grottier rooms. You normally pay a bit extra for the Himalayan views.

The *Pheasant Lodge* has some pretty standard rooms from Rs 40 and Rs 50 but also a few individual bamboo-walled cottages with

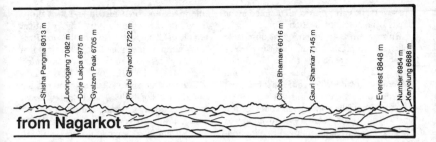

Shisha Pangma 8013 m | Leonpogang 7082 m | Dorje Lakpa 6975 m | Gyalzen Peak 6705 m | Phurbi Ghyachu 5722 m | Choba Bhamare 6016 m | Gauri Shankar 7145 m | Everest 8848 m | Number 6954 m | Kenyolung 6688 m

from Nagarkot

attached toilet for Rs 100. These are probably the nicest rooms to be found here.

The lodge's wonderfully named *Restaurant at the End of the Universe* has great views and atmosphere. With its carpeted bench around the low tables it's a popular gathering place in the evening. The food is pretty good; you should try their Nepalese rice pudding which is delicious.

The *Galaxy Hotel*, just below the Pheasant Lodge, has rooms at Rs 80, Rs 90 and Rs 120. The rooms have attached toilets and the extra cost gets you a view. Some of the upstairs rooms at Rs 120 are very pleasant while some of the downstairs ones are distinctly second rate. The Galaxy also has a popular restaurant. Next to the Galaxy is the *Sunrise Resort* with rather basic and spartan rooms at Rs 40 or Rs 50 with a very fine view.

Continue beyond the Mahakali Temple, skirting the bank official's house, and you come to the *Peaceful Cottage* which, like the Galaxy, has rooms of varying standards. The good ones have fine views and are clean and well kept, the grotty ones are definitely second best. The prices start from Rs 40 and Rs 50. Topping the rise here, above the level of the rooms, is the *Cafe du Mont* with panoramic views.

The new *Mt Everest View Hotel* is just below the Peaceful Cottage, on the outer edge of the ridge. It was under construction in late '89 by Nagarkot's *pradhan panch*, the Nepalese equivalent of a town mayor, and looks like it will be a little more up-market.

Separated from this group of lodges by a couple of hundred metres is the *Niva Home* with simple, spartan rooms at Rs 50 downstairs and Rs 60 upstairs.

Near the Army Camp The third group of places is close to the end of the motor road. Right at the very end, beyond the army encampment, is the other place at Nagarkot with electricity, the government-operated *Taragaon Lodge*. Singles/doubles here cost US$20/26 plus tax and it has a distinctly 'run by the government' air to it. Electricity and attached bathrooms or not, it's hard to justify the cost, although the restaurant is pleasant

The other places are between the army encampment and the main group of lodges. First there's the *Star Guest House*, right by the road and the *Blue Heaven Guest House*, which has rooms at Rs 30 and is down below the road and ridge line on the valley (no view) side. The *Nagarkot Sunrise/Moonbeam Guest House* offers extremely basic rooms at Rs 30 for a double, and is on the view side of the ridge.

Continuing from these lodges back towards the main hilltop group around the Mahakali Temple is the new and very pleasant looking *Holiday Resort Restaurant*.

Getting There & Away

There's a road right up to Nagarkot from Bhaktapur so you can take a bus or taxi all the way there. You don't even have to stay overnight as Kathmandu tour operators run dawn trips to Nagarkot to catch the sunrise. Walking to or, preferably, from Nagarkot is, however, an interesting alternative and there are several possible routes, all detailed in the Treks from Nagarkot section.

Buses operate to a somewhat unreliable schedule from Bhaktapur, departing every few hours and costing Rs 6. The bus can be very slow (can take at least an hour) and extremely crowded. The roof is not only less crowded but also offers fine views.

A taxi from Bhaktapur costs about Rs 300 one way or Rs 400 return. Pre-dawn tours to Nagarkot from Kathmandu will cost about Rs 150.

TREKKING ROUTES FROM NAGARKOT
There are a number of trekking routes to or from Nagarkot. As always with trekking it's easier to go down than up so if you only want to walk one way it's a good idea to take the bus up and walk back down. The following walk descriptions are all written heading downhill from Nagarkot.

Nagarkot-Bhaktapur
Until the road was built up to Bhaktapur this was the only way to go. Now with buses running back and forth it's neither necessary nor all that enjoyable. You would be better off taking one of the alternative routes but if you do want to walk back down it's relatively easy to take the wide, easy trail which shortcuts across the road turns. The trail eventually joins the road on its final gradual ascent to Bhaktapur; you can follow this and turn off at the eastern end of the town or simply catch a bus, should one come by. It takes about 2 hours to walk down, and perhaps twice that walking up.

Going down you leave the main road to descend steeply through a pine forest, then follow a stream to a cluster of bamboo trees near the city water reservoir where you rejoin the main road. From here you enter the town at the eastern end and continue to Tachupal Tole. Coming up from Bhaktapur there are signs to Nagarkot in the town.

Nagarkot-Changunarayan Temple
From Nagarkot it is very easy to see the long spur which extends into the Kathmandu Valley. At the very end of the spur the ridge

line gives one final hiccup and then drops down to the valley floor. The beautiful temple of Changunarayan is on the top of this final bump on the ridge line. Walking down to Changunarayan is a much more interesting alternative to the walk down to Bhaktapur.

The road down to Bhaktapur follows the ridge for most of the way, finally turning down from the ridge at a sharp hairpin bend and then running across the valley floor the final distance into Bhaktapur. Rather than walking all the way down to Changunarayan it's easier to take the bus down to this hairpin bend. The fare is Rs 3 and the ride saves you the tedious part of the walk, where the walking trail runs close to the road.

From the bend, the trail climbs uphill through a pine forest for about 20 minutes until it reaches the top of the ridge and then it simply follows the ridge line undulating gently down to Changunarayan. The walking trail passes through small Chhetri villages with wonderful views over the valley to the Himalaya beyond. Finally the shining roof of Changunarayan appears above the village of Changu itself from where a stone-paved street leads to the temple. From the point where you leave the Nagarkot to Bhaktapur road to go to the temple, it takes about 1 to 1½ hours.

From Changunarayan you can descend to the Manohara River to the north and take the road back to Bodhnath and Kathmandu. Alternatively you can continue south to Bhaktapur, either by the direct trail or by the road running slightly to the east. See the Changunarayan section in the Kathmandu Valley chapter for full details.

Nagarkot-Sankhu
Fewer walkers follow the trail to Sankhu, just north of the Nagarkot to Changunarayan ridge line in the north-east of the valley. The picturesque Newari town is surrounded by rich agricultural land and is easily visible from Nagarkot or from the trail down to Changunarayan. The trail follows a ridge line then drops steeply down the hillside in a north-westerly direction, joining the main Helambu to Sankhu trail and passing a group of teahouses where you can ask directions to

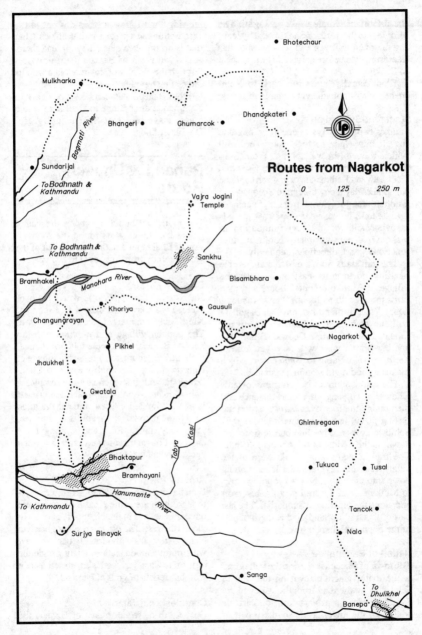

Around the Kathmandu Valley

Bhotechaur

Mulkharka

Bhangeri
Ghumarcok
Dhandakateri

Bagmati River

Sundarijal

To Bodhnath &
Kathmandu

Vajra Jogini
Temple

Routes from Nagarkot

0   125   250 m

To Bodhnath &
Kathmandu

Sankhu

Bramhakel
Manohara River

Bisambhara

Khoriya
Gausuli

Changunarayan

Pikhel

Nagarkot

Jhaukhel

Gwatala

Ghimiregaon

Tabya Kosi

Bhaktapur
Bramhayani

Tukuca
Tusal

To Kathmandu

Hanumante River

Tancok

Surjya Binayak

Nala

Sanga

To
Dhulikhel

Banepa

the important temple of Vajra Jogini. The temple is to the north of Sankhu and by leaving the main trail you can walk west to this interesting site before completing the descent to Sankhu.

From Sankhu buses run back to Kathmandu via Bodhnath every couple of hours.

Nagarkot-Sundarijal

It takes two easy days or one very long one to walk from Nagarkot to Sundarijal on a trail which follows the valley rim. From Sundarijal you can take the road to Gokarna, Bodhnath and Kathmandu or you can continue for another day along the rim to Sheopuri and Budhanilkantha. Some trekking agencies operate treks on this valley rim walk but it is also possible to find accommodation in teahouses. There are many confusing trail junctions so ask directions frequently.

The trail starts from the Mahakali Temple heading north-north-east and passes the village of Kattike (about 1 hour) and then turns more north to Jorsim Pauwa (about 1 hour). Walk further down through Bagdhara with its teahouses to Chowki Bhanjyang (about 1 hour). From Chowki Bhanjyang another hour's walk will take you further north through Nagle to Bhotechaur, which makes a good night stop in a teahouse.

The walk continues by returning towards Chowki Bhanjyang for a short distance and then taking the fork by a *chautara* (porters' resting place) uphill and then more steeply uphill to cross a ridge line before dropping down on the middle of three trails to Chule. The trail contours around the edge of the valley, crossing several ridge lines running down into the valley, before dropping down to Mulkarka and the trail past the reservoir and along the pipeline to Sundarijal. The last part of this trail to Sundarijal is the first part of the popular Helambu trek.

Nagarkot-Banepa

The town of Banepa is outside the valley and is the major junction town on the way to Dhulikhel on the road from the valley to the Tibetan border. From Nagarkot, you start this walk near the tower at the southern part of

the ridge and follow a steep descent to the east. Following a precise trail is difficult, but that is no problem since they all lead there. A few km north of Banepa the trail passes through the old Newari town of Nala with its interesting temples.

From Banepa, you can take a bus back to Kathmandu or continue to Dhulikhel where many travellers stay in the delightful Dhulikhel Lodge.

Panauti & Dhulikhel Route

The route to Dhulikhel outside the valley passes by Thimi, skirts round the southern side of Bhaktapur and then climbs out of the valley before dropping down to Banepa.

BANEPA (26 km)

Just outside the valley, the small town of Banepa is a busy crossroads with a statue of King Tribhuvan marking the centre of town. The popular village of Dhulikhel is 5 km beyond Banepa; the temple town of Panauti is about 5 km south; the interesting village of Nala is just to the north-west; and Chandeshwari, with it's legendary old temple, is only a km or so north-east – yet Banepa itself is of very limited interest. Indeed the main road through town, all that most visitors see, is a dusty, noisy affair and waiting for a change of bus at that busy crossroads is often decidedly unpleasant.

Around Town

Banepa has few buildings of interest although there are some pleasant squares and quieter laneways in the older part of town to the north-west. The old town square has two Narayan temples with virtually back to back worshipful Garuda statues. Right beside the turn-off to Chandeshwari is an attractive tank with bas reliefs of gods at one end.

Chandeshwari Temple

Only a km or so north-east of Banepa the

temple to the goddess Chandeshwari perches on the edge of a gorge. The road out of Banepa runs gently uphill then just as gently downhill through open fields and then a short village street, past an old tank right to the arched entrance gate to the temple.

The people of this valley were once terrorised by a demon known as Chand and when Parvati, in her demon-slaying mode, got rid of the nuisance she took the name Chandeshwari, 'slayer of Chand', and this temple was built in her honour. The temple is entered through a doorway topped by a brilliantly coloured relief of Parvati disposing of the demon. The triple roofed temple has roof struts showing the eight Ashta Matrikas and eight Bhairabs but the temple's most notable feature is on the west wall which is painted with a huge and colourful fresco of Bhairab at his destructive worst.

The temple also has a Shiva shrine complete with lingam, and Nandi and Ganesh also makes an appearance. The ghats below the temple, beside the stream, are an auspicious place to die and people come here when their end is nigh.

Getting There & Away
Regular buses leave from the Central Bus Station (Bus Stop 6) and the trip to Banepa takes about an hour and costs Rs 6. Buses continue on from Banepa to Dhulikhel and further towards Kodari on the Chinese border. There are also regular services south from Banepa to Panauti.

NALA
The interesting small town of Nala is about 4 km north-west of Banepa. Nala's Bhagwati Temple dominates the central square of the town and is one of the very few four-tiered temples in the valley area. On the edge of the settlement is the Buddhist pagoda temple of Karunamaya, dedicated to Avalokitesvara.

PANAUTI
Standing in a valley about 6 km south of Banepa, the small town of Panauti is at the junction of the rivers Roshi Khola and Pungamati Khola. Like Allahabad in India a third 'invisible' river is said to join the other two at the confluence. The town is relatively untouched and has a number of interesting temples, one of which may be the oldest in Nepal. Panauti once stood at the junction of important trading routes and had a royal palace in its main square. Today it's just a quiet backwater, but all the more interesting for that.

Festivals
Panauti celebrates a chariot festival at the end of the monsoon each year when images of the gods from the town's various temples are drawn around the streets in temple carts. The festival starts from the town's old Durbar Square.

The Makar Sankranti festival in the Nepalese month of Magha, around mid-January, is a river bathing festival in honour of Lord Shiva. Like the great mela cities of India the festival becomes a Makar Mela every 12 years when it draws enormous crowds. The next occasion will be in 1998.

Indreshwar Mahadev Temple
The three storey Indreshwar Mahadev Temple in the village centre is a Shiva temple. The temple was originally built in 1294 over a Shiva lingam and was subsequently rebuilt in the 15th century. In 1988 an earthquake caused serious damage and there are plans to renovate it. In its original form it may well have been the oldest temple in Nepal – Kathmandu's Kasthamandap may predate it but Kasthamandap was originally built as a dharamsala, not as a temple.

Around the temple are many shrines including one dedicated to Ahilya, the beautiful wife of a Vedic sage. Legends relate that she was seduced by the god Indra who tricked her by assuming the shape of her husband. When the sage returned and discovered what had happened he took a bizarre revenge upon Indra by causing his body to become covered in yonis, female sexual organs! Naturally Indra was somewhat put out by this and for many years he and his wife Indrayani repented at this auspicious confluence of rivers. Eventually Parvati, Shiva's consort, took pity upon Indrayani and turned her into the invisible river which joins the two visible ones in Panauti. More years passed and eventually Shiva decided to release Indra from his strange problem. Shiva appeared in Panauti as a great lingam and when Indra bathed in the river the yonis disappeared. The lingam is the one which stands in the temple.

Whatever the legends, the temple, run-down though it may be, is certainly a fine one and the roof struts depicting the various incarnations of Shiva and some discreetly amorous couples are said to be masterpieces of Newari woodcarving. The courtyard has numerous smaller shrines apart from the stone pillar to Ahilya. To one side of the main temple is a rectangular Bhairab Temple with faces peering out of the three upstairs windows, rather like the Shiva-Parvati Temple in Kathmandu's Durbar Square. A small double roofed Shiva temple stands by the north-western corner while a Vishnu shrine with a 2 metre high image of the god faces the temple from the west. Look for the pots and pans hanging under the roof eaves of the main temple. They're donated to the temple by newlyweds to ensure a happy married life.

Other Temples

Across the Pungamati Khola is the 17th century Brahmayani Temple; a suspension bridge crosses the river at this point. Brahmayani is the chief goddess of the village and her image is drawn around the town each year in the chariot festival. This temple was restored with French assistance in 1982-83.

On the town side of the river, actually at the junction where the two rivers meet, is a Krishna Narayan Temple with some woodcarvings of similar age and style to the Indreshwar Mahadev Temple. The riverbank stone sculptures are also of interest but unfortunately the late '80s were cruel to Panauti: apart from the earthquake there were also severe floods which swept away the cremation ghats at the river junction.

Getting There & Away

Buses between Dhulikhel and Banepa cost

Rs 1.50. From the junction by the king's statue in the middle of Banepa, buses run regularly to Panauti and cost Rs 1.50. See the Dhulikhel section for information on walking to Panauti.

DHULIKHEL (32 km)

Only 5 km beyond Banepa is the interesting small town of Dhulikhel. It's popular as a Himalayan viewpoint, in part because the road to Dhulikhel is easier than the steep and winding road up to Nagarkot, but Dhulikhel is also a good centre for short day treks. Many visitors come here to stretch their legs before setting off on longer treks.

Dhulikhel is the district headquarters and has a number of government offices, a high school and even a small jail. Its population is Newari although there are people of many other groups in the surrounding villages. The prime Himalayan viewpoint is the parade ground, on the ridge just east of the centre. In the late '60s Dhulikhel was a hippy gathering point and they even planned to build their own temple here! An even better view can be found from the hill topped by a Kali temple, about 30 minutes walk along the Namobuddha trail.

Dhulikhel has a very popular budget lodge right in the town and two excellent but more expensive places nearby.

Temples

The old part of the town, west of the bus halt and the Dhulikhel Lodge, is an interesting area to wander around with some fine old Newari buildings and several interesting temples. The town's main square has a tank, a small triple roofed Harisiddhi Temple and a Vishnu temple fronted by two worshipful Garudas in quite different styles. One is a kneeling stone Garuda topping a low pillar while the second Garuda is in bright metal, flanked by two kneeling devotees, and is more like the bird-faced Garudas of Indonesia than the conventional Nepalese Garudas. The triple roofed temple has been decorated with brightly coloured ceramic tiles.

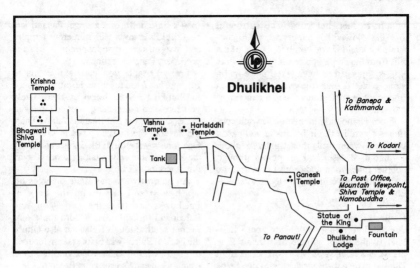

Beyond the square, the western end of the town is marked by a hill topped by a modern Krishna Temple and the Bhagwati Shiva Temple.

Walking in the other direction from the Dhulikhel Lodge you pass the post office, the mountain viewpoint and reach the junction where the road turns south to Namobuddha. Continue straight on from there and dip down to a picturesque little Shiva Temple at the bottom of a gorge. Water flows through the site where the main sanctum is a squat, square block decorated with coloured tiles and topped with a metal dome with four nagas arching down from the pinnacle. The temple is fronted by figures of Nandi on pillars and kneeling devotees. To one side is a fine image of Ganesh while in a second small shrine only the feet remain of three images, the result of art thieves' work. Below that is a tank but this is a temple with everything – if you look around you can find images of Hanuman, Saraswati, Shiva and Parvati, lingams, tridents and much more.

Dhulikhel's final temple attraction is the Kali Temple high up the hill towards Namobuddha. Climb here for the view, not the temple which is of little interest.

Namobuddha Trek

The trek from Dhulikhel to Namobuddha or Namura is a fine walk in itself and also a good leg stretcher for longer treks. It takes about 3 hours each way so it makes a good day walk and the Dhulikhel Lodge has a sketch map of the route. The walk can be made either as a return trip or as a loop walk to avoid backtracking. If you start early enough you can even continue on from Namobuddha to Panauti and return from there via Banepa by bus.

Namobuddha is a relatively easy trek which can even be made during the monsoon. From Dhulikhel the trail first climbs up to the Kali temple lookout then drops down through the village of Kavre and past a number of teahouses. It then climbs again through pine woods past Phulbari and up and down a couple more hills before reaching the Namobuddha hill. Asking directions is no problem, any Westerner heading in this direction is assumed to be going to Namobuddha!

Surprisingly little is known about the stupa at Namobuddha although it is an important destination for Buddhist pilgrims. A legend relates that a Buddha came across a tigress close to death from starvation and unable to feed her cubs. The sorrowful Buddha allowed the hungry tigress to consume him, and if you climb to the top of the hill from the stupa you reach the site where this is supposed to have taken place and a stone tablet depicts the event. There is an important festival at this site in the month of November.

From Namobuddha the circuit walk continues downhill through Sankhu and past a couple of water mills then climbs for about 1 hour to Batase. Next it passes through another pine wood and drops down to cross a stream before climbing up again to Dhulikhel.

Panauti Trek

Another interesting walk leads from Dhulikhel to the small village of Panauti. The pleasant 2 hour stroll starts off south from Dhulikhel then turns west, crosses rice fields and runs along the course of a small stream. It eventually meets the Banepa to Panauti road a little north of the town. Panauti is a beautiful little town with numerous temples and magnificent woodcarvings – see the preceding Panauti section.

From Panauti you can take a bus to Banepa, just 6 km north, and from there back to Dhulikhel or to Kathmandu. Alternatively you can keep on walking west to Godavari in the south of the Kathmandu Valley. There are several alternative routes to Godavari. One runs west through Bhaleswar and along the Roshi Khola valley, taking about 6 hours direct to Godavari.

An alternative to this route diverges off south-west and climbs up the back of Pulchowki then takes the road down from Pulchowki to Godavari. A third route runs further south through Kalar but also climbs the back of Pulchowki before taking the road down to Godavari. Either route via Pulchowki entails a long day's walk from Panauti.

Places to Stay & Eat

Dhulikhel has three places to stay – one in the town itself, one about a km before the town and one several km beyond the town. In Dhulikhel itself, the *Dhulikhel Lodge* (tel 011-61114) is a very popular place for shoestring travellers with a fine old building, a pretty good restaurant and a pleasant open courtyard.

Single/doubles cost Rs 35/70 and are very simple but quite comfortable. If you've got a room in the front you don't even need to climb out of bed to enjoy the Himalayan view, although Dhulikhel can be a surprisingly noisy town and front room occupants can find the street activity a little disturbing.

The Dhulikhel Lodge is a wonderful place to just laze around and talk to people. The food can be quite good and over the years the lodge has collected a veritable library of guest books with lots of interesting information interspersed with the usual dreamy raves! The showers and washroom facilities beside the garden have hot water and there is electricity.

The same people also operate the *Himalayan Horizon Hotel* (tel 2-25092 in Kath-

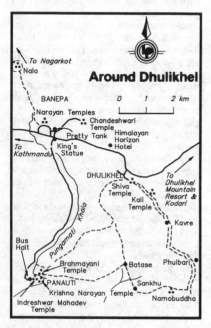

mandu or 011-61296), about a km back towards Banepa. It's also sometimes referred to as the *Sun-n-Snow Hotel*. Singles/doubles with attached bathroom in this very comfortable hotel are US$30/40. All the rooms face straight out on to the Himalayan peaks and there's a grassy area in front of the hotel with equally good views plus a beautiful garden running in terraces down the hill. The restaurant here has excellent food but you should order from the menu rather than opting for the accommodation prices inclusive of meals which are not very good value. The menu features an interesting variety of Nepalese dishes.

Dhulikhel's third accommodation option is the *Dhulikhel Mountain Resort* (tel 2-20031, 2-26779), 4 km beyond the village towards the Chinese border. The Himalayan views from here are equally superb and singles/doubles cost US$42/44. There's no electricity at the attractive resort but the bathrooms have solar-heated hot water. Both the Himalayan Horizon and the Dhulikhel Mountain Resort are popular meal stops for day-trippers from Kathmandu.

Getting There & Away

Regular buses go from the Central Bus Station (Bus Stop 6). The journey takes about 1½ hours and costs Rs 7. The buses skirt Bhaktapur at the eastern end of the valley and then climb over the Sanga Pass out of the valley, before dropping down to Banepa then climbing again to Dhulikhel, 32 km from Kathmandu.The fare is Rs 1.50 for the short ride from Banepa to Dhulikhel. A taxi from Kathmandu will cost about Rs 350, or from Bhaktapur about Rs 250.

The walk to Dhulikhel from Nagarkot is an interesting alternative. After watching the sunrise at Nagarkot you can walk down through Nala to Banepa, from where you can take a bus the last few km to Dhulikhel. See the Treks from Nagarkot section for more information. Tours to Dhulikhel to catch the sunrise operate regularly from Kathmandu and cost about Rs 160.

Godavari & Pulchowki Route

The road to Godavari is sealed and there's quite a bit of traffic, so this is not one of the best bike rides around the valley. There are quite a number of things to see, however. If you have access to a car it is worth considering a trip to the top of nearby Pulchowki, especially in spring (March, April and May) when the rhododendrons are in bloom.

HARISIDDHI (10 km)

This is a small Newari village with a four tiered pagoda temple to Harisiddhi Bhavani.

BISHANKHU NARAYAN (15 km)

If you're looking for an excuse to get off the beaten track, the shrine of Bishanku Narayan will do nicely. The shrine itself is something of a disappointment, despite the fact that it is one of the most important Vishnu shrines in the valley. A steep stairway leads to a tiny cave – more a fissure in the rock – and there's nothing much to see. On the way, however, you pass through an attractive village, and there are some good views from the shrine itself.

Getting There & Away

The unsealed road to Bishankhu Narayan takes off to the north from the undistinguished village of Bandegaon then veers to the south-east and crosses a small stream. After 1 km you come to a small village. The road forks at the 'village green'; take the left fork and the shrine is another km away.

GODAVARI (22 km)

Godavari is not really a proper town, although there are a number of points of interest in the vicinity. This is home to the Royal Botanical Gardens, St Xavier's College, Godavari Kunda, Pulchowki Mai and a controversial marble quarry. The sealed road from Kathmandu continues virtually to the foot of the hills and St Xavier's College – the awful scars from the quarry are also clearly visible. At this point an unsealed road continues to the south and the sealed road veers to the left (north-east) to the botanical gardens.

Royal Botanical Gardens
The main entrance to the gardens is flanked by white-painted walls. It's a quiet and peaceful spot but, unfortunately, few of the trees and plants are labelled so unless you already know what you're looking at you won't end up any the wiser. There really aren't many persuasive reasons for visiting unless you're a keen botanist. They're open from 10 am to 4 pm and entry is Rs 1.

Godavari Kunda
A dirt road continues past the entrance to the botanical gardens and after 100 metres or so you come to the Godavari Kunda – a sacred spring – on your right. It's a curious spot, and although none of the architecture or sculpture is particularly inspiring it is revered by Hindus. Every 12 years – next in July 1991 – thousands of pilgrims come here to bathe and gain merit. Clear mountain water collects in a pool in an inner courtyard, then flows through carved stone spouts into a larger pool in the outer courtyard.

Pulchowki Mai
If you return towards the marble quarry and take the dirt road to the south, Pulchowki Mai is a couple of hundred metres past St Xavier's College and virtually opposite the main gates to the quarry. The site is dilapidated and somewhat overshadowed by the quarry. There's a three tiered pagoda to a Tantric mother goddess flanked by a temple to Ganesh. There are two large pools before the temple compound fed by nine spouts that represent the nine streams that flow off Pulchowki.

Getting There & Away
There are local minibuses and several Saja Sewa buses. They leave from Lagankhel in Patan and the 1 hour journey costs Rs 3.50. It would be quite feasible to ride a mountain bike – the road is good – but there are more interesting rides in the valley.

PULCHOWKI
This 2762 metre mountain is the highest point around the valley and not surprisingly there are absolutely magnificent views from the summit. This is also home to one of the last surviving cloud forests in central Nepal. The mountain is famous for its spring flowers, in particular its magnificent red and white rhododendrons.

Unfortunately, there's a transmission tower on the summit and an army camp. The open shrine to Pulchowki Mai, may once have been a pretty spot, but it's now covered in rubbish. The views and the superb forest, however, make the journey worthwhile.

Getting There & Away
The unsealed road is rough in places but quite OK for a normal car if you take it slowly. It takes about 45 minutes from the bottom. You would need to be very keen to undertake the climb on a mountain bike, although it could certainly be done.

Chapagaon & Lele Route

The road to Lele is an ideal mountain-bike trip. It's sealed to Chapagaon and there are great views and some attractive villages along the way. Take the turn-off from the Ring Rd signposted to the Leprosy Mission. By bicycle it's quite a stiff climb in places – which is all the better for the return trip. Allow the best part of a day, although it's only an hour from the Ring Rd to Chapagaon.

SUNAKOTHI (10 km)
This small village is strung out along the road. There are two temples – one to Jagannath and the other to Bringarshwar Mahadev.

THECHO (12 km)
Thecho also has two temples, the brightly coloured Balkumari Temple and a two tiered pagoda to Brahmayani.

CHAPAGAON (13 km)
Chapagaon is a prosperous village with a number of shops and temples and shrines strung along the road. Near the entrance to the village is a Ganesh shrine. There are two dilapidated two-tiered temples (one looks as if it has been hit by a truck) dedicated to Narayan and Krishna and a shrine to a Bhairab that has erotic carvings on its struts.

Vajra Varahi
A small temple complex – an important Tantric site – lies about 500 metres east of the main road. When you enter Chapagaon take the path on your left after the two-tiered temples. Notice the disused irrigation system, with stone channels and bridges, behind the village. The temple lies in a grove of trees and was built in 1665, but is now surrounded by less-distinguished shelters and an unfortunate amount of litter. Nonetheless, it's an interesting and atmospheric place that has probably been a centre for worship for millenia. Photography is banned.

Getting There & Away
Local minibuses and a Saja Sewa bus leave from Lagankhel in Patan and the 1 to 1½ hour journey costs Rs 4. By mountain bike, Chapagaon is about an hour (note the comparison with the bus time!) from the Ring Rd. About 10 minutes after Chapagaon the road starts to climb into the foothills. The sealed road continues to the Leprosy Mission and Tika Bhairab in the Lele Valley. If you are running out of enthusiasm an unsealed road takes off to the left – there's a pipal tree and chautara. The road is in poor condition but you are rewarded with fantastic views across the valley to the Ganesh Himal. If you keep going you cross a saddle and enter the tranquil Lele Valley.

LELE (19 km)
The Lele Valley seems a million miles from the hustle and bustle of Kathmandu, and there are few visitors. It's a peaceful, beautiful valley that in many ways seems untouched by the 20th century.

Tika Bhairab
The Tika Bhairab is a huge, multicoloured painting on a brick wall. The shrine lies at the confluence of two rivers and is marked by a huge sal tree.

Bungamati Route

The road to Bungamati, one of the most picturesque small towns in the valley, provides yet another ideal mountain-biking expedition. The road to Bungamati is the continuation of the main road that runs through Jawlakhel (the Tibetan refugee camp on the outskirts of Patan), on the other side of the Ring Rd.

BUNGAMATI (10 km)
Bungamati is a classic Newari village dating from the 16th century. It is perched on a spur of land overlooking the Bagmati River and it's shaded by large trees and stands of bamboo. Fortunately, the village's streets are too small and hazardous for cars. Visitors are rare, so tread gently.

Rato Machhendranath Temple
Bungamati is the birthplace of Rato Machhendranath, regarded as the patron of the valley, and the large shikhara-style temple in the centre of the village square is his home for 6 months of the year. He spends the rest of his time in Patan. The process of moving him around Patan and backwards and forwards to Bungamati is the centrepiece to one of the most important annual festivals in the valley. See the Rato Machhendranath section in the Kathmandu, Patan & Bhaktapur chapter and the Festivals & Holidays

section in the Facts about the Country chapter for details.

The *chowk* around the temple is one of the most beautiful in the valley – here one can see the heart of a functioning Newari town. There are many chortens, and a huge prayer wheel, clearly pointing to the syncretic nature of Newari religion.

Karya Binayak Temple

Between Bungamati and Khokna, the Karya Binayak Temple is dedicated to Ganesh. The temple is not particularly interesting and Ganesh is simply represented by a natural stone but the view is spectacular. From this point, surrounded by trees, you can look over the Bagmati Valley to the foothills, or back to Bungamati, tumbling down the opposite hill.

Getting There & Away

Continue over the Ring Rd from the main road through Jawlakhel. After you cross the Nakhu River, veer left. The right fork takes you through to the Chobar Gorge where you can cross the river and return to Kathmandu by a different route. It's a pleasant ride along a gradually climbing ridge to get to Bungamati.

Approximately an hour after leaving the Ring Rd you'll come out at a viewpoint marked by a single, large tree. It's worth pausing here to take in the lie of the land. To the left lies Bungamati, then swinging to the right comes Karya Binayak then about 1 km away, Khokna. Follow the road down to Bungamati and take the right fork which passes to the left of a large pond. The footpath then veers to the left and climbs up to the distinctive, white shikhara temple and the town square.

Buses leave from Jawlakhel, take half an hour and cost Rs 2.

To get to Karya Binayak, retrace your steps to the first pond you came to, follow the path around it and take the right fork. It's a 5 minute walk across the rice paddies to the temple.

KHOKNA

Khokna is not as appealing as Bungamati, partly because it was seriously damaged in the 1934 earthquake, but it has retained many traditional aspects of Newari life. It is famous for producing mustard oil. There is no central square, as in Bungamati, but there's plenty of action in the main street, including women spinning wool. The village's main temple is a two tiered construction of little interest, dedicated to Shekali Mai a mother goddess.

Getting There & Away

From Karya Binayak Temple, Khokna is a 10 minute walk across the paddy fields. Take note of the water tank surrounded by a low brick wall on the outskirts of the village, because if you don't want to retrace your steps to Bungamati, the track that returns to the main road takes off here.

Kirtipur, Chobar & Dakshinkali Route

KIRTIPUR (5 km)

Strung out along a ridge south-west of Kathmandu the small town of Kirtipur is a relatively neglected and timeless backwater despite its proximity to the capital. At one time it was associated with Patan and then became a mini-kingdom in its own right. During the 1770 conquest of the valley by Gorkha's King Prithvi Narayan Shah it was clear that Kirtipur, with its superbly defensible hilltop position, would be the key to defeating the Malla kingdoms so it was here the Gorkha king struck first and hardest.

Their resistance was strong but eventually, after a bitter siege, the town was taken and the unfortunate inhabitants of the town paid a terrible price for their courageous resistance. The king, incensed by the long struggle his forces had endured, ordered the nose and lips cut off every male inhabitant of the town. Fortunately, for a small minority, he was a practical as well as a cruel king and those

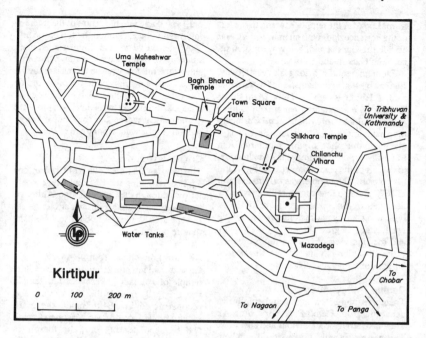

Kirtipur

0   100   200 m

Uma Maheshwar Temple

Bagh Bhairab Temple

Town Square

Tank

To Tribhuvan University & Kathmandu

Shikhara Temple

Chilanchu Vihara

Water Tanks

Mazadega

To Chobar

To Nagaon

To Panga

who could play wind instruments were spared. It is said that the news of this barbaric act considerably reduced thoughts of resistance amongst the inhabitants of the other valley towns and Patan, Bhaktapur and Kathmandu quickly fell.

At one time there were 12 gates into the city and traces of the old city wall from that time can still be seen. Today the Kirtipur Cottage Industry Centre is a major industry for the town. As you wander through Kirtipur you can see dyed yarn hanging from many upstairs windows and hear the clatter of the town's nearly 1000 handlooms in the background. Many of the town's 9000 inhabitants are weavers or farmers; the lower caste people generally live outside the old city wall, lower down the hill. Kirtipur's hilltop position offers fine views over Kathmandu with the Himalaya rising behind.

Tribhuvan University

The campus of Nepal's university, named after King Tribhuvan, stands below the Kirtipur hill. The university library has the best facilities to be found in Nepal, but many Kirtipur farmers lost their land to the university site and have had to turn to other employment.

Temples

Kirtipur's ridge is actually two hills, with a lower saddle between them. The Chilanchu Vihara tops the southern hill and has a central stupa with four smaller stupas, numerous statues and bells and the buildings of a number of Buddhist monasteries around it.

At the bottom of the saddle where the hills meet is the Bagh Bhairab Temple, sacred to both Hindus and Buddhists. This famous triple roofed temple is decorated with swords and shields from the Newari troops defeated by King Prithvi Narayan Shah. They can be seen attached to the walls of the temple, sheltered by the upper roof. The temple's principal image is of Bhairab in his tiger form. Look for the temple's torana to the left of the entrance door with an image of Vishnu astride the Garuda and, below him, Bhairab between Ganesh and Kumar.

From the saddle a long stone stairway, flanked by stone elephants, leads to the triple roofed Hindu Kvath or Uma Maheshwar Temple. The elephants wear spiked saddles to keep children from riding them! Curiously the main image of Shiva and Parvati is a standing one, not in the standard Uma Maheshwar pose, that image is a smaller one, to the left of the central image of the god and his consort. The temple was originally built in 1673 and had four roofs until it was badly damaged by the great earthquake of 1934. Following its recent restoration the temple itself is not of great interest – the stairway and the fine views from the top are better. From this hilltop you can see the nearby villages of Panga and Nagaon.

Getting There & Away

There are numerous buses and minibuses departing from Ratna Park (Bus Stop 4). They take around half an hour and cost Rs 2. They terminate at the university from where you can stroll up the hill to the town itself. Alternatively it's a short trip by taxi and not far by bicycle.

Instead of simply returning the same way you can continue from Kirtipur to Chobar and the Chobar Gorge then back through Patan, an interesting walk. From the Chilanchu stupa at the south-eastern end of the town go down the hill by the mound known as the Mazadega, it was built with the intention of being the foundations of a stupa. At the base of the hill follow the Ring Rd round and take the trail leading towards Chobar, it's very easy to find since Chobar tops the prominent hill to the south-east.

A diversion further south will take you through the small village of Panga with a number of temples, none of great age or interest. A path continues from Panga to Nagaon, an even smaller village. The trail to Chobar meets a wider road just before the base of the hill, but you can turn off this and follow a narrow footpath straight up the hill

until you come into the centre of the interesting small village, right on the top of the hill.

After you've visited Chobar's Adinath Lokeshwar Temple continue down the other side of the hill towards the river. Aim for the large cement works, clearly visible beside the river. The Chobar Gorge and the Jal Binayak Temple are immediately to the north of the cement works. See the Chobar Gorge section for the walk from there to Patan.

CHOBAR (6 km)

The picturesque little village of Chobar tops a hill overlooking the Bagmati River where it flows through the Chobar Gorge. Although the gorge is a regularly visited attraction far fewer people come to Chobar itself. Perhaps they're put off by the steep hill.

Adinath Lokeshwar Temple

Chobar's main attraction is the Buddhist temple of Adinath Lokeshwar. The temple was originally built in the 15th century and reconstructed in 1640. Inside the main sanctuary the face of Rato Machhendranath can be seen peering out, the temple is dedicated to this popular valley deity and is sacred to both Hindus and Buddhists. Six Buddha faces are lined up beneath the temple's golden torana but the most interesting feature is the many metal pots, pans and water containers which are fixed to boards hanging all around the temple roofs. These kitchen utensils are donated to the temple by newlyweds in order to ensure a happy married life.

Getting There & Away

Transport to Pharping and Dakshinkali runs by Chobar, but see the Kirtipur and Chobar Gorge sections for details of walking between Kirtipur and Patan via Chobar and the Chobar Gorge.

CHOBAR GORGE (6 km)

Eons ago the Kathmandu Valley was the Kathmandu Lake. In that long-ago time the hill of Swayambhunath was an island; gradually the lake dried up to leave the valley we see today. Legends relate that the change from lake to valley was a much more dramatic one, for Manjushri is said to have taken his mighty sword and with one blow cut open the valley edge to release the pent-up waters. The place where his sword struck rock was Chobar on the southern edge of the valley and the result was the Chobar Gorge.

Countless snakes were washed out of the valley with the departing waters but Kartotak, 'King of the snakes', is said to still live near the gorge in the Taudaha pond. Whether or not the great serpent is still there the pond is certainly a place where ducks pause on their long annual migration from Siberia to India. A hill known as Dinacho (which means 'meditation point') or Champa Devi rises beyond the pond.

The Chobar Gorge is south of Patan and the Bagmati River cuts through the edge of the Chobar Hill, the highest hill along this side of the valley. The pretty village of Chobar tops the hill and a stone-paved track runs from the river's edge right to the top of the hill where the Adinath Lokeshwar Temple forms the centre of the settlement. Down by the river, just south of the gorge, is another important temple, the Jal Binayak. The valley's first cement factory is a more recent and less pleasing addition to the scenery. A neat little suspension bridge spans the river; it was manufactured in Aberdeen in Scotland in 1903. From the bridge there are fine views of the gorge on one side and the Jal Binayak Temple on the other.

Jal Binayak Temple

Just below the gorge one of the valley's most important Ganesh shrines stands on the riverbank. The triple roofed temple dates from 1602 although there was probably a temple here even earlier. On the temple's platform there is an aged and worn image of Shiva and Parvati in the Uma Maheshwar pose which predates the temple itself by 500 years.

The temple's Ganesh image is simply a huge rock, projecting out the back and bearing very little likeness to an elephant-

headed god. The temple's roof struts depict eight Bhairabs and the eight mother goddesses or Ashta Matrikas with whom Ganesh always appears. On the lower roof Ganesh himself appears on some of the struts, with beautiful female figures standing beside him and tiny, brightly painted erotic depictions below. A bronze figure of Ganesh's 'vehicle', in this case a shrew rather than a mouse, stands respectfully in the temple courtyard, facing the shrine.

Getting There & Away

The Chobar Gorge is usually visited en route to Pharping and Dakshinkali by road. A more interesting way to reach the gorge is to walk there from Kirtipur via the village of Chobar. See the Kirtipur section for more details. From the gorge you can cross the bridge and walk up the hill turning north towards Patan. A road suitable for cars ends at a small village at the top of the hill and you can follow this road, past the Nakhu jail and across the Nakhu River, finally crossing the Ring Rd and entering Patan at Jawlakhel.

SEKH NARAYAN TEMPLE (18 km)

The small Sekh Narayan Temple is the centrepiece in an interesting collection of temples, pools and carvings. The pools are beside the road to Pharping, at a point where it makes a sharp left-hand turn (coming from Kathmandu) and they are often used by local women for washing clothes. The main temple is above the pools and is sheltered under a multicoloured, overhanging cliff. It forms an interesting juxtaposition between the work of man and god. In true Nepalese style, a Buddhist monastery has been built next door.

The temples and carvings have suitably diverse ages. The Sekh Narayan Temple, one of the most important Vishnu temples in the valley, was built in the 17th century, but it is believed the cave has been a place of pilgrimage for much longer than this. Beside the shrine is a bas relief of Vishnu Vikrantha, also known as the dwarf Vamana. This possibly dates from the Licchavi period, or the

5th or 6th century. Vamana was a dwarf who miraculously changed into a giant, the 'long strider', and crossed the world in three gigantic steps.

Half submerged in one of the crystal-clear ponds is a sculpture of Surya, the sun god, framed by a stone arch and with a lotus flower at each shoulder. This dates from the 12th or 13th century. Finally, the Tibetan gompa is a recent 20th century addition. Hindus believe that Gautama Buddha was Vishnu's 10th incarnation, but I don't know if this is the connection!

Getting There & Away
Sekh Narayan is close to Pharping and is probably best reached by foot from the village if you haven't got your own transport.

VAJRA JOGINI TEMPLE (18.5 km)
On a hillside overlooking Pharping is the 17th century Vajra Jogini Temple, dedicated to the same goddess as the Vajra Jogini Temple near Sankhu and built at about the same time. See the Vajra Jogini section for a discussion on the goddess' origins. The pagoda-style temple is in a courtyard surrounded by relatively modern two storey, Newari-style living quarters. Vajra Jogini is featured in the temple's toranas.

Getting There & Away
The temple is just a short walk behind Pharping on the hill that overlooks the town, behind a relatively new gompa. The main gompa at Gorakhnath is only a few hundred metres to the west up a flight of steps. It is possible to do an interesting walking circuit from Dakshinkali to Gorakhnath to Vajra Jogini to Pharping and back to Dakshinkali in less than 2 hours. See the Dakshinkali section.

Coming from Kathmandu and after Sekh Narayan, you approach Pharping past a soccer pitch. The main road swings left around the pitch, but if you continue straight ahead you will come first to Vajra Jogini (on the side of the hill) then Gorakhnath.

GORAKHNATH (19 km)
Several gompas and temples have sprung up around Gorakhnath cave behind Pharping. The white Tibetan gompa is particularly interesting. It's perched high on the hill like an eagle's nest, at the centre of a web of prayer flags.

There are magnificent views overlooking Pharping, the Bagmati River and the valley. You can even see the Himalaya on a clear day. Somewhere in the complex is a cave which the Tibetans associate with Padmasambhava, the Bodhisattva sometimes credited with introducing Buddhism to Tibet.

Getting There & Away
Gorakhnath is an easy walk from Pharping and Vajra Jogini, and a bit of a scramble from Dakshinkali. It can be combined with an interesting walk that takes in all these places (see the Dakshinkali section) or reached by road.

Coming from Kathmandu and after Sekh Narayan, you approach Pharping past a soccer pitch. The main road swings left around the pitch, but if you continue straight ahead you will come first to Vajra Jogini (on the side of the hill) then Gorakhnath.

PHARPING (19 km)
Pharping is a thriving, traditional Newari town, surprisingly untouched by the swarm of tourists that visit Dakshinkali. The main road skirts the village so there are few vehicles in the village proper. Before King Prithvi Narayan Shah unified Nepal this was another tiny city-state.

Getting There & Away
See the Dakshinkali section for details on transport. Dakshinkali is 1 km away – and if you're on a bike, you'll be pleased to know it's all downhill.

DAKSHINKALI (20 km)
At the southern edge of the valley, in a dark, somewhat spooky location in the cleft between two hills and at the confluence of two rivers, stands the bloody temple of

Dakshinkali. The temple is dedicated to the goddess Kali, Shiva's consort in her most bloodthirsty incarnation, and twice a week faithful Nepalese journey here to satisfy her blood lust. The six armed main image of Kali in the temple is of black stone and she tramples upon a male figure.

Sacrifices are always made to goddesses, and the creatures to be sacrificed must be uncastrated males. Saturday is the major sacrificial day of the week when a steady parade of buffaloes, chickens, ducks, goats, sheep and pigs come here to have their throats cut or their heads lopped off. Tuesdays is also a sacrificial day but the blood does not flow quite so freely as on Saturdays. During the festival of Dasain in October the temple is literally awash with blood and the image of Kali is bathed in it.

After their rapid despatch the animals are butchered in the stream beside the temple and their carcasses will later be brought home for a feast, or a picnic may be held on the hillside. Non-Hindus are not allowed into the compound where Kali's image resides, but it is OK to take photos from outside. The temple itself is not particularly interesting, although there are some fine brass nagas forming a canopy over the compound.

This is one of the most important sites in the valley so on the sacrificial days it is crowded with Nepalese families – and tourists. Most of the big hotels and the tour companies cart busloads of camera-laden visitors along. Tours to the 'exciting animal sacrifices' are big business for Kathmandu travel agencies. As a result, there are a number of teahouses, and a good number of hustlers selling souvenirs and goodness knows what else. Be prepared to pay picturesque sadhus for the privilege of taking their photograph.

Despite the carnival spirit, witnessing the sacrifices is a strange and, for some, a confronting experience. The slaughter is surprisingly matter of fact, but it creates a powerful atmosphere. Unfortunately, many tourists behave extremely poorly, hanging from every available vantage point in order to get the most gory possible photos. They are reminiscent of that most unattractive creature – the vulture. However extraordinary the sights might seem, this is a religious ceremony, and the participants should be treated with respect, not turned into a side-show.

Getting There & Away

Buses are very crowded on Tuesdays and Saturdays – the most important days for sacrifice – even though there are plenty of them. After you pass the police checkpoint on the Ring Rd you can sit on the roof and enjoy the spectacular views. Buses leave from Martyrs' Gate (Bus Stop 9). There are minibuses, although they only run in the mornings, normal buses (Rs 5, 1½ hours) and express buses (Rs 15, 45 minutes). Tours will cost around Rs 160. If you have a car allow 45 minutes for the journey.

It is an enjoyable, but exhausting 2 hour bike ride from Kathmandu. The views are exhilarating, but it is basically uphill all the way – so mountain bikes are the way to go. Tuesday is probably the best day to pick as the traffic is not too heavy. Make sure you get an early start, as the shrine is busiest early in the morning. You're advised to pay someone a couple of rupees to mind your bike in the car park.

It's possible to make an interesting 2 hour circuit walk from Dakshinkali to Gorakhnath, Vajra Jogini, Pharping and back to Dakshinkali. Take the path that runs above the left (southern) side of the sacrificial compound. This will bring you out into a cleared part of the gorge where there are several picnic shelters. There's a steep scramble up a goat track that follows a ridge on the right (north-western) side of the gorge. When you get to the top you come out on a plateau and you'll immediately see the white monastery surrounded by prayer flags on the nearby hill. Make your way through the paddy fields, on the narrow paths between the rice. It will take you about 40 minutes to get to Gorakhnath. Vajra Jogini is a few hundred metres down some steps to the east of the gompa, and a short walk to Pharping. From Pharping follow the main road about 1 km downhill to Dakshinkali.

The Terai

When people think of Nepal they think of soaring mountains and crisp, clear air – not hot, subtropical plains. However, the majority of the country's population now lives on a narrow strip of flat and fertile land, between the Indian border and the mountains, that is known as the Terai.

With the Kathmandu Valley and the world's highest mountains little more than a night's bus ride away, it is not surprising that this is often just a transit zone for those travelling overland to and from India. Although there is nothing quite as startling as 8000 metre mountains, there are dramatic sights in this region.

The most important attractions are the magnificent Royal Chitwan National Park, famous for its elephants, tigers and rhinoceros; and, to a lesser extent, Lumbini – the birthplace of Buddha; and Janakpur – the birthplace of Sita.

Travellers should not miss the Chitwan, and in the cool season (November to February) it is definitely worth travelling during the day and seeing the country, even if you do have to stay in a grubby border town overnight.

Nobody could forget riding an elephant through forest as the sun rises and coming upon a rhinoceros standing unconcerned only metres away, or frightening a wild peacock out of the grass so that it flaps into the trees.

Those who do take the time to explore some of the Terai will find it a rewarding and enjoyable place to visit. There is the beauty of quiet villages and bright saris amongst endless expanses of vivid-green rice.

Then there is the strange waterlogged world in the channels of the Sapt Kosi – with its thousands of water birds, thatched villages, and hectares of water hyacinths and lilies. This is just one of the massive rivers, grey and turbulent with snow-melt and silt, that hit the plains 100 metres above sea level and over 1000 km from the Bay of Bengal.

While many people from the hills have settled the region – there are representatives of almost every ethnic group in Nepal – the largest groups speak languages and live in ways similar to their cousins across the Indian border. Despite this, the people of the Terai remain distinctively Nepalese – unhurried, good-humoured, courteous and friendly – and many view their vast and riotous neighbour with an awe tinged with fear.

Unfortunately, most of the border towns are new, dirty and unattractive – with Dickensian-looking industries on their outskirts, streets choked with buses and trucks, and with no views, history or culture to redeem them. The exceptions are ancient Janakpur, a pleasant, well-planned town with numerous temples and tanks; and Lumbini, which is more significant for what it was than what it is.

HISTORY

Over the centuries, parts of the Terai have come under the sway of both Nepalese and Indian empires. Some regions have been centres of civilisation for thousands of years, but most have only been opened up for development since the success of malaria eradication programmes in the late 1950s.

Without doubt the Terai's most famous son is Siddhartha Gautama – Buddha – who was born in 624 BC at present-day Lumbini. Siddhartha was the son of a King Suddhodana who ruled a small kingdom, Kapilavastu. The ruins near Taulihawa to the west of Lumbini are believed to be those of his capital.

The Terai's most famous daughter is Sita, who is believed to have been born where present-day Janakpur now stands, the daughter of Janak, the king of Mithila (also known as Videha). Sita is famous for her faithful marriage to Rama, the hero of the Hindu epic the *Ramayana*. The first version of this story was written in Sanskrit in the 1st or 2nd century BC. The kingdom of Mithila lives on in the rich Maithali culture and language of the eastern Terai and northern Bihar.

By 321 BC the Mauryan Empire based at Patna was on the rise, swallowing the small principalities around it. Under the great Ashoka, the empire controlled more of the subcontinent than any subsequent ruler until the British.

Ashoka was one of Buddhism's greatest followers and missionaries, so it was perhaps inevitable that he would visit nearby Lumbini, then a thriving centre. In 249 BC he erected a stone pillar at Lumbini that can still be seen today. Some believe he travelled as far as Kathmandu.

The next great empire to rise in the region was the Gupta Empire, again originally based in Patna, which flourished between 300 and 600 AD. The empire extended its influence to Kathmandu and beyond. In the early 13th century invading Muslims occupied northern India and the Gangetic basin, driving many Hindu refugees towards Nepal and the Kathmandu Valley. There, it is believed, one of these refugee groups founded the Malla dynasty which by the 15th century under King Yaksha Malla had extended its power from Kathmandu south to the Ganges River.

The next and current Kathmandu-based dynasty, the Shahs, won power in 1768 and continued to expand Nepal until it was twice the size it is now. Eventually the Shahs and their famous Gurkha soldiers ran up against the British East India Company. In 1816, after 2 years of relatively inconclusive war, a treaty was ratified. This took much of the Terai from the Nepalese and established Nepal's modern borders.

Most of the Terai was heavily forested until the 1960s. However, the drainage and spraying programmes started in 1954 markedly reduced the incidence of malaria and this allowed mass migration both south from the hills and north from India. Fertile soils and easy accessibility led to rapid development. The Terai is now the most important region for agricultural and industrial production in Nepal, and the fastest growing.

GEOGRAPHY

The Nepalese Terai lies at the northern rim of the great Gangetic plains, ranges from 60 to 300 metres above sea level and never exceeds more than 40 km in width. The plains run table-flat from deep in India to the foothills of the Himalaya, which abruptly jump 1000 metres.

Several flat, wide 'valleys' known as the inner Terai lie behind the first range of hills. These include the valley along the Narayani River (including much of the Chitwan) and the Rapti River (near Nepalganj).

The border with India is artificial; it does not conform to any particular geographic barrier. To further blur the demarcation, the inhabitants on both sides come and go as they please – sometimes to the chagrin of both governments.

The Terai accounts for only 17% of Nepal's total area, but it is, in effect, the country's granary. In general the soils are highly fertile and this, in addition to abundant water resources, permits the intensive cultivation of a wide variety of crops.

Unfortunately, the native forests are rapidly disappearing and the soil itself is worked very hard. In some regions fallow land is unheard of and no sooner is a crop harvested than a new one is planted. This has already resulted in declining crop yields in some areas. The consequences of rapid population increase, deforestation and overworking the land are likely to be disastrous.

Parts of the Terai are still subject to serious flooding. The relationship between deforestation in the hills and increased siltation and flooding on the plains is controversial. However, there is no doubt that population growth in the hills, nonexistent sewage treatment and the development of industry in the Kathmandu Valley is beginning to have a serious impact on downstream water quality. This is exaggerated in the dry season when many streams become mere trickles or dry up completely. Water flows are much reduced on even the major rivers.

CLIMATE

The Terai has a humid, subtropical climate

with well over 1500 mm of rainfall in most places. The most pleasant time to visit is November to February when you can expect maximum temperatures to average in the mid to high 20°Cs, and cool nights. From March to September temperatures in the high 30°Cs are common and this combines with the additional discomfort of the monsoon from June to September.

ECONOMY
As it is elsewhere in Nepal, agriculture is the major contributor to the economy, although the Terai is also home to the majority of the

---

FLORA
The Terai is subtropical, and the flora & fauna reflect this. Rapid development has led to large scale deforestation but, fortunately, a surprisingly large amount of forest remains.

Substantial areas are still cloaked in sal (*Shorea robusta*) forests. These forests characteristically grow on well-drained soils and form relatively homogeneous communities. Sal is a magnificent, highly valued hardwood. It grows straight and true (averaging 30 metres when mature), and it has long been used by builders and woodcarvers. The longevity of the buildings and the carvings in the Kathmandu Valley is due to the strength and durability of this wood.

On swampier ground there are scrubby forests of *khair* (*Acacia catechu*) and *shisham* (*Dalbergia sissoo*). *Simal* trees (*Bombax ceiba*) stand out above the others. They are notable for their spring display of large red flowers and when they are old they develop huge buttresses at their base.

There are also grasslands that form a diverse and complex community of over 50 species. Elephant grasses (*saccharum* family) can grow up to 8 metres high, but there are also shorter species like *khar* that are vital for thatching.

FAUNA
The fauna of the Terai is striking although, as always, shy. From the road, the most obvious species are the handsome black-faced, grey langur monkeys (*bandar*) and the common, brownish-red rhesus monkeys. You may also catch a glimpse of some of the many species of deer – including the spotted (*chital*), barking (*mirga*) sambar (*jarayo*), hog (*laghuna*) and swamp deer. The blue cow (*nilgai*), Asia's largest antelope, is also quite common, but you won't see this unless you make an effort.

The largest mammal is the Asian elephant, although it is likely there are now only a few individuals surviving in the wild at the Royal Bardia National Park and Sukla Phanta Wildlife Reserve. Not far behind in scale and impressiveness is the great Indian one-horned rhinoceros, which can be seen at the Chitwan.

There are a number of carnivores, the most magnificent being the Royal Bengal tiger (*bagh*) that, thanks to the Terai's national parks, seems to have escaped extinction. There are also leopards (*chituwa*), wild dogs, jackals, civets, various species of mongooses and cats.

You might also find sloth bears (*bhalu*), wild boars, porcupines, hares, bats, squirrels and snakes (*sarpa*) – some of which are poisonous (cobra, krait and viper).

The rivers and lakes are home to small numbers of mugger and gharial crocodiles, and the extraordinary Gangetic dolphin.

The Terai is also a bird-watcher's delight with over 400 migrant and local species recorded. There are cormorants, herons, egrets, storks, cranes, ibis, ducks, kites, goshawks, hawks, eagles, osprey, falcons, kestrel, quail curlews, sandpipers, snipe, gulls, terns, pigeons, parakeets, cuckoos, owls, kingfishers, woodpeckers, swallows, orioles, drongos, babblers, flycatchers, wharblers...

The invertebrates range from butterflies to mosquitoes! ■

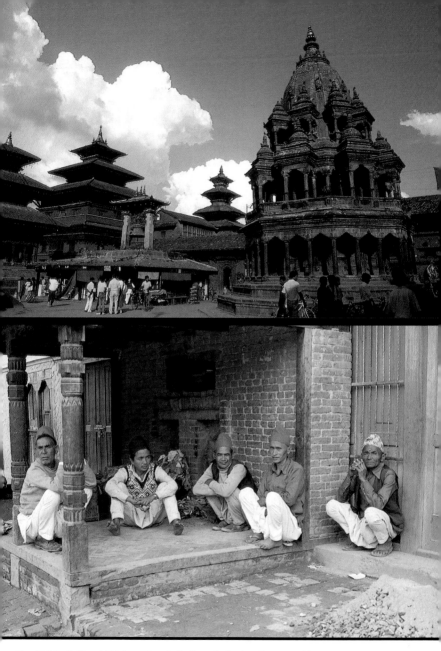

Top: Taleju Bell and Krishna Temple in Patan's Durbar Square with
     Royal Palace in background (TW)
Bottom: Patan men (SB)

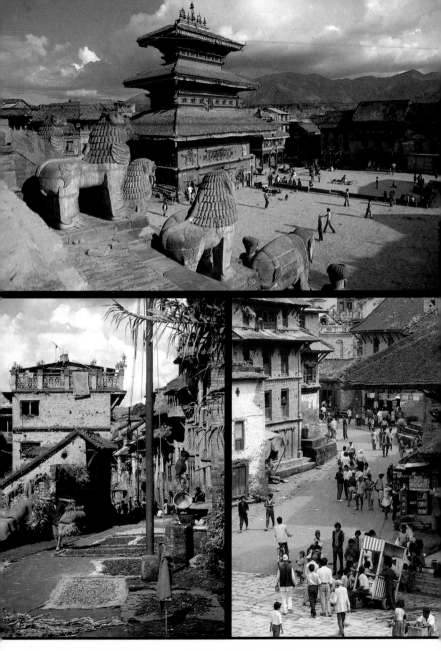

Top: Taumadhi Tole, Bhaktapur, Kathmandu Valley (SB)
Left: Bright red chillies are spread out to dry in Bhaktapur, Kathmandu Valley (TW)
Right: Taumadhi Tole, Bhaktapur, Kathmandu Valley (TW)

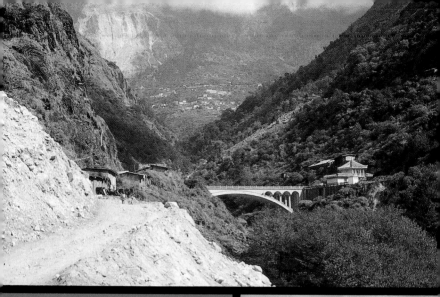

Top: The road to Lhasa and the Friendship Bridge between Nepal and Tibet (RE)
Left: Amongst the eagles – the ancestral home of the Shah dynasty perches
    over Gorkha (RE)
Right: Father and child, Nagarkot (SB)

country's manufacturing industries. More than half the gross domestic product is produced in the Terai.

Many of the Terai's advantages come back to a single fact: it's flat! Development has been assisted by the relative ease with which roads and services can be established. Apart from making industrial development possible, there are less obvious benefits. Health and education services can be delivered more easily, fertilisers and improved seeds are more widely available, and agricultural surpluses can be transported mechanically.

Cash crops like sugar cane, jute, tobacco and tea are grown alongside staples like rice, wheat and maize. Land holdings are much larger than in the hills, but the average size is still under 2 hectares – hardly a Texan cattle ranch. As the population increases holdings shrink. A declining surplus of food is sold, some for export, but much of it currently finds its way to less fortunate relatives and markets in the Kathmandu Valley or the hills.

Mechanised transport, proximity to Indian raw materials and the Indian market, and the availability of hydroelectric power has allowed the development of some industry. This is largely concentrated between Birganj and Hetauda, and around Biratnagar. Amongst other things there are jute mills, a sugar refinery, tanneries and leather factories, biscuit and cigarette factories, and drug manufacturers.

POPULATION

The population of the Terai has increased rapidly since the 1950s. At the time of the last census in 1981, 45% of the population, or over 6.5 million people, lived in the Terai. Due to internal migration from the hills and a high birth rate, the population of the Terai was estimated to be increasing at 4.2% annually, as opposed to a 1.6% increase in the hills.

If these figures are extrapolated, the population of the Terai will now have surpassed that of the hills, and may indeed have doubled by the end of the '90s. Unfortunately, it is now clear that the Terai will not be able to absorb excess population from the

hills indefinitely (and in fact the hill population has continued to grow anyway). Population pressures are mounting at an alarming rate.

PEOPLE

Internal migration has meant that the indigenous people of the Terai have been joined by representatives of almost every ethnic group in the country. However, and not surprisingly, many people are closely related to Indian groups in Bihar and Uttar Pradesh: Indo-Aryan subsistence farmers with dark skin, and Hindu beliefs that are sometimes combined with forms of animism. Although throughout Nepal the common language is usually Nepali, in the Terai, people are just as likely to use Maithali or Hindi. There is a close correspondence between language and ethnicity.

Maithali

The most widely spoken language of the Terai (excluding Nepali) is Maithali, a language and culture shared with people on the Bihar side of the border. It is spoken by around 2 million Nepalese, especially around Janakpur and Biratnagar. Maithali is the language of old Mithila and has its own script, Tirhuta, and a celebrated literature. Most of its speakers are farmers and orthodox Hindus.

Bhojpuri & Abadhi

The next most common language, Bhojpuri, is also used on both sides of the border and is spoken by around 1.5 million people in Nepal, especially around Birganj, though it mingles with Maithali.

Abadhi is another Indian-based language, spoken by around 250,000 Nepalese especially around Bhairawa and Lumbini.

Tharu

One of the most visible groups in the Terai is the Tharu, a race who are believed to be the earliest inhabitants of the Terai (and immune to malaria!). Approximately 700,000 Tharu speakers inhabit the length of the Terai, including the inner Terai around the Chitwan, although they primarily live in the west. There are caste-like distinctions between different Tharu groups or tribes. Most have mongoloid physical features.

Nobody is sure where they came from, although some believe they are the descendants of the Rajputs (from Rajasthan) who sent their women and children away to escape Muslim invaders in the 16th century. The women later married into local tribes. Another belief is that they are descended from the royal Sakya clan, Buddha's family, although they cannot be described as Buddhist.

Customarily the women were heavily tattooed, although these days this is unusual and tattoos are rarely seen on young women. Some groups wear simple white saris, others colourful calf-length dresses and a bodice or *cholo*. Tharu houses have mud-rendered walls and thatched roofs; they are high, dark and cool, with few if any windows. Reliefs of domestic animals are often moulded on the mud walls.

Apart from farming, the Tharu are enthusiastic hunters and fishing people. In particular, groups of young women and children will often be seen heading off on fishing expeditions. Their beliefs are largely animistic, although increasingly influenced by Hinduism, and they live a life that is cleverly adapted to their environment.

Other People

There are quite a number of smaller ethnic groups, none exceeding 40,000 people. They include the Danwar, Darai, Djanghar, Koche, Majhi, Rajbansi, Satar and Tajpuri.

INFORMATION
Tourist Information

There are tourist information centres at the borders at Kakarbhitta, Birganj (tel 2083), Bhairawa (tel 1304) and Janakpur (tel 20755).

General Information

Most services, including post, telephone and electricity are more widely and efficiently available in the Terai than in the rest of the country.

Health

Malaria is the main worry. Make sure you take preventative medication. If you're coming from Westernised Kathmandu you may have been lulled into a false sense of security. Don't drink water or use ice unless you know it has been boiled or properly treated. Skip the dairy products (with the exception of curd) and salads, and peel the fruit. Wash your hands before eating.

ACCOMMODATION

The main towns all have accommodation ranging from hotels of reasonable standard, renting rooms with fans and mosquito nets for around Rs 150, or with air-con for about Rs 250, to grimy, basic places catering to local demand for around Rs 30. Some of the cheap places will only have tattered mosquito nets, if any at all, so if you're on a tight budget and want to sleep at night, bring one with you.

With the exception of the main border towns and Sauraha on the edge of the Royal Chitwan National Park, tourists are basically unknown so there are no lodges specially designed for the discriminating backpacker. Small towns and villages rarely have formal places to stay as there is little or no demand. If you do want to stay off the beaten track it will be necessary to make an arrangement with a restaurant owner or family.

FOOD

Although dhal bhat tarkari (rice, lentil soup and curried vegetables) is the rule, in the small roadside teahouses (*chiyaa pasal*), the quality is high and the prices are low – say around Rs 10 per person. A reasonable variety of vegetables is available in the Terai and in general the dhal bhat tarkari is good, just a trifle repetitive if you eat it at every meal.

Most roadside stalls will be able to find a spoon with a dubious past if you insist, but the custom is to eat with your right hand. As with most Eastern countries, the left is strictly reserved for unclean tasks.

The better class hotels all have restaurants. These range widely in quality and you may be better off eating with the local people. Check out the restaurant and if it looks as if you're going to be the only guest and if, in fact, you might be the first to sample the cuisine in some time, discretion is the better part of valour. Somewhere nearby, you can be almost certain, is a place where the local big-wigs go.

In general, you're considerably safer to stick with Indian vegetarian dishes, despite the fact that there is guaranteed to be a 'Continental' menu. Indian food will arrive quicker and the cook usually knows how to prepare it.

Breakfasts are not really understood. Most Nepalese eat twice a day: in the late morning and just after dark. You are advised to follow suit if you want freshly cooked food that doesn't take an age to arrive. This also means you will be synchronised with any Nepalese you spend time with. If you eat breakfast at 8 am you won't be ready for lunch at 11 am when Nepalese are ravenous, and they won't be hungry at 1 pm, and so on. If you do eat breakfast, make it something light that can be prepared quickly: maybe chai and toast.

GETTING THERE & AWAY
The Terai is easily accessible from West Bengal, Bihar and Uttar Pradesh in India and from Kathmandu and Pokhara. Bus and plane services are frequent and usually cheap. The long distance express buses are even reasonably comfortable. The Indian narrow-gauge railway system runs up to the border at several points (even continuing into Nepal near Janakpur), but most people use the buses because they are much quicker.

See the Nepal country map at the beginning of this book for the location of major places within the Terai.

Air
Royal Nepal Airlines flies to a number of towns in the Terai from Kathmandu. Services include Biratnagar (US$70, daily), Janakpur (Rs 620, three times a week), Bhairawa (US$65, four times a week), and Nepalganj (US$90, daily). See the Getting There &

Away sections of those towns for more details.

Road
Roads enter the Terai at numerous border crossings in the south. Most travellers going to or from Nepal cross the border at one of three places: Raxaul Bazaar (India) to Birganj (Nepal), south of Kathmandu; Nautanwa (India) to Sunauli and Bhairawa (Nepal), south of Pokhara; or, in the extreme east of the country, from Uttar Bagdogra (India, near Darjeeling) to Kakarbhitta (Nepal). Travel on these routes is covered in the Getting There chapter.

GETTING AROUND
Royal Nepal Airlines services all the major cities, but buses are the way most normal mortals travel. This can be a serious penance for although the price is not high in terms of rupees, it can be in terms of comfort and sanity! The express buses are usually OK, although wherever possible check with a local as to which are the best companies.

Unfortunately most day buses are of the stopping-all-stations variety and they can be horrifically crowded. Every cm of the buses may be occupied or clung to by a human being. Under these circumstances, the best place to be is the roof, although you will need to protect yourself from the elements. There is one exception to this – the distinctive blue, government-run Saja Sewa buses. These run to timetables and are not overcrowded.

The problem is that if you don't travel by day, you miss the views and if you do travel by day you run the risk of missing the views (because you are jammed inside a bus) and suffering extreme discomfort. If you are travelling in a group, or if you have the necessary funds, it is worth considering hiring a car and driver. This is certainly not cheap at around US$70 per day for a Toyota Corolla (which would seat three passengers comfortably), but it has plenty of advantages.

See the Getting Around chapter for more details.

Royal Chitwan National Park

In the early part of this century, the Chitwan was a centre for the hunting exploits on which British royalty was so keen. King George V and his son the Prince of Wales, later Edward VIII, never made it to Kathmandu but they did slaughter wildlife in the Chitwan forests. In 11 fun-packed days during one hunting safari in 1911, they killed 39 tigers and 18 rhinos.

Occasional hunting forays into the park did not decimate the Terai's tigers and rhinos however. That was left to malaria, or rather to the malaria eradication programme which began in 1954. Until the late 1950s, the only settlements in the Chitwan Valley were scattered Tharu villages, inhabited by people whose apparent immunity to malaria was rumoured to be the result of their heavy drinking!

After the malaria was defeated, land-hungry people from the hills were quick to see the potential wealth of the region. The jungle was rapidly transformed into farm-

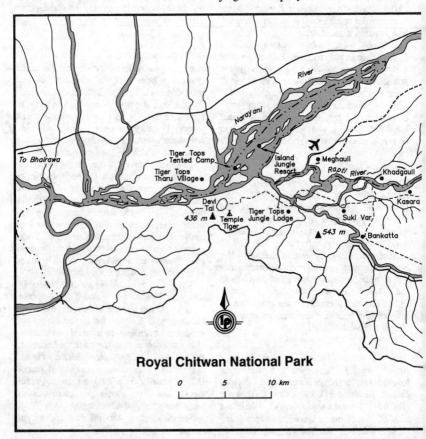

Royal Chitwan National Park

land and as their habitat disappeared so did the tigers and rhinos. By 1973 the rhino population of the Chitwan was estimated to have fallen to 100 and there were only 20 tigers left. Compare those numbers with the British royals' epic hunting trip 60 years earlier.

Fortunately this disastrous slide was reversed when the park area was delineated in 1964 and 22,000 people were removed from within its boundaries. The park actually became a national sanctuary in 1973 and since that time the animal population has rebounded. The Chitwan now contains an estimated 400 rhino and 80 tigers, quite apart from 50 other species of mammals and over 400 different types of birds.

As with many other national parks in the Third World there is local opposition to the park, and the park authorities have to tread a careful path to keep people living close by content. Apart from tying up potential farming land, people living around the sanctuary have to face the depredations of the park's animals.

Rhinos have not been trained to respect the Chitwan's boundaries. They wander out in November to wreak havoc on rice crops, and

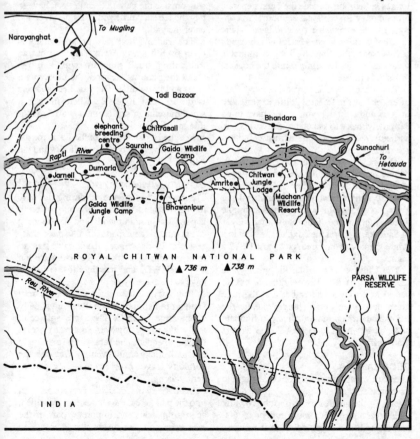

then again in February and March to attack mustard, lentils and wheat. Deer, monkeys and wild pigs also cause a great deal of damage to crops. The little lookout towers (*machan*) you see in many fields outside the park are used by watchmen who spend their nights in the fields waiting to scare off encroaching animals.

In February each year, however, neighbouring villagers are allowed into the park to harvest the high elephant grass, which is used for roof thatching and is a valuable cash crop. Working for the park lodges also provides local employment though the many budget lodges in Sauraha, outside the park, generate more money for the local economy. In contrast to the expensive park lodges, where much of the money goes back to Kathmandu or overseas, the Sauraha lodges funnel a great deal of money straight into the pockets of local families.

Today the Royal Chitwan National Park offers one of the finest wildlife experiences in Asia and although you would have to be extremely lucky to see one of the park's rare and elusive tigers you are almost certain to see rhinos.

The park is easily accessible from Kathmandu or Pokhara and offers something for every budget. At one extreme you can spend US$250 a night to stay at the famous Tiger Tops Lodge, while at the other a simple double room in one of the many small lodges in Sauraha, right on the edge of the park in a prime game viewing area, costs just US$2 a night.

The Chitwan is not like the great game reserves of Africa. The wildlife is not so varied or so great in number and the high grass and often dense jungle means the animals are much more difficult to find and observe. For most, a visit of 2 or 3 days is quite sufficient.

GEOGRAPHY

The park comprises a strip of flood plain to the north, along the Narayani, Rapti and Reu rivers. To the south it rises into the Siwalik Hills, reaching a maximum height of 600 metres, and then drops down to the plains.

Usually the Siwalik Hills continue straight into the higher Mahabharat Range, but here the Chitwan Valley forms a dividing zone, known as the inner Terai, between the two.

There are a number of *tal* or lakes; Devi Tal near Tiger Tops is the largest and most interesting.

The park, including the Parsa Wild Life Reserve, covers 98 sq km.

INFORMATION

The park entry fee is Rs 250. If you're staying at a lodge in the park this will usually be included in your overall charge, but if you stay outside the park in Sauraha you have to pay the fee each time you cross the river and enter the park.

The Park Visitors' Centre at Sauraha is open from 8 am to 5 pm daily and has an interesting small museum with exhibits about the park, its creation, the problems it faces and its wildlife. The park headquarters is further west at Kasara where there is a small museum of skulls and a gharial crocodile breeding project.

See the Books section in the Facts for the Visitor chapter for books on wildlife and the park.

CLIMATE & WHEN TO GO

The park lodges are closed during the May to August monsoon months when visibility is poor, the ground muddy and the flooding rivers make large parts of the park inaccessible. In September the lodges start to re-open, although at first the rivers are too high for 4WDs and transfers to the lodges have to be made by elephant.

The best time to visit the Chitwan is from October to February when the average daily temperature is 25°C. There are still cold, misty mornings, however, so a warm jacket is recommended. The Terai can be extremely hot and sticky, and even in October the humidity leaves everything feeling permanently damp.

In February the local villagers are allowed into the park to cut the elephant grass which, apart from being an important part of the local economy, also makes it much easier to see the game. So from February through May is a prime time for game viewing, although the weather can be uncomfortably hot. Sporadic thunderstorms begin in April.

FLORA & FAUNA
Flora
The park has three basic vegetation types – open grasslands, riverine vegetation and hardwood forests, dominated by sal trees. The forests also have shishan, kapok, flame-of-the-forest (palash), pipal, strangler fig and the scarlet-flowered kusum trees.

Fauna
The Chitwan has over 50 different species of mammals; bird spotters can search for 400 different bird types; and in 1987-88 butterfly spotters identified 67 different types of butterflies at the Machan Resort. Some of the most interesting creatures to be seen in the Chitwan include:

Elephants Although you're likely to see more elephants (*hathi*) than any other Chitwan animal, there are no wild elephants in the park. The Chitwan's elephants are all trained Asian, or Indian, elephants. Training an elephant takes about 2 years and the Chitwan elephants are usually acquired when they're 15 to 20 years old, and can be expected to work until they are 40 or 50.

A trained elephant is not cheap to purchase or to maintain. Typically they cost US$20,000 to US$30,000 to buy and then have to be provided with 270 to 300 kg (over 600 pounds) of food a day.

When you're out on an elephant safari you'll see how even that isn't enough; they're constantly pulling up clumps of grass or other tasty vegetation, and shaking it around to dislodge any insects or dirt before stuffing it thoughtfully into their mouths. Their drinking capacity is just as impressive, 50 litres (10 gallons) a day is what an elephant needs.

Keeping each elephant happy requires a support team of two or three people. The elephant's rider or master, commonly known as a mahout, is a *phanit* in Nepali. He's backed up by one or two *patchouas*, or assistants, whose main task is gathering the fodder to cater for an elephant's healthy appetite. They also assist the phanit when he saddles up the elephant with its howdah, the platform on which passengers ride.

Notice the different fashions in which elephants are ridden. At some lodges the

howdah will be a square railed-in platform carrying one passenger at each corner, while at Sauraha the elephants carry just the phanit and two passengers, all three sitting astride the elephant's back.

If you have aspirations of becoming a phanit you'll first have to learn some elephant commands, although each phanit will have his own particular words and ways of saying them:

sit	*baith*
lie down	*sut*
stand up	*maile*
hold your trunk out for me to climb up	*utha*
stop	*rhaa*
go	*agat*
shower me	*chhop*

The elephant has one of nature's most versatile appendages, a combination of nose and upper lip. The trunk has 100,000 muscles and can hold over 9 litres of water.

It is not simply the size of the ears that distinguishes the difference between Indian (Asian) and African elephants. In actual fact the two species are, scientifically speaking, not closely related.

The Indian elephant is noticeably smaller (males reach an average height of 2.75 metres and females grow to 2.45 metres), has smaller ears, a bulbous head and convex back. Only the males, but not all of them, have tusks. The African elephant has enormous ears, a sloping head, concave back and both the male and female have tusks. The Indian elephant has four nails on each hind foot where the African has only three.

Another major difference, as far as humans are concerned, is the domestication of these huge creatures. Indian elephants are easily trained, African elephants are not; though some people say, that any elephant can be trained and it is simply that training elephants has not been widely attempted in Africa.

Elephants have a gestation period of 22 months and the mother is always assisted by another female in looking after the young calf. In the wild the elephants live in a basically matriarchal society; the bulls do not travel with the herd.

Rhinoceros While elephants are the creatures you see most often in the Chitwan, it's the rhinoceros (*gaida*) you spend most time looking for, and with most hope of success.

There are two types of rhino in Africa and three in Asia. The great Indian one-horned rhino, found in the Chitwan, is larger than the African black rhino although smaller than the African white. A fully grown great Indian rhino can reach 180 cm at the shoulder and weigh more than 2 tonnes.

Rhinos are generally solitary creatures although several may occupy the same area. Their diet is chiefly grass and they have very poor eyesight although their sense of smell and hearing is good. It's their poor sight which leads to the rhino's reputation for bad temper. Since they cannot see very well rhinos are prone to assume almost any shape might be dangerous, so they charge it just in case.

Fortunately for the Indian rhino, its horn is not as large as the African variety and therefore not so valuable to poachers. Nevertheless there are many superstitions about rhinos and almost every part of the creature is of value – the urine is considered a charm against diseases and ghosts, a rhino-skin bracelet wards off evil spirits, rhino blood cures menstrual problems, and the horn is used for medicinal purposes, and is famed as a sexual stimulant. Its value for Arab dagger handles has led to the disastrous decline in rhino numbers in Africa. Along the riverbanks in the Chitwan a rhino would mark its territories by dropping excreta in mounds. Since they walked backwards to approach these mounds a waiting poacher had easy prey.

Tiger The Chitwan's tigers are probably the most elusive of the park's wildlife. Without artificial assistance, such as staking a young buffalo calf out as live bait, you would have to be very lucky to see a tiger (*bagh*) in the Chitwan. Though their numbers have increased considerably since the park was opened, tigers are solitary creatures and they mainly hunt by night.

Tigers require an enormous amount of space. A male commands a territory of about 60 sq km, and a female about 16 or 17 sq km. Both sexes occupy an exclusive territory although a male's territory may overlap with

several females. The Chitwan is simply not big enough to support the 50 breeding adults which is felt to be the minimum number to prevent interbreeding. This is part of the reason why an adjoining wildlife reserve has been proclaimed.

Other Mammals The Chitwan is also known for more than 50 other mammals. Leopards (*chituwa*) are as elusive as tigers and the night prowling sloth bears (*bhalu*) are also rarely seen.

The Chitwan has four types of deer and you will often catch a fleeting glimpse of them as they dash through the undergrowth. There's the tiny barking deer (*mirga*), the attractive spotted deer (*chital*), the hog deer (*laghuna*) and the big sambur deer (*jarayo*). Gaur, the world's largest wild cattle, are also found in the park.

Langur monkeys (*bandar*) are a common sight, chattering noisily in the tree tops or scattering vegetation down below. The spotted deer often follow the langurs around, taking advantage of their profligate feeding habits. The smaller macaque monkeys are the monkeys commonly found at temples in Nepal and all over the subcontinent. Freshwater or Gangetic dolphins are found in some river stretches in the park but they are rarely seen.

Reptiles The Chitwan has snakes (*sarpa*) of course, including some impressive pythons, plus turtles and two types of crocodiles. The marsh muggers are found in marshes, lakes and occasionally in rivers while the rarer gharial crocodile is exclusively found in rivers. The gharial, which grows to 7 metres in length and is a harmless fish eater, was in danger of extinction and is still very rare. A gharial hatchery project, however, is raising them to a reasonable size before releasing them into the Chitwan rivers.

PLACES TO STAY & EAT

Basically you can stay in the park or outside the park, and the division between cheap places to stay and expensive places to stay is almost equally straightforward – the expensive places are inside, the cheap ones outside. The expensive lodges may offer greater luxury than the cheap places but when it comes to seeing the wildlife there's little difference.

Sauraha, the budget accommodation village, is right on the park boundary and there's more wildlife just across the river than around some of the more expensive lodges. You've got just as much chance of seeing a rhino whether your room costs US$2 or US$200 a night.

Places to Stay – In the park

Most visitors to the park lodges will be going there on a package from Kathmandu, often as part of a larger tour of Nepal or the region. The lodges usually quote either an all-inclusive daily charge, which covers park entry fees, activities and all meals, or a total cost for 2 or 3 days including transport from Kathmandu. The only additional expenses will be for drinks and tips. Costs quoted here are per person on a double occupancy basis. There's usually a big price jump for single occupancy.

Tiger Tops (tel 2-22706, GPO Box 242, Kathmandu – on Durbar Marg), the pioneer Chitwan jungle lodge, is the best known and easily the most expensive of the lodges. There are actually three Tiger Tops. In descending order of cost they are: the well-known *Jungle Lodge* (US$270 a night), a *Tented Camp* (US$191 a night) and the *Tharu Village* (US$133 a night).

If you're by yourself there's an additional single supplement, and in the case of the Lodge the cost jumps to US$430 a night! They sometimes have special offers outside peak season.

Accommodation at the Lodge and Tharu Village is in twin-bed rooms with attached bathrooms and solar-heated water. At the Tented Camp it's in African-style safari tents. All three are towards the western end of the Chitwan. Tharu Village is actually across the Narayani River, just outside the park boundaries.

Temple Tiger and Island Resort are also at the western end of the park. *Temple Tiger* (tel 2-21585 in Kathmandu) has accommodation

in safari tents (complete with dressing room!) and costs US$160 per night. *Island Jungle Resort* (tel 2-26022 in Kathmandu) is a tented camp on an island in the Narayani River which costs US$140 a day.

Further east is *Gaida Wildlife Camp* (tel 2-20186 in Kathmandu), just outside the park boundaries near the village of Sauraha, and *Gaida Wildlife Jungle Camp*, within the park. The wildlife, particularly rhino, is said to be particularly easily seen in this area of the park. Guests have even seen rhinos from their rooms! Packages from Kathmandu to Gaida including transport cost from US$300 for 2 nights.

At the eastern end of the park is *Chitwan Jungle Lodge* (tel 4-1091, 2-22679 in Kathmandu) which has rooms, with attached bathroom, of traditional mud-walled and thatch-roofed construction. There's no electricity but otherwise the rustic lodge has all mod cons including a restaurant and a very pleasant open-air bar. The forest is relatively undisturbed in this part of the park and a river with a terrific swimming (and elephant bathing) hole runs close by. Costs at the Chitwan Jungle Lodge are US$240 for a stay of 2 nights and includes surface transport from Kathmandu. If you want to get there by raft then the cost increases to US$290. Additional nights cost US$80 per person.

Finally at the extreme western end of the park, close to the boundary of the adjoining Parsa Wild Life Reserve, is *Machan Wildlife Resort* (tel 2-25001, 2-27001 in Kathmandu).

WILDLIFE RESORT
ROYAL CHITWAN NATIONAL PARK

The wildlife is said to be not so prolific at this end of the park but the Machan Resort compensates by offering excellent facilities including a natural swimming pool and a video library of wildlife films. The rooms are timber-frame bungalows with attached bathrooms. There's also a Machan Tented Camp with safari-style tent accommodation. At the Machan Resort a 2 night stay costs US$290 travelling by surface from Kathmandu, US$335 including a rafting trip. In the Tented Camp the costs are US$188 and US$233 respectively. Additional nights are US$102 in the resort, US$55 in the camp.

Places to Stay – outside the park

Accommodation outside the park is in the village of Sauraha, right on the park border beside the Rapti River, about 8 km south of Tadi Bazaar on the main road

Sauraha is a simple, quiet little village – the sort of place nobody would usually visit – so staying here is a good opportunity to observe Nepalese rural life. There are glowing rice fields, neat and clean houses, little barns with cattle, and a village well close to the entrance of the Elephant Camp Lodge in the 'centre' of town.

Ox carts rumble by and there's a constant background scene of ducks, chickens and smiling children. It all looks amazingly attractive and tidy, in part because there's so little garbage – plastic junk, bottles and

1	Tharu Lodge
2	Rapti Lodge
3	Chitwan Guest House
4	Hotel Holiday Inn
5	Chitwan Wildlife Camp
6	Hotel Shiva's Dream
7	Jungle Express Camp
8	Bicycle Hire
9	Jungle Holiday Camp
10	Jungle Sunset Camp
11	River View Hotel & Lodge
12	Traveller's Jungle Lodge
13	Rhino Lodge
14	Jungle Tourist Camp
15	Cake & Pie Restaurant
16	Tiger Restaurant
17	Christabel's Lodge
18	Restaurant Paradise
19	Bicycle Hire
20	Rhino T-shirt Corner
21	Wendy's Lodge
22	Hotel Park Cottage
23	Park Visitors' Centre
24	Elephant Camp Lodge
25	Jungle Safari Camp
26	Chitwan Safari Lodge
27	Mother Nature Lodge
28	Sauraha Jungle Lodge
29	Annapurna View Lodge
30	Crocodile Safari Camp
31	Smithsonian Nepal Terai Ecology Project

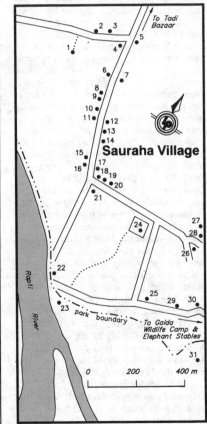

Sauraha Village

scraps of paper have yet to make an impact on Sauraha. Nor is there any electricity.

Sauraha has an enormous number of lodges, all very much out of the same mould. They offer a simple mud-walled, thatched-roof room for Rs 60 a double.

They're usually individual cottages with a small verandah out front and, especially if the garden is pleasant, they can be quite good places to stay. It can get very hot here, but the mud-wall architecture keeps things surprisingly cool. Toilet and bathroom facilities are shared but the rooms have insect screens on the windows and mosquito nets on the beds. Although there are a handful of small restaurants in Sauraha – like the *Tiger Restaurant* or *Restaurant Paradise* – most people eat at their lodge.

The Sauraha map shows more of the town's many lodges but a few places worth mentioning include the *Crocodile Safari Camp* which is east of the visitors' centre, some distance from the centre of the village. Budget organised tours from Kathmandu often use this pleasant lodge with its well-kept central garden area.

Hotel Park Cottage is very pleasantly situated right by the river, just across from the visitors' centre. The *Traveller's Jungle Lodge*, *Jungle Tourist Camp* and the *Chitwan Wildlife Camp* are also pleasant, neatly kept lodges.

Christabel's Lodge is right by the junction at the centre of the village and *Wendy's Lodge*, one of the long-term survivors at Sauraha, is nearby. *Mother Nature Lodge*, run by a former park warden, and the adjacent *Sauraha Jungle Lodge* are further out in the fields, east of the junction. With so many places offering such similar standards the best advice is simply to look into a few places and choose one you like.

A few lodges are slightly up-market; they're still built with the traditional mud-on-thatch construction but they have glass in the windows and attached bathrooms. They include the *Rhino Lodge* and *Jungle Express Camp*, both with doubles at Rs 150. These lodges are also popular for a budget-priced 2 or 3 day package to the Chitwan from Kathmandu.

Rhino Lodge and Jungle Express Camp both have offices in Thamel in Kathmandu and lakeside offices in Pokhara. Their typical 2 night, 3 day package cost less than US$100 by bus, or around US$150 by car. This is still very expensive compared to the costs of doing it yourself. They also have combined rafting/Chitwan trips. These are competitively priced and can be as low as US$130 for 2 nights and 3 days rafting on the Trisuli followed by 2 nights at the Chitwan.

There is one more expensive lodge in

ROYAL CHITWAN NATIONAL PARK
NEPAL

Sauraha, the *Elephant Camp Lodge* (tel 2-22823, 2-23976 in Kathmandu), which offers a 2 night package from Kathmandu for US$180 by road, or US$220 including a rafting trip down the Trisuli River. Their two 3-day packages cost US$230 and US$265 respectively, and additional nights cost US$50.

Like the lodges within the park all activities and park entry charges are included in these costs, although compared to the other lodges in Sauraha the prices look very steep! Because it is right in the village it's easy for night-time activities like the Tharu stick dances to be put on at Elephant Camp. Rooms are simple but comfortable and there's electricity and erratic hot water. There's a bar and a restaurant which can turn out good Nepalese food but usually sticks to providing truly awful Western cuisine!

ACTIVITIES

The greatest thrill at the Chitwan is the traditional elephant-back safaris in search of wildlife; and seeing a rhino from atop an elephant is an experience not to be missed.

All the park lodges have their own stables of elephants to take their guests out into the park, and at Sauraha there's a government-operated elephant stable where a 2 hour excursion into the park costs Rs 200. At times the number of visitors to Sauraha exceeds the supply of elephants so it's wise to book your elephant ahead of time; the Sauraha lodges will generally offer to do this for you. Elephant safaris are usually made in the early morning or late afternoon, prime game viewing times.

You won't want to spend your entire time aboard an elephant. For one thing it's a less than totally comfortable mode of travel and your first 2 hour ride is likely to leave you with aches in muscles you didn't know you had, not to mention an interesting selection of bruises!

The park offers a variety of other experiences, including jungle walks. The lodges' naturalists lead these walks and at Sauraha there are plenty of experienced walk leaders. These young locals may not have formal training but they're often surprisingly knowledgeable about the park's wildlife and where to find it. Often the walks are nothing more than a pleasant stroll through the jungle, but meeting a rhino when you're both on foot can be even more exciting than seeing one from the lofty safety of an elephant's back.

Jungle walks from Sauraha usually cost Rs 50 per person; you're advised not to venture into the jungle on your own. Some of the park lodges organise longer overnight treks into remote parts of the park.

Canoeing trips along the Rapti and Narayani rivers are another way of seeing the wildlife, although the park's two species of crocodiles and the freshwater dolphins are as rare a sight as the tigers. Canoe trips down the river from Sauraha cost Rs 25 per person.

Bird-watching is another popular park activity and the Chitwan also has an amazing selection of colourful butterflies.

The numerous rivers in the parks have some fine swimming holes and if you're staying at one of the park lodges don't pass up the opportunity to lend a hand at elephant bath time. On a hot day in the Terai there's no better way of cooling off than to sit on an elephant's back in a river and shout *chhop*. If your accent is right you'll be rewarded with a cold shower! Visiting the elephant stables to see how they're fed and cared for is also interesting.

Finally the park lodges regularly organise traditional dances by the Tharu people who originally settled the Terai. The Tharu stick dance, with a great circle of men whacking their sticks together, is quite a sight.

WHAT TO BRING

Park visitors should come prepared for every eventuality. At times the Terai can be stiflingly hot so cool clothes are essential; however, because the sun can be fierce and there's little shade when you're sitting on an elephant's back, long sleeves, a shady hat and a good sunscreen are necessary. At the other extreme, the winter months can be surprisingly chilly, particularly if you're out on foot or elephant back at dawn, so from

November to February you should come prepared for the cold with sweaters and a jacket. Good walking shoes (that you don't mind getting wet) are essential at any time of year and you'll want a swimsuit for the rivers.

Neutral colours are best to ensure you blend into the background and are less likely to alert the wildlife. Reds, yellows and whites are particularly conspicuous.

Insect repellent is another Terai necessity. Malaria may have been wiped out but there are still plenty of mosquitoes and a wide variety of other voracious insects. They're a surreptitious and crafty lot as well. Even people who are normally immune to insect attack may discover later that while they were propping up the bar in the evening a full scale attack was being mounted on their ankles.

Come prepared for Nepal's famous jukha as well. These leeches come out in force during the monsoon and will still be waiting for unwary jungle walkers during the first month or two of the dry season. See the leech instructions in the Health section of the Facts for the Visitor chapter for how to deal with these pests.

In addition to camera gear, preferably with a telephoto lens, binoculars are invaluable.

GETTING THERE & AWAY
Air
Royal Nepal Airlines has daily flights to Meghauli, near the Tiger Tops, Temple Tiger and Island Jungle Resort lodges, for US$65 each way. There are three flights a week to Bharatpur (Narayanghat) for US$45 each way. The flights only take about half an hour.

Road
Bus Travellers intending to stay outside the park in Sauraha, the budget accommodation centre for the Chitwan, have to get to Tadi Bazaar (sometimes spelt Tandi Bazaar), on the main east-west highway about 15 km south-east of Narayanghat. Buses to Tadi Bazaar cost about Rs 35 from Kathmandu or Pokhara and the trip typically takes about 7 hours. From Birganj or Sunauli on the Indian border it takes about 4 hours.

Tadi Bazaar is just a junction town, about 8 km from Sauraha which is on the banks of the Rapti River. You can walk there in a couple of hours. On the way, you have to cross a small river at the village of Chitrasali (also known as Gauthali). If the river is high you'll have to cross in one of the dugout canoes which shuttle back and forth. Alternatively you can hire an ox cart for about Rs 75 – they simply ford the river. Another alternative is to rent a bicycle at Tadi Bazaar, which will not only give you transport from the main road to Sauraha, but also for while you are in the village. There are a couple of bicycle rental shops right at the junction.

Car Visitors to the park lodges usually get there by car from Kathmandu or Pokhara and this is usually arranged by the lodge operators. A car typically costs around US$70 to US$100 round trip and the 160 to 180 km trip (depending where you're going) takes 4 to 5 hours. The driver hangs around for the 2 to 3 days his passengers are in the park.

If you're looking for transport from the park to Kathmandu or Pokhara it's often possible to negotiate a deal with these drivers, who will take you there and then return to pick up their round-trippers.

If you are coming or going from Kathmandu, you should try to convince your driver to take you one way via the Tribhuvan Highway between Hetauda and Naubise. This route will cost extra as the narrow, winding road will add at least an hour to your travel time.

The road itself, an engineering feat courtesy of the Indian Government, is sealed the whole way and is in good condition. The views along the way are stupendous. From Daman, about 80 km from Kathmandu, you can see the Himalaya stretching almost 180° from Dhaulagiri to Everest – weather permitting.

The cars usually drop you at the turn-offs from the main road, from where your lodge vehicle will pick you up for the final trip into the park and across the river. This short trip is usually made by 4WD although in the first month or two after the monsoon ends, September and October, the river may still be too high for vehicles and the transfer may be made by elephant. It's quite a surprise when you arrive at the Chitwan Jungle Lodge turn-off, for example, and find an elephant waiting for the final 7 km amble to the lodge!

River

The third way of getting to the Chitwan is by river and numerous Kathmandu rafting operators offer trips down the Trisuli River to the Chitwan. The park lodges will all organise a rafting trip in conjunction with your stay in the park.

The rafting trips start from Mugling, where the road to Narayanghat and the Chitwan turns off from the Kathmandu-Pokhara Highway, or from further up the Trisuli. It takes 2 or 3 days to raft down to the Chitwan but don't expect white-water thrills on the final stretch from Mugling. On that part of the river it's more a gentle drift, although there are some fine views and the sandy beaches along the riverside offer great camping spots.

Prices range from around US$30 to US$75 per day, but combination rafting/Chitwan trips (4 nights, 5 days) can be priced as low as US$130. Shop around and establish details before you hand over your money: Where does the rafting trip begin? What size groups are there? What activities are included at the Chitwan? What transport is there from the river to your accommodation at the Chitwan?

The Terai from East to West

There are quite a number of choices that travellers can make travelling to and from India and Kathmandu, so it is not possible to present this chapter in an order that will suit everyone. Places are described from east to west, from Kakarbhitta to Mahendranagar. The main east-west link is the Mahendra Highway, which is basically sealed between Kakarbhitta and Nepalganj although it varies in quality from good to abominable. West of Nepalganj the road quickly becomes a dry-season-only dirt track, although work is proceeding and it may not be long before it is sealed all the way through to the western border. During the monsoon it is quite possible for sections of the road east of Janakpur to be temporarily cut by floods.

There are a number of attractive hill towns accessible from the Mahendra Highway, or en route between the Terai and Kathmandu and Pokhara, and for the sake of convenience they have been included in this chapter. They are Dharan Bazaar and Dhankuta, which are accessible from Biratnagar; Daman, which is between Hetauda and Naubise; and Tansen, which is between Bhairawa and Pokhara.

KAKARBHITTA

The sole reason for the existence of Kakarbhitta is its proximity to India. This is the border post for road traffic going to or from Siliguri and Darjeeling. In fact, it's not much more than a glorified bus stop and it's difficult to imagine that anyone would want to stay longer than to make a bus connection.

The surrounding countryside is attractive, however, and you can tell you're not far from Darjeeling when you see the tea plantations on the outskirts of town. If you are going through to Darjeeling you'll need a permit in addition to your Indian visa – see the Visas section of the Facts for the Visitor chapter.

Information & Orientation

There's a helpful tourist office just inside Nepal, past customs on the north side of the road, the right if you're coming from India. The Nepal Rastra Bank isn't signposted, but it's the unmistakable pink monstrosity on the left (south) side of the road.

The border is open from 6 am to 7.30 pm and the bank is open from 7.30 am to 6 pm every day (well, that's the way I understood it!).

As you continue away from the border the main bus parking area is a dusty (or muddy, as the case may be) quadrangle on your right, followed by the bazaar and village.

Places to Stay & Eat

There are plenty of cheap but basic places to stay around the bazaar, like the *Rajdoot Hotel* with singles/doubles for Rs 30/40 or the *Nowdurga Hotel* which charges Rs 20 for a dorm, Rs 25/30 for singles/doubles.

If you want to give yourself an even chance of getting a decent night's sleep there are two reasonable, though more expensive, places. The *Shere Punjab Hotel* just past the tourist office has reasonable rooms with a bathroom attached for Rs 70; there's parking and most importantly a decent restaurant. The best, however, is the *ABC Hotel* which is very clean and comfortable with doubles for Rs 80. It's a trifle difficult to find as it's a 3 minute walk from the bus stop, in the village behind the bazaar – which also means it's nice and quiet.

Getting There & Away

There are plenty of land connections to destinations both in Nepal and India.

To/From India The cheapest and slowest method is to catch a rickshaw from one side of the border to the other (Rs 2) then a bus to Siliguri (Rs 5). From Siliguri you can catch a bus on to Darjeeling for around Rs 25. Or you can catch a taxi to Siliguri for Rs 120 and on to Darjeeling for another Rs 500. See the Getting There chapter for more information.

To/From Nepal There is plenty of competition for your business if you plan to buy a bus ticket, so it's worth shopping around. The prices won't vary much but the departure times and the quality of the buses will. If you plan on trying to get to Kathmandu in a single trip, Chandeshwari and National Deluxe have been recommended as having comfortable new buses.

Night buses for Kathmandu and Pokhara generally leave between 3 and 4 pm and take 17 or 18 hours. Not only would this be an epic and unpleasant experience, but you'd miss the views. If time and weather allow,

consider catching a day bus to Janakpur (6 or 7 hours) and spending a day there. The road is particularly interesting between Itahari and Janakpur; it runs across the flood plain of the massive Sapt Kosi. See the Getting There chapter for a description.

There are numerous night buses to Kathmandu and Pokhara for around Rs 170. There are three day buses to Janakpur for Rs 60 and two night buses for Rs 80. There are three day buses to Birganj that leave very early in the morning and cost Rs 109.

From Kathmandu, buses for Kakarbhitta leave from Ratna Park (to the left as you enter). The night express buses leave between 4.30 and 5.30 pm, but they are often full, so book a day or two early.

BIRATNAGAR & JOGBANI

The observation that Biratnagar is the second largest city in Nepal, and an industrial centre, actually makes the place sound worse than it is! It's an energetic bustling place with the crowds and shops you would expect of a city with several hundred thousand inhabitants. There's just nothing much to keep you here, unless you are particularly interested in Nepal's somewhat shaky industrial development.

It is possible to cross to or from West Bengal at the nearby border post Jogbani (also known as Rani Sikiyahi). This would take you to places like Forbesganj, Purna, English Bazaar and Calcutta. Jogbani is 6 km south of Biratnagar and a major crossing point for Nepalese-Indian trade. Amongst other things, jute is an important local industry.

Since the Kanchenjunga area was opened to organised trekkers, an increasing number of groups have come through town on their way to Dharan Bazaar and points north.

Information & Orientation

Reflecting its unpopularity with travellers, there's no tourist information centre at Jogbani. The border's open 24 hours every day, but the bank (diagonally across the intersection on the left when you cross the border – look for the blue sign and barred

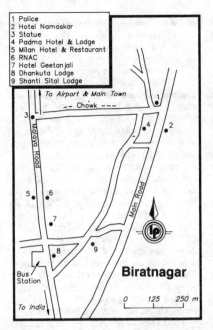

```
1  Police
2  Hotel Namaskar
3  Statue
4  Padma Hotel & Lodge
5  Milan Hotel & Restaurant
6  RNAC
7  Hotel Geetanjali
8  Dhankuta Lodge
9  Shanti Sital Lodge
```

To Airport & Main Town

--- Chowk ---

Malaya Road

Main Road

Bus Station

Biratnagar

0   125   250 m

To India

frequented by the local notables, with car parking, and a uniformed guard to salute you as you enter.

A little less formal, but still comfortable, the *Hotel Geetanjali*, also across from the bus station on Main Rd, is set in a pleasant garden. There's no restaurant, but they serve decent Indian food. A double with/without attached bathroom is Rs 150/100. I would have been happier with a mosquito net, but they do supply electric mosquito thingos. The nearby *Milan Hotel & Restaurant* is not quite in the same league.

Getting There & Away
There are daily flights to Kathmandu for US$70 and to Lukla (a few days walk from the Mt Everest base camp) for US$60.

You can find plenty of buses to Kathmandu, Kakarbhitta and Janakpur, but I didn't find any that went to Pokhara. There was one day bus that went to Birganj (Rs 90), so I guess you could connect from there. Night buses to Kathmandu leave in the late afternoon and cost Rs 150. There are many day buses to Kakarbhitta (Rs 30), Janakpur (Rs 50), Rajbiraj (Rs 25) and to Dharan Bazaar (Rs 10), a departure point for the hill town of Dhankuta, and for Kanchenjunga treks.

From Kathmandu, night buses leave from Ratna Park and the Central Bus Station around 4.30 pm.

Getting Around
It's 6 km from Biratnagar to Jogbani at the border. A bicycle rickshaw will cost Rs 7 to Rs 10, a bus Rs 3.

ITAHARI
Itahari is an undistinguished town at the intersection with the Mahendra Highway and the north-south road that runs between Biratnagar on the border and Dhankuta in the hills. There is an interesting market held along the dusty lanes south-east of the main intersection.

Places to Stay
There's one passable hotel in Itahari, though

window) is only open from 7.30 am to 7 pm. Both Biratnagar's major roads end up at Jogbani; Main Rd is the more direct route back to town (straight ahead over the border).

Places to Stay & Eat
There's quite a range of places at varying prices. Bear in mind that anywhere on Main Rd or near the bus station will be pretty noisy.

Dhankuta Lodge opposite the bus station is a clean and decent cheapie with singles/doubles for Rs 45/60 with attached bathrooms, or Rs 25/30 without. The *Shanti Sital Lodge* and *Padma Hotel & Lodge* are very basic, with rooms around Rs 30.

Up-market, the best value is *Hotel Namaskar* on Malaya Rd, a 15 minute walk from the bus station, which has a range of rooms from Rs 150 to 300. At the top price you get air-con and an attached sitting room, but the cheaper rooms are clean and quite adequate. There's a good, reasonably priced restaurant

it's not particularly clean. The *Jaya Nepal Hotel* has doubles with attached bathrooms for Rs 75.

Getting There & Away

There are numerous buses – all the long-distance, east-west buses stop here. There are also plenty of local buses which go to Biratnagar (Rs 8, 1 hour) and Dharan (Rs 5, half an hour).

DHARAN BAZAAR

Dharan lies right at the foot of the hills, but the transformation from the Terai is dramatic. This is unquestionably a hill town with hill people – there are scarcely any dark-skinned plains people to be seen. Dharan is a bustling bazaar town that has grown rapidly. There are no particular sights of note and nothing to keep you here, but if you're heading into the mountains (say to Kanchenjunga) this will be your best chance for final purchases.

Places to Stay

There are two possibilities, but they'll only look good if you've been trekking for at least 2 weeks! Coming from Itahari, turn right at the statue of the king. The *Hotel Yug Lodge* is labyrinthine, gloomy and not terribly clean. Singles/doubles/triples with attached bathrooms are Rs 45/75/100. There's also a dorm for Rs 15. The *Hotel Evergreen* is a notch above in cleanliness and price Singles/doubles are Rs 65/90.

Getting There & Away

Dharan Bazaar is 75 km from the attractive hill town of Dhankuta. There are numerous buses on a spectacular road for Rs 23.

DHANKUTA

Although Dhankuta is only 75 km by excellent road from the Terai, it seems more like a million miles. The largest flattest spot in the nearby vicinity is the bus station – it soon becomes virtually impossible to believe that flat, water-logged plains exist. Dharan is quite a large town, and although there is no specific attraction, there are good views, a mild climate and plenty of interesting walks

in the surrounding area. It is an ideal escape from Biratnagar and there is a collection of small, but decent, lodges which cater to a largely Nepalese clientele.

The town owes its prosperity to the fact that it was a major recruiting centre for the Gurkha regiments of the British Army and quite a bit of British aid money has been spent in the vicinity. The most obvious legacy is the magnificent, but totally incongruous road. It's one of the best in the country and all of 20 vehicles a day must use it!

The town is strung along a ridge that basically runs north-south; the bus station is below the ridge. The sad remnants of the forest that once covered the hill are at the north end of town.

As you walk downhill (south) along the main street the road forks: the right fork goes down to the bus station; the left fork to a spur where there are fine views of the Himalaya. The latter is a pleasant 45 minute walk. After about 15 minutes the main track veers to the left and there is a stile over a barbed wire fence. Climb the stile and follow the ridge line up to the left. Eventually you'll come to a small shrine. There are plenty of flowers and birds along the way and good views.

Places to Stay

A number of small, clean, decent lodges are on the main street. The *Shah Lodge* and the pleasant *Sanglo Lodge* have doubles/triples for Rs 25/35 with shared facilities.

The best of them all – and it would be a pleasant place to stay while you explored the surrounding hills – is the *Hotel Parichaya*. It's clean and sunny and there are superb views. To find it, walk north up the ridge until you get to a large pipal tree in the middle of an intersection. The hotel is on the right; 'reception' can be found in the restaurant beside the hotel. A single/double is Rs 20/30 and there's a dormitory for Rs 7.

Getting There & Away

There are plenty of buses along the spectacular road to Dharan Bazaar. They cost Rs 33 and take 2 hours. From Dhankuta unsealed road continues to Basantpur and there are plenty of buses that make the 35 km trip for Rs 30. The road is being pushed through to Terhathum.

KOSHI TAPPU WILDLIFE RESERVE

The Koshi Tappu Wildlife Reserve protects a section of the Sapt Kosi's flood plain that lies behind the Kosi Barrage. The Sapt Kosi is one of the Ganges' largest tributaries, and the Kosi Barrage is designed to minimise destructive annual floods. Most of the reserve is surrounded by 8-metre-high embankments that control the spread of the river and funnel it towards the barrage.

The main highway skirts the reserve and crosses the river at the barrage. It's a beautiful, fascinating water world. Small thatched villages perch on what little high ground there is and wherever you look there are water birds, and ponds full of flowering plants, all overwhelmed by fields of rice stretching to the horizon.

Behind the dykes the river continuously changes course and during the monsoon regularly floods, although only to shallow depths. The vegetation is mainly tall grass, with some scrub and riverine forest. Local villagers are allowed to collect grass for thatching every January.

The reserve is home to the last surviving population of wild water buffalo (*arna*), various deer, blue bull (*nilgai*), gharial crocodiles and Gangetic dolphins. It is also either a permanent or temporary home to 280 different species of water birds (migratory and otherwise). These include 20 species of ducks, ibises, storks, egrets and herons.

Information & Orientation

The reserve headquarters is at Kusaha, where all visitors must pay a Rs 250 entrance fee. Kusaha is a 3 km walk from the highway, just outside the eastern embankment, on the eastern side of the barrage.

If you can't find the official signpost just before Laukhi, back-track towards the barrage and cut across to the embankment as soon as you can. A track runs along the top of the embankment and depending where you started, Kusaha should not be more than 5 km away. Laukhi is accessible by local buses from Biratnagar and Rajbiraj.

If you do plan a visit, especially if you want to stay, contact the Department of National Parks & Wildlife Conservation (tel 2-20912), PO Box 860, Babar Mahal, Kathmandu, to get the latest information on access and the availability of facilities.

RAJBIRAJ

Rajbiraj is a dusty uninteresting little town, but it lies on the edge of the Sapt Kosi flood plain, so the countryside and villages to the east are fascinating. Rajbiraj lies to the south of the main highway, but if you have your own vehicle it's definitely worth the detour. You'd have to be pretty keen to build it in to your itinerary if you are using local buses, but it could be done.

Place to Stay

There's only one place to stay – the *Sinha Lodge* – on the main road. It's very, very basic and singles/doubles are Rs 20/30.

Getting There & Away

Local buses from Janakpur and Biratnagar are frequent and cost Rs 25. The road starts to fall apart east of Rajbiraj and there are some very slow sections before the Kosi Barrage.

JANAKPUR

Janakpur is an interesting, attractive town of temples, pools, pedestrians, sadhus, rickshaws and rainbow-coloured saris. Its religious significance lies in the fact that it is the legendary birthplace of Sita (also known as Janaki), the revered heroine of the *Ramayana*, and the place of her marriage to Rama.

Sometimes Janakpur feels like a big village, but when you stand in the broad square before the Janaki Mandir, it also has a definite grandeur. The bus station is as ugly as the best of them, but if, at dusk, you take a long rickshaw ride to a temple or *kunda* (water tank) on the town outskirts you'll experience a subtle, peaceful beauty that will leave you speechless.

Janakpur is a Terai city that works: it's green and clean and it has a sense of history. The farsighted city panchayat (assembly) has kept heavy traffic out of the centre of town – you rarely even see a car or motorbike. Perhaps its age has something to do with this

civic pride and confidence, for Janakpur is an ancient centre of the Maithili language and culture, which has its own script, and is spoken by large numbers of people, both in Nepal and Bihar.

If you do have the time and the inclination to experience something of the Terai, Janakpur should be at the top of your list. It would

---

Ramayana

The *Ramayana*, or romance of Rama, is amongst the best loved and most influential tales of all Hindu literature. Handsome Rama embodies chivalry and virtue, and his wife, the beautiful Sita, is devotion and chastity. Together with Rama's ally, the faithful monkey god Hanuman, they are heroes and exemplars of immense popularity. Like all great mythical archetypes, they have somehow found an enduring place in the human psyche.

It's likely the legend has at least a basis in reality, and was first retold around village hearths in much the same way that Homer's *Iliad* and *Odyssey* began. In the case of the *Ramayana*, the story was first permanently recorded in Sanskrit, possibly as long as 2400 years ago by a sage and poet, Valmiki. Since then it has become a part of people's lives and consciousness throughout India, Nepal and, in various forms, as far as Bali, where to this day it features in puppetry and dance.

Rama was a reincarnation of Vishnu, born at the request of the gods to do battle with the ghastly demon king Ravana, King of Lanka (Sri Lanka). He was reincarnated at Ayodhya (400 km west of Janakpur) as the eldest son of a wealthy king. Handsome, virtuous and strong, he grew up the idol of the people and especially one of his half-brothers, Lakshman.

In the kingdom of Mithila, good King Janak discovered baby Sita, the reincarnation of Lakshmi, lying in a furrow of a ploughed field. She too grew up to be wise and beautiful and so many men wanted to marry her that Janak set a test – a successful suitor had to bend the divine bow of Shiva. Rama, of course, drew the bow and he and Sita looked into each other's eyes and knew divine love.

Rama and his three half-brothers were married in a single ceremony – the brothers to neighbouring princesses – and there was much feasting, flowers falling from heaven, gorgeous processions across the plains, and so on. But this is where things took a turn for the worse.

After returning to Ayodhya, Rama and Sita were forced to leave the palace because of the intrigues of the detestable hunchback Manthara. During their exile Sita was kidnapped and carried off to Lanka by the demon king, while Rama and Lakshman were distracted by a golden deer. Imprisoned, Sita defended herself from the disgusting advances of Ravana.

Meanwhile, Rama and Lakshman formed an alliance with a monkey kingdom. In particular they were served by the indomitable monkey god Hanuman. With Hanuman's loyal assistance Sita was rescued and the demon king Ravana destroyed.

Unfortunately, life didn't improve much for Sita who was forced to undergo an ordeal by fire to prove her chastity. Although Rama, now King of Ayodhya, believed her innocence, his people didn't so Sita found herself in exile again. Sita gave birth to Rama's twin sons and the family was later reunited, but Sita decided she had had enough and was swallowed up by the earth.

Of course, trying to imagine the power and subtlety of the complete story by reading this condensation is a bit like trying to imagine a tree by looking at a match. There are many versions of the story recorded in many art forms and many different languages, including English. ∎

also be an interesting alternative route to or from India (for details see the Getting There chapter).

The only railway in Nepal connects Janakpur to the Indian narrow gauge railway system and runs to Jaynargar. There is also a road connection to Sitamarhi in Bihar. The Nepalese border post, 22 km to the south-west, is called Jaleshwar and it is a recognised entry point.

Information & Orientation

Janakpur is a hopeless tangle of mostly narrow streets, so the best way to get your bearings is from the telecommuication tower and the large concrete water tank on stilts. The town itself lies to the east of the main road that runs through to Jaleshwar at the border. There is a Tourist Information Centre (tel 20755) at Bhanu Chowk.

The Janaki Mandir is just to the south of the water tank and the bus station is to the south-west of the temple near the telecommunications tower. The train station is about a 20 minute walk to the north-east of the water tank.

On the fifth day of the waxing moon in late November or early December, thousands of pilgrims arrive to celebrate a re-enactment of Sita's marriage to Rama (*Bibaha Panchami*). This is also the occasion for an important fair and market that lasts a week. Rama's birthday (*Rama Navami*) in late March or early April is also accompanied by a huge procession.

Janaki Mandir

Sita's temple is believed to be built over the spot where her father, King Janak, found her lying in the furrow of a ploughed field. It's impressively large although, surprisingly, you come across it from the winding Janakpur streets almost without warning.

Although it has no great architectural or historical merit – it was built in 1912 and might be described as baroque Moghul – it is nonetheless a fascinating place. There are instances of fine work, especially in some of the carved stone screens, and beautiful silver doors to the inner sanctum.

The inner sanctum is opened from 5 to 7 am and 6 to 8 pm, to reveal a flower-bedecked statue of Sita that was apparently miraculously found in the Saryu River near Ayodhya. She is accompanied by Rama and his half-brothers Lakshman, Bharat and Satrughna.

During the day, there are few people in the temple – some priests, sadhus and, if you're lucky, perhaps some musicians playing in the cloisters – but it comes alive in the evenings when Sita is displayed.

Ram Sita Bibaha Mandir

Virtually next door to the Janaki Mandir, but built with the traditional Nepalese roof, this rather bizarre temple is built over the spot where Rama and Sita were married. There's a bit of a scam at the gate – you pay to take in a camera, or to have it looked after. The temple itself has glass walls so you can peer in at the life-sized models of Sita and Rama, his half-brothers and sisters-in-law.

Other Tanks & Temples

There are several tanks in the town itself, but it is worth hiring a bicycle rickshaw to see the tanks and temples on the outskirts. Allow a couple of hours and expect to pay around Rs 20. There are a number on the western side of the main road, and you could track them down on foot if you were energetic. They're reached by brick paved roads that wander off into the paddy fields. Two of the most interesting are Bihar Kunda and Ratan Saga Kunda. The countryside is lush and tropical with coconut palms and huge trees framing the temples and ponds that are scattered across the fertile plains. Dhanusa, 15 km to the north, marks the spot where Rama drew Shiva's bow.

Places to Stay & Eat

The best hotel in town, the *Hotel Welcome*, will cater to almost every budget (what you get is what you pay for) and it does a thriving trade. It's very clean, and the staff are helpful. At the bottom end they have a dormitory for Rs 35 per person. Next up is a double with a shared bathroom for Rs 65, or with an attached bathroom for Rs 100. At the top end they have suites with air-con for Rs 350.

The *Rama Hotel* is quite atmospheric, and it's quite OK and the food's decent, but it has definitely seen better days. Its main advantage over the Hotel Welcome is that it has off-street parking. Singles/doubles with attached bathrooms cost Rs 55/110.

Getting There & Away
To/From India There are numerous buses to the Indian border at Jaleshwar.

The train station is a 20 minute walk or a Rs 5 rickshaw ride to the north-east of town. There are daily trains between Jaynargar and Janakpur for the princely sum of Rs 8. You change the nationality of the train at Bijolpura. The train leaves Jaynargar at 9 am, Janakpur at 7 am. Once in Jaynargar you could hook up with the painfully slow Indian narrow gauge.

To/From Nepal There are three flights a week to Kathmandu for Rs 620.

There are half a dozen express buses to and from Kathmandu (day and night) that cost around Rs 105 and take about 12 hours, as well as slower local buses for Rs 85. In Kathmandu most leave from Ratna Park and the Central Bus Station; a Saja bus leaves from near Bhimsen Tower at 6.30 am and costs Rs 85.

There are three day buses to Kakarbhitta for Rs 60, two night buses for Rs 80 and the day journey takes 6 or 7 hours. The Sapt Kosi flood plain are particularly interesting, so if you can, take the day bus.

BIRGANJ
Birganj is one of the most popular entry points for Nepal, and one of Nepal's most important industrial cities. This is an unfortunate combination. Birganj is one of the least attractive places on the planet, let alone in Nepal. The main highway runs right through the centre of town so the overwhelming impression of the city is one of dust (or mud in season), heat, trucks, poverty and squalor.

There are also a large number of depressingly run-down factories, as the 'corridor' between Birganj and Hetauda is, along with Biratnagar, the most important centre for industrial development in Nepal. Amongst tanneries and other unattractive places there's a sugar factory and an agricultural implements factory.

Birganj is probably the most important entry point for Indian imports, but most travellers now enter through Sunauli to the west. Birganj remains the most convenient entry point, however, for those coming from Patna or Calcutta.

Fortunately, there are plenty of day and night buses to and from Kathmandu and Pokhara and points south (in India) so there should be no necessity to stay more than a night – hopefully not even that.

Information & Orientation
Birganj and Raxaul Bazaar (on the Indian

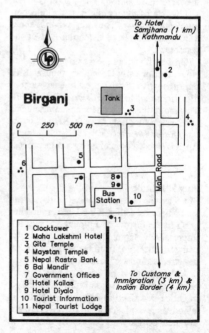

1 Clocktower
2 Maha Lakshmi Hotel
3 Gita Temple
4 Maystan Temple
5 Nepal Rastra Bank
6 Bal Mandir
7 Government Offices
8 Hotel Kailas
9 Hotel Diyalo
10 Tourist Information
11 Nepal Tourist Lodge

side of the border) virtually run together, although it's a 30 minute rickshaw ride from one bus station to the other. Basically Birganj is strung along the north-south highway, with the bus station one block to the west. There's a classically kitsch Nepalese-style clock-tower towards the northern end of town. Nepalese immigration is open from 4 am to 10 pm. There is a Tourist Information Centre (tel 2083) beside the bus station.

Things to See
If you do find yourself with a couple of hours to kill in Birganj you could hire a rickshaw for an hour or two (at around Rs 15 an hour) and have a bit of a wander. The town has a certain gruesome fascination and there are a couple of modern temples and some muddy tanks. The most interesting is the Bal Mandir, a modern Buddhist temple about a km west from the main road.

Places to Stay & Eat
The cheap places are, as per usual, clustered around the bus station. They aren't inspiring, to say the least, but they would do at a pinch. The *Nepal Tourist Lodge* is basic and not all that clean; singles/doubles with attached bathrooms are Rs 40/45. The *National Guest House* is in the same category. There's a slightly better cheapie, the *Maha Lakshmi*, a km or so away, near the clocktower. It has double rooms with an attached bathroom for Rs 35.

If you can afford it, especially if you're travelling in the hot season, go for something a bit more comfortable. The *Hotel Diyalo* (tel 22370) also fronts the bus station, but it's clean and comfortable and there's a good restaurant and even a pleasant roof garden. Singles/doubles with attached bathrooms range from Rs 90/125 to Rs 375/400 if you want air-con.

Virtually next door (going away from the bus station), *Hotel Kailas* is also clean and it has a good tandoori restaurant. Rooms vary in price from Rs 35/70 a singles/double without an attached bathroom to Rs 125, depending where you are in the building.

The *Hotel Samjhana* (tel 22122) is quite a distance from the bus station, but it has parking and decent food. A double room with an attached bathroom is Rs 150; air-con will add another Rs 150 to the bill.

Getting There & Away
To/From India It's a 30 minute, Rs 10 rickshaw ride to Raxaul where you pick up Indian buses. Expect to pay around Rs 55 for the 4 to 5 hour journey to Patna. It's possible to make a single all-inclusive booking for the trip between Patna and Kathmandu (which includes overnighting at Birganj) for Rs 250. See the Getting There chapter for more details.

To/From Nepal There are plenty of day and night buses to and from Kathmandu. Despite the fact that the Tribhuvan Highway from Hetauda to Naubise looks like the best route, all buses travel west to Narayanghat before they climb into the hills. The night buses leave at around 6 pm, cost Rs 75 and take 11 hours. Day buses leave early and take an hour or two longer, but the views make this worthwhile.

It is possible to catch a bus from Hetauda to Kathmandu that traverses the Tribhuvan Highway – it's slow, but there are superb views. See the Hetauda section following, and the Getting There chapter.

From Kathmandu, the night buses leave from the GPO, Central Bus Station and Ratna Park, between 6 and 7 pm; day buses leave from the GPO and Ratna Park from 6.30 to 9 am. Companies to look for include Siddi Overland, Sita Travel and New Rakta Chandra Coach.

There are day/night buses to Pokhara for Rs 60/70 and day buses to Narayanghat for Rs 40. If you're going to the Royal Chitwan National Park get off at Tadi Bazaar (Rs 30, 4 hours).

HETAUDA
Hetauda is the starting point for a cableway that carries bulk goods (especially bulky items like cement, fertiliser, etc) from the Terai to Kathmandu. It's quite an amazing construction (reminiscent of a ski lift). The

current cableway dates from 1958 and can carry 25 tonnes per hour. Unless you want to catch a bus over the superb Tribhuvan Highway, there's no need to stop. Normally, buses turn west to Narayanghat.

Places to Stay & Eat

The *Motel Avocado* on the way out of town on the Tribhuvan Highway has quiet, motel-type accommodation, with parking, for Rs 150. The *Hotel Rapti* (tel 20482) is cheaper and more basic.

Getting There & Away

A Saja Sewa bus runs over the magnificent Tribhuvan Highway via Daman. There are spectacular views and this route is well worth considering. The Saja bus leaves from near the Bhimsen Tower in Kathmandu at 6.30 am (Rs 35, 8 hours). The privately run company Bhagmati Sewa also run on this route; they leave from Ratna Park. Saja buses also travel via Narayanghat and Tadi Bazaar, leaving at 6.45 and 7.30 am (Rs 49).

DAMAN

Daman is 2322 metres above sea level, midway between Kathmandu and Hetauda. Its claim to fame is that it has, arguably, *the* most spectacular outlook on the Himalaya – there are unimpeded views of the entire range from Dhaulagiri to Mt Everest. The view from this ridge is quite simply awesome. If you have the opportunity it should not be missed.

There is a viewing tower, with a telescope, a restaurant and not much else. On the Hetauda side of Daman there is a magnificent rhododendron forest – which would be particularly worth seeing in spring – then great views over the Terai to India.

Places to Stay

At one time it was possible to stay in the viewing tower – the *Everest View Tower & Lodge*. Unfortunately it is now very rundown – replete with broken windows. If you were prepared to rough it, you could certainly not find a better view, especially for only Rs 20!

Getting There & Away

Daman is about 2½ hours from both Kathmandu and Hetauda. Unless you're on your way to Birganj hiring a car and making a day trip from Kathmandu is the ideal way to get to Daman – but it won't be cheap. Think in terms of US$60. If you had a group and it was clear weather, it would be worth it.

Saja Sewa buses come this way – they leave from near the Bhimsen Tower at 6.30 am and, to Daman, cost Rs 35.

TADI BAZAAR

In the Chitwan Valley between Hetauda and Narayanghat, the small town of Tadi Bazaar (sometimes spelt Tandi Bazaar) is nothing more than a junction town for Sauraha, the budget accommodation centre for the Royal Chitwan National Park. For more details see the separate section on the park.

Getting There & Away

Buses to Tadi Bazaar cost about Rs 35 from Kathmandu or Pokhara and the trip typically takes about 7 hours. You can catch any of the buses that run south through to Birganj or points east. Saja Sewa buses leave from near the Bhimsen Tower; the day bus leaves around 6.30 am. From Birganj or Sunauli on the Indian border a bus takes about 4 hours and costs around Rs 30.

Sauraha is about 8 km away, and you can walk there in a couple of hours. For more details see the Getting There & Away section of the Royal Chitwan National Park.

NARAYANGHAT & BHARATPUR

Narayanghat is a fast-growing new town on the banks of the massive Narayani River, just downstream from the junction of the Kali Gandaki and Trisuli rivers. Its importance has grown because it lies at the intersection between the Mahendra Highway, which runs the length of the Terai, and the main road to the hills that joins the Prithvi Highway, from Kathmandu to Pokhara. It is the main administrative and trading centre for the district. Bharatpur is contiguous with Narayanghat, and has an airport.

Although on the map the most direct route

from eastern Nepal to Kathmandu is the road from Hetauda to Naubise, almost all traffic takes the better road from Narayanghat to Mugling. The so-called Rajpath from Hetauda to Naubise is a magnificent drive, but its endless narrow corners mean it is not appropriate for trucks and buses.

Narayanghat will, for most people, simply be a chai stop en route to the Chitwan or India, and apart from the river there's not much of interest. There are some modern temples on the bank of the river, some cheap

hotels, and the up-market Hotel Narayani Safari. It could be used as a base for trips to the Chitwan and to Dev Ghat at the confluence of the Kali Gandaki and Trisuli rivers.

There's an ancient hermitage at Dev Ghat, which is the site for an annual pilgrimage for the festival of Magh Sankranti. This generally takes place in mid-January and celebrates the gradually lengthening days.

Places to Stay

There are a number of cheap lodges and res-

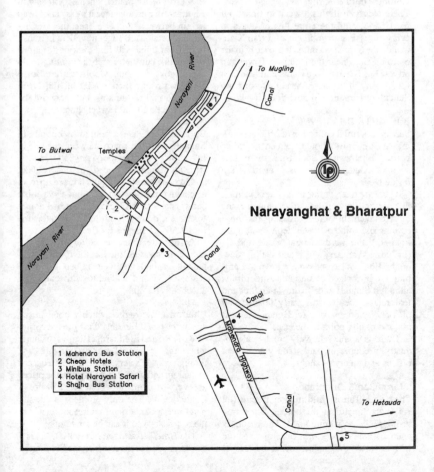

Narayanghat & Bharatpur

1 Mahendra Bus Station
2 Cheap Hotels
3 Minibus Station
4 Hotel Narayani Safari
5 Shajha Bus Station

taurants just over the bridge on the Mahendra Highway. There's nothing much to separate them; expect to pay around Rs 35.

The up-market *Hotel Narayani Safari* (tel (056) 20130, 20634) is primarily used as a base for trips to the Chitwan. It has air-con, a swimming pool and a tennis court. Singles/doubles with full board cost US$51/83. The hotel has a 3 night, 4 day Chitwan package that includes elephant rides, a visit to a Tharu village and so on for US$310.

Getting There & Away

There are three flights a week to Bharatpur for US$45. And there are lots of buses to every accessible town in Nepal. From Kathmandu the Saja Sewa buses leave early in the morning from near the Bhimsen Tower and private buses leave from Ratna Park and cost Rs 35. Any of the buses heading to or from Sunauli or Birganj will drop you off.

SUNAULI & BHAIRAWA

Sunauli is a small collection of official buildings and a couple of hotels right on the Indian border. Bhairawa is somewhat more substantial, a dusty, bustling town nearly 4 km inside Nepal.

There are three points in favour of visiting this part of the world. Firstly, Sunauli is the most convenient border crossing for those coming and going between Nepal (especially Pokhara) and northern and western India (including Varanasi, Agra and Delhi). Secondly, Bhairawa is the closest town to Lumbini, the birthplace of Buddha. And thirdly, although Sunauli and Bhairawa are hot and featureless, they're still fairly relaxed and pleasant by comparison to Birganj, the next major crossing point to the east.

There is some relatively small-scale industry, a couple of banks and government offices and plenty of shops.

Information & Orientation

There is a Tourist Information Centre (tel 1304) in Sunauli at the border. Their free *Visitors' Guide* is quite good. The border is open 24 hours every day, but most visitors will have to change money at the Nepal

Rastra Bank, which is only open from 7.30 am to 7.30 pm. Bhairawa is a 20 minute rickshaw ride to the north.

Most shops and businesses in Bhairawa are strung along Narayan Path or Bank Rd. The Siddhartha Highway runs along the eastern edge of town to the border.

Lumbini is 22 km to the south-west, but there are frequent buses, and most people stay in Bhairawa if they plan to visit the site.

Places to Stay & Eat

It doesn't really matter whether you stay in Bhairawa or Sunauli since it's easy and cheap to go between the two (see the Getting Around section). Budget travellers in transit to or from India will find their best options in Sunauli, but there really is *nothing* to do there, so I for one would rather be in Bhairawa where there's a bit of life. There are no formal restaurants, but there are the usual street stalls and sweet shops.

Sunauli There are a couple of options in Sunauli, with not much between them. My first choice would be the *Nepal Guest House*, which is reasonably priced, reasonably clean and has reasonable food. It's hooked up to an artesian bore so you can have warmish showers any time. There are four bed dorms for Rs 65, doubles with bathroom attached for Rs 50 and singles for Rs 35.

Across the road the *Hotel Mamta* (tel 20512) is also OK and has the flashiest restaurant. A single bed in a six bed dormitory costs Rs 35 and a double with bathroom attached is Rs 80.

Bhairawa The highest quality hotel in the area is the *Hotel Yeti* (tel 20551) on the corner of Bank Rd and Siddhartha Highway. This is where the occasional tour groups that pass through stay. It's very clean, there's a decent restaurant and, for what it delivers, the prices are very reasonable – Rs 200/250 for a single/double. The only problem is that the hotel overlooks a main intersection (where the buses stop) so it can be a bit noisy.

The *Hotel Himalayan Inn* (tel 20347) is a bit out of town to the north on the Siddhartha

Highway. Although it has been left behind by the Hotel Yeti and is struggling a bit, it's still just OK. There is off-road parking. The restaurant is cavernous, and empty, and the food distinctly average. Singles/doubles with attached bathrooms are Rs 150/200.

The *Sayapati Guest House*, which is convenient to the bus station on Bank Rd, is a decent, cheap place to stay. Singles/doubles are Rs 35/70. The *Shree Pashupatinath Lodge & Hotel* on the Narayan Path is a good 10 minute walk from the bus stop, but it's clean and it wins on character. A double with

attached bathroom is Rs 66, and a single with common bathroom Rs 27.

Getting There & Away
There are plenty of bus connections to destinations in both Nepal and India.

To/From India You catch buses to Indian cities on the Indian side of the border. There are direct buses to Varanasi for the equivalent of Rs 90 and the journey takes about 8 hours. See the Getting There chapter for more information.

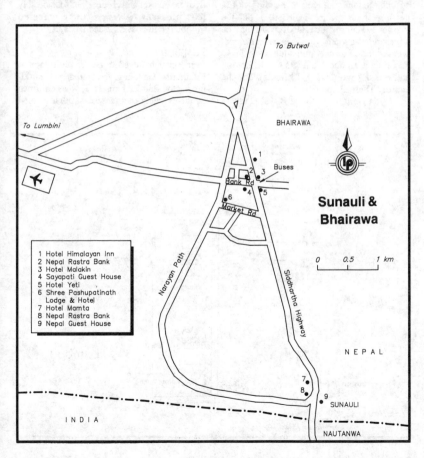

1 Hotel Himalayan Inn
2 Nepal Rastra Bank
3 Hotel Malakin
4 Sayapati Guest House
5 Hotel Yeti
6 Shree Pashupatinath Lodge & Hotel
7 Hotel Mamta
8 Nepal Rastra Bank
9 Nepal Guest House

Sunauli & Bhairawa

To/From Nepal There are four direct flights a week between Kathmandu and Bhairawa for US$65. Travelling north, most buses start their journey in Sunauli, stopping in Bhairawa. It's best to join the bus in Sunauli. In Bhairawa the bus companies' offices are around the intersection of Bank Rd and the Siddhartha Highway.

There are several night and day buses to Pokhara and Kathmandu. The day buses are a bit quicker and cheaper, plus you see the views. The road to Pokhara (Rs 50, 9 hours) is particularly beautiful (for great views of Machhupuchhare if you're heading north, get a seat on the left-hand side), but the journey to Kathmandu is also rewarding. The government-owned, blue Saja buses are recommended. From Kathmandu they leave Ratna Park around 7 am (Rs 65, 12 hours), and 6 and 7 pm (Rs 80, 13 hours). See the Getting There chapter.

If you want to go to the Royal Chitwan National Park, there's a Birganj bus (Rs 65, 7 hours) you could take that leaves at 5.30 am. Get off at Tadi Bazaar if you're heading to Sauraha (Rs 30, 4 hours). There is a night bus to Kakarbhitta (Rs 180, 17 hours).

See the Lumbini Getting There & Away section for transport possibilities.

Getting Around
The only time you'll need transport will be to go between Sunauli and Bhairawa – it's 4 hot, flat km. A rickshaw will cost around Rs 10 and take 20 minutes. The other alternatives are quicker and cheaper, but considerably less pleasant. A *tempo* (three wheeled minibus) will cost Rs 2 and a bus, Rs 1.

LUMBINI
Lumbini is believed to be the birthplace of Siddhartha Gautama, the founder of Buddhism – the Buddha himself. This is confirmed by the existence of an inscribed pillar erected

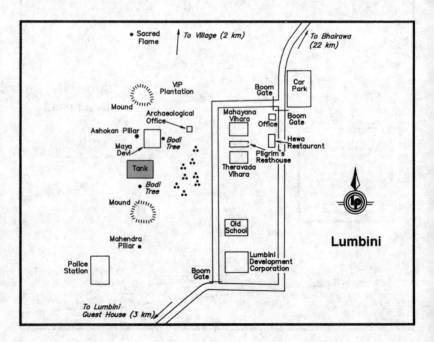

To Village (2 km)

To Bhairawa (22 km)

• Sacred Flame

VIP Plantation

Mound

Ashokan Pillar •

Archaeological Office

Maya Devi

• Bodi Tree

Tank

• Bodi Tree

Mound

Mahendra Pillar •

Police Station

Boom Gate

Car Park

Mahayana Vihara

Office

Boom Gate

Hewa Restaurant

Pilgrim's Resthouse

Theravada Vihara

Old School

Lumbini Development Corporation

Boom Gate

To Lumbini Guest House (3 km)

Lumbini

370 years after the event by the great Buddhist emperor Ashoka, and the presence of a number of ancient ruins.

Fittingly, Lumbini is an example of how illusory and futile human effort is. There's not much to see and it requires a serious effort of the imagination to conjure up the ghosts of the past. Lumbini is not a Bethlehem or Mecca – there is no city, no impressive architecture, no pilgrim-jammed carpark, no heavily armed soldiers, no hustlers, not even a postcard stand.

In the end, it is the absence of all these things, and the peacefulness of Lumbini that make a visit worthwhile. Whatever the surroundings, it would be interesting to visit the birthplace of such a great religious leader, especially if you are interested in his teachings. It's interesting that the Buddha should have been born on this fertile tropical plain, a place of such contrast to the deserts of the Middle East from which so many religious leaders have come; strange that he should have been born a wealthy prince; and strange that this privileged life and rich countryside should have inspired a belief that suffering is synonymous with existence.

Allow yourself an hour or two to wander around and soak in the atmosphere. The important sights don't take long to cover – the Maya Devi Temple, the Ashokan Pillar, the Sacred Pond and the Mahayana and Theravada viharas. Then find a shady spot where you can watch the parrots squabbling in the branches of the massive bo trees.

Two large mounds on either side of the site are not impressive stupas, as you might suspect, but simply the spoils from modern archaeological digs.

Some people don't feel that it is essential to visit the Mahendra Pillar or the eternal flame. The latter was lit by the Chairman of the Lumbini Development Trust, HRH Prince Gyanendra Bir Bikram Shah, on the occasion of the International Year of Peace on 1 November 1986. It marked the silver jubilee year of the Partyless Democratic Panchayat System.

There are grandiose plans for the development of Lumbini, with the aim of creating a place of pilgrimage and a tourist attraction. It will be interesting to see whether this can be achieved by government decree. A plan by the Japanese architect Kenzo Tange was adopted in 1978 – it involves canals, gardens, a library and museum, monastic zones, a pilgrim lodge and a four star hotel. There has been some slow progress, but there's nothing open for visitors yet. The major earthworks, are complete, and there are a couple of buildings quite a distance from the site proper.

Ashokan Pillar

Emperor Ashoka is one of the greatest figures in Indian history. Throughout his massive empire he left pillars and rock-carved edicts, which to this day delineate the extent of his power. They can be seen in Delhi, Gujarat, Orissa, Uttar Pradesh, Madhya Pradesh – and Lumbini.

Buddha's Birth

The birth of the Buddha has been idealised by a number of suitably miraculous Buddhist texts. It is generally accepted, however, that he was born in 624 BC, the son of King Suddhodana who ruled a small kingdom, Kapilavastu, and Queen Maya Devi, originally of the neighbouring Koliya principality. The ruins near Taulihawa to the west of Lumbini are believed to be those of Kapilavastu (but there is not much to see).

Lumbini lay between the two kingdoms and it was on a journey to visit her parents when, legend has it, Maya Devi stopped at Lumbini, then a beautiful garden surrounded by sal trees. In one version of the story, Maya Devi was bathing when labour pains began, and the branches of an overhanging tree bent down to support her while she gave birth. ∎

Ashoka converted to Buddhism and in 250 BC he visited Lumbini and erected a pillar, which is inscribed:

King Ashoka, the beloved of Gods, in the twentieth year of the coronation, made a royal visit. A stone railing and a stone pillar were erected in honour of Buddha who was born here. Because Buddha was born here the village of Lumbini was freed from paying tax.

The Chinese traveller Hiuen Tsang visited Lumbini in the 7th century AD, and described how he saw the pillar struck by lightning and split in two. Apparently the area was already in decline and the site eventually completely disappeared. The pillar was rediscovered in 1895 by a German archaeologist.

Maya Devi Temple

The most important building in Lumbini, the temple of Maya Devi, is believed to be over 2000 years old, perhaps built over a stupa erected by Ashoka. It is not, however, architecturally or artistically interesting in any way. The temple itself is attended by a Hindu priest, and Hindu women in particular revere a stone nativity scene, now protected by a wooden screen. Dating from the Malla dynasty (approximately 13th century AD) the sculpture was the centre of a fertility rite. There is a modern marble copy on view, along with a number of small sculptures left by devotees.

Other Attractions

The square pool is believed to be the spot where Maya Devi bathed. The foundations for a number of stupas and viharas (monasteries) dating from the 2nd century BC to the 9th century AD lie in the vicinity. There are also two modern viharas although, unfortunately, neither are particularly interesting or well maintained. The Mahayana Vihara is built in distinctive Tibetan style.

Places to Stay & Eat

The *Lumbini Guest House* has clean and comfortable rooms. Double rooms are US$10 but the food is limited and rather expensive. If the price doesn't make you twitch, I think this would be a pleasant, if lonely, place to stay. Most people choose to stay in Bhairawa.

There's very, *very* basic pilgrim accommodation in the block between the two viharas. Literally all you get is a roof over your head and a bed (no mattress). If you've got food and camping equipment and you do stay, pay a donation.

Getting There & Away

There are regular buses that make the 22 km journey from Bhairawa to Lumbini for Rs 6. If you are in a group it would be preferable to hire an autorickshaw (about Rs 250) or a taxi (about Rs 500). Make sure this includes waiting time – a couple of hours are more than sufficient.

BUTWAL

Lying at the very foot of the Siwalik Hills, Butwal is an unattractive, dirty town. The approach from Tansen, to the north, is dramatic: one moment you're in a narrow mountain gorge, the next you pass through a pleasant mango grove, and suddenly you are on the plains with people, dust, rickshaws and Hindi film posters everywhere. There's no apparent reason to stop, but if you did have to for some reason, try the *Hotel Sindoor*.

TANSEN

Tansen is just off the Siddhartha Highway, between Pokhara and Bhairawa/Sunauli. Prior to the unification of Nepal under the Shahs this was the capital of the Palpan kings and it is still the administrative centre for a large region. It's a bustling town that sees few visitors. There are great views from the town itself and from the nearby hills. It would be a pleasant place to break a journey – it's about 3½ hours from Pokhara and 2 hours from Bhairawa.

The town sprawls over a steep ridge and quite a few of the main streets are too steep for cars, which helps to keep some of the less pleasant aspects of the 20th century at bay.

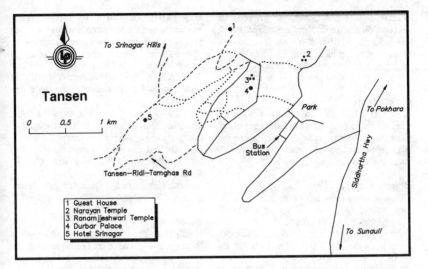

Tansen

To Srinagar Hills

0   0.5   1 km

Park

To Pokhara

Bus Station

Siddhartha Hwy

Tansen—Ridi—Tamghas Rd

To Sunauli

1 Guest House
2 Narayan Temple
3 Ranamjjeshwari Temple
4 Durbar Palace
5 Hotel Srinagar

There are some fine old buildings lining the cobbled streets and there are two interesting temples: a classic Narayan temple (near a large fruit bat colony) which is one of the most beautiful outside the Kathmandu Valley; and the Ranamjeshwari Temple that was built in 1815 to commemorate a short-lived victory over the British. There's also an ugly, pink, Rana-style palace now used as government offices. It's worth exploring the bazaars – Tansen is famous for topis (Nepalese hats) and metalware.

There are also some interesting walks in the nearby hills, including a 2 hour trek to the banks of the Kali Gandaki River and the vast, deserted Ranighat Palace.

Places to Stay

There are some ordinary, simple hotels around the bus station with singles/doubles for around Rs 30/40. The best is the *Siddhartha Hotel*. There's a town plan at the bus station showing directions to the *Hotel Srinagar* (tel 20425) which is perched above the town. The hotel has comfortable accommodation and magnificent views. It's about 3 km from the bus station and singles/doubles are US$15/20.

Getting There & Away

There are two buses a day from Pokhara for Rs 35 and five per day to Bhairawa/Sunauli for Rs 20. The road is magnificent, so if you can, find a place on the roof so you can appreciate the views. If you're inside and coming from Pokhara try to get a seat on the right side of the bus.

NEPALGANJ

The most important town in western Nepal, Nepalganj at times feels more Indian than Nepalese. It's a border town that owes as much to trade as it does to its position as a major administrative centre. It has more of an air of permanence than some other border towns and planners have had the good sense to run the highway to the west of the main town.

The old part of town has a temple honouring Shiva and a large pool. There's a vibrant bazaar selling everything except kitchen sinks (although I'm sure one of the metal workers could knock one up if you needed it).

A steady trickle of travellers come through Nepalganj on their way to the Royal Bardia National Park, the site for Tiger Tops Karnali

Lodge and Tented Camp (see the separate section on the Royal Bardia National Park), or to Jumla. Politics allowing, it could be a very interesting back door into Nepal, connecting with a narrow-gauge railway on the Indian side of the border in Uttar Pradesh.

Orientation

The airport is about 5 km to the north of town and the town is about 6 km from the border. The old, interesting part of town lies to the east of the main road, although virtually all the hotels are on the highway.

Places to Stay & Eat

There are two reasonable hotels, both on the way to the Indian border on the highway. They're set back from the road so noise and parking aren't problems. The older and more popular is the *Hotel Sneha* (tel 20119, telex Attn Hotel Sneha 8001 PCONGNP) with large clean rooms and helpful staff. Singles/doubles are Rs 125/175 and there's a chance you'll get hot water. Deluxe rooms (with air-con) are Rs 250. There's a decent restaurant with good vegetable thalis for Rs 40, beer for Rs 60.

Virtually next door, the *Hotel Batika* (tel 20827) is new, very clean, well designed, and quite unexpected in this part of the world. I couldn't work out why those with expense accounts weren't staying here. Singles/double are Rs 250/350 and the hot water is guaranteed.

The cheapies are around the main intersection (and the inevitable statue). Best of the lot, but nothing to write home about, the *Shanta Shakya Lodge* has singles/doubles with a shared bathroom for Rs 30/50, double with an attached bathroom for Rs 80. Ask for clean sheets.

On the other side of the road, the *Narayani Guest House*, and nearby the *Shital Guest House*, would be worth considering if you wanted something *really* cheap.

Getting There & Away

This is Royal Nepal Airlines' western headquarters, so there's a modern airport, plus housing for pilots and their families. Unfortunately this doesn't mean that you are any more certain to arrive or depart on the promised hour or day than you are anywhere else in Nepal. The usual possible disasters apply – weather, VIPs, or a group booking for Karnali or Jumla. There are daily flights to Jumla for US$40 and to Kathmandu for US$90.

If all else fails, there's always the bus. There are four night buses to Kathmandu (14 hours, Rs 150), and one to Pokhara (10 hours, Rs 130). You can get to Narayanghat for Rs 107, and if you really had to, Kakarbhitta for Rs 200.

From Kathmandu, Saja buses leave from Bhimsen Tower at 4 pm.

Getting Around

It will cost around Rs 10 by rickshaw from the airport to town, or the border to town .

ROYAL BARDIA NATIONAL PARK

The Royal Bardia National Park is the largest untouched wilderness area in the Terai. It's bordered to the north by the crest of the Siwalik Hills and to the west by the Geruwa River, a branch of the mighty Karnali, one of the major tributaries of the Ganges.

You stand a better chance of seeing a tiger here than anywhere else in Nepal (including the Chitwan). It's a stunning place that seems a very long way from the 20th century – watching the sun rise over the forest from the back of an elephant is like having a box seat at the dawn of time.

Most of the reserve is covered with open sal forest, with the balance a mixture of grassland, savannah and riverine forest. The grassed areas (*phanta*) are excellent for game viewing. Most people will visit in the hope of seeing a Royal Bengal tiger, but there are also leopard, jungle cats, mongoose, sloth bears, blue bull (*nilgai*), langur and rhesus monkeys, and sambar, spotted, hog and barking deer. The Asian one-horned rhinoceros was reintroduced from the Chitwan in 1986, and although they are breeding successfully there are only small numbers. There's at least one wild male elephant.

The Geruwa (Karnali) River rushes pell-

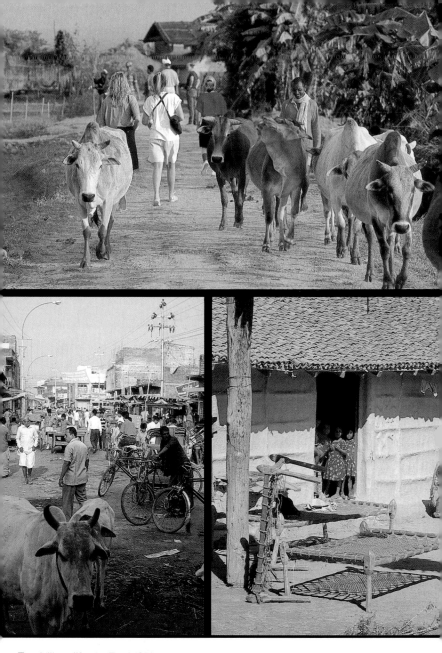

Top: Village life, the Terai (SB)
Left: Sacred cows and an unholy mess, Birganj (RE)
Right: Curiosity gets the bettter of Tharu girls, western Terai (RE)

Top: Hopes in the balance – rice is weighed at Itahari, eastern Terai (RE)
Bottom: Terai village afloat on Sapt Kosi's floodplain, eastern Terai (RE)

mell through a gap in the hills at Chisopani, grey with silt and snow melt. It's home to the famous mahseer game fish, gharial and mugger crocodiles, and the strange Gangetic dolphin.

More than 30 different mammals and over 250 species of birds have been recorded in the park. Birds include numerous species of herons, storks, geese, ducks and parakeets as well as endangered birds like the Bengal Florican and Sarus Crane.

In some ways Bardia is like the Chitwan; the major difference is the degree of isolation and the limited number of visitors. Those that do make the effort to get here will never forget it.

Information & Orientation

The park headquarters are at Tharkurdwara, an 8 km walk from Motipur. Private vehicles can enter the park at East Chisopani, 8 km north of Kohalpur on the Nepalganj to Surkhet road. After completion of the Mahendra Rajmarg the park entrance will be at Motipur. The entrance fee is Rs 250 and camping is possible, with prior permission.

There are no shops, medical facilities or petrol stations, so if you come independently, come prepared. Most people, however, will stay at the superb lodge at Chitkaiya or a luxurious tented camp on the banks of the Churia.

Places to Stay

Tiger Mountain, the same company that runs the famous Tiger Tops Lodge in the Chitwan, runs all-inclusive tours. The *Tiger Tops Karnali Lodge* and *Tented Camp* are simply outstanding. Although they aren't cheap, at US$150 and US$120 a night respectively, they offer an extraordinary experience and are worth every cent. Bookings can be made through Tiger Mountain (tel 222706), PO Box 242, Durbar Marg, Kathmandu. Those that have been to both the Chitwan and Karnali almost unanimously vote Karnali superior.

The Lodge is on the edge of the park, a short walk from a fascinating Tharu village. It's built from traditional materials – thatch and mud – and is extremely comfortable. The

staff is knowledgeable and helpful, without being intrusive. It's a place where you can abdicate all responsibility, relax and just enjoy. The principle activity is exploring the forest from elephant back, but the staff will also organise walks to the nearby village or through the bush.

The Tented Camp is beautifully sited on a cliff overlooking the Churia River, in the shadow of the Siwalik Hills – the peace and quiet is almost overwhelming. A camp it might be, rough it is not. The beds are comfortable, the food is good and the water is hot. Again activities revolve around the elephants, but another highlight is a float down the river – a bird-watcher's delight.

The disadvantage (advantage?) of Karnali is that it takes a day of travelling to get to or from Kathmandu. This means you need a minimum of 4 days: day 1 – Kathmandu to the Lodge; day 2 – elephant rides and walks; day 3 – to the Tented Camp, rafting and elephant ride; day 4 to Kathmandu.

Getting There & Away

Although the park is accessible from the Mahendra Highway, most people fly to Nepalganj (US$90) where they are then picked up by the Tiger Tops people. The road soon deteriorates to a very rough track and the drive to the Lodge takes at least 4 hours. It's an interesting drive past thriving villages and fording several rivers. When the highway is completed the travelling time from Nepalganj will be halved.

ROYAL SUKLA PHANTA WILDLIFE RESERVE

Sukla Phanta is smaller and even more isolated than Bardia, although in some respects it is similar. In the extreme south-west of the country, it covers 155 sq km of riverine floodplain, which includes open grass plains (phanta), forest (primarily sal), a lake and a river.

It is home to tigers, leopards, various species of deer (including an important colony of swamp deer), gharial and mugger crocodiles, otters and a wide variety of bird life.

Places to Stay

Silent Safari is currently the only company operating in the park. They have a number of tours, a minimum of 5 days long, leaving from Mahendranagar, or Dhangardi. Accommodation is in comfortable tented camps or *machans* (tree platforms for watching wildlife). Wildlife viewing is undertaken by vehicle, elephant canoe or on foot. In addition to the wildlife, visits to local Tharu villages are arranged.

Silent Safari (tel 227236, fax 225524), GPO Box 1679, Kathmandu, has an office in Kathmandu in the Jyatha-Thamel area near the Hotel Blue Diamond. The cost is US$65 per person per night, with the flight to Mahendranagar and booze, etc extra.

Getting There & Away

Silent Safari picks guests up from the airport at Mahendranagar or Dhangardi. Royal Nepal Airlines flies to Mahendranagar every Friday (Rs 1125, 1½ hours) and to Dhangardi on Thursdays and Saturdays (Rs 1365). Silent Safari can also arrange road transport through to New Delhi, which is about a 9 hour drive away.

MAHENDRANAGAR

Mahendranagar is in the far west of Nepal – the westernmost entry point to the country. This looks like a fascinating route into the mountainous north-eastern corner of Uttar Pradesh (much of which belonged to Nepal until 1815) and to famous hills stations like Almora. Lonely Planet has not made it to this isolated corner of the world, so we'd appreciate hearing from someone who has.

Places to Stay

According to the Department of Tourism there is a *Hotel Mahakali*, and that's all we know.

Getting There & Away

The road from Nepalganj is being improved, but work came to a halt in late 1989 because of a border dispute with India and the difficulty of getting materials. Until work on surfacing the road is completed it will be a strictly dry-season proposition, and even then it is a very rough, slow and dusty road. Buses do make the journey from Nepalganj but, once again, that's all we know – I would expect the bus to take at least 12 hours and cost around Rs 70. It is, apparently, a 9 hour drive to New Delhi, although a bus may well take longer.

There is also one flight a week to Kathmandu for Rs 1125 and to Nepalganj for Rs 495.

Pokhara

The Pokhara area is the most popular destination in Nepal after Kathmandu. It's an area of natural beauty rather than historic or cultural interest and is also the starting point for some of the most popular treks in Nepal. The roads linking Pokhara with Kathmandu and the Indian border are a comparatively recent innovation and as a result the Pokhara region is still an area of rapid change.

Kathmandu to Pokhara

It's 206 km from Kathmandu to Pokhara. The road follows the Trisuli River for most of the distance to Mugling, where the Marsyandi River joins the Trisuli River. The road then follows the Marsyandi River as far as Dumre and from Damauli to Pokhara it follows the Seti Gandaki River.

The road is known as the Prithvi Highway and the section from Naubise to Pokhara was built with Chinese assistance in the early '70s. Naubise, 29 km from Kathmandu, is where the Indian-built Tribhuvan Highway, or Tribhuvan Rajpath, turns south and winds its often spectacular way down to Birganj on the Indian border.

The scenery along the road is a constantly changing treat for the eye – there are rock gorges and rivers, rolling hills, tiered rice paddy terraces and glimpses of the Himalaya in the background.

The clear, dry season days from October through the winter months frequently allow tantalising views of the mountains. As you get closer to the peaks, on the stretch of road from Mugling to Pokhara, it's often possible to see the Annapurnas, Himalchuli, Manaslu and other mountains.

Kathmandu to Naubise
The road climbs out of the Kathmandu Valley and drops down into a fertile valley where guavas and sugar cane are grown. The road passes through Gajuri and Benighat before reaching Naubise where the Tribhuvan Highway to India branches off.

Naubise to Mugling
From Naubise, the road follows the small Mahesh Khola to the point where it joins the Trisuli River at Galchi Bazaar, 22 km further on and 51 km from Kathmandu. The Pokhara road continues along the Trisuli Valley through the small town of Gajuritar to Benighat, where the large Bidhi Gandaki River flows into the Trisuli from the north. The road continues to follow the westward flowing Trisuli River to Mugling where it meets the equally large eastward flowing Marsyandi River.

MUGLING
Mugling is the halfway point and a popular lunch stop for buses operating between Kathmandu and Pokhara or Kathmandu and Narayanghat. Mugling, at an elevation of just 208 metres, is the lowest town between Kathmandu and Pokhara. The road south from Mugling to Narayanghat and the Royal Chitwan National Park was also built with Chinese assistance. Atop a 1700 metre hill about 15 km north of Mugling is the sacred Hindu temple of Mankamana.

Mugling is the launching place for shorter rafting trips down the Narayani River to the Chitwan. The Narayani is the river formed by the confluence of the Trisuli and the Marsyandi and is a major tributary of the Ganges.

Places to Stay & Eat
There are many cheap and basic hotels in Mugling with rooms for around Rs 30. The *Laxmi Nauli Hotel* is a decent European-style hotel with doubles for Rs 70. On the Pokhara side of town, just past the bridge, the pleasant *Motel du Mugling* (tel 2-25242, 2-21711) is more expensive at US$23/33 plus 10% tax.

View of Himalayan Ranges from Pokhara

Mugling is a favourite meal stop for Kathmandu to Pokhara buses so there are many small eating places in the centre of town.

Mugling to Gorkha & Dumre

Leaving Mugling, a long suspension bridge crosses the Narayani River just below the junction of the Trisuli and Marsyandi. The road then follows the course of the Marsyandi River as far as Dumre, where the river turns away to the north.

Eight km from Mugling is the turn-off north to Gorkha, the old capital of the Pokhara Valley. It's a further 18 km to Dumre from the Gorkha turn-off.

GORKHA

Gorkha was the home of eight generations of Shah kings before the ninth in the line, King Prithvi Narayan Shah, began his ultimately successful attempt to conquer the Kathmandu Valley.

Gorkha was also the name given to the fearsome soldiers (mostly Thakuri, Magar and Gurung) under his command. The *Gurkhas* were later recruited from throughout the country, not just Gorkha, and many served in the British and Indian armies, where they confirmed their reputation for bravery and toughness in two world wars, and numerous other conflicts, most recently in the Falkland Islands.

Gorkha lies 18 km north of the Prithvi Highway accessible by a good-quality sealed road that intersects with the highway 8 km west of Mugling. The countryside is spectacular and Gorkha itself is well worth visiting.

To commemorate his conquest of the Kathmandu Valley, King Prithvi Narayan Shah built Gorkha Durbar, a fort, palace and temple complex high on a ridge overlooking the town, probably on the site of much older constructions.

The complex is a triumph of Nepalese architecture – perched like an eagle's nest high above the town in a perfect defensive position – with superb views of plunging valleys and the soaring Himalaya. You can easily imagine an ambitious prince looking out over this dramatic landscape and dreaming of ruling all he could see – and more.

To get to Gorkha Durbar walk north from the bus station until you come to several small temples (to Vishnu, Krishna and Ganesh) surrounding a tank. Head to your right until you come to a square, to the right of which is Tallo Durbar, which apparently predates the conquest of Kathmandu. It is probable that this was the administrative centre for the kingdom, and the royal family is quite likely to have lived here. Tallo Durbar is being renovated.

You pay for the impressive view from the Gorkha Durbar with a good steep 1 hour walk from Tallo Durbar. Return to the square from Tallo Durbar and continue to the east. The town itself is inaccessible to cars, so it's quite pleasant to wander the cobbled, shop-lined streets.

On your left after about 100 metres you'll see some well made steps heading directly up to Gorkha Durbar (there is a 2 metre long arrow on the side of a building). If you get to the gully where village women are washing clothes you've gone too far.

The hillside has a network of paths and retaining walls that must have cost a fortune to build. When you get to the big pipal tree, the path forks and though you can take either path the gentlest ascent is to the left. After about 200 metres there is another junction; again head to your left. When you get to the

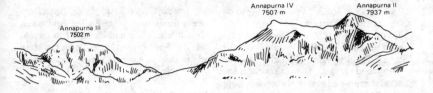

Annapurna III
7502 m

Annapurna IV
7507 m

Annapurna II
7937 m

ridge you are greeted with stupendous views of the Ganesh and Annapurna Himal.

From the ridge, you obviously turn right to the palace, but if you turn left you soon come to Tallokot, a small, old fort now used as a sacrificial site.

Photography is not permitted once you are inside the Gorkha Durbar complex, and this is strictly enforced by soldiers, so you may want to try to capture something on film from here. You are not allowed to wear leather inside the complex, so wear sandshoes or a

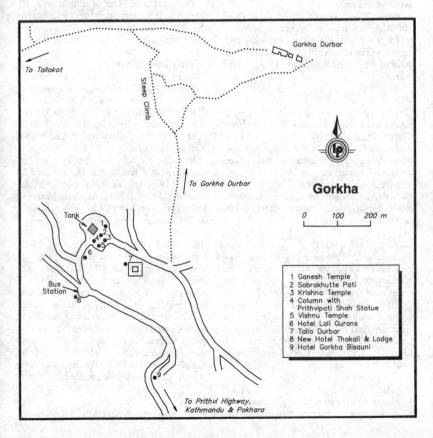

Gorkha Durbar

To Tallokot

Steep Climb

To Gorkha Durbar

Gorkha

0   100   200 m

Tank

1
2
3
4
5

6

7

Bus
Station

8

9

1 Ganesh Temple
2 Sobrakhutte Pati
3 Krishna Temple
4 Column with
  Prithvipati Shah Statue
5 Vishnu Temple
6 Hotel Lali Gurans
7 Talio Durbar
8 New Hotel Thakali & Lodge
9 Hotel Gorkha Bisauni

To Prithvi Highway,
Kathmandu & Pokhara

thick old pair of socks if you are going to do some serious exploration.

If you enter from the west, the first building on your left is a Kali temple (note the 'Star of David' window), which has some superb wood carving. The main palace has latticed windows all around the top floor, but unfortunately you are not allowed to enter, so you can only imagine what lies behind: beautiful breezy rooms, perhaps, from where you could look down on eagles.

Next, go up a few steps. There is a priests' house on the left and two bells on the right. Between the latter are stairs descending to a cave where a reclusive saint named Gorkhanath once lived.

Beyond the priests' house is a four faced shiva lingam. You can descend to servants' quarters and a temple on the next level, then down again to a crude but dramatic repainted carving of Hanuman and six carved stele.

Places to Stay

There are some cheap, basic places to stay near the Gorkha bus station. The *New Hotel Thakali & Lodge* has doubles for Rs 30 and a dorm for Rs 7. The *Hotel Lali Gurans* costs about the same, but is further from the buses, and therefore quieter.

At the entrance to the town the *Hotel Gorkha Bisauni* is quite a decent place with doubles with attached bathrooms for Rs 100 and reasonable food.

Getting There & Away

There are five buses a day to and from Pokhara for Rs 28, and six buses to and from Kathmandu for Rs 35. There are also direct buses from Gorkha to Birganj for Rs 46.

If you are driving, turn right at Majawa Khirene, a village 8 km after Mugling. If you were dropped off at Majawa Khirene you would find local minibuses, which cost Rs 6 to Gorkha. It's an enjoyable drive on a good road.

DUMRE

Dumre, a new town which only came into existence after the construction of the road,

is a typical, dirty roadside town. Apart from being the starting point for the Annapurna Circuit trek it has nothing at all to recommend it. For circuit trekkers it's the last place where there is a decent range of supplies at reasonable prices.

Places to Stay & Eat

Annapurna Circuit trekkers may have to spend the night at Dumre if they arrive late. If so the best option is the basic *Hotel Mustang*, right in the middle of town opposite the roadside temple. A double costs Rs 40 but beware the steep 50 metre climb to the outside toilet, and keep a torch handy!

There are a number of alternatives, although none are very inspiring. You could try the *Hotel Chandrag* or the *Ravi Hotel & Lodge* which have rooms for Rs 30.

Getting There & Away

Dumre is about 5 hours from Kathmandu and 2½ hours from Pokhara. A public bus from Kathmandu (they leave from Bhimsen Tower) will cost Rs 33 and could take longer; from Pokhara it costs Rs 17. The tourist buses that travel between Pokhara and Kathmandu cost around Rs 100.

Many people start their trek by catching shared jeeps to Besi Sahar, but the road is incredibly rough and it's questionable whether the time saved is adequate compensation for the discomfort! It will cost around Rs 2000 to hire a jeep to Besi Sahar.

BANDIPUR

Overlooking Dumre from its hilltop position, Bandipur is a beautiful Newari town just south of the Kathmandu-Pokhara (Prithvi) Highway. Before the construction of the road, Bandipur was a major trading centre, and its bazaars still hint of those days. Stone-paved roads pass between temples and multistoreyed houses, and along the way there are excellent views of the Annapurnas and Machhapuchhare. It takes about 2 hours to walk up to Bandipur from Dumre.

DAMAULI

From Dumre it's just 16 km to the district

headquarters of Damauli which has a bustling bazaar. The main road in the town leads to the panchayat building, while a path to the left drops down to the junction of the Madi Khola and Seti Gandaki River. If you walk upstream about 100 metres you will find a beach which is good for swimming.

Damauli to Pokhara

Soon after Damauli the road crosses the Madi Khola, via a large bridge, and follows the Seti Gandaki River for the remaining 54 km to Pokhara. The next town is Khaireni, where a West German assisted agricultural project is based.

After Khaireni, the road passes the turn-off to Rupa Tal and Begnas Tal, which are the second and third largest lakes of the Pokhara Valley. Sisuwa, only 12 km from Pokhara, is the last place before you arrive at the Pokhara bus station which is immediately north of the airport and some distance south of the busy bazaar area of the town.

Pokhara

Viewed from Pokhara, the Himalaya is indeed a mighty mountain range, looming over the horizon much closer than it does in Kathmandu. Only foothills separate Pokhara from the full height of the Himalaya, and the magnificent 8000 metre peaks of the Annapurna range utterly dominate the view to the north. In the Kathmandu Valley the high temples are all around you, in Pokhara it is the mountains.

The Pokhara Valley has three large lakes. Two of them, Rupa Tal and Begnas Tal, are slightly to the east of town while the third and largest, Phewa Tal, is the focal point of Pokhara's tourist centre.

Pokhara stands at 884 metres above sea level, about 700 metres lower than Kathmandu. The autumn and winter temperatures in Pokhara are generally much more comfortable than in often chilly Kathmandu but the monsoon rains are twice as heavy.

Although the Pokhara Valley is chiefly inhabited by Brahmins and Chhetris, the country around Pokhara is predominantly inhabited by Gurungs. These sturdy tribal people continue to play an important part in the Gurkha troops in India and overseas, while Gurkha earnings have a major impact on the local economy.

Pokhara's development has been recent and rapid. Only with the eradication of malaria in the 1950s did it become safe to live here. The construction of the airstrip in the '50s, the hydroelectric power dam (with Indian aid) in 1968 and the building of the roads to Kathmandu and the Indian border in the early '70s, catapulted Pokhara into the 20th century.

ORIENTATION

Pokhara is a surprisingly sprawling town, stretching in a north-south direction for something like 5 km. Starting from the north there's the busy bazaar area which also contains the oldest part of Pokhara – the town as it was before the airport, electricity and roads totally transformed it. South of the bazaar is the bus station and south again is the airport.

West of the bus station and airport is Phewa Tal, the lakeside tourist centre where Pokhara's great and growing number of hotels and restaurants are predominantly located. It's a long walk from place to place in Pokhara and if you go from south to north it's uphill all the way.

Most of Pokhara's local shops and the post office are around the Mahendrapul (or Mahendra Pool) Bridge in the bazaar area. The bazaar is a long, strung-out affair and the campus of the Pokhara college is also found in that area.

The tourist office and two of the town's larger hotels are beside the airport while a number of government buildings, including the immigration office, are between the airport and Phewa Tal.

At the airport end of the lake in the Pardi area is the hydroelectric power dam. There are many hotels in the Pardi area although the lakeside has even more.

Finally there's the lakeside area itself, also

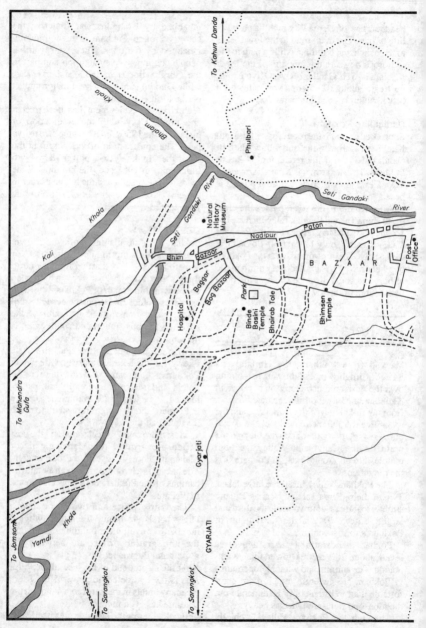

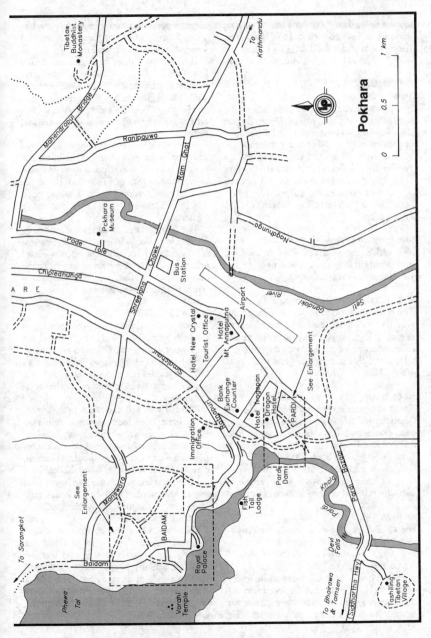

Pokhara

known as Baidam, where the overwhelming majority of foreign visitors to Pokhara stay. Along the lakeside road there's a continuous stretch of small hotels, restaurants and shops.

INFORMATION
Tourist Office
Pokhara's tourist office is right across the road from the airport terminal. Depending on the Nepalese calendar the office is open approximately mid-February to mid-November from 10 am to 5 pm, and mid-November to mid-February from 9 am to 4 pm. On Fridays, however, it closes at 3 pm and it's closed completely on Saturdays and public holidays. The office has some limited information.

Immigration Office
The office, for visa renewals or trekking permit applications, is convenient to the lakeside and dam area hotels.

Post & Telecommunications
The post office, on the other hand, is a long way away in the bazaar area near Mahendrapul Bridge. If you want to make phone calls overseas or to Kathmandu there's a telecommunications building east of the post office along the bridge.

Bookshops
There are numerous bookshops along the lakeside road offering both new and second-hand books and maps. Good shops include the Pokhara Bookshop, the As You Like It Bookshop, the Kiwi Book Shop, the Collectors Bookshop and the Holy Bookshop. The Bongsor Valley in Han Suyin's *The Mountain is Young* is based on the Pokhara Valley.

PHEWA TAL
Phewa Tal, or Phewa Lake, is the tourist centre of Pokhara and the second largest lake in Nepal. Only Rara Lake in the far west of the country is larger.

From Phewa Tal you can set off on walks or bicycle rides, or take to the lake in one of the numerous canoes available for rent, for around Rs 20 an hour, from the lakeside

canoe operators. You can simply paddle yourself lazily around or jump overboard for a swim in the pleasant waters.

Baidam, the village by the lake is mainly inhabited by Chhetris although these days there is a great deal of outside influence as well. Although there have been recent efforts to clean out Pokhara's drug pushers, this area still has a bit of the old hippy scene feel about it.

Along the lakeside are a number of banyan and pipal trees with *chautaras* built around them. These stone platforms were designed to provide a resting place and shade for walkers, and building them was one good way of improving your karma for future existences.

The lakeside area is somewhat arbitrarily divided into east and west. The dividing line is either the Royal Palace, used as a winter retreat by the Nepalese royal family, or the nearby open 'square' which is the tourist centre for lakeside activities.

MOUNTAIN VIEWS
The wonderful Annapurna panorama forms a superb backdrop to Pokhara. You can see the mountains clearly from the lake, while from the other side of Phewa Tal, by the Fish Tail Lodge, you can actually see them twice if you count their reflection in the often placid waters.

Alternatively you can climb to Sarangkot or one of the other lookout points around the valley and enjoy a closer uninterrupted view.

The incredible Annapurna massif includes mountains like Lamjung Himal, Hiunchuli, Varahashikhar, Khangsar Kang, Tarke Kang and Gangapurna; but it's the five Annapurna peaks, Annupurna I to IV plus Annapurna South, and the magnificent Machhapuchhare which are best known.

Machhapuchhare means 'fishtail' and if you walk several days west along the Jomsom Trek route you will find that the mountain actually has a second peak, and from that side it does indeed look like a fishtail. From Pokhara, however, it's simply a superb pyramid; a Himalayan Matterhorn, only much higher.

Machhapuchhare stands out not only because of its prominent shape and lonely position, but because it is closer to Pokhara than the other peaks. In actual fact, at 6993 metres, it is lower than the five Annapurnas. Remarkably it has never been successfully climbed.

A 1957 attempt, led by the legendary Mountain Travel founder J O M Roberts (who, incidentally, settled in Pokhara after his retirement), got to within 50 metres of the top but turned back when the Sherpas refused to conquer such a holy summit.

Climbing is now not allowed on this mountain. Robert Rieffel in *Nepal Namaste* questions how Machhapuchhare acquired its holy image: if it's so significant, why on earth is it called 'fishtail' when so many other unholy Nepalese peaks are named after gods and goddesses?

The other peak with a mountaineering tale to tell is Annapurna I which, at 8091 metres, is the highest in the range. It's also part of a long ridge line and because it's further north appears less conspicuous.

Annapurna I's claim to fame is that when a small French expedition, led by Maurice Herzog, reached the summit in 1950 it was the first time an 8000 metre peak had been climbed.

Herzog's book *Annapurna* is a classic of mountaineering writing, which traces the hardships of organising a climb in what was then a remote, inaccessible and little known area. The harrowing aftermath of the climb, when a severe storm caught the retreating mountaineers, resulted in Herzog losing most of his fingers and toes from frostbite.

To the west of the Annapurnas is Dhaulagiri, at 8167 metres. The Kali Gandaki River, which cuts the deepest gorge in the world, flows between Dhaulagiri and the Annapurnas and actually predates the rise of the Himalaya. For a while, before more precise measuring methods were available, it was thought that Dhaulagiri was the world's highest mountain.

TEMPLES

Pokhara, unlike the towns of the Kathmandu Valley, is not noted for its temples. In fact there are very few of even the most minor note.

In the lake there's a small island with a double roofed temple dedicated to Varaha, who is Vishnu in his boar incarnation.

In the northern part of the bazaar area, is the small, double-roofed Bhimsen Temple with some small and not very notable erotic carvings on the roof struts. The streets of the bazaar area become steadily more attractive and traditional as you move north from the newer area around the bus stand to what was the centre of the original settlement of Pokhara. Bhimsen Temple, very much in the Newari style of the Kathmandu Valley, is right in the main road in the oldest part of town.

Slightly further north, atop a small hill with a park at its base, is Pokhara's best known temple, the Binde Basini Temple. Its pleasant and shady setting is actually more impressive than the white painted shikhara style temple itself. The temple is dedicated to Durga (Parvati) in her Binde Basini Bhagwati manifestation, and interestingly the image of the goddess is a saligram. These black ammonite fossils of marine animals date from the Jurassic period over 100 million years ago and are found in the Himalaya, north of Pokhara. Saligrams, which make nice souvenirs of the Pokhara region, provide scientists with clear proof that this region was once under the sea. They also have a religious significance to the Nepalese, as this temple shows.

MUSEUMS

Pokhara has two museums. The Pokhara Museum is north of the bus station on the main road and has exhibits on local history. It's closed on Tuesdays. At the northern end of town, on the university campus, there's a Natural History Museum, also known as the Annapurna Regional Museum. Its principal attraction is an extensive collection of Nepalese butterflies and moths.

SETI GANDAKI RIVER

The Seti Gandaki River flows right through

Pokhara but in places it runs completely underground, sometimes dropping to 50 metres below ground level. *Seti* means 'white' and the water's milky colour comes from limestone in the soil.

There's a good view of this elusive river from the bridge near the Mission Hospital at the northern end of the bazaar; though an even more dramatic view can be found just over the airport runway. Cross the runway by the terminal, it's a busy thoroughfare and a warning is sounded when an aircraft approaches, and follow the trail to the river where a footbridge crosses the canyon. The bridge is only about 10 metres wide but the river flows past a good 30 metres below.

Another good view of the river can be found at Mahendrapul Bridge in the main bazaar area.

DEVI FALLS
Also known as Fadke, Devin's or David's Falls, this waterfall is about 2 km south-west of the airport on the main Siddhartha Highway and just before the Tashiling Tibetan Village.

The Pardi Khola is the outflow from Phewa Tal and at Devi Falls it suddenly drops down into a hole in the ground and disappears.

One of its alternate names comes from a tale that a tourist named David disappeared down the hole as well, taking his girlfriend with him! There's a Rs 3 admission charge to the falls – if there's anyone there to collect it.

The river emerges from its subterranean hideaway 200 metres away and then joins the Phusre Khola before flowing into the Seti Gandaki River.

TIBETAN SETTLEMENTS
There are a number of Tibetan settlements around Pokhara and you see many Tibetans around the lake selling their crafts and artefacts. The Tashiling Tibetan village, where they weave Tibetan carpets, is only a couple of km south-west of the airport.

There's a larger settlement known as Tashipalkhel at Hyangja, a short drive or an hour or two's walk north-west of Pokhara on the start of the Jomsom Trek route.

TIBETAN BUDDHIST MONASTERY
Cross Mahendrapul Bridge from the bazaar area and follow the road, at first paved, to this hilltop monastery. It's a comparatively recent construction with a large Buddha statue and colourful wall paintings.

WALKS
The Pokhara area offers some fine walking possibilities ranging from day walks like the climb up to Sarangkot to short 3 or 4-day treks. See the Around Pokhara section for full details.

PLACES TO STAY
There are four accommodation areas in Pokhara. One area is around the bus station and bazaar but there's no attraction in staying there. Another area is by the airport, where a couple of Pokhara's larger and more expensive hotels are. The dam area, or Pardi, has numerous bottom end and middle range hotels.

The major accommodation site is by the lakeside, where you'll find the best hotel in Pokhara and an enormous number of budget to middle range lodges and guest houses. If you're staying in one of the really rock bottom budget lakeside places take care of your valuables, as theft is not unknown.

Bazaar Area
There are numerous cheaper hotels around the bus station and near the Mahendrapul Bridge in the bazaar area. It's a much less pleasant place to stay than the lakeside and there's no real reason to do so.

By staying in the bazaar area you may be a little closer to the start of the Jomsom and Annapurna trekking trails, but these days you can travel some distance out of Pokhara by road before you start walking, so being a km or two closer will make no difference at all.

Airport Area
Two of Pokhara's large hotels are directly

opposite the airport terminal, as is the Pokhara's tourist office.

The *Hotel Mt Annapurna* (tel 20027, 20037) is decorated in Tibetan style; the murals in the restaurant showing Tibetan traders and other scenes are particularly impressive. There's also a fine view of the Annapurna skyline from the roof, and a pleasant garden area. Rooms all have attached bathrooms and cost US$18/25 for singles/doubles, plus 12% government tax.

The *Hotel New Crystal* (tel 20035, 20036) has singles/doubles with air-con for US$31/45 plus some rooms without air-con, in an annex, for US$17/22. All rooms have attached bathrooms and there's a 13% government tax. Also opposite the airport is the *Hotel Taragaon* (tel 20255) with rooms from US$15.

Dam Area

South-west of the airport, at the dam which marks the eastern end of Phewa Tal, is the dam area or Pardi. There are numerous lodges and hotels here, many of which are run by Thakalis from the Kali Gandaki Valley.

The *Dragon Hotel* (tel 20391, 20052) has singles/doubles, all with attached bathrooms, for US$25/35, plus 12% government tax. There's a restaurant, bar and roof garden.

Cheaper hotels in the dam area include the popular *Hotel Garden* (tel 20870) and the adjacent *Hotel Peaceful* (tel 20861) with singles at Rs 150 to Rs 200 and doubles at Rs 200 to Rs 300 with attached bath, or Rs 50/75 without; all plus 10% tax. Some rooms have views of the mountains or the lake. Next to these is the popular *Hotel Mt View* (tel 20860) which has rooms with and without attached bathroom, and a small sunny garden.

Near the lake is the *Ashok Guest House*, which is slightly more expensive and has a new building and a pleasant garden. The

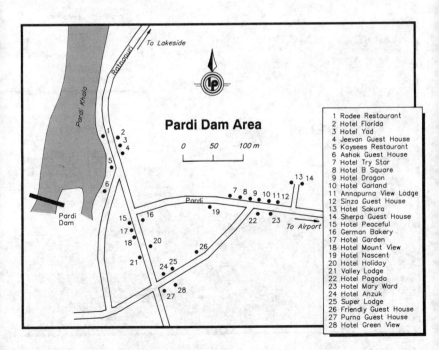

1 Rodee Restaurant
2 Hotel Florida
3 Hotel Yad
4 Jeevan Guest House
5 Kaysees Restaurant
6 Ashok Guest House
7 Hotel Try Star
8 Hotel B Square
9 Hotel Dragon
10 Hotel Garland
11 Annapurna View Lodge
12 Sinza Guest House
13 Hotel Sakura
14 Sherpa Guest House
15 Hotel Peaceful
16 German Bakery
17 Hotel Garden
18 Hotel Mount View
19 Hotel Nascent
20 Hotel Holiday
21 Valley Lodge
22 Hotel Pagoda
23 Hotel Mary Ward
24 Hotel Anzuk
25 Super Lodge
26 Friendly Guest House
27 Purna Guest House
28 Hotel Green View

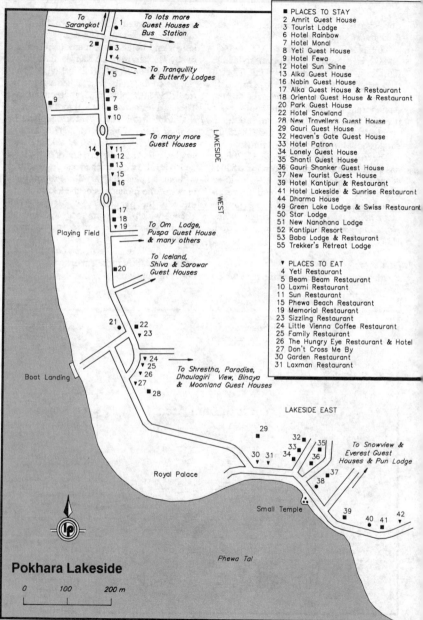

■ PLACES TO STAY
2 Amrit Guest House
3 Tourist Lodge
6 Hotel Rainbow
7 Hotel Monal
8 Yeti Guest House
9 Hotel Fewa
12 Hotel Sun Shine
13 Alka Guest House
16 Nabin Guest House
17 Alka Guest House & Restaurant
18 Oriental Guest House & Restaurant
20 Park Guest House
22 Hotel Snowland
28 New Travellers Guest House
29 Gauri Guest House
32 Heaven's Gate Guest House
33 Hotel Patron
34 Lonely Guest House
35 Shanti Guest House
36 Gauri Shanker Guest House
37 New Tourist Guest House
39 Hotel Kantipur & Restaurant
41 Hotel Lakeside & Sunrise Restaurant
44 Dharma House
49 Green Lake Lodge & Swiss Restaurant
50 Star Lodge
51 New Nanohana Lodge
52 Kantipur Resort
53 Baba Lodge & Restaurant
55 Trekker's Retreat Lodge

▼ PLACES TO EAT
4 Yeti Restaurant
5 Beam Beam Restaurant
10 Laxmi Restaurant
11 Sun Restaurant
15 Phewa Beach Restaurant
19 Memorial Restaurant
23 Sizzling Restaurant
24 Little Vienna Coffee Restaurant
25 Family Restaurant
26 The Hungry Eye Restaurant & Hotel
27 Don't Cross Me By
30 Garden Restaurant
31 Laxman Restaurant

To Sarangkot
To lots more Guest Houses & Bus Station
To Tranquility & Butterfly Lodges
To many more Guest Houses
LAKESIDE WEST
Playing Field
To Om Lodge, Puspa Guest House & many others
To Iceland, Shiva & Sarowar Guest Houses
Boat Landing
To Shrestha, Paradise, Dhaulagiri View, Binaya & Moonland Guest Houses

LAKESIDE EAST
To Snowview & Everest Guest Houses & Pun Lodge
Royal Palace
Small Temple

Pokhara Lakeside
Phewa Tal

0   100   200 m

Hotel Green View is another comfortable alternative with a garden and good restaurant. Singles/doubles are mostly around Rs 150/250.

Hotel Tragopan (tel 20073) is in an intermediate position between the dam and lakeside areas, which means it isn't very convenient for either! There's a nice garden and the rooms are pleasant though rather expensive at US$25/30. Finally the dam area also boasts the wonderfully named *Yak & Yuppie Guest House*.

Lakeside

The road running alongside Phewa Tal is the real visitors' centre for Pokhara. Not only does it have the largest number of hotels, guest houses and lodges it also has the widest selection of shops, bookshops, restaurants, travel agents, bicycle rental places and so on. Although the overwhelming majority of the lakeside places are firmly in the budget price range there are a few exceptions, including Pokhara's most expensive hotel.

DRAGON HOTEL

P.O. BOX NO. 15
'PARDI LAKE SIDE
POKHARA
WEST NEPAL

Many of the budget lodges and guest houses along the lake are very similar in facilities and price. There are so many of them that making specific recommendations is really redundant; looking into a few is probably your best bet. Prices tend to vary with demand, rising and falling with the season and the number of travellers passing through.

Standard double accommodation costs around Rs 40 for a room without attached bathroom, or from Rs 120 to Rs 200 with attached bathroom. There's usually hot water available and many places offer very pleasant garden areas, often right in front of your room. The rooms are usually quite simply furnished, but good Pokhara guest houses are clean and well kept.

Location may be the major deciding factor for most travellers. You can stay close to the centre of things, on or near the main lakeside road, or opt for a quieter location either back from the main road or way down at the western end of the lake. The price for the peace and quiet is a longer walk to get to the restaurants and other activities by the water.

The following suggestions are just a handful of standard places, plus some of the

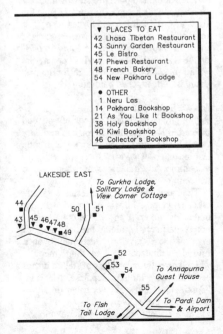

▼ PLACES TO EAT
42 Lhasa Tibetan Restaurant
43 Sunny Garden Restaurant
45 Le Bistro
47 Phewa Restaurant
48 French Bakery
54 New Pokhara Lodge

● OTHER
1 Neru Las
14 Pokhara Bookshop
21 As You Like It Bookshop
38 Holy Bookshop
40 Kiwi Bookshop
46 Collector's Bookshop

LAKESIDE EAST

To Gurkha Lodge,
Solitary Lodge &
View Corner Cottage

44
43
45 46 47 48
49
50
51
52
53
54
55

To Annapurna
Guest House

To Fish
Tail Lodge

To Pardi Dam
& Airport

smaller number of pricier alternatives. They're described in order as you move along the lakeside from east (bus station end) to west. The Royal Palace is the arbitrary dividing line between Lakeside East and Lakeside West.

Lakeside East

Pokhara's most expensive hotel is the wonderfully located *Fish Tail Lodge* (tel 20071). It's actually across the lake on the southern side, at the eastern end where it narrows down towards the dam. Guests are shuttled over to the hotel by a rope drawn raft.

The hotel takes its name from Machhapuchhare, the 'Fishtail Mountain' which dominates the skyline of Pokhara. From the hotel there are superb views of Machhapuchhare and the Annapurnas, which are particularly beautiful at dawn when the mountains are reflected in the still waters of the lake. The rooms cost US$40/55 for single/doubles, with all the usual luxury mod cons. There's a pleasant bar and restaurant although the food is only average.

All the other lakeside places are on the northern side of the lake and one of the first you come to is the popular and budget priced *Baba Lodge & Restaurant*.

Right behind it is one of Pokhara's few middle range places, the very pleasant *Kantipur Resort* (tel 20886) which has excellent rooms with attached bathrooms for US$28/35. A little further along the lakeside is the older *Kantipur Hotel* (also tel 20886) with rooms at US$10/14 with bathroom, or deluxe rooms for US$20/27.

Budget priced places offering rooms in the standard Rs 40 to Rs 200 bracket include the *Green Lake Lodge, Hotel Lakeside, New Solitary Lodge, Gauri Shanker Guest House, Lonely Guest House, New Tourist Guest House, Star Lodge* and many others. The popular *Gurkha Lodge* is back from the lake and is a slightly more expensive place with rooms from around US$10. It's run by an ex-Gurkha soldier and his British wife and has a beautiful garden.

Near the Royal Palace the popular *New Travellers Guest House* has camping and parking areas as well as rooms at the usual rock bottom rates.

Lakeside West

Beyond the Royal Palace there's the *Snowland Hotel* (tel 20384), a long time favourite by the open area that forms the real centre of lakeside activity. Rooms cost from around Rs 100, or more with an attached bathroom.

The *Alka Guest House* is a newer building with rooms starting from Rs 40 but going up towards Rs 200 for the better ones. Behind it is the clean and well kept *Puspa Guest House* with singles/doubles at Rs 100/125 with a bathroom.

Further along, the superbly situated *Hotel Fewa* is right on the edge of the lake and has rooms from around Rs 75 to Rs 200; the more expensive rooms have attached bathrooms. The *Yeti Guest House* has rooms at Rs 100 or there's the *Hotel Monal* which is 'under Nepali-German management' and has rooms from Rs 150 to Rs 325.

There are more places to stay on the lakeside beyond the junction or from the junction back towards the bazaar. Places along this road include the *Cordial Guest House* and the *Hotel Mandir*. The *Hong Kong Hotel* is on the road to the bazaar and has rooms from Rs 50 to Rs 100 or Rs 150/225 for singles/doubles with attached bathroom.

PLACES TO EAT

Pokhara may not match the variety of food offered in Kathmandu but you can certainly eat well although, as usual in Nepal, a little caution is always wise. Upset stomachs are as common in Pokhara as anywhere else in the country.

The bazaar area has local restaurants, and other eating possibilities are found in the big hotels or amongst the numerous cheaper hotels particularly along the lakeside. At most of these travellers' restaurants you'll find the standard 'try anything' menu – which currently means lots of Italian dishes backed up by Indian, Nepalese, Mexican, 'Continental' and whatever other possibilities present themselves.

There are not so many restaurants in the

dam area although *Kaysees Restaurant*, right by the lake, is particularly popular (it's no relation to the KC's in Kathmandu). In the same area, the *Rodee Restaurant* does Chinese dishes or you can get a simple dhal bhat tarkari in the *Hotel Garden* or *Hotel Mt View*.

Most Pokhara dining is done along the lakeside starting with the *Baba Restaurant* with its fine terrace overlooking the lake. There are good breakfasts there.

Continuing on you come to more places, all with the standard Nepalese traveller's menu and with open eating areas overlooking the lake.

The *Phewa Restaurant* is pretty good although the sign proclaiming that the food is 'prepared under the supervision of a French chef' may raise some expectations a little too high! *Le Bistro* has everything from Mexican, Italian, Chinese and Indian to Nepalese and they seem to do a pretty good job of all of it. Their apple pies are not bad either!

The *Sun Rise Restaurant* is another popular lakeside place and claims to have the best steaks in town. Their Rs 30 chicken biriyani, with a bit of everything mixed in, is certainly good value. The *Hotel Kantipur*'s restaurant has a varied menu and does good curries. Its pizzas are said to be good too.

Further down beyond the palace the adjacent *Don't Cross Me By* and *Hungry Eye* are Pokhara gathering places and good for an afternoon snack or a meal. Don't Cross Me By has a great selection of pies and cakes and even makes a pretty fair cappuccino. *Hotel Snowland* has a rooftop restaurant and sometimes chronically slow service. There are more places, like the *Sizzling Restaurant*, around this central lakeside area and many more further on down the road.

At the top end of the restaurant spectrum the *Fish Tail Lodge*'s bar and restaurant could be a fine place for a more expensive night out but the food is only average and the service, once you depart from the fixed meals, is appallingly slow. The fixed breakfast costs Rs 165, dinner is Rs 265, plus 12% in each case. Ordering à la carte is cheaper

but the lakeside restaurants can turn out good food in half the time for half the cost.

ENTERTAINMENT

The *Fish Tail Lodge* puts on a nightly cultural programme featuring Nepalese dancing by the Danfe Dance Club. It runs from 6 to 7 pm in winter, 6.30 to 7.30 pm in summer and the admission charge is Rs 50.

Similar programmes are sometimes put on at the *Hotel Dragon* or the *Hotel New Crystal*. Otherwise Pokhara is not the place to go if you're in search of evening entertainment.

THINGS TO BUY

Pokhara's large Tibetan population sells many crafts and artefacts. Carpet weaving is a major local industry for these people.

Saligrams, the fossilised sea creatures found north up the Kali Gandaki Valley, are a popular souvenir.

GETTING THERE & AWAY
Air

There are daily Royal Nepal Airlines services between Kathmandu and Pokhara; the flight takes less than an hour and costs US$55. There are great Himalayan views if you sit on the right-hand side of the plane from Kathmandu to Pokhara, and on the left side from Pokhara to Kathmandu.

Bus – To/From Kathmandu

The bus trip between Kathmandu and Pokhara takes 7 or 8 hours and departures are early in the morning. The first stretch of road out of Kathmandu is in appalling condition and for a couple of hours the trip is a tedious and uncomfortable lurch from pothole to pothole. The road gradually improves and the Mugling to Pokhara section is fine.

Public buses depart from the foot of the Bhimsen Tower near the post office or from the Central Bus Station in Kathmandu and cost Rs 45. From Pokhara they depart from the bus stand north of the airport. Uncomfortable is probably the kindest way to describe these public buses.

The more expensive tourist buses and minibuses cost Rs 110 to Rs 120. Tickets are sold from offices around Freak St and Thamel in Kathmandu or lakeside in Pokhara. Apart from being more comfortable these buses make fewer stops to pick up passengers along the way; usually the rest and refreshment stop at Mugling is the only halt. They also take you right to the lake at Pokhara rather than terminating at the bus station. Whichever bus you take it's wise to book at least a day ahead.

Bus – To/From Chitwan
Buses between Pokhara and Tadi Bazaar cost Rs 35. See the Royal Chitwan National Park section of the Terai chapter for more details.

Bus – To/From Indian Border
Buses to Bhairawa depart from the main Pokhara bus stand and cost Rs 55.

The road to India is called the Siddhartha Highway because it ends close to Lumbini where the Buddha, Siddhartha Gautama, was born. See the Getting There & Away chapter for more details.

GETTING AROUND
It's a long way between the bus station or the bazaar and the lakeside; a taxi will probably cost around Rs 40. Small taxis and minibuses shuttle between the lakeside, airport and bazaar with per person fares of about Rs 2 to Rs 5 depending on how far you are going.

There are lots of bicycle rental places along the lakeside, by the dam or by the airport. Bikes typically cost Rs 15 to Rs 20 per day. You can also rent children's bicycles. Pokhara looks deceptively flat but actually it slopes steadily uphill as you move north. If you ride a bicycle from the lake to the Binde Basini Temple at the northern end of the bazaar area you'll find it's a wonderfully long freewheel on the way back.

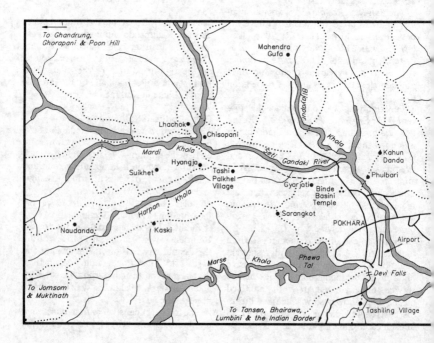

Around Pokhara

Pokhara is the starting or finishing point for some of Nepal's most popular treks like the Annapurna Circuit, the Jomsom Trek and the Annapurna Sanctuary Trek.

For those with limited time, less enthusiasm for walking or with small children in tow, the Pokhara area also has some fine short treks ranging from half day and day walks to longer treks lasting anything from 2 or 3 days to a week.

DAY WALKS
The following walks can all be made in a day or less.

Sarangkot
This very pleasant walk up to Sarangkot, at an elevation of 1592 metres, is probably the most popular short excursion from Pokhara.

It can be a good, pre-breakfast stroll to admire the mountain views, a leg stretcher before you start out on a longer trek or a place you pass through on the first or last hours of one of the longer treks from Pokhara.

There are a number of places to stay or eat at Sarangkot – like the *Didi Lodge, Restaurant Sarangkot, Trekking Lodge* or *New Tourist Lodge* – so you can climb up to Sarangkot in the evening, stay overnight there and catch the view at dawn, or simply walk up for breakfast.

There are a number of routes to Sarangkot but the easiest way is to walk up from the Binde Basini Temple in Pokhara Bazaar and then head straight down from the top to the lake.

As you approach the temple from the bazaar, ignore the sign to Sarangkot just south of the temple and continue a little further to look at the temple before you start the walk.

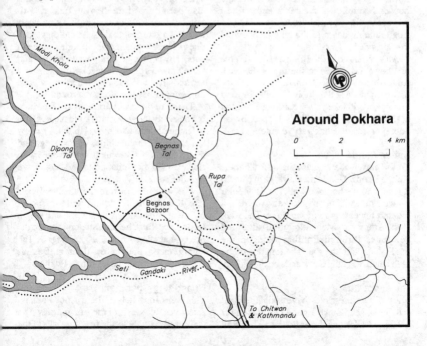

From the temple head directly east and follow the vehicle track which runs most of the way up. You can short cut many of the sharp corners and from where the vehicle track ends there is virtually a stairway to the top. On the way up you pass several places where women work at handlooms. It takes about 1½ to 2 hours to walk to Sarangkot from Binde Basini Temple, versus 3 or 4 hours from the lakeside *if* you don't get seriously lost!

Sarangkot once had a fort or *kot* and its remains can be seen on the very top of the ridge above Sarangkot. There is a lookout point actually inside the old fort walls and the view of the Annapurnas to the north is superb.

The view back down over Phewa Tal is equally fine and from the top it only takes about 2 hours to walk down to the lake. It's easy to get lost on the way up from the lake but going down is straightforward. The walk down is very pleasant; you pass fields and houses then follow a stream through a forest and across flat rice paddies to the snout of a ridge running down to the lake just beyond the lakeside lodge area.

An alternative to the Binde Basini Temple or Phewa Tal routes to the top is the walk from Bhairab Tole in Pokhara via the village of Gyarjati. Another hour's walk beyond Sarangkot will take you to Kaski or Kaskikot at 1788 metres. The hill is topped by an unprepossessing Bhagwati Temple.

Kahun Danda

To the east of the bazaar area of Pokhara is Kahun Danda. *Danda* means ridge in Nepali. It takes about 3 hours to walk to this popular viewpoint at 1560 metres and there's a lookout tower on top of the ridge. The walk starts from the Mahendrapul Bridge and continues through Phulbari and up the gradual slope to the top. The remains of the 18th century Kanhu Kot stands on the hilltop.

Mahendra Gufa

These limestone caves have stalactites and stalagmites and make a good destination for a 2 hour walk north from Pokhara. The trail

to the caves crosses the bridge just north of Bagar at the end of the bazaar and heads toward the village of Batulechaur. Batulechaur was once an important centre for growing citrus fruit until an epidemic killed all the citrus trees in the Pokhara Valley.

Rupa & Begnas Tals

These two lakes are the second and third largest in the valley, but few travellers visit them even though they're only 15 km east of the town. Buses run regularly from Pokhara to Begnas Bazaar, the small bazaar centre at very end of the ridge which divides the two lakes. From there it's a pleasant stroll along the ridge to the other end of either lake.

SHORT TREKS

The following short treks all last less than a week.

Annapurna Skyline Trek

The 3 or 4 day Annapurna Skyline Trek has also been dubbed the 'Royal Trek' as Britain's Prince Charles walked it a few years ago. It's a fine trek to do with children, as it doesn't reach any great altitudes, doesn't entail any particularly long walking days and there's always plenty to see. It's not a heavily trekked area, however, so there is no village inn accommodation along the route.

There are several variations on the route but basically the walk starts from the Pokhara to Kathmandu road (Prithvi Highway), a few km east of Pokhara, climbs up to a ridge and then for most of the walk follows ridges with fine views of the Annapurnas and back down into the Pokhara Valley.

The walk passes through small villages like Kalikathan, Shaklung and Chisopani before it drops down to the stream which feeds Rupa Tal. The final stretch is along the ridge separating Rupa Tal and Begnas Tal, emerging on the valley floor at Begnas Bazaar from where buses run to Pokhara.

Ghandrung-Ghorapani Trek

This week-long trek to the west of Pokhara also gives fine views of the Annapurnas. The walk essentially links the first few days of the

Annapurna Sanctuary Trek as far as Ghandrung with the first few days of the Jomsom Trek as far as Ghorapani, then crosses between those two villages.

Near Ghorapani is Poon Hill, one of the finest lookout points in the region.

Ghachok Trek

An interesting 2 day trek goes north from Pokhara to the interesting Gurung villages around Ghachok. The walk starts from Hyangja, with its Tibetan settlement, and crosses the Mardi Khola to Lhachok then Ghachok before turning south and returning to Pokhara through Batulechaur.

Naudanda Trek

This 2 day walk, a shorter variation of the Ghandrung-Ghorapani Trek, takes you from Hyangja to Suikhet then to Naudanda and back to Pokhara through Kaski and Sarangkot. Naudanda has a variety of guest houses and shops.

The Himalaya & Mountaineering

The word *Himalaya* is Sanskrit for 'Abode of Snows' and Nepal's stretch of the Himalaya includes eight peaks over 8000 metres, including the highest of them all, mighty Mt Everest. Known to the Tibetans as Chomolongma and to the Nepalese as Sagarmatha the world's highest place was the overpowering attraction which drew in Nepal's first modern tourists – the mountaineers. During the 1950s and 1960s most of the important Nepalese peaks were conquered, but just because it is no longer possible to be the first to set foot on top has certainly not diminished the attraction of Himalayan mountaineering. Climbing these giants today is often an adventurous sporting activity, where 30 years ago it required huge and well-sponsored expeditions.

Nepal's magnificent mountains can be enjoyed in three distinctly different fashions. The easiest way is to simply look at them. This can be done by flying past them – either on regular flights or the daily tourist season mountain flights. Or you can admire them from the various popular mountain viewpoints such as Nagarkot or Dhulikhel near Kathmandu or Sarangkot above Pokhara. Getting to these viewpoints is covered in the appropriate chapters. If simply looking at the mountains isn't enough you can get right in amongst them by trekking. Trekking is not mountain climbing: apart from high passes on certain treks and the approach to the Everest Base Camp you are unlikely to go above 3500 metres. Trekking, however, does provide breathtaking views. Full details on trekking are covered in the Trekking chapter.

Finally there is real mountain climbing and while getting to the top of an 8000 metre peak is strictly for the professionals there are plenty of 'trekking peaks' which small scale amateur expeditions can readily attempt. This is not to say that mountaineering in Nepal can be easy, climbing mountains this high always involves an element of risk, but getting to the top of a worthwhile Himalayan peak doesn't necessarily require millionaire status or big commercial backers.

The Highest Mountains

There are 14 peaks over 8000 metres and of the 10 highest no less than eight are in Nepal, although some of the peaks actually straddle borders – Everest is in Nepal and China for example, Kanchenjunga is in Nepal and India. The heights of the 14 highest peaks, followed by the highest peaks in other regions are in the diagram opposite at the top.

The Mountain Flight

Every morning during the clear dry-season months Royal Nepal Airlines' mountain flight offers panoramic dawn views of the Himalaya. The hour-long Boeing 727 flight from Kathmandu costs US$85 and flies along the Himalaya in both directions. If the weather's clear and you have a good window it can provide some stunning views.

MOUNTAINEERING
History

Origins Mountaineering became a fashionable pursuit in Europe during the second half of the 1800s and, mountaineers having knocked off the great Alpine peaks, the much

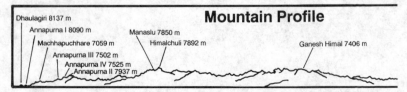

Mountain Profile

Dhaulagiri 8137 m
Annapurna I 8090 m
Machhapuchhare 7059 m
Annapurna III 7502 m
Annapurna IV 7525 m
Annapurna II 7937 m
Manaslu 7850 m
Himalchuli 7892 m
Ganesh Himal 7406 m

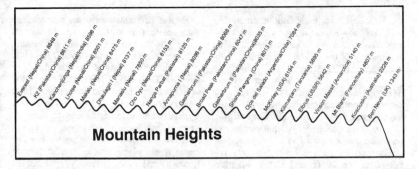

Mountain Heights

greater heights of the Himalaya were an obvious new challenge. An English gentleman named W W Graham made a mountaineering visit to Nepal in 1883 and managed to reach the top of a 6000 metre peak. Tom Longstaff, another Englishman, climbed 7215 metre Trisuli in 1907 and for the next 20 years this remained the highest summit reached anywhere in the world. An Italian attempt on K2 in Pakistan 2 years later was the first of the huge Himalayan expeditions with hundreds of porters.

First Attempts on Mt Everest During the 1920s and 1930s reaching the top of Mt Everest came to be seen as the major goal, but apart from the difficulties inherent in reaching such heights there were also political constraints. Nepal continued to be a totally secluded country and attempts on Everest were all made from the Tibetan side of the range.

British assaults in 1921, 1922 and 1924 fell just 300 metres short of the top, reaching 8572 metres in 1924 and without the use of oxygen. The 1922 expedition had used oxygen to reach 8326 metres and these huge expeditions set a pattern which was to continue until recent years. Apart from numerous climbers and support staff the 1924 expedition utilised no less than 350 porters.

One of the enduring mysteries of mountaineering history has its origins in 1925 when the British climbers Mallory and Irvine disappeared within sight of the top. Did they reach it? We will never know. However, Mallory did leave behind that famous explanation for why mountaineers do what they do – he said he was climbing Everest 'because it's there'. Further expeditions followed through the remaining years of the '20s and '30s but no real progress was made, although the 8000 metre level was breached on a number of occasions. Maurice Wilson added his name to the Everest legends, and the Everest death roll, when he died during a bizarre solo attempt on the mountain in 1934.

After WW II The West's new-found affluence after its recovery from WW II, together with more modern equipment, vastly improved oxygen apparatus, new mountaineering skills and the reopening of Nepal led to a golden age of Himalayan mountaineering. There hadn't been any Himalayan mountaineering in the 1940s, and through

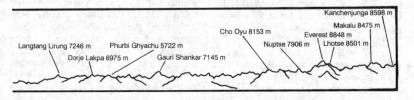

the '30s only two significant summits had been reached – Kamet at 7761 metres in 1931 and Nanda Devi at 7822 metres in 1936. Interestingly the Kamet summit group included H W Tilman and the Nanda Devi group included Eric Shipton, whose descriptions of their trekking and mountaineering experiences helped to spark the current interest in trekking. Shipton was said to have planned his lightweight expeditions on the back of an envelope.

The pre-war failures were abruptly reversed in the 1950s and it was Maurice Herzog's valiant French expedition on Annapurna in 1950 which turned the tide. His team's horrific storm-plagued struggle down the mountain turned an extremely difficult climb into an epic of human endurance – but for the first time mountaineers had reached the top of an 8000 metre peak. After descending the mountain they then had a month-long struggle through the monsoon with the expedition doctor having to perform amputations of frostbitten fingers and toes as they went. Herzog's book *Annapurna* (Jonathan Cape, London, 1952) remains a classic of mountaineering literature. It's indicative of how things have changed in Nepal that Herzog had trouble even finding his way to the mountain! Today thousands of trekkers pass by the Annapurnas every year and, where Herzog once had to search desperately for supplies for his hungry climbers, there are now comfortable lodges offering bed and breakfast to trekking parties.

Conquest of Everest Everest was also getting its share of attention, and in 1951 a climber who would soon become very famous took part in an exploratory expedition to the mountain – he was New Zealand climber Edmund Hillary. Another name, soon to be equally famous, appeared on the list of climbers on the Swiss Everest expedition of 1952 when Sherpa climber Norgay Tensing reached 7500 metres. The conquest of Everest finally took place in 1953 when the British team led by John Hunt put those two climbers, Tensing and Hillary, on top of the world's highest peak.

Repeat performances came much easier than the first time and the second success came in 1956 when a Swiss party reached the summit. In 1960 it was the People's Republic of China who managed the feat, this time from the Tibetan side. A huge US expedition with the climbers backed up by nearly 1000 porters got to the top in 1963 and in 1965 it was the turn of an Indian expedition. Another huge party, this time from Japan, was on top in 1970 and one utterly fearless climber ensured his place in the Everest history books by making an extremely rapid descent on skis! Further attempts included the massive Italian expedition which reached the summit in 1973 and the victorious Japanese women's party which celebrated International Women's Year by putting a woman climber on top.

The success of the 1953 British expedition to Everest had started a trend for larger and larger expeditions. Proponents of this form of 'siege' mountaineering believed that this was the only way to conquer the great Himalayan peaks. A series of camps would be established higher and higher up the mountain with constant 'carries' of supplies eventually resulting in climbers reaching the top. This theory of Himalayan climbing reached its ultimate expression with the '73 Italian Everest expedition when 64 climbers were backed up by 100 sherpas and nearly 2000 porters! Helicopters ferried supplies and, hardly surprisingly, this massive effort put nine people on the summit in two parties.

The few climbers who did reach the summit from these expeditions required a huge pyramid of supporters below them. The effect on the country could be devastating as forests fell to provide firewood for the expeditions and vast amounts of mountaineering equipment and garbage were left behind. The Everest Base Camp has been aptly titled the 'world's highest garbage dump'. Lightweight expeditions had been successful, but Helmut Bhul's solo climb to the summit of Nanga Parbat in Pakistan and his lightweight expedition to the top of Broad Peak were looked upon more as aberrations requiring superhuman effort than as pointers towards a different way of doing things.

New-Style Mountaineering Inevitably a reaction set in and, while the checklist of important summits was methodically knocked over by huge and expensive expeditions, young climbers were perfecting a wholly different style of climbing on the peaks of Europe and North America. Getting to the top was no longer the sole aim, you had to reach the top with style.

The 'easy' ridge routes to the top were ignored while climbers scaled the most difficult faces using a combination of athletic skills and high technology equipment. British mountaineer Chris Bonnington was the chief protagonist for this style of climbing and his brilliant conquest of the southern face of Annapurna in 1970, followed by an expertly organised race up the hitherto unthinkable south-western face of Everest in 1975 were supreme examples of this trend.

Lightweight Expeditions Attempting the difficult faces and routes was one trend but lightweight expeditions were another. In 1978 the Austrian expedition to Everest put Reinhold Messner and Peter Habler on top without the use of oxygen. Once this 'impossible' feat had been achieved other climbers also found they could reach the top without oxygen and, freed from the necessity of carting heavy oxygen cylinders up the mountains, much smaller parties could attempt the big mountains. Only 2 years later Reinhold Messner made a solo ascent of Everest, climbing the North Face on the Tibetan side in the fastest ascent ever made.

In early 1990 Tim McCartney-Snape went several steps further. He walked and climbed from sea level at the Bay of Bengal, to the top of Mt Everest, alone and without oxygen.

Mountaineering Today Himalayan mountaineering today not only provides a great deal of free publicity for tourism to Nepal, it's also a very useful source of income for the government. If you want to attempt a Himalayan peak there's a fee to be paid to the government before you get your climbing permit, and the higher and more famous the mountain the higher the fee that must be paid. Everest is currently about US$6000 and is usually 'booked out' for years ahead. Annually 600 to 900 climbers come to Nepal to try their luck, but there are still many sizable peaks which have not been successfully climbed, and some which haven't even been attempted.

Today mountaineering is a sport pure and simple – there's no noise made about its scientific value. In fact the successes and failures of the various expeditions are regularly reported on the sports pages of the *Rising Nepal*. Of course it's also a decidedly dangerous sport: over 200 climbers have reached the top of Everest (some of them three, four and even five times), but nearly 100 climbers have died in the attempt. Some other mountains in Nepal have an even worse record: almost as many climbers have lost their lives climbing Annapurna as have managed to reach the top.

Trekking Peaks
There are many smaller mountains in Nepal which keen trekkers can climb. Most Everest Base Camp trekkers make the ascent of Kala Pattar for the view of Everest and at 5545 metres this would be a substantial peak anywhere else in the world. In his book *Many people come, looking, looking* (The Mountaineers, Seattle, 1980) Galen Rowell tells of a little jaunt up a 6500 metre peak as a pre-lunch sidetrip while crossing the Thorong La pass on the Annapurna Circuit trek.

Nepal also has 18 'trekking peaks' which are open to mini-expeditions. To climb a trekking peak all you need is US$300 for one of the 12 Group A peaks or US$150 for the six Group B peaks. The fee for a big 'expedition' peak will be more than 10 times as much. The peaks range from 5587 metres to 6584 metres so these are not little mountains. Nor are they day trips: a series of camps will have to be established and the climb can take from a few days to a few weeks. The permit is issued by the Nepal Mountaineering Association and allows up to 10 climbers.

Climbing gear can be bought or rented in Kathmandu, although socks, shoes, clothing and freeze dried food are likely to be harder to find while tents, stoves, sleeping bags and down gear should pose less problems. Bill O'Connor's book *The Trekking Peaks of Nepal* (Crowood Press, 1989) gives a detailed description of climbing each of the peaks plus the trek to the mountain. Equipment, applications, procedures, weather, health and other matters are also comprehensively covered.

Trekking

For the people in the hills of Nepal walking has always been the main method of getting from A to B. There were no roads into the hill country from the Terai and India until the Tribhuvan Highway to Kathmandu was constructed in the 1950s. Pokhara was not connected to the outside world by road until the 1970s. Even today the vast majority of villages can only be reached on foot, although every year the roads penetrate further into the hills and mountains.

The Nepalese people, making their way from village to village on the well-worn trails, were only joined by Western visitors when Himalayan mountaineering came into vogue. It was the accounts of those pioneering mountaineers, who had to make their way to the base of the great peaks on foot, which inspired the first trekkers. The word 'trekking' first started to be applied to Nepalese hiking trips in the 1960s and the enormous popularity of trekking today has developed since that time.

Trekking in Nepal means a walking trip following trails, many of which have been used for communication and trade for many years. Trekking is not mountaineering. Some of the popular trekking trails are used by mountaineering expeditions on their approach marches, but most are used by Nepalese for everyday travel and trade. A trekking trip can be any length you choose – there are popular short treks around the Kathmandu and Pokhara valleys which only take a day to complete, there are short treks of 2 or 3 days or there are longer treks lasting from a week to a month. You could even string a series of popular treks together and walk for months on end.

Two major attractions account for trekking's enormous popularity and for the many trekkers who find they are soon planning a repeat visit – the scenery and the people.

The Scenery

There is no question that Nepal offers some of the most spectacular and beautiful scenery in the world. Of course it's the mountains that are best known, and the exploits of mountain photographers have made Machhapuchhare, Everest, Ama Dablam, and other mountains instantly recognisable to keen walkers all over the world. Nepal has a near monopoly on the world's highest peaks – eight of the 10 highest are found in Nepal and a number of the popular trekking routes offer you wonderful views or even visits to the base camps used by mountaineering expeditions. Mountain flights may give you superb views, but there is absolutely nothing like waking up on a crystal-clear Himalayan day and seeing an 8000 metre peak towering over you, seemingly just an arm's length away.

The mountains may be the most obvious scenic attraction, but trekkers soon find there are plenty of other treats for the eye. The hill country is often breathtakingly beautiful with pretty little villages, attractive houses, neat fields and interesting temples. As you climb higher the semitropical lowlands give way to meadows, stretches of forest, swift-flowing rivers and deep canyons before you reach the cold and often barren regions at the foot of the great peaks. The views change with the seasons, whether it is the cycle of planting and harvesting or the brilliant displays of wild flowers late in the dry season.

The People

Nepal is a country of contrasts and this extends to the people as well as the landscape. Trekking in Nepal is not like hiking through the often uninhabited countryside of a North American, Australian or European national park. People are constantly passing by on the trails, and along many routes there are regularly spaced villages to pause in. The villages and their people can be as interesting as the scenery, as you meet people from many of Nepal's wide diversity of ethnic groups. The outgoing nature, general friendliness and good humour of the Nepalese is often commented on by trekkers. Colourful festivals can make trekking at certain times of year even more enjoyable.

Of course your trekking companions can be another important part of the trekking experience. A long trek can be a great opportunity to enjoy yourself with good friends. Despite stories you may have heard about the Himalaya being overrun with hordes of trekkers the reality is very different. Certainly there may be many trekkers on the most popular routes, particularly the Pokhara to Jomsom trek, but compared to the crowds visiting national parks in the West the numbers are often minuscule. The trails of Nepal are a long way from being overcrowded.

ALL ABOUT TREKKING

Although Nepal offers plenty of opportunity for short treks lasting a day or less, most treks last considerably longer. From Pokhara or around the Kathmandu Valley you can make a variety of 2, 3 or 4-day walks, but Nepal's most popular treks take at least a week. For the very popular Everest Base Camp Trek and Annapurna Circuit Trek you have to allow 3 weeks. Don't take on one of these classic long treks too lightly: the end of the first week is not the ideal time to discover you're not keen on walking.

The Trekking Seasons

Put very simply the best time to trek is from October to May (the dry season) and the worst time is from June to September (the monsoon). This generalisation does not allow for the peculiarities of individual treks, however. Some people even claim that the undeniable difficulties of trekking during the monsoon are outweighed by the lack of crowds.

The first 2 months of the dry season, October and November, are probably the ideal period for trekking in Nepal. The air, freshly washed by the monsoon rains, is crystal clear, the mountain scenery is superb and the weather is still comfortably warm. At

Onlookers watching the finish of the biannual Everest Marathon

low altitudes in October it can actually be quite balmy, and trekkers may find they complete a whole trek in T-shirt weather.

December, January and February are still good months for trekking, but the cold can be bitter at high altitudes. Getting up to the Everest Base Camp can be a real endurance test and the Thorung La pass on the Annapurna Circuit trek is sometimes blocked by snow.

March and April offer better weather but at the price of hazy visibility. By this time of year the weather has been dry for a long time and dust is starting to hang in the air. The poorer quality of the Himalayan views is compensated for by the superb wild flowers, particularly Nepal's wonderful rhododendrons.

By May it is getting very hot, dusty and humid, and the monsoon is definitely just round the corner. From June to September the trails can be dangerously slippery due to the monsoon rains, and raging rivers often wash away bridges and stretches of trail. Nepal's famous leeches (jukha) are an unpleasant feature of the wet season, but with care trekking can still be possible in the wet season and there are certainly few other trekkers on the trail.

The Trails

Most trekkers want to get away from roads as quickly as possible, and although roads reach further into the hill country every year, it is still possible to leave them quickly behind. Nepalese trails are often steep and taxing. Trekkers often feel that the old adage that the shortest path between two points is a straight line has been firmly drummed into the Nepalese, irrespective of any mountains which may get in the way! In compensation the trails are often very well maintained. Busy trails up steep slopes are often flagged with stones every step of the way.

Walking the trails of Nepal often entails a great deal of altitude gain and loss, and it is as well to remember that even the base of the great mountains of the Himalaya can be very high. Most treks which go through populated areas stick to between 1000 metres and 3000 metres, although the Everest Base Camp

Trek and the Annapurna Circuit Trek both reach over 5000 metres. On high treks like these ones it is wise to ensure adequate acclimatisation, and the old maxim of 'walking high, sleeping low' is good advice: your night halt should be at a lower level than the highest point reached in the day.

The Walking Day

A typical day's walk lasts from 5 to 7 hours and involves a number of ascents and descents. It's rare to spend much time at the same level. On an organised camping trek the day is run to a remarkably tight schedule. A typical pattern would be: up at 6 am, start walking at 7 am, stop for lunch at 10 am, start after lunch at noon, stop walking at 3 pm. The Nepalese rise early, eat very little for breakfast, eat a large lunch in the late morning and a second meal before dark, then retire early – you are best off following a similar schedule. Although a little rudimentary knowledge of Nepali will help to make your trek easier and more interesting, finding your way is rarely difficult on the major trekking routes and English is becoming more widely spoken.

Accommodation & Food

Organised treks camp each night and all you have to do is crawl into your tent. Even erecting the tent is handled by the trekking group who put it up for you at the site selected by your *sirdar* or group leader.

Independent trekkers usually stay in the small lodges, guest houses or village inns which have appeared along almost all the main trails. At first this sort of accommodation was simply a matter of local teahouses letting you unroll your sleeping bag on the floor. Today along some of the most popular trails the lodges are quite luxurious and offer private rooms, extensive menus and even showers. It's even possible to make quite long treks without bringing a sleeping bag with you.

On a typical organised trek your only concern with food is sitting down to eat it. The porters carry all the food along with them, and there will be a cook with well-drilled assistants who can turn out meals of often stunning complexity. Baking a cake on a campfire is just one of the tricks trekking party cooks like to perform to display their virtuosity.

Independent trekkers will usually find places to eat along the most popular trails, although it's often wise to carry some emergency food supplies like cheese, dried fruit or chocolate bars. Food on the trail may vary from dhal and rice at simple teahouses to surprisingly good meals on particularly popular trails.

The standards of cuisine on the Pokhara to Jomsom trek are so high that it has been dubbed 'The Apple Pie Trail' as that dish features on so many village inn menus. It's surprising how many places even have cold beer available as well; before you complain about the price contemplate the fact that somebody had to carry that bottle of beer all the way there and will probably have to carry the empty bottle back again!

If you're going right off the beaten track and exploring areas which have only recently been opened, like Makalu and Kanchenjunga in the east or Jumla and Dolpo in the west, you must be very self-sufficient. In these relatively untouched areas there is probably very little surplus food for sale and the practice of catering to Western trekkers will not yet have developed.

Hill ambulance service

Health

See the Health section in the Facts for the Visitor chapter for more information on trekking health. Acute mountain sickness or altitude sickness is the major concern on high altitude treks, but for the majority of trekkers health problems are likely to be minor ones, such as care in avoiding stomach upsets.

Basic rules for healthy trekking include taking care that water is always boiled (usually at least for 10 minutes) or adequately treated. Diarrhoea is one of the comparatively minor problems which can ruin a trek so take care in what you eat and make sure your medical kit has some sort of antidiarrhoeal medication. The food on an organised trekking expedition is unlikely to cause any problems, but village inn trekkers

may be slightly more at risk. At high altitudes the burning power of the sun is much stronger, so have good sunglasses and a high protection factor sunscreen for your skin. Blisters can take the fun out of trekking so make sure your shoes and socks are comfortable and come prepared with band-aids and moleskins just in case they aren't.

Make sure you are in good health before departing as there is very little medical attention along the trails and rescue helicopters are not only very expensive but usually must be paid for in advance! See the individual treks for more information on possible medical assistance. In general Himalayan hospitals can offer only very limited facilities and expertise. The Himalayan Rescue Association can offer valuable advice on trekking medical matters and have an excellent pamphlet on acute mountain sickness. Its

Kathmandu office is in the Kathmandu Guest House compound and is well worth a visit.

Safety

In the mid-70s it was possible to claim that Nepal was totally immune from theft, assaults and other assorted vices of contemporary Western 'civilisation'. Unfortunately that claim can no longer be made and in a number of places in Nepal it would not be wise to trek alone, and a sharp eye should be kept on your possessions.

Usually the further you get from roads and population centres the fewer problems there will be, but several basic rules should be followed. Don't trek alone, don't make ostentatious displays of valuable possessions and don't leave lodge doors unlocked or valuables unattended. If you hire porters make sure they are reputable by hiring them through an agency or with good recommendations. A porter or guide found at a street corner can easily disappear along the trail with all your gear.

Minimising Your Impact

Recently the ecological impact of trekkers in the Himalaya has become a major concern. Everest pioneer Sir Edmund Hillary has even suggested that the number of trekkers to the Solu Khumbu region should be limited. While trekkers certainly contribute to the problems of firewood use and the appearance of rubbish along the trails they are not the only culprits. The depletion of forests is a severe problem throughout the Himalaya and, as modern non-biodegradable packaging becomes increasingly common in Nepal, garbage is starting to appear along village trails untravelled by Western trekkers.

Trekkers can definitely do their part to aid Himalayan conservation. You can minimise the use of firewood by staying in lodges that use kerosene or fuel-efficient wood stoves and solar heated hot water. Avoid using large open fires for warmth – wear additional clothing instead – and keep showers to a minimum if wood is burnt to produce the hot water.

Trekkers should always carry their garbage out or burn it, although you should remember that the fireplace in a Nepalese home is a sacred institution and throwing rubbish into it would be a grave insult. Toilet paper is a particularly unpleasant sight along trails: if you must use it, carry it out in a plastic bag until you can burn it. Better yet, carry a small plastic trowel to bury the shit (well away from any streams) and a small plastic container so that – like the vast majority of people in the world – you can clean yourself with water instead.

Trekkers should also respect Nepalese culture and traditions. Dress modestly – women should not wear short or revealing clothes and men should not go shirtless. Don't put down what you may see as shortcomings in the Nepalese life style; remember life in the West has many problems and drawbacks as well. Don't encourage begging children; tell them *Na raamro*, 'Not good', and remember that hand-outs can create dependence and other negative side effects.

PREPARATIONS
Trekking Permits

Travel in Nepal is still highly restricted and your visa only allows you to visit the areas around the Kathmandu and Pokhara valleys, Royal Chitwan National Park and the routes followed by the main roads. Elsewhere in the country – this essentially means the places which can only be reached by aircraft or walking – requires a trekking permit which is stamped in your passport.

If you are trekking with an organised group this will be arranged for you. If you're doing it yourself it is possible to obtain the permit the same day – if you arrive at the office early. It's best, however, to budget for a rather longer and distinctly tiring battle with bureaucracy. Some of the trekking agents around Thamel will, for a fee of around Rs 50, handle this task for you, which is worth considering if you have a low tolerance for queues. Make sure you get a receipt for your passport.

Trekking permits must be applied for in Kathmandu or Pokhara at the same office that handles visa extensions. In Kathmandu the office is on Tridevi Marg near Thamel; in Pokhara the office is between the airport and the lakeside. The permit costs Rs 90 per week for the first month, Rs 112.50 per week for the second and third month and you need two identical passport photos. Your trekking permit also acts as a visa extension (when necessary), although you will need to fill in another form.

In addition, you must *officially* change US$10 per day for the duration of your trek, so you'll need an exchange receipt. There is a bank counter in the Thamel office, so you're best off changing the money there. Finally, if you plan to trek through a national park, wildlife reserve or conservation area – this will be necessary in the case of the Mt Everest, Langtang and Annapurna treks – you will need to pay a park entrance fee, which is roughly equivalent to US$10. Currently, there is a Rs 250 entry fee to the Sagarmatha and Langtang national parks and a Rs 200 entry fee to the Annapurna Conservation Area, which encompasses the main treks from Pokhara.

The trekking permit specifies the route you will be following so make sure you include any possible variation you might take along the way. Permits can be extended at the offices in Kathmandu or Pokhara or, for a maximum of 7 days at a time, at a police station.

Trekking Companions

For safety reasons you should not trek alone, but if you're intending to trek independently and don't have a partner it's usually relatively easy to find one. Notice boards around Kathmandu or Pokhara often have signs up from people looking for partners. In Kathmandu the Himalayan Rescue Association office in the Kathmandu Guest House compound has a notice board specifically for trekking partner requests. Despite warnings and scare stories the chances of theft or physical assault on the trail are remote, but you can take a fall, suffer some illness or sprain your ankle at any time.

Trekking Equipment

It's always best to have your own equipment since you will be familiar with it and should know for certain that it works. If there is some equipment which you do not have, however, it can probably be bought or rented from one of Nepal's many trekking shops. The equipment available is usually of excellent quality and the rental charges are generally not excessive, but large deposits are often required. There may be a US$100 deposit required on equipment which costs only US$1 a day to rent.

Shoes are probably the most essential piece of equipment, but these days many trekkers, particularly at low altitudes, just wear running shoes. In winter or at high altitudes a high-quality sleeping bag, down jackets and down pants may all be necessary, and if you don't have your own they can all be rented in Kathmandu. If you are going on an organised trek check exactly what equipment is supplied: it's a waste of time bringing your own sleeping bag if the company supplies one.

Kathmandu is still the centre for trekking equipment and there are many outlets around Thamel. These days Pokhara also has some trekking equipment places and so do popular destinations like Namche Bazaar. The equipment available in Nepal used to be mainly expedition leftovers and at Namche Bazaar, the important 'last stop before Mt Everest', that will still be the case. In Kathmandu, however, there is now a great deal of new equipment obviously brought into the country purely for resale purposes.

Books & Maps

Books and maps are readily available in Kathmandu and Pokhara bookshops. See the Lonely Planet *Trekking in the Nepal Himalaya* book by Stan Armington for the complete story on trekking. It has considerable advice on equipment selection, an excellent medical section oriented towards trekking and the mountains, and comprehensive route descriptions not only of the popular treks covered more briefly in this book, but also of a number of interesting but less heavily used treks.

The Schneider Maps, named after their

Top: Typical farmhouse in the hills near Pokhara (TW)
Bottom: Mother and daughter near Dumre (JL)

cartographer, are the best available trekking maps but they're mainly for the Everest trek and they're expensive. The locally produced Mandala series now has colour maps for *Round Annapurna* and *Helambu & Langtang* as well as their older dyeline maps for other regions.

All the trekking maps, including the Schneider maps, suffer from a number of problems. For a start the trails change faster than the maps: you may well find a new trail in use or a route change necessitated by an avalanche or flood. Equally disorienting is the fact that Nepalese villages are often hard to pinpoint (they sprawl over hills and down valleys) and often have very different names depending on which map you look at or whom you ask. Treat any map with suspicion.

Clothing & Other Equipment

The clothing you require depends on where and when you trek. If you're going up to Everest Base Camp in the middle of winter you must be prepared for very cold weather with down gear, mittens and the like. On the other hand if you're doing a short low altitude trek early or late in the season the weather is likely to be fine for T-shirts and perhaps a sweater to pull on in the evenings.

Apart from ensuring you have adequate clothing to keep warm the important considerations are that your feet are comfortable and that you can keep dry if it rains or snows. Uncomfortable shoes or blistered feet are the worst possible trekking discomfort. Make sure your shoes fit well and are comfortable for long periods. For most trekking running shoes are quite adequate, but they're inadequate if you come to snow or wet weather. Rain is unlikely in most of the trekking season, but waterproof gear or at least an umbrella is necessary if there is rain or snow, particularly if it's cold. The rainy season also brings leeches and it's nice to have some salt or matches to deal with them.

Take a torch (flashlight) for those inevitable calls of nature on moonless nights.

Money

Except perhaps on the Pokhara trail changing foreign money is likely to be very difficult if not impossible. Bring enough money for the whole walk and carry it in small denominations.

Bringing Gifts

Cigarettes and matches are popular small gifts, but beware of encouraging children begging for 'one rupee' or a 'school pen' – see the earlier Minimising Your Impact section.

ARRANGEMENTS

Essentially you can trek by yourself or in a group, but there are many variations on those two possibilities.

Independent Trekking

At one extreme, independent trekking can mean simply trekking from lodge to lodge along the main trekking trails with one or more friends. All you need is your trekking permit and your walking gear and off you go. The popular trekking trails all have accommodation along their entire length. People have even walked the complete Annapurna Circuit without a sleeping bag, although this is not recommended.

For most moderately fit people guides and porters are not necessary on the Annapurna or Mt Everest treks. A good guide/porter may enhance your experience, but a bad one will just make life more complicated.

There are many factors that influence how much you spend on such a trip. In most places accommodation costs around Rs 10, a simple meal of rice and dhal around Rs 15. After a long day hiking, however, most people will weaken when confronted by a cold beer or an apple pie and these will start to add to your costs. Even with luxury items thrown in, however, it will be difficult to spend the US$10 you were forced to change. According to some studies, competition on the Annapurna Circuit is so intense, and the need for money so desperate, that lodges have been known to provide food and accommodation at below cost. Remember this – and the real value of the rupee – if you start to get carried away with bargaining.

Guides & Porters If you can't (or don't want to) carry a decent-size pack, if you have children or elderly people in your party, or if you plan to walk in regions where you have to carry in food and tents, help should be considered. It's fairly easy to find guides and porters, but it is hard to be certain of their honesty and ability. Unless you have first-hand recommendations, you're best to hire someone through an agency. Arranging expeditions where guides, porters, tents and food are required can be very time-consuming and can quickly become extremely complicated. In such cases you're definitely best off putting this in the hands of a professional.

There is a distinct difference between a guide and a porter. A guide will speak English, know the terrain and the trails, and supervise porters, but will probably not be interested in carrying a load or doing menial tasks like cooking and putting up tents. A porter is generally hired strictly for load carrying, although an increasing number speak

some English and know the trails well enough to act as a guide.

If halfway through a trek you decide you do need some help (illness, problems with high altitude or ordinary old blisters might contribute) it will generally be possible to find someone. A large village or a hill country airstrip would be a good place to look. At airstrips like the ones in Lukla or Jomsom there are often porters who have just been paid off from a trekking party and are looking for another load to carry. Large organised trekking parties carry most of their own food and as the food is used up fewer porters are needed and the extra porters are paid off along the route – so you can find experienced porters in the most unlikely places.

Whether you're making the arrangements yourself or going through an agency, make sure you've very clearly established where you will go, how long you will take, how much you are going to pay and what you will be obliged to supply along the way. Most agreements provide that guides and porters pay for their own food and accommodation out of their wages, but this means you will have to stay in villages that supply such services. Arrangements where you pay for the porter's accommodation and food can end up being surprisingly expensive. The amount of food a hungry Nepalese porter can get through, when you're footing the bill, can be simply stunning.

You may also be responsible for outfitting guides and porters to cope with cold and snow. If you are going above the snowline you must make absolutely certain that porters have goggles, shoes, shelter and appropriate clothing. There are still regular horror stories about ill-equipped porters tackling the Thorung La (the pass between Manang and Muktinath on the Annapurna Circuit). Frostbite, snow blindness and death have resulted.

If you make arrangements with one of the small trekking agencies in Kathmandu expect to pay US$10 per day for a guide, US$7 per day for a porter. If you find a porter yourself, the costs will be much lower – say

Rs 75 to Rs 100 per day. See the following section for a list of local agencies.

Organised Trekking

Organised trekking can also have many variations in standards and costs. At one extreme there are the big international adventure travel companies in the West. You book your trek through them and everything is organised and arranged before you leave home. Your cost will probably include flights to and from Nepal, accommodation in Kathmandu before and after the trek, tours and other activities as well as the trek itself. A fully organised trek will provide tents, sleeping bags, food, porters and an experienced English-speaking sirdar or trek leader. All you need to carry is your day pack and camera.

Companies organising trekking trips in Nepal include well-known names like Mountain Travel or Wilderness Travel in the USA, World Expeditions or Peregrine Adventures in Australia, and Sherpa Expeditions in the UK. Although the trek leaders may be experienced Western walkers from the international company the actual organisation in Nepal will probably be by a locally based trekking company.

It's quite possible to join a fully organised trip when you get to Nepal (and save a lot of money), but unless you have a decent-size group or have made arrangements in advance, you will be dependent on whether there is a vacancy on a trip with pre-established starting and finishing dates. With the best of these companies a trek may cost upwards of US$60 a day and you'll trek in real comfort with tables, chairs, dining tents, toilet tents and other luxuries which seem quite incompatible with walking in the wilds! Some of the large Nepal-based organisations include:

Ama Dablam Trekking
    Lazimpat (tel 4-10219)
Mountain Travel Nepal
    Naxal (tel 4-14508)
Malla Treks
    Malla Hotel (tel 4-18389)
Sherpa Co-operative Trekking
    PO Box 1338, Durbar Marg (tel 2-24068)

Tiger Mountain
    PO Box 170, Durbar Marg (tel 4-14508)

There are more than 80 trekking agencies in Nepal, ranging from the big ones tied up with international adventure travel companies, down to small agencies who specialise in handling independent trekkers. These small agencies will often be able to fix you up with individual porters or guides. A group trek organised through one of these smaller trekking agencies might cost US$40 to US$60 a day. Group treks staying at village lodges along the route, like those run by Sherpa Co-operative Trekking, can be cheaper still (around US$25 a day).

Trekking agencies in this category include:

Above the Clouds Trekking
    Thamel (tel 4-16909)
Adventure Jungle Camp
    Thamel (tel 4-17184)
Asian Trekking
    Thamel (tel 4-12821)
Glacier Safari Treks
    Thamel (tel 4-12116)
Himalayan Journeys
    Kantipath (tel 2-26138)
Kanchenjunga Travel
    Thahiti Tole
Mandala Trekking
    Kantipath (tel 2-14700)
Machhapuchhare Trekking
    Thamel (tel 2-27207)
Nepal Tashi Taki Trekking
    Thamel (tel 4-15920)
Sherpa Co-operative Trekking
    Durbar Marg (tel 2-24068)
Sherpa Trekking Services
    Kamaldi (tel 2-22489)
Wilderness Experience
    Kantipath (tel 2-27152)
Yangrima Trekking
    Kathmandu (tel 2-25608)

TREKS

There are countless long treks in Nepal, many of which still see only a handful of Western walkers each year. Two new routes have been opened up, but only for trekkers in organised groups: in the Dolpo region west of the Kali Gandaki Valley and to the

Kanchenjunga Base Camp in the north-east of the country.

The six very popular longer treks, described in detail, are:

Everest Base Camp Trek

The Everest Base Camp Trek takes about 3 weeks and reaches a maximum height of 5545 metres at Kala Pattar, the small peak offering fine views of Mt Everest. Although the final part of the trek is through essentially uninhabited areas, these days small lodges operate in the trekking season so it's quite suitable for independent trekkers. The flights in or out of Lukla at the start and/or finish of the trek can be a real problem.

Helambu Trek

This 1 week trek can start and finish straight from the Kathmandu Valley and, although it does not offer superb mountain scenery, it is culturally interesting. The maximum height reached is only 2800 metres and there is plenty of accommodation along the route.

Langtang Trek

The Langtang Trek lasts 10 to 12 days if you walk in and out but it can be varied by flying out or by crossing a high pass down to the Helambu region. There are fine views, interesting villages and although there are some relatively uninhabited stretches ac-

commodation is available. The maximum height attained is 3800 metres.

Jomsom Trek

The trek up the Kali Gandaki Valley from Pokhara is one of the most popular in Nepal with superb scenery, interesting people and the best trailside accommodation in the country. It takes a week to reach Muktinath, the end point of the trek. Walking back takes another week or you can fly from Jomsom. Muktinath, the high point of the trek, is at 3700 metres.

Annapurna Circuit

It takes nearly 3 weeks to walk the entire Annapurna Circuit but for scenery and cultural diversity this is the best trek in Nepal. It crosses to the north of the main Himalayan range, on to the Tibetan Plateau, and crosses a 5400 metre pass. The last week of the trek is the Jomsom trek in reverse.

Annapurna Sanctuary

Also commencing from Pokhara, the walk into the centre of the Annapurna mountains offers unparalled mountain scenery. The trek takes 10 to 14 days and reaches a maximum height of 3000 metres. Finding shelter in the uninhabited sanctuary area was a real problem at one time, but recently numerous lodges have sprung up along the route.

The Yeti

Like Big Foot in North America, the Loch Ness monster in Scotland or even the elusive bunyip in Australia, the yeti or abominable snowman is much hunted but little seen. The yeti is a shy humanoid creature which lives high in the most remote regions of the Himalaya. There are countless yeti legends told by the Sherpas and other hill peoples. They tell of its legendary strength, its ability to carry off yaks and even abduct people.

Nobody has ever managed to get a clear photograph of the yeti: footprints in the snow are generally the only indication that a yeti has been by, although hastily gnawed yak bones also add to the yeti legend.

Of course there are plenty of scientific explanations for yetis. The footprints may have been a human print or some other natural footprint which has appeared to grow larger as the snow melts. Rigorous studies have been made of the yeti scalps found in various monasteries, in particular the one at the Pangboche monastery, and they have all turned out to be fakes. Keep your camera loaded though, a good photo of a yeti (even a small yeti) will probably be worth a fortune. ■

Everest Base Camp Trek

Everybody knows of Mt Everest and that's the simple reason why the Everest Base Camp Trek is so popular. The trek has a number of stunning attractions, but it also has some distinct drawbacks which might well deter potential trekkers were it not for the undeniable plus point of being able to say you've been to the base of the highest mountain in the world.

The attractions include spectacular scenery and the outgoing Sherpa people of the Solu Khumbu, the region where Mt Everest and its attendant lesser peaks are located. The drawbacks include the long, hard slog to get there and the acclimatisation problems caused by the region's considerable altitude.

It's not until you get right into the Solu Khumbu region that the Everest trek really gets interesting. The first part of the trek is not only a hard slog, but is also pretty sparse in the breathtaking views department. The hard slog comes about because the trek doesn't follow valleys – like the Annapurna treks – instead the Everest trek cuts across the valleys. So for day after day it's a tiring process of dropping down one side of a steep valley and climbing up again on the other. The popular figure is that by the time you reach the base camp your ascents will tote up to just about 9000 metres, the full height of Everest from sea level!

The Everest trek starts in the Nepali-speaking Hindu lowlands and ends in the Tibetan-Buddhist highlands where the Sherpas are renowned for their enterprise, hard work, civic responsibility and devotion to the practice of Buddhism. In their often inhospitable land, the potato, a relatively recent introduction, is the main crop, but these days trekking and mountaineering is the backbone of the Sherpa economy. More than half the population in the region is now involved with tourism and Namche Bazaar looks more like an alpine resort than a Sherpa village.

Most Everest trekkers opt to fly one way

to avoid having to repeat all those ups and downs. This introduces its own problems as the Lukla to Kathmandu flights are notorious for cancellations, waiting lists and short-tempered trekkers. Kathmandu to Lukla flights are less heavily used (more people fly out than fly in) but it's preferable to walk up and fly back in order to aid the acclimatisation that is necessary for the extreme altitudes encountered.

The Everest trek may not be quite as good as the Pokhara area for village inn treks, but these days accommodation is available during the trekking season even in the normally uninhabited areas around the high peaks.

Medical Assistance

There are small hospitals in Jiri, Phaphlu and Khunde, while the Himalayan Rescue Association has a medical facility in Pheriche and the Edmund Hillary Hospital is at Khumjung.

EVEREST BASE CAMP TREK
Day 1: Kathmandu-Lamosangu-Jiri

The Everest trek has been getting steadily shorter over the years. The members of the 1953 British expedition which put Hillary and Tensing on the top started their walk to Everest at Bhaktapur in the Kathmandu Valley. Today you can take the Kodari road to Lamosangu, 78 km from Kathmandu, and turn off there to Jiri, a further 110 km. Buses

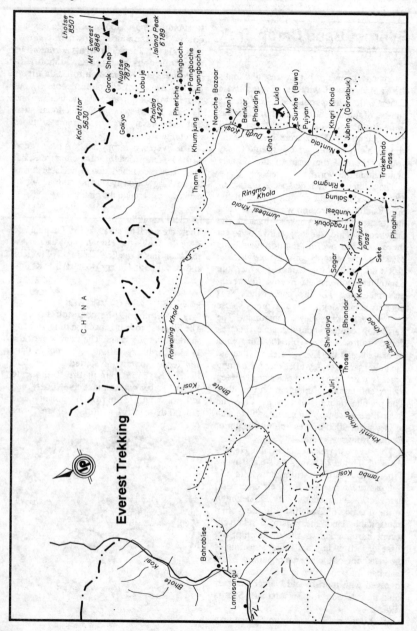

Everest Trekking

to Jiri go two or three times daily from the main bus park in Kathmandu and the 12 hour trip costs Rs 66.

Jiri at 1860 metres is a relatively new town which has developed since the road was completed. There's a STOL field and a hospital and you can fly here to save the long bus trip. Jiri has a weekly market on Saturdays and there are several hotels in town.

Day 2: Jiri-Bhandar

The walk starts with a climb to the ridge top at 2400 metres then drops down to Shivalaya at 1800 metres. Before the Jiri road was opened the trek used to go through Those, which at that time was the busiest market town between Lamosangu and Namche Bazaar. It's still possible to walk from Jiri to Those and Shivalaya.

From Shivalaya you climb again to Sangbadanda at 2150 metres and already you start to see the mani stone walls which indicate you are entering a Buddhist region. Walk to the left side of these walls. You reach

Kosaribas at 2500 metres, then a pass at 2705 metres before descending again to Bhandar at 2200 metres. This Sherpa settlement has a gompa and a number of hotels. It's possible to take a detour between Sangbadanda and Bhandar to visit Thodung at 3090 metres where there's a cheese factory, established with Swiss aid in the 1950s.

Day 3: Bhandar-Sagar or Sete

The trail drops down to the Likhu Khola and crosses the river at 1580 metres, climbs through Kenja and then rises steeply to a fork where you choose the route to Sagar at 2440 metres or Sete at 2575 metres. If you're in a group Sagar is preferable (the camping site is better), but if you're not camping then Sete offers a better choice of hotels. From here on the villages are almost all inhabited by Sherpas (alternative village names are given in brackets).

Day 4: Sagar or Sete-Junbesi

It's a long but gradual climb to the Lamjura pass at 3530 metres. You're rewarded with frost and often snow along the trail in winter or with flowering rhododendrons in the spring. Goyem at 3300 metres on your way to the pass is a good lunch stop. The pass is the highest point between Jiri and Namche Bazaar and from the top you descend to Tragdobuk at 2860 metres, then to the pretty Sherpa village of Junbesi at 2675 metres. It has a monastery, some good hotels and is a good place for a rest day with some interesting walks in the vicinity.

Day 5: Junbesi-Nuntala

The trail drops to Phaphlu where there is an airstrip, then climbs to a ridge at 3080 metres where for the first time you can see Everest. The route then descends to Salung at 2980 metres and the Ringmo Khola at 2650 metres. This is the last chance to wash in a river, as the Dudh Kosi is much too cold! Then it's up to Ringmo where apples and other fruit are grown. The new trail from here to Namche Bazaar was built in the '80s and avoids many of the steep descents and ascents of the old route.

A local Jiri woman

A short climb from Ringmo Khola takes you to the 3071 metre Trakshindo pass, drops down past the monastery of the same name, and on down to Nuntala (Manidingma) at 2320 metres where there are a variety of hotels offering a variety of standards.

Day 6: Nuntala-Kharl Khola
The trail descends to the Dudh Kosi at 1500 metres and crosses it to follow the other bank. The trail climbs to Jubing (Dorakbuk) at 1680 metres and continues up to Khari Khola at 2070 metres. The old trail along the Dudh Kosi to Namche Bazaar usually required a stop here, and if you're walking with porters this may still be the traditional stopping place. If not you can push on to Bupsa (Bumshing) on Day 6 and then reach Ghat (Lhawa) on Day 7 and Namche Bazaar on Day 8, saving a day's walk.

Day 7: Khari Khola-Pulyan
The trail first drops to 2010 metres then climbs to Bupsa at 2300 metres. From here the trail climbs gradually, offering views of the Dudh Kosi 1000 metres below at the bottom of the steep-sided valley, until it reaches a ridge at 2900 metres overlooking Puiyan. Puiyan is at 2730 metres in a side canyon off the Dudh Kosi valley.

Day 8: Pulyan-Phakding
The trail climbs to a ridge at 2800 metres then drops down to Surkhe (Buwa) at 2293 metres. Shortly beyond Surkhe is the turn-off to Lukla with its airstrip. It continues to climb through Mushe and Chaunrikarka at 2680 metres to Chablung, then drops to Ghat at 2550 metres. Another climb takes you to Phakding at 2650 metres and from here on the trek is pretty much up, up, up.

Day 9: Phakding-Namche Bazaar
The trail climbs to Benkar at 2700 metres, then Chomoa, with the curious *Hatago Lodge* run by a resident Japanese gentleman, and Monjo before dropping down to cross the Dudh Kosi. On the other side it's up to Jorsale at 2850 metres where there are a number of good places to eat and stay. Here

A salt tradesman at the Namche Bazaar market

you enter the Sagarmatha National Park and must pay the entry fee.

It's a steady climb from here to Namche Bazaar at 3440 metres. This is the main centre in the Solu Khumbu region and has shops, restaurants, a bakery, hotels with hot showers, a national park office, a police checkpost where your trekking permit will be inspected and even a bank. Namche Bazaar even has hydroelectricity, mainly used for lighting. There is a colourful market each Saturday.

Day 10: Namche Bazaar
There is plenty to do around Namche Bazaar and a day should be spent here acclimatising. Remember that the victims of altitude sickness are often the fittest and healthiest people who foolishly overextend themselves.

Day 11: Namche Bazaar-Thyangboche
The slightly longer route from Namche

Bazaar to Thyangboche via Khumjung and Khunde is more interesting than the direct one. It starts by climbing up to the Shyangboche airstrip at 3720 metres. Above it is the *Everest View Hotel*, a Japanese scheme to build a deluxe hotel with great views of the highest mountains on earth. The idea fell flat on its face, since flying straight up to nearly 4000 metres is not good for people's health, especially for the elderly folk who were generally the ones who could afford it.

From the hotel or the airstrip you continue to Khumjung and then rejoin the direct trail to Thyangboche. The trail descends to the Dudh Kosi at 3250 metres where there is a small teashop and a series of picturesque water-driven prayer wheels. A steep ascent brings you to Thyangboche (Tengpoche) at 3870 metres. The famous monastery, a photographer's favourite with its background of Ama Dablam, Everest and other peaks, was burnt down in 1988; although it's being rebuilt, 1989 was not an auspicious year for building things so a start wasn't made until 1990. There's a camping area, a number of places to stay and at the November-December full moon the colourful Mani Rimdu festival is held here with much singing and dancing.

Day 12: Thyangboche-Pheriche
Beyond Thyangboche the altitude really starts to tell. The trail drops down to Devuche, crosses the Imja Khola on a frightening bridge and climbs past superb mani stones to Pangboche at 3860 metres. The monastery here has a 'yeti scalp' and the village is a good lunch stop.

The trail then climbs to Pheriche at 4240 metres where there is a trekkers' aid post and possible medical assistance. Pheriche has a number of hotels and restaurants which usually feature exotic dishes left over from international mountaineering expeditions.

Day 13: Pheriche
Another acclimatisation day should be spent at Pheriche. You can either laze around the settlement or make a day trip to Nangkartshang Gompa or up past Dingboche. Either walk offers good views.

Day 14: Pheriche-Lobuje
The trail climbs to Phalang Karpa at 4340

Selling produce at the Saturday weekly market, Namche Bazaar

metres then Duglha at 4620 metres before reaching Lobuje at 4930 metres. The lodge accommodation here is all dormitory-style and the altitude, the cold and the crowding combine to ensure less than restful nights. The views, however, are superb!

Day 15: Lobuje-Gorak Shep
The trail continues to climb to Gorak Shep at 5160 metres. You reach there by lunch time and in the afternoon can rest or continue to Kala Pattar (Black Rock). At 5545 metres this small peak offers the best view you'll get of Everest without climbing it. Although there is usually accommodation at Gorak Shep it's nothing to write home about. Making the Lobuje, Gorak Shep, Kala Pattar, Lobuje circuit in a single day is a better idea if you're not on an organised trek with camping equipment.

Day 16: Gorak Shep-Lobuje
After a sleepless night at Gorak Shep, the altitude hits nearly everybody; getting back down to Lobuje or even better to Pheriche makes a real difference. If you want to actually get to the base camp then it's about 6 hours round trip from Lobuje, and there's no view, so if you only have the energy for one sidetrip on day 16 or 17 then make it Kala Pattar. It's downhill, but tiring, back to Lobuje.

Day 17: Lobuje-Dingboche
Staying the night at Dingboche instead of Pheriche makes an interesting alternative. It's a 'summer village' at 4360 metres.

Days 18, 19 & 20: Dingboche-Lukla
The next 3 days retrace your steps down to Lukla via Thyangboche and Namche Bazaar. You have to arrive at Lukla the day before your scheduled departure in order to re-confirm your flight. Lukla has a number of places to stay including the relatively expensive *Sherpa Co-operative Hotel*, and life revolves around wondering whether flights will come in and who will manage to get on them.

Day 21: Lukla-Kathmandu
If the gods are with you, your flight comes in and your reservation hasn't been cancelled. Then, after it took you so many days to get here by road and foot, your aircraft only takes 35 minutes to fly you back.

VARIATIONS & SIDE TRIPS
See the Other Treks section later in this chapter for information on the long trek south from the Solu Khumbu region to Dhankuta, an interesting alternative to going straight back to Kathmandu. Alternatives to hanging around in Lukla waiting for flights or walking all the way back to Jiri are also possible but not very satisfactory. Going down to Phaphlu, 2 or 3 days south of Lukla, is unlikely to get you out any faster. It's 4 or 5 days walk down to Lamidanda from where there are several flights a week to Biratnagar and Kathmandu.

Experienced trekkers could take the little-frequented Barabise to Shivalaya route in, avoiding the Jiri road completely. It's an interesting 6 day round trip from Namche Bazaar to Gokyo and back. This trek ends at another Kala Pattar with fine, but different, views of Everest. You can even combine both Kala Pattars by crossing the 5420 metre Chola La pass, but you had better bring your ice axe and crampons and know how to use them.

A shorter side trip from Namche Bazaar is to Thami, the gateway to Tesi Laphcha and the Rolwaling Himal. You can do a round trip to Thami in a day, although it's better to stay overnight in order to catch the morning views.

Helambu & Langtang Treks

Although they are not as well known and popular as the Everest Base Camp trek or the Annapurna Circuit trek these two treks offer a number of distinct advantages. The treks are north of the Kathmandu Valley, so both

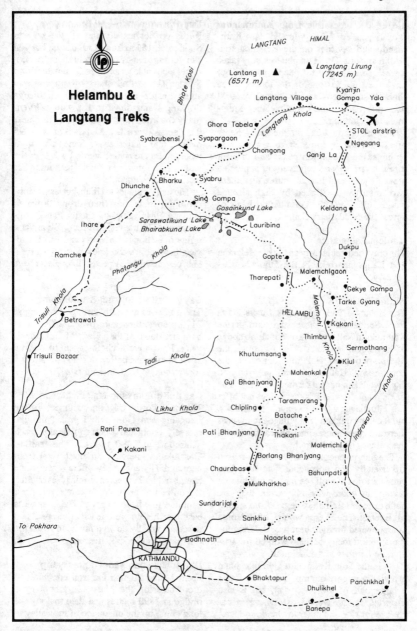

**Helambu &
Langtang Treks**

are easily accessible from Kathmandu. Indeed you can leave your hotel in Kathmandu and set foot on the Helambu trail within an hour. The Helambu trek only takes a week so it is ideal for people who do not have the time for one of the longer treks. Since it stays at relatively low altitudes it does not require fancy cold weather equipment and clothing.

The Langtang trek, on the other hand, gives you the opportunity to get right in amongst the Himalayan peaks and to walk through remote and relatively unpopulated areas. If you want real adventure then these two treks can be linked by high altitude passes, either via the Gosainkund lakes or across the 5000 metre Ganja La pass.

Medical Assistance

The only medical facility on the the Helambu and Langtang treks is the Dhunche dispensary.

HELAMBU TREK

The Helambu Trek only takes 7 days, starts from Sundarijal at the eastern end of the Kathmandu Valley and does not climb above 3500 metres. It makes a loop through the Sherpa-populated Helambu region to the north-east of Kathmandu and only the first day's walk is repeated on the return trip. The trek's main drawback is that it does not offer fine Himalayan views, like some other treks, but it can be trekked on a village inn basis as there are guest houses and lodges in many of the villages along the trail.

The Sherpa people of the Helambu region are friendly and hospitable, just like their better known kinfolk of the Solu Khumbu region. In other ways, however, they are quite different from the Sherpas from around Mt Everest. The Sherpa women of Helambu are renowned for their beauty and during the Rana period many of them worked for aristocratic families in Kathmandu.

As in the Solu Khumbu region the potato is a vitally important crop. It not only forms a large part of the local diet, but is also exported to the Nepalese lowland in exchange for rice and other lowland produce.

Day 1: Kathmandu-Pati Bhanjyang

Buses do not usually run all the way to Sundarijal, 15 km from Kathmandu, but you can get to the start of the trail there by taxi, or get a bus at least as far as Bodhnath. From Sundarijal the trail starts off up concrete steps beside the pipeline which brings drinking water down to the valley. Eventually the trail leaves the pipeline from near the dam and reaches Mulkharkha at 1895 metres, 600 metres above Sundarijal, from where there are superb views back over the valley and some convenient teahouses for rest and refreshment.

The trail continues to climb, but less steeply, through Chaurabas then drops down to Borlang Bhanjyang and finally Pati Bhanjyang at 1770 metres. Borlang Bhanjyang offers fine Himalayan views and Pati Bhanjyang has a police checkpost where your trekking permit will be inspected. Both places have hotels.

Day 2: Pati Bhanjyang-Khutumsang

The trail rises and falls through Chipling at 2170 metres, then goes over a 2470 metre pass and down to the village of Gul Bhanjyang. From here it climbs again to reach a 2620 metre pass before descending along a rocky route to Khutumsang at 2470 metres.

Day 3: Khutumsang-Malemchigaon

The trail follows a ridge line, with views of the Langtang and Gosainkund peaks, through sparsely populated forests to finally reach Tharepati at 3490 metres. The trail to Gosainkund branches off north-west from here and Tharepati only offers a few stone huts, used by herders in summer, as shelter. If you're not prepared to camp you must continue to Malemchigaon. The trail turns east just before you reach Tharepati and descends rapidly down a ravine to reach the Sherpa village at 2530 metres.

Day 4: Malemchigaon-Tarke Gyang

From Malemchigaon the trail continues to drop, crossing the Malemchi Khola by a bridge at 1890 metres and then making the long climb up the other side of the valley to

Tarke Gyang at 2743 metres. This is the largest village in Helambu and the prosperous Sherpas who live here specialise, amongst other things, in turning out 'instant antiques' for gullible trekkers.

Day 5: Tarke Gyang-Kiul
From Tarke Gyang there is an alternative route, described after the final day of this trek report. On the loop trek the wide and well-used trail descends through rhododendron forests, past Buddhist chortens and mani stone walls to Kakani at 2070 metres and Thimbu at 1580 metres. By the time you reach Kiul at 1280 metres you have left the Sherpa highlands and entered the warmer lowland areas where rice is grown. Kiul is at a lower altitude than Kathmandu.

Day 6: Kiul-Pati Bhanjyang
The trail descends along Malemchi Khola, crossing it on the second suspension bridge at just 1190 metres, then joining a roadway at Mahenkal and following it to Taramarang at 940 metres. Here the trail leaves the road and climbs steeply to Batache and then Thakani, on the ridge top, at 1890 metres. From here the trail follows the ridge to Pati Bhanjyang where the Helambu circuit is completed.

Day 7: Pati Bhanjyang-Kathmandu
The final day retraces the first day's walk to Sundarijal, then back to Kathmandu.

Alternative Route from Tarke Gyang
An alternative route can be followed from Tarke Gyang through Sermathang to the road at Malemchi, south of Taramarang. This route shortens the walk by a day, but the final stretch is along a dusty roadway and it brings you out on the Kathmandu to Kodari road at Panchkhal, from where you will have to take a bus 55 km back to Kathmandu. It's certainly more convenient ending the trek at Sundarijal if you intend to head straight back to Kathmandu. If, however, you are continuing on or starting from Dhulikhel then this could be an interesting alternative.

Another Helambu alternative is to start

and finish from Panchkhal on the main road, completing the shorter loop through Malemchi, Taramarang, Kiul, Tarke Gyang, Sermathang and back to Malemchi. It's also possible to walk on from Bahunpati to Sankhu or Nagarkot, completing a loop which starts and finishes in the Kathmandu Valley but does not retrace your steps at any point.

Day 5: Tarke Gyang-Sermathang The easy
trail descends gently through a beautiful forest to Sermathang, the centre of an important apple-growing area. Sermathang is more spread out than the closely spaced houses of Tarke Gyang and there are fine views of the valley of the Malemchi Khola to the south.

Day 6: Sermathang-Panchkhal From
Sermathang the trail continues to descend to Malemchi where it meets the road. You should be able to get a ride from there down to Panchkhal on the Kathmandu to Kodari road. From there you can catch a bus to Dhulikhel or Kathmandu. If you can't find transport it's another day's walk down the roadway, following the Indrawati River, to Bahunpati and Panchkhal.

LANGTANG TREK
Langtang Lirung (7245 metres) is visible to the north of Kathmandu on clear days. The Langtang Trek takes up to 2 weeks and leads to a glacier in the valley at the foot of Langtang Lirung, close to the peak's base camp. The trail passes through Tibetan and Tamang villages and offers fine views of the Ganesh Himal range. The trek passes through comparatively lightly populated and undeveloped areas, but it is still possible to stay at village inns along the route. Ascending from just 541 metres at Trisuli Bazaar to 3800 metres at Kyanjin Gompa, the trail passes through an ever-changing climate and offers trekkers an exceptionally wide diversity of scenery and cultural areas.

Day 1: Kathmandu-Trisuli-Dhunche
It's 72 km from Kathmandu to Trisuli Bazaar,

taking about 4 hours by car or 6 hours by bus. The road is sealed but very winding and offers some fine mountain views. Rani Pauwa is the only large village along the route. From there the 50 km road to Dhunche is steep, winding and rather hairy; it passes through Betrawati and Thare. Transport can be problematic from Betrawati, only 8 km beyond Trisuli Bazaar. If you can't find transport for the 4 hour drive you have a 2 day walk to face. There is now a daily bus from Kathmandu to Dhunche; the 12 hour trip costs Rs 80.

Dhunche is a pretty village at 1950 metres where you have your trekking permit checked and must pay the entrance fee to the Langtang National Park. Eventually the road will continue beyond here towards the Ganesh Himal.

Day 2: Dhunche-Syabru

Soon after Dhunche the trail leaves the road and follows the Trisuli Khola, crossing it and climbing steeply, then leaving the Gosainkund trail and following a ridge to Bharku at 1860 metres. Most of the Trisuli Khola's water comes from the Bhote Kosi, from Tibet. Bhote Kosi means 'river from Tibet'. From Bharku there are alternative routes to Langtang village but the newer southern route through Syabru is better than the longer northern route through Syabrubensi and Syapargaon.

From Bharku you climb to 2300 metres and enter the Langtang Valley with views of Himalayan peaks to the west, north and east. The trail descends rapidly to Syabru at 2130 metres where there are good hotels.

Day 3: Syabru-Chongong

The trail descends through forest to the Langtang Khola at 1890 metres and then follows the river upstream, crossing from the southern to northern bank to reach Chongong at 2380 metres. Some maps show this as *Lama Hotel*, the name of one of the places to stay here.

Day 4: Chongon-Langtang Village

The trail continues to follow the Langtang Khola, climbing steeply, at times very steeply, to Ghora Tabela at 3000 metres where there are fine views of Langtang Lirung. Although there is no permanent settlement there is a good lodge and your trekking permit and entry permit to the national park will be checked here.

From here the trail climbs more gradually to Langtang village at 3500 metres. The national park headquarters is here, and Langtang and the villages around are in Tibetan style with stone walls surrounding the fields and herds of yaks.

Day 5: Langtang Village-Kyanjin Gompa

It only takes the morning, passing through small villages, to climb to Kyanjin Gompa at 3800 metres where there is a monastery, a lodge and a cheese factory. There are a number of interesting walks from the gompa, and if you are intending to continue over the Ganja La pass to Helambu you should spend some time here acclimatising. From the gompa you can climb to 4300 metres on the the glacial moraine to the north for superb views of Langtang Lirung. Day walks can also be made to Yala or further up the valley for more spectacular views.

Back to Kathmandu

There are a number of alternative routes back to Kathmandu. The quickest is the flight by Pilatus Porter from the nearby STOL airstrip, but a charter usually must be arranged in advance. Alternatively you can simply retrace your route back down the valley to Dhunche or, if the season and weather permits, attempt the high routes over the Ganja La pass or via the Gosainkund lakes to Helambu.

ACROSS THE GANJA LA

Walking from the Kyanjin Gompa at the end of the Langtang route south to Tarke Gyang in Helambu involves crossing the 5106 metre Ganja La pass. The pass is usually blocked by snow from December to March and at any time a bad weather change can make crossing the pass decidedly dangerous. This is one of the more difficult passes in Nepal and should not be attempted without local advice, adequate acclimatisation, good equipment and some experience. The walk takes 4 days and from leaving the gompa until you reach the Gekye Gompa, shortly before Tarke Gyang, there is no permanent settlement.

Some altitude acclimatisation around the Kyanjin Gompa is a very wise idea before commencing the crossing. Day 1 from the gompa involves a short walk to Ngegang at 4000 metres, the last good place to camp before the pass. Staying here shortens the crossing over the pass and also increases your acclimatisation.

From Ngegang the trail climbs steeply and crosses a snow slope to the pass, marked by rock cairns and prayer flags and with a spectacular view of the peaks to the north and the hills to the south. A steep and dangerous descent follows to Keldang at 4270 metres. Coming the other way over the pass the long ascent from Keldang means you must spend an additional night on the southern side of the pass. From Keldang it's a long day's walk to Dukpu at 4080 metres and another day from there to Tarke Gyang at 2743 metres. The last day's walk offers tremendous views of the Himalaya as you cross a 4020 metre pass soon after leaving Dukpu.

GOSAINKUND LAKES

The trek via the Gosainkund lakes is another way of crossing between Langtang and Helambu. Again adequate preparation is necessary and finding food and accommodation along the way is not always possible. It takes 4 days to walk from Dhunche, at the start of the Langtang trek, to Tharepati in Helambu. The trek can also be made from Helambu or by turning off the Langtang route from Syabru.

Gosainkund Lake is the site for a great pilgrimage in August each year – this is the height of the monsoon, not a pleasant time for trekking. The large rock in the centre of the lake is said to be the remains of a Shiva shrine and it is also claimed that a channel carries water from the lake directly to the tank at the Kumbeshwar Temple in Patan, 60 km to the south.

Day 1 takes you from Dhunche at 1950 metres to the Sing Gompa at 3350 metres. The route from Syabru to the gompa can be confusing. The second day's walk climbs steeply, offering fine mountain views, then drops down to Saraswatikund Lake at 4100 metres, the first of the Gosainkund lakes. The second is Bhairabkund Lake, and the third is Gosainkund Lake itself at 4380 metres. There are stone shelters at Gosainkund, used by pilgrims during the festival at the August full moon.

From the lake the trail climbs still higher to the four lakes near the Lauribina pass at 4610 metres, then drops down to Gopte at 3430 metres where you can shelter in a cave. The final day's walk descends to a stream and then climbs to Tharepati at 3490 metres.

Jomsom Trek, Annapurna Circuit & Other Pokhara Treks

Pokhara is the starting or finishing point for some of the best trekking in Nepal and the long Annapurna Circuit Trek is the most popular trek in the country.

The reasons for the area's popularity are numerous. You can start your trek from Pokhara itself: no long, uncomfortable bus rides or problematic flights are required to get to the starting point. You are in the mountains immediately: the Annapurna range is very close to Pokhara. The treks in this part of the country offer a great deal of cultural and geographic diversity; indeed the Jomsom and Annapurna Circuit treks both go to the north of the Himalayan watershed, into the dry desert area which is properly part of the Tibetan Plateau. Finally these treks are the best in Nepal for independent trekkers and a network of lodges and guest houses can be found along all the main trails. The Annapurna Circuit has even been dubbed 'The Apple Pie Trail'.

The Pokhara area also offers a number of 1-day treks or short 3 or 4-day treks. These are covered in the Around Pokhara section of the Pokhara chapter. There are three popular longer treks from Pokhara, all of which follow the same route at some point. The Annapurna Sanctuary Trek takes you right in amongst the mountains of the Annapurna range to the Machhapuchhare Base Camp. This trek takes about 8 days. The Jomsom trek takes about 7 days in each direction, but it is possible to fly back to Pokhara from Jomsom. Most trekkers continue a day further to the holy temple of Muktinath, well to the north of the main Himalayan range. Finally the Annapurna Circuit takes a full 3 weeks and completely encircles the Annapurna range. The last 7 days of the circuit walk from Muktinath to Pokhara are the same as the Jomsom trek, but in reverse.

The Annapurna range is the centre for all these Pokhara treks. For most of Nepal's length the Himalaya form the border between Nepal and China. The Annapurna mountains are different in that the border is well to the north so the Jomsom and Annapurna Circuit treks both go north of the Himalayan watershed, into the high altitude desert which is characteristic of the Tibetan Plateau.

Medical Assistance

Around the Annapurna Circuit the only facilities are the small hospital at Jomsom and the government dispensaries on the Manang side of the Thorung La pass.

JOMSOM TREK

The Jomsom trek is essentially the final third of the Annapurna Circuit. It follows the Kali Gandaki Valley between the soaring peaks of Annapurna and Dhaulagiri and finally emerges to the north of the main Himalayan range, on the dry, desert-like Tibetan Plateau. The final destination is the holy temples of Muktinath, a further day's walk beyond Jomsom. The return to Pokhara can either be made by retracing your steps down the Kali Gandaki Valley or by flying from Jomsom to Pokhara or Kathmandu.

Day 1: Pokhara-Naudanda

Like many other treks in Nepal this one is getting shorter as the road gradually extends further into the mountains. Eventually it will probably go all the way to Jomsom. It's already possible to get as far as Phedi although it only turns a 3 hour walk into a lurching 1 hour ride. The route goes from Pokhara through Hyangja at 1070 metres, Suikhet at 1125 metres and on to Phedi. From there the trail climbs relatively gradually to Naudanda's ridgetop position at 1430 metres. There are fine views of the whole Annapurna range and back over Pokhara and Phewa Tal from this large village. Naudanda has a choice of hotels and a trekking permit checkpost, so for day trekkers without a permit this is the end of the line.

It's also possible to reach Naudanda by walking through Sarangkot (see the Pokhara chapter for details) and along the ridge to Kaski, which has the ruins of a small principality's palace, and on to Naudanda.

Day 2: Naudanda-Tirkedungha

From Naudanda the trail climbs to Khare at the top of the Yamdi Khola Valley at 1710 metres. The trail then drops down to Lumle at 1585 metres, where there are a number of hotels and a British-aided agricultural project. Don't take the wrong turning here and get on the Dhorpatan, Baglung and Beni trail. The next village is Chandrakot at 1550 metres where there are more fine Annapurna views and again more hotels and good places to eat.

From Chandrakot the trail drops steeply to the Modi Khola and crosses it at 1065 metres to the large village of Birethanti where you can really see how civilised this trek is. Birethanti even has sidewalk cafes! Trails to Ghandrung turn off from Chandrakot or Birethanti. Birethanti has excellent hotels but you may want to continue further to shorten the next day's long climb. Sticking to the northern side of the Bhurungdi Khola, the trail climbs to Hille and nearby Tirkedungha at 1525 metres. Hille and Tirkedungha both have places to stay.

Top: Trekkers on Poon Hill viewing the Annapurnas (SB)
Left: Beliefs before boots – barefoot saddhus approach Muktinath in the snow (RE)
Right: Trekkers campsite, Debarto (SB)

Top: Trekking scene in the Mt Everest region (JR)
Left: Trekking porter (SB)
Right: On the trail from Namche Bazaar to Thyangboche (TW)

Day 3: Tirkedungha-Ghorapani

From Tirkedungha the trail climbs very steeply to Ulleri, a large Magar village at 2070 metres. It continues to ascend, but more gently, through fine forests of oak and rhododendron to Bahunthanti at 2250 metres and then Nayathanti at 2460 metres. Another hour brings you to Ghorapani at 2775 metres.

Only a short walk beyond Ghorapani is the Deorali pass (*deorali* actually means 'pass') with spectacular views. An hour's climb from here will take you to Poon (or Pun) Hill, one of the best Himalayan viewpoints in Nepal. There are hotels at Ghorapani and at Poon Hill. *Ghora* means 'horse' and *pani* means 'water' and indeed long caravans of pack horses are regularly seen all along the Jomsom trek. A trail also runs from Ghorapani to Ghandruk. This part of the trek is plagued by leeches during the monsoon and there may be snow on the trail in the winter.

Day 4: Ghorapani-Tatopani

The trail descends steeply to Chitre at 2390 metres where there are more lodges offering accommodation. From here the hills are extensively terraced as the trail drops down through Sikha, a large village with shops and hotels, at 1980 metres and then descends gently to Ghara at 1705 metres. A further steep descent of 500 metres takes you to the Ghar Khola where the trail crosses the river on a suspension bridge and then climbs up above the Kali Gandaki River before crossing that too.

Turning north the trail soon reaches Tatopani at 1189 metres. It's a busy population centre where you will find some of the best food along the whole trail, and you can even get a cold beer to go with it. *Tato* means 'hot' and *pani* is 'water', a name earned courtesy of the hot springs by the river. Tatopani is a popular destination for a shorter trek out of Pokhara.

Day 5: Tatopani-Kalopani

The trail follows the Kali Gandaki Valley all the rest of the way to Jomsom. The river cuts a channel between the peaks of Annapurna I

and Dhaulagiri, thus qualifying the Kali Gandaki Valley for the title of the world's deepest gorge. The two 8000 metre mountain tops are only 38 metres apart and the river flows between them at a height of less than 2200 metres. The Kali Gandaki Valley is also the home for the Thakalis, a group noted for their trading and business expertise, particularly in running hotels and lodges not only here in their homeland but also in Pokhara and elsewhere in Nepal. The Thakali women are very liberated and many of the lodges are run by women, whose menfolk have been taken elsewhere by business.

From Tatopani the trail climbs gradually to Dana at 1400 metres. This is where the difficult track branches off to Maurice Herzog's base camp, used for his historic ascent of Annapurna in 1950. The trail continues to climb to Rukse Chhara and at one stage takes a precarious route through a very steep and narrow section of the gorge. Another suspension bridge crosses the river at 1935 metres and the trail then goes through Ghasa at 2000 metres, the first Thakali village reached. A steep climb through forest takes you to the Lete Khola, then to the village of Lete at 2470 metres with a superb view of the western flank of Dhaulagiri and finally to Kalopani at 2560 metres. Kalopani has great mountain views and some comfortable lodges to view them from.

Day 6: Kalopani-Jomsom

For a distance from Kalopani there are trails on both sides of the river to choose from. Larjung on the west bank at 2560 metres has interesting alleyways and tunnels between the houses, an attempt to avoid the fierce winds that often whistle down the Kali Gandaki Valley. Khobang is the next village, with a gompa above it, and the mountain views on this stretch are the best to be seen. Tukche at 2590 is one of the most important Thakali villages, once a meeting place for traders from Tibet. Despite the growth of tourism in this area Tukche is still a quieter, smaller place than it was during the era of trade with Tibet.

From here the landscape changes as you enter the drier and more desert-like country north of the Himalayan watershed. It also gets windier: gentle breezes from the north in the morning shift to a gale from the south every afternoon. Marpha at 2665 metres virtually huddles behind a ridge to keep out of the wind! The village also has some of the most luxurious accommodation facilities to be found along the trail and is a good alternative to staying in Jomsom. A government-established project between Tukche and Marpha grows fruit and vegetables for the whole region.

At 2713 metres Jomsom is the major centre in the region and has a hospital and the inevitable trekking permit checkpoint. If you're heading in the opposite direction on the Annapurna Circuit you must get your permit stamped here as it will be checked further south. This is the last Thakali village, those further north are inhabited by people of Tibetan descent. Jomsom has regular flights to Kathmandu (US$75) and Pokhara (US$45), but the Kathmandu to Jomsom flights can be problematic since in winter Kathmandu is often closed by fog in the early morning while the wind stops flights into or out of Jomsom later in the morning. Pokhara to Jomsom flights are less likely to be effected.

Day 7: Jomsom-Muktinath

If you have time it's worth making the sidetrip to the mediaeval-looking village of Kagbeni at 2810 metres. This very Tibetan-influenced settlement is as close as you can get to Lo Monthang, the capital of the legendary kingdom of Mustang further to the north. From here the trail climbs steeply to rejoin the regular trail before Khingar is reached at 3200 metres. The trail climbs through a desert landscape then past meadows and streams to the interesting village of Jharkot at 3500 metres. A further climb brings you to Ranipowa, the accommodation area of Muktinath, at 3710 metres.

Muktinath is a pilgrimage centre for Buddhists and Hindus. You'll see Tibetan traders as well as sadhus from the far south of India. The shrines in a grove of trees include a Buddhist gompa and the Vishnu temple of Jiwala Mayi. An old temple nearby shelters a spring and natural gas jets which provide Muktinath's famous eternal flame. It's the earth-water-fire combination that accounts for Muktinath's great religious significance.

Saligrams

The black fossils of marine animals known as saligrams are found in the area north of Jomsom. These ammonite fossils date back to the Jurassic period over 100 million years ago and are dramatic proof that the Himalaya were indeed once under water. Saligrams have a religious significance in many Nepalese homes, but you will find many on sale in Pokhara or along the trail. Think twice before buying them here: they're often overpriced, and adding rocks to your backpack is never a good idea! ∎

From Muktinath you can retrace your steps to Pokhara, or simply to Jomsom and hope to catch a flight from there. It is possible to continue beyond Muktinath and cross the Thorung La pass to walk the rest of the Annapurna Circuit but this long walk is better made in the opposite direction.

ANNAPURNA CIRCUIT

Since it opened to foreign trekkers in 1977 the 3 week Annapurna Circuit has become the most popular trek in Nepal. It passes through country inhabited by a wide diversity of peoples, it offers spectacular mountain scenery and it goes to the north of the main Himalayan range on to the high and dry Tibetan Plateau. To many independent trekkers it also offers the considerable advantage of having accommodation available each night. Some trekkers even walk the circuit without a sleeping bag, although that is not wise since there is always the possibility of finding no beds available at some village or other.

The circuit is usually walked in a counterclockwise direction because of the difficulties of crossing the Thorung La pass.

Travelling clockwise the longer ascent and shorter descent from west to east is too much for many people to manage in 1 day. The Thorung La pass at 5416 metres is closed by snow from mid-December to mid-April and bad weather can move in at any time. Trekkers should be prepared to turn back due to the weather or if they suffer from altitude sickness. If you take porters over this pass you must make sure they are adequately equipped for the cold weather.

The circuit is usually started from Dumre, on the Kathmandu to Pokhara road. These days there are usually jeeps north from Dumre as far as Bhote Odar. Some treks now walk the circuit starting directly from Pokhara by walking from Begnas Bazaar, by Begnas Tal and Rupa Tal, through Karputar to Besi Sahar. Although this route avoids some tedious road travel it does cross country where you will have to camp since village inns are not (yet) available. Another variation at the beginning of the trek is to start from Gorkha and walk across to intersect the route up from Dumre, again avoiding that tedious initial stretch of road.

After you cross the Thorung La pass from Manang to Muktinath the final 7 days of the circuit trek are the same as the Jomsom trek from Pokhara, but in reverse.

Day 1: Kathmandu-Dumre-Besi Sahar
It's a long and somewhat tedious drive from Kathmandu to the turn-off at Dumre. Starting from Pokhara is much easier since Dumre is 137 km from Kathmandu but only 70 km from Pokhara and, more importantly, the first stretch out of Kathmandu is in very bad condition. From Dumre at 440 metres 4WDs run regularly to Bhote Odar, which is about 3 hours walk from Besi Sahar at 790 metres. If you can't get a 4WD up the road then an extra day must be added.

Day 2: Besi Sahar-Bahundanda
The trail drops, then climbs to Khudi at 790 metres. This is the first Gurung village that you reach (many of Nepal's Gurkha soldiers are Gurungs). From Khudi the trail offers fine views of Himalchuli and Peak 29 (Ngadi

Chuli) as it climbs to Bhulbhule at 825 metres; it then goes to Ngadi before reaching Lampata at 1135 metres and nearby Bahundanda at 1310 metres. Both Lampata and Bahundanda have hotels although Lampata probably offers a better choice.

Day 3: Bahundanda-Chyanje
From Bahundanda the trail drops steeply to Syange at 1070 metres. The trail crosses the Marsyandi River on a suspension bridge and then follows the river to the stone village of Jagat before climbing through forest to Chyanje at 1400 metres.

Day 4: Chyanje-Bagarchhap
The rocky trail follows the Marsyandi River steadily uphill to Tal at 1675 metres, the first village in the Manang district. The trail crosses a wide, flat valley then climbs a stone stairway to 1860 metres before dropping down to another stairway. The trail continues up and down to Dharapani at 1890 metres, which is marked by a stone entrance chorten typical of the Tibetan-influenced villages from here northwards. Bagarchhap at 2160 metres has flat-roofed stone houses of typical Tibetan design although the village is still in the transition zone before the dry highlands.

Day 5: Bagarchhap-Chame
The trail, often rough and rocky, climbs to Tyanja at 2360 metres and then continues through forest, but near the river, to Kopar at 2590 metres. Chame at 2685 metres is the headquarters of the Manang district and its buildings include a bank. There are fine views of Annapurna II as you approach Chame and two small hot springs by the town.

Day 6: Chame-Pisang
The trail runs through deep forest in a steep and narrow valley, crosses a river on a long bridge at 2910 metres and then another bridge at 3040 metres. Views include the first sight of the soaring Paungda Danda rock face. The trail continues to climb to Pisang which sprawls between 3200 and 3300 metres and has many hotels.

Day 7: Pisang-Manang

The walk is now through the drier upper part of the Manang district, cut off from the full effect of the monsoon by the Annapurna range. The people of this area herd yaks and raise crops for part of the year, but they also continue to enjoy special trading rights gained way back in 1784. Today they exploit these rights with shopping trips to Singapore and Hong Kong where they buy electronic goods and other modern equipment to resell in Nepal. Not surprisingly they are shrewd traders and hard bargainers.

From Pisang there are alternate trails north and south of the Marsyandi River which meet up again at Mungji. The southern route by Ongre with its airstrip at 3325 metres involves less climbing than the northern route via Ghyaru. The trail continues from Mungji past the picturesque but partially hidden village of Bryaga at 3475 metres to nearby Manang at 3535 metres where there are a number of hotels.

Day 8: Manang

It's a good idea to spend a day acclimatising in Manang before pushing on to the Thorung La pass. There are some fine day walks and magnificent views around the village. The Manangbhot people's legendary trading skills are seen at their keenest here – buy with caution!

Day 9: Manang-Phedi

From Manang it's an ascent of nearly 2000 metres to the Thorung La pass. The trail climbs steadily through Tengi, leaving the Marsyandi Valley and continuing along the Jarsang Khola Valley. The vegetation becomes steadily more sparse as you reach Ledar (or Lathar) at 4250 metres. Finally you descend to cross the river at 4310 metres and then climb up to Phedi at 4420 metres. There are hotels here and the range of accommodation is being expanded. At the height of the season as many as 100 trekkers a day may cross over the Thorung La pass and beds can be in short supply. Some trekkers find themselves suffering from altitude sickness symptoms at Phedi. If you find yourself in a similar condition you must retreat downhill; even the descent to Ledar can make a difference.

Day 10: Phedi-Muktinath

Phedi means 'foot of the hill' and that's where it is, at the foot of the 5415 metre Thorung La pass. The trail climbs steeply but is regularly used and easy to follow. The altitude and snow can be problems: when the pass is snow covered it is often impossible to cross it. It takes about 4 hours to climb up to the pass, marked by chortens and prayer flags. The effort is worthwhile as the view from the top is magnificent. From the pass you have a tough 1600 metre descent to Muktinath.

Days 11-17: Muktinath-Pokhara

The remaining 7 days of the trek simply follow the Pokhara, Jomsom, Muktinath route but in the opposite direction. Completing the Annapurna Circuit in 17 days allows for only one rest and acclimatisation day at Manang. It's very easy to slot a few additional days into the schedule.

ANNAPURNA SANCTUARY

The walk up to the Annapurna Base Camp is a classic walk right into the heart of the mountains. The walk ends at a point where you are virtually surrounded by soaring Himalayan peaks. At one time this trek was a real expedition into an uninhabited wilderness area, but now there are a string of temporary lodges set up during the trekking season. The return trip takes 10 to 14 days and the walk to the base camp can be tacked on as a sidetrip from the Jomsom or Annapurna Circuit treks.

There are several routes to the sanctuary, all meeting at Ghandrung. The diversion from the Jomsom and Annapurna Circuit treks is also made from Ghorapani to Ghandrung.

Day 1: Pokhara-Dhampus

The walk from Pokhara leaves the Jomsom and Annapurna Circuit routes at Phedi. From Phedi the trail climbs to Dhampus which

stretches for several km from 1580 to 1700 metres and has a number of widely spaced hotels. Theft is a real problem in Dhampus, so take care.

Day 2: Dhampus-Ghandrung
The trail climbs to Pothana, descends steeply through a forest to Bichok and finally emerges in the Modi Khola Valley. It continues to drop to Tolka and then the Gurung village of Landrung (or Landruk) at 1650 metres. The trail continues to descend to a suspension bridge at 1370 metres, then climbs steeply to join the trail from Birethanti and climb a long, long stone stairway to Ghandrung. There are many hotels in this large and confusing village; the biggest ones are near the top. From here Machhapuchhare really does begin to have a fishtail.

Day 3: Ghandrung-Chhomro
The trail climbs to a pass at 2220 metres, then descends steeply to the Khumnu Khola at 1770 metres before climbing up again to Khumnu (or Kimrong). The trail continues to climb higher before dropping down to Chhomro at 1950 metres, the last permanent settlement in the valley. There are a number of places to stay and to stock up on supplies.

Day 4: Chhomro-Khuldi
The trail drops down to the Chhomro Khola, then climbs to Khuldi at 2380 metres. There

are many leeches around here early and late in the trekking season.

Day 5: Khuldi-Hinko
The trail climbs through bamboo, then rhododendron, forests to Hinko at 3020 metres and on past the Machhapuchhare Base Camp (which isn't really a base camp since climbing the mountain is not permitted) to the Annapurna Base Camp. This area is called the Annapurna Sanctuary since it is totally surrounded by mountains.

Back to Pokhara
On the return trip you can simply retrace your steps, or you can divert from Ghandrung to Ghorapani to visit Poon Hill and follow the Annapurna Circuit or Jomsom route back to Pokhara.

POKHARA AREA VARIATIONS
The Ghorapani to Ghandrung walk is becoming increasing popular as a way of linking the Annapurna Sanctuary Trek with treks up the Kali Gandaki Valley. It's also used for shorter loop walks out of Pokhara (see the Around Pokhara section of the Pokhara chapter for details of these walks).

There's an alternative route between Pokhara and Tatopani, via Kushma and Beni, that comes out on the Bhairawa road south of Pokhara.

Other Treks

The Everest Base Camp Trek in the east, the Langtang and Helambu treks to the north of Kathmandu and the three Pokhara area treks in central Nepal between them are used by the vast majority of all trekkers. There are other alternatives taking you to areas still relatively unvisited.

KANCHENJUNGA BASE CAMP
The trekking route up to the Kanchenjunga Base Camp in the extreme north-eastern corner of the country has recently been opened to trekkers, but you have to go with

a recognised agency. The starting point can be Ilam by road, or Tumlingtar or Taplejung by air.

MAKALU BASE CAMP

It's a long but fine trek from Hile or Tumlingtar up the Arun River to the Makalu Base Camp in eastern Nepal.

SOLU KHUMBU TO DHANKUTA

As an alternative to flying back to Kathmandu from Lukla, or walking back to Jiri, the Everest Base Camp Trek can be extended by walking for 11 days south to Hile. From here you can travel by road through Dhankuta and Dharan to Biratnagar from where there are buses and flights to Kathmandu.

DOLPO

Trekking to the Dolpo region has only been permitted since mid-1989. The region lies to the west of the Kali Gandaki Valley. Permits are still not easy to get and from Pokhara it's a tough 14 day trek to Phaksundo Lake and beyond. You can only trek there with a recognised agency.

RARA LAKE

The 8 day round trip trek from Jumla to the Rara Lake and back still gets less than 50 trekkers a year. Trekking here requires real planning since flights are difficult to get on, porters are hard to find and little food is available.

Rafting & Mountain Biking

At times Nepal and the Himalaya seem to be one big adventure playground for Western visitors. First it was mountaineering, then trekking, then chasing wildlife in the Royal Chitwan National Park, then in the late '70s rafting became the rage. Many people now combine a trek with a rafting trip and a wildlife expedition in the Chitwan. Recently, mountain biking has become a craze.

Surprisingly, there are few skiing possibilities in Nepal – the snowline is too high and the mountains too steep. Of course some people do bring their skis, and there have been some amazing feats, including ski descents of 8000 metre mountains. It helps if you've got a kamikaze streak and a parachute strapped to your back. Small numbers of hang-gliders have also tried the Himalayan thermals.

Rafting

Nepal has plenty of dramatic mountain rivers so it's hardly surprising that rafting has become so popular. The rafting trips mainly take place on the Sun Kosi, the Trisuli and the Kali Gandaki rivers although trips to more remote locales have also been introduced. *Adventure Travel Magazine* rated the Sun Kosi as one of the world's top 10 rafting rivers. There are numerous rafting companies in Kathmandu and rafting down the Trisuli and Narayani to the Royal Chitwan National Park is particularly popular. Most Chitwan expedition organisers offer you the option of getting to the national park by road or river.

ALL ABOUT RAFTING
Rafting means floating down Nepal's swift flowing rivers in inflatable rafts. The trips can vary enormously: from short and exhilarating white-water runs, to gentler trips lasting a number of days, all the way to long expeditions in remote parts of the country.

The Rafting Seasons
Rafting is highly dependent on the seasons and the best times are very similar to those for trekking. The monsoon is the worst time to hit the walking trails and also the worst time for rafting. Conditions are damp and miserable and the rivers are often simply too high. In October when the monsoon ends, however, conditions are near perfect. The weather is superb, the scenery is green and lush and the rivers are still running high from the monsoon runoff.

As with trekking, the winter months are OK for enthusiasts, but the weather can be uncomfortably cold in December and January. Spring brings ideal rafting conditions as the weather is warmer and the melting snow means fast-flowing waters. By April the rivers are lower and rafting trips can involve lots of paddling, which is uncomfortably hot work by this time.

Preparations
So long as you don't mind getting wet you're OK for a rafting trip. No prior experience is necessary and the rafting companies supply all the necessary equipment.

Rafting Permits
The government now issues rafting permits much like trekking permits. They cost US$5 and are issued by the Ministry of Tourism at Tripureshwar, unlike trekking permits which are issued by the immigration office.

Operators
As with trekking, there are a wide variety of operators and standards. Typical rafting trips cost from US$25 to US$75 per day. Every trip will have an experienced leader, but at one extreme you paddle yourself and fix the food; at the other there will be Nepalese paddlers and cooks and all you have to do is sit back and enjoy yourself. The trips generally take between 3 and 9 days.

As always, it is important to establish

clearly what you will get for your money — before you part with it. The rafting business is very competitive, but in addition to slick sales pitches there can also be important differences. Check exactly what you will be supplied, what kind of land transport will be used, and the itinerary and distance to be covered.

A disgruntled rafter pointed out some of the potential problems:

Rafting trips can cost as little as US$15 a day although this involves travelling by local bus to the starting point. I have been white-water rafting in '84, '86 and '89 and feel qualified to talk about the major changes. There were once just a few booking agents and companies where now there are maybe 50 booking agents who basically know nothing about the trips and tell you all sorts of shit which is usually wrong.

I knew where the major rapids were and nearly all companies start 2-day trips from *below* the major rapids; excuses vary from 'government regulations' to 'rivers being too low'. They then set up camps too far apart and most of the day is spent paddling to get to camp. We arrived at 5 pm, another group at 6 pm, in December when it is very cold and there's a real danger of hypothermia. The only reason for these long days is for the guides to have an early finish on the last day and leave back for Kathmandu around 1 pm.

No bookings are made on local buses: it's a case of rolling up at the bus station and hoping to buy tickets. On cheaper trips the gear is probably hand-me-down from major companies and comes complete with air leaks. Gear from one 3 day trip was actually taken away back upriver to meet the next trip, leaving eight large Westerners in a smaller boat, with tiny jackets and not enough paddles. Due to this cost cutting a lot of the fun is now missing.

Stephen Currie, Australia

The message is obvious — if you go on a low-price rafting trip you should make thorough inquiries beforehand about standards. Satisfied customers are the best advertisement a company can have.

THE RIVERS

The Trisuli, Sun Kosi and Kali Gandaki are the rivers most used for rafting trips and they provide a range of possibilities to suit most rafters. As rafting continues to grow in popularity more rivers will be tried. Already some trips are being run on the Tamur and Arun rivers in eastern Nepal, the Marsyandi River in central Nepal and the Karnali and Bheri rivers in the far west.

Trisuli River

Probably the most popular rafting river in Nepal, the Trisuli River starts north-west of Kathmandu and flows south and then south-west to Mugling, on the Kathmandu to Pokhara road, where it joins the eastward flowing Marsyandi River. It then flows south into the Terai as the Narayani River, meeting the mighty Kali Gandaki River before it flows through the Royal Chitwan National Park. Many people combine a rafting trip with a visit to Chitwan, and a number of packages that combine both are available.

The Trisuli River is a relatively easy, gentle one – good for inexperienced rafters. Expeditions typically take 3 to 7 days, although day trips are also possible. Flexibility in the length of trips is possible because the highway follows the river reasonably closely for much of its length, so you can start or finish a trip at a number of points. The 3 day trip to the Chitwan is very popular, but longer Trisuli River trips involve more exciting waters in the narrower, steeper reaches of the river to the north.

The Trisuli River trips usually start along the Kathmandu to Pokhara road between Naubise and Mugling. Narayanghat is the usual end point (especially for those going on to Chitwan). Along the way the river flows through areas of Gurung and Magar population.

Sun Kosi

If the Trisuli River appeals to rafters looking for an easy float then the Sun Kosi is the river for exciting, heart stopping white-water adventures. The Sun Kosi flows southward from the Himalaya then turns west and flows right across Nepal before finally turning sharply south again and crossing the Terai near Dharan and Biratnagar and flowing into India.

The Sun Kosi and the rivers which join into it flow down from some of the highest mountains of the Himalaya. Rafting trips go through a variety of country, including wide valleys and deep gorges, and past small villages where dugout canoes are used as transport across the river. From the mountainous pine forests in the high country you eventually emerge in the green and fertile lowlands of the Terai.

The Sun Kosi is not as accessible as the Trisuli River so there is not so much flexibility in the length of trips you can make. Day trips are done on the section of the river north of Dolalghat (55 km north-west of Kathmandu on the road to the Chinese border). After Dolalghat you're committed for 8 to 10 days until you get to Chatra, near Dharan Bazaar on the Terai.

The long trips usually consist of a couple of days of easy paddling, followed by a half-dozen days of white-water adventure as more and more southward flowing rivers join the westward flowing Sun Kosi. Finally there are a couple more days of easy floating across the Terai before reaching Chatra, about 200 km downstream from the starting point.

Kali Gandaki River

The Kali Gandaki River, flowing south between the Annapurnas and Dhaulagiri and then turning west to meet the Narayani just north of Narayanghat, is not used as much as the Trisuli River and Sun Kosi.

Other Rivers

Trips are also made on the Karnali and Bheri rivers in the west of the country, starting on the Bheri River between Nepalganj and Surkhet and visiting the Royal Bardia National Park (see the Terai chapter). In the east of Nepal runs are also made on the Tamur and Arun rivers.

Mountain Biking

Mountain bikes started to appear in Nepal in the mid-80s, and by the end of the '80s in the Kathmandu Valley they were nearly as ubiquitous as the old Chinese and Indian single-speeders. Most of the mountain bikes are cheaper Taiwanese bikes but for charging about the hills around Kathmandu they're just fine. Of course you pay more for having 12 or more speeds under your control: a straightforward bike rents for Rs 15 to Rs 20 a day, but a mountain bike costs from Rs 75 to Rs 100.

You can make your own tours around the valley or head out with a specialist operator like Himalayan Mountain Bikes (tel 4-

13632, 4-18733) in the Kathmandu Guest House compound, but for real enthusiasts, the sky is the limit. For a while the ride over the Himalaya from Lhasa in Tibet to Kathmandu was *the* ride for mountain bikers who had done it all.

VALLEY TRIPS

There are plenty of superb mountain biking opportunities around the Kathmandu Valley or close to it. See the Around the Valley chapter for numerous possibilities. You can ride up to Nagarkot via Bhaktapur and come back down on a dirt trail through Sankhu. A longer ride takes you out of the valley to Dhulikhel and on to Namobuddha. Any of the valley's remote temples are an easy day trip.

Himalayan Mountain Bikes offers a 1 day valley trip for US$20, a 2 day trip to Nagarkot for US$80 or a 3 day trip to Dhulikhel and Namobuddha for US$130. Longer trips go right round the valley rim.

FURTHER AFIELD

Himalayan Mountain Bikes also organises mountain bike trips to other areas of Nepal. A 12 day expedition to the Royal Chitwan National Park and Pokhara with the usual Chitwan elephant safaris and a short trek included will cost US$1140. They also have a trip from Pokhara down into the Terai to the Royal Bardia National Park in the west of Nepal. Rabid enthusiasts have even attempted some trekking routes by mountain bike; reportedly the Langtang trek is 70% rideable (the rest of the time you carry your bike!).

Glossary

Beware of the different methods of transliterating Nepali and the other languages spoken in Nepal. There are many and varied ways of spelling Nepali words. In particular the letter 'b' and letter 'v' are often interchanged. The god Bhairab becomes Bhairav or the thunderbolt symbol changes from Vajra to Bajra.

Adi Buddha – the original self-generated Buddha of Tantric Buddhism who created the Dhyani Buddhas.

Aditya – ancient Vedic sun god.

Agni – ancient Vedic god of the hearth and fire. He rides a chariot drawn by parrots and his four arms hold flames, a ball of fire, a trident and a rosary.

Agnipura – Buddhist symbol for fire.

Aksobhya – the Dhyani Buddha of the east; his vehicle is an elephant and he is often seen with one hand touching the ground in the gesture known as subduing Mara.

Amitabha – the Dhyani Buddha of the west, Amitabha's animal is the peacock.

Amoghasiddhi – the Dhyani Buddha of the north, his consort is Green Tara and in Nepalese stupas he sits under a seven-hooded snake canopy.

Ananda – the Buddha's chief disciple

Ananta – the cosmic serpent upon which Vishnu reclines.

Annapurna – the goddess of abundance and an incarnation of Mahadevi.

Arak – a fermented drink made from potatoes or grain.

Ashoka – Indian Buddhist emperor who spread the religion throughout the subcontinent.

Ashta Matrikas – the eight mother goddesses.

Asla – river trout.

Avalokitesvara

Asuras – demons ruled by Rawana, King of Lanka. The name can be a suffix as in Mahishasura.

Avalokitesvara – as Gautama Buddha is the Buddha of our era, so is Avalokitesvara the Bodhisattva of our era. In Nepal he has become a Hindu/Buddhist god of mercy whose incarnation is Machhendranath or Manjushri.

Avatar – an incarnation of a deity living on earth.

Bahal – a Buddhist monastery, usually two storeys high and built around a courtyard. There are a great number of bahals in the Kathmandu Valley towns but few of them continue to function as monasteries. Many are used as schools.

Bahil – a simpler version of a bahal.

Bakba – Tibetan clay mask.

Bajra – see vajra or dorje.

Balarama – Krishna's brother.

Balkumari – one of Bhairab's consorts.

Bazaar – market area; a market town is called a bazaar or bazar.

Bell – Tantric female symbol equivalent to the male thunderbolt or dorje. The bell handle usually looks like one end of a dorje. See ghanta.

Bel Tree – it is a Newari custom to 'marry' young girls to a bel tree so that they can never be widowed.

Betel – mildly intoxicant concoction of areca nut and lime which is wrapped in betel leaf and chewed. The red splashes you see on the ground throughout south Asia are spat out by betel chewers. Regular betel chewing leads to dark-red stained teeth.

Bhairab – the 'terrific' or fearsome Tantric form of Shiva in Nepal. Bhairab has 64 manifestations.

Bhadrakali – a Tantric goddess who is also a consort of Bhairab.

Bhagavadgita – Krishna's lessons to Arjuna, part of the *Mahabharata*.

Bhati – term for a teashop in the west of Nepal.

Bhimsen – a deity noted for his strength and bravery.

Bhot – high altitude desert valleys north of the Himalaya bordering Tibet. In Nepal Tibetans are known as Bhots.

Bhote – Nepali for Tibet.

Bodhi or Bo Tree – pipal tree under which the Buddha was sitting when he attained enlightenment.

Bodhisattva – a near-Buddha who renounces the opportunity to attain nirvana in order to aid humankind.

Bon – the animist religion of Tibet prior to Buddhism.

Bon-po – follower of the Bon religion.

Brahmins – the highest Hindu caste, said to originate from Brahma's head. Priests are drawn from this caste although Brahmins may have many other occupations.

Caste – Nepalese Hindus have four castes which originate from, in descending order, Brahma's head, arms, thighs and feet.

Chaitya – small stupa which usually contains a mantra rather than a Buddhist relic.

Chakra – Vishnu's disc-like weapon, one of the four symbols he holds.

Chang – Tibetan rice beer.

Chappati – unleavened Indian bread.

Chaturmukha – Shiva lingam with four images of the god's face.

Chautara – stone platforms around trees which serve as shady places for porters to rest their dokos.

Chenrezig – Tibetan name for Avalokitesvara.

Chhetris – the second caste of Nepalese Hindus. It is the prince and warrior caste to which the Ranas and the Shah kings belonged. They are said to originate from Brahma's arms.

Chirag – ceremonial oil lamp.

Chomolongma – 'Mother Goddess of the World', the Tibetan name for Mt Everest.

Chortens – Tibetan Buddhist stupas.

Chowk – a courtyard or marketplace such as the Kumari Chowk (courtyard of the living goddess' home) or Indra Chowk (the old market area of Kathmandu).

Chuba – long woollen Sherpa coat.

Chura – beaten rice.

Crore – 10 million.

Crow – messenger of Yama, the god of death.

Curd – yoghurt.

Dalai Lama – incarnation of a Bodhisattva who is the spiritual leader of Tibetan Buddhists.

Damais – a caste of tailors who perform music at weddings.

Dattatraya – deity who is thought of as an incarnation of Vishnu, Shiva's teacher or the Buddha's cousin.

Deval – temple in Nepali.

Devanagari – Sanskrit Nepali script.

Devi – the short form of Mahadevi, the shakti to Shiva.

Dhal – the lentil soup that is the main form of protein in the Nepalese diet.

Dhami – priest claiming occult powers, a sorcerer.

Dharma – Buddhist teachings.

Dharamsala – rest house for pilgrims.

Dhoka – door or gate.

Dhwaja – metal ribbon streaming out from the roof of a temple and acting as a pathway for the gods.

Dhyana – meditation.

Dhyani Buddhas – the original Adi Buddha created five Dhyani Buddhas who in turn create the universe of each human era. Amitabha is the Dhyani Buddha of our era. See Swayambhunath in the Kathmandu Valley chapter for more information.

Dighur – Thakali cooperative economic system where members of a group pool their money to support one person's plans.

Doko – basket carried by porters.

Dorje – Tibetan word for the 'thunderbolt' symbol of Buddhist power. See also vajra.

Durbar – palace. Each of the Kathmandu Valley towns has a palace in front of which is the Durbar Square.

Durga – fearsome manifestation of Parvati, Shiva's consort.

Dwarapala – door guardian figure.

Dyochhen – a form of temple enshrining Tantric deities.

Dzopkyo – male cross between a yak and a cow.

Dzum – female offspring of a yak and a cow.

Dzu-tch – large yeti that eats cattle.

Earthquakes – despite the fact that the Himalaya are still rising earthquakes are rare, although disastrous tremors destroyed many buildings in the Kathmandu Valley in 1833 and 1934. In 1989 a serious earthquake caused major losses of life and property in the east of the country.

Ek – Nepalese number one, a symbol of the unity of all life.

Ekamukha – Shiva lingam with one image of the god's face.

Everest – the world's highest mountain was named after George Everest, the Surveyor General of India.

Flag – Nepal's curious double triangle flag is the only one of its type in the world.

Freaks – '60s term from the overland era for the young Westerners who wandered the East and could be found congregating in Bali, Kabul, Goa and Kathmandu.

Gaines – beggar musicians.

Gajur – bell-shaped top to a bahal.

Ganas – Shiva's 'companions'.

Ganesh – Shiva and Parvati's son, instantly recognisable by his elephant head.

Ganga – goddess of the River Ganges.

Ganja – hashish.

Garuda – the man-bird vehicle of Vishnu. A statue of the Garuda often kneels before Vishnu temples.

Gautama Buddha – the Buddha of our era.

Gelugpa – yellow-hat sect of Tibetan Buddhism. This is the reformed sect headed by the Dalai Lama.

Ghada – club-like weapon of Vishnu.

Ghanta – Tantric bell which is the female equivalent of the dorje.

Ghat – steps beside a river. A 'burning ghat' is used for cremations.

Ghee – clarified butter.

Gompa – Tibetan Buddhist monastery.

Gopis – cowherd girls. Krishna had a lot of fun with his gopis.

Gorakhnath – 11th century yogi now said to be an incarnation of Shiva.

Gurkha – Nepalese mercenaries who have long

formed a part of the British army. The name comes from the region of Gorkha.

Gurkhali – British army name for the Nepali language.

Gurr – traditional Sherpa potato dish.

Gurungs – western hill people, predominantly from around Gorkha and Pokhara.

Guthi – Newari community group offering mutual support to its members.

Hanuman – monkey god.

Harisiddhi – a fearsome Tantric goddess.

Harmika – eyes on a stupa which face the four cardinal directions or the 13 steps of a stupa steeple, symbolising the 13 stages to enlightenment.

Hashish – dried marijuana plant resin.

Hiti – water conduit or tank with water spouts.

Hookah – water pipe for smoking.

Impeyan – pheasant which is Nepal's national bird.

Incarnation – a particular life form; in the case of mortals, determined by karma. Vishnu has 10 different incarnations.

Indra – king of the Vedic gods, god of rain.

Jagannath – Krishna as 'Lord of the World'.

Jambhala – god of wealth; look for his money bag and his attendant mongoose.

Jamuna – goddess of the River Jamuna.

Janai – sacred thread which high caste Hindu men wear looped over their left shoulder and replace once each year.

Jatra – festival, as in Indra Jatra.

Jaya Varahi – Vishnu's consort when the god takes on his boar incarnation.

Jhankri – sorcerer.

Jogini – mystical goddesses, counterparts to the 64 manifestations of Bhairab.

Jukha – Nepali word for leech.

Kala – see Mara.

Kalakuta – the poison which Shiva swallowed when he was in the form of Nilakantha.

Kalasa – a pot, or a pot-shaped top to a temple.

Kali – most terrifying manifestation of Parvati.

Kali Gandaki River – major river which flows between the Annapurnas and Dhaulagiri.

Kalki – Vishnu's 10th, and as yet unseen, incarnation when he will come riding a white horse and wielding a sword to destroy the world.

Kalpa – a day in the age of Brahma.

Kam Dev – Shiva's 'companion'.

Karkotak – chief naga of the Kathmandu Valley.

Karma – Buddhist and Hindu law of cause and effect which continues from one life to another.

Kartikiya – god of war and son of Shiva, his animal is the cock or peacock and he carries a variety of weapons. Also known as Skanda or Kumara.

Kata – the Tibetan prayer shawl which should be presented to an important Buddhist personage when introduced.

Kaukala – a form of Shiva in his fearsome aspect, he carries a trident with the skeleton of Vishnu's gatekeeper impaled upon it: a result of banning Shiva from Vishnu's palace!

Khas – Hindu hill people.

Khas-khura – language of the Khas, ie Nepali.

Khola – stream or tributary.

Khukri – traditional curved knife of the Nepalese.

Khukri

Kinkinimali – temple wind bells.

Kosi – river.

Krishna – the fun-loving eighth incarnation of Vishnu.

Kshatriyas – Indian equivalent of the Chhetri caste.

Kshepu – snake-eating figure often seen on toranas.

Kubera – see Jambhala.

Kundalini – female energy principle.

Kumara – see Kartikiya.

Kumari – the living goddess, a peaceful incarnation of Kali.

Kunda – water tank fed by springs.

La – mountain pass.

Lakh – 100,000.

Lakshmi – goddess of prosperity and Vishnu's consort.

Laliguras – Nepalese word for rhododendron, the national flower.

Lama – Tibetan Buddhist monk or priest.

Leeches – blood-sucking creatures that plague walkers during the monsoon.

Lingam – phallic symbol of Shiva's creative powers.

Locana – consort of the Dhyani Buddha, Aksobhya.

Lokesvara – Lord of the World, an aspect of Avalokitesvara but often mingled with the Hindu gods in Nepal. He appears as Nilakantha, an aspect of Shiva, and as Natesvara, much like Natraj, the dancing Shiva whose cosmic dance created the world.

Machhendranath – patron god of the Kathmandu Valley and an incarnation of Avalokitesvara or Lokesvara.

Mahabharata – one of the major Hindu epics.

Mahadeva (Mahadeo) – another name for Shiva; *maha*translates as 'great', *deva* as 'god'.

Mahadevi – great goddess, sometimes known simply as Devi, the shakti to Shiva.

Mahakala – Great Black One, protector of the Mandala and a Tantric equivalent of Shiva.

Maharishi – means great teacher.

Mahayana – large-vehicle Buddhism, prevalent through East Asia, Tibet and Nepal.

Mahayuga – each day of Brahma (see Kalpa) is divided into 1000 Mahayugas or Great Ages.

Mahishasura – buffalo demon killed by Durga.

Mahseer – game fish of the Terai rivers.

Maitreya – a Buddha who will come in a future era.

Makara – mythical water monster, often appears as a water spout on buildings.

Mali – Newari gardener caste.

Malla – royal dynasty of the Kathmandu Valley which was responsible for most of the important temples and palaces of the valley towns.

Mandala – geometrical and astrological representation of the world.

Mandap – roofless Tantric shrine.

Mandir – Nepali word for temple.

Manjushri – god who cut open the Chobar Gorge so that the Kathmandu Lake could become the Kathmandu Valley.

Mani Stone – stone carved with the Tibetan Buddhist chant *Om mani padme hum*.

Mani Rimdu – Tibetan dance drama.

Mani Wall – wall built of mani stones; walk by one with the wall on your right.

Mantra – prayer formula or chant.

Mara – Buddhist god of death, has three eyes and holds the wheel of life.

Math – Hindu priest's house.

Mela – a country fair.

Mirror – usually found on temples to help devotees place their tikas.

Mithuna – couple, usually refers to depiction of gods engaged in intercourse in erotic art. Yab-yum is the Tibetan equivalent of this Sanskrit term.

Moksha – spiritual release, Hindu equivalent of nirvana.

Momo – Tibetan dim sum.

Monsoon – wet season from mid-June to late-September when there is rainfall virtually every day; there is also a very short winter monsoon, lasting a day or two, usually in late January.

Mt Kailash – Shiva's home in the eastern Himalaya in Tibet.

Mukha Lingam – lingam with four faces.

Mudra – symbolic hand gesture.

Munja – see Janai.

Naga – serpent deity. There are eight of them and they have control over water. Nagas are often seen over the entrance to a house in order to keep evil spirits away.

Nagini – female naga.

Nagpura – Buddhist symbol for water.

Nak – female yak.

Namaste – Nepalese greeting.

Names – Sherpa boys are named after the day of the week they were born; Monday – Dawa, Tuesday – Mingma, Wednesday – Lakpa, Thursday – Phurbu, Friday – Pasang, Saturday – Pemba, Sunday – Nyima.

Nandi – the bull, vehicle of Shiva.

Narayan – Vishnu as the sleeping figure on the cosmic ocean. From his navel Brahma appears and goes on to create the universe. Narayan is Vishnu's most important appearance in Nepal but it is simply another name for Vishnu, not another incarnation.

Narsingha (Narsimha) – man-lion incarnation of Vishnu.

Newaris – people of the Kathmandu Valley.

Nilakantha – blue-throated form of Shiva, a result of swallowing poison that would have destroyed the world.

Nirvana – final escape from the cycles of existence.

Nriteshwar – god of dance.

Nyingmapa – one of the three red-hat sects of Tibetan Buddhism.

Om Mani Padme Hum – sacred Buddhist mantra which translates as 'hail to the jewel in the lotus'.

Oriflammes – prayer flags; the wind carries off the prayers written on them.

Padma – lotus flower.

Padmapani – literally 'lotus in hand'; a manifestation of Avalokitesvara as he appears in many Nepalese viharas, holding a tall lotus stalk.

Padmasambhava – Bodhisattva who founded Nyingma-pa Buddhist sect.

Pagoda – multistoreyed Nepalese temple. This style was later exported from Nepal to China and Japan.

Panchayat – the non-party parliament of Nepal until 1990.

Panduravasini – consort of the Dhyani Buddha Amitabha.

Parvati – Shiva's consort.

Pashmina – goat's wool blanket or shawl.

Pashupati – Shiva as Lord of the Animals.

Patakas – see dhwaja.

Path (Pati) – small raised platform to shelter travellers.

Patuka – waistcoat to carry things.

Pith – open shrine for a Tantric goddess.

Prajna – female counterparts of male Buddhist deities.

Pokhari – large water tank.

Porters – hill people who carry goods along the trails.

Prajapati – Vedic creative power, forerunner of Brahma.

Prajnaparamita – consort of the Dhyani Buddhas Vairocana and Aksobhya.

Prasad – food offering.

Prayer Flags – like prayer wheels, prayer flags each carry a sacred mantra and, as spinning the wheel says the prayer, so does fluttering the flag.

Prayer Wheels – cylindrical wheel inscribed with a Buddhist prayer or mantra. Spinning the wheel says the prayer. There are even water-driven prayer wheels.

Prayer wheel

Prithvi – Vedic earth goddess.
Puja (Pooja) – religious offering or prayer.
Puranas – Hindu holy books of around 400 BC which heralded the shift from the Vedic gods to the Hindu trinity of Brahma, Vishnu and Shiva.
Puri – town.

Radha – Krishna's wife.
Rajpath – road or highway, literally 'king's road'.
Rakshi – rice spirit.
Rama – Vishnu's seventh incarnation and hero of the *Ramayana*.
Ramayana – Hindu epic which recounts the adventures of Rama, Sita, Hanuman and the demon king Rawana.
Rana – hereditary prime ministers who ruled Nepal from 1841 to 1951.
Rath – the temple chariot in which the idol is conveyed in processions.
Ratnasambhava – Dhyani Buddha of the south.
Rawana (Ravana) – the demon king of Lanka in the *Ramayana*.
Refugees – Nepal has many Tibetan refugees who fled the Chinese invasion of their land.
Reincarnate Lama – lama who is believed to be the reincarnated form of a predecessor.
Rhododendron – the national flower. In March and April above 2000 metres, rhododendrons flower as huge and colourful trees.
Rikhi Doro – golden thread worn around the waist by Shiva devotees.

Rimpoche – abbot of a gompa.
Ropeway – since 1929 a ropeway has been used to transport goods from Hetauda in the Terai to the Kathmandu Valley.
Rudra – Vedic god of lightning, an early version of Shiva.

Sadhus – wandering Hindu holy men, generally Shaivites who have given up everything to follow the trail to religious salvation. Many sadhus come from India to visit Pashupatinath, the great Shiva temple of Nepal
Sagarmatha – Nepalese name for Mt Everest.
Sakyamuni – another name for Gautama Buddha.
Sal – tree of the lower Himalayan foothills.
Saligrams – black ammonite fossils of Jurassic Period sea creatures, proof that the Himalaya was once under water.
Sankha – conch shell symbol of Vishnu.
Sanyasin – religious ascetic who has cut all ties with normal society.
Saranghi – small violin played by the Gaines.
Saraswati – goddess of learning and the creative arts. She can often be identified by the flute-like instrument which she plays called a *vina*. Saraswati is Brahma's consort.
Satai – pilgrim's house.
Shaivites – followers of Shiva, they cover their faces in ashes, paint three horizontal lines on their forehead and carry a begging bowl and Shiva's symbolic trident.
Shakti – dynamic female element in male-female relationships, a goddess.
Shantipura – Buddhist symbol for the sky.
Sherpas – literally 'people from the east', the Sherpas are Buddhist hill people famed for their stalwart work with mountaineering expeditions. With a small 's' sherpa means trek leader.
Sherpanis – female Sherpas.
Sheshnag – some believe that this snake, not Ananta, is the one which Vishnu reclines on.
Shikhara – Indian-style temple with tall corncob-like spire.
Shitala Mai – ogress who became a protector of children.
Shiva – most powerful Hindu god, the creator and destroyer.
Shivaratri – birthday of Shiva.
Simhanada – a form of Avalokitesvara who rides a lion.
Sindur – red dust and mustard oil mixture used for offerings.
Sirdar – leader/organiser of a trekking party.
Sita – Rama's wife in the *Ramayana*.
Skanda – see Kartikiya.
Solu Khumbu – Everest region of eastern Nepal where the majority of the Sherpas live.
Sonam – the karma acquired through successive incarnations.

STOL – Short Take-Off and Landing aircraft used on mountain airstrips.

Stupa – hemispherical Buddhist religious structure; always walk around stupas clockwise.

Sudras – the lowest Nepalese caste, they originate from Brahma's feet.

Sundhara – fountain with golden spout.

Surya – see Aditya.

Suttee (sati) – practice of throwing widows on their husband's funeral pyre.

Tabla – hand drum.

Tahr – wild mountain goat.

Taleju Bhawani – Nepalese goddess, an aspect of Mahadevi and the family deity of the Malla kings of the Kathmandu Valley. There is a Taleju Temple in the old royal palaces of Kathmandu, Patan and Bhaktapur.

Tantric Buddhism – form of Buddhism which evolved in Tibet during the 10th to 15th centuries.

Tara – as White Tara she is the consort of the Dhyani Buddha Vairocana, as Green Tara she is associated with Amoghasiddhi. Either way she is a very popular figure in the Buddhist pantheon and may also be adopted by the Hindus as Shiva's wife in her peaceful mood.

Tempos – small Indian three-wheeled transports commonly used in Kathmandu – similar to a Thai *samlor*.

Terai – flat land south of the Himalaya in Nepal.

Thakalis – people of the Kali Gandaki Valley who specialise in running hotels.

Thangka – rectangular Tibetan paintings on cotton, usually of mandalas or Tantric deities.

Third Eye – symbolic eye on Buddha figures, used to indicate the Buddha's clairvoyant powers.

Tika – red sandalwood paste spot marked on the forehead, particularly for religious occasions.

Thukba – thick Tibetan soup.

Tole – street or quarter of a town, sometimes used to refer to a square such as Kel Tole in Kathmandu or Tachupal Tole in Bhaktapur.

Topi – traditional Nepalese cap.

Torana – portico above temple doors which can indicate the god to whom the temple is dedicated.

Tribhuvan – king who ended the Rana period and Nepal's long seclusion in 1951.

Trident – see trisul.

Trisul – trident weapon symbol of Shiva.

Tsampa – barley-flour porridge of the Sherpas.

Tulku – Tibetan Buddhist reincarnation of a great lama.

Tulsi – sacred basil plant.

Tunal – carved temple strut.

Tympanum – crest beneath the triangular peak of a roof.

Uma – one of the peaceful incarnations of Shiva's consort Parvati.

Uma Maheshwar – Shiva and Parvati in a pose where Shiva sits cross-legged and Parvati sits on his thigh and leans against him.

Upanishads – ancient Vedic scripts, the last part of the Vedas.

Urna – the bump on the forehead of a Buddha or Bodhisattva.

Usha – Vedic goddess of the dawn.

Vahana – a god's animal mount or vehicle.

Vairocana – the central Dhyani Buddha and the 'embodiment of perfection'.

Vaisya – caste of merchants and farmers, they originate from Brahma's thighs.

Vaishnavites – followers of Vishnu.

Vajra – Nepali word for thunderbolt. See dorje.

Vajra Jogini – a Tantric goddess, shakti to a Bhairab.

Vajrapani – literally 'thunderbolt in hand', a manifestation of Avalokitesvara holding a thunderbolt.

Vajrayana – literally 'vehicle of the thunderbolts', it's a variety of Buddhism involving magical spells.

Valley – usually the Kathmandu Valley, at one time virtually synonymous with Nepal.

Vamana – see Vikrantha.

Varahi – Vishnu's boar incarnation.

Varuna – ancient Vedic god of wisdom and morality.

Vasudhara – wife of Jambhala the god of wealth, she rides a chariot drawn by a pig!

Vasupura – Buddhist symbol for the earth.

Vayapura – Buddhist symbol for the air.

Vedas – ancient spiritual texts, the orthodox Hindu scriptures.

Vedic Gods – ancient Hindu gods of the Vedas.

Vehicle – the animal which a Hindu god is associated with. Shiva's vehicle is a bull, Ganesh's is a mouse while Vishnu's is the man-bird Garuda.

Vihara – Buddhist religious buildings and pilgrim accommodation.

Vikrantha – Vishnu's fifth incarnation when he appeared as a dwarf, then grew so large that he could cross the universe in three strides.

Vishnu – the preserver, one of the three major Hindu gods.

Vishnu Chaturmurti – Vishnu with four faces of a lion, a boar, a human and a demon.

Wheel of Life – held by Mara, the god of death, the concentric circles of the Wheel of Life show a stage of existence, those who are chained to the cycles of existence, the forces which keep the wheel turning or the desires which keep humankind chained to the cycle.

Yab-yum – Tantric erotica.

Yak – main beast of burden and form of cattle above 3000 metres.

Yakshas – attendant deities.

Yama – Vedic god of death, son of Aditya or Surya.

Yeti – the abominable snowman.
Yi-dam – protective deities of the Buddhas, they have a fierce form in contrast to the peacefulness of the Buddhas.
Yoni – female sexual symbol, equivalent of a lingam.
Yuga – each Mahayuga is divided into four Yugas.

Zamindar – absentee landlord.
Zhum – variant spelling of dzum, female offspring of a yak and a cow.

Index

MAPS

THANKS

Many thanks to the following people:

Anil Agarwal (Nep), Ian Arnold (UK), Arjun Bahaduz Aryal (Nep), Keshaba Nanda Baidya (Aus), D Bailey (Aus), Colin Barnes (Aus), Dr Buddha Basnyat (Nep), Susan Bellass (UK), Jim Bird (Can), Sven Bjorge (Nor), Joyce Brown (PNG), J & G Brown (Aus), Romano & Caryl Cassar (?), Julie Charles (UK), Matthew Cloudsdale (Aus), Rosamund Collins (UK), Jonathan Conroy (UK), James Coury (?), Kauyo Crawford (Can), Charles Crouch (Aus), A L Crozier (NZ), Stephen Currie (Aus), Louise De Raeve (Aus), Leonard Di Tono (USA), Joe Doherty (Ire), Chris Doran (USA), Ciaran Downey (Ire), Brian Eales (Aus), Ursulawev Eiselin-Ladek (Swi), Alan Erlich (Thai), C Fontana (It), Mike Freeman (UK), Courtney Gaertner (USA), Monica Gallagher (Can), John Garlick (NZ), Arthur Glickman (USA), John Glynn (Aus), Mike Guest (Can), Som Gurung (Nep), Martin Hammond (USA), Joseph Heathcote (Aus), Simon Hicks (Pak), Francis Wall Higgins (Nep), Patrick Holden (UK), Pamela Jaison (USA), Mishka Jambov (Aus), Eric Janigian (USA), Hazel Jones (UK), Scott Kramen (Chi), S Lapham (NZ), Jay Lathan (?), Karen Liebreich (UK), Kim Mackay (Aus), Rebecca Malzard (Aus), Paul & Margo McCutcheon (?), Janet McIntyre (Can), Kip McKay (Nep), Todd Miller (USA), Boris Minnaert (Nl), Peter Mitchell (UK), Ronald Nachtegaal (Nl), Ariane Nick (?), Henrik Nielsen (Dk), Fred Norris (UK), Michael Olwylet (USA), Jenny Paxton (Aus), Stephen Pead (Aus), Lars Perison (Swe), Lois L Perry (?), Jacqueline Peters (Aus), Marcia & Robert Popper (USA), J M Reidy (NZ), H Raun & C Riise (Dk), David Robbins (USA), Tey Roberts (USA), Laura Saxton (USA), Kevin Seaver (Aus), Thomas Seguine (USA), Dawa Sherpa (Nep), Prem Shrestha (Nep), Tony Smales (Aus), B C Smith (UK), Colin Smith (UK), Patrick Smith (Aus), Pauline & Ian Smith (UK), Joann Song (USA), Jack Sonnabaum (Jap), Pamela Steele (Aus), C Steele-Davies (Swi), Bruce Tamagno (A), Rishab Lal Timila (Nep), Patrick Wallerrand (Bel), Louis Waters (USA), Alan Watson (UK), Allon Weisselberg (Isr), Pat Williams (USA), David Willis (UK), Amanda Wood (UK), Peter Young (?), Malcolm Young (Aus), Karen Young (Aus), Steven Zimmerman (USA)

A – Austria, Aus – Australia, Bel – Belgium, Can – Canada, Chi – Chile, Dk – Denmark, Ire – Republic of Ireland, Isr – Israel, It – Italy, Nl – Netherlands, Nep – Nepal, NZ – New Zealand, Nor – Norway, Pak – Pakistan, PNG – Papua New Guinea, Swe – Sweden, Swi – Switzerland, Thai – Thailand, UK – United Kingdom, USA – United States of America

MAP LEGEND

BOUNDARIES

–·–·–·–·– ....International Boundaries

–··–··–··–·· ....Internal Boundaries

·–··–··–··– ....National Parks, Reserves

– – – – – – – – ....The Equator

· · · · · · · · · · · · · · · · · · ....The Tropics

SYMBOLS

◉ NEW DELHI ....National Capital

● BOMBAY ....Provincial or State Capital

● Pune ....Major Town

• Barsi ....Minor Town

🏤 ....Post Office

✈ ....Airport

ℹ ....Tourist Information

⊖ ....Bus Station, Terminal

66 ....Highway Route Number

☪ ♰ ♰ ....Mosque, Church, Cathedral

∴ ...Temple, Ruin or Archaeological Site

🏠 ....Hostel

✚ ....Hospital

※ ....Lookout

⚑ ....Camping Areas

⌓ ....Picnic Areas

⌂ ....Hut or Chalet

▲ ....Mountain

⊷⊷ ....Railway Station

⫝⫝ ....Road Bridge

⫝⫝⫝ ....Road Rail Bridge

⇗ ⟵ Road Tunnel

⇘ ⟵ ....Railway Tunnel

⫟⫟⫟ ....Escarpment or Cliff

⌇⌇ ....Pass

⌇⌇ ....Ancient or Historic Wall

ROUTES

——————— ......Major Roads and Highways

- - - - - - - - - ....Unsealed Major Roads

——————— ....Sealed Roads

- - - - - - - - - ....Unsealed Roads, Tracks

——————— ....City Streets

+++++++++++++++ ....Railways

■—●—■ ....Subways

· · · · · · · · · · · · · · · · ....Walking Tracks

- - - - - - - - - - ....Ferry Routes

—⊢⊢—⊢⊢—⊢⊢— ....Cable Car or Chair Lift

HYDROGRAPHIC FEATURES

〰〰〰 ....Rivers, Creeks

- - - - - ....Intermittent Streams

◑ ⟨⟩ ....Lakes, Intermittent Lake

〜〜 ....Coast Line

◖ ....Spring

⟩⟩ ⊢⊢ ....Waterfall

⊻⊻ ⊻⊻ ....Swamps

▦ ....Salt Lakes, Reefs

▦ ....Glacier

OTHER FEATURES

▦ Parks, Gardens and
....National Parks

▦ ....Built Up Area

▦ Market Place and
..............................Pedestrian Mall

▦ ....Plaza and Town Square

✛✛✛✛
✛✛✛✛ ....Cemetery

Note: Not all the symbols displayed above will necessarily appear in this book

Facing Page 16 - Things for Sale

a. Puppet shop, Durbar Square, Kathmandu (TW)
b. Fruit cart, Pokhara (TW)
c. Potters' Square, Bhaktapur (TW)
d. Coloured powder, Patan (TW)
e. Pottery near Wakupati Narayan Temple, Bhaktapur (TW)

Facing Page 17 - Buddha Eyes

a. Swayambhunath Stupa (TW)
b. Chabahil Stupa (TW)
c. Bodhnath Stupa (TW)
d. Swayambhunath Stupa (TW)
e. Bodhnath Stupa (TW)

Facing Page 32 - Signs

a. Bicycle, Kathmandu Valley (TW)
b. The spoilt country, Pokhara? (TW)
c. Sauraha, Royal Chitwan National Park (TW)
d. Yak & Yuppie Hotel, Pokhara (TW)
e. Family planning, Panauti (TW)
f. Thamel signs, Kathmandu (TW)

Facing Page 33 - Temple Struts & Erotic Art

a. Temple strut, Patan (RE)
b. Minanath Temple, Patan (TW)
c. Shiva Temple erotica, Kathmandu (TW)
d. Shiva Temple erotica, Kathmandu (TW)
e. Changunarayan Temple, Changunarayan (TW)
f. Jal Binayak Temple, Chobar Gorge (TW)

Facing Page 48 - Nepalese Art

a. Lion at Vajra Jogini Temple, Sankhu (RE)
b. Hanuman Statue, Gorkha Durbar, Gorkha (RE)
c. Peacock Window, Bhaktapur (TW)
d. Bhaktapur Wrestler reproduction (TW)
e. Chandeshwari Temple gate, Chandesh-wari (TW)

Facing Page 49 - Porters

a. A hill country ambulance, near Pokhara (TW)
b. Loading up at the end of a trek, near Pokhara (TW)
c. Waiting for the ferry, Sauraha, Royal Chitwan National Park (TW)
d. Delivering pots, Bhaktapur (TW)
e. Delivering onions, Kathmandu (TW)

Facing Page 64 - Agriculture

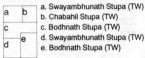

a. Rice fields, Sauraha, Royal Chitwan National Park (TW)
b. Winnowing grain, Panauti (TW)
c. Working in the fields, near Dhulikhel (TW)
d. Harvest time, Kathmandu Valley (TW)
e. Piles of grain, Panauti (TW)
f. Children in the fields, near Dhulikhel (TW)

Facing Page 65 - People

a. Village boy (SB)
b. Girl, near Besi Sahar (JL)
c. Monk, Gorakhnath Tibetan Temple, Kathmandu Valley (RE)
d. Children, Pangboche (CG)
e. Family in the Terai (SB)
f. Shiva sadhu, Dakshinkali (RE)
g. Village children & man (SB)
h. Man, Kali Gandaki Gorge near Tatopani (RE)

Facing Page 80 - Transport

a. River crossing by dugout canoe, Sauraha, Royal Chitwan National Park (TW)
b. Nagarkot to Bhaktapur bus (TW)
c. Travelling by ox cart, Sauraha, Royal Chitwan National Park (TW)
d. RNAC aircraft, Pokhara - Annapurnas in the background (TW)
e. Bus station, Tansen (RE)
f. Bicycle rickshaw, Kathmandu (TW)

Facing Page 240 - Wildlife

a. Rhino & elephant, Royal Chitwan National Park (SB)
b. Elephant riding, Royal Chitwan National Park (TW)
c. Crossing a river by elephant, Royal Chitwan National Park (TW)
d. Elephant bath time, Royal Chitwan National Park (TW)
e. Elephant, Royal Bardia Wildlife Reserve (RE)
f. Rhinos, Royal Chitwan National Park (TW)

Facing Page 304 - Mountains

a. The Himalaya (SB)
b. Machhapuchhare from Pokhara-Tansen road (RE)
c. Machhapuchhare with the fishtail showing (SB)
d. Machhapuchhare from east of Pokhara (TW)
e. Full moon rising over Manaslu Himal (TW)
f. Sun rising over Dhaulagiri from Poon Hill (JL)

cm	in
0	0
1	
2	
	1
3	
4	
5	2
6	
7	
	3
8	
9	
10	4
11	
12	
13	5
14	
15	6

Temperature

To convert °C to °F multiply by 1.8 and add 32
To convert °F to °C subtract 32 and multiply by .55

Length, Distance & Area

	multiply by
inches to centimetres	2.54
centimetres to inches	0.39
feet to metres	0.30
metres to feet	3.28
yards to metres	0.91
metres to yards	1.09
miles to kilometres	1.61
kilometres to miles	0.62
acres to hectares	0.40
hectares to acres	2.47

Weight

	multiply by
ounces to grams	28.35
grams to ounces	0.035
pounds to kilograms	0.45
kilograms to pounds	2.21
British tons to kilograms	1016
US tons to kilograms	907

A British ton is 2240 lbs, a US ton is 2000 lbs

Volume

	multiply by
imperial gallons to litres	4.55
litres to imperial gallons	0.22
US gallons to litres	3.79
litres to US gallons	0.26

5 imperial gallons equals 6 US gallons
a litre is slightly more than a US quart, slightly less than a British one

C | F
50 — 122
45 — 113
40 — 104
35 — 95
30 — 86
25 — 75
20 — 68
15 — 59
10 — 50
5 — 41
0 — 32

Guides to the Indian Subcontinent

Trekking in the Nepal Himalaya
Complete trekking information for Nepal, including day-by-day route descriptions and detailed maps — a wealth of advice for both independent and group trekkers.

Trekking in the Indian Himalaya
All the advice you'll need for planning and equipping a trek, including detailed route descriptions for some of the world's most exciting treks.

India - a travel survival kit
Widely regarded as the guide to India, this award-winning book has all the information to help you make the most of the unforgettable experience that is India.

Kashmir, Ladakh & Zanskar - a travel survival kit
Detailed information on three contrasting Himalayan regions in the Indian state of Jammu and Kashmir — the narrow valley of Zanskar, the isolated 'little Tibet' of Ladakh, and the stunningly beautiful Vale of Kashmir.

Bangladesh - a travel survival kit
Travel is easy in Bangladesh, with only short distances between markedly different environments — tropical forests and beaches, wooded marshlands and jungles, ancient ruins of temples and palaces, and fascinating remnants of colonial cultures.

Karakoram Highway the high road to China - a travel survival kit
Travel in the footsteps of Alexander the Great and Marco Polo on the Karakoram Highway, following the ancient and fabled Silk Road. This comprehensive guide also covers villages and treks away from the highway.

Pakistan - a travel survival kit
Discover 'the unknown land of the Indus' with this informative guidebook — from bustling Karachi to ancient cities and tranquil mountain valleys.

Sri Lanka - a travel survival kit
Some parts of Sri Lanka are off-limits to visitors, but this guidebook uses the restriction as an incentive to explore other areas more closely — making the most of friendly people, good food and pleasant places to stay — all at reasonable cost.

Also available:
Hindi/Urdu phrasebook, *Nepal* phrasebook, *and Sri Lanka* phrasebook.

Lonely Planet Guidebooks

Lonely Planet guidebooks cover virtually every accessible part of Asia as well as Australia, the Pacific, Central and South America, Africa, the Middle East and parts of North America. There are four main series: 'travel survival kits', covering a single country for a range of budgets; 'shoestring' guides with compact information for low-budget travel in a major region; trekking guides; and 'phrasebooks'.

Australia & the Pacific
Australia
Bushwalking in Australia
Papua New Guinea
Papua New Guinea phrasebook
New Zealand
Tramping in New Zealand
Rarotonga & the Cook Islands
Solomon Islands
Tahiti & French Polynesia
Fiji
Micronesia
Tonga
Samoa
New Caledonia

South-East Asia
South-East Asia on a shoestring
Malaysia, Singapore & Brunei
Indonesia
Bali & Lombok
Indonesia phrasebook
Burma
Burmese phrasebook
Thailand
Thai phrasebook
Philippines
Pilipino phrasebook

North-East Asia
North-East Asia on a shoestring
China
China phrasebook
Tibet
Tibet phrasebook
Japan
Japanese phrasebook
Korea
Korean phrasebook
Hong Kong, Macau & Canton
Taiwan

West Asia
West Asia on a shoestring
Trekking in Turkey
Turkey
Turkish phrasebook

Indian Ocean
Madagascar & Comoros
Maldives & Islands of the East Indian Ocean
Mauritius, Réunion & Seychelles

Mail Order

Lonely Planet guidebooks are distributed worldwide and are sold by good bookshops everywhere. They are also available by mail order from Lonely Planet, so if you have difficulty finding a title please write to us. US and Canadian residents should write to Embarcadero West, 112 Linden St, Oakland CA 94607, USA and residents of other countries to PO Box 617, Hawthorn, Victoria 3122, Australia.

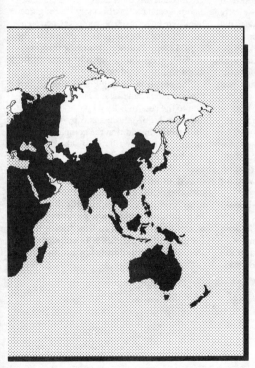

Europe
Eastern Europe
Trekking in Spain

Indian Subcontinent
India
Hindi/Urdu phrasebook
Kashmir, Ladakh & Zanskar
Trekking in the Indian Himalaya
Pakistan
Kathmandu & the Kingdom of Nepal
Trekking in the Nepal Himalaya
Nepal phrasebook
Sri Lanka
Sri Lanka phrasebook
Bangladesh
Karakoram Highway

Africa
Africa on a shoestring
East Africa
Swahili phrasebook
West Africa
Central Africa
Morocco, Algeria & Tunisia

North America
Canada
Alaska

Mexico
Mexico
Baja California

South America
South America on a shoestring
Ecuador & the Galapagos Islands
Colombia
Chile & Easter Island
Bolivia
Brazil
Brazilian phrasebook
Peru
Argentina
Quechua phrasebook

Middle East
Israel
Egypt & the Sudan
Jordan & Syria
Yemen

Lonely Planet

Lonely Planet published its first book in 1973. Tony and Maureen Wheeler had made an overland trip from England to Australia and, in response to numerous 'how do you do it?' questions, Tony wrote and they published *Across Asia on the Cheap*. It became an instant local best seller and inspired thoughts of a second travel guide. A year and a half in South-East Asia resulted in their second book, *South-East Asia on a Shoestring*, which they put together in a backstreet Chinese hotel in Singapore in 1975. The 'yellow book', as it quickly became known, soon became the guide to the region and has gone through six editions, always with its familiar yellow cover.

Soon other writers came to them with ideas for similar books - books that went off the beaten track, books that 'assumed you knew how to get your luggage off the carousel' as one reviewer put it. Lonely Planet grew from a kitchen table operation to a spare room and then to its own office. Its international reputation began to grow as the Lonely Planet logo began to appear in more and more countries. In 1982 *India - a travel survival kit* won the Thomas Cook award for the best guidebook of the year.

These days there are over 70 Lonely Planet titles. Over 40 people work at our office in Melbourne and another half dozen at our US office in Oakland, California.

At first Lonely Planet specialised in the Asia region but these days we are also developing major ranges of guidebooks to the Pacific region, to South America and to Africa. The list of walking guides is growing and Lonely Planet now has a unique series of phrasebooks to 'unusual' languages. The emphasis continues to be on travel for travellers and Tony and Maureen still manage to fit in a number of trips each year and play a very active part in the writing and updating of Lonely Planet's guides.

Keeping guidebooks up to date is a constant battle which requires an ear to the ground and lots of walking, but technology also plays its part. All Lonely Planet guidebooks are now stored on computer, and some authors even take lap-top computers into the field. Lonely Planet is also using computers to draw maps and eventually many of the maps will be stored on disc.

The people at Lonely Planet strongly feel that travellers can make a positive contribution to the countries they visit both by better appreciation of cultures and by the money they spend. In addition the company tries to make a direct contribution to the countries and regions it covers. Since 1986 a percentage of the income from each book has gone to aid groups and associations. This has included donations to famine relief in Africa, to aid projects in India, to agricultural projects in Central America, to Greenpeace's efforts to halt French nuclear testing in the Pacific and to Amnesty International. In 1990 $60,000 was donated by Lonely Planet to these projects.